Adventures with a Historian
The Life and Times of John R. "Jack" Hubbard

by
John R. Hubbard

Edited by
Elizabeth A. Hubbard
and George U. Hubbard

Denton, Texas

Cover design and maps by Marcela Roberts

Photos and Illustrations are provided by family members and the University of Southern California except where noted.

Photos of the formation of US Navy Aircraft (Chapter 13) and the mushroom cloud above Hiroshima (Chapter 12) used by permission of the Navy Heritage Command, U.S. Department of the Navy. Emil Zátopek leading the marathon (Chapter 15) used under license from dpa Picture-Alliance GmbH, Frankfurt, Germany.

Roots & Branches
An imprint of AWOC.COM Publishing
P.O. Box 2819
Denton, TX 76202

©2014 by Elizabeth A. Hubbard
All Rights Reserved.

No part of this publication may be reproduced, stored in a retrieval system, or transmitted in any form or by any means, electronic, mechanical, recording or otherwise, without written permission, except in the case of brief quotations embodied in critical articles and reviews.

Manufactured in the United States of America.

ISBN: 978-1-62016-050-3 Paperback
ISBN: 978-1-62016-051-0 Ebook

Table of Contents

Foreword 7
Part I – Watershed Adventures 15
   CHAPTER 1 – A Liberal Education 17
   CHAPTER 2 – Louise, We've Got to Go! or Elements in a Liberal Education 49
   CHAPTER 3 – The Summer of 1938 54
      Addendum I 87
      Addendum II 87
      Editor's Addition 89
   CHAPTER 4 – Just Try to Be Ready 90
      Addendum I 112
      Addendum II 113
Part II – Adventures in Naval Aviation 115
   CHAPTER 5 – Anacostia Elimination Base 117
   CHAPTER 6 – Jacksonville Naval Air Station 138
      Ensign Joseph P. Kennedy, Jr., (AVN) USNR 153
      Editor's Addition 154
   CHAPTER 7 – Instrument Flight Instructor's School ... 156
      Editor's Addition 174
   CHAPTER 8 – Bermuda 176
   CHAPTER 9 – From Hutch to Crow's Landing 189
   CHAPTER 10 – Crow's Landing to Palau 208
   CHAPTER 11 – The Route to Tokyo: Tinian, Iwo Jima, Okinawa 218
      Editor's Addition 239
   CHAPTER 12 – The Bombs and VJ-Day 241
      Editor's Addition 252

Part III – Academic, Athletic, and Politically Eclectic Adventures 259
  CHAPTER 13 – The Road Not Taken 261
    Editor's Addition 271
  CHAPTER 14 – Hi'yuh Tex: Scandinavian Research Adventures 275
  CHAPTER 15 – Finland and the 1952 Olympiad 302
    Editor's Addition 328
  CHAPTER 16 – Interlude at Yale 331
  CHAPTER 17 – The Newcomb Years 354
    Editor's Addition 389
  CHAPTER 18 – A Cajun Compliment 393
  CHAPTER 19 – India (1965) Huge Plans 411
  CHAPTER 20 – India (1966-1969) A Change of Plans 448
    Editor's Additions 477
  CHAPTER 21 – Expanding the Liberal Arts at the University of Southern California 486
  CHAPTER 22 – USC without Football? 517
  CHAPTER 23 – USC - A Bastion of Independence 543
  CHAPTER 24 – India (1988—1989) A Dream Come True 566
    Editor's Addendum 593
  Chapter 25 – Sunset 594
Bibliography 599

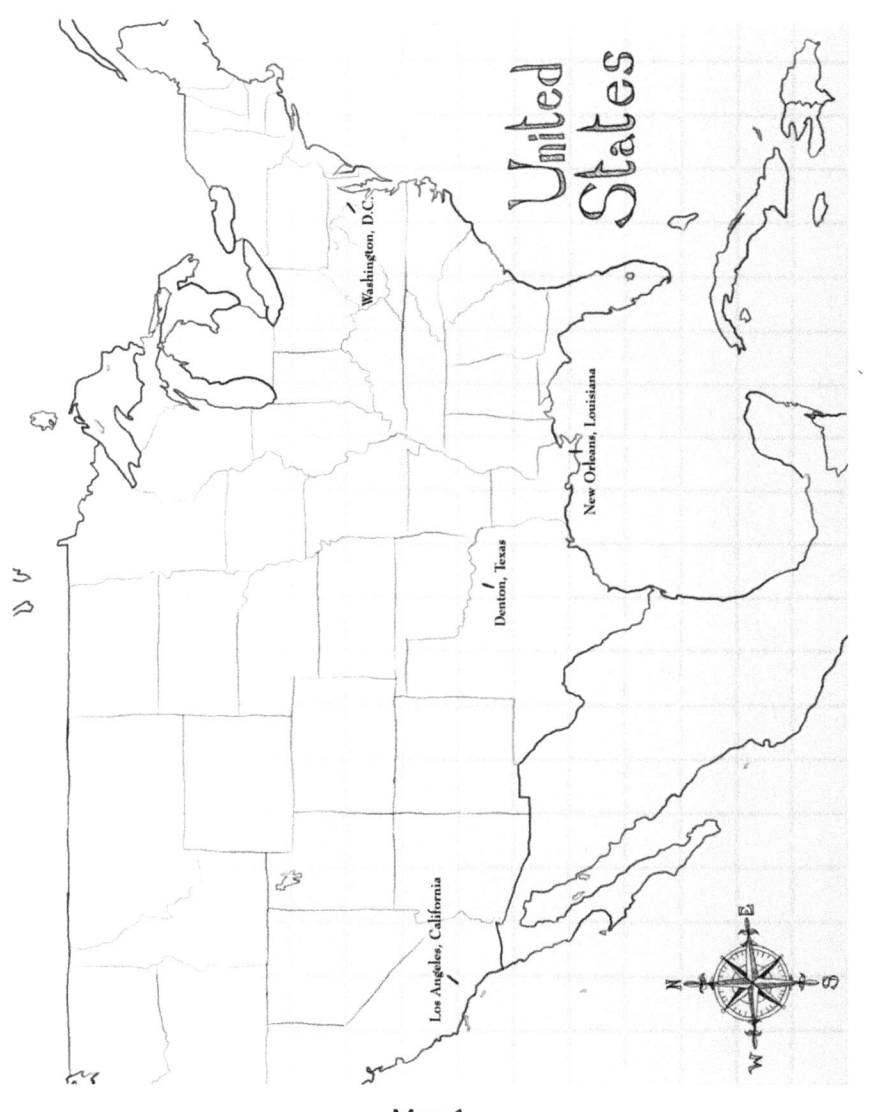

Map 1
Key Adventure Launch Points

Foreword

An educated person is not defined by a recitation of facts and figures. The world has machines staffed with memory cards which store more facts and figures than any single human will ever want to know or access. During the past decade, advanced search engines developed by companies such as Microsoft and Google have negated the need for individuals to memorize streams of data. Today's high school teachers and college/university professors grapple with the challenge of educating their students so they can be successful and productive contributors to the continuance and promulgation of mankind and its multiple spheres.

An educated person has learned—under the careful tutelage of those who have gone before—to look for, analyze, and understand interrelationships; to formulate and then test hypotheses; to correlate seemingly disparate variables; to afford basic human dignity to all people regardless of race, creed, or color; to stand in awe at the beauty, mysteries, and wonders of nature; to recognize a power greater than oneself; that there is no limitation to the sources of knowledge because data is infinite; that what is true may change over time as new information is gleaned; and to acknowledge to all that the search for knowledge and truth never ends. John Randolph "Jack" Hubbard was an educated man and an educator. More specifically, Jack was a historian, and he knew that history is more than just dates, places, times, and events.

Jack lived during the years when the world at large was undergoing many of the most significant geo-political, socio-economic, and industrial changes in world history. Born a few days after the official end of World War I, he grew up during the roaring 20s, Prohibition, and the Great Depression. During his teenage years, the Spanish Civil War raged, Hitler came to power and began expanding the German empire as did Mussolini in Italy, and Japan waged war against China.

Following adventuresome and formative years as a youth and a student, Jack commenced his formal career as a historian at the time of the evolving Cold War in Europe and the "police action" in Korea (aka Korean War of 1950 - 1953). Both situations pitted the burgeoning Soviet Union against the United States. Jack had a passion for pursuing historical understanding wherever it could be found, and these endeavors and their related travel quickly made him a recognized international figure. It was inevitable, therefore, that the major movements of his time—the Viet Nam War; the civil rights movement; the race to the moon; the Yom Kippur War; Watergate; the Arab oil embargo; the advent of the birth control pill; the women's liberation movement; the Iranian Revolution and the Iran Hostage Crisis; affirmative action; the Soviet-Afghan War; nuclear proliferation; the development of the silicon chip, semi-conductors, and rapid expansion of high technology as both a new and separate industry, and high tech innovations revolutionizing virtually all other industries; and the widening gulf between developed and under-developed nations—all impacted Jack's career to varying degrees.

Jack's historical interests, however, began early in his life and led to his being a student of history at The University of Texas. And as a pursuer of historical understanding he had an uncanny knack of being in the right place at the right time to see history in the making. As examples, Jack was present at one of Hitler's famous rallies in Nuremburg, Germany in 1938. Jack was also present in the Labor Department Auditorium in 1940 when the "then Secretary of War, Henry Stimson, stood blindfolded before the fishbowl on the dais and withdrew the first fateful draft number." Jack then had to make a decision: Would he wait to be drafted or would he enlist early in the military branch of his choice? He made his decision, and he survived World War II as a decorated naval aviator.

Following World War II, Jack's career choices segued into two divergent paths—Naval Aviation which he now loved or Academia which he had always loved—between which he had to choose. Robert Frost's immortal poem *The Road Not Taken* underscores Jack's dilemma.

> *Two roads diverged in a yellow wood*
> *And sorry I could not travel both*
> *And be one traveler, long I stood*
> *And looked down one as far as I could*
> *To where it bent in the undergrowth;*
>
> *Then took the other, just a fair,*
> *And having perhaps the better claim,*
> *Because it was grassy and wanted wear;*
> *Though as for that that passing there*

Had worn them really about the same,

And both that morning equally lay
In leaves no step had trodden black.
Oh, I kept the first for another day!
Yet knowing how way leads on to way,
I doubted if I should ever come back.

I should be telling this with a sign
Somewhere ages and ages hence:
Two roads diverged in a wood, and I –
I took the one less traveled by,
And that has made all the difference.

Jack's memoirs reflect the two roads and as such, we, the editors, have sectioned the book into three parts. Part I, *Watershed Adventures* are remembrances of events and adventures during the formative years of Jack's physical and intellectual development from picking cotton to growing up on university campuses. Jack's adventures in Europe during the summer of 1938 could lead the reader to speculate that Jack would be one of the first Americans to go to Canada or England to join the fight against Hitler even before the United States officially entered the war.

The dilemma is quickly resolved as the reader turns to Part II and reads *The Route to Tokyo* which climaxes with his team flying air search and rescue support for the Enola Gay on its fateful trip to and from Hiroshima. Jack understood the importance of incorporating personalities, activities, and interpersonal relationships into his World War II story for it is only through this integration that the audience can begin to grasp the enormity of the world stage on which his story is played out, where the dichotomy of the invincible champion of freedom and the mantra that there may be no tomorrow belied the caliber of men with whom Jack served.

Adventures With a Historian, Part III, presents Jack's academic and political career—the other road—which he took after the war. The watershed for this career choice was Jack's upbringing on the campuses of The University of Texas and Texas Woman's University. As Jack tells the story of his own travels through academia, into the political fringes, then back into academia, he sheds light on adventures he shared with colleagues providing a rare insight into the greatest challenges of higher education in the United States, and he gives the reader tastes of life in various parts of the world by allowing the reader to travel with him on exotic—and sometimes dangerous—adventures.

Although Jack was an able and effective administrator, as evidenced by his years as Dean of Sophie Newcomb College and President of the University of Southern California, his primary love was teaching. Jack loved teaching—primarily British History—through story-telling. He often told his students that they never needed to memorize dates or places. He encouraged them to think. Think about the events, the personalities, the cultural setting, and the economy, and then put them in context with the strategic objectives of the nation and its leaders. In both the classroom and the board room, Jack was considered an educational innovator. In the end, however, many in the board room considered Jack too much of a maverick to remain USC's president despite the potential upsides of his innovative thought.

When Jack decided that he wanted to write his memoirs, he wanted an environment that offered him the peace and quiet needed to focus on the task at hand without having to give up all of the accoutrements to which he was accustomed. During the summers of 1996 and 1997, Jack packed a manual typewriter, boarded a freighter, and sailed around the world documenting the most propitious and important parts of his life. As he wrote, he expounded upon events and activities surrounding him which had significant impact on him, yet he also wrote with the education of the reader in mind. For example, as Jack recounts some of his experiences with USAID in India during the 1960's, he gives the readers the historical backgrounds—which always involved the British—so that the reader would have a greater appreciation of the situations in which Jack found himself.

In the twilight of his life, Jack handed his rough manuscript to his brother, George, with the request that it be edited, completed, and published under George's direction. At the time, George did not realize that his brother had not given him a complete book in the traditional sense of the word. As George scanned each chapter of Jack's typed manuscript into a computer using optical character reader (OCR) software and began the editing and formatting process into Microsoft's Word.doc documents, he realized that Jack had written each chapter as an independent story. Therefore we the editors (me and my father George) made the decision to edit the chapters as required to facilitate natural segues from one chapter to the next. Duplicate passages, redundancies, and passages that might cause embarrassment to those referenced were deleted. At the same time we made it a point to preserve Jack's phenomenal vocabulary and writing style that make his writings such a pleasure to read.

Jack did not write an autobiography in the purest sense of the word. He did not write much about his family—either while growing up or the family he created upon his marriage. He wrote primarily of the many highlights of his life as he reminisced, and these highlights are presented here in his own words. All photos, maps, and other graphics included in the books were selected and added by the editors. A special thank you goes to Jack's eldest nephew and namesake, John Randolph "Randy" Paine, M.D. for contributing letters and photographs Jack sent home to his family over the years which Randy's mother, (Jack's sister) Louise Hubbard Paine, passed on to Randy for safe-keeping..

Jack's own writings ended with his arrival at the University of Southern California in 1969. We are not sure why he never completed his memoirs—or if he did complete them, we do not know what happened to them. Therefore, after considerable research by us, the editors, we have written the final chapters covering the last forty years of Jack's life. These chapters, though heavily documented, should not be considered a biography as they are very specific to Jack's tenure at the University of Southern California and his service as United States Ambassador to India.

When George accepted the request of his brother to edit and publish his memoirs, he stated that he wanted to add a little bit to Jack's manuscript about his accomplishments as the president of the University of Southern California, and about his time as ambassador. George wanted to know why Jack was ambassador for such a short period of time, and what he accomplished as ambassador. The search for the answers to those two questions led to the development of the three chapters we wrote about Jack's tenure at USC as well as the chapter we wrote about his ambassadorship to India. Since Jack had written about his youth in the first chapter of his memoirs we wrote a closing chapter for the book addressing his final years.

The normal adjectives seem inadequate for describing Jack's impact on the people with whom he associated or for assessing him many achievements. Perhaps the word "special" is as good as any. It is hoped that the reader of these memoirs will find the man that his intimate friends and family knew.

Where we, as editors, have found or had access to documents that would add credence to Jack's recollections, or additional information that may be of interest to the reader, we have included them in Editor's Additions at the end of the respective chapters. Jack had his adherents and he had some critics, with the former greatly outnumbering the latter. However, just as beauty is in the eye of the beholder, so too is the perception of truth in the eye of the observer, for each observer may view the same incident from a different position or line of sight. All must agree, however, that he was "special."

Every effort has been made to check names, titles, dates, events, and locations as recorded by Jack for accuracy in order to avoid claims of incompleteness, inaccuracy, libel, etc. We acknowledge and are grateful to those who have provided interviews, assisted with research, technical review, photos, editing, and fact-checking: Col. Brad Hildreth, Aviation, US Army (Ret); Reagan Savoie; Lt. Cmdr. James Sitton, USNR; Linda Pinkerton; Mark White, USN; John Randolph Paine, MD; Rachel Wood; University of Southern California Archivist and Manuscripts Librarian Claude Zackary; former University of Southern California (USC) football players Charles Young, Sam Dickerson, Pat Haden, John McKay, Jr., and Anthony Muñoz; USC Football Coach John Robinson; USC alum and author Steve Travers; USC Sports Information Director Tim Tessalone; Dr. John K. Hubbard; President Ronald Reagan's Director of Personnel Robert Tuttle; President George H. W. Bush's Director of Personnel Chase Untermeyer; USC Band Director Art Bartner; Billie Hubbard; U.S. Military Academy Research Library; U.S. Naval Academy Research Library; National Museum of Naval Aviation; the Office of Congressman Michael Burgess; and documents received under the Freedom of Information Act.

—Elizabeth Hubbard

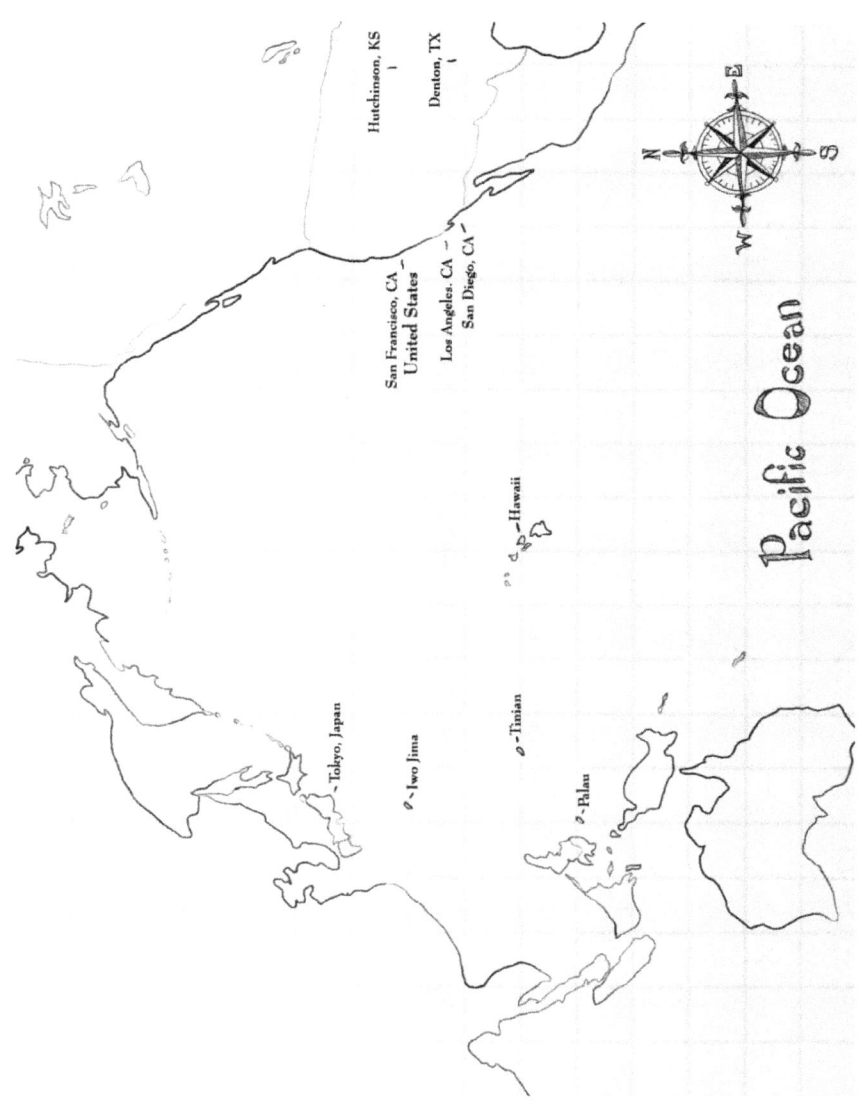

Map 2
Key Pacific Adventure Launch Points

Map 3
Key Eurasia Adventure Launch Points

Part I
—
Watershed Adventures

John R. "Jack" Hubbard, circa 1925

CHAPTER 1
—
A Liberal Education

The tale of some of my most memorable adventures begins with a brief background of my father, Louis Herman Hubbard—the most influential person in my life. Dad was born February 10, 1882, in Mayaguez, Puerto Rico, where his father, Gorham Eustis Hubbard—a proper Bostonian, was U. S. Consul General, and had married a noblewoman, Louisa Mendez-Monsanto. Following termination of his consulate duties, my grandfather moved his family, which now consisted of four small children—Mercedes, Edward, Alice, and Dad—to El Paso, Texas, where he operated a wholesale fruit and grocery business. After about four years in El Paso, my grandfather succumbed to cancer, and his widow eked out a meager living subsisting on a small government pension, abetted by her proclivity at sewing and lace-making, and Dad's paper route and employment as a part-time Western Union messenger.

Dad's most vivid memory of those days, which he was fond of retelling, was the evening he delivered a telegram to John Wesley Hardin, one of the Southwest's most dangerous outlaws and gun-fighters, who Dad found drinking at a saloon bar: "I was speechless with fright as I handed him the wire, whereupon he reached in his pocket, tipped me a dime, patted me on the head and said, 'Son, don't you ever do what I am doing.'" After reading the telegram, Hardin strode toward the swinging door, and as he stepped into the dusty street, he was shot dead by a rival, who, knowing Hardin's drinking habits, had sent the wire and was waiting outside in ambush.

After finishing high school in El Paso, Dad went to The University of Texas in Austin, working his way through but finding time to make the varsity football team and being named All-Southwestern right end in 1902. He was proud of his nickname, Choo-choo: "I hit the ball carriers like a runaway train!" But his real loves were music and literature, especially 19th century English literature. Upon graduation, he began a career as a high school teacher of English in various Texas towns including

San Angelo and Sulphur Springs, before being called back to Belton as Principal of the high school (having taught there in previous years).

Belton was important to the Hubbard family. A small community in central Texas, 60 miles north of Austin and the county seat of Bell County, it had its brush with fame when it came within one vote in the Texas Legislature of being named capitol of the state. It was there that Dad met Bertha Altizer, a true First Family of Virginia (FFV) lady reared on a plantation between Roanoke and Salem, Virginia, who had accompanied her father, a gentleman cotton fancier, on a business trip to the Lone Star State. Using his father's Boston Brahmin background and diplomatic career as arguments, Dad convinced Mr. Altizer of his social acceptability and Bertha of the sincerity of his ardor; they married and began their family with the arrival of Martha Louise in June 1916 and John Randolph in December 1918, by which time the Principal had become Superintendent of Schools.

Cedar Crest

We lived in a spacious frame house on a ten-acre plot called Cedar Crest on the northern outskirts of Belton which melded a small farm atmosphere with a small town urbanity, and as a youngster I reveled in the presence of pigs, chickens, milk cows, and a cedar break with plenty of room to roam and a swimming hole. We had become a joint family of nine with the inclusion of Dad's deaf sister, Mercedes, having lost her hearing as a young child due to scarlet fever, and Bertha's sister, Frances, who with her three children had been deserted by her husband Vin Moore, in Tucumcari, New Mexico, a strange location for a Virginia belle. So in effect I began life with a father, two mothers, an aunt, two older brothers and two older sisters, and my rearing began in a milieu of books, music (all the females played the piano and everyone loved to sing), great cuisine (the Altizer women were marvelous cooks), farm chores, persistent light-hearted banter between adults and siblings, stern strictures on gracious manners and morals (Bostonian and FFV style), and plenty of breathing space. My tenure at Cedar Crest was short, but the memories remain and are still vivid and pleasant.

Me (Jack), a tough Texan, circa 1921

As the name implied, Cedar Crest was perched atop a hill with a sharp slope to the east beyond which ran the Leon River about an eighth of a mile away. Between the hill and the river was wonderfully high bottom land planted in cotton which, when in bloom, formed a veritable sea of white. It was there I found my first gainful employment. At picking time field hands came from miles around to enjoy the princely wage of 25¢ per hundred pounds, and the really expert could garner a dollar a day. My cousins Bert and Vin had joined in the year before, and this time they said I could go with them. Mother took a dim view of this notion, suggesting (correctly) that I would probably just get in peoples' way, but she relented and made me a little sack that I could sling over my shoulder and hopefully fill with cotton. The next morning we reported to the field boss and were assigned a row to pick. After a cursory demonstration to me of how to separate the cotton from the boll, my cousins took off, saying they would leave enough cotton in their wake for my sack. So off I started down the row on my hands and knees.

It was hard going; the sun was boiling, and as I made my way up the row, my trousers split and my knees began to bleed, then my hands as I clumsily tried to work the bolls, and worst of all I was putting precious little cotton in my sack. After about an hour of this, the whole thing seemed hopeless, and I did what I suppose was not unnatural for a thoroughly frustrated five year old—I just sat down in the middle of that cotton field and started crying. About that time a colored family working the adjacent row drew alongside. They were a man, his wife, and four children, all covered with sweat, but with cotton fairly flying into their sacks.

They paused at this bedraggled sight, and the woman said, "What's the matter, white boy? Where's yo folks? Dis yo first time in de patch?"

"Yes, ma'am," I blubbered, "and my cousins are up ahead somewhere."

And the man observed, "Seems they doan left much cotton for you."

Then the woman suggested, "You come with us and my kids'll show you what to do."

But the man objected, "Dea's no way he can keep up and we got cotton to pick." With that he took my sack, and reaching into his, he filled mine to the brim. "Yo take that down to the scales. De's bound to give you sumpin. And you grows a little fo you come back next year."

I was so relieved that I could barely mumble my thanks. I hoisted the sack over my shoulder and made my way back to the weighing-in wagon, where a man took it, pretending to stagger under the weight, threw it on the scales, emptied it into the wagon, and spoke to the checker. In a few moments he came back and handed me a dime. That was not a great sum, but the lesson of that colored family's compassion was enormous.

In 1924 the Hubbards departed Belton (leaving the Moores at Cedar Crest) for Austin and The University of Texas (UT), whose then President, W.M.W. Splawn, had created a new post of Dean of Students and asked Dad to be the first occupant. We traversed that sixty miles south in a Model-T Ford touring car in something over four hours, passing through Salado and stopping for lunch in Round Rock at the Sam Bass Cafe, named after another fabled outlaw and reminding Dad of his encounter with John Wesley Hardin. We settled comfortably in a large frame house on Wichita Street, abutting in the rear of the Beta Theta Pi fraternity house. Dad was exhilarated at returning to his beloved alma mater and launching a new career in higher education, and he continued work on his Ph.D. in English Lit while defining the parameters of his new position.

Austin, the state capitol, was, and is to me, the loveliest community in Texas, what with its rivers, springs, lakes, and hills, temperate (for Texas) climate, and verdure. And for me the University was a wonderland with its forty acre campus, spacious buildings, and teeming student body. Austin then, as now, prospered as a seat of government and university community, being referred to at times as a place with no visible means of support and as such being marvelously attractive as a place to live.

As son of the Dean of Students, I had the run of the campus, and my parents saw to it that I was immersed in the multifaceted attractions concomitant to university life. Having earned his "T" in football as a varsity letterman, Dad had a lifetime pass to all the stadia, and it was here that I was introduced to collegiate athletics and the rivalries of the Southwest Conference. I have never met a person more interested in and knowledgeable about sports than my father, and it was rare indeed that we missed a football, baseball or basketball game. I well remember old Clark Gymnasium, the arena for varsity basketball and intramural games which doubled as the venue for the university's Fine Arts series. It was there that I marveled at the lithe dexterity of Sandy Esquival, UT's great sports hero of the '20s, and it was there that I first heard in solo, without really comprehending, the artistry of Enrique Caruso and Mme. Galli-Curci. It was also at this time that I met my first political luminary.

Dad had somehow become acquainted with "Ma" Ferguson, first woman Governor of the state, who was serving out the term of her husband, Jim, who had been impeached and found guilty of malfeasance. One day Dad took the family down to the Capitol to meet the great lady, and I remember her formidable appearance and her patting me on the head, telling me to let her know if I found anything wrong with her administration. Needless to say, she had my vote—such as it was.

The thorniest problems encountered by Dad in his administration of student life were posed by the Greeks, that is, the fraternities and sororities. In our back yard fence there was a convenient knothole that afforded me a good view of the rear of the Beta house. I was fascinated by their Saturday bashes, and with my eyes glued to the knot hole, I was amazed at the variety of contortions boys and girls could assume, although I did not understand the game. I recall that after dark there was what seemed to me an awful lot of giggling. But the worst of the lot was Delta Kappa Epsilon, often referred to as the "drunken Dekes."

I remember a Saturday midnight when our household was awakened by a jangling telephone, and I heard Dad on one end telling a frantic sorority housemother on the other to stay calm and he'd be right over. It seems that the Dekes had acquired a new house which they had moved into that afternoon, having sold their old premises to the Phi Mu sorority. To celebrate this transaction, the brothers had gone down town en masse to a dive called the Brazos Buffet, known to serve tolerable home brew in Mason jars. After a huge evening, the brethren began unsteadily to wend their way home when they became confused, and instead of going into their new house, they went into their old one, finding in their accustomed beds unaccustomed bedmates. Amid shrieks of chagrin or delight, bedlam ensued which prompted the telephone call and greeted Dad's arrival. He got it sorted out. His first inclination was to kick the fraternity off campus, but after much pleading by distinguished alums, he simply grounded them for a year with no social privileges. When some years later I entered the university and went through fraternity Rush Week, I called home to tell my parents of the result.

"Did you pledge?" Dad asked.

"Yes, sir."

"Which house?"

"DKE."

It was the only time in my life I ever heard my father curse.

It was in September 1925, when at age 6, I began my own academic career, enrolling in the first grade at Woolridge School very near the UT campus. Mother walked me over and left me almost in tears because my classmates, including girls, all seemed so much bigger than I. This was not, however, my first experience in a classroom.

Shortly before we left Belton, Dad had taken me to the high school to hear a veteran describe his experiences in the Great War. He dwelt at length on life in the ghastly trenches, filled most of the time with water and pestilential rats grown swollen by feeding on corpses. But, he said, they did perform one signal service.

"What was it?" he asked the audience.

I instinctively blurted out, "They could smell gas coming."

I shall never forget all eyes in the room turning on this toddler sitting atop a desk in the back row so he could see the speaker. I wanted desperately to disappear. Apparently I was red as a beet as described by Dad when he related the incident at home, adding his relief that at least I knew the right answer. That had posed no problem for I remembered it from an earlier family discussion on the late war at the dining table (between mouth-fulls of Virginia spoon bread). But from then on it was petulance that I had to worry about.

The Austin idyll ended all too soon when in June 1926, after only two years in Austin, Dad was named president of the women's College of Industrial Arts (CIA) at Denton, 250 miles to the north. So once again the Hubbards were on the move, this time in a 1924 Model-T roadster driven by Dad and a new 1926 Dodge sedan with mother at the wheel.

In Denton, Texas, a town of some 5,000 people forty miles north of Dallas and Fort Worth, the College of Industrial Arts (now known as Texas Woman's University) was the state-supported residential college for women, and as its name indicates, its mission was to prepare females for appropriate roles, limited as they were, in an industrial society. Its strongest academic discipline was Home Economics, although its general curriculum had liberal arts pretensions leading to Bachelor of Arts and Bachelor of Science degrees. The student body numbered about 1,500 on a pleasant, spacious campus.

The Hubbard family packed hat and baggage into our two cars for our hegira to—for us—the uncharted land of north Texas. There were six of us: Mother, Dad, his deaf sister, Mercy, my elder sister, Louise, and my Airedale mutt, Dan. We spent the first night with the Moores at Cedar Crest in Belton, where the adults decided that if things went well in Denton, we should probably sell Cedar Crest if the two families were to see each other, for the 200 mile distance between was not a journey to be undertaken with any regularity. Three hard-driven days later, with only two flat tires and one skid into a ditch, we arrived.

The highways north from Fort Worth and Dallas converged at Denton, prompting the city fathers to call it the gateway to North Texas.

Denton was a languid, easy-going community, the county seat, and along with CIA, the home of the North Texas State

Teachers' College (now known as the University of North Texas). With Dallas and its Southern Methodist University an hour to the southeast, and Fort Worth and its Texan Christian University an hour to the southwest, this was by no means an intellectually barren region, and local pride had the three communities as the cultural triangle and northern gateway to Texas proper.

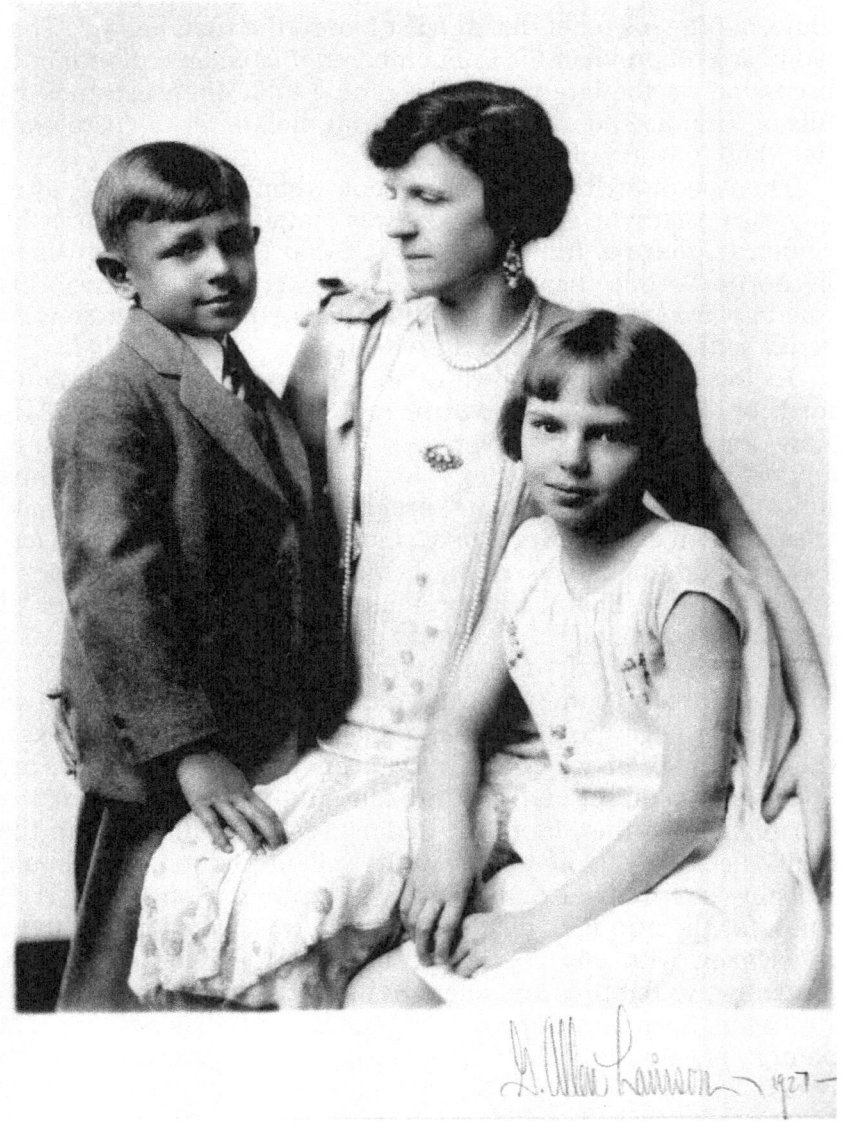

Me (Jack), Mom & Louise in 1927

On a rise in Denton's central area was the town square dominated by an imposing Court House and bordered by retail establishments and two cinemas. Off the square two main streets ran to the north and two to the west through the principal residential areas, while to the east was the railway depot, the Interurban station, granaries and warehouses, and with sparse low-income housing to the south. CIA was located on the northern edge of town, while on the western edge was the North Texas State Teachers' College, even larger than CIA and a rival for the support and affection of the community. So Denton had some legitimate pretensions to the life of the mind, and, like Austin, its principal intellectual, social and commercial activities revolved around government and higher education.

Oakland Avenue ran in a sweeping curve along the western edge of the CIA campus, and as we drove its length for our first glimpse of our new environs, Dad pointed out the principal landmarks: four red brick dormitories housing some 300 girls each, the power plant, laundry and commissary, the president's home, the Main Building with its classrooms and administrative offices perched on a hill to survey the scene, the library, other academic buildings dwarfed by Home Economics, and finally the freestanding auditorium, wherein resided the music and drama departments.

So once again my milieu was a college campus of seemingly boundless space, faculty children for companions, and students who were invariably nice to that "precocious little boy." It never occurred to me that being the president's son had anything to do with my reception, but one thing was evident—my mother would never lack for baby sitters.

The president's home, a commodious frame two-story affair right in the center of the campus, was a delight for there was enough space upstairs for Aunt Mercy and Louise to have separate bedrooms with bath, a guest room, a master bedroom, a study, and a sleeping porch, which was my bailiwick. Downstairs, connected by a front and a rear staircase, featured a large entrance hall flanked on one side by a formal dining room, breakfast room and kitchen, and on the other by a spacious living room on which abutted a sun porch. Behind were the servants' quarters of a bedroom and bath on each floor of the two-story structure which was attached to a double garage above which was a large unfinished room ideal for storage and arts and crafts. (In later years after the Moore family moved to Denton, my cousins found it an ideal spot to store home brew.)

But for all these comfortable surroundings, my first year in residence was surely my most miserable, although it had begun with a considerable challenge. I was enrolled in the Stonewall Jackson Elementary School, a short walk from the CIA campus, where I had taken a battery of tests which indicated I might safely enter the third grade rather than the second. (This was not especially heartening news to me, for it meant that the disparity of my physique compared to my classmates would only be magnified, and I did not relish the moniker of "Pee Wee.") My problem was that somewhere, somehow, I had contracted an almost lethal case of recurring malaria, and a week each month as regular as clockwork I spent in bed, ravaged by fever and too listless to do much but take quinine and have an enlarged spleen massaged by my gentle, distraught mother. Yet in retrospect it was a crucial time in my intellectual development for it was a year of reading and being read to by a dutiful family. Dad introduced me to his great love, English poetry, with a careful explication of texts, and though I did not always grasp the point, I was fascinated by the rhythms, the juxtaposition of words, the various meters. It was my first exposure to the Romantic movement, and in prose, it was then that I met Tom and Aunt Polly, Huck and Jim, Kipling's Kim, not to mention the Rover boys and Tom Swift. I devoured a boy's illustrated adventure magazine which featured the aerial exploits of World War I, with a description of our hero having stuck in my mind to this day: "And as he flung his flimsy aircraft among the Fokkers of the Hun, his chattering Vickers drummed a threnody of death across the Argonne sky." Wow!

The College of Industrial Arts was Dad's first command of an institution of higher education. To be sure, he had to answer to the Board of Regents on major policy initiatives and to the Texas Legislature for biennial appropriations. But to all intents and purposes, it was his ship and his bridge, and he reveled in the challenge and the responsibility. He took his time surveying the situation, meeting personally with every member of the faculty and staff. As a family we frequently ate in the two major dormitory dining rooms until he had made the rounds of each table which seated ten students, beginning a relationship with the student body which I have never seen equaled in terms of warmth and trust. There was a compulsory assembly once a week in the college auditorium which variably opened with the singing of *Moonlight and Roses*, with Dad directing his favorite ballad which became his campus signature.

Dad was dedicated to the idea of the liberal arts, for he was first and foremost a professor of English literature and then a college administrator. Indeed, Dad's principal administrative efforts had been the strengthening of the faculties in the arts and sciences and beefing up the library holdings in support of those disciplines, legitimizing the B.A. and M.A., as well as the B.S. and M.S. degrees.

Yet from the outset there were things which Dad did not admire about the place. To begin with was the name—the College of Industrial Arts—with all its connotations of a trade school, whereas Dad's vision was of a first-class liberal arts college. And in a relatively short time the Board and the State Department of Education approved a change to the Texas State College for Women. So it was TSCW, or "Tessie," as the girls fondly referred to her for the next twenty-five years.

The dress code was another matter. The compulsory wearing of uniforms on campus was stoutly defended in some quarters as preventing discrimination by reason of pecuniary affluence. But it rubbed my mother, among others, the wrong way, for she hated regimentation, and she argued that the code robbed the girls of any individual stylistic expression which they would have to contend with daily once they left college. Why not let them cultivate good taste now was the FFV's contention. Dad was too sanguine to get in the middle of this one; he simply bided his time until slowly but surely a consensus in the student ranks was reached some years later that the uniforms must go. I always regretted that, for I felt that somehow it was for the Tessie girl a badge of distinction. As will be seen, the decision also did severe damage to my economic well-being.

Three of the residential halls were located some distance from the college laundry. I was the possessor of the proverbial little red wagon, and it occurred to me that I might do a brisk business by collecting the students' laundry bags at the dormitories and returning the finished parcels a week later, Saturday being the laundry's designated day for both receipt and delivery. The students' uniforms were then not dry cleaned but washed and ironed and then folded neatly into the laundry package, so business was assured, and at 10¢ a roundtrip I envisaged a small fortune. Dad blessed the enterprise so long as I was polite, issued receipts, and, of course, did not enter the students' living quarters. The idea caught on, and before long I had more business than I could say Grace over. When my sister declined a partnership, I enlisted help from two neighborhood chums, and we kept three wagons fairly flying. Then, crisis!

One Saturday morning there appeared on the scene the neighborhood bully with a wagon more capacious than ours. She was Frances M, two years my senior, tall and gangly with a very pretty face, of French descent, smart as a whip, tough as a boot, and mean as a snake. Her widowed mother eked out a modest existence as a seamstress, abetted by whatever income Frances could bring in through odd jobs, including a paper route which she had taken away from one of my pals by threatening physical mayhem. Unknown to us, she had been observing our laundry delivery service and decided to horn in.

We were furious, not only because of our proprietary claim but also as a girl, she could go inside the dormitories, solicit business from room to room, and offer portal to portal service which was beyond our mandate. I threatened her with every kind of quo warranto proceeding I could think of, including transgression of state property. She in turn threatened to break our wagons—and our heads, if need be, and besides my father didn't own that campus, and she and her mother needed the income more than we did. The situation was salvageable because there was enough business for all, but when the Tessies abandoned the wearing of uniforms and dry cleaning became the vogue, my laundry delivery business went *kaput*.

But my life was so active that I never missed it, except for the income. I found this business of growing up so much fun and so full of surprises that I seemed to run out of time every day. Our home, situated as it was on a college campus, was comfortable and secure and a perpetual source of challenge. Mother with her Virginia upbringing set the tone for gracious living; good manners for her was simply an expression of consideration for others, and we children deviated at our peril.

Early on she heard of a colored family, cotton farmers, with a plethora of children in Pilot Point, a rural village just north of Denton. I drove up with her in the Dodge to introduce herself and state her mission: she badly needed domestic help and could provide lodging, food, a generous salary, uniforms, and an extended horizon. Could she meet the younger children, please? Five of them were called in from the field and lined up according to age: Olivia-20, Eddie Mae-18, William-17, Bessie-15, and Idelle-13. Mother explained that because of her husband's position, there would be a lot of visitors and entertaining but that she would teach them all they needed to know about running a household. A deal was struck: Olivia would come immediately as cook and house-keeper, Bill as houseboy and butler. In the event during our 25 year tenure at TSCW, the girls succeeded one another and Bill went the route. They were without exception bright, willing, superb human beings, and we had in effect yet another joint family.

Further alleviating Mother's household regimen was the fact of the college commissary which supplied the foodstuffs for the campus dining halls. The Purchasing Agent, Claude Castleberry, a tall, pleasant accommodating fellow, presided over one of the largest food accounts in the state, and he knew a good thing when he saw it; he skimmed enough to satisfy his creature comforts but never too much to alarm the auditors. He early on ingratiated himself with Mother, showing her in what form to submit her weekly requirements and assuring her the freshest of this and the most tender of that delivered to her kitchen door. Before long Olivia did all the ordering herself according to the menus that she and Mother concocted. I spent quite a little time in Mr. Castleberry's warehouse, where he always regaled me with how much money he was saving the college and the taxpayers through his shrewd bargaining with the bulk suppliers, and I soon learned the difference between the insiders who called him Claude and the others who addressed him as Mr. His oldest son, a couple of years older than I, was a classmate in high school. Later among the first to be drafted, he was a seaman aboard the USS Arizona at Pearl Harbor thus becoming Denton's first casualty of the Second World War. His father never recovered and actually became demented in his excoriation of draft dodgers, who for him was anyone of age not in uniform.

The education of Olivia and Bill in the refinements of a genteel household was also a great learning experience for Louise and me. Slowly but surely Mother was able to bridge that vast chasm between a cotton patch and the President's Home. Cleanliness and personal grooming, polite responses, "Yes, sir" and "Yes, ma'am" instead of "Yasser" and "Yessum," "You're welcome" if any thanks were proffered. Louise worked with Olivia and I with Bill on reading and writing skills. Preparations for a formal dinner were the most fun, a game which we all played. Flower arrangement, table setting, cutlery, the folding of napkins, glasses, which knife, fork or spoon in what order, soup bowls to be tipped away from, not toward you, service from the left—retrieval from the right, seating arrangements, helping women with their chairs.

To help everyone's perspective, we would reverse roles, with Olivia, Bill, Louise and me taking turns as guests of honor. The drill was to go outside and walk up to the front door, ring the bell, and on being greeted, to identify yourself, enter and take seats in the living room, and with the announcement of dinner, to take your seats as directed, and wait for the blessing. The first time Bill and Olivia were guests, Louise and I were hosts. The bell rang and I opened the front door to find them dressed to the nines.

Bill cleared his throat and announced, "I is tha Revrund William Smith of the Ebenezer Afro Baptist Church, and this is ma best girl fren. Weez come to batize you white sinnuhs."

Amid gales of laughter we carried the thing through, sitting briefly in the living room and then to the dining room where I sat Olivia on my right and Louise did the same with Bill, after which I asked the Reverend Smith to say the blessing. Mother observed the whole proceeding, making suggestions here and there but was generally pleased. She was in deadly earnest about these rehearsals, and before long we all became comfortable with our roles and assured in our responses. For years to come, dinners at the Hubbard home were known to be elegant affairs.

To these young eyes, the CIA campus was a marvelous expanse of greenery, tree-shaded buildings, and ample room for Dan and me to roam. There were 1,500 students in residence, and indeed the college was a self-contained and sufficient community with its own dormitories and dining halls, power plant, laundry, commissary and health service, plus gymnasia, a swimming pool, tennis courts, and even a riding stable. The Main Building, which housed Dad's office, sat atop a small hill and dominated the campus architecturally.

But the building which intrigued him most was the Auditorium, to me a cavernous structure which housed the Music Department and had a seating capacity of 3,000 in its main arena, the site of the once weekly student assemblies and, artistically speaking, of student voice and piano recitals and stage productions of the Speech Department. I well remember during our first year going there frequently with Dad after hours, who would position me at the podium in center stage with a book to read aloud while he stationed himself at various places on the main floor and in the balcony, instructing me to speak normally, loudly, softly, as he checked the acoustics. He generally did not like what he heard, or more properly the difficulty of hearing in too many areas my normal enunciation, and so it was that his first capital project at CIA was the interior renovation of the Auditorium to make it as acoustically perfect as the then state of the art could produce. Since, apart from the assemblies, the student performances played at best to sparse audiences, such a major fiscal outlay became known in several less favored academic areas as "Hubbard's Folly."

On the eve of the annual Texas-Oklahoma football game held in conjunction with the State Fair in Dallas, tradition had it that the OU band would stop en route at CIA for a concert and supper, an event eagerly anticipated by the girls and reveled in by the young musicians, especially the après concert festivities. With the completion of the Auditorium project, and after several dry runs by Dad and me which had pleased him mightily, the first public concert was by this aggregation. To a nearly full house, the OU band—which was usually much better than its football team—gave a spirited performance, after which everyone agreed that the acoustics were superb. So in a sense Dad was vindicated, although seldom were that many people attracted to the place.

It was not long afterwards that while sitting at breakfast Dad made his momentous announcement. He was going to New York City, mission and length of absence unspecified, although the lack of demurral by Mother indicated that she knew what was up. But for Louise and me, just the thought of that kind of journey to that kind of place seemed a tremendous undertaking. On the appointed day we drove Dad to Denton's little depot, which surprising enough was a station stop on the Katy railroad which connected Texas with the Midwest and East. The train was on time, and when its great engine ground to a stop with great emissions of steam, we watched Dad give his luggage to the Pullman porter, wave good-bye, and disappear inside. I was confused by excitement and sadness, and finally consoled by Mother's assurance that he really would return in due course. Which he did.

At dinner that night, he related with considerable fervor the purpose of his trip and its denouement. He had gone to New York to meet with Sol Hurok, America's leading impresario, who had under contract practically every leading performing artist and lecturer on tour in the United States, controlling their appearances through his booking agency. His negotiation with Mr. Hurok went something like this:

"Sir, you have the artists, and I have the seats, 3,000 of them in an acoustically perfect auditorium in a pleasant college setting. As your performers make their way from coast to coast across the southern United States, Denton, Texas, will provide the same kind of convenient and lucrative stop-over as do Chicago and St. Louis farther north. Furthermore, if you will agree that an appearance by one of your artists in Denton precludes another within a 150 mile radius, I will guarantee that every one of those seats will be filled."

The deal was struck, and so it was that the cultural life of the Hubbard family, the students at CIA, and the citizenry of North Texas were magically transformed. I can remember hearing Galli-Curci and Enrico Caruso at The University of Texas without the slightest notion of who or what I was listening to. But now my baptism in the arts was about to begin, and it was total immersion. The parade of the world's greatest performers began in the fall of 1928 and continued unabated for the twenty-three years that Dad was president of the institution, and it wrought major changes in the life of the college and all of those who were privileged to partake.

More intimately, there was also a change in the Hubbard household. The President's home was a spacious, rambling but comfortable two-story frame structure in the center of the campus, presided over with exquisite grace by my mother, Virginia bred and as patrician as ever came down the pike. Denton at this time boasted only one hotel, nondescript in character and frequented mainly by travelling salesmen. Mother realized immediately that these accommodations were quite unsuitable for the likes of Lily Pons, Rosa Ponselle and other luminaries in the Hurok galaxy likely to appear on our campus, so she supervised an extensive renovation of our home, converting an upstairs wing into an apartment with a small sitting room, a commodious bedroom and a modern bath.

So it was that the individual artists, with or without spouse, who generally arrived the day before and departed the day after the performance, briefly became part of the Hubbard family, which meant among other things exposure to the Hubbard children. That was what Louise and I reveled in, for with rare exception we were more than tolerated. Dinners were memorable. Not only was the table laden with the exceptional Southern fare that only our gifted cook, Bessie, could produce—Virginia ham, fried chicken, spoon bread, black-eyed peas, yams, mustard greens (which for some unfathomable reason today is called "soul food"), the conversation was exhilarating. Dad was no mean raconteur, and on each occasion the faculty department chairman—be it piano, voice, speech, dance, literature, history, political science—most relevant to our guest would be present. And after dinner we would all repair to the living room for coffee and more talk until our guest retired. Naturally, each visitor was different—but exciting, and no two kids ever got a more liberal education.

Dad, Mom, Amelia Earhart, and her husband, George P. Putnam

Robert Frost became an annual fixture, sometimes staying for a week. William Cowper Powys talked of things I really didn't understand. John Butler tucked me in bed one night with anecdotes of American history, including the dubious authenticity of Paul Revere's ride. Lily Pons simply sparkled. Vladimir Horowitz in his American debut gave his second concert with us, and some years later on his return after his struggle with tuberculosis insisted that Denton be on his itinerary. Amelia Putnam, nee Earhart, with her unbelievably stuffy husband, en route to California for her last, tragic flight, insisted on taking her coffee sitting on the living room floor—but only if I would sit next to her. Lord Robert Cecil talked about the futility of the League of Nations—partially his creation—without the presence of the United States. And so it went.

My first exposure to Shakespeare on stage was by the Ben Greet Players, and I liked Falstaff far better than Hamlet. I could barely await the return of the Vienna Boys Choir, listening enthralled until intermission, when I wandered backstage and saw a furious Herr Director slap one of his prodigies until the tears came, presumably for missing a note. So I was not always titillated by what I saw and heard in that wondrous auditorium, although it had become a mecca of the performing arts for a vast region. The 150 mile prohibition ensured that every seat was at a premium, and the good people of Dallas and Fort Worth and even as far north as Oklahoma City found their way to Denton if they were lucky enough to procure tickets. Indeed, John Rosenfield, the distinguished arts critic of the *Dallas Morning News*, almost had to take up permanent residence with us. Still, a Saturday afternoon matinee by Ted Shawn and Ruth St. Denis had a baleful effect on my private life.

Apart from these formal occasions, which steadily increased in frequency, life at home was a relaxed affair. Without guests, the meal hours were inviolable—breakfast at 7, lunch at 12, dinner at 6—and following dinner, family prayers. Then the games began, much to the delight of my deaf Aunt Mercy, who was very good at Flinch, Hearts, Fan Tan, Rummy, and Dominoes. Mother and Dad were especially keen on auction bridge, and Louise and I had no option but to learn, which was no chore for we both took to the game avidly and before long formed a pretty tough partnership against our parents.

Another game Dad thoroughly enjoyed was billiards, and there was a table in the Faculty Men's Lounge, where he introduced me to the use of chalk to put English on the cue ball and the delicacy of the masse and carom. He was good and I seldom beat him, but he taught me enough to make a few bobs at snooker when I went to college. He was also an avid if not accomplished golfer, and since Denton boasted a Country Club with a decent nine-hole course, he joined for his infrequent games with me, of course, as his caddy. He gave me a set of cut-down clubs, and I played more often with Shorty Knox, the Junior High football coach, who installed me as his quarterback largely, as I suspected, because of my access to the golf course. The club on occasion hosted a caddie tournament with invitations issued to towns in the vicinity. I played in it just once, when I was thirteen. I found myself paired against a dour, beady-eyed little cuss from Fort Worth named Ben Hogan, and although I soon discovered his game was from another planet—I did halve one hole—what I most vividly recall is that even then he was a relentless competitor who never smiled or spoke a word during the massacre and looked at me only to glare.

On occasion Dad would invite Claude Castleberry and Prof. Jackson over for a male evening of dominos. Prof, a fine teacher of Political Science, was locally famous as a raconteur and tippler, and Dad would invariably remind him, "Prof, you can't take a drink in this house on this campus because it's against the State law," with the invariable rejoinder, "Don't worry, Prexy, I've already had enough to get me through this domino game." As a matter of fact, Dad never claimed to be a teetotaler, but ever mindful of his position, he said simply that he would "never take a drink in this county." To my knowledge he broke that rule only once, on the occasion of my return from a summer sojourn in Europe, lugging an Edam cheese, which he loved, from Amsterdam and two bottles of genuine French champagne.

"We should ice it quickly," he said, "for it would be a shame to waste it after you have brought it so far, and it does go well with Edam."

This is not to say, however, that there was never any alcohol on the premises. Some years later after the Moore family had moved to Denton, Bert and Vin, my cousins, had learned how to make home brew, set up a small still in the woods east of town, bottled the stuff and stored it in the attic of our garage with the connivance of Bill and me. One hot Sunday afternoon I was up in my little carpenter shop over the garage, and suddenly I thought I heard machine gun fire. The whole batch of home brew had blown and bottle caps were flying in every direction. Fortunately my parents were not at home and Bill and I managed to clean up the stinking mess. As for Bert and Vin, they were merely sore as hell at the loss of their labor but did agree that another cache might be more suitable.

As previously mentioned, my father had played football at The University of Texas where he earned the sobriquet of "Choo Choo" (he hit you like a runaway locomotive), and in 1902 he was selected as All-Southwestern end. He remained the most avid sports enthusiast of my acquaintance. So it was probably in subliminal emulation of my father's devotion to sports that upon entering Denton Senior High School I tried out for the varsity football team, bringing with me little talent and less hope. I, too, soon had a sobriquet, although slightly different from Dad's: one afternoon at practice the coach remarked that because I was such a lightweight, if I ever stepped on a piece of chewing gum on the football field, I would be stuck to the spot for the rest of the game. From then on I was called "Double Bubble."

Coach Stanton, who was also our mathematics teacher, was a kindly but forlorn man because the paucity of ability among his reserves left him no option but to install me as the quarterback of the second team. In truth, I was more like the team mascot than an effective participant. Nonetheless, we had a pretty good first string with Johnny Stovall and Shorty Hester as mobile running backs and Owen Hussey anchoring a decent line. The big game of the year was against the hated Highland Park High, those snobbish city slickers from a posh Dallas neighborhood and perennial contenders for the state championship. We were not given much of a chance, but local interest was so great that the game venue was shifted to the North Texas Teachers' College stadium to accommodate the anticipated crowd.

It was on the Wednesday before the game that Dad fired his salvo. I was informed that I would not be with the team on Saturday but rather that my presence was required at the Ted Shawn-St. Denis recital. It was an incredulous dictum, and I think in all my life I was never more stunned and furious. What could I tell my coach and teammates—that I had to miss THE game because I was watching some sissy in tights leap around the stage like a banshee! But protestations were to no avail. Dad calmly pointed out that I had the rest of my life to play football, but I might never have another opportunity to see America's premier classical dance duo. There was some amelioration to my total exasperation—but not much—when I humorously informed Coach Stanton of the situation, who observed that Dad was probably right and that he would simply tell the team that I was under the weather.

So there I sat fuming in the President's balcony box. "Afternoon of the Fawn" my aching back; although I secretly had to admit that Mr. Shawn was beautifully muscled and proportioned and would probably do very well in the high jump.

Intermission, finally, and it happened. Dad said to me, "It should be about half time at the stadium. Here are the keys to the car which is parked right behind the auditorium. Get out there, and if you get in the game, play well." I flew, suited up in the locker room, and got to my accustomed place on the bench by the start of the third quarter. The first half had been disastrous for us, and the second half began the same way, with Highland Park returning our kickoff for a touchdown. Shortly thereafter, unbelievably, a chant emanated from the stands, "Put Hubbard in! Put Hubbard in!" I couldn't believe my ears, and I looked around to see Dad and two of his friends standing and shouting at the top of their lungs. It seems that he too had fled the Shawn scene after me to meet his friends who were waiting in their car, and here he was—rooting for me. Incidentally, with the game hopelessly lost, Coach Stanton put me in for the last five minutes. Playing safety on defense, I fielded one of our opponent's few punts of the afternoon and returned it twenty yards. In our huddle for the next play, Owen Hussey said, "Bubble, fake a handoff and follow me over right guard," which I did for another ten yards. And that was all that was reportable of my cameo appearance. The important thing was that for Dad and Ted Shawn and Ruth St. Dennis, all was forgiven.

Sunday morning was a busy time for most of my family. We were all duly "baptized" and confirmed Episcopalians, which gave us a distinctly minority status shared with Catholics and Jews. We enjoyed a neat little parish church, St. Barnabas, but because of our small congregation a priest appeared only on alternate Sundays, with a Lay Reader, which my father was, presiding in between. I began my organized religious experience as a lighter of candles and carrier of the cross, then acolyte serving the visiting priests, teacher in Sunday School and then superintendent, and finally as a Lay Reader myself. So St. Barnabas acquired a distinctly Hubbard flavor with Mother chairing the Altar Guild, Louise in the choir, cousin Mary Jane at the organ, and my alternating with Dad in conducting the service. By far our best attended service of the year was the Choral Mass at midnight on Christmas eve, with many of Denton's citizenry outside our congregation present, including our leading dentist, Dr. Hawley and his strikingly beautiful blond daughter, Joy, an older high school classmate and later one of Vogue's leading models.

Some other experiences with the Episcopacy were not so pleasant. Our diocesan see was Dallas, presided over by a jolly toper, Bishop Moore, who became a great friend of my father and honored me occasionally by inviting me to be one of his acolytes in the celebration of High Mass at the Cathedral. In the summer the diocese sponsored a camp for Bible study for two weeks, and I attended once. We used the campus of a preparatory school adjacent to the Cathedral, and we were housed in the school dormitory, vacant for the summer, with the boys on the first floor under the eye of Father Thaxton and the girls on the second floor under the piercing gaze of the redoubtable Deaconess Crain. I had served Father Thaxton, a finely drawn young priest, on his occasional visits to St. Barnabas, so I was not surprised when he invited me to his quarters one evening after dinner. I was surprised and indeed frightened to death at his subsequent laying on of hands; I didn't know much but enough to get the hell out of there. So I struck out at the Cathedral.

In fact, organized religion and I were never much of a match. To be sure I enjoyed my duties as acolyte and lay reader and I liked the service rituals, especially those of High Church. But in terms of creed and belief, I never could buy the Creation, and the Bible for me was simply an exposure at times to great literature, Ecclesiastes being my favorite. But in terms of the church as a refuge for healing and compassion, the Methodists ruined it for me.

The Methodists were by far the largest and most affluent congregation in Denton, and to preside over that flock was a sure stepping stone for advancement. Their manse was a large, comfortable house across the street from our Junior High School, and Billy Tittle, the minister's son, enrolled there at the same time as I. We became close pals, and at lunch break four of us brown-bagged in his room, formed an ultra-secret society, and used congealed gelation as a mimeograph for our cryptic notes which we circulated at school. But three years later his father took a larger calling in Fort Worth. He was replaced by a Reverend Mr. White, whose baggage included an efficacious wife and an unbelievably pretty daughter, Louise, only a year my senior. Louise was perfectly aware of her physical attractions and, as the saying goes, flaunted them, and since we seemed to have in our midst the proverbial preacher's daughter, there was a long line of suitors, including me, in and out of the White residence seeking her favors. Her mother, too, was much in evidence, seeking to convince the male community, at least, that she was also quite a dish. So in staid little Denton, the new minister's arrival had tongues wagging, and White *fille mère* provided plenty of grist.

Toward the end of the high school year, Louise White and some of her chums came up with the idea of the junior class giving a dance in honor of the seniors, which seemed like a splendid notion. The principal of the high school, Red Calhoun, agreed but ruled that since it would not be an official school function, the gymnasium could not be used. No one's home was commodious enough, and since most churches, especially the Methodists, held dancing to be a deadly sin, their properties were out of the question. What to do?

Louise came up with an ideal solution: the Denton Country Club, some five miles south of town, had the requisite space, and as Dad was a member, would I get him to use his good offices, for which she would consent to be my date. He and the Club agreed, with the strict proviso that there be adequate chaperonage. And without a by your leave, Mrs. White took over the arrangements: decorations, refreshment, the music—a jazz combo from North Texas State—and the chaperones. It was a splendid affair, the chaperones were vigilant, and there was very little to-ing and fro-ing to inspect the putting greens. But there was a deep chill in the Methodist community.

The canon against dancing had been wantonly violated, and under the brazen leadership of none other than the minister's wife. Her comportment in the community from the outset had been at best questionable, but this was unforgivable. The demon must be exorcised. The sinner must be publically rebuked and cast out. There were protest meetings, letters to the bishops, and letters to the editor. A few brave souls came to her defense, but the storm would not abate. Finally the beleaguered minister announced an open meeting of the congregation, at which he would address the issue. I accompanied Louise.

Normally when I went to church with her we would concentrate on how many ways we could hold hands undetected during her father's sermon, but that did not seem appropriate now. With his wife sitting in the first row with space notable on each side of her, Mr. White took the pulpit in an atmosphere charged with anticipation. Yes, his wife had sinned. The sin was grievous. The sin could not be forgiven. But as Christians, look into your hearts and souls. Does all this mean that she is beyond redemption? *Ad nauseum, ad nauseum.* He finally ended with this pathetic plea, "Do not condemn her. Pray for her."

Sullen silence.

This was my first exposure to organized hypocrisy. Louise, in tears, and I walked out. The transfer came in six months, but Louise stayed on to finish high school.

My last appearance at St. Barnabas was equally sour. I was home on leave during the war, and on Sunday the whole Hubbard clan, now augmented by another son, ten years my junior, who was much impressed by my naval uniform and its wings of gold and an odd medal here and there, attended services together. Our parish had grown and was now graced with a priest in residence who, after the hymns and prayers for the safety of our armed forces, directed his sermon to me in an effort to impress his most prominent parishioners. It was for love of country, family, and Jesus Christ that I had taken up arms against the Philistines, and if, despite the prayers of everyone assembled, I should not make it, I could pass on secure in the knowledge that as an Anglican, I was a member of the one true church in all the world and as such my salvation was assured.

I did not need my graduate work in the English Reformation to rail against the asininity of such a statement, and I was saddened that my Anglicanism had come to this, after so many pleasant experiences in the companionship of beliefs relatively free of dogma. But ever since I have been in debt to the earnest vicar for providing me with a ready answer to any question about my religious preference, "Oh, I belong to the one true church, the Anglican, with which that splinter group in Rome has never made its peace."

Not all my Catholic friends are amused, but one who gladly enters into the repartee is the Monsignor Clement Connelly, one of my favorite golf companions, who recently accompanied Archbishop Maloney of the Diocese of Los Angeles to the Holy See for his elevation to Cardinal. During the course of a round in which we were partners and in pretty tough competition, he described with wonderment the pomp and circumstance of the ordination ceremony and its utter sublimity, and after he missed a crucial putt, I said, "Jesus, Clem, the next time you visit the Vatican I hope you'll come home by way of Canterbury and get detoxed."

Through a system of academic advancement called "double promotion," I missed the fourth grade as I had the second, so I was fairly sailing through grammar school. One of the classes I liked most was music appreciation, which meshed nicely with my family's proclivity, and I really did not object to my mother's insistence that I take up the piano. The college music department offered a splendid source of instruction, and Miss Kanouse nervously undertook the tutelage of the president's son, neither one of us then comprehended the odds against. I got to the point of at least a recognizable Chopin sonata and produced a spirited rendition of *Pollywog Cakewalk* for my recital in the college auditorium, but two things precluded further progress. In the first place, some obtuse portion of my brain refused to learn how to read music with facility, and only a good ear had got me this far. In the second place, I had discovered baseball.

Every Saturday morning five of us would gather at the home of Roland Laney, which abutted the city park, and whose father owned the Texaco filling station. The others were Robert Goode, whose father was a cobbler; Robert Spear, whose father was our leading surgeon; and Billy Tittle. Membership in this august group required the reading of a book a week, and we would bring our volumes, discuss them, exchange them, and read for an hour. Then we would head for the park with our baseball gear to be joined by our mentor, an older, strapping kid named Wally Craddock, whose dream was to be a major leaguer. We would have pepper games, infield practice, shag fly balls, and take our cuts at Wally's pitches, and I was amazed to find I had some talent for the game. Wally lived right across the street from me, and he would join me after school on weekdays hitting fly balls which I would shag by the hour. We had some neighborhood football games, too, in which I was fair. And all this was at the expense of any systematic piano practice, which today I regret as much as anything I have failed to do.

Junior High School consisted of the seventh and eighth grades, and by the time I got there at age eleven I was a pretty active kid and considered by many of my peers as a smart aleck, first class. The only mitigation was the fact that my sister Louise who preceded me always made the best grades in her classes, so maybe being a smart ass was an inescapable Hubbard trait, and a fawning home room teacher, Margaret Calhoun, didn't help my popularity any. At any rate, Mrs. Calhoun was the school impresario, and she delighted in putting her precocious charges on display at "pay assembly" where for a dime the kids could admire all the talent in their midst. I still had a pretty true soprano voice, and I was matched up with various girls, including Christine Smith, in the rendition of duets such as *Tiptoe Through the Tulips*. Robert Goode and I were popular for our *When Its Springtime in the Rockies* in harmony worked out by my cousin Mary Jane who was our accompanist. And the next year I was paired with a new girl in school with real talent, Louise Tobin, in a catchy new tune, *I'm Confessing*, in a daring routine choreographed by Mrs. Calhoun which involved our holding hands. This was such a hit that we were invited to present it at a Senior High School assembly. Louise and I also represented the school in declamation in the Texas Interscholastic League statewide competition. My rendering of Jeremy Bentham's *Skeleton in the Closet* got mixed reviews, but Tobin won second place with what I thought was the best-modulated voice I ever heard. She went on to become Benny Goodman's featured vocalist and later joined Harry James as vocalist and wife. If she had listened to me, she might have amounted to something as a declaimer.

Another spirited event was the choosing of Junior High's most popular boy and girl. This usually pitted home room against home room, but other pressure groups entered in. Selection was done at an assembly with each vote costing one penny. On this occasion our football team, on which I was the second-string quarterback, was heavily involved because our captain and guard, Owen Hussey, the biggest boy in school, was gaga over one of the girl nominees. Owen had taken me under his wing, and on this occasion, I lobbied earnestly for his candidate. Finally the winner was announced and it was our girl, Miss Clara Lou Sheridan.

Much later during the war when I was stationed on the West Coast, I called Clara Lou (now known as Ann) in Hollywood to remind her of my role in her first step towards stardom. My cousins Bert and Vin and I also spent a lot of time at the Blondell household where the son was a pal of theirs but whose real attraction was his sister, Rosebud, who Hollywood was later to greet as Joan. And on our side of town, the leading student in our Drama Department was a lithesome brunette named Brenda Marshall, whose cinema career was interrupted by her marriage to William Holden. So Denton was not lacking in pulchritude.

Senior High School fairly flew by, and as all schools should be, every day was an adventure. There were wonderful teachers: Miss Tevis in Latin, Sam McAllister in History, Cara Boswell in English Literature, Mrs. Martin in Writing and Composition. Latin was tough going, and Miss Tevis was patiently fighting a losing cause. Indeed, I wound up as the only student willing to tackle a third year, which meant Ovid and Virgil and Cicero. My mastery of composition and grammar was very much like my reading of music—I never really got it, and I managed to spoil Miss Tevis' heroic effort when as Denton High's only entrant in the State Latin contest, I finished dead last. Mr. McAllister, who doubled as basketball coach, raised the red flag of bias in the writing of history, pointing out that the accepted popular versions of Texans at the Alamo and San Jacinto, among other things, would not stand up to scholarly scrutiny. Miss Boswell and Mrs. Martin, who shared a reputation for being humorless and demanding, simply would not tolerate superficial interpretation and shoddy exposition in their classes and any felicity in language with its beauty and precision I owe to them.

I went out for varsity football and still paraded as second string quarterback; it was good discipline and a lesson in teamwork, but Coach Stanton was no magician when confronted with my dearth of skills. There was no organized team, but Saturday mornings I was busy with pick-up games and shagging flies. I worked my way up to become co-editor of the school yearbook, and my opposite number, Mary Lewis, graduated as

Valedictorian and I as Salutatorian. Commencement was held in, of all places, the Methodist church, and afterwards Louise White and I took our diplomas and drove out to Lake Dallas, but the pain was still there. We never met again.

Summers were times to look forward to. One of the great pleasures of the academic calendar was the three-month hiatus, June to September, between the regular scholastic sessions, and as much of this time as his duties permitted, Dad set aside for extended motor trips. An added attraction was the opportunity for Louise and me to improve our driving proficiency since there was relatively sparse highway traffic in those days. The first trip I really remember was to Colorado, driving through the Texas Panhandle, stopping at the fabled Carlsbad Caverns, then across New Mexico and up to Denver, where we had relatives who were really close friends. A week there, and then on to Pike's Peak and finally Estes Park, where we took a spacious cabin for a month of trout fishing, horseback riding, hiking and the like. Glorious.

The next summer we went in the opposite direction to Florida, stopping along the way at various colleges and universities that Dad wanted to look at, such as the Alabama State College for Women at Montevallo, which was headed at the time by President Oliver Carmichael, one of Dad's close friends and colleagues, who later became chancellor of Vanderbilt University and then President of the Carnegie Foundation for the Advancement of Teaching in New York. The next summer was back to Colorado, stopping for a heavenly two weeks at the Canejos Fishing Lodge near Durango, with its large central communal and dining facility surrounded by log cabins set among the aspens and a meandering mountain stream that sang us to sleep at night.

But it was the summer of 1932 that became indelible— California and the Olympic Games. No more ardent sports enthusiast ever lived than my father, and as soon as Los Angeles had been determined as the venue for the Olympiad, Dad secured tickets for the two of us, although the hegira to and from was to be a family affair. So it was up to Denver again for our first stop, then across the Great Divide, the sulphuric run from Needles to Barstow, a week's pause at Yosemite and its glories, then Lake Tahoe and its fabled Emerald Bay, San Francisco, then inland down the San Joaquin Valley all the way to San Diego before turning north up the coast to Long Beach. On the peninsula were only a few scattered home sites and that vista of sky and sea was the most enchanting place I had ever seen. In Long Beach we leased an apartment for a month right on the strand, and there began one of the most exciting times of my existence. Long Beach in itself was a delight, what with its surf, boardwalk, amusement park, and 10¢ cinemas. I had brought along my home-made surf board and just managed not to drown. The Navy was much in evidence, with the aircraft carriers Lexington and Saratoga lying just offshore in honor of the games and taking aboard hundreds of visitors every weekend. Then there were the excursions into the big city, the movie studios, Hollywood and Vine, Pickfair, Grauman's Chinese Theater, The May Company for the ladies, the Hollywood Bowl, the campuses of UCLA, USC and Cal Tech, Pasadena and its orange groves. Endless delight, with the climax yet to come.

Me (Jack), Mom, Dad, Louise, and George, circa 1932

Our Olympic tickets, which were issued in passport-like holders, cost Dad and me $22 and $11 respectively, and gave us entrée to every event held in the Coliseum, which had been enlarged to seat 100,000 spectators. Our seats were on the top row of the southwest sector, a long distance from the track and field, but with the advantage of overlooking the swimming and diving stadium if we stood up and turned around, thereby getting to witness the heroics of Buster Crabbe, Gertrude Ederle and company. I kept a meticulous record of each event, which I perused for years afterward, but in my mind's eye today I can still recall the unfolding drama: Babe Didrikson, the 18 year old girl from Texas, setting records in the 80 meter dash and javelin throw and being disqualified from one in the high jump for using the Western Roll, a technique reserved for males. Eddie Tolan beating Ralph Metcalf, the world record holder, at the tape in the 100 and 200 meter sprints. The effortless grace of Bill Carr in the 400 meter drubbing Blazing Ben Eastman who should have been in the 800 meter, his best distance, and won by Tom Hampson, an unknown from Great Britain. Luigi Beccali of Italy emerging from the pack with a furious finish in the 1500. The fanfare over the public address system announcing the *Ceremonie Olympique Protocolaire*, with flags raised as anthems played for the awarding of medals.

In each Olympiad the host nation selects two demonstration sports as exhibitions, and in this case they were lacrosse and American football. It was my first experience with lacrosse, where an all-star Canadian team mostly of Indians engaged American collegians from Johns Hopkins. The amazing speed, dexterity and endurance of the players was enlivened by the very amusing commentary by Will Rogers on the public address microphone. In the football game, I got my first look at a legendary USC Trojan, Gus Shaver, as he led his Western seniors to a narrow victory over the East. From beginning to end it was heaven for this 13 year old who enjoyed the spectacle almost as much as his father. All in all, and despite my good fortune in attending five subsequent Olympiads, the '32 Games remain the most impressive of my sports-watching career.

The encore summer, 1933, was also memorable and not just because Franklin Roosevelt was in Washington, which would have been reason enough. This time the destination was the World's Fair in Chicago, and then fishing in the Canadian lake country, with the added attraction for me of the presence of my cousin/brother, Bert Moore, by then a collegian at North Texas State. Chicago was an education in itself, what with the Academy of Fine Arts, the Field Museum, the Shedd Aquarium, Soldier's Field, the University, and especially the Adler Planetarium, where for the first time I began to have some conception of the universe. We stayed at the world's largest hotel, the Stevens, and took Lakeshore Drive north past Grant's tomb to Evanston to see the Edgewater Beach Hotel and Northwestern University. Busy days, indeed.

One highlight was a Saturday afternoon double header at Wrigley Field between the Cubs and the St. Louis Cardinals, who were locked in a heated pennant chase. I had cut my teeth on organized baseball in the Texas League, which included the nearby Fort Worth Cats, a Brooklyn Dodger farm team, and the Houston Buffalos, a Cardinal franchise. Whenever they got together in Fort Worth, Dad and I tried to be there because our favorite players were Dizzy Dean, Ducky Medwick, and others of the Gas House Gang who were coming up through the Cardinal chain. Later I remember seeing a 19 year old rookie outfielder named Duke Snyder make his debut for the Cats; his strike outs were thunderous. At any rate, on this particular afternoon in Chicago, Charley Root and Burleigh Grimes, pitching to Gabby Hartnett, were facing Wild Bill Hallahan and Dizzy Dean. Not anticipating the sell-out crowd, we got to the park later than we should have, and the long lines before the ticket windows made it doubtful that we would get inside. Dad gave me some money and told me to try to slip into line closer up, which I managed to do and got the last three tickets sold, which entitled us to sit on the outfield grass with the overflow crowd. I certainly didn't mind for I found myself not ten feet from the famed slugger, Hack Wilson, when the Cubs took the field. Wild Bill was true to his name in the first game, but Dizzy restored order in the second, during which we found some seats in the grandstand—a perfect ending to my first major league games. Could life ever be sweeter?

Every day at the Fair was an adventure in glimpsing at the future, what with the wonders of science and technology presaging things to come. Bert introduced me to my first taste of legal beer at the Schlitz pavilion while I reminded him of our misfortune with his home brew; and Louise and I danced to the music of Ben Bernie at the Pabst Blue Ribbon Casino. One of the highlights was the landing in Lake Michigan of a squadron of Italian seaplanes under the leadership of the colorful Italo Balboa, greeted by the tumultuous cheers of thousands of spectators. Chicago, Chicago, a wonderful town, indeed.

We bid a reluctant farewell and headed north to Ely, Minnesota, gateway to Canada's fishing paradise and where we made our arrangements to stay at the Lodge on Basswood Lake. There were boats and guides who introduced us to the adventure of trolling for great northern and walleyed pike, and pulling into little coves for a lunch of fresh fillets broiled over an open fire. Once to my positive delight we were joined by a real Canadian Mountie in his resplendent uniform. We did not know that this was the last such outing for the Hubbard household, but it had been such a wondrous summer that we were all saddened when it came time to begin the long trek back to Texas. I was, however, looking forward to my senior year in high school.

Upon graduation in June 1934, my summer was quite different from the previous two. The father of one of Dad's favorite students at TSCW was a cattle rancher in west Texas who operated a small spread south of San Angelo. She arranged for me to be taken on as a hired hand, and so for a couple of months I was to be a cowboy, no less.

The bus from San Angelo south to Rock Springs and Del Rio dropped me off at the gate into the ranch, with the main house about a quarter of a mile from the highway, where my new employer was waiting for his daughter and me with a wagon. The house was a rambling frame structure which featured a long veranda in front with a swing and some rocking chairs. I was given a small bedroom with a chest of drawers and an adjacent bathroom, and I was to eat with the family at the table at one end of a large kitchen. There was one other hand on the place who lived in the bunkhouse, and he showed me the barn and stable area, outlined my chores such as milking and feeding the two cows, and then introduced me to my horse and saddle gear. The ranch was about 200 acres, running some white face cattle but mostly sheep, and the next morning the rancher and I took a ride over the layout, where he pointed out that my principal duties were a daily inspection of the fences, noting repairs to be made, and to inspect the stock, especially the calves and lambs, for any infestation of the dreaded screw worms, the plague of every ranch in west Texas. This was all very exciting, and I was going to live closer to the land than at any other time since Cedar Crest. But it didn't last long—two days, as a matter of fact.

My new boss was a short, wizened, sunburned, tobacco chewing son of the soil with a limited vocabulary, his daughter being the only member of the family with a formal education, and a rock-ribbed conservatism stemming from inclination and circumstance, and also, I discovered, a monumental temper. It all began at the supper table the second evening when the conversation got around to President Roosevelt and what seemed to me to be the courageous and enlightened measures such as the NRA in an attempt to alleviate the depression and restore the nation's confidence. My peroration had caught him with a mouthful on which I thought he would choke. His bronzed face became red as a beet, he began to splutter and finally found his voice that spewed out a torrent of invective against those citified professors who'd never done a day of honest work taking over Washington and conjuring up insane legislation which forced honest farmers and ranchers to plow under their crops and slaughter their livestock. They were thieves, that's what they were, no, they were worse than thieves because you could shoot a thief. They were a bunch of ignorant high-binders with nothing but contempt for the folks who worked their asses off to feed this country. And if I thought they were so almighty wonderful then by God I could get the hell off his property because no smart-assed little punk of a New Dealer was going to sleep under his roof.

His wife and daughter tried to calm him to no avail, and still livid, he stormed into my room, seized my meager belongings and suitcase and threw the whole passel out on the veranda. Scared out of my wits and fearing physical mayhem, I scurried out of the kitchen door and headed for the barn, where I spent the night after watching the ladies retrieve my bits and pieces. The next morning the daughter, embarrassed to tears, took me in the wagon to the highway, where I hailed the first bus for San Angelo.

CHAPTER 2
—
Louise, We've Got to Go!
or
Elements in a Liberal Education

I was a sophomore in college, home on Spring break, when Edna St. Vincent Millay made the first of her three appearances at TSCW. Louise and I met her and her husband, a pheasant fancier from Connecticut, at the depot and collected their mountain of luggage. At the President's home, Mother greeted them with her customary warmth and led them directly upstairs to the guest quarters. I was following with two suitcases, so I witnessed what happened.

After a cursory inspection of the rooms, Miss Millay turned to Mother and said, "My dear, this simply won't do. I find the place utterly claustrophobic." The touch of crimson in Mother's cheeks told me of the depth of the wound to her FFV rearing, but without hesitation she apologized for the inadequacy of the apartment, especially since it was the best she could offer but that other arrangements would be made to their satisfaction and in the meantime would they try to make themselves as comfortable as possible and would they like any nourishment before her appearance at 8 o'clock.

"Some ice, if you please, and perhaps sandwiches and tea around seven."

After we retreated, Mother's only comment was, "Well, never in my born days!" and instructed me to get busy with Plan B. We knew that a grand new hotel, the Blackstone, had recently opened in Fort Worth, and I called to reserve its most sumptuous suite and to alert them to the celebrity of their guests-to-be. Louise and I would drive them over after her performance. In the meantime, Miss Millay sequestered herself while Louise gave her husband a walking tour of the campus, finding him most amiable.

At the appointed time we walked to the auditorium, which was jammed with a standing room only crowd. Naturally every Tessie who was ambulatory was there. Dad and Miss Millay walked on stage together, and after his introduction, the house lights were dimmed and she stood alone at the podium, illuminated by a single spotlight.

She wore a black velvet full length gown which accentuated the paleness of her features. Indeed she seemed positively fragile except for blazing piercing eyes that seemed to penetrate every niche and cranny of the vast hall. Without having spoken a word, hers was a mesmerizing presence that pervaded the place; she knew it and we wanted her to sense our obeisance. I said to myself that I wouldn't have missed this for all the football games in the world. And then she began to read. From "The Harp Weaver," from "Fire and Ice," etc, etc, etc.

After each passage she explained the circumstances leading to that particular composition and the message she hoped to convey. The timbre of her voice was clear as crystal with a resonance remarkable for so slight a figure, and her enunciation and modulations were superb. In the midst of one reading, a gentleman in the audience began to cough. She stopped, clutched her gown with her right hand—and stared. The poor fellow did not realize that because of the spotlight, she could not see beyond the proscenium, but he was painfully aware of the fixity of her gaze; a shuffling of feet told of an embarrassed exit.

For forty-five minutes she held her listeners in thrall, and after a short intermission she came back to the podium and turned to her sonnets, especially those—perhaps because of the Tessies present—dealing with the joy and agony of love. My God, how she could write, and how she could read. At the end the applause was rapturous and continued until Dad had to come on stage and beg her to leave explaining that she still had a journey to make that evening. Miss Millay had certainly appeared before more sophisticated audiences, but none would ever receive her more warmly.

After we walked home, she and her husband changed to their traveling clothes, and we gathered in the dining room for a light supper. She was, of course, seated on Dad's right and asked that I be seated on her right, telling Mother with a laugh that she liked being surrounded by the Hubbard men. I don't know what Dad thought of that remark, but it perked me up considerably. Her whole demeanor had changed: she was in high spirits, chatty, even elfin, like a little girl who had just finished successfully her first recital. She smoked a lot while dabbling at her food, but there was no reason to doubt her protestation that she hoped she could return. After coffee, and with the luggage stowed in the car, she thanked everyone, being particularly solicitous to Mother, who might just have forgiven her. We then went out to our new Hupmobile, with Louise and the husband sitting in back and Miss Millay in front with me.

The night was dressed for the occasion. A huge, luminescent full Texas moon was just clearing the horizon, and it lay directly in our path to Fort Worth, making my headlights redundant. From the rear I could hear the conversation about the travails of raising pheasants, but up front there was silence. She sat very quietly against the car door with the window rolled down, apparently lost in some reverie and moving only to light cigarettes two at a time, one of which she gave to me. Maybe it was the moon. Except for one hill halfway *en route*, the highway traversed a perfectly flat plain, and when we topped that hill, we could suddenly see the lights of Fort Worth sparkling in the distance. She gasped, slid over against me as close as she could get, and grasped my leg just above the knee with both her hands.

"What is that?" she asked, with lips trembling. "What are those lights?"

I was also startled, but only by her propinquity, and I replied in as normal a voice as I could muster, "Why, those are the lights of Fort Worth, our destination, and somewhere among them is your hotel."

Silence. And then, "Jack, wouldn't it be strange that when we get to those lights, Fort Worth isn't there?"

It was not a question I had anticipated, but I replied as convincingly as I could, "Yes, ma'am, it would be strange indeed, but I don't think we have anything to worry about. I've made this trip many times, and Fort Worth has always been there."

And so it was. But for the remainder of the journey, she never budged an inch nor relaxed her grip except to light our cigarettes.

Although it was nearly midnight when we reached the Blackstone, the hotel manager and his staff were there to roll out the red carpet. After the fulsome greetings and with the luggage whisked away, it was clearly time for Louise and me to take our leave. But at the mention of it, Miss Millay turned on me.

"You will not go now," she commanded. "You must come up for a desperate cigarette!"

I looked at Louise, who suggested that at this late hour and after such a long and demanding day, our remaining would be an imposition.

"Nonsense, my dear," replied the great lady, "I have asked you to stay."

Whereupon she led us inside. In the elevator I surreptitiously held Louise's hand, seeking some assurance against a growing sense of unease.

We decamped at the Executive Suite. This was my first experience with hotel accommodations so luxurious and spacious, and I could now understand the discomfiture at the relatively meager digs we had offered. Louise and I were directed to a large sofa while Edna scoured around for glasses and her husband lugged a sizeable portmanteau and laid it flat on the coffee table. Then she undid the straps, flipped it open, and there on top of the clothes was a bottle of White Horse Scotch. Now thanks to my older cousins I had been exposed to home brew and white lightning, but this was another first for me, a genuine bottle of Scotch whisky. She poured out four dollops with no ice, no nothing, and raised her glass. Louise tasted, I swallowed, and only my cigarette dampened the fire in my throat. My eyes began to water and I turned my head to try to avert her gaze, but she just smiled, poured more Scotch in my glass and said, "Now, now, Jack, this lovely stuff is to sip, not gulp. Bring your drink into the bedroom and help me with the suitcases." Not being sure I could, I was happy to stand up and follow her. In my growing confusion, I guess I would have followed her anywhere.

There was indeed a bed, seemingly larger than life—and off the bedroom, a balcony staring straight at that moon. We stood there gazing out on a sleeping Fort Worth that was still in place, and then with a cigarette in one hand and the Scotch in the other, I turned to her, unbelieving. For how long I'm really not sure when she excused herself, telling me not to move, and I was thankful for the balcony rail. I only sensed the soft, gliding rustle of her return, but there she was in that delicate white lacey stuff. Jesus Christ, what to do now? My stomach was churning, my heart throbbing, my throat ablaze, my head a confusion of emotion, Scotch and fear. She put her hands on my shoulders, holding me at arms-length, looked up at me, closed her eyes, and began:

> *What lips my lips have kissed and where and why*
> *I have forgotten, and what arms have lain*
> *Beneath my head til morning . . .*

I could stand it no longer, and like a frightened lamb desperate for its mother, I broke and ran.

Bursting into the sitting room where my sister and the husband were still quietly talking, I blurted, "Louise, we've got to go!" Seeing my distress, she arose immediately, apologizing for such an unseemly departure. The husband—who knew all along what I was up against—was the gentleman to the end, thanking us for our courtesies as he opened the door. In the corridor waiting impatiently for the elevator, I was afraid to look back. But no one followed us.

When we got to the car, Louise took the wheel, found an all-night café for coffee, and drove us home. I told her as best I could what had happened, and at the end she could only say, "What an extraordinary evening! Not that it matters, but who will believe us?" In the depth of my humiliation of the moment, how could I know that it would matter to one pilgrim for a long time to come. Her own words had told me:

> *Time does not bring relief. You all have lied.*
>   *Who said that time would ease me of my pain?*
> *I miss her in the weeping of the rain,*
>   *I want her at the shrinking of the tide.*
> *The old snows melt on every mountainside*
>   *and last year's leaves are smoke in every lane,*
> *But last year's bitter loving must remain*
>   *Heaped on my heart, and my old thoughts abide.*
>
> *There are a hundred places where I fear*
>   *To go, so with her memory they brim.*
> *And entering with relief some quiet place*
>   *Where never fell her fact or saw her face,*
> *I say there is no memory of her here –*
>   *And so stand stricken, so remembering her.*

CHAPTER 3
—
The Summer of 1938

At the Harvard commencement exercises on 5 June 1948, General George C. Marshall, then Secretary of State, was awarded an honorary degree. He chose this occasion to enunciate a daring program of massive economic assistance to war-ravaged Europe, since styled the Marshall Plan, which Churchill would later ascribe as "one of the least sordid acts in history." Dean Acheson, our brilliant Under-Secretary of State at the time and a Yale man, had objected to the selection of this venue for a policy statement of such import, not because it was Harvard, but for the very sensible reason that no one ever listened to commencement addresses, especially those for whom they were intended. And I can personally attest to the soundness of Mr. Acheson's logic, for of the hundred or so commencement speeches that I have either delivered or been forced to listen to, there is only one that remains steadfastly in my memory.

The time was 5 June 1938, ten years to the day before General Marshall's pronouncement. The occasion was my own undergraduate commencement from The University of Texas at Austin. The speaker was Howard Mumford Jones, Distinguished Professor of Literature at Harvard and himself an alumnus of UT.

As the Class of '38 ruminated about the kind of world we would be stepping into, our prospects seemed dreary at best. At home, the nation was still in the throes of the Great Depression, despite all rhetoric and attempted nostrums of the New Deal. Most of my male classmates had had to work their way through college at whatever odd jobs they could find. My salvation was a Magnolia filling station where my average wage was $2 a day, for which I was thankful, and the stakes at my Saturday night poker forays were whether I could afford a date next week. But I was among the fortunate; my father was a college president with a handsome annual salary of $7,500 from which he happily provided my room and board, but as an object lesson, spending money was mine to earn. And during those four collegiate years, whenever foreign affairs intruded into a conversation, our elders were for the most part isolationists, unpersuaded by President Roosevelt's progressively determined but carefully understated warnings that grave dangers for the free world, including us, lay ahead if totalitarianism continued unabated.

Our class was not loathe to look abroad as part of the world we were entering, but there our prospects seemed even dimmer. The world we saw was dominated by dictatorships: Hitler in Germany, Mussolini in Italy, Stalin in Russia, and Tojo in Japan. Just in our collegiate lifetime we had seen Japan launch her Greater East Asian Co-Prosperity Sphere by seizing Manchuria by the throat and then invading China proper, culminating in the capture of Shanghai and the unspeakably cruel rape of Nanking.

We had seen Mussolini avenge an old Italian defeat at Adowa by swarming into Ethiopia and derisively demonstrating that tribesmen on horseback were no match for aerial bombardment, tanks, machine guns, flame-throwers and poison gas. We watched in despair the League of Nations' reaction to these events, proving itself worse than useless by convincing the dictators that there would be no organized resistance to future aggression. Indeed, we watched and heard on the newsreel when Haile Selassie, the only head of state ever to address that hapless body, after pleading for air, pronounce the League's epitaph with his pathos-ridden last sentence, "... God and history will remember your judgment."

We had seen Austria disappear in the Anschluss under the goose-stepping boots of Hitler's Reichswehr. We had borne witness to the formation of the Rome-Berlin Pact, the Anti-Comintern Pact. We were watching General Franco and his Fascist allies decimate republican Spain, aided only by Russia's spurious support; and after Guernica, the first city ever wholly destroyed from the air, and this by the Luftwaffe's Condor Legion, we saw more than one of our colleagues driven by despair to the futility of the International Brigades.

And what of our erstwhile democratic allies? There was Great Britain, still trying to recuperate from horrendous losses in the Great War, impoverished in physical, material and emotional resources, still trying desperately to hold together Empire and Commonwealth, her Royal Throne barely surviving the assault of an American tramp, dangerously under armed, especially in the air, and now under the tutelage of an honest, sincere, strait-laced, able but totally unimaginative Prime Minister, Neville Chamberlain, who had become convinced that appeasement of the dictators held the only glimmer of hope for his nation's security.

And there was France, also trying to recover from even greater losses in the 1914-1918 holocaust and having totally misread all the lessons of that war, now standing numbly in defensive posture behind the vaunted unassailability of her Maginot Line, backed by supposedly the best army in Europe under the leadership of the most brilliant General Staff extant. Yet any disinterested observer of the French scene in the 1930's could discern that she was floundering, that the venality of her politicians and the endless succession of governments had robbed her of any sense of national unity and purpose, that her army was a hollow shell, lacking organization, discipline and élan, and that the General Staff was a mere congeries of ego-driven, posturing charlatans, an embodiment of their chief, General Gamelin, himself.

Hitler's first great gamble, the invasion of the Rhineland in 1934 in direct violation of the Treaty of Versailles, without the slightest counter-response, proved beyond peradventure the lack of French—and British—resolve. So Britain and France, individually and collectively, seemed to us bewilderingly slender reeds in the defense of democracy. And this, less than twenty years after the guns had gone silent in November 1918, less than a month before I was born.

All this Professor Jones had in mind as he addressed us in our black gowns and mortar boards on that sunny June morning. He went straight to the point. We were facing a world that seemingly grew more irrational day by day, but we must not lose faith in and forsake the enduring qualities of reason. If their ends, as well they might, seemed totally irrational to us, the dictators were establishing their noxious tyrannies by rational means. When Hitler, for example, at a Nazi party congress, launched into one of his impassioned, mesmerizing tirades, his arguments had been rationally chosen and rehearsed for their effectiveness. Herr Goebbels' masterful propaganda machine was a model of rational organization, application, and the effectiveness of repetition. Mussolini's flamboyant gesturing and the stridency of speech as he bounced along the balcony of the Palazzo Venezia were rationally calculated to inflame the Italian hubris. The simplistic slogan: "He made the trains run on time." was a rational palliative to deep-seated discontent. Stalin's brutal programs and mass butcheries, such as the massacre of the Kulaks, though terrible to contemplate, were a rational means to silencing dissent. Japan's ascendency in the Far East was the result of meticulous planning and execution. The results, Professor Jones paused to note, could not always be anticipated; the rape of Nanking, for example, was nothing but the sheer, unadulterated orgy of innate cruelty gone berserk, illustrative of the frightfulness abroad in our world.

"So the problem that your generation—and what is left of mine—faces is not the disappearance of reason, per se," he continued, "but that the dictators have abandoned reason in determining not their means but their ends. Here the operative words are greed and guile, the voracious lust for power. History, however, tells us repeatedly that irrationality cannot withstand the rule of reason, steadfastly applied. The Inquisition, for example, no longer awaits the non-believer. The sole objective of your formal education thus far has been to endow you with the tools of reason, and your presence here today indicates that at least you have begun the mastery of those tools. Now the future depends entirely on the persistence, the passion with which you apply those tools in defense of the free world."

So, our future was to be a dogfight, and what we had unmistakably heard was an intellectual call to arms and a battle flag on which was writ large, "The tools of reason and the passion for the fray." And I wanted to shout. "Take that, Messrs. Chamberlain et Daladier. Take that, Senators Burton and Wheeler, Take that, Joe Kennedy and Charles Lindberg!" And what added immeasurably to my excitement was the knowledge that before long I would be seeing the "battlefield" at close hand.

Harry Fulweiler was a fraternity brother in Delta Kappa Epsilon and one of my closest friends, who at age 21 was two years my senior. He stood barely 5' 7" but had a stocky build, with a shock of wavy blond hair, an infectious smile, and was fairly bursting with energy. Short girls thought he was a dream, and taller ones wanted to give him elevator shoes. His 1938 red Ford convertible did not diminish his popularity. Sober, he was about as attractive as a guy could be, but like many people of short stature, he carried a chip on his shoulder which became evident when he got on the outside of too much beer, and he would invariably try to pick a fight with the "biggest man in the bar". What saved him from utter destruction was his well-practiced habit of choosing a sufficient number of tall and muscular chaps as his drinking companions. At any rate, sometime during the course of our final semester we conceived the idea that the perfect graduation gift from our parents would be a trip to Europe, and during the Easter break we drove in his car first to his home in Abilene and then to mine in Denton to promote a "poor students' grand tour." We had done our homework and had discovered what seemed to be a perfect vehicle in a tour sponsored by the Students' International Travel Association (SITA) which would take us to Britain, Holland, Germany, Italy, Switzerland and France for $699 for everything, including ocean transportation on the Holland-American Line's new flagship, the *SS Nieuw Amsterdam*. Our parents had not only been amenable but enthusiastic, and so it was that as Harry and I sat together listening to Professor Jones, it was with a heightened sense of self-interest.

Our tour group was to rendezvous in New York before our sailing day of 16 June, which gave Harry and me time for a fairly leisurely drive through the Southeast and then up the East coast. We fell into a speed trap in a North Carolina hamlet, where we were hauled up before a drunken county judge who demanded $25 or a night in jail, but otherwise the trip went well. Thanks to my father's penchant for extended summer automobile tours, I was a pretty seasoned traveler, but this was my first experience in the Northeast. We stopped for two days in Washington, D. C. which we found astonishingly impressive and worked very hard at seeing the sights. It also gave me the chance to call upon Commissioner Walter Splawn, a former president of UT. who had appointed Dad as his Dean of Students and who had been subsequently named by Roosevelt to the Interstate Commerce Commission. Our families had remained close, and on this occasion he invited me to return to Washington the following year as his private secretary, on the proviso that I would have completed my M.A. degree. Then the drive into New York City was a real adventure, but we finally made it to our hotel without injury, Holland Tunnel and all.

Dad had suggested that we stay at the Biltmore Hotel at 43rd and Madison, noted for its reduced rates to collegians and under whose fabulous clock God knows how many Ivy Leaguer's had begun their amorous adventures. The first thing we did was get rid of the car—New York was awesome enough without having to drive in it, and we found a garage in the vicinity which would store it for the summer. Then, armed with a map, we took to the streets—two fresh young college graduates on the loose in the world's greatest city.

We first headed for Broadway and there, within sight of the clock on the Woolworth Building, we found a little bistro called the Silver Dollar which was notable for three things: a huge shrimp cocktail for 25¢, draft beer for 10¢ a copious mug, and a jukebox loaded with Benny Goodman's latest releases. This, we concluded, was about as near to Heaven as we were likely to get and the Silver Dollar became our headquarters. Yes, we did all those things we were supposed to do—the Met, Carnegie Hall, the Public Library, Central Park, up the Chrysler Building, up the Empire State, Rockefeller Center, St. Patrick's. We mastered the subway to the Polo Grounds to see the Giants play the Cardinals. It was hard work but it was glorious, every minute of it.

The highlight of this adventure was to be the return bout at Yankee Stadium between Joe Louis, the Detroit Brown Bomber and Max Schmeling, the German heavyweight champion who in their first fight had given his younger opponent a memorable boxing lesson. This return engagement was being billed as the fight of the decade, of the century, maybe of all time, and the sporting world was transfixed at the prospect. Harry's father through a banking friend in New York had somehow managed tickets for us, and we scrambled aboard the uptown express at Grand Central about as excited as two youngsters can get. Why, just to see Yankee Stadium would have been thrill enough. The crowd disgorged at 125th Street station, sweeping us with it. We had trouble finding the right entrance, and then the right section, and then the right aisle, all the while hearing the announcements and introductions booming from ringside. Never had we seen such an arena and such a crowd. Finally we were headed for our seats when the bell sounded for Round 1. But before we could get to them, the fight was over; Louis had come out of his corner like a panther and demolished the German in something like two minutes, and we had never seen a blow struck! But the whole spectacle had been worth it, we concluded back at the Silver Dollar, for we had been physically present where history was being made even if we hadn't actually seen it.

The day before departure we met our tour group, headed by Dr. Collie Sparkman, a kind of Chipsean professor of French at the University of Alabama and a SITA veteran; there were nine girls and six boys, all recent graduates and the rest were parents of some of our group who had decided to come along. It all seemed amiable enough, but as Harry was quick to observe, pulchritude was in very short supply; one red-head seemed promising but, of course, she was one of those with parents.

The next morning Harry and I joined Dr. Sparkman in a cab for the Holland-American berth in Hoboken, and as we drove up, there rode our ocean liner sparkling in the sun, immense, beautiful. For two country boys from Texas, this was breathtaking, the simple act of going aboard memorable. Given the price of our passage, our cabin had to be deep in the ship's bowels; it was small, with two bunks one above the other, two chairs, some hanging space, a basin and a toilet, with the baths and showers not too far away; but it was so neat and trim that after four years of living in a fraternity house, we decided it had to be uncomfortable.

Then the loudspeakers blared the "going ashore" signal, there was the usual last minute flurry of activity but it was all new to us—the hurried good-byes, the band, the confetti, the frantic waves to those ashore, and finally the deep-throated blast from her foghorn as the tugs eased her out into the Hudson River. And, of course, no one left the rails until one of the greatest sights in the world hove into view, our Lady of Liberty. "Harry," I said, "honest and truly we are on our way!"

We sized up our travel group pretty quickly as being nice enough but without much sparkle, so we saw little of them except at mealtime; and although we must have seemed much of the time as typically loud, boorish Texans, we found plenty of fun-loving Rovers aboard who put up with us. We were into all the deck sports, usually as partners, and we won more than our share of matches. I suppose we were typical neophytes on our first ocean voyage, all over the place and into everything, and we ran out of time every day.

There were a lot of recent college graduates aboard, most of them from the northeast. I was really smitten by a stunning blond from Boulder, but alas she was 24 and out of my league, being far more interested in the ship's younger officers. But nowhere could I find any expression of real concern for the state of the world. These were essentially people on a summer holiday and for most of our age group this was their first trip to Europe, the Europe of the guide books, and all anticipating the wonders of London and Paris and Vienna and Rome that lay ahead. Spain, of course, was out of bounds, but as far as anyone knew, Americans were still welcomed everywhere else. War, or the possibilities thereof, apparently was the last thing on anyone's mind, if, indeed, the thought occurred at all. So with this glorious ship, calm seas and bright skies, the festive mood was genuine and unabated.

As the social patterns began to shake down, Harry and I found ourselves more and more in the company of three comely Wellesleyites who had also just graduated; they were not part of a structured tour but were to follow an itinerary worked out by a New York travel agent which reflected their parents' tastes and means. It was our first exposure in depth to the Ivy League ethos and their first to Texans, and despite some uncomfortable fits and starts, we decided they weren't really snobs and they decided we weren't really crude bumpkins. In stature, one of them just fitted Harry, while either of the others suited me just fine, but it early became apparent that they had taken an oath, probably in blood, that no two of them were going to walk the deck with prospective swains and leave the other unattended. So in the evenings, at the bar or while dancing in the lounge, we were constantly on the lookout for a compatible third mate, but we never seemed to find one with any staying power. At any rate, the five of us became fast friends, and as we neared Plymouth, where we were all disembarking, we sat up one night for a serious comparison of itineraries in the hope of finding points of juncture along the way, particularly since they had considerable flexibility which we lacked. We found that early on we would have a two-day overlap in London, but the next possible rendezvous would depend on their willingness to see less of Berlin and its environs in favor of a trip down the Rhine. If so, we could meet at Mainz and pick up a river steamer there; and secure in the feeling that Thomas Cook could do the needful for them, we agreed on the Hotel Adler in Mainz on 16 July.

 We went ashore at Plymouth, and by the time our luggage was sorted out and stowed aboard our chartered bus it was nearly 9 p.m. when we reached our hotel. After depositing our overnight bags in our room, Harry and I left immediately to collect our Ivy friends at their much posher digs up the street and headed for the nearest pub, entering just in time to hear a bell ring and the publican chant, "Time, gentlemen, please; the law is no longer on our side."

 Having no clue as to English licensing laws, we asked for beer, only to be told that the pub was closed, whereupon we pled that we had just got off the ship, this was our first night on British soil and our first visit to a pub about which we had heard so much, and could we please have just one beer? Our girls were especially pitiful and convincing, and the publican smiled and explained that he must perforce lock up his establishment to the public but that he could invite us to remain as his "personal guests" for "A bit of a dram." Included in this invitation were a couple of the "regulars," and thus we were introduced to pints of warm beer and lovely people. In retrospect I couldn't think of a grander start for us five pilgrims or to what became my life-long love affair with what I consider the most singularly satisfying social organization ever devised by man, the English pub.

The only Britain I knew came from the history texts and the shared devotion with my father of some of its literature, especially Shakespeare and the Romantic poets, Dickens and Galsworthy and Conrad and Kipling. And as we made our leisurely way inland in our comfortable bus, we had our first exposure to the English countryside, and I began to get that feeling I have never lost for the "rain and the shine and the green of that blessed land." Eastbourne, Bath and its Victorian Crescent, Wells and the cherubic voices at Evensong in that vast Cathedral.

But as we made our progress, something began to nag at the back of my mind: did I detect a sense of apprehension among the British people, particularly as dusk approached, or was it merely a trick of thought? At Oxford, which we reached on the fourth day, we were to spend two nights; we were quartered in private lodgings which during term catered to students not housed in the colleges. Our particular address was Wellington Square, and we got our first glimpse of domestic arrangements with few basic amenities: tiny rooms, no hot water, and pretty primitive WCs, all of which faded before the glories that awaited us the next day. We had already learned that if there was one thing the British could do, it was breakfast, and filled the next morning with eggs, rashers of their wonderful bacon, broiled tomatoes, and jams and preserves on hot scones, we went off to have our first look at this fabulous university setting.

From my father I had long known about the Rhodes scholarships, but since as an undergraduate I had not been nominated by my university for the competition, I could only look with envy at the colleges, the courtyards and the quads, the Bodleian, the playing fields. My college would have been Magdalen, where Harry and I tried a punt on the Isis with little success. Our hosts had insisted that we be back for tea, having invited their niece to come see what Texans looked like, and it was certainly welcome after a long day of sightseeing.

The niece, as it turned out, was a nurse, about 25 and most attractive in her white uniform and, I noted with relief, much too tall for Harry. Their notions of America and Americans had been gleaned almost entirely from the cinema, and they were actually disappointed that we Texans were not wearing boots, and that we were university graduates rather than cowboys. Surely we must have pistols in our belongings. At least we had our own horses, and were Indians still a problem?

It was all great fun, but as it began to darken outside, the three of them—the husband and wife and niece—rose almost in unison; they were going to step outside for a moment and we could join them if we liked. As we stepped out into the Square, other householders were appearing. Not a word was spoken, and they all faced the east, looking into the sky and listening intently. And then it dawned on me. Oxford was considerably farther east than Plymouth and only fifty miles from London, and what these people were listening for was the sound of German bombers.

After we went back inside, the husband, half in apology, explained that he had been in the navy and his wife a nurse during the last war, which had ended only twenty years ago, and they knew what war was like, and they knew that Hitler and Germany were bent on revenge, and, yes they did this every night since the fall of Austria only two months ago, and that moonlit nights were dreaded most. The niece arose, saying she had to return to her nursing home about a mile away, and despite her objections I insisted on walking with her, saying that if I got lost, my "pardner" would come and find me. We had to cross two fields, but there was a distinct enough path, and at the end of the first field we stopped at a stile that enabled one to cross the rocky boundary.

"Tell me," I asked, "is what I saw tonight going on all over Britain?"

She couldn't speak to that, but certainly along the Channel coast and in all the towns close to London.

"You see, we know what the Germans did to Guernica from the air, and Mr. Churchill speaks in Commons everyday about how ill prepared our aerial defenses are. We all hope like our Prime Minister that Hitler will come to his senses, but who can tell. We also know that if another war should begin soon, you Yanks, even if you were willing, could not get here in time to save us."

"What about the French?"

"Rotten to the core."

The moon was beginning to rise, desolate and she looked so beautiful and discouraged and helpless, and to try to change the subject, I recited a couple of Elizabeth Barrett Browning's sonnets as if to prove that Texans weren't complete barbarians. Then we just sat there, holding hands. When she stood to leave, she took my other hand and faced me, and I'll swear there was a touch of Madeleine Carroll, still the most beautiful woman I have seen. I stammered something about wanting very much to kiss her good night, and she replied that she would like that—and meant it.

"Will you come to tea tomorrow?"

"I don't think I can get away, but I shall try."

"Please!"

In the meantime, Harry and her uncle had gone to a pub, where with much urging and a few pints, he had related some of his experiences in the Great War.

They say London is a man's town, a town comfortable as an old shoe, but there is no way adequately to describe its effect on five young Americans exposed to its wonders for the first time. Harry and I gathered up our Ivy girls and first off did Buckingham Palace and gawked at Queen Victoria. Then we strolled through Green Park up to Piccadilly, decided to throw caution to the winds and climbed aboard a double-decker bus and scrambled up to the top deck in the open air. We flew down Piccadilly, turned right on the Haymarket, across Trafalgar Square, up the Strand and Fleet Street to pause at St. Paul's, then down the Embankment to Big Ben, the Houses of Parliament and Westminster Abbey. There we decided that each of us should go his own way and take his own time, and we would reassemble at the west exit just beyond the tomb of the Unknown Soldier. Back outside, we had our first meeting with a Ploughman's lunch at a nearby pub, and were off again. Walking north, we passed the Foreign Office and Clive's statue, on past the Home Office and onto the Horse Guard's Parade, where on the right stood Kitchener "with his back on Downing Street," and at the eastern entrance, Field Marshals Wolseley and Roberts, with their exploits on behalf of Empire etched in stone. And just beyond these worthies, in their full uniforms sitting at rigid attention on their chargers, were the two ever-present members of the Household Cavalry.

Then we faced west, towards St. James Park, with the Admiralty on our right, and there stood the white marble Cenotaph, Britain's principal monument to the 1914-1918 War, with the bronzed figures of Tommy Atkins standing at Parade Rest, the inscriptions of every unit that made up the B.E.F., and in chronological order the principal engagements it fought, beginning with Mons. For some years the Cenotaph had been considered little more than a tourist attraction, but now it had suddenly become a grim reminder of the dangers Britain might again be facing.

That evening we went to the theatre to some farce at which the British are unexcelled, and then to Soho, for a late supper. Quite at random we chose a likely looking bistro on Greek Street named "L'Escargot," which quite lived up to its promise. There our companions announced that they had done their homework and secured confirmed reservations at the Hotel Adler in Mainz, after which it was back to their hotel and good-bye until, God willing, 16 July.

Dr. Sparkman had arranged for a briefing at our Embassy on Grosvenor Square, and he took Harry and me with him. His objective was to report our itinerary and find out if any unusual precautions need be taken, particularly in Germany and Italy. A young First Secretary ushered us into his office, and he seemed to be on top of his game. U. S. tourists, on the surface at least, were welcome in both countries, and if we were careful not to trammel on native sensibilities, we would be cordially treated. Recent American returnees, however, were reporting what seemed to be an increasing sensitivity as to our impressions about what was going on. In public places such as restaurants, bars and beer gardens, we might well be politely approached by apparent civilians but who were Nazi party members announced by the swastikas in their coat lapels. They would probably ask if they might join you for a moment, which you should always agree to, and after offering to buy a round of drinks, they would begin to ask you how you liked their country. Had you ever seen a happier people, a greater sense of purpose and orderliness, public pride and the like. The trick is to humor them, to praise Germany and its leaders to the high heavens, to indicate that you have never been so impressed by a country before, and if you do it convincingly, I am told that your restaurant and bar bills will be significantly diminished. And you had better get accustomed to "Heil Hitler," now the standard substitute for "Good morning" and "Good night;" the words which Germans now used to start and end the day, and you will be well served to reply in kind, and better still with your arm upraised. Just play their game, and try to seem sincere.

Our SITA group made its way to the Continent via the ferry from Dover to Ostend, where we were met by a new and even roomier bus, a new driver, and a travel companion for the rest of our tour in Europe. Her name was Hilda Mueller, a linguist who made her living, she explained, through translations, private language lessons and turismo. She was in her mid-fifties and ugly as sin, skinny, flat-chested, uneven teeth stained from chain smoking, clothes barely hanging on her scrawny frame, disheveled hair splotched with gray, but with an intensity about her and a piercing gaze that caught one's immediate attention. She introduced herself with the admonition that if we paid attention to what she was saying, we might learn something on this journey. Our driver was a quiet little man in obvious awe of our interlocutor.

Belgium did not detain us long, but we spent a remarkable day touring the battle fields of Flanders, working out of Ypres and the Menin Gate, white crosses everywhere, British, French, Canadian, Australian, New Zealand, Indian, and now black crosses, too, in the beautifully reconstituted German cemeteries by order from Hitler. And then it was into Germany proper.

The walled cities of Nuremberg and Rothenburg were our first major stops, then Frankfurt and its sausage stalls along the banks of the River Rhine. After Mainz, we headed for Heidelberg on the River Neckar with its university, Heidelberg Schloss, and dinner in the Zum Rhoten Ochsen, the fabled student inn. Then there was the jewel-like Dinkelsbühl, where Harry and I plagiarized Wordsworth's opening paragraph of his "Preface to the Lyrical Ballads" by substituting our word "Bier" for his word "Poetry" and leaving it in the guestbook of the little hotel where we spent the night before arriving in Munich.

It had been in Nuremberg, however, where our high adventures began. After our customary bus tour of the city, with Hilda doing her best to enlighten us, Harry and I wandered off in the early afternoon in search of a bierstube. We found one, a nice one with a dark interior of polished oak and tables set up alfresco in a sizeable garden. We took a table outside and had no sooner placed our order than here they came, three well-dressed gentlemen, the tell-tale swastika on their coat lapels, greeted us with "Heil Hitler."

"Heil Hitler," we returned, with right arms up. They paused beside us and asked us from which country we came.

When we replied "the United States" they asked if they might join us for a moment. Then they began, and we were flabbergasted at the accuracy of our First Secretary in London.

How did we like Germany?

The most beautiful country we had ever seen.

How had we been treated?

Our reception could not have been more cordial.

What did we think of Hitler?

He must be a remarkable leader to have taken a nation so debilitated by war and depression and the dictates of the Treaty of Versailles and brought about its rebirth as a great power.

What do you think of the Jews?

We despise them for the money grubbers they are and we hope Hitler puts them in their place.

What are you going to say about Germany when you return to your country?

Why, compared to Britain and France, Germany is the one great hope for an orderly and prosperous Europe.

"Herr Ober, Herr Ober," one of them fairly shouted to a waiter, "bring these gentlemen whatever they wish, for they are our guests." With that they rose to take their leave, in all geniality, but I asked them to stay for a few minutes because we had some questions.

We had noticed an almost festive air about the city and what seemed to us an unusual number of people in uniform, brown, grey, black and green. "Was this a national holiday?"

"Not exactly, but tonight is the meeting of the National Socialist Party Congress which will be held in the Sportplatz."

"Is this their annual rally?"

"Nein. That is in September but this is still a very important meeting. Der Führer is coming to address us."

"Could we attend?"

That stopped them cold. After a hurried discussion among themselves, they decided it would be quite impossible. But, we argued, think of what an impression it would create at home if we could say that we had actually seen and listened in person to your Great Leader and that we could describe the enthusiasm of his reception. And remember, the U.S. never tried to punish Germany for the last war, we did not ratify the Treaty of Versailles, we did not join the League of Nations. And besides, we could wear our lederhosen so we wouldn't be too conspicuous. Another huddle, and it was finally agreed that they would take us; we must be in front of this restaurant at 6 p.m.

The Sportplatz was a huge, cavernous steel and concrete horseshoe of a stadium that seemed as though it could seat a hundred thousand spectators, but tonight there would be double that number for every inch of the infield grass would be covered by the uniformed battalions of the Nazi faithful. The festivities were to begin at dusk to accentuate the hundreds of burning torches that rimmed the stadium and the searchlights that were beginning to play on the infield and podium. The stadium was filling rapidly and we were happy to have found seats in the section reserved for the Hitler Jungend. The steady, muffled beat of the drums setting the cadence for the goose-stepping units of the brown shirted SS, the black shirted Waffen SS, and the field grey of the Wehrmacht had already begun as they filled the infield in an atmosphere designed to emulate the medieval aura of the Teutonic knights of old. The crowd was tense with excitement and anticipation of what was to follow, and in the event, Harry and I could have been sitting there naked and no one would have noticed.

As darkness settled in, suddenly the drums went silent and every searchlight was extinguished, leaving the stadium bathed in only the flickering of the burning torches. Then a single spotlight riveted the podium and onto the dais strode the gangling figure of Goebbels, Hitler's Propaganda Minister who exerted totalitarian control over the media, the arts, and information of any sort. "Sieg Heil," he screamed into the microphone, and "Sieg Heil" was the thunderous response.

Now my German was far from fluent, but I could follow Goebbels' peroration well enough to realize that this was the old vaudeville shtick of warming up the crowd. He damned those envious of Germany's growing strength, damned those who opposed the absorption of every German who wanted to be part of the Third Reich. "Our answer to them is our answer to Austria: Anschluss!" He damned the Poles, the Czechs, the Russians, the French, the British, all conspirators against Germany in the last great trial of arms. Most of all he damned the Jews and encouraged spontaneous violence against them. "We have risen from the ashes of Versailles and today we have a leader who will not be deterred from reaching our rightful destiny." He stopped, quickly stepped aside, and standing before us was Adolph Hitler.

Nuremberg Rally

For the next ten minutes all that could be heard was the feverish "Sieg Heil" from every throat in that vast assemblage. And then when he raised his hand, silence. He started slowly, as if a father talking to his family. But then his practiced technique asserted itself, and by intonation and gesture, he worked his way up to fever pitch. The central theme was the Sudetenland, the harassment and persecution of the Sudeten Germans by the Czechs and Slovaks that was becoming intolerable.

But had I not understood a word, I still would have succumbed to this mesmerizing display of passion and guile, this consummate artist in jack boots bamboozling his people with controlled fury. What a frightening performance, and what a frightening response. Harry and I both had to admit later fighting against the impulse to join in the "Sieg Heils." At any rate, the next item on the Reich's agenda had been announced to the world.

When our escorts dropped us off at our hotel, they told us there would be a parade the next day featuring Hitler and his entourage, and that our beer garden would be a good place from which to view it. So having alerted our SITA group, we all assembled there for lunch. The street was already being lined with excited spectators, and when the first strains from the distant band could be heard, the cafe emptied, lock, stock and barrel. We were pressed against the restaurant windows by the exuberant crowd, but by standing on tiptoe, we could still manage to view the proceedings. That is, all but Harry, who went back inside and brought out a chair to stand on. We could follow the parade's progress by the swelling roar of the viewers, and in good time the first units began to appear: the Army band, a platoon of Storm Troopers, a company of light tanks, personnel carriers, and motorcyclists. And then there they were, in a huge open touring car with its top down: Hitler, Goering, Himmler, Goebbels, and Hess—the architects and prime movers of a Reich designed to last a thousand years. The crowd was quite beside itself with the frantic waving of flags, the weeping and the shouting for joy.

With the passing of the principals, our group went back inside, but not so the Germans, who stayed in the street transfixed. With the place all to ourselves, Harry and I took over the bartending, and when much later the restaurant began to resume normal operations ours was a jolly company, but no one paid the slightest notice, so transported were they by the sight of their leaders.

Our day, however, was to end on a dreary note. From time to time we had all seen the sign "Juden Verboten" plastered on an occasional storefront, cafe, or public building. But that afternoon we witnessed for the first time Nazi goon squads in action. Seemingly inspired by the spectacle they had witnessed the night before, they burst into Jewish shops and places of business, dragging the occupants into the street, beating, kicking, cursing and urinating on them. It was nauseating, loathsome, and I had seen nothing like it since witnessing the lynching of an innocent black man years ago in Texas.

We left the charms of Nuremburg and arrived in Mainz, from whence we were to embark on a week's tour of the Rhineland and its castles by steamer and bus. Harry and I had already explained to Dr. Sparkman that we had invited the Wellesley girls to accompany us on this segment, and furthermore, if we found an inviting spot en route, the five of us might just leave the steamer and stop for a spell, but not to worry for we would meet the tour back in Mainz at the appointed time. When we told Hilda, who by this time was a member of the family, what we had in mind, she suggested that there was a charming little village just below Koblenz that was noted for its vineyards.

"It might just suit your needs, whatever they are," she said, her eyes smiling. But the great question was, of course, would anyone be waiting to meet us at the Hotel Adler? No one was, but they had booked a room for that night. We waited up for them, and I must say we all seemed mightily pleased to see each other. They were travel weary and they readily embraced our notion of stopping a spell in some quiet, out of the way spot, and we agreed to travel as lightly as possible, with only our overnight things in our rucksacks, in case we did any hiking.

So buoyed by the prospect of a happy reunion, we boarded our steamer the next morning to begin our cruise up the Rhine Valley. The weather was gorgeous, the river fairly glistening and alive with traffic; the steep hills rising abruptly from each side of the river all seemed given over to vineyards, which at this time of the year were lush in green vegetation. The castles high above stood like immense guardians, which I suppose was their original intent. Nuremberg seemed to be on another planet. After a splendid lunch with a goodly sampling of the regional wines, Hilda told me Bacharach would be coming up in about an hour's time; the stop was brief so have our gear ready. Leaning over the rails, we saw this tiny, picture post-card village slowly slide into view, nestled beneath its towering vineyards that came right down to the water's edge. We couldn't have gone ashore with lighter hearts.

A short walk from the pier took us to the town center, a little square with a small band pavilion and surrounded by little business houses, A green grocer, a butcher shop, and the like. At one corner there was a larger building, the town hotel, and in we went to inquire about lodgings. The manager's English was better than our German, happily, but he explained that he was fully booked and would be for some time, the town being unusually full of visitors and we would be better off by taking the next steamer to Koblenz. Pensions? None that he could recommend. That was all very discouraging, but on leaving I spotted the post office, which is usually the font of all wisdom in a small town. There, a jolly, plump post-mistress told us she knew of one pension that might be suitable; if we would walk down the street off the square that parallels the square, in about an 1/8th of a mile, almost to the edge of the village, we would come to a small park on our right, directly across from which was a row of small houses, one of which was the pension, which had a sign. So down the street we went.

The town certainly didn't appear to be crowded; few people were on the streets although I did notice occasional men in uniforms that I was not familiar with. We found the pension without difficulty where we were warmly greeted by the proprietor and his wife; yes, they could take us for the night or even longer if we wished; yes there were places to hike; yes, they would give us breakfast; yes, the town was famous for its wine, and there was a noted weinstube that also served good food to which they would direct us.

"But," said our host, "are you sure you want to say with us. We are Jewish, and Jews are not liked in many parts of Germany."

We merely replied that now we were even more certain that we wanted to stay. Our two rooms were larger than expected and neat as a pin, and there was a separate WC which adjoined a bath with two basins and an inviting tub. So after dumping our rucksacks and washing up, we set out to explore "our village."

They were an attractive threesome, attired now in light sweaters, shorts and sandals, and it looked as though that Eastern reserve was beginning to thaw. I asked Harry if he had noticed the pure pleasure in his friend's eyes when she first spotted him in the Adler, and I was sure she was the one who had insisted that they keep the rendezvous with us.

Road into the vineyards in Bacharach

"Anytime you two want to peel off, don't hesitate," I told him. "I'll try to manage the other two."

But for the moment we were enjoying immensely this outing together. We guessed Bacharach numbered about 2,000 souls, and in an hour we made the circuit of the town's periphery. From the elevation behind the village we could just make out the battlements of a castle above us and towards Mainz, and then down to the water's edge we sat in the grass watching the ebb and flow of the river traffic. We were as happy and carefree as five fresh American college graduates abroad in Europe for the first time could be, laughing, joking, and Harry and I telling lies about growing up in the wilds of Texas. Finally we felt the need for sustenance, so we strolled back to the town square, and following directions we had got from the pension, we found the weinstube just off a little street to our right.

This weinstube was the genuine article: leaded glass windows, beamed ceilings, burnished copper fixtures and braziers, oak paneling, heavy oaken tables and chairs and bar stools, solid wooden floors. The main room, the principal room was quite commodious, featuring a long curving bar, padded benches lining the walls, where there were niches for holding your glass if you preferred to drink standing up. Off this there opened two smaller rooms, separated by a stairwell, for the dining patrons, in one of which a string ensemble was softly playing familiar waltzes. The stairs led down to a cellar housing assorted tubs and barrels and two large WCs side by side, with the doors leading into them appropriately marked "Herren" and "Damen".

We assembled at the bar and bade the vintner to introduce us to the beauties of the local grape. The wine was fresh and light and delicious, and we leisurely drank our share before ordering dinner. When called to the table, in the middle of which stood a large pitcher of our wine, we sat down to a wonderful meal of wiener schnitzel, pounded paper thin, vegetables, and a salad, followed by a warm apple strudel swimming in thick cream and a cheese board. Then the vintner came and asked us to return to the bar for his best local after dinner brandy. As I recall there were four or five older couples also dining.

We were sitting at the bar, happy as clams, warming our snifters in our hands, when it happened. Bursting into the weinstube were ten of the best looking young guys you will ever see, tall, lithe, ruddy cheeked, blond and blue-eyed for the most part, wearing their uniforms as though they had been poured into them, their jodhpurs fairly crackling on the wood floor, and over each left breast a pair of embroidered silver wings. Clearly these were Luftwaffe pilots, and they looked every inch of it. Seeing us at the bar, they came up immediately and greeted us with "Heil Hitler" which we returned.

One of them asked, "Engländer?"
"Nein."
Another ventured, "Swedish?"
"Nein."
Then one said, "Amerikaner?"
"Ja."
"Wohin in Amerika?"

When the girls said Massachusetts, it made no impression whatsoever, but when Harry and I said Texas, one of them pretended to draw his six-shooters and fire into the air, saying something like Cowboys and Indians to their great amusement. Despite the medley of fractured German and English, young people can usually find a way to communicate, and before long it was Heinrich and Johann and Hans and Pam and Sally and Lisa and Harry and Jack. But almost immediately their arrogance began to manifest itself. They ordered the vintner from behind the bar and one of them took his place; and it became quickly apparent that this was now *their* weinstube and the staff and everyone else was there by sufferance. But for a while it all seemed good natured enough, a real bash.

The only German drinking song that Harry and I knew seemed appropriate for the occasion, and we struck up with "In München Steht ein Hofbräuhaus, oans, zwoa, g'suffa—." I then asked them to sing "Horst Wessel" and "Unter den Linden" their patriotic songs most in vogue at the time, and they responded with enthusiasm, and we answered with "A Band of Brothers in DKE" and "The Goddamned Dutch." It was all very gay and spontaneous, and the wine and beer continued to flow. But then I heard something strange. I could swear two of the flyers were conversing in Spanish. Now my Spanish was not that good but considerably better than my German, and I turned to them.

"*¿Hablo Español?*"

"*Si, si,*" they replied, "*con mucho gusto.*"

Where did they learn their Spanish?

"Why, in Spain, of course."

They had been stationed there for the past year, and had just returned to Germany on home leave. Bacharach was one of their rest and recreation areas. So that was why the hotel was full. But wasn't there a civil war going on in Spain?

"Yes, yes, that is why we were there—to fight the Spanish communists and their Russian comrades."

Everyone was listening to us now.

"How did it go?"

"Very well indeed." He smiled, threw out his chest and touched the Iron Cross on his uniform jacket. "Guernica," he beamed, and all ten of them snapped to attention. "We must drink to that!"

I had just enough presence of mind to agree.

"To Guernica," I replied, and we all lifted our glasses.

Jesus Christ Almighty! So that's who they were—the Condor Legion, the lads who just the prior year bombed Guernica in the Basque section of northern Spain into oblivion in support of the Spanish Nationalists led by Franco—Nazi Germany's newest heroes! These were the lads whom Hitler was using in Spain for live-action developing and testing the Luftwaffe's new plane designs, aerial tactics, and ace fighter pilot training. That explained the Iron Crosses. My God, no wonder they were arrogant! In a low voice, I quickly explained the situation to Harry and the girls, ending with the premonition that this party could get rough. It had become apparent that Harry and I were incidental to the proceedings as the young German studs clustered around the girls vying for individual attention. And now with Spanish as an aid to conversation, I was asked to relay terms of endearment and increasingly lewd suggestions.

"Ladies," I said, "they are well and truly after you."

"I know," whispered Pam, because the touchy-feely stuff had already started. Claiming the need for fresh air, Harry and I stepped into the street. We were worried as hell, for it was now clear as crystal that our Germans intended to bed those girls by whatever means it took; they were certainly not going to let them walk out of that weinstube with or without us. Knowing Harry's predisposition, I said we might have to start a fight as a distraction, but first let's try to get them to sing some more while I see if there is any other way out of here.

Needless to say, the WCs had been busy places, and that was my excuse for going down to the cellar; but what I was desperately looking for was an exit from there, but there was apparently no way out except back up the stairs. I used the Herren, and for some reason I decided to look into the Damen. To my surprise and joy, there was one of those leaded glass windows above the toilet which, by standing on the sides of the commode, I could barely reach and pry open far enough to see that it opened onto an alley or street of some sort. Closing it gently, 1 stepped back down, closed the door and went back up stairs.

"The drinks are on me!" I shouted, laughing, and while the steins and glasses were being filled, I managed to get the girls off to the side and hurriedly told them what I wanted them to do. "When we start singing, first one of you, and then the other two excuse yourself for the Damen and once inside, talk, giggle and flush the thing as often as you can, and when I come down and knock twice, let me in." Then I turned to the group, catching Harry's eye, raised my arms and burst out with "In München Steht" with Harry joining in immediately, and soon we were all singing and parading all over the place. Lisa was the first to drop out, disappearing down the stairs, and in a couple of minutes, Pam and Sally followed her. We continued our snake dance until I abruptly stopped, put my hands to my mouth as though ill and, much to their amusement, disappeared into the cellar.

The girls let me in, and pointing up, I said, "You're going out that window which opens up onto some kind of passageway. The town square is on your right somewhere not too far. Walk as softly as you can til you get to the band stand, and then take off like hell straight down the street to the pension and don't stop til you get inside. Come on, Pam, you're the lightest. Up on my shoulders, push the window open, get out and then help pull your sisters up. Last one out, close the window."

In a trice they were up and out. I then went into the Herren and vomited for all I was worth and as loudly as I could. Back upstairs, and trying to look appropriately shaken, I called for a beer and gulped it down. It was not the same happy group; for all of their youth and manliness, their speech was becoming slurred, one of them had fallen off his barstool, and their mood was turning sour.

Perhaps ten minutes elapsed before one of them slammed his stein on the bar and glowered, "¿Donde estan las señoritas?"

I looked at Harry with a quizzical gesture, and he replied, "Yo no se, abajo, yo creo."

Then I suggested that perhaps they, too, were ill and that we ought to go down and see if we could help them.

"Ja. Ja," they chorused and started lurching toward the stairwell.

But Harry stopped them in their tracks: "Primero, yo quiero brindar saluda por Guernica" at which they retrieved their glasses and struggled to attention.

"To Guernica," we intoned. And then, as the last of their heads disappeared below, Harry and I broke and ran. At the pension, completely out of breath, we knocked, heard the peephole open and shut and the door open as our Jewish friends came outside to listen.

"Are the girls here?"

"Yes."

"Then you know what happened."

"Yes."

"Thank God, we're safe!"

"But you're not safe," said the wife, her voice desperate. "You don't know them. They think they are gods and can do as they please. But they are nothing but savages who will come here, break into our home, drag those girls out into the street, and rape them before your eyes. You must all leave, now, out the back. I've told the girls where to go!"

Harry and I had thought, given their state, that it would take our erstwhile comrades some time to figure out what had happened, but suddenly on the night air we could hear a full-throated roar of disbelief, disgust and rage, and soon they would be charging over the cobblestones like hounds at full cry. We ran upstairs to pack our rucksacks and found that the girls had done it for us. Fortunately they had changed into slacks and their pea coats. By the time we got downstairs with all our belongings, the pack had arrived and was beating on the door which fortunately held firm. The last thing I saw, as I peeked through a curtain, was four of them crossing the road and seizing a park bench which they could use as a battering ram.

Out the back we flew, turned into the alley which took us to the narrow path we had taken that afternoon between two vineyards to the top of the ridge behind the town, where there was a little roadway. Reaching that, we simply had to stop and catch our breath. We sat there, looking down on Bacharach and its few lights still to be dimly seen, and from the direction from which we had come, tongues of flame began to lick the night sky.

Park benches in Bacharach

"My God," cried Sally, bursting into tears, "there goes our pension, and our friends are probably still in it!"

Our directions were to follow the road eastward in the general direction of the castle we had seen in the distance and to move only at night, hiding in the vineyards during the day. The next village was 15 miles up the river, where we could catch a little mail steamer that made all the stops but would eventually get us to Mainz. We ought to be able to cover the distance in two nights. So thinking of what was happening below, it was a sad and frightened group that began its trek. The girls were game as could be, but it was slow, tough going, and we welcomed the first signs of daylight so we could get off our feet. When we could see what we were doing, we stepped off the road into the vineyard on our left and worked our way down among the leaves until we were reasonably sure we couldn't be seen from any direction. The foliage was thick enough so that by moving a few yards we could relieve ourselves with some privacy, and having accomplished that, we sat huddled together, counting our sorrows and our blessings. Despite our frantic departure, our sainted landlord had managed to stuff a bottle of cognac into my rucksack, and I figured it would never do more good than right now.

"Take it slow and easy, girls, or you'll gag," advised Harry as we passed the bottle around, "but it will help keep out the chill."

After the second round we pepped up a little, but the fact was that we were just plain, dogged tired. Harry and Pam curled up together, and I stretched out so that Lisa and Sally could put their heads in my lap. How very strange, I thought before I dropped off, that this was the first time we had physically touched each other since dancing on the *Nieuw Amsterdam*.

It was past noon when we woke, stiff and sore and hungry, but the sun was pleasantly warm, which was a blessing. We heard what we thought were farmer's carts occasionally pass by above us, but there was no vehicular traffic and, thank God, no sound of dogs in hot pursuit. There was nothing to do but just sit it out awaiting the dusk and moving about as little as possible. We figured that we had covered maybe five miles and that one more night ought to do it. Finally we ventured out back on the road and began stumbling along at an even slower pace than the night before and with rest stops more frequent.

It was about 2 a.m. that we began to see enough lights flickering below to indicate that there must be the village we were seeking. Not daring to grope around in the vineyards in the dark, we found a place to rest until the first light of dawn at which time we began our descent through the steep slope toward the village. None of us spoke much—not only for fear of being heard and arousing suspicion so early in the morning, but from shear emotional and physical exhaustion.

As we reached the edge of the village, it was decided that Harry and the girls would hide while I found a safe route to the river. In the doing of such I was also on the lookout for the baker—assuming he would be the first up and working in the village—from whom we could buy some bread as we had not eaten since fleeing Bacharach. Perhaps it was the adrenaline that had been working overtime that heightened my sense of smell for it was only a few minutes after I entered the village that my nose led me directly to the baker near the center of town. I explained that I had been on a trek up to the castle the day before but had become separated from my group when I set off to explore the beautiful countryside on my own and that I was hoping to catch the mail barge to Mainz where I could meet up with my group, and I was also very hungry so could I please buy some bread—even if it was yesterday's.

In the event, I learned that the mail barge would make a very brief stop around 10 a.m. He then suggested the best place to wait for the barge. As I paid him for the bread, he said, "Aren't your friends hungry as well?" I just stood there dumbstruck. How did he know? What did he know?

"You know of us from Bacharach?"

"Ja und der Condor Legion," he replied.

"Do you know what happened to our friends at the Pension?"

"Ja." With that simple response and the immense look of sadness in his eyes I knew that our Jewish friends—who had done nothing wrong except help us escape what was sure to have been unspeakable brutality to the girls—had themselves been tortured.

With the five small loaves of bread and a bottle of wine safely in my rucksack, I returned to Harry and girls. After eating we quietly made our way to where the baker had suggested and we waited until the mail barge arrived at almost exactly 10 a.m. Once on the barge we began to relax a little. I was tempted to tell all, but I decided not to say anything until we were safely in Mainz.

After depositing the girls safely at the Hotel Adler in Mainz—with their constant reassurance that they would be fine and that they would continue with their original itinerary—Harry and I made our way back to the SITA group. It was only when we were dining al fresco at a small restaurant near our hotel that I dared tell Harry what I had learned. We both hoped the girls were okay and that they were more resilient than we at the moment. It had been the German version of a Mexican stand-off, Harry and I reckoned; we had got them into it, and we had got them out, but the doing of it had exacted a terrible price. Maybe our friends were doomed anyway, but that was no consolation to us. At least we knew now, without wholly grasping it at Nuremberg, what a ghastly Germany the world had on its hands.

Freudenstadt, which lay about 90 miles south of Heidelberg and 150 miles south of Mainz and the girls, was the next major stop on the SITA itinerary. It did not belie its name; it was a beautiful little town in the center of a resort area that abutted on the Black Forest, mercifully free, it seemed, of gauleiters and demigods and so a welcome relief from the Bacharach ordeal. The only person we told about our Bacharach adventure was Hilda, who by now was our trusted confidant, and we hers. At the outset, she had been disgusted at our seeming political insensitivity and ready acceptance of the Nazi regime, our Sieg Heiling all over the place and the like until we told her about our briefing in London. After that she never missed a chance to describe the horrors that had befallen Germany, the wreckage of the universities, the carnage among German intellectuals, the assault on the Jews and any other minorities not measuring up to the Aryan image. She told us for example, about how in her army of occupation in the Rhineland after the Great War, the French had deliberately included battalions of Senegalese soldiers, black as the ace of spades, as an affront against the Germans, and how Hitler's first act after becoming Reich Chancellor had been to exterminate the issue of the inevitable union between the Senegalese and German women, including every mother he could get his hands on. When she described the rape of human dignity, her frail body shook with fury. She loathed the Nazis with a pure passion, and now, after Bacharach, we had a common bond.

But this was Freudenstadt, under a glorious summer sky; there was a large swimming pool to which we had access, there were soccer games at which we tried our hand, there was the Forest itself, with its inviting paths. But best of all there was an abundance of young people, some on holiday, some as members of a Hitler Jungend troop on its annual summer encampment, some, like us, just plain tourists, so the evenings were alive with singing and dancing and tall steins of beer.

Harry and I found a riding stable, and we invited our tour group to come along as we demonstrated the art of horsemanship a la Texas. We mounted our horses in the indoor arena, for the proprietor wanted to observe our proficiency before turning us loose, but, alas, we could not get those animals to budge an inch. We jiggled the reins, we patted their necks, we prodded their jowls, we swatted their rumps, we whistled, but those dumb animals just stood there as though cast in concrete, and our spectators were bent over with laughter. Finally a stable girl took our reins and began to lead us slowly around in a circle, and even she joined in the merriment. We were without question the most embarrassed Texans ever to set foot on German soil. When she finally handed the reins back to us and the horses still refused to budge, we surrendered. But all was not lost.

The stable girl, Herta by name, even in her bib overalls and mucky boots, would turn any young man's head. She finished her chores at noon, and yes, she would join us at the Schwimmbad after lunch. She brought along her older brother and his girlfriend, both of whom were at the youth encampment, and we all got along famously. So Harry and I again found ourselves as part of a five-some.

We decided that next day we would take a picnic lunch into the Black Forest, and we spent a lovely afternoon hiking and lying in the grass watching the clouds. Harry and I tried to explain American university life and that, yes, we really could ride horses if they spoke English. They all wanted to know about Hollywood, of course, and Helmut, the brother told us about the Hitler Jungend and what a wonderful opportunity it was for city kids to get out into the countryside, do some hard physical labor, and learn to enjoy nature.

That night we all went to a bierstube that catered to our age group, and we sang and tried to dance the polka and had such a good time that on parting, we agreed to repeat the program the next day. After our picnic in a sunny little glade we had discovered, Helmut took his leave, saying he hoped to join us that evening, and the rest of us hiked and then went back for a swim, the only sad note being that Harry and I had to leave with our group at noon the next day. It was another fun evening, although Helmut did not show up.

The next morning Harry and I went to the stables to say our good-byes to Herta, and we asked her to tell Helmut how much we had enjoyed his company. She then explained his absence: he was a reserve sub-lieutenant in a Waffen SS company and yesterday had received his orders to active duty. Herta kissed us warmly with tears in her eyes, and after leaving her we were walking along a narrow foot path towards the town center and our bus. We looked up and saw a young officer, resplendent in his black uniform, coming towards us. It was Helmut. We were all smiles, but he approached us without a tint of recognition, staring straight ahead, and when we did not make way for him, he put out his left arm and without a word pushed us aside. Apparently, we were now the enemy, and when we later told Hilda about it, she merely spat and replied, "Now you've seen it again. When those animals put on the uniform, they are insufferable. There is no limit to their arrogance."

Of all the cities on our route, Munich made the most lasting impression and was beyond doubt our favorite. In Germany, Bavarians are a breed apart, with a lighter, gentler touch, a more fully developed aesthetic sense, a less frenetic pace which is characteristic of the southern climes of every nation, and their capitol city was a reflection of this *joie de vivre*. The broad avenues, abundant parks, airy public buildings, music halls and opera, open air markets all bore testimony to a people who understood the good life. And, of course, for kids our age, there was the storied Hofbräuhaus.

It was a cavernous, three-storied place with a brass band and Amazonian waitresses muscling foaming liters of lager to the crowded tables. There were hot sausages of all kinds to be had, and roast chicken and kraut and hard rolls. Harry and I had our pictures taken in our lederhosen and perky Tyrolean hats, holding our mugs while sitting on a huge beer barrel. About once an hour the band, its tubas blaring, would launch into the signature song and a thousand voices would join in shouting "Oans, zwoa, g'suffa!" We ran into some fraternity brothers from Yale and immediately began parading all over the place to the rendition of the "Phi Marching Song." It was a grand evening in a brilliant city. Who could have dreamt of the tragic denouement which would unfold there in scarcely a month's time.

Driving south from Munich, our bus began getting caught up in all sorts of military traffic, columns of tanks and motorized artillery and personnel carriers moving southeast towards the Czech frontier. None of this was surprising to Harry and me since we had heard it from the Führer himself at Nuremberg, but we had never seen an army on the move before. At one point the advance motorcyclists of a Panzer division ordered our bus to pull off the road and stop.

Craning our heads out of the open bus windows, we could see coming up a long line of tanks moving slowly towards us with an open staff car carrying the regimental officers in the lead. As it passed us, Harry and I shouted out in what we called the Unknown Tongue at our fraternity house but was actually meaningless gibberish. Suddenly the staff car slammed on its brakes and the whole armored column ground to a halt. What must have been the commanding general was standing in the car, his face flushed with anger and gesticulating wildly towards us, and before we knew it two orderlies came up and ordered Harry and me off the bus. Hilda, in near panic, was translating all this, and she came with us as we were marched up to the staff car.

The General demanded to know who we were and what we had said. Hilda, bless her soul and with the aid of our passports explained that we were American college students who had never seen the German army before and were trying to tell them what a wonderful sight we thought it was. The General, mollified, waived us back to the bus, and Hilda, Harry and I raised our right arms and said in unison, "Heil Hitler." We had not been so terrified since Bacharach, and we promised a distraught but relieved Hilda not to be so foolish again. The next day we crossed the frontier into Switzerland with a profound sense of thanksgiving.

My first glimpse of the majestic Alps was awe inspiring. Switzerland was Switzerland, prosperous, peaceful, prim and proper—"very hygienic" as one of our group observed—and Harry and I had no difficulty staying out of trouble. In Zurich I visited the Cafe Voltaire, which had seen the spawning of the Dada movement during the Great War, and could almost see Lenin and his cohorts, who as exiles were nightly visitors, sitting at their back table, watching and listening to the madness and becoming ever more confirmed in their belief that capitalism equated with insanity, before the Germans whisked them off in a sealed train to the Finland Station in St. Petersburg and all the gruesome consequences for Russia and the world.

The ride through the Brenner Pass, along the Austria-Italy boarder was spectacular. Italy for the most part was a delight, and we did what all first-timers were supposed to do. Florence—with its Uffizi, David and the Arno bridges, Venice—with its canals and St. Mark's Square and the pigeons, Pisa—with its tower, which we climbed and which did indeed lean, and, of course, "The Last Supper." Rome was overwhelming, but we worked hard at it: the Sistine Chapel and the Vatican, the Victor Emmanuel memorial, the Coliseum, the Catacombs, the Via Veneto. We were amused at the huge murals recently erected outside the Coliseum depicting that the Roman Empire at its height encompassed far less territory than Mussolini's, which was true if one included all the useless Italian holdings in North Africa.

There was plentiful evidence of the dictatorship. Mussolini's portraits were plastered everywhere along with his deathless exhortations. The Blackshirts, with their often garish uniforms, strutted about like the toy soldiers they actually were.

One day at noon we happened to be in the vicinity of the Palazzo Venezia when a huge crowd began to assemble, clearly the beginning of a Fascist rally, and we inched as close to the building as we could. Suddenly a huge roar went up as Il Duce himself stepped out on his famous balcony, arms akimbo, jutting jaw, bald head reflecting the sunlight as it bobbed up and down, eyes blazing, as he began pacing up and down, glowering over the throng. Silence. Then he began his harangue with a voice becoming increasingly shrill, clenched fists flailing the air, pauses for effect, a really splendid, well-rehearsed *tour de force*.

When he finished, the roar of the faithful went up, clenched fists held high in the air, "Vive Il Duce! Vive Il Duce!" on and on. And then I felt something prodding me in the back, and I turned to see a member of the Carbonari poking me with his carbine. He pointed to my right arm. My God, I had forgotten my instructions. That arm shot up into the air, and at the top of my voice I joined in the clamor. But compared with Nuremberg, this was comic opera. This performance was in the daylight in an open square, not in a darkened arena lit by torch light echoing the steady cadence of muted drums. Here there was no feeling of suffocating menace, no sense of deadly determination, no clutching of the throat, no call to an avenging angel.

In Mussolini's Italy, to be sure, there were disappearances in the night, there were goon squads, there was an army, a navy, and an air force, all of which had fired shots in anger. But in bars, at dinner parties, in bordellos, here one could still hear the merits of the regime debated, and often with fervor, and in many quarters the feeling persisted that Italy was held in thrall not so much by a madman as by an egotistical buffoon. Nevertheless, the presence of Rome in a Berlin dominated axis made the menace to democracy even more formidable, and it might lead to a feeling of martial overconfidence that would make the casting of the die inevitable. Leaving Italy by way of the lake district of Como and Maggiore, which I thought the most exquisite scenery of my experience, did not dispel my conviction that our times were in dangerous disarray.

France made me feel no better although Paris, if not the Parisians, did its best. I was better versed in French history than of any other nation on the Continent, and to walk the cobblestones and boulevards of Paris made it all come to life. There was the Church of the Madeleine, where my paternal grandfather had married his first wife (who died before he was posted to Puerto Rico). There was St. Chapelle, exactly as my father had described it—"the loveliest chapel in all of Christendom." There was Sacré-Coeur, with its breathtaking view of the city, and Montmartre. There was the Folies Bergere and fending off the courtesans as you left the theater, and I thought about how much French women could learn about the refinements of passion from their Italian sisters. But my favorite spot was atop the Arc de Triomphe at the Etoile, with its sweep over the Champs de Mars to the Invalides, and down the Champs Elysées·to the Place de la Concorde, the Tuileries Gardens and the Louvre. Standing there, I could be with Napoleon at Wagram and Lodz at the Nile. From my perch I could later see von Moltke lead his grey-clad, jack-booted legions down that long avenue between crowds of stunned, sullen Frenchmen witnessing the investment of their beloved capitol by the enemy for the first time in its glorious history, a tableau ending at their own Louis XIV's Versailles, where in the Hall of Mirrors, Bismarck proclaimed the new German Empire, with Alsace-Lorraine to be included therein.

"But you can't take those provinces," plead the French. "They are the key to our house."

"I can and will," retorted the Iron Chancellor. "They are indeed the key, but they are the key to *our* house!"

And later still I could look down as another victory parade passed through the arch, but this one led by Foch and Haig and Pershing, and again the tableau ending in the Hall of Mirrors at Versailles where Georges Clemenceau, the "Tiger of France," solemnly intoned, "The time has come for a reckoning."

The Place de la Concorde is surrounded by the huge marble busts of ten female figures representing the queen cities of France. I had my picture taken beneath the one labeled "Strasbourg," the capital of Alsace. After its loss in 1871, the Parisians had draped the entire statue in black crepe as a constant reminder of France's defeat and disgrace, and to remain so until the "Lost Provinces" had been regained. But in this August I could find no defiance in the people of Paris, rather a kind of forced gayety that failed to mask the mood of grim resignation.

Hitler's announced determination to tear up the Versailles Diktat could be tolerated so long as he continued to face the East, the "Drang nach Osten." By now a Franco Spain seemed a certainty, but that posed no threat of invasion. The Rhineland had taken us by surprise, but what was so venal in a nation wishing to reclaim its historic frontiers? But now Hitler's ambitions seemed to lie in the other direction. The Anschluss had been nothing but the absorption of a handful of Germans from the cadaver of the Austro-Hungarian Empire. If Czechoslovakia seemed to be the next target of opportunity, so what—the intention was simply to protect the Sudentan Germans from a bastard state hacked out of the same corpse. And if he should be so demented as to have designs on the Poles, it would only serve him right, for what sane person would want to mix the vermin of Europe into his own flesh and blood. Poland, furthermore, would bring him face to face with the Soviets, and to have those two go at each other would be the best of all possible worlds.

But for the sake of argument, what if Hitler decided not to pose a threat to Stalin but instead turned to the West? He wouldn't dare. Daladier is no Clemenceau but he is a clever man and a match for the Nazi mentality. But more to the point, we have in the French army what everyone acknowledges to be the best equipped, best trained ground forces in Europe, and with the same elan that stopped the Boche in his tracks at Verdun and twice at the Marne. Foch is gone, but in Gamelin we have a master strategist. And our army is now shielded by the engineering miracle of the 20th century, the Maginot Line, the most complex and complete series of fortifications ever devised by man. We also understand that even the Brits are beginning to rearm. So let him have his little bits and pieces that will sate his appetite. The last thing he wants is war, East or West.

From Paris we took our last bus ride down the valley of the Seine, where we said goodbye to our faithful driver and promised Hilda that we would spread her message to anyone who would listen. The *Nieuw Amsterdam*, grand as ever, deposited us in Hoboken, after which we reclaimed the red convertible from storage and, carefully avoiding North Carolina, reached Texas during the first week in September.

Once home, I presented my father with a large ball of Edam, his favorite cheese, and mother with four bottles of Piper-Heidsik champagne, the real stuff; and sitting on our sun porch, we had a small welcome-home party while I talked about our fabulous trip. My favorite edifice—Saint Chapelle, with the sun lighting those incomparable rose windows. My favorite scenic spot—Lake Como, which I would gladly revisit tomorrow. I did not mention Bacharach, but I talked at length about Nuremberg and our other encounters with the Nazis and the buffoonery of Mussolini. At the end of my long recital, I summed it all up with a prediction: Harry and I were convinced that within a year, there would be another war in Europe. Nothing could save Czechoslovakia, and Poland would probably be next, and after that who knows, but inevitably, sooner or later, France and Britain would be under attack. How could I be so sure?

"I don't know, Dad; perhaps it's just the obstinacy of youth."

Unspoken but not forgotten was the sheer inadvertence by which Harry and I had flicked the tail of the dragon and seen it breathe fire. Nothing and no one was going to deter Hitler's attempt at the Mastery of Europe. That Harry and I knew. And I thought of my beautiful nurse in Oxfordshire.

Addendum 1

In September of 1938, Harry and I returned to The University of Texas to begin work on our Master's degrees. Later in the fall, when news came of Czechoslovakia's dismemberment, giving the lie to the Munich agreement, we drove out to Eisenheiser's, ordered two large steins of beer, and drank to the fact that we were probably the only two Americans in all of history who had personally faced up to and been shouted at by the Panzer general who commanded Hitler's occupation forces.

Addendum II

In the summer of 1975, while I was president of the University of Southern California, I went to take a look at the educational programs we were conducting for American personnel at our military bases throughout Germany. With me was my wife, Lucy, and Professor Ross Berkes, chairman of our Department of International Relations under whose aegis these courses had been developed. There we traveled by car with a bright young German and his fiancé who were based in Munich from where they coordinated our academic efforts.

After visiting one of our larger bases in Wiesbaden, Fran told us that it would be a pleasant diversion to drive down the Rhine valley where certain of the castles had been refurbished to take paying guests and that he had booked us into one of them for two nights. Arriving at this regal establishment perched high on the ridge overlooking the river, and looking down we could see little villages at the water's edge nestled in the vineyards that rose behind them. Suddenly I thought I knew where I was, and by consulting our road map, I confirmed that one of those villages was, indeed, Bacharach. Then I told the group about Harry Fulweiler and me having stopped there on that long ago post-graduation trip and how we had found this marvelous old weinstube.

"We ought to drive down there after dinner and if it's still in existence, we can get a dollop or two of fine local brandy."

So after our meal we drove down a narrow winding road and before long we parked the car in the town square just before dusk. Nothing seemed to have changed. Looking upward towards Mainz, there was the dim outline of our castle, just as before, and then without a moment's hesitation I started walking in the direction I remembered. There was my weinstube. We entered the main room, as warm and inviting as ever, and sat at one of the tables in the bar area.

"Now before you do anything else," I said, "I want the four of you to go down those stairs over there, and in the cellar you ought to find two WCs side by side, the first one marked Herren and the other, Damen. All of you look inside both of them and then come back up here, and I'll tell you what you saw." They dutifully responded, disappearing into the cellar, and in about ten minutes were back at our table.

"In the Herren," I said, "you saw nothing out of the ordinary, but in the Damen, above the john you saw a leaded glass window high enough to open out onto the street."

They looked at me in some amazement, Lucy complimenting me on my memory and then wanting to know said, "Pray do tell!"

I told them about my ordeal here some thirty-eight years earlier with Harry and the Wellesleyites—and the Condor Legion's night of terror.

Bacharach and the castle Stahleck as seen from a hill on the other side of the River Rhine

Editor's Addition

In 2012, while working on my own bucket list, I (George) traveled to Bacharach, Germany, with the hope of taking a photo of the weinstube my brother, Jack, described in this chapter and to retrace his escape route. The pension at which they stayed was at the southern end of Bacharach at the foot of the hill, but I was unable to determine its exact location.

The weinstube described by Jack no longer stands, but the park benches in Bacharach, one of which the Condor Legion used as a battering ram, still exist. As can be seen from the photograph I took and included in this chapter, they are made of hewn logs, and are quite heavy and solid.

I gained a greater appreciation of the difficulty Jack and his friends had fleeing Bacharach when I observed the extent and steepness of the slopes bordering the village. There are three roads into Bacharach, one from the north along the Rhine, one from the south also along the Rhine, and a third from the west which runs through the valley between these two slopes. The steepness of the south-facing vineyards appears to have a 40 - 45° rise. The wooded slope facing north is just as steep. Overlooking the village on the north facing wooded slope is the castle Stahleck. Behind the castle are the vineyards traversed that fateful night. This photo taken from www.bacharach-germany.net provides a much clearer view of the rise than does the photo I took.

—G.U. Hubbard

CHAPTER 4
—
Just Try to Be Ready

Jack, circa 1940

On 15 September 1938, I was back in Austin at The University of Texas (UT) to enter graduate school—and quite frankly I was glad to be back in tranquil Texas after my summer experiences though I knew it would be short lived if Herr Hitler had his way. The best I could hope for was to be able to apply what I had learned from my European adventure to a M.A. in history. To my eternal good fortune, the History Department at UT at that time ranked with the best in the land; in each area of concentration there was a giant in his field: Thad Riker in Modern Europe, Milton Gutsch in Modern Britain, Fredrick Duncalf in Ancient and Medieval, Charles Ramsdell in Latin America, Eugene Barker in Texas and the Southwest, Oliver Radkey, a brilliant newcomer in Modern Russia, Walter Prescott Webb in the Great Plains and the West, and each of them developing library resources to match. My exposure to them as an undergraduate had been just that in generally crowded lectures, but now to sit in their seminars gave me my first inkling of what serious scholarship was about. "Facts, facts, facts," repeated Dr. Gutsch as he pounded the podium. "If you can't master the facts, then you can become a philosopher."

Because of my concern with contemporary Europe, Professors Gutsch and Riker became my principal mentors, and I came to them not as a stranger because they remembered President Splawn and Dad's tenure with him as Dean of Students. I told them about my summer in Europe and that now Commissioner Splawn of the ICC had offered me a position as his private secretary in Washington next September if I could bring my Master's degree in hand. They agreed it was possible but we had to choose a topic for the thesis immediately. Might I do something about Britain's confrontation with Hitler, and muttering something about their thinking I wanted to do history, not current events, they decided to let me take a crack at Britain's reaction to the Anschluss of the previous March, rationalizing that an M.A. thesis was but an introduction to research methodology, data compilation, and rational presentation, and that technique was more important than topic in such an exercise. Since the Texas library was rich in its British newspaper and periodical collections, I could take a crack at it. Just to complicate matters, as an undergraduate I had taken enough courses in Education to qualify for a second major, lacking only a session of practice teaching to qualify for a Permanent Teacher's Certificate for the State of Texas. Dad had insisted that I get that little chore attended to as an insurance policy, so I duly signed on for an eighth grade civics class at the University Junior High

School, which, incidentally, I thoroughly enjoyed. With those matters taken care of, I returned to the Deke House, where I had reserved a room for the year, and began the life of a full-fledged graduate student.

One of the pure delights of fraternity life in the Deke House was our cook, Adelaide Williams, a negro lady in her late thirties whose mother had been a fixture there for twenty-five years and whom Adelaide as a youngster had come in to help on special occasions, and had now succeeded. Not only was she superlative at her trade, but she also brought with her an inquiring mind and prodigious common sense and a feeling for people that was truly remarkable. To all of her "boys" she was surrogate mother, as tender when mending broken hearts as she was disapproving when ministering to hangovers. The one thing she could not abide was the waste of time and talent by those among us who viewed the university as some vast playground and classes as something to be avoided whenever possible. For most of us we feared her glower of disapproval more than parental strictures, and I give her full credit for making me stick to a work schedule that enabled me to beat the deadline for my completed thesis.

But with her insatiable curiosity, she was perhaps the best student in the Deke House. Whenever she could spare the time, she would ask me to come down to the kitchen and explain what was going on in Europe.

"Mister Jack, how can you be so sure there is going to be another war? All those people running things over there were in the last war, like my father was, and the last thing he wants is another one."

So with my map of Europe spread out on her work table, I would point out the demilitarized zone of the Rhineland, a severely diminished Austria forever forbidden to unite with Germany, Czechoslovakia with its Sudeten Germans, a resurrected Poland with its corridor separating East from West Prussia, all of these things dictated, not negotiated, by the victors at Versailles.

"Now, Adelaide, think of Versailles as a chicken coop full of big fat fryers, and Hitler as the sly fox who has a covetous eye on those chickens. Believing the farmer will be too frightened to oppose him, the fox slips into the henhouse and carries off the Rhineland, and sure enough, the farmer is too afraid to reach for his shotgun. So the fox comes back and carries off Austria, and still the farmer is paralyzed. And so it will go until the farmer realizes that he must reach for his gun or face an empty chicken coop. That is why the war is inevitable."

"But what about the Munich Agreement?" Adelaide protested, "Didn't Mr. Chamberlain say that this is 'peace for our time'?"

"At Munich," I replied, "the fox said all he wanted was a little pullet, the Sudetenland, and that would be enough chicken to last him for 25 years, and when the farmer said O.K. if that's a promise, the fox grabbed not only the pullet but the mother hen as well. Now there's just one chicken, Poland, left in the henhouse, and I promise you that before the end of summer, the fox will go after that one as well. What the farmer will do then no one knows, but I predict he will finally reach for his gun."

"I hear you, Mr. Jack, but I still don't believe grown men can be that stupid," she protested. "Why, the boys in this house, even the ones who do nothing but play, have more sense than that!"

"Adelaide," I replied, "I hate to say this, but I'm afraid most of the boys in this house are going to find themselves defending the henhouse before this is all over." The Molotov-Ribbentrop Pact in April 1939 made that look like better than an even bet.

At the end of the term in May, appearing before my august Faculty Committee, I managed to pass my oral exam and successfully defend my thesis, which now needed only minor revisions and re-typing. Taking it with me, I was off to Denver to visit relatives with my parents and sister, who had attended the University of Colorado at Boulder for two years before graduating from TSCW.

I had last seen Louise when we came home for the Christmas break and stayed over for the annual Cotton Bowl game in Dallas on New Year's day, which this year matched the University of Colorado Buffaloes against the Rice Institute Owls from Houston, the first major bowl appearance for both teams. The Owls were favored because of two excellent running backs, Johnny Nance and Frank Steen, and greater team speed and depth, but the Buffaloes featured one of the greatest all-purpose players of the era, the All-American Byron "Whizzer" White, who had a sensational first half leading Colorado to a 14 point lead, only to see Rice finally prevail 28-14.

During the festivities attendant to the game, Louise had introduced me to one of her college chums, a statuesque Pi Phi who had been Colorado's Homecoming Queen that year. Her name, Ruth Lelani Drinkwater, did not belie her beauty, and if my English nurse had reminded me of Madeline Carroll, Ruth could have been her twin. I was just plain bedazzled, and in my subsequent letters to Louise concerning our summer plans, I invariably asked about Ruth, who lived in Denver—would she be around, what were my chances of seeing her? And my good honest sister invariably reminded me that Ruth was the most popular co-ed on campus, that her would-be swains formed a lengthy line, and that the most earnest contender for her favor was a guy named Whizzer White! Oh well, I had met her and I liked to think I had detected a slight smile when we were introduced.

On reaching Denver, I holed up for three days with my thesis, attending to the revisions, then engaged a typist to make a clean copy, had it duplicated and sent the original back to the university in time to make the deadline for the Summer Commencement. Then I turned to important things.

"Louise?"

"Yes."

"Is Ruth in town?"

"I think so."

"You think so. You mean you haven't seen her lately?"

"No. I haven't seen her lately. I told you we weren't the closest of friends."

"You mean you haven't told her I'm here?"

"Yes, I mean I haven't told her you are here or that you were even coming, so I don't think she's expecting you."

"What a sister!"

"What a pest!"

But sometimes the gods do smile, however briefly. Louise had a boyfriend, Tom, a congenial, humorous guy, who, as it happened, loved to play bridge. Louise loved to play bridge, as did I. It also so happened that Tom was a good friend of Ruth's. So when one day Louise and Tom and I were wondering who we could get for a fourth, I asked him if by any chance one Ruth Lelani Drinkwater played bridge, he replied that she did and was very good at it.

"Would you then convey a message to her?"

"Be glad to. What is it?"

"Would you tell her that the tall, handsome, brilliant Texan who she could not take her eyes off of at the Cotton Bowl party would aspire to be her bridge partner and no later than tomorrow?" And by the Lord Harry, she accepted!

We played at my cousin's house the following afternoon, and when she walked in, I was bedazzled all over again. As her partner I had an astonishing run of cards which I somehow managed not to screw up, and we really had a fun game. After finishing the last rubber, I took the bull by the horns. Louise had told me about a famous amusement park on the outskirts of

Denver called Elitch's Gardens which among other things had two large dance casinos where all the big bands stopped over on their way to the West Coast, in short, a wonderful place to eat hamburgers, drink draft Coors, and enjoy the best swing music to be heard anywhere. I had also read that Ray Noble and his orchestra were beginning a four day stand tonight. So I suggested that we all go out there tonight and introduce me to the wonders of Elitch's, adding that although I realized that Coloradans didn't know much about playing football, I did presume that they could dance. Sometimes brass serves better than brains, for I got away with it and that's exactly what we did.

For me Elitch's was a pleasure dome—no hamburgers ever tasted so good, no beer was ever better, the dance floor was spacious, no band ever had a sweeter rhythm, and I was sharing it all with Ruth. It was inconceivable that she had come with me on such short notice; it was inconceivable that she had come with me under any circumstance. In the beginning it was I who was least adept on the dance floor. Louise and I had grown up on the "crowded floor" technique imposed by the postage-stamp spaces in the Adolphus and Baker Hotels in Dallas when the name bands stopped by, but here there was room galore and Ruth patiently coaxed me to extend my steps until I was comfortable in what I dubbed the "Rocky Mountain Glide." But the only thing that really mattered was that I was with Ruth and we were comfortable with each other, and we had already begun a crash course in "getting to know you."

Her father was a respected physician who had once practiced in Honolulu where she was born and hence her name. She had an older brother, Terry, who had just finished law school and gone to California to seek his fortune. She was going back to Boulder to get an M.A. in social work. Yes, she was older than I, by a year and a half, but that seemed inevitable since I had never been out with a girl who was not older than I. She got the short version of my European junket, at least feigned some interest in my thesis topic, took exception to the certainty of my gloomy predictions for the future, and envied my prospects with Commissioner Splawn in Washington, which she had once visited and found awesome. Eventually we got to the critical question.

"How long are you going to be here?" she asked.

"Ten days," I replied, explaining that I had to get home to work in my cousin Bert's filling station to get some pocket money before heading East, where I was expected on 15 September.

"Ten days," she repeated. "Gosh, that means I'll have to make some changes in my calendar," she said, squeezing my hand.

That did it, like the lark at heaven's gate. Tom and Louise brought me back to earth with the motion it was time to leave. I did not argue but countered with the suggestion that tomorrow night we ought to try the other pavilion, Lakeside, where Ted Weems was featuring a young vocalist named Perry Como. Ruth said she would try but wasn't sure and Louise demurred, but at least we agreed that the night following we would resume the bridge game.

At her front door, Ruth said that some way she would manage about tomorrow night, gave me a quick kiss, and stepped inside. There was not much sleep for me that night as I tossed and turned in my excitement and disbelief. And at lunch the next day with my family and relatives, I apparently was not masking my elation very well when Louise referred to me as "God's latest gift to the Pi Phis." Mother, who had looked in on our bridge game and met Ruth, tried, as always, to come to my rescue.

"Well, she is beautiful and she seemed perfectly nice."

To which Louise replied, "Granted she's all that and more, but I ought to remind my goo-goo eyed little brother that it would be hard to count the number of fraternity pins that have adorned her palpitating bosom—briefly; we used to refer to them as her 'sudden enthusiasms,' and since two days ago she didn't even know you existed, this one may set a new record for suddenness. So just relax and enjoy, while it lasts."

"Meow, meow," I snarled at her. "Spoken like a true Alpha Phi. She's probably been offered more pins than your whole chapter of crones put together."

Dad, who liked to trot out a literary quip on any occasion, chimed in. "And perhaps we ought to remind our young swain of A. E. Housman's advice to an English lad with a similar affliction—

When I was one and twenty, I heard a wise man say
'Give crowns and pounds and guineas, but not your heart away
Give pearls away and rubies, but keep your fancy free.'
But I was one and twenty. No use to talk to me.

When I was one and twenty, I heard him say again
'The heart out of the bosom is never given in vain.
Tis sold with tears aplenty, and bought with endless rue.
Now I am two and twenty, and oh, tis true, tis true.'

"Thank you all very much," I retorted with all the haughtiness I could muster, "but Mr. Housman's opinion has no relevance for me. May I remind my dear parents that their son won't be one and twenty until next December?" Fraternity pin. Gosh, I hadn't even thought of that. I wondered if I brought mine along. So after lunch I rushed upstairs and rummaged in my kit bag. There it was.

Ruth called to say she'd be able to do Lakeside after all, and would I like a guided tour of Denver beforehand. She picked me up in her pert little British Triumph convertible, which seemed an appropriate vehicle for so elfin a creature, and we drove all over the place including Cheeseman's Park, an oasis in the middle of the city, "enfolding sunny spots of greenery" with its lake and riding trails and picnic nooks galore. Lakeside was wonderful; Ted Weems was in great form and young Como was obviously a vocalist with a future, but we both decided that we liked Elitch's better and that we shouldn't miss Ray Noble's last night on Saturday.

Driving back to the city I wondered aloud how Cheeseman's Park might look in the moonlight, and without demurrer she agreed there was only one way to find out. I don't know how long we sat there but it was glorious and my recitation of Elizabeth Barrett Browning's. "How do I love thee? Let me count the ways . . ." seemed the perfect evocation of how we felt.

The next night Tom and I thoroughly trounced the girls at the bridge table, and Dad and Mother added to the evening by sitting in for a rubber, with Ruth being perfectly at ease with them and they with her. When I asked Louise if she and Tom would like to join us for Noble's last night, she suggested that we would probably have more fun by ourselves, and she was even nice about it.

Dancing to Noble's rendition of "The Lamps Are Low" we decided that was "our song," and he must have sensed how we felt when he graciously agreed to repeat it as his last number. We said little or nothing on the way to Cheeseman's, but once there I let Edna St. Vincent take over. "Love is not all, it is not meat nor drink . . ." And after fumbling in my pocket, I produced my treasured Deke pin.

Would she?
She would.
May I?
I might. I even managed to pin it to her blouse without dropping it. I looked at it, resting there. In all the world I could not imagine a more elegant setting for that pin. I couldn't stand

it. I had to get out of the car and move about in sheer exultation. She joined me, and hand in hand we walked down to the lake shore.

The last week was a mélange of happiness, or giddiness, as my sweet sister would put it—we did everything but have breakfast together. One afternoon while listening to her Debussy records, Whizzer White, already armed with a Rhodes scholarship and a professional football contract, dropped by to tell Ruth of his acceptance to Yale Law School and so, as he put it, he would be out of pocket for some time while trying to do his balancing act. They were old friends, maybe more, for all I knew, but if this was goodbye, they certainly didn't need me around and so I excused myself. She thanked me for that small courtesy that night, but in truth, our own goodbye was fast approaching, and elation was giving way to more somber thoughts. It seemed our earliest chance of reunion would be Christmas in either Denver or Washington, and neither of us was sure we could even manage that. So our last night was sadness, to say the least, and Elizabeth Barrett Browning's premonition of her death seemed all too apt.

> *Go from me . . . the widest land*
> *Doom takes to part us, leaves thy heart in mine*
> *With pulses beating double. What I do*
> *And what I dream include thee as the wine*
> *Must taste of its own grapes. And when I sue*
> *God for myself, He hears that name of thine*
> *And sees within my eyes the tears of two.*

She handed me two framed pictures, reminding me that the telephone lines ran in both directions, and I departed.

Driving back to Texas with my parents was one mood swing after another, happy at the thought of her but depressed by the separation. For no good reason on one of my highs, I ventured to my father, "Well, I've got the M.A. under my belt, I've pinned the most beautiful girl in all captivity, and in a couple of months I'll be taking on Washington. How's that for growing up!"

"Jack," he replied, smiling, "you're a very promising young man. The problem is that you'll promise anything. You remind me of the old hunter who took his young puppy for its first romp in the fields. The whelp dashed this way and that, wildly chasing everything he could see or hear or smell; and when he came back to his master panting heavily from near exhaustion, the hunter patted his head and said, 'Tiger, you're gonna be a good 'un, but so far you ain't treed nuthin'."

At 5 a.m. on Sunday morning, 1 September 1939, I was opening up my cousin Bert's Magnolia service station on Locust Street in Denton, Texas. I turned on the radio for some music, only to hear "We are interrupting our scheduled program to bring you the latest news bulletins. Hitler's Panzer divisions have crossed the Polish frontiers, and in response to their treaty obligations to Poland, Great Britain and France are expected momentarily to declare war on Germany ..." So much for Munich and "peace in our time"; the Molotov-Ribbentrop Pact had announced what was in store for Europe, and this news bulletin had removed the last bit of guesswork. The time was now. And what added immeasurably to my excitement was the knowledge that before long I would be seeing the "battlefield" at close hand.

That it should come to this was no surprise to Harry and me, but it was not a bet we wanted to win. My first instinct was to dash off a note to Ruth—this was Stalin's war as much as Hitler's, and now he might be able to realize his fondest dream, that Germany and the democracies might be able to bleed each other to death and then he could step among the carcasses and snatch any bit of the remains he chose. All of which made my Washington prospects seem a waste of time and what I ought to do now is what I should have done a year ago and that is sign up with some branch of our military. Repeating these thoughts to her on the phone that night, she fairly exploded; she wanted no more of that kind of talk, and until the issue of our involvement in this mess became clear, for her sake I would go as far and as fast as I could doing something useful. She must have been talking to my Dad.

I knew there was no time to waste and that Dad was right. "You should just try to be ready and that means getting as much formal education under your belt and as much experience of this world as quickly as you can. Play a little game with Hitler—see if you can get your Ph.D. before he screws everything up."

So that is why I arrived in Washington's Union Station on the morning of 14 September. Mother and Dad had taken me to the same depot from which he had departed ten years earlier for his fateful interview with Sol Hurok. Within walking distance of the station was the Dodge Hotel, where I checked in to freshen up before reporting in to my place of work. Then I took a taxi to the Interstate Commerce Commission (ICC), housed in a handsome building facing onto Constitution Avenue at 14th Street and directly across from the Mall and the Washington Monument. Across 14th Street was the Department of Justice with the Capitol in the distance, while in the other direction the ICC abutted on the Labor Department, and then the enormous Department of Commerce building which bordered on the White House grounds. There was no doubt about it—I was in the big middle of official Washington. The Commissioner's suite of offices occupied the southeast corner of the third floor along 14th Street and Constitution. I had been there briefly en route to Europe fifteen months earlier when I had been offered the position, but I had forgotten how imposing a place it was, and the thought of presiding over its activities was almost overwhelming.

Upon entering I introduced myself to the page in the reception area, and in short order I was made welcome and taken on the rounds to meet my associates. Reporting directly to me were the page, then Martha Blossom, senior stenographer and a formidable spinster with some thirty years as a civil servant, and then Glenn Kidd, administrative assistant, three years older than I and bright as a penny who was attending law school at night. Then there were those who reported through me—three senior examiners, transportation economists who, with their research assistants, handled the rate cases before the Commission over which my Commissioner had primary jurisdiction. In all of this I learned that one of my principal office functions was to be the traffic cop controlling access to the Commissioner, handling the appointments calendar, the log of impending hearings, time and place, and making sure that the Commissioner was thoroughly briefed on time on all the matters over which he had to pass judgment. What complicated all of this was the fact that Commissioner Splawn was blind.

My sojourn in Washington—from 14 September 1939 to 1 July 1941, 21 ½ months, to be exact—was a distinctive watershed in my life, and for three principal reasons. The first was the character of my employer, Dr. Splawn. The second was the fact that in this period, the State of Texas dominated Washington politically, and I was a Texan. The third is that because of the unique demands of my full-time position and my enrollment full-time in night school, my intellectual capacity was never more severely tested or stimulated.

Walter Marshal William Splawn was in many respects the most remarkable man I have ever known. An economist by profession, in the field of transportation he was the country's leading scholar, and his meteoric academic advancement in short order found him President of The University of Texas. He left that position to become Chairman of the Texas Railroad Commission, the state's most respected regulatory agency, where his reputation for mastery of the issues, probity and independence of mind became legendary. So it was not difficult for President Roosevelt, when the vacancy occurred, to heed Sam Rayburn's advice and appoint Dr. Splawn to the ICC.

In Austin our two families had become warm friends; his two daughters, Zoe and Mary, were the same age as Louise and I, and we frequently played together. But somewhere down the line his eyesight began to fail, and by the time he took his seat on the Commission, he could only discern light from darkness. But in a structured physical environment with which he was familiar, he could move about and comport himself with such assurance that many a visitor to his office and many a lawyer who pled his brief at a hearing were unaware of his debility. He knew the exact number of steps from his desk to his private bathroom, from his office door to the elevator, from the elevator to the hearing room, from the hearing room door to his seat on the bench, from the garage elevator to his car, and the same for his apartment at the Kennedy-Warren and at his country home in Lincoln, Virginia. His retentive capacity for facts and figures was more than extraordinary, it was magical. Before each hearing I would read him page after page of numerical comparisons and statistical analyses over which he had full command on the bench. So in that sense it was my responsibility to assure that he was at ease in his professional environment at the ICC. Outside of it, I was, of course, his eyes and the proverbial "fly on the wall" whether it was to the Oval Office, where he was summoned with some frequency as a member of Roosevelt's "kitchen cabinet" or to Capitol Hill to visit with his Texas cronies, it was I who took him and sat quietly in the corner taking notes of the proceedings. He enjoyed having lunch at the Cosmos Club with old friends, and he told me the old saw about Washington's clubs: The Metropolitan had the money, the Cosmos had the brains, and the Army-Navy had the chef. So my role with this remarkable man gave me an exceptional exposure to the inner workings of our national government.

And this experience was accentuated by the "movers and shakers" that I was exposed to. Probably never before nor since has one State exercised such influence in Washington as did Texas at this point in time. John Nance Garner of Uvalde was Vice President of the United States. He lived up to and enjoyed his sobriquet of "Cactus Jack," as he did his visits to a small, sparsely furnished room in the Capital marked simply on the door as Office of Education, and inside of which was a table and chairs and a refrigerator holding a goodly supply of ice and

Mount Vernon Rye. This was where the VP liked to relax with friends and colleagues and, as he put it while pouring the drinks, "Gentlemen, we're gonna strike a blow for liberty." The two ranking Senators by seniority were both from Texas, Morris Sheppard and Tom Connolly, who respectively chaired the Senate's two most powerful committees, Appropriations and Foreign Relations. So the Senate side of the Hill was in good hands.

On the House side, the Speaker was the venerable Sam Rayburn of Bonham, and no more honest, tougher, wiser, abler man ever dominated that assembly than "Mr. Sam." But before anyone could hope to do business with the Speaker, he must first pass the cynosure of "Miss Alla," who presided over his office. Mr. Rayburn was a bachelor, and Alla Clary, from Sherman, was a spinster, but their celibate relationship, based on long years of friendship, loyalty, respect and complete trust, was really a "marriage made in Heaven." And in those days when seniority was the *sine qua non* for influence on the Hill, they presided over a state congressional delegation that was cohesive and potent, for Texas had long since learned the importance of continuity of representation. So things boded well for the political fortunes of the baby member of the delegation, a brash, wild-eyed liberal named Lyndon Johnson, who had just preceded me to Washington.

And not only on the Hill were there Texans in high places; besides Commissioner Splawn, there was Marvin Jones, Chief Justice of the U. S. Court of Claims, and Luther Evans was librarian of Congress. Texans were also the heart and soul of another enterprise fundamental to the city's sense of well-being and civic pride: Sammy Baugh of TCU was the legendary quarterback of the Washington Redskins throwing touchdown passes to Dick Nolan and Charlie Malone of Texas A&M against the detestable New York Giants and the unspeakable Chicago Bears. So in the Washington of those halcyon days there was a hint of truth in the old saying that it was tough to be humble if you were a Texan.

Finally for me, already exhilarated by my crash course on "inside Washington," there came the icing on the cake. The Wilcox family of Sherman had grown up with the Rayburn's, and their son, Billy, a friend of mine at UT, had just been appointed as the junior member of the Speaker's staff. His arrival in Washington coincided with the fact that Miss Clary had just purchased a home in a lovely rural community in Virginia called Falls Church, a drive of some thirty minutes from the city. She loved the tranquility, but the house was really too large for a single person and there was a sense of isolation. Would Billy and I like to share one of her spare bedrooms? Would we ever! So here was I, not yet one and twenty, the private secretary of a member of the President's "kitchen cabinet" living with a woman who in her way was far more influential than Virginia Cafritz, the reigning hostess of the capital's social scene.

The third element in my Washington equation was my academic race with Herr Hitler. After hostilities had been declared in September, Britain had sent an expeditionary force to bolster the French, but neither had been able to do anything to help the hapless Poles, and in the West the lack of military activity had been dubbed the "phony war."

Dad had discussed with Dr. Splawn my restiveness, and they had agreed that one of the conditions for my coming to Washington was that I would enroll in night school, which I had done immediately upon my arrival. The Evening Graduate Division of American University at its "downtown campus" was a full-fledged academic program geared to the needs of government employees and manned by a creditable faculty drawn largely from government specialists. I needed advanced hours in my major subject matter areas of British and European History and International Relations, and in my minor fields of American History and Economic Statistical Analysis, all of which were readily available. But perhaps the most formidable hurdle between me and the Ph.D. was the foreign language requirement which meant, for my area of concentration, that I must demonstrate an absolute reading proficiency in both French and German, thus enabling me to do research in original archival sources. For some reason Spanish had been my undergraduate foreign language, and though it had been useful at Bacharach, it was of no help toward the Ph.D., and so I now needed crash courses in French and German. Happily in the Washington area there were language tutors in abundance who would work with me at odd hours, such as lunchtime, and that is the route I chose. So Monday through Thursday nights from 7 to 10 p.m. found me in the classroom at American U. The weekends I had to reserve for the Commissioner—on Friday afternoons in good weather I would drive him to Springdale, his country place in Virginia near Purcellville, for the weekend, returning early Monday morning.

I learned to love the place almost as much as he—the long walks through the countryside, accompanied by Dan, the colored hand who maintained the place, who helped me describe the texture of the grass, the seasonal colors of the foliage, the rate of flow in the streams, the wild flowers, the fences needing repair—and on Sunday mornings the meeting of the Friends in the little Quaker chapel. On Saturdays nights we were always joined by the Commissioner's youngest daughter, Mary, my erstwhile Austin playmate, a 1938 Vassar graduate who had married a gentleman farmer named Tom in the community, a graduate of Guildford, and they lived in a restored farmhouse just up the road. Among other things Tom was quite an athlete, and he and I played on the Purcellville semi-pro baseball team on Saturday afternoons, after which we would enjoy a couple of beers at the local tavern, and sometimes his home-brewed elderberry wine. A fine old oak tree graced the front lawn of Springdale and its trunk exactly fitted the curvature of my spine, and three hours a day I leaned against it and struggled with my wretched reading assignments, my French and German dictionaries close at hand. Busy, glorious days, with Sunday nights reserved for briefings for Dr. Splawn's Monday schedule.

Besides being the seat of our nation's government, Washington had myriad other attractions, if one could find the time to partake. There was, for example, Constitution Hall which, despite being owned and operated by the DAR, had a splendid concert series, and my Sunday matinee season ticket brought me the New York Philharmonic and solo artists like Melchior and Flagstad. The National Theater brought some of the best and some otherwise from Broadway. The epic screen presentation of all time, *Gone With The Wind* almost brought the government to a standstill with the number of grandmothers in urgent need of attention.

Griffith Stadium was home to the beloved Redskins, and at the end of the 1940 season I witnessed their two classic battles with the Chicago Bears. In the first, the Redskins won 7-3, stopping the Bears at the one foot line on the last play of the game and thus denying them a single touchdown, all of which set up the re-match two weeks later for the League championship and forcing Billy Wilcox and me to stand in line for four hours to get our tickets. Receiving the opening kickoff, it was clear that Luckman, McAfee, Bulldog Turner, et.al. were out for blood, marching straight down the field to lead 7-0; but then the Redskins took the ensuing kickoff and mounted a drive of their own with Baugh hitting a wide-open Charlie Malone in the end zone, only to see him drop the ball. The end result, 73-0, made professional football history. Griffith Stadium also provided comic relief as the home of the hapless Senators, forever immortalized by the inspired quip of a sportswriter: "Ah,

Washington, first in war, first in peace, and last in the American League." But when DiMaggio's Yankees or Ted Williams' Red Sox came to town, the place was worth a visit.

There was also a monthly luncheon of DKE alumni in the District, which was pleasant and considerably enlarged my social contacts. I was introduced to the group by Hallan Huffman, by then my best friend in the ICC, an Examiner in Commissioner Mahaffie's office and an expert in the trucking industry. He had been a Deke at the University of Minnesota and remains the only man I ever knew who hailed from Bemidji. He and his wife were serious bridge players, and whenever they need a fourth, I was their man. I mention him here because some three years later, it was he who inadvertently tipped me off to the existence of the Manhattan Project.

So with work, school, and whatever extracurricular activities that time permitted, I really had more on my platter than I could say Grace over, which was fortunate for another reason. I hadn't seen Ruth since June, and the letters and telephone calls did little to ease my pain; I missed her so much that at times I literally ached and was sustained only by the prospect of a possible Christmas in Denver. But by November the change had begun, her letters were less frequent and less fervent, and only a complete dunce could have failed to sense what was coming next. She did her best to be gentle—she wanted so badly to see me, she knew I was one person who would make a difference in this world and she was proud to have been a tiny part of it, she would forever be grateful for the perfect moments we had shared, but she was making no commitment that would take her away from her beloved mountain milieu and being together again would only prolong the agony, so the only sensible thing was to end it here and now, and on this she would insist.

It stands to reason that the receipt of one's first "Dear John" letter must be the most unnerving, and this one was numbing. My desperate reply, intended as a passionate rejection of her proposal, was most certainly puerile, but it was the best I could muster at the time. In the event, I did spend Christmas in Denver, but it was because of Louise. She was working there and in December had contracted viral pneumonia, being released from the hospital the middle of the month, and my parents hoped I could be with her during the holidays; indeed, they had explained the situation to the Commissioner, who insisted that I go. When I called Ruth, she said by all means come and of course she would see me but, please, no illusions about the future.

So that is how I found myself aboard two of America's storied trains, B & O's Capitol Limited from Washington to Chicago and Union Pacific's new Zephyr on to Denver. Louise was much improved but still weak, and I was glad I had come. Ruth and I spent an afternoon and evening together; Elitch's was closed for the winter and Cheeseman's Park was icy, but we managed. It was as incredible as ever until the end, when she handed me back my fraternity pin, and that was that. Yes, Mr. Housman, I was now one and twenty. On returning to Washington, I wrote my father the briefest of letters:

Dear Dad,

If in future you would advise another young man to grow up in a hurry, tell him to fall in love in Cheeseman's Park. Louise is fine.

Your obedient son,

For me and much of the world, 1940 was the year of decision. When Hitler, with Poland under his heel, turned westward, the "phony" war was revealed in all its savagery. Churchill and Reynaud replaced Chamberlain and Daladier, but nothing could stop the breakthroughs of the Wehrmacht with the Luftwaffe in close support, thus revealing the horrid truth that Germany's was the only General staff in the whole world to have learned the tactical answers to the siege conditions of the Great War. So there followed in quick and tragic order the refugees streaming across the saddened fields of fallen France, the British Expeditionary Force (BEF) driven into the sea at Dunkerque, and then Britain's turn herself as Goering launched his all-out offensive against the RAF and her air defenses. The single relief from this unmitigated gloom was the indomitable voice of Churchill still hurling his defiance.

In the United States in general and in Washington in particular there were two burning questions, quite different in detail but inextricably linked: what would be the official reaction to the plight of our erstwhile Allies, and would President Roosevelt seek a third term of office? And thanks to my fairly strategic placement in the capital scene, I was able to witness these developments at first hand.

As to the first question, thanks to Miss Alla Clary and Billy Wilcox of the Interstate Commerce Commission (ICC) staff, I always had a seat in the Observers' Gallery in the House of

Representatives, and the Commissioner was invariably generous in granting me the time to go to the Hill. Thus I heard the questions raised, the key debates, and the actions taken—armed neutrality and the arming of our merchant ships; destroyers for bases; Lend-Lease; national conscription under a Selective Service System—that moved us inexorably closer to the war, with Churchill's impassioned plea of "Give us the tools and we will finish the job!" as a backdrop. The nay-sayers, the America Firsters—Borah, Couglin, Lindberg, Joe Kennedy—were in full voice but were no match for the Administration as emergency measures were sent up for the President's eager signature. Sometime later, I was present in the Labor Department Auditorium when our Secretary of War, Henry Stimson, stood blindfolded before the fishbowl on the dais and withdrew the first fateful draft number—but by this time it was all academic as far as I was concerned.

As for the third term issue, I was present when the President publically answered the question himself for anyone accustomed to his penchant for oblique phraseology. The occasion was the laying of the cornerstone for the Jefferson Memorial at the Tidal Basin. At the close of the expected eulogy and with trowel in hand, the President concluded the ceremony by remarking how honored he was to have laid the cornerstone at what would be a lasting tribute to this extraordinary statesman and how much he hoped, like everyone else present to be there for the dedication of the completed edifice. When I got back to the office I fairly burst into the Commissioner's room to announce that I had heard it with my own ears—the President is going to run again, although I caught myself just in time to add, "but I'm sure you knew it all the time."

In any event, it was the Battle of Britain that decided everything for me. The fall of France and the supreme irony of the picture of Hitler standing in the circular balcony of Les Invalides gazing down on Napoleon's sarcophagus spelled disaster but held no surprise for me. Dunkerque, although mitigated by the miraculous salvation of the BEF, was nonetheless a disaster, albeit a part of the anticipated French miracle. But the Battle of Britain had an emotional impact that hit me right in the middle of the solar plexus. Perhaps it was the unparalleled gallantry of Sir Hugh Dowding's storied "few." Undoubtedly a large part of it was the nightly wail of London's sirens and Ed Murrow's terse commentary that brought it all into our homes. Without question it was Mr. Churchill's evocation of

Tennyson's elegy on break of day, which he directed straight at me,

> *And not through Eastern windows only,*
> *When daylight comes, comes in the light.*
> *In front the sun climbs slow, how slowly,*
> *But westward look, the land is bright.*

It was the clarion call, but what branch of the service had I considered? That stumped me. With all my pious mouthings about the need to do something, I had really never given any serious thought as to precisely what, which seems clear evidence that my response to world events had been far more visceral than intellectual.

"How about the RAF (Royal Air Force)," I suggested to the Commissioner.

The Commissioner's smile was worth the price of admission: that benign face would light up, the eyes would sparkle, and if he disagreed with you, he would raise them toward Heaven, which he now did.

"Oh," he answered, "I'm sure you would be welcome, but the problem is your nationality. Were you Canadian, you could join the Royal Canadian Air Force (RCAF), were you Polish you could join Sikorski's group, or were you French you could join DeGaulle: but as an American in some other nation's armed forces, you would always be a maverick. No you would be much better served, and you would better serve your country, if you joined an American unit."

And as proof that he had given more thought to my future than I had, he asked, "Have you given any thought to military intelligence? With your academic background, you know a great deal more about Europe than most people your age, or my age for that matter, and if you continue to work on your language proficiency, I should think you have a great deal to offer to our intelligence people."

I literally jumped at the idea, and he told me to put through a telephone call to his friend and colleague, Henry Stimson.

That is how I found myself a week later in the War Department seated at the desk of Colonel Robert Johnson, an Army Intelligence officer, armed with my diploma and my academic records, and recounting briefly my one foray into Europe. I asked him if he thought I could be of use to his operation. After actually studying my transcripts, he began to ask me questions to test my grasp of the contemporary European scene, such as political and military leadership, command systems, relative Army, Naval, and Air Force strengths in being, and the like. Finally he asked me in what regional geographic area I felt most competent and comfortable with. I stated that I had a pretty good grasp of the general 19th and 20th century European panorama, particularly its political, diplomatic and military aspects, but where I felt most at home was Great Britain and her empire, partly by predilection and obviously because of language.

"You should understand, Sir, that although I am working on my French and German, my competence there is at best minimal."

"Don't worry about that," he replied, "for we have methods for speeding that up." And then he got to the point. "How soon do you think you could join us? We also have ways of speeding up the commissioning process."

Not even trying to mask my astonishment and elation, and shaking my head in disbelief, I managed an answer. "Sir, I would guess within a month at the outside. It all depends on how long it takes me to leave the Commissioner's office in good working order. Were it not for that, I would be here tomorrow!"

Colonel Johnson stood up, and I assumed the interview was over. Instead, he stepped from behind his desk and went to each of his office doors to make sure they were securely closed, and resumed his seat. He looked me straight in the eye and in a lowered voice said, "Young man, I am impressed with your record and I like the cut of your jib. So in all honesty, I must tell you that in my professional opinion, on the basis of the quality of its personnel, I consider the finest branch of all our armed services to be the Naval Air Corps. Have you given it a thought?"

Considering the source, I was dumbfounded. "No Sir, I have not. I know absolutely nothing about aviation. I have never been up in a plane. I have never been near a plane. I know no one who flies a plane. The very idea of flying is foreign to me."

"But," he retorted, "You told your Commissioner you wanted to join the RAF."

"That, Sir, was a mere stab in the dark." But now it was clear that Dr. Splawn had discussed me in some detail with Mr. Stimson.

Colonel Johnson continued. "Right across the Potomac River is the Anacostia Naval Air Station. Why don't you go over there and see if you are physically qualified for flying duty, but you should know that their standards are very, very rigorous. Now don't misunderstand me; I am not trying to get rid of you. We badly need persons of your caliber in our work here, and should you not pass the Navy physical, you come right back to me and my offer stands. So what do you have to lose?"

Thinking that I should never meet a more honest man, I thanked him and departed.

It took something over a month to get my appointment for a physical at Anacostia, and then two days of the most exhaustive testing I had ever undergone. Not a portion of my anatomy went unprobed. I was told I should get the results within two weeks. Finally, I received a summons to report to the Medical Department at the Air Station, where I was informed that I was of sound body and the psychiatrist had attested to reasonable sanity. Would I please take these papers and report to the yeoman in the Administrative Office. There I was handed another sheaf of papers to be filled out but with the injunction that before I could proceed I would have to produce my birth certificate.

"I don't have one. Why is that so important?"

He fixed me with that superior stare that all yeomen instinctively cultivate when dealing with civilians.

"The papers you just handed me indicate you are alive, but we have no proof that you were born, and the Government insists on proof."

So there went another two weeks until the sacred document arrived from the Office of Vital Statistics of Bell County, Texas. Back to the Air Station where I handed the yeoman the certificate which I had barely glanced at and proceeded to fill out the forms. In a few minutes he came over to check my progress.

"Jesus Christ," he ejaculated, "don't you even know your own birthday?"

"What the hell are you talking about? According to my mother it is December 2, 1918, and I've been celebrating it for 21 years!"

"Well," he retorted, "with all due respect to your mother, your birth certificate says December 3, 1918, and from this day forward that's what Uncle Sam will say."

It then dawned on me that old Doc Ferguson must have reported my arrival a day late, but why argue. So from that day on I have celebrated both the 2nd and the 3rd, pointing out to my friends that presents are appropriate on either day. When all the papers were finally completed, I was told to await orders to active duty and to report any interim change of address without delay. So at long last, the die was cast. I had kept Colonel Johnson informed of all of this, and now I made my last call to thank him again. It was now the end of October, 1940.

At this particular point in time there was no apparent sense of urgency on the part of the U.S. Navy; I did not report for active duty until 1 June 1941. Although I wondered more than once at the wisdom of my decision, the interim was useful for me in many ways. For one thing, it enabled me on 21 January 1941 to join Miss Clary and Billy in choice seats at the inauguration of FDR as the first third term President in the history of our Republic. It was a clear, bitterly cold day, but a sense of high drama pervaded the shivering spectators, and as I witnessed the President and his running mate, Henry Wallace, take the oath of office, I got a tincture of satisfaction in remembering that I had got his message at the Jefferson Memorial. Afterwards we attended a large reception of jubilant Democrats in the Capitol building hosted by Speaker Rayburn.

Of larger importance was the fact that my wait for orders enabled me to complete another full semester at American University. The greatest relief of all was that I somehow managed to fulfill my foreign language requirements, aided by the fortuitous selection of the passages I was required to translate. For French I was given a selection dealing with the defense of Verdun in 1916, and for German, the siege of Paris in 1871, events that I was familiar with which helped enormously with my translations. So from September 1939 to June 1941 in two full terms and one summer session I had completed all of my course work plus the languages, so that all that stood between me and the Ph.D. was the dissertation. I had even decided on my topic— Great Britain's reaction to the Spanish Civil War, 1936-1939, which was to include the effect of the bombing of Guernica on British attitudes. So in academic terms, I had fallen short of the target, but I had given it my best shot.

What I had not fallen short of was a dazzling exposure to the art of government in our nation's capital during one of the most critical periods in our country's history against the backdrop of a world in turmoil. I had witnessed our slow climb as a nation from the depths of isolationism to a clear commitment to the defense of the Western democratic tradition, and I had been at the nerve-center of the process. In all of this I had finally found a role for myself in that commitment. The most profound personal lesson of my Washington experience however was the opportunity to observe how sheer strength of intellect can defeat the debilitating vagaries of nature. In President Roosevelt I could watch it sometimes at close hand but mostly from a distance. But given my uniquely intimate relationship with Commissioner Splawn, his ability to cope was part of my daily existence, and I shall be forever grateful to this remarkable human being for allowing me to be useful in his personal and professional life.

Dad and me in our living room, 1941

Now, whether the U. S. Naval Air Corps and I were meant for each other remained to be seen, but I was two and twenty and ready for the courtship.

Addendum 1

In 1970 when I became President of the University of Southern California, one of my prerequisites was membership in the Los Angeles Country Club. On my first visit there I was introduced to the current Club President, Terry Drinkwater, who had just retired as CEO of Capitol Air Lines and who, I learned later, was a notable wit and raconteur.

"May I presume," I asked, "that you are one of the Denver Drinkwaters?"

"You may," he replied, "but how do you know the Denver Drinkwaters?"

"Well," I said, "in the summer of 1938 I paid court to a beautiful girl named Ruth Lelani."

"Oh, I heard about you," and with that he took me into the Men's Grill and announced, "Hey fellows, I want you to meet the new President of USC, and the guy who tried to screw my sister."

Nonplussed, I replied, "Mr. Drinkwater, I won't deny your allegation, but there must be a more elegant way to phrase it!"

Addendum II

One of the annual highlights of the USC Law School is the Moot Court competition, when senior students argue hypothetical cases before sitting judges who have been invited for the occasion, one of whom is generally from the U.S. Supreme Court. In 1975 that dignitary was Associate Justice Byron White. As President of the University it was my function to open the proceedings by introducing the distinguished panel of judges and the competing teams. Afterwards I was walking with Mr. White to luncheon, and I said, "Mr. Justice, there is no reason for you to remember me, but I remember you on two distinct occasions. My sister went to Boulder and I took her to the 1939 Cotton Bowl game, and I have not forgotten your brilliant first half against Rice. The second time I saw you was that summer in Denver. I was sitting in Ruth Drinkwater's living room the afternoon you came to say goodbye to her before heading East. She introduced us and I excused myself, but if you noticed that strange fraternity pin she was wearing, it was mine."

"I certainly remember that game—Rice was just too much for us, but we scared them. As for Denver, I recall saying goodbye to Ruth, but I don't remember you. She was a beautiful girl, but she must have been smarter than both of us thought because she didn't marry either of us."

Part II
—
Adventures in Naval Aviation
Enroute to Tokyo

Lt. Commander John R. "Jack" Hubbard, U.S. Navy Reserves, Air Corps

CHAPTER 5
—
Anacostia Elimination Base

Throughout the country there were some Naval Air Stations which bore the designation of "E Base," the "E" standing for the elimination of those deemed unfit for further flight training. It was to these bases that civilian aspirants, having successfully passed the rigorous physical examination, first reported for active duty, where they were duly sworn into the Navy as Seamen 2nd Class, issued perfectly plain khaki uniforms, assigned quarters, and then turned over to Marine drill instructors. Anacostia Naval Air Station, located along the Potomac in Southeast Washington, District of Columbia, was one of these, and it was here that I reported on 1 June 1941, along with sixteen other candidates for a new flight class. We were all volunteers, having signed up at various times during 1940 but only now called up, an indication that at this point the Naval Air Corps was in no great hurry to augment its numbers. The drill at each E base was exactly the same and very simple: we were each to receive up to ten hours of flight instruction, after which we must demonstrate our ability to fly the airplane solo, although we could solo anytime at our instructor's discretion. In our group, the average time for solo was seven hours. If one failed to solo, he could re-enter civilian life or he could ask for assignment to another branch of the Navy. If he successfully soloed, his designation was changed to that of Aviation Cadet (AVCAD) and he could await assignment to the traditional flying school at Pensacola, Florida, or to the one newly commissioned at NAS Jacksonville, Florida. In the meantime, between instructional flights, we were introduced to the strange and wonderful world of the Navy, which included learning a whole new language.

So that is how, the morning after our induction, we found ourselves on our hands and knees with pails of soapy water swabbing the decks of the Administration building. I was galloping along at a great rate until I backed into one of my new colleagues, a hulking Jewish lad with a craggy face and voice to match.

"What's the matter, Bud?" he snarled. "Isn't this place big enough for you?"

Which is one way friendships are formed.

Then the Drill Instructors, with innate disgust punctuating their commands, introduced us to the rudiments of marching in unison. There were lectures on Naval history, manners, and morals. We got our first taste of semaphore signals and Morse Code. Our lecture on the use of a parachute ended with the admonition that this was one drill we never practice since it was strongly recommended that we be perfect the first time if we had to bailout. We learned what bulkheads, ladders, and the head were. At our mess we began the endless regimen of carrots at breakfast, lunch and dinner, which supposedly would sharpen our eyesight. It was all very strange, and while not quite wonderful, different enough to be interesting, something akin to one's first summer camp. And just then, as at the outset, it seemed unlikely that this motley crew could ever be shaped into a cohesive unit of happy campers.

My flight instructor, Ensign Shawn Brios, was right out of Central Casting. Of medium height with a supple frame, a shock of curly black hair presiding over a dark, handsome visage punctuated by piercing black eyes, perfect teeth set in a mouth that seemed trying without success to mask a sneer, he was perfectly accoutered in a well-tailored uniform over burnished jodhpurs, and with those wings of gold pinned neatly over his left breast tunic pocket. He was by designation, as well as by aura, a fighter pilot. He had just returned from fleet duty aboard one of our storied carriers, the *USS Saratoga*, and he must have been wondering at the cruelty of the detail officer who had condemned him to shore duty which involved trying to teach the likes of me how to fly. In all the fleet there was no ignominy like coming a cropper at the hands of some ham-handed flying cadet.

We all met our instructors outside the hangar on the flight line with our training planes aligned in a neat row. These were Stearman single-engine bi-planes, affectionately known as "Yellow Perils" because they were all painted a solid bright yellow so they could more easily be spotted from the air in the event of a forced landing at sea or on the land. In the event, it was marvelously stable and air worthy, and for its purpose I suggest no better aircraft was ever designed. We had each been issued a parachute and a flying helmet with a gosport, which was a speaking tube issuing from each ear flap extending into the front cockpit and thus permitting one-way communication from the instructor to the student.

Stearman single engine on display at Pima Air & Space Museum

Ensign Brios' first question established the fact that we were beginning from absolute ground zero—that I had never flown, been up in, or even close to an airplane before. If that be true, he wondered, why had I chosen this branch of the service? Not mentioning Colonel Johnson, of course, I replied that I guess I wanted to see if I had "that something extra." I was referring to Naval Air Corps recruiting posters that were beginning to appear on billboards around the country which asked the question. "Have you got that something extra? Then wear those wings of gold!"

"Well," he replied, "we'll soon find out."

Checking to see that my parachute was correctly buckled, he bade me to climb into the rear cockpit and secure my seat belt; then he pointed out the essentials—first the controls, such as stick, throttle, rudder bar and brake pedals, and then the instrument panel of compass, airspeed indicator, and needle and ball turn and bank indicator, and last but not least, the ignition switch. He then climbed into the front cockpit, signaled to the plane captain to crank up the engine accelerator, switched on the ignition, and when the engine caught, he warmed it up by setting the throttle up a bit. When all was ready, he stuck out his left fist with thumb up as a signal to pull the parking chocks. With that, he began to taxi to the active runway, guiding the airplane with the brake pedals. At the end of the runway he set the brakes and revved up the engine to full throttle, checking the magnetos for any drop in revolutions per minute (rpms), and satisfied, taxied into for-take-off position, and off we went. It was a lovely cloudless morning, and our initial flight path took us towards DC; there it was as I had never seen it, the Capitol, the Washington Monument, the Lincoln Memorial, the Reflection Basin—surely the most capital of ALL Capitals. Then we swung south down the Potomac estuary, over Mount Vernon and the wooded countryside until there emerged a clearing in the forest that contained a graveled landing strip with a ramshackle building at one end. This was Hybla Valley, an outlying training field from which we would operate, and where, God willing, we would make our first solo flights.

Before landing, however, Brios, through the gosport, explained that one of the keys to flying was to have confidence in your aircraft and to understand its limitations, so he was going to perform some maneuvers to show me what the Stearman was capable of. We would find ourselves in some unusual positions but try not to be frightened and should I become ill to so indicate by wiggling the stick. First, though, I had to make sure my seat belt was tightly fastened. Not knowing what to expect I could hardly be frightened, but an alarm bell certainly went off. We started innocently enough with some gentle wing-overs, and then came a relatively simple and graceful loop. So far, so good. But then in succession came a split-s, a snap roll, and a slow roll, and I did not know which end was up. Finally we climbed up to 8,000 feet, and he explained to me how an airplane through loss of flying speed might stall and fall off into a spin, and in that event, how to recover. So saying, he put us into a spin and, talking to me all the time, he then pulled us out of it by thrusting the stick forward and kicking the opposite rudder from the direction of the spin. It worked like magic. The upshot of all of this was that I had every confidence in the Stearman but none whatsoever that I would ever be able to put it through its paces.

On our way back to the Hybla Valley for what was to be my first landing, Brios explained that we would be making a carrier approach and that he would talk to me throughout the whole procedure. The key, he explained, was control of the airspeed throughout the landing pattern, and until one mastered that, everything else was futile as far as a precision landing was concerned, that is to say, the ability to touch down at a given spot.

Me (Jack) in flight training outfit—Anacostia, DC, Summer 1941

(It may be useful to point out here that at this time that basic to the Navy's flight training procedures was the assumption that every pilot at some stage of his career would operate from a carrier, and critical to that operation was the landing—the ability to hit the back end of the carrier deck tail down and as slow as possible so that the tail hook could engage the arresting cable and so stop the aircraft in a very limited space. Landing on water excepted, it follows that regardless of the airstrip from which you are operating, and regardless of the type of aircraft you are flying, every landing approach should be a simulated carrier approach, and every landing should be designed, within the limits of safety, to use as little of the runway as possible, even if a 10,000 foot strip stretches out before you. To reinforce this concept until it becomes absolutely second nature, at all of our advanced training bases for squadrons assigned to carrier duty, the dimensions of a carrier deck were painted on all the active runways, and seemingly endless touch-and-go landings were practiced, complete with a Landing Signal Officer. I was never carrier-based, although I did qualify for that duty with three landings in an SNJ trainer aboard the old *Wright* off Pensacola, the only three I ever made. My combat assignments were for the most part in land-based multi-engine patrol bombers. But it was my ability to handle short airstrips in our 4-engine PB4Ys, particularly on Iwo Jima, that accounts for my presence today. And it all began with that first landing at Hybla Valley.)

As the airstrip came into view, Ensign Brios descended to 500 feet, and with our port wing following the starboard edge of the runway, he began our downwind leg at exactly 60 knots. Through the speaking tube came the admonition, "When I say 60 knots, I don't mean 61 or 59!" When we passed the end of the strip, he eased the throttle, lowered the nose to maintain his airspeed, and began his u-turn onto the final approach; then with the strip dead ahead, he eased off more throttle to an airspeed of 58, 3 knots above stalling speed, and gliding over the fence marking the field boundary, he eased the nose up, cut the throttle, and we touched tail down in a full stall—ker-plop—with very little forward momentum left to us. Simple. The key to the last stage of any landing is, of course, depth perception, the measurement of which being such a key part of our physical exam. And I describe Brios' movement of the stick and throttle as having been done with "ease," for there was nothing herky-jerky about his procedure. When he taxied up to what served as an administration building and cut the engine, I followed him out of the cockpit and took his leave; I badly needed to visit the head, but that accomplished, I seemed none the worse for wear.

Next came an hour's practice with a yeoman sending and receiving Morse code, then we went back into the air. Leveling off at 5,000 feet, Brios patted himself on the head, put his hands in the air, and said, "You've got it." And just like that I was handling the controls of an airplane for the first time in my life. "Clutching" would be a more apt description for what I was doing, for I had stick and throttle in a death grip. "Relax, relax," came through the Gosport, "you're not driving a truck. Just try to keep her straight and level." And I must say that didn't seem so hard to do. "Try a 90° turn to the right and maintain your altitude." So-so. "Now to the left." A little better. "Climb 500 feet and level off." Not bad. "Climb 500 more in a 90° right turn, and level off." Sloppy, very sloppy. "Let's try that again. You didn't pull enough power in the turn." A little better. "Now, straight ahead and put her in a glide." I didn't know what he meant by "glide" and I started shaking my head. "Glide, dummy." More shaking of my head. "For Christ's sake, ease back on the throttle and let the nose go down." Having got that sorted out, we began our drills on air speed. Straight and level at 100 knots. Climb at 85. Glide at 90. Climb and turn, glide and turn, 90°, 180°, 360°, at a constant air speed. Then stalling characteristics, discovering the stall point at 55 knots, and noting which way the plane fell off. Each flight we repeated these maneuvers until he was satisfied that I had at least mastered the minimum essentials of the principle involved. Then it was back to the air strip for touch-and-go landings, he at first, then together on the controls, then with his hands in view to emphasize that it was my landing. Finally, there was taxi drill: land, come to a full stop, taxi back to take-off position, and repeat the procedure. So it was that after my seventh instructional hour, the magic words were spoken, "I think you're safe for solo," and so saying, he climbed out of the plane, and I was on my own. There really wasn't much to it: take off, one circle of the field, land, and taxi back to the line. But the rewards were tremendous, beginning with Brios' smile of genuine pleasure as he walked up to the fuselage to shake my hand, and then jumping into his cockpit, saying, "Take us home." The flight up the Potomac was much too brief and the traffic pattern at Anacostia was much too cluttered for me to handle, but I had flown Ensign Brios home.

 It was the custom in our mess during Happy Hour for those who had soloed to stand the drinks, and so it was now my happy turn. At this juncture there were five of us still to go, four of whom were to make it, so our batting average was a respectable 16 to 1, and the one remained in the Navy in another slot. These pre-prandial gatherings in the bar before chow were also the occasions for getting to know one another, for sizing up, for getting at the why and wherefores of how we happened to be gathered together in this particular outfit at this particular time. Evenings were spent poring over ground school assignments designed to hasten our familiarity with things Naval: nomenclature, etiquette, dress, ranks and chain-of-command, fleet components, fleet configurations, types of aircraft and their missions, uniforms, in sum, the physical, sociological, behavioral and historical characteristics of our brave new world. Occasionally we would all gather together after dinner for a lecture or a training film, and one evening we were given time off to listen to the Joe Louis-Billy Conn heavyweight championship fight and were stunned as the cocky young Irishman clearly outboxed the champion and was comfortably ahead on points until the Brown Bomber caught up and knocked him out in the 13th round, thus restoring order. And order was what this regimen was all about. We were being shaped to take our places in a rigidly structured society clear and confident about its mission, permitting no deviation from its code of honor and performance, permitting no debate in its decision-making, and demanding sublimation of self to "the good of the Service." We had joined on our own free will which had then been checked into cold storage for the duration. With no personal decisions to be made, we were free to succeed or fail, win or lose as a team on which no one could command until he had proven he could obey.

It was at the Happy Hour that we recaptured our individuality. There, like small children, we began probing, testing, measuring our "shipmates" and began the inevitable process of forming alliances within the group. By any measure we were an unusual group, with disparate backgrounds, abilities, temperament and experience, and joined together only by the initial bond that we were all present by our own volition, perhaps our last pure expression of free will for the duration. We were all of the same age group 20 to 24, white, and literate, and in general we could be described as being "full of piss and high purpose." But as individuals, of course, the genes took over. At any rate, here follows my remembrance of the nine who became my closest companions.

George H. Charno, Jr.
Education: BA, LLB, University of Missouri.
Position at Enlistment: Member of the Missouri Bar; practicing attorney in the Kansas City law firm of Charno and Charno, founded by his father.
Professional Ambition: Partnership in the firm; eventual succession of his father; a Federal judgeship.
Motivation for Enlistment: "I don't like what they are doing to my people in Germany."
Flying Experience: Nil.
Demeanor: Very bright, but with no particular literary bent, rather the logician that the law demands. Quick tempered but

no harborer of grudges, one always knew where he stood. Absolutely dependable, free from pretense and guile, if he flew wing on you, you would never have to worry about your flanks or rear end. He perfectly fitted my grandfather's description of the man "who ain't fit much but who ain't scairt." He never wore his religion on his sleeve, but Hitler never had a more committed foe. A man of conviction, but with an impish sense of humor that made him a delightful companion. Solid. A rock.

Draft Classification: One-A, but deep in the list.

William Schuler Burns

Education: BA, Phi Beta Kappa, Rhodes Scholar Nominee, Washington and Lee University; LLB, University of Virginia.

Position at Enlistment: Member of the Virginia Bar; had just been elected from his home district of Lexington as the youngest member ever of the Virginia House of Burgesses.

Professional Ambition: U. S. Senator from Virginia; and then (why not?) President of the United States.

Motivation for Enlistment: Since our entry into the war seemed inevitable after Lend-Lease and the arming of our merchantmen, he decided to believe the Navy ad that "the pay is good and the life glamorous," and besides, we had the best looking uniforms in the armed services.

Flying Experience: Nil.

Demeanor: Very bright, indeed, sometimes to the point of insolence with those less gifted. But his intellect had no sharp edge to it, no distinctive focus; it was as though he had put the life of the mind on "hold", now that he was off on a kind of boisterous holiday that was to be savored without the baggage of reflection. He was supremely confident that his cream would rise to the top in these surroundings; even his walk, with a slight hitch in his gait, resembled a strut. With all the airs of a snob he really wasn't—he was generous about picking up tabs and with the use of his car—and I suspected that his bravado was a mask for his anxiety about being able to cut the flying mustard. At any rate, at his wetting down party following his solo (in 7 hours) he grandly proclaimed to our little gathering, "I am the complete master of that aircraft!" It became our rallying cry.

Draft Classification: Exempt from military service by reason of his seat in the House of Burgesses, it would have been like ignoring the call from Fort Sumter for this representative of the First Families of Virginia. His only comment, however, about relinquishing that exemption was, "What would the ladies have thought of me in civilian clothes?"

Frederick Clark Durant, III
Education: BS and MS in Engineering, Lehigh University; Phi Beta Kappa
Position at Enlistment: Working in the research laboratory of the Keystone Telephone Company of Pennsylvania, of which his father was founder, owner, and CEO.
Professional Ambition: To work his way up to the succession of his father; election to the National Academy of Engineers.
Motivation for Enlistment: Convinced of the inevitability of our entering the war, he was urged by his father and family friends in high places, that as the scion of a Philadelphia Main Line family, he should enter an elite branch of the service.
Flying Experience: Private pilot's license.
Demeanor: Complex. Exceptionally bright, the only one in our group who had any real grasp of the abstractions of science, but widely read for an engineer. A great help in explaining the mysteries of aerodynamics. But he was a snob, by rearing, education and experience. He had that Ivy League diffidence; his speech had that Main Line affectation; he was ill at ease in his badly fitting G.I. uniform, and one knew that when commissioned, he would be accoutered only by Brooks Brothers or J. Press. In the larger areas of science and industry, he was the best informed; but in the communal, often bawdy informality of our present milieu, he was with us but not of us. But bless his heart, he tried, and he became far more companionable when he realized the level of erudition in his colleagues.
Draft Classification: One-A, but deep in the list. Would most likely have been granted an exemption because of his engineering skills, but declined to request it.

William Sean Perkins
Education: Choate School; BA and MA, Yale; Phi Beta Kappa; Candidate for the Ph.D. in English Literature, Yale.
Position at Enlistment: Teaching fellow in English Literature in the Yale Graduate School.
Professional Ambition: Arial. He loved flying so much that had he lived, I feel certain he would have made the Naval Air Corps his career.

Motivation for Enlistment: His father was in the publishing trade, an editor and collector of rare editions, but by this time Perk had found bookishness too tame and the folk ways of academe too restrictive. Not particularly enchanted with pedagogy, though I would have gladly enrolled in any course he offered. The impending war was a godsend for him, offering as it did the prospect of orgiastic action, and had already discovered his affinity for the air. His anathema: dictatorship.
Flying Experience: Private pilot's license.
Demeanor: Our cheer leader; the bon chance was always just ahead. We would be caught up in his enthusiasms, lifted above the banal, and feeling better about everything. Our collective literary tastes were centered for the most part in nineteenth century Britain—the Romantics through Tennyson and Kipling, Dickens through Conrad—and Perk was our doyen, leading us through polished explication of texts in our off-duty hours. His stories were endless, both ribald and subtle. There were no fits of depression, no hang ups, no dwelling on what might have been. He reveled in our companionship, and most especially he reveled in the peculiar freedom afforded him by the Naval Air Corps. Whoever wrote "Don't Fence Me In" must have known a one like him. Blithe spirit. Every one of us who remains still mourns his passing.
Draft Classification: One-A, but deep in the list. But he never hesitated and couldn't believe his good fortune at having found the right service at the right time.

Vincent K. Hull, Jr.
Education: BA, University of Montana
Position at Enlistment: Management intern at NYC naval architectural firm, founded by his father, recently deceased.
Professional Ambition: Ski instructor, Stowe or Sun Valley. Plan B: beachcombing.
Motivation for Enlistment: His father had been a principal designer of U. S. Naval vessels, including aircraft carriers, so the Naval Air Corps seemed a logical branch of the service for him.
Flying Experience: Nil, unless one included sailing down a ski slope.
Demeanor: Bright, articulate to a fault (long winded), he was our rebel, our philosopher, our mystic. A product of an affluent household in Short Hills, New Jersey, now presided

over by an aristocratic mother but dominated by two older sisters both Bryn Mawr, both married to investment counselors, one Harvard, the other Princeton, who commuted daily to Wall Street. His first sign of revolt manifested itself upon graduation from a very good if not top-drawer prep school, when he eschewed the Ivy League for the most improbable University of Montana in Missoula. His reasons were two: good skiing for most of the year, and the unlikelihood of meeting any representatives of the Eastern Establishment. But his father's death and family pressures brought him back into the milieu he professed to despise and, for his mother's sake he had joined the firm. Now fate had freed him again, and he could once more become an honest man.

Draft Classification: One-A, and high on the list.

Robert Gillespie

Education: BBA, University of Maryland.
Position at Enlistment: Insurance salesman in Baltimore, Maryland; attending law school at night.
Professional Ambition: Making money, and the more of it the better.
Motivation for Enlistment: Already adept at flying, being a commissioned officer with flight pay was the best option available.
Flying Experience: Private pilot's license, with over 100 hours.
Demeanor: Clever; street smart; a born gambler; never burdened by the greater questions of our age. Happy-go-lucky, and absolutely confident of his destiny as a flying ace. Gregarious and never in awe of his colleagues. Accepted life as it came so long as there were opportunities for earthy expression. Not exactly the person that Durant would invite to dinner in Rittenhouse Square, he was a menace to no one except himself—and unsuspecting innocents.

George Bisbee

Education: BA, University of Michigan.
Position at Enlistment: None. Although his father presided over a law firm in Jackson, Michigan, he, who had been an All-Conference third baseman at UM, aspired to play professionally. Had signed a minor league contract with the Atlanta Crackers but couldn't hit the curve ball and was released.

Professional Ambition: A career in professional baseball, at the managerial or front office level. His father had persuaded him that a law degree might be useful in getting him into baseball administration, but he was too high on the draft list to begin legal studies.

Motivation for Enlistment: A friend had suggested aviation as an alternative to the draft, and having seen the Navy billboards, he decided to have a go.

Flying Experience: Nil.

Demeanor: No great intellect, but no dummy; had thoroughly enjoyed his collegiate experience without taking up a lot of space in the library, although to his great surprise, even chagrin, he had made the Dean's List one semester. Cocky, good looking, well-proportioned and coordinated, a cat-like grace of movement, to no one's surprise he quickly exhibited an aptitude for flying. He was a pleasant companion who would, if you let him, talk baseball by the hour, and he avoided Hull like the plague. But there was a far away look in his eye, as that of a young man in love. It seems that while he was in Atlanta, he had been taken by a former classmate and fraternity brother to a society function at the Piedmont Drive-In Club—which was later to host the likes of Tyrone Power and Robert Taylor when they were on flight duty in that fair city. There he had met one of the belles for which Georgia was famous, and that was that. (They later married, and he was the first in our group to have a child.) So at Anacostia he was no social butterfly. But he was our All-American boy.

Draft Classification: One-A, and very high on the list.

Russell Childs

Education: BS in Physical Education, University of West Virginia, which he attended on a basketball scholarship.

Position at Enlistment: High school teacher of Phys Ed in Charleston, West Virginia.

Professional Ambition: To be basketball coach and athletic director at UWV.

Motivation for Enlistment: Ed Murrow's nightly broadcasts from London during the Battle of Britain, and Winston Churchill's pleas for assistance from the West. Had first considered the Canadian Royal Air Force but was dissuaded by his parents. Had been the second among us actually to enlist in August 1940, and was despairing of ever being called up.

Flying Experience: In preparation for active duty, he had taken flying lessons and obtained his Private Pilot's License.

Demeanor: Intelligent; inquisitive. Clean cut, tall and lithe with the physical grace of Bisbee; a natural athlete whose first love was basketball. Reared on a West Virginia farm by solid, God-fearing parents, he was first in his family to have attended a university, where he first discovered the world of books, and in his spare time off the playing fields, read voraciously if without focus. He never missed our little seminars with Perkins, who suggested a reading list for him beginning with *Huckleberry Finn*: and it was here that he was first introduced to poetry. That he could fly for the Navy was obvious from the beginning, and he was most comfortable with the order and discipline of military life. He was the consummate team player. What mystified him at the outset was the apparent worldliness of his colleagues, which he mistook for sophistication. It was he who discovered in a news column that loveliest of all sonnets describing what we were all about, "High Flight," and he first committed it to memory. He was special, someone to be protected. He was our little brother, and to a man, we loved him.

Draft Classification: One-A, but he was far ahead of that game.

Thomas Morgan

Education: BA, Bowdin; enrolled briefly in Yale Graduate School of Drama.

Position at Enlistment: At loose ends, but had most recently been what he described as an "Assistant Stage Manager" for the Old Vic in London.

Professional Ambition: Undefined, but reasonably sure that it would not be in the performing arts.

Motivation for Enlistment: Survival. Had been in London during the Blitz and was certain he wanted no part in a European war; reasoned that our Naval Air Corps was not likely to be much involved there; by the same token he did not want to be drafted.

Flying Experience: Nil.

Demeanor: Adonis, no less, with a goodly dose of hauteur; medium build; fluid motion in a ballet torso; strikingly handsome aquiline features with brown eyes and ample wavy hair. Witty conversationalist with perfect diction made distinctive by a sedulously cultivated touch of Oxbridge accent. Shocked to discover that the Old Vic was not an

institution which had penetrated the consciousness of most of us. His parents had a theatrical background, having trod the boards with modest success before opening a casting agency for Broadway productions; it was through their intervention that, while in England on a summer break from Yale, he had managed the Old Vic connection and become a backstage grip, which was not his idea of high drama. But the Blitz was, and having escaped that, his principal concern was to manipulate the war, if it came, to his own advantage. To that end we might conceivably be useful, so he maintained a perfectly civil relationship, but tinged with diffidence. So he was with us but not of us, and the last to volunteer.
Draft Classification: One-A, and high on the list.

So what had the Naval Air Corps got on its hands with this particular batch of fledgling flyers? Were we unique in the level of talent and motivation and human qualities which we brought to this totally alien enterprise? In comparison with the groups which had been assembled at Squantum, or Gross Ile, or Los Alomitos and other E Bases in the six months since the NAVCAD program had been initiated, the answer is "No": we were all volunteers who had passed the same rigorous mental and physical exams. But in comparison to the total enlistment pattern in all ranks and branches of the armed forces during the same period of time, the answer was "Yes." We were an elite vanguard; elite in an exceptional level of formal higher education; elite in the diversity of already proven professional competencies; elite in our perception of the positive evil inherent in the totalitarian systems; elite in our conviction that our nation must inevitably enter the lists alongside the British Commonwealth and what was left of France in armed combat against those systems; elite in that we had been adjudged capable of attempting the mastery of the most demanding aviation program extant. We were bringing a lot to the table, and at this stage of the game, we were a confident, cocky bunch.

At the level of fun and games, as evidence of our puckish ingenuity, we initiated a form of diversion I warrant was unique in the annals of the armed forces. It was Perkins who fathered the notion. It was ten days before the 4th of July, a day of celebration in more ways than one for us, for by then all would have completed our solos and finished the rudimentary ground school syllabus. The E Base would shut down its normal operations and we would have a 24-hour liberty, returning on the 5th to receive our august designation as Naval Aviation Cadets, and orders to report to NAS Jacksonville, Florida, the newly-opened flight training companion to Pensacola, with two weeks leave and travel time for the transit. It was at Happy Hour that Perk unveiled his grand design that we ought to turn the 4th of July into a Shakespeare Festival! Sipping on his rum and Coke, he fleshed out his proposal.

Cadet John R. Hubbard, November 1941

First we would gather together whatever female companionship we could muster, the only caveat being that she ought to be able to read, and then we would repair to a leafy glen in some Virginia Forest of Arden. Then after a serious bout with steaks and ale, we would jointly present one of the Bard's masterpieces—*Much Ado About Nothing* might be a suitable vehicle for our inaugural—after which, filled with exultation at the magnificence of our performance, we would lose ourselves in the forest's fastness to woo our damsels with sonnets of love—but no slipping off at intermission, thank you. Almost to a man we bought it, with only Bisbee opting out; to our mild surprise even Morgan thought it might be fun, and we immediately appointed him as impresario, casting director and supervisor of elocution. Since we had some time, Burns was sure his charmer would come up from Richmond; Durant hoped his would come down from Bryn Mawr, and Gillespie grandly volunteered to make up any deficiencies with Baltimore smashers. I was, of course, broadly acquainted in Washington, and I promised Childs someone he would be comfortable with. Happily we had enough cars and station wagons among us to handle our logistical needs.

I took charge of local arrangements with help from Billy Wilcox, my erstwhile roommate at Alla Clary's residence in Falls Church. As chief of staff for Speaker Rayburn, Miss Clary knew everyone in Washington worth knowing, and when I explained my need for a secluded picnic spot, she came up with the owner of a farm southeast of Tyson's Corner with plenty of grassy plots and wooded areas. Then she and Billy gathered together all of our provisions, including two kegs of beer, from her suppliers in Falls Church. I also persuaded Billy to join us so he could see warriors at play and report to the Speaker that the nation's defenses were adequately manned. Last but not least, he acquired ten paperback copies of Shakespeare's plays from a second hand book store.

When the day arrived, we departed the Air Station about ten in the morning, clad in mufti of various design, gathered up our companions from their various abodes of the evening before, and headed for Miss Clary's home in Falls Church. She and Billy had performed nobly, laying in all the comestibles and accoutrements for an outdoor feast. So with Billy and his girl in tow, we set sail for our farm past Tyson's Corner, where we were met by the foreman and directed to what he suggested as an adequate picnic site, admonishing us only not to disturb the livestock and assuring us that there were no neighbors within earshot. And what a lovely spot it was: a green carpet sloping down gently into a little valley through which a freshet meandered and surrounded on three sides by pines and hemlocks. Arden, indeed! And there was even the promise of a full moon.

The stage design was Morgan's department: he decreed that our centerpiece would be a bonfire, around which we would spread our blankets lengthwise, creating the effect of a wheel with ten spokes, while on the periphery we would place our two beer kegs and our two barbeque grills equidistant from each other so that we could minister to our gustatory needs without disturbing the loci of dramatic action. (Although it was William Perkins, an English Literature teacher at Yale, who suggested the drama, it was Thomas Morgan, a graduate student in drama at

Yale, who supervised the staging of the play.) Finally we parked the cars a little farther out around the circle so their headlights would abet the illumination of the bonfire. Had a stranger stumbled upon the scene after dark, he might have sworn he had intruded upon the tribal rites of the Ku Klux Klan.

The first action, of course, was the tapping of the beer kegs, and after that celebratory ritual, the guys set about the physical arrangements, gathering firewood, laying out the blankets, setting up the grills, and sorting out our provisions for a lunch of hamburgers and a dinner of steaks. While that was going on, Morgan gathered the gals around him, issued them their paperbacks, and marched them to the other side of the valley to read for their parts after sternly admonishing them that unless they spoke trippingly, they would be banished to the woods without food or drink—or companionship. They were something to see, for never before had Bryn Mawr been joined by Baltimore smashers in common cause. With the beer continuing to flow we began to get into the spirit of the thing, roaring with laughter at Morgan's periodic bursts of pain and disgust from across the way as the smashers mauled the language. At the end of a long and bibulous lunch, Burns rose to his feet and, holding his flagon of beer on high, regally proclaimed that henceforth he was Prince Hal and that his first command was that his Faery Queen join him for a romp in the hay. By common consent, Perkins was our Falstaff; and when I pointed out that his man had never encountered Boca Chica, he replied that he wouldn't be at all surprised if the old imposter wouldn't sample a wee drop or two before the night was over. He had, not so incidentally, drawn the lustiest and bustiest of the Baltimore contingent who he promptly dubbed Mistress Quickly as a hopeful omen for the evening. Gillespie was our Aeriel, a most incongruous bit of casting, as he began to frolic around on his tiptoes and titter in his squeaky voice something about "Geez, Louise." We had our Desdemona and Lady Macbeth and Juliet and Ophelia too, although some so named hadn't a clue as to their new personas.

The afternoon was given over to siestas and wanderings around the farm in search of secluded trysting places which our locale provided in abundance—with mixed results. Prince Hal was furious with his Queen for her refusal to bow to his commands, but Falstaff and Mistress Quickly were all smiles when we reassembled. By 1700 hours all the stragglers had returned, the circle of blankets reformed, the flagons refilled, and each couple took its place with its paperback at the ready. With the lighting of the ceremonial bonfire, the performance began under Morgan's stern direction. We tried, we really did, and despite the mixed cues and Morgan's frequent pleas to re-read and this time with feeling, we got through Act 1 in reasonably good shape under the circumstances, and everyone agreed the game was worth the candle. But by this time food and drink and other urgings took precedence; and after the "toings" and "froings" had run their course, we policed the place thoroughly and so left our Arden unsullied. Fortunately, there was enough sobriety available in each vehicle to assure a safe passage. And so was born a tradition of sorts: for the duration of our war which still lay ahead. Whenever two or three of us were gathered together, we would produce our paperbacks, grab whatever damsels were available, and head for the open spaces.

The next morning we stood at attention before our Base Commander, who wished us well and dismissed us forever from Anacostia. We were now on our way to the real proving grounds. That afternoon I took Charno, Burns, Durant and Childs on a quick tour of Capitol Hill, visiting the Supreme Court and the Library of Congress before ending up in Speaker Rayburn's office. There Miss Alla and Billy introduced them to Mr. Sam who, since the House was in recess, took them into the Chamber and up to the dais where he presided. As we gazed out over the empty seats, he said, "Mr. Burns, I understand that you have already been elected to public office. When you return from wherever the good Lord is going to send you, it would give me great pleasure to swear you in as a Representative of the Commonwealth of Virginia." It was one of the Speaker's endearing little gestures, and Bill fairly glowed with pride and pleasure. From there I took them down Constitution Avenue to the Interstate Commerce Commission, my old bailiwick. The chairs in the Commissioner's office had been, per usual, carefully aligned, and he had been briefed as to who would sit where. When I ushered them in, Dr. Splawn arose from behind his desk and came forward to shake their hands and bid them to be seated. He then returned to his own chair and turned to face them.

He looked first towards Charno and then Burns, saying, "I understand that you two gentlemen are lawyers, and that you, Mr. Burns, won a seat in the Virginia House of Burgesses. And I believe that you, Mr. Durant, are an engineer, and that you, Mr. Childs, are a teacher."

They all nodded in agreement as though he could see them; and when I asked him to describe our Commander-In-Chief as a person, he responded with a little homily on the democratic imperative and the quality of leadership our nation enjoyed, on life in Washington in these trying times, and on the virtues of public service in the public good.

"And I shall tell the President when I next see him of how encouraging this meeting has been for me, of your extraordinary perception of the dangers we face, and of the exceptional talents you bring to your commitment to the national defense. Perhaps he will worry a little bit less about our future, as will I. Thank you so much for coming, God speed, and take good care of Jack, who has become a member of my family."

He rose and began to accompany us towards the door. Suddenly he stopped, his face radiant in a smile. "Young men, after talking to you, it has just dawned on me that the dictators have no notion of what they are up against."

They all knew they had been in the company of a formidable presence, and I am not sure I really convinced them that he was blind. Childs was thunder struck; he simply could not believe that in one afternoon he had been warmly received by two members of President Roosevelt's "Kitchen Cabinet." Charno brought him back to earth. "Thank God they didn't see us silly bastards yesterday!" With that we took leave of each other until reconvening at Jacksonville.

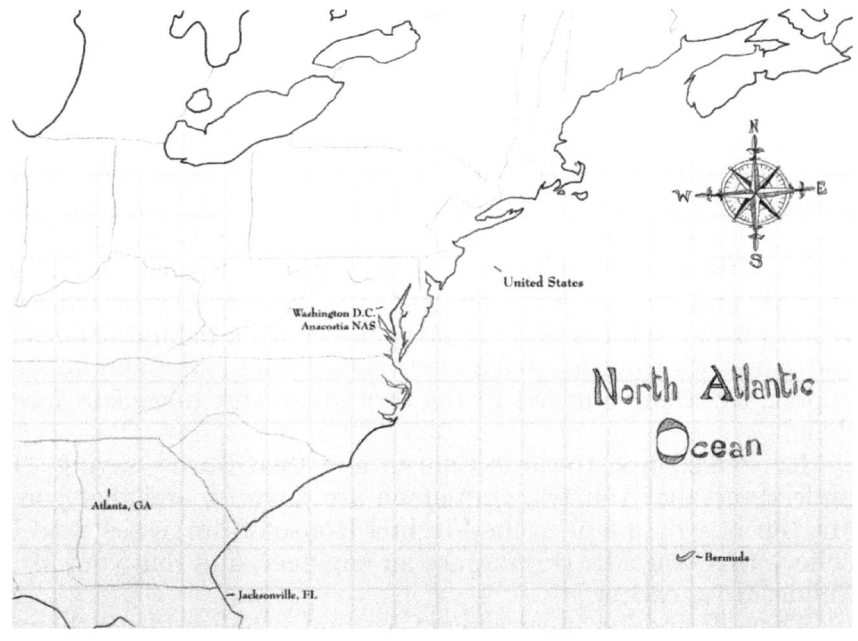

Map 4
Key Launch Sites for Early Naval Aviation Adventures

That night I went back to Falls Church for a farewell dinner with Miss Alla and Billy, and a last sleep in my old bed. The next day Billy and I left early for old Griffith Park where the Yankees were in town for a double header with the beleaguered Senators. The local club in its accustomed last place was stirring up slight attention, but this day was something special. Joe DiMaggio was within two games of tying the major league consecutive game hitting streak, and Bucky Harris was sending out his two wily veterans, knuckle-ballers Dutch Leonard and Johnny Niggling, to try to stop the Yankee Clipper. There was a large and enthusiastic crowd on hand pulling almost to a man for DiMaggio. He had no trouble in the first game, going two for five against Leonard, but it was not until his last at bat in the ninth inning that he got to Niggling for a clean single to left. High drama, indeed. And for me as good an omen as one could ask for.

CHAPTER 6
Jacksonville Naval Air Station

The Naval Air Station at Jacksonville, Florida, had recently undergone a massive expansion and transformation into the Navy's second major aviation training facility, becoming a more modern version of the storied Pensacola, where heretofore every naval aviator had won his wings of gold. (A third such base at Corpus Christi, Texas, was on the drawing boards.) JAX had taken its first class aboard on 1 June 1941, and it was now the destination of all the NAVCADS who had made it through the eastern and north central E Bases. Located some fifteen miles south of the city proper, it was a huge, sprawling base laid out alongside the St. Johns River which provided an ample operational area for our seaplanes. There were hangars for every type of aircraft, repair facilities, storage depots, commissaries, a hospital, a library, and recreational areas. The comfort level of the living arrangements was determined strictly by rank, from the senior married officers' individual units (Officers Country) to the enlisted barracks; and each identifiable unit, such as we NAVCADS, had its own club, wardroom, and messing facilities.

"We go by the numbers here, Mister, and don't you forget it!" This was, in short, the Navy.

When I left the Washington area, a trip home to Texas before reporting to Florida was too great a distance for my allotted time, so Durant had invited me to Philadelphia over the weekend to meet his family, after which we would drive south together in his car. They were people of substance who I liked immensely, gracious hosts in their elegant Rittenhouse Square apartment. One night we dined at Bookbinders with his girlfriend, who claimed almost to have recovered from her strange encounter with Shakespeare, and we even went out to old Shibe Park to watch the futile Phils. Then we headed south, rendezvousing with Burns in Virginia, and proceeded toward Jacksonville en caravan.

We stopped overnight in Savannah where resided a girl Burns had known when she attended Sweet Briar. Her parents were prominent Southern aristocrats from the Old School, and they had arranged a dinner party for us at their ancestral plantation residence with several local belles in attendance. The mint juleps were much in evidence, and the wine flowed at a gorgeous dinner served by colored butlers. Our host toasted us with glowing words about splendid young men who had recognized their duty to their country, to which Burns made a slurred response. Shortly after dinner he and his friend excused themselves for a walk in the garden, with our hostess in a hushed aside suggesting that he might do with a bit of fresh air as she invited Fred and me for a brief tour of the premises. In about half an hour Bill and the girl reappeared; he was clearly furious, his face livid, and she was upset almost to the point of tears, it being evident that after a struggle she had managed to defend her honor. He ordered a scotch and soda, took a long pull, managed to stand and face our hostess, and blurted out, "Madam, our duty calls and we must depart. Don't think it hasn't been charming, because it hasn't." With that, he passed out. After profuse apologies, we got him out of there and back to the motel to sleep it off. All I could think of was Commissioner Splawn's remark about the dictators not knowing what they were up against. Had Bill been mine, I'd have shot him then and there.

At JAX we were assigned to our barracks, lectured on air station procedures, and given the class designation of 8A-41J, which meant that our flying status would begin on 1 August 1941 at NAS Jacksonville. Until then we were thrust into a tightly structured indoctrination program designed to first shape us up as respectful members of the U.S. Navy, and second to make us aware of the unique demands of the Naval Air Corps. In short, it was glorified boot camp designed to ready us for effective participation on the team; so we needs must know the drill, the history, customs and traditions, the parlance, the command structure, the ship classifications and their missions, the same with the airplanes, the order of rank, the proper attire—all those things that lead to homogeneity, singleness of purpose, and pride in the establishment. We gladly immersed ourselves in the routine, and slowly but surely we began to acquire a military mien. But the critical question remained unanswered: could we fly, and well enough to meet the most exacting standards ever set for military aviation?

Each day began with reveille at 0500 hours, followed at 0530 hours by muster and a half hour of outdoor calisthenics, then breakfast (complete with carrots), then a clean sweep down and beds made in our quarters, then off to drill, or machine gun watch atop the hangars, or a cleaning detail, followed by ground school. In order to preserve at least a tincture of intellectual freedom for our little Anacostia coterie, Perk worked up a set of assignments in our Shakespeare paper- backs for those standing watch, a soliloquy or a sonnet to be committed to memory and recited at the Happy Hour. And as soon as we discovered enough willing, femme fatales among the local gentry, we revived our impromptu theatrics in the countryside. Our principal recruiting depot was the Hotel Seminole in downtown Jacksonville which happily catered to the likes of us. We became such regular Saturday overnighters that an understanding management set aside the most spacious salesmen's display area on the top floor as our rumpus room, a fact which became well known through the local grapevine and attracted all sorts of would-be thespians, including the cashier and the manageress of the hotel coffee shop, but not at the same time.

An alternative playground was Jacksonville Beach, a Florida cracker version of Coney Island about thirty miles due east on the Atlantic shore which afforded a large rambling frame hotel and a couple of good seafood restaurants for a change of pace and scenery, with the beach providing a congenial spot for one of our performances around a fire with the breakers rolling gently ashore. So our existence was more than drab, and 1 August arrived before we knew it.

The flight line at the Main Station abutted onto a huge hard surfaced circular mat that assured that flight operations would always be into the prevailing wind, and about half of the hundreds of daily flights took off and landed here. In addition JAX utilized outlying fields such as Lee to the south at Green Cove Springs, and Cecil and Middleburg to the east. The flight syllabus was divided into three phases: Primary, during which you really learned how to fly the Stearman; Advanced, in which you graduated into operational-type aircraft; and Final, wherein you got the finishing touches, such as instrument and formation flying. Each phase was punctuated with check flights in which an instructor other than your own, and usually a total stranger, put you through your paces to assess your progress. In between your instructional flights, you went out on your own to practice, practice, practice. The Great Divide, the Rubicon was the 25 hour check in the Yellow Peril, which included everything in the Primary syllabus: touch and go landings, wingovers, small field procedures, slips to a circle, aerobatics, and emergency landing field selection. If at the end of it the check pilot said, "I'll take it in," it was back to the drawing board for one more chance; but if he said, "You take us in," those were the sweetest words in any language, for there were very few washouts beyond this stage of the game.

AT-6B at the Pima Air & Space Museum

Our group drew Lee Field as the venue for the Primary flight operations, and that meant leaving the Main Station at 0630 hours each morning in elongated vans on a trailer hitch with bench seats running along the sides and canvas flaps that could be raised or dropped according to the weather. Each van accommodated 50 cadets, and after a thirty minute ride we routinely passed through the main gate and its Marine guards and debouched at the flight line to check the schedule. If one flew in the morning he spent the afternoon in ground school, and vice versa, mustering again at 1700 hours for the ride back. Our flight instructors resided on the base in comfortable quarters and so were spared the commute, which pleased us mightily for there was nothing worse than going up with a disgruntled pilot who had missed his morning coffee, especially if it happened to be a check flight.

Fortune continued to smile on me, for my instructor, a full lieutenant and fleet veteran, was a wiry, laconic Texan, very deliberate in speech and movement, and possessing an exquisite touch at the controls; our only disagreement in the month that followed was his avid espousal of the Yankees while I remained a loyal Cardinal fan. Under his patient tutelage my skills and confidence increased markedly, and I sailed through the syllabus and every check flight without a "down." Sad to say, I lost track of his subsequent career, but to this day I remain in his debt.

Me (Jack) in AT-6 at JAX

Then came the great leap forward—from the lowly Stearman to operational-type aircraft, that is to say, planes much larger with relatively powerful engines, variable-pitch propellers, cowl and wing flaps, retractable landing gear, and a much more complicated instrument panel. We had two types of these advanced trainers: the old, reliable SN-J, produced by North American (and known in Army parlance as the AT-6), and the newer, sleeker, faster, and more maneuverable SN-C, produced by Curtis and recently arrived on the flight line. Parked next to the staid SN-J, the SN-C was a thing of beauty, and in the air it was pure poetry, but its ground characteristics were abysmal; its big engine made it nose-heavy, and its braking system was so sensitive that if applied too abruptly, the pilot found himself hanging on his safety belt with the nose buried in the deck and the tail pointed skyward, if, indeed, he wasn't on his back. Thus, every landing was an adventure, everyone hated it, and eventually it was withdrawn from service, like most Curtis productions thereafter. But not soon enough for me, for I drew it rather than the SN-J, and there followed the most miserable, most tentative flying of my career. The plain fact was that I was afraid of it. I dreaded taking it up and was petrified taking it down, and how I passed my final check I can only attribute to the generosity of my check pilot who was so grateful that we were able to walk away from the landing.

But having cleared this hurdle, which for me was monumental, there followed the first steps towards specialization. The first division was between sea-based or land (eventually carrier) based aircraft, with various categories within each division: if sea based, observation and scouting planes working off of cruisers and battleships, or multi-engine patrol bombers; and if land-based, fighters, dive bombers, or torpedo bombers. Each cadet was given a sheet of paper on which to state his preferences, an exercise of futility if ever there was one because the ultimate determinants were the needs of the fleet at that point in time, which were far beyond our ken. At any rate, our group without exception opted for land-based, with fighters, dive bombers and torpedo bombers in that order. When the selections were announced, Charno, Durant, Hull, Childs and I found ourselves in patrol bombers, Morgan in scouts, Perk and Gillespie in fighters, Bisbee in dive bombers, and Burns in torpedo bombers. So the inevitable parting of the ways began, but for the time being we were reunited at the Happy Hour or the rumpus room with different experiences to relate.

In fact on a Saturday not long thereafter when we all had liberty, we had a reunion of our theatrical group, but instead of going to the beach, we gathered up our ladies and chartered an excursion boat for a cruise on the St. Johns River. We stocked our craft aplenty with food and drink, helped our ladies aboard, and slipped anchor on a warm and bright November day. Burns was suffering from a terrible hangover, but after three quick beers he began to feel better about everything.

Bill Perkins, Bob Gillespie, & Me (Jack), Jacksonville, FL Nov. 3, 1941

When we gathered on the bridge, he stepped forth and announced in stentorian tones, "Men, I shall assume command of this man o' war because I know these waters well!"

The Burns' bravado was happily intact. We had, for us, enticed a remarkably comely group of young ladies to venture out on what we called the high seas, for this was the first time in our budding Naval careers that we had ever left dry land. Perk's companion was especially eye-catching, a statuesque, unbelievably well-proportioned blond who I could swear I had seen and admired before. Then I remembered. With the Naval Air Station now going full bore and chock-a-block with Naval personnel, Jacksonville had become a favorite stopping-off place for the courtesans from the northeast on their autumnal hegira to the warmer climes of Miami, and I had noticed this biddy last weekend patiently sitting in the Seminole lobby awaiting a customer. Getting Perk aside, I asked him how he had persuaded her to join him on an outing such as this, and he replied that there was nothing to it: she had told him that she loved to make love for a living but had never done it at sea, and he had convinced her that it was high time she lost her virginity. We had decided to do *A Merchant of Venice* on this little voyage, and Perk, of course, insisted on casting her as Portia. To our amazement and amusement, she entered right into the spirit of things and read her lines with astonishing felicity, putting quite to shame our more socially acceptable effete comrades.

Those of us assigned to multi-engine training were introduced to the venerable old PBY, or Catalina, with a long, boat-like fuselage with two gun turrets amidship and one in the nose beneath a huge single wing on which were mounted twin radial engines and a pontoon affixed to each wing-tip. A model of stability, it was remarkably easy to fly, and our major challenge was to learn how to take off, land, and taxi on water. The PBY was the "donkey" of the Naval Air Corps, being utilized mainly for the transport of supplies and personnel. Years later we had one assigned for logistic support to my squadron of PB4Y-2s on Peleliu in the Palau Island group. One day I took it with only a co-pilot and plane captain aboard over to Ulithi, our principle fleet anchorage in the South Pacific at the time, to replenish our beer supply, and we loaded her to the gills. About midway on the flight back I lost an engine, and unable to maintain altitude, I ordered the plane captain to jettison five cases. Since that did not do the trick, I then ordered him to throw out all but five. In the event, however, I still had to ditch, a simple maneuver on a mercifully glassy sea, we got off a distress signal and our position, threw out the sea anchors, and with our five remaining cases, climbed up on the wing to await developments. By the time we were taken in tow, we couldn't have cared less. The PBY in its combat mode was also our only initial response to the German submarine scourge of our Atlantic and Gulf coasts which lay ahead. And it was the PBY "Black Cat" squadrons, working at night out of secret bases, that played havoc with Japanese coastal shipping at New Guinea and the Solomons, and where Childs met his gruesome fate. So she was a proud old bird, and we did not mind at all the appellation our kind colleagues hung on us of "truck drivers." When we passed our final check in the left seat, we were well on our way to becoming PPCs, or Patrol Plane Commanders.

Our group was united for the last time for the final and most demanding phase of the advanced syllabus –aerial gunnery. We were flying OS2U2 scout planes with twin .30 caliber machine guns mounted in the nose, and for a week we chased after big white target sleeves attached by cable to tow planes which crisscrossed in the sky. We made simulated runs from every conceivable angle trying to get the hang of it for a week until Friday, the day that counted, rolled around. On that day the ammunition in each of our planes was color coated, so that the referee could assess the hits, and by whom. After the firing runs the sleeves were cut loose over a designated area close to the Main Station, so they had to be retrieved and brought into the hangar area before the results could be tabulated. So it was not until Saturday morning that we gathered in the hangar, the sleeves lined up on the Gunner's Mate deck, to learn our fate from a grizzled, salty old Chief Gunner's Mate who was in charge of the tally. The Chief took his own sweet time, checking each sleeve for the color codes, and after finally totaling up the tally sheets, he turned to us and growled, "Well, you sure as hell wouldn't scare a pigeon with this kind of gunnery, but you all passed." Perk had registered the most hits, followed by Gillespie and Bisbee, but the multi-engine boys hadn't done too badly. No matter, we all stood transfixed and let it sink in; we had just cleared the last major hurdle between us and those wings of gold.

The Chief, however, was not through with us. "Now let me tell you kids what real gunnery practice was like," he intoned, fixing us with a steady eye. "When I was with the Pacific Fleet, we'd move our battle wagons just as close into Japanese territorial waters as the law allowed, and then we'd tow our target sleds just over the horizon and let our 16 inchers knock out the bull's eye on every one of them. And then we'd wait til the tides were just right and cut them loose to float onto the mainland so the Japs could see what real gunnery looked like. Now I don't know who you whipper-snappers are getting ready to fight, but I'll guarantee you one thing: it won't be the Japs, cause those slant-eyed little bastards don't want anything to do with Uncle Sam's Navy!"

The date was 6 December 1941.

Needless to say, that night was given over to a monumental celebration. Our good ladies, knowing the import of the exercise we had just been through, had congregated at my girl's house and were prepared to lay on either a great victory party or a wake. The only two things I remember with any clarity was that Burns was beside himself for having lost his bet that he would score highest in the drill and that Maureen was especially tender. I have no notion how or when we found our bunks, or even the Air

Station, for that matter, but I was apparently fully clothed and spread out like a week's washing trying to sleep it off. What I do remember is that about 1400 hours Sunday afternoon, Charno burst into my room and began shaking me.

"Tex, Tex wake up, wake up. We're at war, we're at war! The Japs are kicking hell out of us at Pearl Harbor!! Tex, God damn it, wake up. We're at war!!!"

Try that on for a wake-up call. I staggered to my feet, getting the message but not fully comprehending, although instinctively knowing we had to get the hell off the base before it was secured. We piled into Burns' and Durant's cars and just made it through the main gate before the Marines shut the place down. We drove to Maureen's, our ears glued to the car radio for the dispatches pouring in from Hawaii and Washington. It was dreadful; the Japs had taken us by complete surprise, Pearl was in shambles, and major units of our fleet were on the bottom. We were a somber bunch, and not even a cold beer tasted good although I was in desperate need. We could hear sirens all over town as the Military Police and Shore Patrol jeeps raced around with their bull horns blasting, "All service personnel return to base!" And the radio spewed forth unrelieved chaos. I looked around the room at George and Bill and Fred and Perk, the carefree thespians of Anacostia no longer. The worst thing that could have possibly happened had happened, and the only alleviation was the knowledge we shared that by whatever intellectual process, we had each of us early on anticipated the threat and had made our move. If in the future anyone asked us where we were on that day of infamy, we had a pretty good answer.

0530 hours Monday morning found us mustered outside our barracks; it was bitterly cold and the calisthenics were welcomed to get the juices flowing. We were entering the Final phase of the syllabus, formation flying, conducted in the less crowded air space of Lee Field, so after breakfast we piled back into the horse vans for the ride south, the canvas flaps closed tightly against the weather. Since no one had slept well the night before, many of us were sprawled out in disarray on the floor of the van, the interior of which was as dark as the inside of Grogan's goat. Among other things on my mind I found myself saddened at the thought of our Gunner's Mate who had been so sure and so proud of his Navy.

Reaching Lee's main gate, through which we had been routinely passing for the last four months, we heard the sharp command to our driver to halt. Lifting the canvas flaps, we could see the Marine guards now in their battle dress, side arms and bayonets bristling, as though expecting a Japanese charge from out of the boonies. Then a tough sergeant stepped into the van, armed with a bull light which he proceeded to flash into every single one of our faces. Finally satisfied that there were no infiltrators aboard, he snapped off the light and started to step outside, when out of the stygian darkness came this high-pitched falsetto voice, "Velly solly, me catchee wrong bus." Back on came the bull light which he waved about furiously, our gales of laughter only increasing his choler. In apoplectic fury he could only hiss, "Smart asses, I hope you get yours," and the van was permitted to enter the field. Somehow I felt this was one war we weren't going to lose. At any rate, the tone was set for the day.

At the flight line we were counted off in batches of six, since we were going to begin the drill in six-plane sections: and then we went into the Ready Room for a briefing on formation flying. On the black board were chalked out the basic configurations, such as the V and left and right echelons, the hand signals for changing from one to another, the proper spacing, and the break-up procedures before landing. We were told that the easiest formations to fly were the tightest ones, wherein changes in relative motion were more easily detected and corrected for, but we would only learn that from experience. Finally, we were taken through the procedure for joining up after takeoff, the hardest thing of all for the beginner. Then out to the flight line and back into our beloved Yellow Perils, ideal for this sort of drill since they were the slowest and least demanding aircraft we had. Then we took off section by section, each of us with an instructor in the back seat, who took the controls for the initial join up and made it look easy. Then we landed and took off again, and this time we tried to join up and wound up with airplanes all over the sky. But we got better at it as we went along, and finally we landed to let our instructors out, who gave us a final briefing and sent us out on our own. I had been designated as the leader of our section, and before taking off, we huddled as I expounded my game plan, to which everyone agreed.

We knew the area we were flying over like the back of our hands, and we had observed that every day at high noon, a Delta DC-3 commercial flight left the Jacksonville airport bound for Miami, flying due south down the coast at an altitude of 6,000 feet. So we climbed up to 8,000 feet in the general direction of Daytona Beach, which lay directly in Delta's flight path and where the Navy had recently opened a new landing strip. I put the section into what might charitably be called a right echelon formation, began a slow circle and waited. Right on schedule we spotted the unsuspecting DC-3, and one by one we rolled on our backs and began our simulated dive bombing runs, flashing down across her nose and fuselage as closely as we dared before pulling up to see what we had wrought. The Delta pilot had begun a series of evasive actions and then headed straight for Daytona for an emergency landing, where he and his panic-stricken passengers reported an attack by Japanese fighters. Within the hour, I was later to learn, the whole Atlantic seaboard had been placed under air alert, and planes from every base from Brunswick, Maine, to Key West were ordered out to search for those Japanese carriers that must be lurking off shore. But there was one man who had divined the truth, and that was the skipper of our Air Station, and since I had brought my group back nearly an hour after the others had landed, he knew who the culprits were. I had no sooner taxied up to the line and cut my engine than I was ordered to his office, on the double. As I stood at attention, he fixed me with a baleful eye, and after what seemed like forever, his face relaxed into a grin and he bid me be at ease.

"Mr. Hubbard," he said, "I admire your spirit, but your judgment is lousy. I know it is insane to think there are Jap carriers in the Atlantic, but you didn't consider the fact that today this country is on the verge of hysteria, and you scared the crap out of some innocent people. In this man's Navy, the one who goofs off has to pay, and since you were the leader of the group, that means you."

So in the future if anyone asks me how I spent the first week of the war, the answer is: grounded and confined to quarters for four days. And there was another result from this little escapade: from the next day and for the duration, all commercial flights in the U.S. were to fly with their window curtains tightly closed, a tiny bit of history for which I am not particularly proud.

This episode had another result with serious consequences for me. I had flown that morning with a terrible cold, which climbing to 8,000 feet hadn't helped, and before the next day was out my right ear had clogged up, I had lost my hearing, and a meaningful ache had developed. At Sick Bay I was diagnosed as having acute otitis media, a serious middle ear infection, and I was dispatched forthwith to the base hospital where I languished for two weeks. My friends were good as gold, one or two of them coming by each day with liquid refreshment and toting away the empty beer cans, at which my kindly nurse turned a blind eye. She was a pretty thing but much too wise in the ways of fledgling aviators to give me any hope of dalliance. They would keep me abreast of their progress through the syllabus, and therein lay the rub; it became increasingly clear that I was getting so far behind that I would not be able to finish with my class. That troubled me mightily, for it seemed only fit and proper that the Anacostia Volunteer Group (AVG), as we had dubbed ourselves, should be commissioned together, knowing that then we would scatter to the four winds. The rites of commissioning were performed on the first Saturday of each month, and our date was less than three weeks away; but if for any reason you missed your scheduled turn, you could but wait for the next one a month hence. That was my situation now, and I had the mullygrubs so bad that not even Nursie's suggestion that as a convalescent I could get shore leave and that we might slip away for a weekend could lift my spirits. Could I have a raincheck, please?

After three weeks I was restored to flying status, and while my group, which had completed the syllabus, was busy with all the paper work and red tape attendant to the change in rank from NAVCAD to Commissioned Officer, I took the lonely ride in the van to and from Lee Field, flying with strangers. Now, coexistent with the thrill of being designated Naval Aviators was the anticipation of our next duty assignments; we had gone through the charade once again of expressing our preferences—everyone opting for fleet duty—and by this time the orders for the class of 8A-41J had been cut, so my set-back had no bearing on what was to be. Our futures were to be revealed to us two days before the January commissioning date, and we were antsy with anticipation.

For the AVG, the tally was as follows: Charno —transition training to four-engine patrol bombers, at Hutcheson, Kansas; Burns—advanced torpedo bomber training—at Fort Lauderdale, Florida; Durant and Hull—Transport Squadron 1 at Pautuxent River, Maryland; Perkins and Gillespie—advanced fighter training, at Miami; Childs—advanced PBY training, at Banana River, Florida; Morgan—Utility Squadron 20, at Quonset Point, Rhode Island; Bisbee—advanced dive bombing training, at Daytona Beach; Hubbard—two weeks at Flight Instructors' School at Cecil Field, then back to Lee Field as a Primary flight instructor. It was a mixed bag with mixed feelings, the unhappiest being I, although my friends tried to assure me that it was a great distinction to be selected for an activity generally reserved for fleet veterans. Before the Great Day at which I was a reluctant onlooker, we managed one more soiree at the Rumpus Room, and that was pretty much the end of our old gang, although throughout the war we would occasionally bump into each other at strange and not so wonderful places, or be saddened by the news of friends we would never set eyes on again.

After their departure from JAX, I stood lonely and thoroughly pissed, brightened only by the raincheck Nursie had granted me. But there was another dividend in store for me that no one could have anticipated. Among my occasional visitors at the hospital had been a member of the class of 9A-41J, who had gone through E-Base at Squantum, Massachusetts, before coming to JAX and with whose class I was now apparently going to be commissioned. He was a fine looking, articulate, unassuming young man whose human qualities were readily manifest—a sophisticated Russ Childs, if you will—whose capacity for leadership had been recognized by his designation as cadet commandant of his group. He had been attracted to our coterie by listening to one of our "literary" sessions during Happy Hour, surprised but wholly approving of the effort.

"It was something," he later told Perk, "that even a Harvard man could appreciate."

He became a welcome fourth for bridge when we needed him, and although we were senior to him by a whole month, we all agreed that he had the right stuff to be co-opted into the AVG. His name was Joseph P. Kennedy, Jr., heir apparent to that famed family's political destiny, and in our last month at JAX we became practically inseparable. He, too, had gone through his advanced phase in PBYs, and now at Lee Field he flew formation a couple of times in my section. Our relationship became so cordial and candid that I had no hesitancy in railing against his father's earlier defense of appeasement, joined in by the likes of Lindberg, in believing that Hitler's Wehrmacht and Luftwaffe were invincible and that we should abandon Britain and France to their fate and withdraw behind the protective cover of armed neutrality. Joe listened to this without the slightest trace of resentment, replying only that his father as Ambassador to the Court of St. James had access to information not readily available to us at home, and that his was an honest assessment. And it was his father who long before Pearl Harbor had suggested the Naval Air Corps to him when he finished Harvard. There we left it and had another beer while I urged him to keep a pocket Shakespeare as his constant companion.

As the February Great Day approached, young Joe was summoned to the office of the base commandant, Captain Charles Perry Mason, an impressive white haired, rosy cheeked veteran with a fine sense for public relations. He had just talked to the Ambassador by telephone and was informed that the whole Kennedy clan would be present for Joe's commissioning. Under those circumstances and for their convenience, Captain Mason had decided to conduct a private ceremony in his office so the family would be undisturbed by the press and the Ambassador could personally present his son's Ensign shoulder boards and wings. This would all be duly recorded on film by the Navy photographer for the family archives and afterwards, of course, there would be ample photo opportunities. Joe's immediate reaction was unequivocally negative: he wanted to be commissioned with his classmates and he did not want to detract from their recognition by being singled out as someone special. Captain Mason, to his credit, must have anticipated such a reply, for he had his response at the ready: these were perilous times and the Navy needed manpower like never before in its history; the publicity attendant to such a ceremony with its personal family touch would be a tremendous boon to Naval recruitment and it would be unpatriotic to miss such an opportunity.

"You will find out, young man, that there are many times when we must do things for the good of the Service. I will not command you, but I ask you to reconsider."

Joe respectfully said that he would but that first he wanted to talk to his family. Having done that, the matter was resolved: he refused to go through the drill alone, but he would acquiesce to Captain Mason's wishes if I were included in the ceremony. The good Captain did not want just anybody included in the tableau with someone of America's most prominent families, so he checked my dossier very carefully; so when Joe and I went to discuss with him the details, he greeted me with some warmth.

"Mr. Hubbard, I note that you have almost completed your Ph.D. and that you are a friend of Speaker Rayburn. You're also the chap that nearly wrecked Delta Airlines, but since no one outside our little family knows that, you'll do."

So it was that on 6 February 1942, there was assembled in the Commandant's office Ambassador Kennedy, Rose, their daughter, John in a new Ensign's uniform, having just been commissioned in a torpedo boat squadron, Robert, and Teddy dressed appropriately in a little sailor's suit, who immediately began romping around the room until his mother threatened him within an inch of his life. With order restored, Captain Mason called Joe and me to attention and read our citations, after which the Ambassador snapped on our shoulder boards and pinned our wings on our tunics. It was a moment I wanted to freeze in time. Rose rushed up to embrace her son and then gave me a friendly kiss, as the rest of them surrounded the brother they clearly adored. It was a happy babble of sibling voices, for none of the Kennedys were ever known to be short on words. Freeing himself for a moment he came up to me, and we needed only a handshake to express our regard for each other and my gratitude for having been included in his family. I paid my respects to each of them and took my departure as the press and photographers, not the slightest bit interested in a supernumerary, crowded into the room.

After commissioning, we each had a 10 day leave, and I went back to the barracks to pack for my first visit home in Denton, Texas, since the Christmas of 1940. Next day the Kennedys very kindly sent their limousine and chauffer to drive me to the Jacksonville airport, where I boarded a Delta flight to Dallas, with the window curtains tightly drawn.

I never saw Joe Kennedy again.

Ensign Joseph P. Kennedy, Jr., (AVN) USNR

The Navy Department, wary of the charge of bowing to political influence were it to assign a member of this family to some posh shore duty, issued to Joe the same orders it had to Charno a month earlier: transitional training at Hutcheson, Kansas, to four-engine patrol bombers. By coincidence they wound up in the same Liberator squadron based in southern England flying anti-submarine missions over the Bay of Biscay, the Nazis principal under-sea route into the Atlantic. It was a tour of duty from which Joe never returned.

Later on Charno told me the story.

The squadron had completed its assignment of 25 missions per pilot and was preparing to return to the States, where the PPCs would begin a tour as flight instructors at Hutch, as far from a combat zone as it was possible to be for a well-earned respite. At the same time, the Allied staffs in Britain were desperately seized of the submarine menace for the wolf packs were making mincemeat out of our Atlantic convoys. Their pens along the Channel coast such as at Peenemünde were so layered with concrete as to be impervious to aerial assault, and we had not yet been able effectively to interdict their passage under the Bay of Biscay. It was at this juncture that someone had come up with the idea for our first "guided missile." The notion was to pack a Liberator from bow to stern with high explosives, and once airborne, it would become a drone, its controls taken over through electronic circuitry by a command plane, whereupon its pilot and mechanic would bail out, leaving the command plane to guide the drone across the Channel into the very mouth of a submarine pen and if not demolish it, at least block its entrance. The date for the great experiment was set for the morrow after Joe's squadron was scheduled to decamp.

The only thing left to be decided was who would take the drone up, retract the landing gear, set the flight tabs, and bail out. When the call went out for a volunteer, Joe never hesitated. Bidding his departing squadron goodbye, he reported the next morning to the flight line. He and his faithful mechanic, who had opted to join him, took the Liberator off and climbed to the designated altitude, but when the command plane signaled that it was taking over, the electronics fouled up and the drone exploded in mid-air with Joe and his mechanic still in their seats.

Joe Kennedy, Jr., as his mother knew tragically well, was everything in huge measure his father and brothers pretended to be, and his loss to America and the post-war world is beyond calculation. For Charno and me, the memory of him still leaves us in utter desolation.

Editor's Addition

In the following excerpt from a letter to his parents, written while still at Jacksonville's Cecil Field, Jack gives poetic expression to the love he has gained for flying.

> It has been said that of all the works of man, the airplane is the nearest to a living being. In this statement I wholly concur. In an airplane one can find expression for any passion, mood or desire. The plane and the pilot blend together to make a harmonious whole that is capable of the purest expression of a man's ultimate goal of freedom. For one is wholly, unalterably free; there are no fetters, no bonds, no mortal vicissitudes that can mar his dance through space. Flying and the weather go hand in hand. Give me a day when the fluffy, white clouds are billowing up in their foamy splendor and let me join them as they dance in the wind. We have a wonderful time, the clouds and I, as we play hide and seek with the sun. Just when he thinks he has me, my friends extend their arms and cloak me in their cooling whiteness, and I can hear them laughing at old Mr. Sun because he cannot find me. And sometimes I tease the clouds as I dart in and out, playing along their fringes, teasing and taunting, but never quite giving myself up to them. When I overdo it and their patience is exhausted, they become dark with anger and toss me around, and I can hear them mock me as I run for home. But my friends the clouds know that I'll be back

tomorrow. Surely I am fortunate in my present work, for up there freedom is not just a word or hope or dream. It is absolute.

CHAPTER 7
Instrument Flight Instructor's School

Cecil Field was one of the outlying bases attached to NAS JAX about 30 miles due east of the Main Station, a self-contained unit with Officer's Quarters, messing and recreational facilities, and aircraft maintenance capabilities, and all in all a not unpleasant posting except its location in the middle of nowhere. A variety of flying activities were conducted there, among which was the Flight Instructor's School, consisting of a dozen veteran pilots and a syllabus designed to put the finishing touches on flying technique and pedagogical guidelines for instructor-designates such as I. It was a relaxed two-week exercise, with the veterans acting the part of students as we went over and over every step of the primary syllabus, and for our own amusement we also spent a lot of time at aerobatics and simulated dog fights. It was too brief a period to establish close relationships, but the person I enjoyed most was Nile Kinnick, a recent Heisman trophy winner from the University of Iowa, who reminded me a lot of Joe Kennedy and who also did not go the distance. Then it was back to Lee Field and my first ever attempt at the fine art of teaching.

By this time the numbers of fledgling aviators were increasing by leaps and bounds, and flight schedules were extended from dawn to dusk. I took considerable pride in getting my first ten students through the entire syllabus without a down check, but the eleventh nearly did us both in, and after an almost disastrous landing attempt that forced me to wrench the controls from him, he agreed with me that flying was not his game. It was tiring, often nerve-wracking, and absolutely essential work, but it was not the Fleet, and I began increasing my correspondence with a friend who was a detail officer in the Navy's Bureau of Personnel in Washington, pleading for a change of duty.

For recreation I only occasionally dropped by the Hotel Seminole, so full of memories it was of the AVG, but Nursie, who remained as faithful as she knew how, and I discovered a new playground at Fernandina, northeast of Jacksonville where the river by that name emptied into the Atlantic and in whose delta there were huge oyster beds under cultivation. The proprietors, simply as a diversion, had laid out a spacious picnic area with grills set over barbeque pits dug in the ground and each customer supplied with a pair of thick gloves and a screwdriver, plus a fork and a receptacle for melted butter. Then for a dollar a person you could get as many pails of freshly harvested oysters in their shells as you could eat, and bowls of crackers for good measure. Then you built your fire and threw the oysters onto the grill and waited impatiently until time to remove them, shuck the shell with your screwdriver, dip them in the hot butter, place them on a cracker, and then plop that succulent roasted bivalve into your mouth, to be washed down with a cold beer at ten cents the bottle. Nirvana! For three dollars we could literally gorge ourselves, and since there was no time limit, and having eaten as much at that sitting as we possibly could, we would take our blankets and stroll along the beach, stopping for a siesta or whatever, and come back to start the drill all over again. Cads that we were, we never told a soul about the place.

It was six months later at the end of August that I received a new set of orders marked Top Secret, and when they were handed to me by an adjutant in the Base Commander's office (where I had reported once before) to be digested and then destroyed in his presence, I read them in disbelief. I was to report to NAS Atlanta, Georgia, to an outfit with the acronym IFIS— Instrument Flight Instructor's School for public consumption.

"Atlanta, Georgia," I inwardly fumed, "now that's an unlikely place for a Naval Air Station, and instead of going to the Fleet, I seem to be going away from it."

The orders concluded with the terse sentence that I was to report ASAP and that I would receive further instructions from the Commandant upon arrival.

"Have you any idea what this is all about?" I asked the adjutant, and he replied in the negative, saying that he didn't even know we had an Air Station in Atlanta. Nor did anyone else I talked to.

When I arrived in Atlanta along with a half a dozen others with the same orders, this is what I learned at our initial briefing. The Navy was determined to add a new strike capability to its carriers and land-based patrol bombers, which would require a crash research and development program, the application of radical new techniques in our advanced training units, and a significant restructuring of our basic flight training syllabi. The ultimate objective was the formation of "all weather" squadrons that could deliver a strike in practically any atmospheric condition day or night at targets which would least expect them and where aerial opposition was calculated to be nil. In other words, a critical mass of Naval aviators would have to acquire the capability of "flying blind," a goal that must obviously remain top secret, as must its corollary, the R and D part of the program, the design and testing of new flight instrumentation, navigational systems such as the embryo Loran, new radio directional finding systems, new ground controlled approach and landing techniques, anything and everything that involved the combat application of what we were trying to do. Since we could not very well hide the fact that a new Naval Air Station was being constructed on the site of an old municipal airport that had heretofore serviced private aircraft, our public posture was simply that we were training instrument flight instructors to accommodate the growing number of NAVCADS at Pensacola, JAX, and now Corpus Christi.

We were the guinea pigs, 24 of us selected on the basis of demonstrated flying skill and also as a result of rigorous psychological testing indicating we would be unlikely to lose our equilibrium while relying solely on the instrument panel as our only visible point of reference while in flight. (We had always assumed that these tests that we had been periodically subjected to were random exercises devised by mad psychologists as their means of avoiding combat duty.) We would be augmented by a group of AV-Ts, (Aviators-Temporary Duty), a group of seasoned commercial pilots experienced in flying the radio beams, the then principal navigational aid utilized by the airlines. Our mission was three-fold: first we ourselves must become acclimatized to instrument flying until we were proficient at it and comfortable with it; second, we must keep a careful record of all the devices and drills which had enabled us to gain that proficiency, and from those records compile a handbook for the teaching of instrument flying; and finally, we would take a batch of trainees through the syllabus to measure the efficacy of our methods. For all this we were allotted three months. We had two indispensable allies: a newly developed gyroscopic instrument called the artificial horizon, invaluable for the maintenance of a given altitude, air speed, and direction while flying "under the hood," and the Link Trainer, a mechanized replica of an airplane cockpit, flight controls and instrument panel by which the controller could simulate any flight condition from which the trainee must extricate himself. And so we were embarked on a demanding, exciting challenge.

There were to be, however, distractions of major magnitude, all unanticipated. In the first place, there was the nascent condition of the Air Station itself, at this point bereft of infrastructure, which was being tasked with accommodating not only a new and complex flying operation, but also two other major training programs—one of which involved the recruits which were arriving daily for the Link Trainer, one of the keys to our success here, but which in the future would be utilized in increasing numbers at every air training facility in the country. Who would be qualified to operate them? It was deemed to be an assignment eminently suited to the talents of the newest recruits to our ranks, the WAVES (Women Accepted for Volunteer Emergency Service), which required the establishment of a WAVE Link Trainer Operators school which ideally would function as an adjunct to our program and thus be located at NAS Atlanta. The other program also involved the ladies, this time the Marine BAMS, (Broad-Axle Marines) who, it had been decided, could easily replace the male flight tower operators, which required the establishment of a BAM Flight Tower Operators school, which for some obscure reason was also to be located at NAS Atlanta. The only problem with all this was that as yet, NAS Atlanta had no housing facilities whatsoever. So the Navy in its wisdom contracted with the staid and fashionable Biltmore Hotel downtown on Peachtree Street for three floors of rooms where we could all be temporarily housed and discretely segregated—the bachelor flying officers on the ninth floor, the WAVES on the seventh, and the BAMS on the fifth. A mess allowance and a shuttle bus service would be provided. It goes without saying that from the first night of this arrangement, the Hotel Biltmore was staid no longer.

Another distraction was Atlanta itself. A sleepy, easy-going, rather charming Southern city, in 1942 it was scarcely affected by the war except for the presence on the outskirts of Fort McPherson, whose rude and crude denizens would swarm in on the weekends and destroy the tranquility of the citizenry. But now in their midst was a strange and wonderful new breed of cat, the Naval aviator, a species never before encountered in this neck of the woods, with his studiously assumed regal bearing, jaunty mien, and uniforms adjudged to be altogether glamorous, and best of all, we were socially acceptable. So from the outset, we were showered with hospitality, and because we were so few in numbers, it became a point of pride with soignee hostesses to snare us for their soirees; and we were welcomed into the exclusive watering holes like the Piedmont Drive-In Club. Thus, in addition to the implications of our quarters at the Biltmore, we were warmly welcomed into a generous and gracious social scene.

Another distraction for me was my designation as Mess Captain for our new Officers Club, which meant that I had to start from scratch in its organization and in the laying in of supplies. Already war-induced shortages were in evidence, particularly among premium brands of spirits, so I had to scrounge for an adequate supply, picking up a case or two here and a case or two there. Sometime later I learned of a Budweiser warehouse that reputedly also stocked off-brands of wine and whiskey so little known that they had few takers. It was noon on a fiercely hot and humid day when I was greeted by the custodian, a portly man of some 300 pounds with a huge stomach protruding from overalls and dripping with perspiration. When I explained my mission, he first insisted that we have a beer and then took me on a tour of the premises. I never saw so many brands that I had never heard of that he seemed to have in ample supply. Finally we came to a deep recess and some shelves where he literally had to scrape off the cobwebs before we could read the labels, one green and the other black which proclaimed "Jack Daniels, Tennessee Sour Mash Whiskey."

"I tried this stuff once and it was mighty tasty," he said, seizing a bottle, unscrewing the cap, and taking a hefty quaff, which went down without any visible repercussion. "Here, you try it."

Now the last thing I needed at this time on such a day was a slug of straight whiskey, but I turned up the bottle, and, apart from a burn sensation, I could not believe how smooth and mellow were its contents. So we made a deal right then and there; he would give me all the Jack Daniels he had in stock and reserve for me all he was likely to get if from time to time I would relieve him of some of the junk in his inventory. Word of this acquisition spread in a remarkably short time, and that is why the Officers Club at NAS Atlanta became the favorite stopping-off place for our ferry pilots going from coast to coast who would depart laden with bottles of this nectar and spread its fame across the land. Someday I hope that distillery at Lynchburg, Tennessee acknowledges my great contribution to its prosperity and rewards me appropriately.

With all of this, the pilot's life became a simple matter of endurance. Getting back to our rooms each evening late and tired, for example, we never knew who would be perched on our bed, a WAVE or a BAM or a member of the local gentry, for the

Biltmore bell hops did a thriving business in the distribution of master room keys. But our flight schedule went on around the clock. As the guinea pigs, most of our flight time was spent "under the hood," a canvas contraption that completely enclosed the rear cockpit, leaving you wholly dependent on your instruments for executing a prescribed drill. Collectively we devised intricate flight patterns stressing precision, the most demanding of which would be rewarded with a bottle of champagne if one could complete it within miniscule margins for error. Then the AV-Ts would work our butts off on the radio ranges, taking us out under the hood into the void and monitoring how we oriented ourselves, found our way home and descended in the proper blind landing approach mode. We even worked out an alternative procedure not dependent on the beam called RDF, Radio Direction Finding, by which we could home in on any transmitter, commercial or otherwise, from any direction provided we knew its location relative to the landing area. Our basic aircraft at the outset were SNJs with a few Vultee Vibrators thrown in, later augmented with Howards with new instruments especially designed for our mission which we had to test out, and twin-engine Beechcraft which we utilized for long cross-country flights at night, taking along an occasional WAVE or BAM who wished to qualify for the Mile High Club. And all the while we worked diligently at the compilation of our handbook and a set of ground school lectures. In sum we became very proficient in the art of flying from takeoff to final landing approach without any natural visual references, and we were ready to try out a syllabus designed to inculcate those skills in others.

In fact we had two syllabi, one for operational carrier units and the other for those slated to become instrument flight instructors, and from the results with each group and their commentary, we managed to iron out the deficiencies in our instructional procedures. Mission accomplished, we were now in business. Imagine our surprise, then, when our next batch of students included 20 Army Air Force types, hand-picked for the establishment of a like school for its own pilots at Bryan, Texas. These were veterans, set in their ways as to basic procedures, as were we, and there was an instant rivalry as to which group was more adept at this flying business. There was a vast difference, for example, in the way we made landing approaches.

When we took them up for instrument instruction, at the end of the drill we would make our customary carrier procedure, downwind hugging the field, flaps down in a sharp turn into the strip a couple of knots above stalling speed, and then the tail down kerplunk on the leading edge of the runway. But when they took each other up on practice hops and returned, they used a long, straight-in approach, never lowering their flaps until squared away with the runway, and touching down at a considerably greater speed which used up more of the landing strip than we thought necessary. We ridiculed their method and they raged at ours, at one point marching en masse to our Chief Flight Instructor, claiming that we were just showing off and that our every landing was a suicide in the making. When he pointed out to them that that kind of landing was second nature to us and that our still being alive was proof of its margin of safety, they became mollified but never comfortable. And they had taken particular umbrage at one of my antics. One day as I neared the field, I called the control tower for permission to enter the landing pattern, and the dulcet voice of the BAM informed me that I would be number three.

"Number three," I protested, "there's not another plane in the sky!"

"But, Sir, yes there is," came the honeyed tones, "two of our Army guests are on final approach."

"Well," I retorted, "I am going to take a nap, so please give me a wakeup call when I am clear to land."

Our "Army guests" were, of course, tuned into the same radio frequency and listening to this banter, and I heard the click of one of their microphones.

"Smart ass," was all that he said. But apart from this little contretemps, a great relationship developed, and we began to admire the consistent quality of their performance.

Our close relationship was abetted by the fact that they, too, were quartered on the ninth floor of the Biltmore, and so our rivalry was extended into the boudoir. We Navy types were now old hat and our Air Force friends brought a new allure to the distaff side of our little community, not to mention the Atlanta natives. So someone devised a contest: once a week at the stroke of midnight randomly chosen, a bugle would be sounded, a signal for every female on the floor, regardless of dishabille, to step out into the corridor and stand at attention while a panel of judges paraded up and down and finally selected the beauty queen of the evening. And this Army-Navy game turned out to be a Mexican standoff. When this foolishness became known, the Base Commander stationed a duty officer on the ninth, seventh, and fifth floors at the elevators and stair wells to stem the flow of traffic, but municipal law prevented the blocking of the fire escapes. It had gotten so bad that some of us long since had pooled our housing allowances to rent a furnished flat in the neighborhood of Georgia Tech nearby. Finally, the completion of the BOQs and barracks on the base put an end to it all, and none too soon. But while it lasted, for frenzy of activity, the good old Seminole Hotel in Jacksonville was not a patch on the Atlanta Biltmore.

There was another aspect of the Atlanta experience that persists in my memory. While I was instructing at Lee Field, George Bisbee had drawn some temporary duty at Cecil Field, and I would fly over occasionally to have lunch with him and his relatively new bride. It seems that when he was returning from commissioning leave in Michigan en route to Daytona, he had stopped over for a night in Atlanta, where through a mutual friend he had been invited to dinner by a socially prominent family. At the table was their most attractive daughter, Nancy, a recent graduate of Agnes Scott, and George, handsome in his dress blue uniform with the golden wings, apparently captured her attention and her heart. Afterwards she went down to Daytona a couple of times to see him, and soon thereafter they were married, and none too soon, for the baby arrived nine months after their first meeting. But by the time I met her at Cecil, the dew was off the roses, and when I flew over to tell them that I had just been posted to NAS Atlanta, she told me she would be there before I for she was leaving George for a trial separation and was going home with the baby. It was all very sad, and I promised I would check on how she was faring when I got there, which I did and was promptly invited for lunch at the family residence.

At the luncheon for my benefit was a young lady named Sally, a childhood friend of Nancy; they had been in high school together but had parted temporarily when Nancy enrolled at Agnes Scott and Sally went off to the University of Georgia at Athens. They were now reunited but under dramatically different personal circumstances; here was Nancy, married with child but now separated; whereas Sally, who had dropped out of the university after one year, had worked her way up to a managerial position in a local insurance company, and was living with her parents. Nancy and I talked of the cruel coincidence that had brought us to this table together, while Sally brought us up to date on life in war-time Atlanta (pretty dull) and bewailed the fact that the only man she had been remotely interested in was now in the Army and stationed at some place called the Presidio in California. I took that bit of information as an invitation to call, which I promptly did and found myself ensconced that evening in her family living room. In short order we became—how does one say it?—an item, and that is how I missed most of the hanky-panky at the Biltmore. We had other fish to fry.

In many ways, Sally was one of the most remarkable human beings I have ever known, certainly the most pleasant. Not statuesque, she was of moderate stature and a mite plump, but in all the right places, with dark curly hair in a boyish bob and luminous deep brown eyes. What set her apart was the uncommon pleasantness of her face, always smiling, and an equable disposition that defined for me what sweetness of spirit was all about. Her very presence in a room made the occupants feel better about themselves and each other, for she was the soul of unalloyed good humor. Her thoughtful awareness of others' feelings was constant; her demands for self-attention non-existent. Her devotion to me was complete and pure as the driven snow, and her every look, smile, and trick of thought were designed only to please, but there was nothing cloying about her abundant good nature. She was, in sum, something else again. She was in love, she freely admitted, and possessive but not meanly so, and she fully understood how tenuous were the times and hence our relationship, but, as she put it, she was willing to take her chances.

If all this be true, then where was the fatal flaw? If never before had I felt so good, so whole, so content by just being with a person, if all the physical and spiritual affinities were there in full measure, fully shared, then what was the rub? In three words, my intellectual snobbery. Sally possessed not a single ounce of intellectual curiosity; she had never finished a book of substance, she had made a mess of her one exposure to formal higher education, there was no evidence that she even comprehended the existence of the life of the mind or had ever been moved by the love she had of learning. There was not a book to be seen in her apartment. It was not that Sally was dim-witted for she was bright as a penny and held her own in parlor games requiring quick responses; it was just that at no time had she been moved to hone her natural gifts. I gave her a reading list and a copy of *Huckleberry Finn* to start, but it evoked no spark. I recited to her all the love sonnets in my considerable lexicon, alternating Elizabeth Barrett's unabashed sentimentality with Millay's bittersweet realism, but though she listened attentively and asked for more, she never picked up *Sonnets From The Portuguese*, another of my gifts to her, on her own. So how could I, I asked myself, with dreams of an academic career, think of a long-term future with her. I could see myself taking her home and walking into the Presidential mansion of Texas State College for Women (TSCW); my aristocratic mother, hiding her disappointment, would have clasped her to her bosom for what she was, but my less gallant father would have merely shaken his head in disbelief. So despite my utter devotion to her, I dismissed all thoughts of *Pygmalion*, rationalizing that until this war was over, in all fairness I ought not think beyond tomorrow with anyone.

Half in jest, I had often proclaimed that apart from her physical allure, my attraction to any woman depended on her affinity with the three Bs—beer, bridge, and baseball. In Sally I had almost hit the jackpot; she abominated bridge, as do most people who have tried it and been found wanting, but her taste for beer was quite the equal of mine, and she loved baseball. Each evening after work, she would pause at a flower stall just outside her office building and take a bus which deposited her at the door of the Biltmore, which in its lower reaches afforded a rathskellar with cold draft beer, a jukebox, comfortable booths and a modest dance floor; and when I arrived in the shuttle bus from the field, there she would be in our booth, her little bouquet in a water glass, and a wonderful smile of welcome. Our foaming steins would appear, and after a kiss, I would plug in Goodman or Dorsey or Harry James, and while we danced I would recount for her my daring deeds of the day, a routine that we never seemed to tire of. Then when we decided where we would eat, she would wait while I went up to the ninth floor to change out of my flying gear. We would often dine at Mammy's Shanty, just up Peachtree Street, or get the next shuttle to the Air Station for drinks and dinner in the Officers Club. In fact Sally became such a familiar sight and was so universally liked that she was acclaimed mascot of our Squadron. But the nights we liked the best were when the Atlanta Crackers, a pretty good Class AA baseball team, were in town; and we would go out to Fulton County Stadium and munch hotdogs and drink beer which by now had skyrocketed to 25¢ the bottle, and Sally would second guess the manager as vehemently as anyone. One night we were impressed by the debut of an eighteen year old shortstop named Roy Hartsfield, who eventually became quite a legend. Baseball was the only sport I had remotely excelled in at college, and I never let her forget my vastly superior knowledge, even though when I got cranked up she would excuse herself to get another beer.

And it was Sally who was vicariously involved in an incident critical to my flying career. Up to now most of my flying time had been accumulated in the Stearman, either learning or instructing, and now I was flying much larger and more powerful aircraft like the SN-J and on up. And although I was technically nearly perfect, I was never completely comfortable in them, being plagued by a psychological hang-up which I attributed to my dreadful experience in the SN-C at JAX. Simply put, in the deepest recesses of my psyche, I felt myself at the mercy of the aircraft; that it was flying me and not the other way around, and try as I did to combat it, the feeling persisted. Late one afternoon I was out in an SN-J with one of our Army friends under the hood in the rear cockpit on his final attempt at a champagne performance. The weather guesser had predicted thunderstorms in the area, but there were plenty of clear patches around and I became so engrossed in monitoring the instruments that I failed to note the darkening clouds in the distance and the field begin to close in. My student had indeed earned champagne, but our elation was diminished as I headed for the base and found myself flying in and out of rain squalls; and when I raised the tower, I was told that the field was being closed and that I would have to find an open area and fly a holding pattern. I replied that I didn't have enough AV gas for a holding pattern and I would have to take my chances on coming in. And inside a little voice said to me, "Okay. Buddy. This is it. You're either going to become a complete master of this aircraft or turn in your suit." Since the wind was gusting in every direction, the tower gave me my choice of runways except the long north-south one which was blocked by the emergency landing of an Army B-26 that had burst its tires. As I circled the field, I could barely pick out the east-west runway through the rain that was now pelting down, and I took what I hoped was dead aim for it. The wind was now squarely off my port beam, and with landing gear and flaps down, all I could do was lower my wing into it, give it full throttle, and bore in.

"Just like slips to a circle," the wee voice said.

Finally I sailed over the end of the runway, cut the throttle, and kicked her straight, and blam, we were on the deck. By now the visibility was zero, and they had to send out a jeep to lead me in to the flight line. We climbed out of the plane, sloshed through the downpour, and stowed our parachutes; and my Army companion patted me on the back, mumbling his thanks and allowing that never again would he complain about a carrier approach.

As we entered the Ready Room, to my astonishment there stood Sally, tears coursing down her cheeks, who had witnessed it all. She rushed up to me and buried her head in my shoulder, her whole body quivering from relief and joy. Our Executive Officer was hosting a small dinner that night to which we had been invited, but unbeknownst to me he had asked Sally if she would like to come to the base early and observe some of our flight operations. While they were chatting in the Wardroom, the tower had called him, apprising him of my difficulties.

Turning to Sally, he had said. "Your friend seems to be in a spot of trouble and is going to try to land in this mess. It may not be amusing, but if you'd like to watch, come up in the tower with me while I try to talk him in," which she did.

"It was dreadful," she later related, "when I saw the ambulance and the fire truck head for your runway. We caught just a glimpse of your final approach and then you disappeared. I was petrified until the tower said you were okay and then we rushed down to meet you."

The next day I took a busman's holiday, checking out an SN-J and telling the BAM custodian of our parachutes to grab one and I'd take her up. Exhilarated by my new self-confidence, I put the plane through every contortion I could think of, completely forgetting about my charge in the rear cockpit until the poor thing, completely wrung out, called me on the intercom, moaning for relief.

"I'll take you in on one condition," I said jokingly.

With relief she replied, "Willingly, if I ever touch the ground in one piece!"

But the only thing important to me was that, by God, I could fly, and from then on I felt I was as good as any pilot who ever lived.

Finally, one of the dividends of NAS Atlanta was the fact that as our reputation grew, pilots from bases all over the country were detailed to go through our drill. So it was that Hull showed up from Patuxent, Morgan from Quonset Point, Perkins from Grand Prairie, and other old acquaintances, including a roommate from the University of Texas and a boyhood chum from, of all places, Denton, Texas, who I did not even know was in the Service. Since none of our AVG ever traveled without his paperback, we were even able for one night to revive our Little Theatre, there being no problem in recruiting distaff readers. After that performance I went to the Visitors BOQ to see Perk safely to his room where right on schedule he produced his favorite bottle, called his wife long distance and whispered lovingly, "Boca Chica, Boca Chica, Boca Chica" as he passed into oblivion.

Another diversion was the fact that when the minor baseball leagues had to fold up because of transportation difficulties, the Atlanta Crackers enlisted in the Navy en masse and were assigned to our Air Station and became our team. Between their boot camp chores they let me work out with them, shagging flies in the outfield and taking batting practice. Their first scheduled service game was with Fort Dix in Chattanooga, and we flew them up in our Beechcraft. In the dressing room they shocked the daylights out of me by issuing me a uniform and announcing that I would start in left field and be the lead-off hitter. What they knew—but I didn't—was that the opposing pitcher would be none other than Johnny Beazley, one of the aces of the St. Louis Cardinal staff who had won two games in the last World Series, and this was their idea of one huge joke. But I was game—foolish but game. As the visitors we were up first, and I stepped into the batter's box as scared as I had been on my first night solo. I never saw his first pitch but heard it pop into the catcher's mitt. As he wound up and let fly again, I closed my eyes and swung, the crack of the bat telling me I had made contact, and before I knew it I was standing on third base, having rattled the right-center field boards for a triple. Beazley just glowered at me, and of course I was stranded there, for we didn't get a loud foul off him the rest of the night. In the bottom of the inning I took my position amid the boos and cat calls of a few thousand G.I.s and WACS, and I did manage to catch the only ball hit in my direction, an easy pop fly, after which I was mercifully replaced. And that is the sum total of my career against major league pitching, so I am still batting 1000. After the game the WACS, most of whom had never seen a Naval uniform before, crowded around our dressing room, and as we made our way to our bus, they closed in on us and we narrowly escaped mass rapine.

 The final test of the radio-beam part of the syllabus was the long cross-country flight, and since the trainee was under the hood for its duration, it made slight difference whether the flight was conducted during the day or at night. Whenever available we would include a Link Trainer operator in the crew of the Beechcraft, the plane most often utilized in this exercise, so she could monitor the instruments and radio beam techniques involved in an actual flight, and in good weather we would let her try her hand at the controls. I personally preferred the night flights, for one could generally count on smoother, more stable air, and I enjoyed the twinkling lights delineating the villages and hamlets passing underneath, plus checking off the radio beacons, which were a boon to the commercial flights. At any rate, we would select a destination, and the pilot under the gun would before takeoff pore over his route maps, noting the terrain, the radio ranges, the call letters and radio frequencies of the transmitters en route and the distances between them, the allowable fuel consumption, while the command pilot would do the same, and also make note of any visual landmarks, such as hills and rivers and railroad tracks, which we called the "iron compass", should our electronic gear go on the fritz. At the end of the outbound leg we would generally land and take a break for an hour or so, and so we let our Army friends pick destinations within hailing distance of their homes, if that were possible, so they could have a quick visit with family and friends.

Then there were the ferry hops. We were taking delivery of our Howards at Midway Airport in Chicago and our Beechcraft from their assembly plant in Wichita, Kansas, and from time to time we would draw the duty of flying commercially to pick them up and ferrying them to Atlanta. One such junket got me into a mess of difficulty. One of the coeds I had dated with some frequency at The University of Texas was a Theta from Childress in the Panhandle named Lois Sager, and she was well and truly what was known in the vernacular as a BWOC (Big Woman On Campus). A journalism major, she was a member of Phi Beta Kappa, president of her sorority, had been elected to Mortar Board, and in her senior year of 1939 (I was then in Graduate School working on my MA) she was one of the nominees for Sweetheart of the University, a selection made annually by the student body of the most popular coed on the campus. In much demand socially, I ranked about third or fourth on her select dating list, but I was her escort at my fraternity's luncheon honoring the nominees. Upon graduation, she became a political correspondent for the *Dallas Morning News*, Texas' most influential newspaper, covering municipal affairs in Dallas, the State scene in Austin, and with occasional spot assignments in Washington, D.C., while I was still there, and I would squire her around town. We had maintained a fairly steady correspondence, not exactly platonic but not dripping in passion, because she used the language so very well and I enjoyed her views on most any topic; but this slackened considerably with the announcement of her engagement to one of my college rivals. I last saw her in Washington in May 1941, just before going on active duty, at which time she said she had broken her engagement and seemed so relieved that she suggested a weekend in New York City. So our relationship took a decidedly different turn; and although I had not seen her since my commissioning leave in February 1942, our letters increased in frequency and became far less prosaic. This was the situation when she called me in Atlanta from Austin, where she was then assigned, telling me that she was due some vacation and could she come to Atlanta for a week leave if she could manage flight reservations, which in those days were not easy to come by, our now having been at war for something over a year. I warned her that she would see precious little of me in the daytime, but if she didn't mind that, to come as soon as she could, and she replied that she would shoot for the second week of February (1943). That night I was duty-bound to tell Sally, and she just sat there and looked at me, biting her lip and forcing back the tears until she uttered the only snide remark I ever heard from her, "Well, I'll try to exist for a week without His Majesty's presence, but I think I can manage it."

Lois' arrival was set for a Monday afternoon, but a week before that date I was issued temporary orders to proceed to Chicago on that Monday morning to pick up a Howard. I called Lois immediately to explain the situation and to see if she could change her reservation, but the next day she called back to say there wasn't a prayer. The upshot was that since I would get back to Atlanta late on Tuesday, she should come on as scheduled and I would have her met at the airport and taken to her hotel, our having lost only one day. So it was that on that Monday morning Sally borrowed the family car and drove me to the airport for the early Delta flight to Chicago, a thoughtful gesture so typical of her and indicating that although not all was forgiven there would be no further mention of my dereliction. Then followed one of those coincidences that seem to mark my life; the Delta stewardess was an old classmate of mine at Texas who had driven one of my fraternity brothers up the wall so enamored of her was he, but she had decided to see something of the world and thus her presence here. Not only that, but she and Lois had been good friends, so I brought her up to date on that score, and since we were both staying at the south side hotel near Midway used by the flight crews, we agreed to meet that night for a drink before her dinner date. After landing, I made straight for the Howard hangar, inspected the aircraft, signed the necessary papers and got clearance for an early morning takeoff; and once in my room at the hotel, I called Atlanta to find Lois comfortably ensconced in the Biltmore, which by then had reverted to its pristine ways, and dressing for dinner with some of my squadron mates. Relieved, I then went down to the bar to meet our mutual friend. At Midway, the weather officer was predicting a cold front for around noon the next day but thought if I got off at the crack of dawn, I would be OK and enjoy a good tail wind for the flight southeast, so I left a wake-up call for 0400 hours.

You could hear the wind gusting at almost gale force, and the snow was beginning to fall thick and fast; since we had been inside all the time we were unaware of the approaching cold front, the leading edge of which was now right on top of us. Four days later I was back in Atlanta, where Lois and I tried to make the best of the two days left to us.

For ferrying the Beechcraft, we used a different procedure, and it, too, led to a strange coincidence. Since it was a twin-engine aircraft, regulations called for a two man crew, so it was deemed to be more economical to wait until several planes were ready for delivery, and instead of using the commercial airlines, to fly our personnel to Wichita ourselves, usually four crews at a time. We would generally arrive there around noon, check in at the Allis Hotel, one of two decent hostelries the town afforded, have lunch, and then spend the afternoon at the air field adjacent to the Beech assembly line, checking out our planes and doing the necessary paper work prior to an early departure the next day. Returning to the hotel late one afternoon, we were sitting around the lobby, and for lack of something better to do, I decided to teach the group a song entitled "The Good Ship Titanic" which had been one of our favorites in the wardroom at Lee Field, and which went, in part, like this:

> *Oh they built the ship Titanic, and when they had got through*
> *They said they had a ship the water would never get through.*
> *But the Lord's almighty hand said that ship would never land—*
> *It was sad when that great ship went down.*
> *It was sad, Lord, sad, it was sad, Lord, sad*
> *It was sad when that great ship went down.*
> *Husbands and wives, little bitty children lost their lives—*
> *It was sad when that great ship went down.*

I had the group repeating that stanza until they got the hang of it, when a lady approached us with determined strides across the lobby floor. She faced us, her face flushed with agitation, but in a calm voice with a distinct British accent, she said, "I am a resident of this hotel, and I ask you not to sing that song; it offends me. It so happens that I am the granddaughter of Captain Smith who was in command of the *Titanic* on that fateful voyage."

Me (Jack) home on leave in Denton, TX, May 1942

Our astonishment was complete, our embarrassment, acute, our apologies, profuse—but by the Lord Harry, who could have predicted that scenario!

On that particular junket, I had got permission to break the flight back and RON (Remain Over Night) in Fort Worth, so I could have a quick visit with my family who lived in Denton, 35 miles to the north. Now I knew that an old acquaintance of mine, Christine Smith, was now living in Fort Worth with her mother; in fact, Chris had been the other half of my first honest to God love affair which had begun in Junior High School and had continued in a sometimes sweet but more often stormy on-and-off again fashion through high school and college, and we had even spent a wonderful New Years together when she had visited me in Washington in 1940. I hadn't seen her since then but I decided to take a chance, and I called her from Wichita. To my amazement and delight she agreed to meet me at Meacham Field, drive me to Denton and then bring me back. When I arrived the next afternoon, she picked me up at the Transit Officers BOQ, and on the way north she told me about her managerial position at the huge Consolidated Aircraft installation at Ramey field, and about her interest in one of the Division Heads, a graduate engineer from MIT who was also a talented musician.

"Well," said I gallantly, "it sounds to me like you've got someone with his feet on the ground and an assured future, unlike some fly-by-nights I know."

"That has occurred to me," she replied without batting an eye.

But on the way back we talked about other things, about how proud she was of me and worried about what might happen to me in this God damned war, and as we lingered in her car outside the BOQ the best of everything came flooding back and the embrace touched just as deeply as ever, and we parted not knowing what to say next or what to do about it all.

"Chris, I can't ask you to wait," was all I could manage.

Her reply just shattered me. "I can't say I will, but oh, Jack, I so much want to."

Surely MacArthur, at a later time, meant first loves—not old soldiers.

The next morning I flew over the homestead, where Dad and Mother and my little brother, George, and the cook and the houseboy were all out on the lawn furiously waving flags; I buzzed them a couple of times, thinking about last night and waggled my wings and headed east, not knowing whether to jump with joy—or weep.

For me, the climax of the IFIS experience was my final editing of our revised handbook, which for years remained the bible for Naval instrument flying, thus adding a new dimension to our attack capabilities. We had more than met our challenge and knew the pride of all those who have been in on the ground floor of a new enterprise and seen it through to a successful conclusion. But for Sally and me, it also meant a new and saddened dimension to our relationship for the end of this phase of it, at least, was clearly in sight. She knew that most of the original cast, now anxious to practice what we had been preaching, had put in for sea duty, with some assurance that, because of our performance here, our requests would be given priority. In a sense it was like breaking up the AVG again, for ours had been a joint effort and all that implies in our respect for each other. For Sally and me the only way out was marriage, and this I could not bring myself to do, a fact that she accepted, but the hurt was as deep as the affection. My puny and futile parting gesture was to leave her with a copy of Wordsworth's poignant sonnet which begins

> *When in disgrace with fortune and men's eyes . . . and ends*
> *For thy sweet love remembered such wealth brings*
> *That then I scorn to change my state with kings.*

It was nearly a year later that I saw her for the last time. On my way home on leave, I stopped off in Atlanta, and we spent a desperate evening together, which only served to lay bare all of our emotional scars, and the pain of that parting I can feel to this day.

Editor's Addition

Although Jack enjoyed his service as a flight instructor, he longed to be in the center of the "real" action. In this excerpt from a letter to his parents, one vicariously flies with him as he gives expression to some of the intricacies of flight instruction. And then we feel his lament for not sharing combat duty with the friends made while doing his own training. (His desire for combat did materialize as will be seen in subsequent chapters.)

> Were this only the pre-war era, I should be quite content with the part I am now playing as an instructor. I am flying around seven hours a day, and to say the least it is a nerve-wracking business. These cadets can give one many an anxious moment as they feebly reach for the ground. Much of our training course consists of precision work close to the ground, particularly in the early stages, for a pilot must be able to land his plane in any given situation if he wants to walk away from it. Believe me, these boys can get themselves in some ticklish situations, and all too often it

takes all of my skill to get them out of them. Still, that is precisely my job, and I am learning much more about the truly fine points of flying than I could anywhere else. Stunt instruction is the most wearing physically because the maneuvers properly executed are intricate in themselves, yet coupled with that one must contend with all the odd positions a cadet can get the plane into. However, this is the least dangerous of all the phases of instruction, because the planes are wonderfully sturdy and because of the most priceless asset of a flyer—altitude. When an airplane loses flying speed the inevitable result is a spin, and drops of 1000 feet are a common occurrence. But when one is originally at 8000 feet, then it is a mere nothing to wind up at 4000 feet. Stunts are the hardest things to teach because of the necessity of acquiring a totally new perspective; that is, one must be able to have absolute control of the plane whether he is on his back, side, etc. The cadets simply get lost once they get turned over, and the result is usually a screaming dive or a spin. But the instructor is always there to right the ship, and away we go again. Fortunately, I remember only too well when I was in their place, and I can fully appreciate what they are going through. Honestly, though so often you have to scream and shout at them, you really get to love them. Then there is formation flying in which I can find relaxation for I enjoy it so much. It is really wonderful when you are flying with your buddies. So I can honestly say that mine is not an easy job, and I hope I can say that I am doing it well. Of course, as with any teacher, the only true indication is the progress of my students, and as yet not one of them has failed a single test flight. Am I knocking on wood?

As I said before, were it not for the war I might think I was doing my part. But the war is going so badly now, and it becomes increasingly difficult for me to think of much else than going into action. I thought that when I became an aviator I would have every opportunity to vent my spleen against the state of the world, but since attaining that goal, I have met with nothing but complete frustration. Many of my buddies that I went through training with have been giving them the devil in the Coral Sea and at Midway, and here I sit . . . Surely the tide will turn soon.

CHAPTER 8
Bermuda

My new assignment was to Utility Squadron 15, attached to the Atlantic Fleet, and I reported to one of its units based at the time in Brunswick, Maine, on Casco Bay and home of Bowdoin College and the Red Lion Inn. Now a Utility Squadron is definitely not one of the glamour outfits of the Naval Air Corps, but, as the saying goes, someone has to do it, the "it" being any chore the Fleet needs having done. The Squadron's combat role was limited to anti-submarine patrols, but the chief requirement for its pilots was versatility, for sooner or later they would fly every type of aircraft the Navy possessed and even some of the Army Air Corps. There was the towing of targets for Fleet units on their shake-down cruise, the ferrying of aircraft, the testing and acceptance of new or updated types that were constantly coming off the assembly lines, familiarization with the characteristics of Army types such as the B-25 which might be used in joint operations as Doolittle demonstrated, everything that might conceivably be utilized, single engine, multi-engine, land based or sea based. Donkey work.

Among our inventory at Brunswick were three land-based PBYs, and as a certified P-Boat pilot, my first assignment was the nightly anti- submarine patrol from Casco Bay down to Martha's Vineyard, with the additional duty of monitoring the blackout along the coast. To this day few people ever realized the monumental losses inflicted by submarines on our coastal shipping after we entered the war against Germany. Her U-boats ranged all the way from Maine down along the Atlantic coast to Key West and into the Gulf of Mexico, a favorite point of concentration being just off the mouth of the Mississippi River. Our undisciplined citizenry for many months blatantly ignored the blackout regulations, and the sub commanders after nightfall would simply surface and sit quietly in wait for a passing merchantman which, perfectly outlined against the shore lights, made an easy target for their deck guns without having to expend their precious torpedoes. There was not a beach from Maine to

Florida that was not slathered with oil and other debris from this kind of carnage, and at JAX we used the protruding hulks of sunken freighters as bombing targets. For nearly a year the U-boats ranged up and down the coast practically unscathed until we forced them at least to stay beneath the surface.

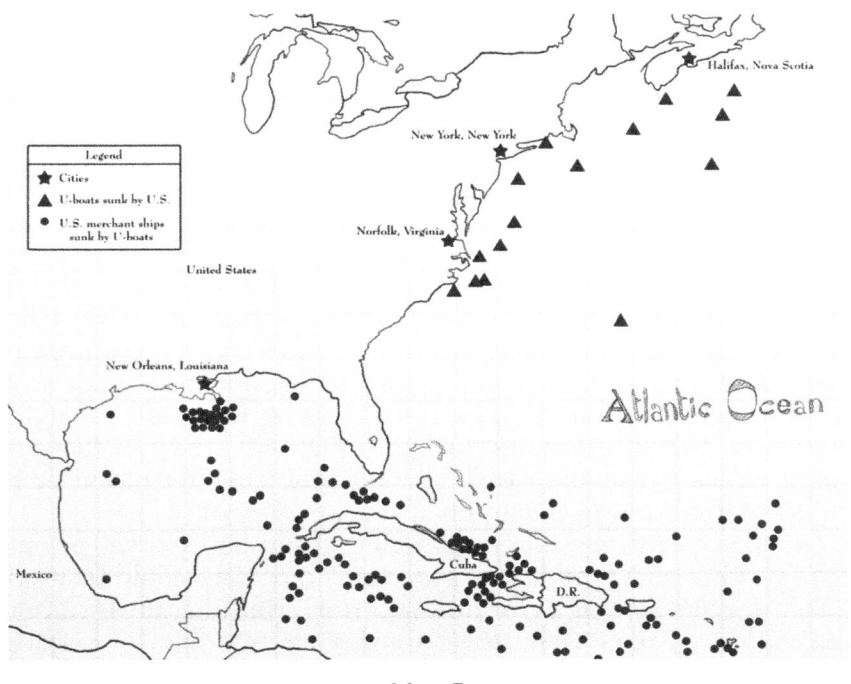

Map 5
Locations of U-Boat Attacks in U.S. Territorial Waters

One day Grumman ferry pilots delivered three TBFs, torpedo bombers, at that time the largest single-engine combat planes in the Navy's arsenal with their powerful Pratt & Whitney engines, torpedo bays, revolving gun turrets mounted aft of the cockpit, and folding wings to abet stowage on carriers. Since no one in the detachment had ever flown one of these contraptions, I volunteered to be the pioneer, one of the few smart moves of my Naval career. One of the Grumman pilots took me out to the plane, gave me a cockpit check, dropped a copy of the Operating Manual in my lap, and wished me good luck. It was a remarkably easy plane to fly, slow but stable and responsive to the controls, and once I became familiar with its higher stalling speed and landing characteristics, which a series of touch and gos took care of, I felt right at home; and since I was now the "ace" of the TBFs, I checked out our other pilots in it.

For divertissement there was the Red Lion Inn, the traditional watering hole of the Bowdoinites, much like the Roten Ochsen in Heidelberg, and for more ribald pleasures there was Lewiston just up the road, an essentially French Canuck community lavish in its earthy hospitality. But as anyone who has been there knows, the positive joy of New England in October is the blaze of color and changing hues of the foliage in the countryside, a sight unmatched anywhere in the world for the purity of its beauty. I was fortunate in finding in the detachment a friend from our Jacksonville days, Paul Gibson, who, with his wife, occupied a cottage in a wooded area just outside the township, where, after duty hours, we would tramp endlessly in those glorious woods, stopping on the way home at the local pier to pick up lobsters fresh from the trap for 25¢ a pound. It reminded me of those days in the past when Robert Frost would make his annual hegira to visit my father's college and read to the students. But the end of October also brought omens of things to come with the chill winds coming off the Canadian flatlands and the issuance of winter flight gear—helmets, mittens, ankle-length leather coats and boots, all fur lined. The one aspect of flying I cared for least was cold weather, and a Maine winter promised a chill factor more severe than I had yet experienced.

In the meantime, our engineering group had worked it out that by adjustments in the torpedo bays, our TBFs could be used to tow targets as well as for anti-sub work, and the needs of our fleet units on their shakedown cruises for this kind of service were increasing. So it was decided to send our TBFs to the squadron's detachment in Bermuda, in whose adjacent waters many of such Fleet exercises were being conducted. In President Roosevelt's 1940 arrangements with Great Britain involving the swapping of destroyers for bases, the U.S. had acquired 99 year leases in Bermuda, enabling us to establish land and air installations 600 miles off shore, a tremendous boon in the so-called battle of the Atlantic. First we had built and manned Fort Bell, an intelligence-gathering outfit concerned with the interception of instructions to enemy submarines, allowing us to plot their location and intentions, which we could do by virtue of having broken the German wireless codes with the help of Enigma. The major aerial operations emanating from Bermuda were centered at the southern end of the islands where our long-range PBM squadrons were sea-based, and the Seabees who had built a magnificent landing strip in a coral lagoon on the northernmost island in St. George's Parish. This was Kindley Field, and its contractors had used much of the same labor force which had dug the Holland and Lincoln tunnels under the Hudson River, many of them Irish and all of them with a low life expectancy because of the toxic inhalations attendant to their perilous profession underground. It was said that these "sand hogs" would daily carry a bottle of whiskey in their lunch buckets, and by night would terrorize the natives; at any rate, one of them was the father of one of the authentic RAF heroes of the Battle of Britain, "Paddy" Finucane, who upon learning of his son's loss, went berserk and drank himself to death. It was on Kindley Field that Squadron 15's Bermuda detachment was based.

At Brunswick, meanwhile, preparations were under way for the ferry flight, which was being billed as the first attempt by single-engine planes to negotiate the Bermuda Triangle. As I had amassed the most hours in the TBF, I was designated to lead the flight, and I could not adequately express my pleasure at the prospect of trading a Maine winter for the Bermuda sunshine. The first leg of the flight was to NAS Norfolk, our jumping-off base, where we were duly briefed on route maps, navigational aids, expected wind velocity and direction, and emergency life boat procedures; a PBM was to precede us, reporting on weather en route, and a destroyer would be on station mid-way in the event one of us had to ditch. It was a piece of cake; the weather on takeoff was CAVU (Ceiling and Visibility Unlimited), and becoming airborne all I had to do was set the automatic pilot on a course of 090, plus having a powerful beam emanating from Kindley Field which I picked up half-way out, and in three hours those beautiful islands passed underneath our bow. With all the station personnel out on the tarmac to greet us, I managed to make one of the worst landings of my life, but except for that embarrassment, all had gone according to plan. It could never be confused with Lindberg's arrival at Le Bourget, but at least it was a tiny first for the Naval Air Corps, and there used to be a plaque there to commemorate it. An Army pilot would have been awarded a ten-day furlough, a raise in rank, and the Distinguished Flying Cross; as it was, I was told that I would be welcome at the poker table that night.

The United States had now been at war for two years, and I found myself detailed to one of the most beautiful spots in the world; it was downright sinful. To fly over the coves and inlets and glistening coral, the lush green vegetation dotted with spotless white stone cottages and picturesque hamlets, the pink beaches and immaculate golf courses, the winding roads free of traffic except for our own jeeps and lorries, the Toonerville

Trolley connecting St. George's with Hamilton was sheer bliss. And there was more than these physical graces; a grateful populace, seeing and hearing our planes take off and land at Kindley Field around the clock felt secure in their conviction that we brave airmen were holding at bay any possible threat to their Eden. What was true was that our small detachment that numbered only 15 pilots in their strange uniforms remained a subject of curiosity, as at Atlanta, especially to the youngsters who crowded up to the fences surrounding our base to marvel at our flight operations, and whose parents tried to outdo each other in their offers of hospitality. Typical was the Board of Governors of the Mid-Ocean Club, that swank establishment to the south of us whose membership read like an international Who's Who; these worthies bade us use their entire facilities, including the golf course, at will as their invited guests, and forbade us to pick up a tab. There were also manifestations of welcome from another quarter. Bermuda had long been one of the playgrounds of America's big rich, some of whom had built lavish pleasure palaces, the most impressive of which was the estate of J. P. Morgan, who had turned it over to the Navy as headquarters for the highest ranking officers and their staffs.

Our quarters at Kindley, however, were strictly run of the mill: Quonset huts for barracks and for a wardroom and tiny bar which opened into the mess hall, which we shared with the officers of a Free French submarine flotilla that was emulating German undersea tactics for the benefit of our Fleet units in training. For amusement we had some card tables, a battered upright piano and a record player, while outside was an area cleared for the showing of movies al fresco. It had become a routine that when I entered the mess hall for the evening meal, someone would ask, "Hey, Tex, what's the movie tonight?" to which my automatic response was, "Hoot Mix in 'Who Shit In My Saddle?'" But one night one of the lads had slipped in a female guest and tucked her away in the corner of the mess hall, where fortunately I had spotted her through a window on the way in to the wardroom; so when I entered the mess area and was greeted with the inevitable question, to their utter disgust I innocently replied, "Hoot Mix in 'Who Stole My Saddle?'"

Another diversion was an agreement with our French comrades that if they would take us down, we would take them up. When it was my turn, I joined my Commander and his crew in a personnel carrier and drove to the slip where their submarines were tethered. Scrambling aboard, we proceeded on the surface until reaching the open sea, when at a given signal we descended the conning tower ladder, battened down the hatches, and the helmsman took us down to periscope depth. My God, it was quiet, and I felt like I had been sealed in a sardine can and must surely suffocate. We made our way forward along the narrowest of passageways to a tiny cubicle that served as the officers' mess for a breakfast of ham and eggs and, to my amazement, tall flagons of red wine, after which things seemed none so bad. And when the ordinary seamen filed past us to the galley each carrying a pail to receive his daily ration of *vin ordinare*, I began to think this wasn't such a bad service after all. Then the captain explained the game plan: three of our carriers with their destroyer escorts were operating in the area, and our sub's target was the last one in line which, if we could escape detection, we would close in on for a broadside point blank torpedo shot. Our captain had been informed beforehand that that carrier would begin launching its aircraft at 0630 hours and would recover them beginning at 0830 hours, which was the moment of closure while the carrier's attention was riveted to the recovery of its planes. The Fleet units, for their part, had been alerted that submarine activities had been reported in these waters. So the game of cat and mouse was on, and for the next two hours we changed depths and courses, sometimes lying silent, anything to evade the destroyers with their sonar and other gear, until finally we made our mock attack and surfaced. The referees topside ruled we had been sunk, but no matter to me; I could breathe fresh air and see the sky again.

The next day I took the French commander up with me. We were 6 TBFs and we too were going to make a torpedo run on the same Air Group, timing our attack for the launching of their planes, skimming the waves and boring in from six different directions. So fitting the Frenchmen in their parachutes and making sure they were securely buckled in, we took off in the pre-dawn blackness, climbed up and away and took up our positions around the Fleet perimeter; and at 0625 hours, with the sun just peeping over the horizon, we started our runs in, zigging and zagging right on top of the waves with every anti-aircraft battery in the Fleet trying to track us, and as we passed the launch point, we stood our planes on their tails, zooming straight up into the morning sky. We regrouped overhead, got a "well done" from the bridge of the flagship, and for the edification of our quaking companions, flew a very tight formation back to the field. In the post mortem, not a single submariner or fly boy was willing to trade places.

Given its location and the reputation of its charms, Bermuda was a frequent destination for USO groups sent out to entertain the troops. The aging siren, Helen Twelvetrees, liked to come out, managing still to look sexy from a distance, and never straying far from the bar. A dramatic troupe featuring the Meadows sisters—one of whom later married Steve Allen, and Nedda Harrigan, once wed to Walter Connolly and later to become Mrs. Joshua Logan—were a great hit. The various officers' messes on the islands vied for the chance to host these groups, and although our primitive digs were bereft of charm, we were the only ones who could provide them *entree* to the Mid-Ocean Club, where the local members enjoyed their presence as much as we did. It is also a fact that some of the associations engendered by these visits carried over into the post-war era.

We were amassing a ton of flight time, what with servicing the Fleet exercises and our ASW (Anti-Submarine Warfare) activities. With regard to the latter, our offensive capabilities were limited, being dependent almost entirely on our luck in spotting a U-boat on the surface; but defensively we were to be reckoned with. Our constant concern was the protection of the Fleet and its environs from the German undersea menace, and we endeavored to fly a picket line around the Fleet, thus putting the Germans on notice that these waters were under a 24-hour surveillance. Of great help, even excitement, was the delivery to our squadron of two sleek JMs, the Navy version of the Army's fastest and most lethal twin-engine medium range bomber, the notorious B-26, which had acquired with considerable justification the reputation of a killer. A thing of beauty in the air, its problem was that its wing-loading was so screwed up when first pressed into service that in its landing mode, it was given to premature stalling out, forcing the Army pilots to make their approaches at much higher speed than specifications called for and land so hot that they frequently burnt out their brakes or blew their tires, and every so often ran out of runway. But the Navy version had a new wing and was stripped of its heavy armament, thus removing the problem altogether, with the result that we had on our hands a hot new airplane that was the most fun to fly in my experience. For our uses, it enabled us to tow targets at a much higher speed, and it increased our range and ability to keep the Fleet encircled. We just loved it. In all of this our greatest enemy was the weather, for the North Atlantic in mid-winter could be treacherous and sometimes viscous, with line squalls and poor visibility abounding, and the IFIS

Handbook, which was now in the possession of every squadron in the Navy, was a great help, particularly for our younger pilots.

Bermuda Railway

The skipper of our detachment was a senior Lieutenant, soon to get his next half stripe, named Chuck Fagan, a veteran PBY jockey who had been in the Midway Island shoot out. Dark visaged, saturnine, strikingly handsome in the Robert Taylor mold, he was relaxed and pleasant. He seldom flew, he loved his poker and the great outdoors, and he dreamed of a post-Naval life perhaps in Alaska. A great guy who the enlisted men all adored, he was due to be relieved three weeks after my arrival. On movie nights and sometimes in the mess, he was in the company of a stunning red head named Helene, who had caught my eye in the mornings when on her bicycle she passed by our compound on the road that took her to Fort Bell, where she was a civilian code clerk with a high security clearance. I had danced with her a couple of times in our wardroom to her favorite record, Artie Shaw's "All The Things You Are," and I knew that another of Lieutenant Fagan's attributes was good taste, and that their regard for each other was genuine. So after his departure, I gave her a day to recover and then intercepted her on her way to work, asking if she would join me that night for dinner and the movie in the hope that her association with our detachment would continue since she had become a pleasant adornment. With only a polite demurrer she accepted, and that night after work she parked her bike in our compound and waited for me in the wardroom while I changed out of my flight suit. We had a drink and ate our delicious bully beef and were just taking our seats outside when it began to rain cats and dogs. We rushed inside to let the squall pass, and I began to worry about her cycling home in the wet when it dawned on me that I didn't know where "home" was. She said it was not too far away but that sometimes Chuck would drive her there in a jeep, which seemed not a bad idea on a night like this if I could manage it. So I checked out one of our trusty vehicles, tossed her bike in the rear, and off we went.

"Home" was some twenty minutes away, and when she directed me through an imposing gateway and down a twisting drive edged with hibiscus, I thought she must be pulling my leg, and I was sure of it when there loomed ahead this palatial edifice. It was the Vincent Astor estate, another of those American showplaces on the islands. I drove up to the garage area and sat there and gaped. She laughed, took me in a side entrance into a room with a solid mahogany bar and said, "Make us a drink and take them up those stairs to the tower. I'll join you in a minute and explain all this and then give you the Grand Tour." Doing as I was bidden, I found myself in a sort of circular turret jutting up from the central structure and affording a magnificent view of St. George's Parish, with Kindley Field in full sight. Looking down, I could see that the main house had been built in the form of an X, with the four appendages joining together in a central core containing the formal reception rooms, dining salon, kitchens, library, an informal sitting room and bar and all sorts of tastefully decorated nooks and crannies with views of the lawns and gardens which surrounded the whole affair. Each of the wings was a self-contained living area, with a master suite and enormous bath and dressing room, two other bedrooms with bath, a kitchenette, and a sitting room which opened onto a spacious balcony at the end of the unit. In the basement there was a game room with billiard table, dart boards and the like, a card room, a finished wine cellar and liquor bins all well stocked. Outside was a four-car garage and bicycle shed, a small machine shop, and on the south side where a gently sloping lawn ended in a crystal clear lagoon, a boat house with three Chris-Craft inboard Runabouts.

When Helene returned, I was still staring at the wonder of it. "I've flown over this place a dozen times," I said, "but never seeing a sign of life, I just assumed it had been closed for the duration. Tell me about all this—and you."

The wind had freshened with the rain squall, now passed beyond us, and under a half moon the white coral reef shimmered as the waves from the lagoon lapped over it. At hand were a pair of binoculars, and I watched our planes taking off on their nightly patrols.

Helene was 35 years old, a native of Winnipeg where, having been orphaned at an early age, she was reared by an aunt and uncle. After finishing secondary school there, she had matriculated at McGill in Montreal but after two years had become disenchanted with the formalities of higher education. As a crossword puzzle addict, however, she had discovered a latent talent for cryptography and eventually went to work for the Department of Defense in Ottawa, where she met and married a pilot in the RCAF. In the meantime, her foster parents had decided to escape the horrors of winter in Winnipeg, and as citizens of the British Commonwealth, they had been welcomed as residents of the Crown Colony of Bermuda and in time had joined the domestic staff of the Astors, the aunt as principal housekeeper, and the uncle as butler/cum/handyman. After Pearl Harbor, the Astors had closed down the estate for the duration, leaving only these two on the premises as caretakers. Back in Canada, meanwhile, in 1943 Helene's ten year marriage ended in a "messy" divorce, and seeking somewhere to heal her wounds and clear her head, she had come to Bermuda to visit her foster parents; and unexpectedly finding a niche for herself at Fort Bell, she had stayed on.

"It was not as though we were sharing crowded quarters," she explained. "I rattle around in the north wing and they in the south, and there are days when we never see each other."

My favorite place was the tower, where nothing much had to be said beyond the poetry it evoked. If I had any talent for poetry, this is where I would write it. Now I finally understand what Duke Senior, driven out of Venice into the pristine countryside, meant when he spoke to his fellow exiles –

> *Sweet are the uses of adversity,*
> *Which, like the toad, ugly and venomous,*
> *Wears yet a precious jewel in his head,*
> *And this our life, exempt from public haunt,*
> *Finds tongues in trees, books in the running brooks,*
> *Sermons in stones, and good in everything.*
> *I would not change it.*

On Christmas Eve the detachment invited our local friends to an Open House; we decorated the tree, hung the bunting and mistletoe, and pooled our Care packages of goodies from home; and with our French contingent supplying the wine, it was a festive affair. For our guests we put on an exhibition of formation flying, taking off and landing in tandem in two-plane sections, and for good measure made torpedo runs on our Quonset huts before landing and partaking of the food and drink. The citizenry, many of whom brought dishes of their yuletide specialties, were dressed to the nines, and we changed into our dress Blues in honor of the occasion. Now I had alerted my co-mates down through the Chief Petty Officers that, as a symbol of our respect for the community and its customs, we were leaving at 2330 hours for St. George's to attend Christmas Eve Mass at the oldest Anglican church in the Western Hemisphere, where the presiding vicar had kindly offered to reserve pews for our contingent. My problem was to keep everyone sober enough to follow the service, and I threatened bread and water to anyone who fouled up the deal. At the appointed time I held a muster to check the uniforms, and satisfied that we were presentable, I herded them on the bus that Helene, who was back in our midst, and I would follow in a jeep. When we disembarked in front of the ancient edifice, it became clear that one of our CPOs, a huge Pole named Balski, was having trouble navigating the stairs leading up to the entrance, but with assistance he managed to make it. But as we filed down the aisle, with all eyes upon us, to turn into our pews, Balski stumbled, and in trying to regain his balance, one foot came down with such force that it went through the thin planking of the floor and he stood there impaled. The crash had at first startled the congregation, but when they realized what had happened, the sight of this giant trying to free his foot was so amusing they could but barely keep their composure; and even the good vicar came shuffling down the aisle to lend assistance. I was livid with shame and embarrassment; but when Balski finally found his pew, the priest, unruffled as he regained the altar, turned to his parishioners and bid us a warm welcome, saying how honored they all were to have England's brave allies present on this solemn occasion, noting, with a perfectly straight face, that since our normal milieu was the wide open spaces, some of us might well have difficulty managing the narrow confines which this humble chapel afforded. So in this true spirit of Christmas, Balski was forgiven and our attempt at hands across the seas had worked out rather well after all.

    Nor was this affair the end of the incorrigible Balski, who seemed able to rise to special occasions. It was St. Patrick's Day, to be exact, a glorious spring day with fleecy clouds dancing in crystal air; we had declared it a holiday, and only a skeleton crew remained aboard, including me as Officer of the Deck. About midafternoon there marched into my cubby hole in the Ready Room Balski and another Chief, dressed in freshly pressed uniforms, their hats on square; at my desk they snapped to attention, saluted smartly, and handed me a chit.

"What the hell are you two doing here?" I demanded sharply. "You're supposed to be in the hangar overhauling that TBF engine."

Unfazed, Balski began, in his best Polish cockney, "Top of the morning, I mean afternoon to you, Sir. My boyhood chum, Selinski here, and I might be wondering, if your good self might find the goodness in your kind heart to sign that chit which would permit us to leave the base and make our way to that wee *kirk* in St. George's—you remember the one, Sir—where we might repent our sins and pay our deepest respect to our Patron Saint on this his name day? Thanking you, Sir, for your consideration of this sacred matter, Sir."

I could not contain myself, and roaring with laughter, I handed him the signed chit, saying, "Now hear this, you miserable Polish frauds, get off this base on the double, but I'm telling you, if I have to send the Shore Patrol for you tonight, it's the brig!"

Christmas was a pleasant day, cold and crisp. Bermuda was alleged by the natives to be the only place in the world where a man sleeping under a rose bush in full bloom could freeze to death. Helene and her foster mother produced a roast goose with all the trimmings, ending with hot mince pie and trifle and a magnum of the Astor's best champagne. We took the Toonerville Trolley to Hamilton and walked around admiring the decorations in the store fronts of the "Forty Thieves," as the affluent merchants had been dubbed. During the next few weeks the only bump in the road was a mail call with a letter with a Fort Worth postmark and I knew before I opened it that it was a "Dear John". Chris had indeed opted for the MIT bloke; there were no recriminations, just regret that I had given her no choice—and thanks for the memories. That I had treated her like a dog in my manger was all too true, but the finality of it hurt like the dickens.

April was a month of celebrations. After St. Patrick's Day, the islands were resplendent in their Easter finery. My promotion to full Lieutenant came through, followed by the traditional "wetting down" party. But the highlight was our gala in honor of Navy Day, for which the Mid-Ocean Club had been put at our disposal complete with a catering staff, and a local dance band had been engaged. I had gone down to Triminghams in Hamilton to be measured for a set of dress whites to display properly my new stripes, and Helene had said she would wear her most elegant gown. For the occasion the Lord Lieutenant and his lady had invited the brass for pre-prandial drinks in their lovely garden, after which we assembled at the Club. The Club was hung with the flags and pennants of the Allies, the food and drink and music were just right, and the happy assemblage caught up in such ambience lingered until the wee hours.

For me, at least, it had been a fitting climax to an improbable dream-like sequence of events, and albeit a war-time anomaly, I went back to squadron headquarters at Quonset Point to await further orders.

CHAPTER 9

From Hutch to Crow's Landing

The mystical Detail Officer abiding somewhere in the bowels of the Bureau of Naval Personnel had apparently decided that it was time for me to pay for my dance in Bermuda, and he was amply justified for that duty had been something out of a fairy tale. I was ordered to report to NAS Hutchinson, Kansas, for transitional training into our land-based four-engine patrol bombers, the heavyweights of the Naval Air Corps. Now Kansas may also seem to be an odd place for a Naval Air Station, but with its perfectly flat topography providing ample space for lengthy runways with unobstructed approaches ala the sea, it was an ideal area for training purposes, and we had long since had an E-Base at Olathe as well as the major installation at Hutch, some fifty miles northwest of Kansas City and twenty miles due north of Wichita. Between duty stations, I made that ill-fated stop-over in Atlanta to see Sally and then spent a ten-day leave at home, arriving at Hutch in the middle of May.

This leave had been revealing in that it was my first real taste of the home front. Denton was a typical community where now the demands of war were everywhere apparent: shortages of this and that, rationing, the absence of able-bodied young men and women now scattered among the armed forces, and many of the older ones dispersed in war-related industries and other activities. Each town had known bereavement, such as Claude Castleberry's son entombed in the USS *Arizona* on the bottom of Pearl Harbor; and each had its heroes, such as Brigadier General Roger Ramey now commanding a squadron of our new B-29s in the Far East and Col. Frank McDonald, formerly head of TSCW's Journalism Department and now on the staff of General MacArthur somewhere in the Pacific. Even I was feted at the Thursday luncheon of Dad's beloved Rotary Club, and a special prayer said in my behalf at our little St. Barnabas chapel on that Sunday.

As in all wars, the perceptions of the home front and the reality of the combat arenas had little relationship to each other, for the civilians were entirely at the mercy of the vagaries of the press and the radio commentators, although there were brilliant exceptions like Murrow and Sevareid, to whose ranks I could now add Lois Sager as a war correspondent for the *Dallas Morning News* now based in England. In this regard I, like every other son, vowed to write Mother more frequently if only to let her know I was alive and kicking. But what was most remarkable about this small example of America as a whole was the unparalleled unity, the conviction that her enemies were clear and present, that her cause was just, that her sons and daughters were engaged in a noble crusade, that this, if ever-possible, was a "good" war.

Consolidated B-24J on display at Pima Air & Space Museum

Good or bad, the aura of war permeated a base like Hutch; this was a hard-nosed dress rehearsal for combat: you knew your destination was the Pacific theatre, that your objective was to put the Japanese fleet out of business, that here you must become thoroughly skilled in using the tools likely to be at your disposal in the quickest time possible, that your instructors were veterans who had been there so you had better listen up, that this was what you had joined up for in the first place so don't screw around. At this juncture, the Navy's basic long-range patrol bomber was the PB2Y-2 built by Consolidated; in Army parlance, it was the B-24 Liberator, a twin-tailed counterpart to the B-17 Flying Fortress produced by Boeing. The personnel complement of a PB2Y-2 was 12, and since it was at Hutch that these crews were assembled, the training program was conducted at various levels befitting the special function of each crew member. Each plane crew consisted of 3 commissioned officers and 9 enlisted men, each with a distinct but sometimes complementary assignment.

The skipper was the Patrol Plane Commander (PPC), assisted in his flying duties by two co-pilots, who also alternated as navigator/cum/bombardier, skills that had required so much specialized training that they had been unable to amass much time in the actual flying of an airplane. So the PPC, once he was checked out in the manifold characteristics of the aircraft, became the flying instructor of his co-pilots until assured that each of them was safe for solo, and thus were the duties of the cockpit attended to. Next in the pecking order was the Plane Captain, who from where I sat was the key to the kingdom; he was the senior enlisted man present in charge of the crewmen but whose ultimate responsibility as the chief mechanic was to see that all the plane's systems were functioning properly before each takeoff, in which he was assisted by the #2 mechanic who doubled as a nose gunner. The chief radioman, also with a #2, could operate a gun turret as well was next. Then came the chief ordnance man who, with his #2, were responsible for the bomb racks and the stowage of the bomb loads which varied with each mission. The last three were primarily turret gunners who could also help out wherever needed. Now these people were rotated in and out of all the training flights so that the PPC was able to get some notion of the skills and personalities of the players before naming his own starting lineup, and they in turn formed their opinions about whom they would like to fly with, including the PPCs, if they should have any choice in the matter.

In its physical aspects, the PB2Y-2 was a new experience. To begin with, there were the four engines to contend with, requiring careful synchronization. There were engine superchargers to ensure full power settings for takeoff and, in case of an emergency, there were mixture controls to ensure optimum fuel consumption, and there were variable pitch propellers. The fuel, hydraulic and electrical systems were much more complex than I was accustomed to. Then there was the plane configuration; the twin tails and the six gun turrets, two top, two waist, and one fore and aft, plus the bomb bay and the arming procedures. But for a utility squadron pilot accustomed to flying two or three different types of aircraft each day, the flying characteristics required only the normal adjustment to power, size and weight because regardless of the type of aircraft, the four vectors governing flight are eternal; thrust, lift, drag, and gravity, and when thrust and lift exceed drag and gravity, one is inevitably airborne, and when the reverse is true, one is not. So the familiarization syllabus was engaged in spades, day and night, interspersed with ground school exercises in advanced navigation and constant drills in the recognition of Japanese and U. S. fleet types and aircraft. It was not the PPCs but the designated co-pilots who were under the severest pressure because their lack of flying time inevitably meant lack of confidence, and here they were trying to master the heaviest and most complex aircraft in the Fleet. Their touch and go drills seemed endless and would have been boring in the extreme except for the all too frequent difficulties they found themselves in, especially the night landings with no lights. Yet their other skills, particularly in navigation, were top drawer, and it was a great comfort to know that two of them would be aboard; after all, I could teach them how to fly in time, but it would be pointless if we couldn't get to where we were supposed to be going.

In many respects, good fortune smiled on me at Hutch; I got the combat squadron assignment I wanted, I put together a plane crew that I never in future would have traded with any PPC, and I was reunited with an old and cherished companion. Imagine my surprise and delight to find among the pilot instructors George Charno, a charter member of the AVG.

Charno had completed a long and tough tour in a Liberator squadron, the one to which Joe Kennedy, Jr. had been attached, in the south of England, and was now in the business of training his successors. He was now the father of a one year old son named Kip, and Hutch seemed an ideal posting since he and his wife were natives of Kansas City, Missouri, which was within easy hailing distance. So on the occasional evenings off it was wonderful to go to their digs in the Married Officers Quarters and play with Kip, have an honest to goodness home-cooked meal, sip brandy and reminisce. I did very little syllabus flying with George on the premise that he might not be inclined to be as critical of my procedures as the situation warranted, but occasionally we'd take a cross country together just for the hell of it, and it was on one of these that he made his pronouncement. Claiming to be fed up with his present assignment, that he was in more daily peril at the hands of these young hot shots who fancied they already knew it all than he had ever encountered in the Fleet, he was putting in for a change of duty.

"Hub, whatever squadron you get I'm going to put in for it too, and I ought to have enough seniority around here to swing the deal. Ever since Anacostia I've thought it would be great to go to sea with you, and besides, I've never seen the Pacific."

I had never known George to go off half-cocked, his decisions generally derived from due deliberation, and although I made them, I knew my arguments about wife and child and prior distinguished service were not going to dissuade him. In the event, we did not get the same squadron but companion squadrons, the next best thing, for wherever we wound up in the Pacific theatre, we would be there together. Inside, I was flattered and elated.

With my luck holding up, I also struck up a new friendship that was to be critical in my Naval career. He was Buzz Lefever, from Oxnard, California, a former football player at the University of Southern California from which he was graduated in 1937 and had gone directly into the Naval Air Corps. He was now a Lieutenant Commander with a plethora of flying time, mostly in multi-engine stuff, who at the very outset of the war had operated out of Perth, Australia, in a PBY squadron. He was at Hutch for the same reason as most of us, familiarization with the Liberator, and he was the epitome of the seasoned veteran, hard-driving and hard-nosed, who had been accepted into the regular Navy as a career officer. His experience tabbed him for at least the #2 spot of Executive Officer in one of the squadrons under formation. Underneath that bluff exterior resided a really gentle spirit and fine sense of humor, but his professionalism demanded that although play should be savored to the hilt, it should never intrude on the central reason for our being here. In sum, he was the kind of man that Commissioner Splawn thought he had in mind on the eve of the AVG's departure, and he was certainly the type I wanted to serve with. Fortunately he somehow felt the same about me, and in the end he co-opted me for his squadron.

Hutchinson was your typical Midwestern burg, God-fearing and unexciting, with the churches far out-numbering the bars and the movie houses, so most of the recreational time was spent on the base. But, occasionally, Buzz and I would go into town for a movie, and on one Sunday we were especially glad we did, for the offering was Bing Crosby and Barry Fitzgerald in *Going My Way*; another time we were in a bar chatting up the local belles when from the jukebox came Mr. Crosby again, this time with the

Andrews sisters in their new hit, "Don't Fence Me In." And in the Ready Room one afternoon we heard for the first time the haunting lyrics of "I'll Be Seeing You." That movie and those songs stayed with us the rest of our long journey. For more manly pursuits we might of a weekend drive down to my old stomping ground of IFIS days, the Allis Hotel in Wichita, which abounded with patriotic riveters from the nearby Beech and other airplane assembly plants, some of whom would insist on repaying the visit; at any rate, the bus line between these two Kansas outposts did a land office business. As an esthetic experience, it was pretty drab, but any just sumptuary law would have ordained it after Bermuda.

As our tenure at Hutch neared completion, the deadline came for the selection of air crews, and in making this critical decision, the PPCs resembled competing football coaches recruiting for their teams. The training process had exposed us to a variety of people in each category of need and I had kept a fairly good log on those who had impressed me. The keys to my particular kingdom were the two co-pilots and the plane captain, who in turn would consult and choose the remainder of the complement, with skill and personality ranked in that order. For some time I had had my eye on two senior Ensigns who I had flown with from time to time, although never in tandem, and I had made tentative overtures to each of them which they now accepted. Myron Hale, a rugged 200 pound six footer with an even disposition and a handsome countenance displaying brilliant white teeth generally etched in a boyish grin, was a graduate of Ohio State with a major in Political Science. Calmly self-possessed and unprepossessingly erudite, he seemed well-equipped to provide a steadying influence on what was likely to be a disparate crew, and in my few flights with him, he had displayed all the right instincts, particularly in simulated emergencies. Martin Moskowitz, a tall, willowy Jewish lad who moved with feline ease, mercurial in mind and manner, a born gambler possessing the best card sense I have ever encountered, was from Upper Derby, Pennsylvania, and a graduate of Drexel Institute with a mathematics major. Not very confident behind the flight controls, he was an absolute wizard with a calculator behind the navigator's table, with an amazing intuition for the vagaries of wind and weather, and I figured that on any mission, he would have us pointed in the right direction if only Hale and I could get us there and back. With his lively imagination and light-hearted patter, he would be our guarantor against ennui. As bombardiers, he and Hale were equally competent, but as things turned out, that would be irrelevant. A common bond between the three of us was our love of sports, a useful conversation piece on the long patrols that lay ahead. So on every count I was pleased to have them join me, and if intelligence mattered in this business, our team had a goodly supply of wits.

That accomplished, next came the really critical choice of plane captain, a selection which Buzz and Charno had impressed on me would be of vital importance. Lady luck remaining steadfast, this decision in effect was made for me. One evening after chow I was playing acey-deucy in the wardroom when a message came that an enlisted man wanted to see me. Outside the BOQ was this chap about my age, dressed in fresh dungarees and nervously twisting his cap, who asked politely if my name was Hubbard and if I came from Texas. I agreed on both counts, and although I didn't know his name, I was sure I had seen him before, and from his soft drawl, he could only have hailed from Georgia.

"Sir," he said, "I've not been in the Navy very long and I don't know how you go about this sort of thing, but with your permission, I would like to be your plane captain. I've flown with you three times, but I know you don't remember me because you were too busy doing your own things."

But now I did remember him and I asked him to come up to my quarters while I looked at my notes.

> *Good mech today-thoro pre-flight check-kept eyes screwed to the gauges- double checked check-off lists.*

His name was J. C. Rivers, who had come straight out of a peanut patch in rural Georgia to become an apprentice in Delta's instrument repair shop in Atlanta. When the war began, he enlisted and went through the Navy's rigorous aircraft maintenance program, did well, and now held the rating of Aircraft Mechanic 1st Class, with no blemishes on his conduct record, and at Hutch he had been clearly marked as someone's plane captain.

"You've flown with a lot of guys here, so why me?" I asked.

"Well, Sir," he replied, obviously searching for the right words, "I just kind of admired the way you did things, easy like, without a lot of bull shit. And you coming from Texas, I figured you understood us Southern boys. In other words, Sir, I just felt comfortable with you in that left-hand seat."

I thanked him for coming, told him about Hale and Moskowitz and that I would have them talk to him, adding, "If you three don't make music together, then we'll all be in the deep fat."

Later on when the three of them shook hands, I told them to fill out the crew, making damned sure we got a good radioman named Wakefield, who turned out to be damned good, saving our bacon on more than one occasion. So the deed was done; I had my starting lineup. Incidentally, from the time we came together I was never again addressed as "Sir"; to Hale and Moskowitz, I was "Coach" and to Rivers and the rest, I was simply "Boss" To some of my Annapolis-type colleagues, such familiarity meant lack of discipline and respect, but that's the kind of outfit we were, a taut but happy ship, and I was proud of it.

With my plane crew now intact, the last but by no means least detail was our assignment to the Pacific Fleet. At this stage of the war, a heavy patrol bombing squadron was made up of 15 aircraft, with their 12-man crews, 3 stand-by crews which would be rotated into the flight sequence, plus a maintenance, supply, administrative, and intelligence officer for a total personnel complement of 220. Buzz and I were assigned to VPB-108, he as the designated Executive Officer, while Charno drew her sister squadron, VPB-105. Both of these squadrons were in—being on the West Coast, and having recently returned from sea duty, they were now in the process of reforming with new planes and personnel. The exciting prospect was that now coming off the Consolidated assembly lines was the next generation replacement for the Liberator, designated the PB4Y-2, the Navy's update comparable to the Army's new B-24 Superfortress, and if the production schedule held, it might be available to us before we shipped out. So now we left the arid Kansas plains behind and headed for California.

George took me with him to Kansas City to meet his parents, who could not have made me more welcome, and it was easy to see from whence George's steadfast nature and sagacity derived. He dismissed his mother's distressed query about the necessity for his going on Fleet duty again with the laconic reply that the war was still going on, and that topic was not raised again. But Mrs. Charno, not an atypical Jewish mother, took me aside at every opportunity to charge me with the well-being of her beloved son, and drew little comfort from my insistence that it would most probably be the other way around. I was shown the impressive law offices of Charno and Charno, and introduced to the fabled Muehlebach Hotel where Senator Truman, from nearby Lamar, was known to break bread with Tom Pendergast, little dreaming of what was soon to happen to the Senator—and to us.

After three wonderful days, sated with thick steaks and jacket potatoes, George's wife June, leaving young Kip with his grandparents, came with us on the flight west. We were booked on a United DC-3, and at the airport we happened to see our pilot, an elderly man wearing thick glasses, checking the weather en route; he was holding the weather report in his hands and pushing it back and forth until he found the range of legibility. We watched him in some amazement, dubbed him "Trombone Eyes," crossed our fingers and went aboard. But he was certainly up to the task, making a deft landing in the early morning fog at Burbank.

It was the Charno's first glimpse of California and Los Angeles, and my first since the 1932 Olympic Games, twelve years before. Unimpressed by "downtown Los Angeles" except for the Biltmore Hotel and the Public Library, we headed west by bus on Wilshire Boulevard, we passed two legendary landmarks, the Astor Hotel with its Cocoanut Grove on the left and the Brown Derby on the right. Hollywood and Vine did nothing for us as we looked for Lana Turner or Bette Grable in vain. Time to go south.

Our destination was Brown Field perched atop Otay Mesa near the town of the same name, about 15 miles southeast of San Diego and sitting right on the Mexican border. San Diego was to the Pacific Fleet what Norfolk was to the Atlantic, a community dominated by the presence of the Navy, with its constant "toing" and "froing" of personnel, for it was here that our carriers and their support screens and our Fleet submarines put in for refitting and replenishment and R&R for their crews. The area was dotted with air strips, such as Miramar for fighters, North Island for dive and torpedo bombers, and Brown for patrol bombers. To the north lay the sprawling mass of Camp Pendleton, the Marine Corps' principal staging base for the Pacific along with the Marine air base, El Toro. San Diego was blessed with a gorgeous natural setting and a nearly-perfect year round climate, and across its sparkling bay in Coronado stood the stately Hotel Del Coronado, the dream of every returning service man for a romantic rendezvous and the pious hope that its walls did not have ears.

The regimen at Brown Field was simple and straightforward: our newly fashioned plane crews must now well and truly come together as effective combat teams, which meant practice, practice, practice. Along with Buzz and George and me there were ten other groups in training, some destined for either 108 or 105, and at our disposal were 20 tired but serviceable Liberators. The days were filled with bombing or gunnery runs over the Mojave desert, low-level attacks on sleds towed in Coronado Bay to simulate submarines caught on the surface, radio intercepts, navigational hops, formation flying—everything designed to put each crew member through his paces, individually and as a unit. Buzz was the SOP (Senior Officer Present) and he was at the same time a hard driver and a mother hen looking after his brood; from time to time he would fly with us as a check pilot, roving up and down the aircraft with an eye on everyone's performance. He was a presence with an acid tongue, and woe to anyone, including George and me, who by reason of attitude or malfeasance incurred his displeasure. Privately he was a big, cuddly bear.

One morning there occurred what we had all been hoping for; taxiing up the runway to the flight line was a prototype of our new aircraft, the PB4Y-2 Privateer, and for the next two hours flight operations were suspended while we took turns inspecting her from stem to stern with the Consolidated pilots who had flown her in. She was something to behold with her blue-gray fuselage and soaring single tail in place of the twin rudders of the Liberator. But it was the state of the art interior that impressed us most. The wider body greatly facilitated the movements and creature comfort of the crew; the pilots' seats had lumbar adjustments to ease the strain of the long patrol; the cockpit instrumentation was less complex with gauges easier to read; the automatic pilot was Sperry's newest model and the bombsight was Norden's latest version.

The six turrets mounting twin .50 caliber machine guns were on smoother swivels and all blind spots had been eliminated because the two waist turrets now moved in a vertical arc that permitted a converging line of fire beneath the plane. And, oh, the new electronic gear: radar, with a 150 mile line-of-sight range at 10,000 feet and scopes which could be finely adjusted for clarity; Loran, a new long-range navigational system whose master and slave transmitters were now operating around the globe; a new master radio with ultra-high frequencies and a newly designed system of internal communication. The bombing systems could accommodate any configuration of missiles up to 1000 pounds; the hydraulic system for flaps and landing gear was much less prone to malfunction, as was the fuel transfer system. And the new Pratt & Whitney engines produced more horsepower for less fuel, providing higher speeds at longer ranges. And so it went. The question on everyone's mind, of course, was when do we get them? The answer was that delivery would take place at Crows Landing where the final squadron configurations were taking place. Needless to say, we could hardly wait to complete this phase of our training so we could get our hands on our new toys.

In the meantime, life at Brown Field was not too shabby. Not only was it a time for getting to know our crews, but it was also a time for the crews getting to know each other. Buzz's plane captain, for example, was from Dallas, and for two Texans who had grown up within forty miles of each other, there was no lack of communication. Buzz also had a Lt. (Junior grade) co-pilot named Tony Jackson from Los Angeles, dapper in appearance and manner, a fledgling lawyer from UCLA with a deep bass voice which was in constant use; Charno couldn't abide him but I found him amusing, especially when at a squadron mixer he invited me to stop over in L.A. on the way north so he could introduce me to the starlets in his stable.

For local transportation, Hale and Moscow and I purchased a third or fourth hand Chevrolet, for which as serving officers we had no trouble acquiring ration stamps for fuel and tires, which came in handy. From Otay Mesa we looked down upon that charming village of Tijuana, where every little urchin in the shabby streets claimed to have a beautiful sister waiting just for us. There were, however, some good restaurants, and we would frequently take what we called a Trans-Mex for lunches of enchiladas and tacos and cold Bohemia beer. For the distaff side, it was Tony Jackson who discovered The Spot in San Diego, a bar called Paul's, or in local lore, Paul's Passion Pit, an apt nomenclature that it lived up to; for no sooner did our carriers put out to sea than many of the bereaved wives and girlfriends made a bee-line for Paul's to wash away their tears, this war being no different from any other, and either as a participant or mere spectator, it was an interesting phenomenon to observe.

For the Brown Field contingent, based as we were several miles away, our rule of thumb was never to indulge unless she could provide her own transportation. All of which made for some interesting weekends. Besides its ptomaine parlors, Tijuana boasted a race track named Agua Caliente which operated on Saturday and Sunday, and in all the Western Hemisphere there was no horse parlor quite as crooked as this one, although devotees of the Fair Grounds in New Orleans might find this hard to believe. On the odd Sunday the ladies from San Diego would pick us up at Brown, and after the good lunch in Tijuana we'd head for the track, a new experience for Hale and me but right down the wily Moscow's ally.

With program and racing form in hand, Moscow would conduct a clinic for us neophytes: classes of races, betting permutations, how to read the pari-mutuel board, and all those good things, ending with the suggestion that if a gray horse showed up, bet on it. So with pockets full of pesos and high hopes, we entered into the spirit of the thing, with the girls making their selections on the basis of cute names, Hale and I through sheer guess work, with Marty after long deliberation making the "scientific" wagers. With all these "systems" being equally unproductive, although Marty did hit on one odds-on favorite, we came down to the last race, and sure enough in the post parade, there was a gray horse. Without even a glance at the tote board, Marty exclaimed, "That's the one for us."

But I, by this time an expert, chose to differ with him, "Moscow, how can you bet on a nag like that? Look at those odds; he was 25-1 in the Morning Line, and now he's 60-1. He'll be lucky just to finish."

There was a pause, and then with one of his aphorisms worthy of immortality, he set me straight.

"Coach, the owner can read those odds, the trainer can read those odds, the handicappers can read those odds, the touts can read those odds, the jockeys can read those odds, the jockey's girl friends can read those odds, but the horses can't read those odds."

We bet him across the board! Our gray was beaten by a head by another long shot, and the prices he paid provided us with enough pesos for a splendid dinner.

At the end of September we left Brown Field and the lovely ambiance of San Diego with few regrets, so anxious were we to acquire our new aircraft. We ferried the Liberators to El Toro for the Marines to play with, and then Hale, Moskowitz and I loaded our car and took off. Buzz and his wife, Jean, had their own car, and at the last minute, George was ordered to remain at Brown; VPB-105 would form there instead of at Crows Landing, but we would hook up with them in Hawaii on our way out. We drove north on the Pacific Coast Highway, through La Jolla which, though now discovered since my first sight of it in 1932, remained one of the most beautiful spots on this earth, past Oceanside and Del Mar where, Moscow informed us, decent horses were known to run. Reaching Santa Monica, we turned east, somehow finding Wilshire Boulevard which took us virtually to the Biltmore Hotel's front door. That night we were scheduled to do the town with Tony Jackson, but since Hale and Moscowitz found him much too precious for their taste, they decided to go it alone. I took a taxi to the Jackson ménage on Van Ness, where I was greeted effusively by his widowed mother, attired in the mode affected by the young. It then turned out that the "starlet" Tony had in mind for me was his sister, Jeannie, and when she made her appearance, to my mind she had all the physical requisites of a leading lady. Recently divorced, she was living with her mother, and it became evident in short order that the light of their present lives was the handsome Tony. He was squiring that evening with a neighbor from across the street, one Kath Heerman, a plump but attractive red head of medium height and quiet demeanor who as evidence of her independent nature had gone East to college and graduated from Smith. The four of us had dinner at a smart little supper club within walking distance of the Cocoanut Grove, to which we planned to repair later in the evening. We entered the club through a bar-lounge area where an excellent instrumental trio was holding forth, and I paused for a moment to hear the closing bars of "I'll Be Seeing You."

"Who is she?" asked Jeannie, with a knowing smile.

"Oh, no one in particular," I replied, "you know the Navy, one here, one there."

During dinner, she and Tony were wholly engrossed in sibling patter, bringing each other up to date, while Kath and I were left to ourselves. I found out that she and Jeannie had grown up together, that she saw Tony only when he could not find anyone more glamorous although she had loved him as the boy next door, that the Jacksons were an attractive, sometimes amusing clan but so self-centered as to generally ignore the feelings of others; but I also learned that she had majored in comparative literature, that her German was fluent, and that she was as devoted to Goethe and Schiller as I was to Shakespeare and Wordsworth. She even listened with amusement and considerable envy as I related the literary antics of the AVG, saying she wished she could have been present.

"What role would you have taken?" I asked.

"Well,'" she said, "had you been Falstaff, I should have been Mistress Quickly," she smiled demurely, and, listening to the Jackson palaver, I wanted to trade horses right then and there. So I was startled when after coffee, Jeannie turned to me, "My goodness, I haven't let Kath say a word to Tony. While they go to the Grove, let's have a drink here in the lounge and we can join them later."

There sitting in a comfortable booth she apologized for her neglect but that she and her mother so adored Tony and were so worried about his going overseas and how glad he was to be in the same squadron with Buzz and me and, taking my hand, would I try to keep him from being a dead hero.

"I'll buy the next round and we'll drink to a safe journey, for both of you."

And even though it was all so superficial, she was attractive when she turned it on. When a racing photographer came by, she even insisted on having our picture taken. Just as we were about to leave, the trio came forth with a soft, haunting rendition of "September Song."

Taking both my hands and looking at me, she said, "Tex, this is September. There's a message for us if you want to heed it."

We then went over to the Grove, and after a few dances, they dropped me off at the Biltmore, where Jeannie came to the entrance with me.

"See you tomorrow?" she asked.

"If you insist."

The morrow was spent with a picnic hamper somewhere in the wilds of Mulholland Drive, and then it was time to resume the journey north. In San Louis Obispo we managed to blow one of our paper-thin tires, and it took a visit to the City Hall with our ration book to get permission to purchase a new one, which upset the delicate balance of our frail machine. Then we turned inland towards Modesto to the northeast.

Crows Landing was a wide place in the road ten miles northwest of Modesto and sixty miles southeast of San Francisco, situated in a wooded area between the San Joaquin and Napa Valleys. For reasons still not clear to me, the Navy had chosen this site to establish an Auxiliary Air Station, whose only distinctive characteristic was a 9,000 foot airstrip. Be that as it may, this was where many of the patrol bombing squadrons were formed up with the medium-range PV-2s and now the long-range PB4Y-2s. Having completed our crew orientation at Brown, here our mission was two-fold: to become familiar with our new planes, and then to learn to operate as a squadron. After checking in and being assigned to our chic wooden barracks, I went to find Rivers and check on my crew's whereabouts, all of whom had managed to find the place. Then I went in search of our squadron office to report all present or accounted for. The Commanding Officer of Squadron VPB-108 was Lieutenant Commander John Muldrow, and I found him in the offices allocated to us on the second deck of one of the hangars, beneath which was our Ready Room. Upon graduation from college in 1934, he had gone straight into the service and now held a regular Navy commission. At Pearl Harbor he had been with a PBY detachment out on patrol that fateful morning, in the wrong sector, as it turned out, but that was a Staff error with which that day was replete. He had subsequently participated in the Tarawa and Guadalcanal campaigns, returned briefly to a desk job, and then gone through Hutch for the four-engine transition before being given this, his first command. As a veteran of the Fleet, he had served as a consultant for modifications in the new 4Y-2s, so he knew that aircraft backwards and forward. And in another of those coincidences that seemed to mark my passage, he had married a graduate of my father's college, TSCW, so going in I was less of a stranger than I normally would have been. He was slender of build and of medium height but agile as a cat, and a shock of brown hair topped an aquiline face with piercing brown eyes, and though his countenance was seldom in repose, the serious mien was belied by his fundamental good nature. Not given to histrionics, he seemed quite content to lead by example, a quiet professional who well merited the respect his officers and men freely gave.

When our personnel roster was finally completed, Muldrow found himself presiding over perhaps the most senior air squadron the Navy had ever assembled for combat. Of our 18 PPCs, four were Lieutenant Commanders—Muldrow as CO, Lefever as Exec, Rogers as Chief Flight, and Ackerman as Engineering Officers—and four more were to attain that rank before our tour ended. Among them they could speak of Pearl Harbor, Wake, Tarawa, Guadalcanal, Eniwetok, Kwajalein, and New Guinea. I, who had got my second stripe within the year, ranked in the lower half in terms of seniority, and despite my 2,000 odd flying hours, all I could speak of was Jacksonville, Atlanta, Brunswick, and Bermuda, in effect a mere rookie in the starting lineup of a veteran ball club. In a non-flying status was Lieutenant Probst, a lawyer from San Francisco, as our Admin Officer, as well as Lieutenant Norman Palmer, a professor of Political Science at Colgate, our Air Combat Intelligence Officer. Shortly after meeting him, I talked to Palmer about academic life in wartime and asked him how he happened to wind up in an outfit like this. His reply was to the point and representative of the conviction of thoughtful Americans, "My teaching specialty is Comparative Constitutional Systems, and unless we win this war, constitutional government will be relegated, like the fall of Rome, to the realm of ancient history, and I didn't want to lose my job."

Lieutenant John R. Hubbard, 1944

The delivery of the Privateers had begun before our arrival, and Consolidated technicians were aboard to lead the plane crews step by step through the Operation Manual on the ground and in the air. Most everyone has known the excitement of getting behind the wheel of his new car for the first time—the power, the smoothness, the new capabilities, the new gadgets and instruments— and it was exactly the same with us, in spades. So the first flight of our crew in our new machine was an adventure in discovery for everyone in his area of responsibility; my first concerns, per usual, were the stalling speeds and the flight characteristics in the event of engine failure. In terms of remaining airborne and with directional control, the loss of one engine on one side presented no problem, nor did the loss of two simultaneously, provided one was on each side, but the loss of two on the same side was a problem; I could pull enough power on the two remaining engines to maintain altitude, but despite the elongated rudder on the huge single tail, it could not neutralize the added thrust on one side and I found myself flying in a circle. Myron and Marty and Rivers were more than casual observers of this phenomenon, and we all agreed that in future, if we wanted to live long and do well we ought not to lose two engines on one side unless we were perched directly over an airstrip. But apart from that, everything worked. Our radio range was vastly enhanced. The automatic pilot was the soul of stability. Myron and Marty worked sedulously to solve the mysteries of Loran. By night we crept into the bays and coves of the Pacific coastline relying solely on our lovely radar. We made bombing runs at high altitude, daily wiping out Fresno and Bakersfield, but we never disturbed a grape in the Napa Valley. At low level we bombed sleds all over San Francisco Bay. In aerial gunnery we paid particular attention to the converging trajectory of our waist turrets. As an exercise in fuel consumption, one day we headed west as though bound for Hawaii until reversing our course just before reaching the point of no return. We flew formation, mostly in two-plane sections, and we figured our combined fire power would be a match for a considerable number of Japanese fighters. And for Hale's and Moscow's benefit, there were the inevitable touch and go landings in which they worked from both the left and the right seats. Slowly but surely we began to gel as an air crew and as a squadron.

For recreation, Crows Landing left us to our own devices. There were softball games, mostly crew against crew and occasionally the men against the officers; my bunch had a pretty good nucleus with Hale at third base and Moscow at first, and I was no slouch in the outfield—but our pitching was pathetic. In the Ready Room acey-deucy was, of course, continuous, and in the evenings Marty and I soon separated the men from the boys at the bridge table; we tried to make a convert of Hale, but he preferred poker where he certainly needed no coaching. Occasionally we would invade Modesto just to gladden the hearts of the local belles, but there was not even a pale reflection of Paul's Passion Pit. Once we made the hegira into San Francisco where, thanks to Probst, we had entree to the Domino Club and the gorgeous nudes that adorned its walls. On three occasions Jeannie and Kath came up from Los Angeles, thanks to our gas ration coupons. On the last visit Jeannie and I found a jukebox in

Modesto with "our song," and there were all the elements for a desperate romance, for it was November and the dashing hero was about to depart for the wars, but somehow the leaves never turned to flame; she was lovely to look at and prodigal with her charms but we never seemed to get much beyond that. The irony was that Kath and I had something to talk about besides the war and each other, but that was not to be.

Scuttlebutt had it that the squadron would be shoving off by the end of November, and when the "go" orders failed to materialize, we got very antsy. We were as ready as a squadron could be; Muldrow and Lefever were a great combination, John not as intense but equally committed, and Buzz filling the role of "holler guy" to perfection, while the veterans had welcomed the less experienced into their ranks. Someone in jest suggested that our orders were delayed because the island we were slated for had not been invaded yet, and in the event he was pretty close to the mark. In our mission briefings, we had come to understand that in the island-hopping campaigns now under way, from the South Pacific towards the Japanese mainland, we would be among the first squadrons into the forward area to minimize the distances involved in our surveillance of the enemy fleet. At any rate, the orders did come in mid-December, establishing 3 January as the day we shoved off for Hawaii, the first leg of our trans-Pacific flight to the Palau Island group.

In order to complete the preparations for departure without interruption, we traded Christmas leave for three days at the end of the month to include New Year's Eve. That arrangement enabled me to spend a last festive evening with Jeannie and on the next day to see my first Rose Bowl game. Merton Ebright, the most senior of the senior Lieutenants, and our Gunnery Officer, had been one of my check pilots in my primary training at JAX, and so we at least had that experience in common. A short, dapper, lively individual, he was the possessor of an Oldsmobile that was in pretty good shape, and it was his suggestion that we drive down to Los Angeles for New Year's and take in the Rose Bowl, which that year was to pit Tennessee against USC. A splendid notion, I agreed, if we could manage some tickets; and it was Buzz, calling on his old USC connections, who solved that problem for us. Neither he nor Tony could be with us for they were departing for Hawaii two days before the rest of us to test the weather en route and see that arrangements were in place to handle our squadron. I called Jeannie, who promised Kath as a companion for Mert, and we left early in the morning of 31 December for the six hour drive. On arrival the Jacksons offered me a bedroom as did the Heermans for Mert. Obviously, this New Year's Eve had a finality about it, for God alone knew if and where we would know another, and we all entered into the spirit of it. Mert was introduced to the Club and the Grove, he and Kath were a frolicsome pair, the champagne flowed, and we apparently greeted the stroke of midnight in fine fettle, though I am not sure of the particulars. Back at Jeannie's house, the last thing I remember is inviting Mrs. Jackson to join us for one more toast. But I do remember the next morning Jeannie slipping into my room in her negligee bearing a pot of steaming coffee, a combination calculated to get the juices flowing in a mummy.

We drove to Pasadena in two cars since Mert and I had to leave right after the game. It was a day of brilliant sunshine, a Rose Bowl tradition, which added to the amazing spectacle of that famous arena filled to its 100,000 odd capacity. Given the wartime travel restrictions, there were precious few spectators from Tennessee, so half the USC student body dressed in orange to root for the Volunteers. But there was little to root for because USC dominated 25-0 with a team featuring an All-American tackle, John Ferraro, and an All-Conference quarterback, Jim Hardy, both of whom in later years became distinguished public servants in Los Angeles, Jim as general manager of the Coliseum, and John as long-time member and president of the City Council.

Indeed, Los Angeles was becoming something of a talisman for me, for now I could add my first Rose Bowl to my first Olympic Games. Who then could have dreamed how many Rose Bowl games in future I would attend, and in what capacity.

Filing out of that cavernous stadium was no easy chore, but we finally reached Mert's car, kissed away a few tears and took off, checking into Crows Landing about midnight.

CHAPTER 10
—
Crow's Landing to Palau

Jack (center) and fellow officers at the Top of the Mark restaurant, Mark Hopkins Hotel in San Francisco, California

One of the problems attendant to the departure of a land-based squadron from the shores of the mother country was the transportation of its liquor supply, which is to say that every squadron hoped to have a supply large enough to be a problem, and VPB-108 did. At the eleventh hour, our enterprising Administrative Officer, Lieutenant Probst had, through the machinations of his San Francisco connections, managed to sequester 50 cases of I. W. Harper bourbon whiskey, a remarkable feat if anyone remembers that day and age, which were duly delivered to our ramp at Crows Landing. They were a beautiful sight to behold, but they raised a monumental question in our wardroom as to which of our plane crews was most likely to get them safely to wherever we were going. Commander Muldrow, in his wisdom, scratched his head and said he would take the matter under advisement. However he reached his decision, he called me in to announce that I had been "elected" and that my plane would be stripped of its armament so it could handle the weight of the precious cargo.

Naturally I considered this to be a great compliment, perhaps the greatest in my Naval career, and inwardly I was quite set up, but I said to him in mock seriousness, "But, Sir, if we should be attacked en route by a massive Jap task force, I will be defenseless."

"Don't worry about that," he grinned, "the rest of us will be covering your plane like a dirty shirt!"

On 2 January, in order to avoid the traffic of the Bay Area, we moved our planes up to an Army airfield north of San Francisco and awaited a signal from Buzz as to the weather he had encountered, and when we got his good report from Kaneohe, our exodus began. At 0100 hours of the morning of the 3rd, we began taking off in five minute intervals in two-plane sections; Rogers and I led off, and when we broke out on top of the light fog, he settled onto his course and I pulled in comfortably close to fly on his starboard wing light. Hale was in the right-hand seat and Moscow was our navigator, and I sent Rivers to check the bomb bay to see that our treasures were riding comfortably. When Marty corroborated Rogers' heading, Myron trimmed up our plane and we settled into the long pull ahead of us. I was particularly pleased at my ability to maintain a constant position relative to Rodgers' wing light, so self-satisfied that I called Marty and Rivers to join us in the cockpit so I could give the three of them a lecture on the finer points of formation flying, stressing the vital importance of relative motion, and they seemed duly impressed because we were hanging right in there. So it was a startling shock to my nervous system when the first light of dawn revealed that Rogers wasn't there; in fact, when I swung my gaze in a 180 degree arc from wingtip to wingtip, there was not a plane to be seen, but the "wing light" on which I had been flying was slowly descending below the horizon. There followed a gentle tap on my right shoulder, and I looked around to see that smart-assed Moscowitz, trying to keep a straight face, had screwed up enough courage to inform me that I had been flying on Sirus, the brightest star in the Western equinox, but since we were right on course, he hadn't wanted to disturb me. Hale and Rivers, not daring to look at me, stared straight ahead.

"Jesus Christ!" was all I could manage, glaring at the three of them. But where the hell was Rogers; had he vanished without a trace?

"Rivers," I commanded, "get up to the top turret and swing it 360 degrees and see if you can see anything."

"Boss," he replied, his sides now splitting with laughter, "I just did, and I counted 13 planes in a nice little tight semicircle behind us." Muldrow had been right as rain, and my chagrin was absolute. From then on I was kindly referred to in the squadron as that celebrated celestial navigator, I. W. Hubbard.

Our flight had taken slightly under 14 hours, and it was a welcome relief to raise Kaneohe Tower for landing instructions. For we first-timers to the Islands, as I circled Oahu, all our eyes were concentrated on two quite disparate landmarks, Diamond Head and the outlines of the battered Arizona as she lay in her shallow grave at Pearl Harbor. Kaneohe was directly across the island to the northeast of Pearl, and its long and broad runways were utilized for the transiting of our patrol bombers. Buzz was on the flight line to greet us as we taxied in one by one, and the first official action of VPB-108 overseas was to secure my plane and place it under guard. Then despite our general weariness, two of our PPCs, old Hawaiian hands, commandeered a jeep and took me over the spectacular Pali into Honolulu for dinner in the establishment of P. Y. Chung, purveyor of the finest steaks west of San Francisco.

Our respite in Kaneohe was notable for two things: the formal christening of our aircraft, and a drastic alteration of its tactical capabilities. By this time it was practically *de regueur* that every Army and Navy pilot emblazon on the fuselage of his plane some personal logo, a name or an aphorism, accompanied, when appropriate, by a pictorial adornment, usually a leggy and buxom blond. The aphorism most favored was "Is This Trip Necessary?" but more generally there was simply the name of someone near and dear; for Charno, as an example, it was "Mr. Kip: after his infant son. But because of my inability to come to a decision, our plane stood there in bleak anonymity, much to the disgruntlement of Rivers and the crew who by now had developed a deep affection for her. I had ruled out anything personal that was meaningful to me alone, and in derision they had vetoed anything that smacked of Texas. Considering our cargo, I suggested "Nectar of the Gods" but Rivers would have none of it on the grounds that the booze wouldn't last very long and that, anyway, the officers weren't likely to share much of it with the men. But it was clear that they did not want to leave

Hawaii nameless, and so I took the bit in my teeth. Early one morning I assembled the crew on the flight line and had them sit in the shadow of our plane upon the tarmac while I paced back and forth before them.

Beginning my sermon with the dictum to Rivers that I didn't want him opening his cotton picking mouth before I finished, I proceed to enlighten them on the Romantic movement in early 19th Century English poetry, how Wordsworth, Byron, Shelley, Keats, Coleridge with their wondrous talents had ushered in one of the epic periods of English literature, and how it was to one of them, Percy Bysshe Shelley, that we would be forever indebted for providing us with a fit and proper name for our beloved aircraft. The hero of his greatest poem was a giant of a man who argued that no individual should be under the arbitrary control of another, but who had been overcome by the forces of Darkness, bound in chains and exiled to a barren rocky promontory where the vulture could pick at his flesh; but one day he had burst his shackles and stood defiantly against his oppressors as the symbol of individual liberty.

"The last stanza of Shelley's epic," I said, stopping and facing them, "goes like this –"

> *To suffer woes which Hope thinks infinite;*
> *To forgive wrongs darker than death or night;*
> *To defy Power which seems omnipotent;*
> *To love, and bear; To hope til Hope creates*
> *From its own wreck the thing it contemplates;*
> *Neither to change, nor falter, nor repent;*
> *This, like thy glory, Titan, is to be*
> *Good, great and joyous, beautiful and free;*
> *This is alone Life, Joy, Empire and Victory.*

"What I am suggesting is that we, you and I, this plane crew, this squadron, this Navy are engaged in the same kind of mission against the powers of Evil, against those ass-hole dictators, Hitler, Mussolini and Tojo, who would enslave the free world. It is we who are defying their power which seems omnipotent. And what was the name of our paragon, our exemplar? He was Prometheus, and Shelley entitled his epic "Prometheus Unbound." That, gentlemen, will be the name of our aircraft."

I ended this peroration by telling Rivers to have copies made of that stanza for every member of our crew and that henceforth I did not want anyone setting a foot in our aircraft without that copy in his possession. With that I dismissed them, and I broke and ran, not wanting to entertain any discussion of the matter which in my mind, at least, was finally settled.

The ultimate depiction of all this on our airplane fuselage is almost beyond description. Rivers, of course, was in charge of the art department, and to his intense disgust he was now going to have to abandon any likeness of Betty Grable. At the same time, he was having difficulty getting a steady fix on Prometheus in his mind's eye.

"Imagine a physique like Tarzan's," I told him, "sitting atop a boulder on this mountain with his ankles chained together and wearing handcuffs which he has broken apart."

He said he would think it over and do his best, adding that he didn't want me near the plane, please, until he had finished his masterpiece. After a couple of days he announced that he was ready for the unveiling, and we all gathered around the nose of the plane in high anticipation. What appeared was, to put it mildly, a revelation. Underneath my cockpit window was etched in bright red capital letters PROMETHEUS UNBOUND, and below that was depicted a rooster with flaming eyes and a prominent yellow beak, garbed in a cowboy outfit with a ten-gallon hat, chaps and boots, and brandishing a smoking six-shooter in the tip of each wing, with a chain around its left ankle running to a stake in the ground, the chain having been broken in the middle, all in all—in the artist's eyes—a dramatic representation of defiance.

We just stood there in mute amazement, and finally I was moved to say, "Rivers, I've never really understood what impels creative genius, but if the poet were with us today, he would say that you have visually captured his message to perfection."

For the rest of the squadron, our plane crew was beginning to take on distinctive characteristics: a PPC who flew formation on the stars, and now an artistic plane captain gone absolutely mad.

That was the good news. The bad news came without warning. In view of the imminent capture of the Marianas, the invasion of which was just about to be launched, there was to be a radical re-deployment of our air forces in the Pacific. Our first operational B-29 squadrons, now based somewhere in China would be shifted to Guam, Tinian and Saipan, 1,500 miles south of Tokyo, as soon as the massive airstrips and supportive infrastructure could be got in place. Moreover, their numbers would be beefed up exponentially by the new Superforts now beginning to flood off the assembly lines, so rapidly, in fact, that serious shortages were beginning to develop in their vital ancillary equipment, to wit, their bombing gear. So the Joint

Chiefs of Staff had determined that the Navy patrol squadrons, whose primary mission was scouting rather than bombing, would be relieved of all their Norden bombsights for use by the B-29s. We were furious, particularly all the co-pilots, who up to now had spent so many training hours perfecting their skills on the Norden, not to mention the fire-eaters like Buzz with dreams of reducing the Japanese navy to scrap iron. The order, however, had been issued; there was no recourse, and all over Kaneohe the dismantling of our bomb sights began, a sorry sight. By the stroke of a pen half of our offensive capabilities had been eliminated, and all that remained were the possibilities of low-level attacks and bombing by what was known in the Navy by "seaman's eye," which is to say, manual instinctive release by the pilot. Buzz, who I thought we were going to have to bury, and the rest of us began to take stock of the situation. Now it seemed that our practice bombing runs on towed sleds had been the most important part of our offensive training regimen, and we determined to resume that kind of activity in spades, flying over to Pearl Harbor and "sinking" every surface vessel in sight from fifty feet. Besides our bomb load, however, such a tactic brought into action only our nose and top forward turrets; how, then, could we increase our fire power? Buzz had the idea of fixing twin 20 mm cannon just below the nose turret, and he set off to convince Ordnance to attempt such an installation; but even if it worked, there was neither time nor guns available to equip the whole squadron, and the rest of us had to live with what was left to us.

On the plus side, we were introduced to a new anti-radar device known as "window," which had been developed by the British—long strips of tinfoil packed in loose bales which came apart when jettisoned and formed a curtain that appeared on radar screens as a massive rain storm behind which attacking planes could penetrate the target area undetected until the last few minutes. Using "window" we carried out surprise "attacks" on Oahu's anti-aircraft emplacements with considerable success, and so it became a part of our arsenal. The least popular drill we were subjected to fell under the heading of self-preservation. Each plane crew was taken by boat five to ten miles out to sea, at which point we jumped overboard along with the kind of life rafts carried on our planes which we had to inflate, clamor aboard, and make our way to shore as best we could with the implements at hand. A soggy drill, to be sure, but mastering it at least gave us a small sense of security. As a kind of recompense Buzz and I flew up to Hilo for a Saturday night at the old Naniloa Hotel and a visit to Hilo Hattie for that cold fresh milk which she served.

Finally, Kaneohe, like all major air depots, had a scrap heap of unserviceable aircraft and discarded gear which was a veritable Flea Market for enterprising plane captains in search of usable bits and pieces. In this regard, Rivers had no superior, and he would take his crew on scavenger hunts, their objective being to make more habitable the tail section of our plane from the bomb bay to the tail turret which served as a rough lounging area for the men between duty stations. Whenever an especially useful cache was discovered, they would latch onto all of it, using what they didn't need for bartering purposes. I, of course, kept a blind eye to their machinations, and *Prometheus* gradually benefitted from carpeting, crockery, cutlery, a sink ingeniously supplied with running water, and other civilizing appurtenances.

"Boss," Rivers proudly announced, "as soon as I get us a hot plate, we'll have a house warming."

After two active weeks of this, we bade "aloha" to Diamond Head and headed for Johnston Island, a long strip of sand and lava southwest of Hawaii which was used as a refueling base and overnight stop for the now continual passage of planes east and west. It was a sad occasion for me, because one of the administrative officers who greeted us was Robert Gillespie, one of our most gifted pilots in the AVG, who had been permanently grounded and exiled to this God-forsaken spot because of his role in a near fatal mid-air collision while allegedly under the influence. He had been on Johnston for nearly two years and apparently would remain for the duration, and he was a miserable figure. As we took a long walk after dinner I tried to bring him up to date on the whereabouts of our old group, but there was nothing I could say that would lift his spirits; and since this was his first glimpse of the PB4Y-2s, I took him through the plane—and only made matters worse. At the end it was all he could do to fight back the tears and murmur, "Jeez, Louise, why did I go up that day?"

Taking off at dawn, our next leg was to Kwajalein in the Marshall Islands, the invasion of which had occupied some of our group the previous year. I was now flying wing on Buzz, and it was on this run that we encountered our first severe weather.

Lying ahead of us was a massive frontal system that defied our ability to top, and there was nothing to do but plow through it, trusting to our radar to help us find the softer spots. In the ensuing mess it was impossible to maintain any visual contact with Buzz, but going into it we had agreed on a heading we would try to maintain, and after breaking into the clear some three hours later, it was a great relief to pick him up on our radar about five miles abaft our port beam. Finally Kwajalein appeared on the horizon, and for all its desolation it was a welcome sight. After landing, I was tempted to dip into my cargo, but there was a make-shift bar in the Quonset hut housing the Officers' mess that supplied our immediate needs.

Guam, the southern-most major island in the Mariana chain, with Tinian and Saipan lying to its north, had been the first objective in the Mariana invasion campaign, which was still in progress, but by the time of our scheduled arrival, it had been deemed secure, the fact that had governed our departure from Kaneohe. But getting there from Kwajalein was a different matter. Our weather briefing before departure convinced me that all Navy weather guessers in the Pacific had been cut from the same piece of cloth, because the forecast was identical with the one we had received at Johnston: you will encounter frontal systems but none that you can't top at 8,000 feet. Even while warming up for takeoff Buzz and I could see the ominous gray cloud masses directly in front of us which we reckoned couldn't be topped at 18,000 feet, but there was nothing to it but go. For lack of anything better to do, we climbed to 8,000 feet, and after about thirty minutes we ploughed into the stuff, which, except for one terrifying instant, was the last we saw of each other until we hit Guam. Fortunately, big Hale was my co-pilot on this run, and the turbulence became so severe that it took both him and me on the yolk plus the autopilot to hold an approximate altitude and heading. Emerging for an instant from a dark patch of clouds, I caught a glimpse of this blue-gray shape just above us as it flashed over our bow; it was Buzz, who of course had never seen us, but we were that close to ending our war then and there.

"To hell with this," I shouted to Myron, "we're heading for the deck."

Now it is an observable fact that in a storm system at sea, no matter how intense, the cloud base never actually touches the water; there is always a space of generally one to two hundred feet between the cloud base and the ocean through which you can fly if you don't mind the white caps lapping at your underbelly, and of course in a rain squall your visibility is nil as it would be at a higher altitude. So if one chooses this option, he is at the mercy of the accuracy of his altimeter and his artificial horizon, just as it says in the IFIS handbook; the one great advantage is a considerable lessening of turbulence despite the down drafts and up drafts, but the margin for error is slim. Given my experience in Atlanta, it was the option I much preferred to the terrible pounding upstairs, and it is to it that I attribute the ultimate survival of *Prometheus*—and her crew. So for the next four hours we flew at 100 feet until we finally broke into the clear and could pick up Guam on our radar; and I landed 30 minutes ahead of Buzz. If nothing else, we had all the proof we needed that the PB4Y-2 was one tough baby.

It was at Guam that we knew we were in the middle of the war zone; the place was littered with all the human and materiel debris of the invasion. Hawaii and Johnston and Kwajalein were now quiet backwater way stations, but this was the forward area, and its grim reality was pervasive. Tight-lipped from fatigue, Rivers and I gave our plane the once-over but found no signs of structural damage. Then the PPCs gathered in the Headquarters shack for a tactical briefing on the Marianas; Admiral Hoover and his staff were moving in to take command of the area, and Tinian and Saipan were in their last throes, with our Seabees already moving north with their heavy equipment to lengthen and strengthen the captured Japanese air strips.

With that, Buzz and I had a couple of drinks while I told him how close we had come to an unscheduled meeting in mid-air, then ate quickly and hit the sack to be ready for another dawn departure on the last leg of our journey.

The Palau Island group, some 400 miles southwest of Guam, consisted of Angaur, with a small native population, and two larger islands, Peleliu and Babelthuap, both heavily garrisoned by the Japanese, and whose harbors afforded a good staging area for her naval units. So in our island-hopping strategy, Palau had to be neutralized as a prelude to the invasion of the Marianas; and because Babelthuap presented such a daunting physical presence, it was decided that Peleliu offered a much easier objective, and with it in hand, we could seal off Babelthuap's harbors and leave its garrison there to rot. So our Marine 1st Division hit Peleliu at Purple Beach in one of the bloodiest encounters of the whole Pacific campaign, and which for some reason got buried in the annals that so glorified the names of Guadalcanal and Iwo Jima. Once the island had been secured and the Seabees had worked their magic on the runways, we moved in, to be followed shortly by two Marine fighter squadrons.

The flight from Guam had taken us over the Ulithi Atoll, now the mid-Pacific fleet anchorage for our ever-growing task forces and where our invasion group covering the Palau and Mariana assaults had returned for refitting. Flying over this galaxy of Men o' War—carriers, battleships, cruisers, and destroyers riding at anchor—was an unforgettable sight and lent a sense of urgency to our mission of keeping the Japanese fleet off their backs.

No sooner had we got squared away in our new operational habitat than our active patrols began. By day the Marines kept Babelthuap under surveillance while we ranged far to the north and east. At night we kept two planes around and over Babelthuap, dropping occasional bomb clusters just to keep the Nips awake. A sobering element in all this was the known presence of Japanese infiltrators holed up in what was called Bloody Nose Ridge, an escarpment that ran across the island just to the north of one of our active runways and from which the Japs would take pot shots from time to time as we crossed over it. But the sense of the real tragedy of this war came from a visit to Purple Beach to see first-hand the devilish ingenuity of the Japs' defensive perimeter that had cost the Marines so dearly despite the pre-invasion point blank bombardment by our Fleet. Tokyo was still many islands and many lives away, and for us the next milestone was Tinian. My hope was that Charno and VPB-105 would rendezvous with us there.

CHAPTER 11

The Route to Tokyo: Tinian, Iwo Jima, Okinawa

Tinian, the middle island in the Mariana chain, has not the slightest promise as some future tourist attraction. Shaped roughly in the form of the human torso sans head and appendages, it is devoid of physical charm, with no towering mountains or lush valleys or exotic beaches, no physical attribute worth description, for the most part flat and arid. What brought it and its sister island to the north, Saipan, onto the world stage in 1945 was their location, exactly 1500 miles south southeast of Tokyo, bringing the Japanese mainland for the first time since Pearl Harbor into the range of our heavy land-based bombers. It is perhaps instructive to note here the monumental difference in the logistical problem of getting at the enemy's heartland between the European Theatre of Operations and the Pacific Theatre. Germany and her minions were but a cross-Channel hop from Britain's myriad air bases, whereas here, after three wearing years, we were ecstatic at having reduced the remoteness of Japan to a mere 1,500 miles, 1,500 up and 1,500 back. The Marianas were now our forward area in our inexorable movement north, and as fast as human ingenuity and materiel permitted, they were literally converted into stationary aircraft carriers, the nesting places for General Curtis LeMay's magnificent B-29s. But now the first squadrons operating out of any new forward area were the PB4Y-2s, whose primary target was not the Jap mainland but the Jap fleet which we were determined to herd into its home waters; so the moment Tinian was declared secure, VPB-108 and her companion groups moved up.

By January, 1945, the offensive capabilities of Japanese naval task forces had to all intents and purposes been obliterated; the mauling of her carriers in the Coral Sea and in the celebrated Mariana Turkey Shoot had pretty well marked paid to Pearl Harbor. But Japan still had a fleet-in-being with menacing defensive potential, as witness the sinking with all hands aboard of our heavy cruiser *Indianapolis* right under our noses; and her submarines remained a threat to our surface ships and to the massive convoys now spread all over the Pacific. So one of our missions was to assure that no surprise sorties in force were launched against our exposed forward areas.

And there was a troubling corollary to the fact that we could now bring the Jap mainland under aerial attack from our Mariana bases. Given the distances involved in the bombing effort, it was impossible to provide the B-29s with fighter cover, and so over the target area they were completely exposed to Japan's superb home defense Fighter Command which ringed her major cities. It therefore required no tactical genius to determine what our next offensive move must be; we desperately needed a base much closer to the mainland from which we could provide protection for the Superforts, and a mere glance at the map indicated precisely where that could be. Seven hundred fifty miles to the north northwest, exactly half the distance between Tinian and Tokyo, lay a group of islands known as the Bonins Volcanoes, principal of which was a mere speck in the ocean called Iwo Jima. Like the Marianas, Iwo's place in history was determined entirely by geography; in Japan's perimeter defensive scheme for the mainland based on outlying islands, Iwo was a critical bastion; nine miles long and three miles at its greatest width, it was completely covered in brown volcanic ash, with a hump-backed ridge down the middle and at its western end its only distinguishing feature, Mount Suribachi, a volcanic cone rising 1,000 feet, and later to be immortalized by Joe Rosenthal's dramatic photograph of our flag being raised on its peak. More to the point, there were three serviceable air strips, two at sea level and one on a mesa of the ridge, 6,000 feet of clay surface with a 300 foot drop off each end. Our intelligence estimate of Iwo's garrison strength was put at 25,000 men under a general famed in Japanese army circles for his tenacity on defense.

By the time VPB-108 began operating out of Tinian, our offensive preparations against Iwo were well in train. One key to the kingdom was Iwo's isolation to prevent any egress or ingress by air or sea, and our patrols to the east, north, and west of the island were designed to keep it that way while the island itself was encircled by our task force which included two carriers and a battlewagon. The Jap fighters had been deemed hopeless in the face of such an armada and had been withdrawn to the mainland, but the garrison had been ordered to resist to the end. For 51 consecutive days Iwo was subjected to aerial assault, bombing and strafing, without opposition, and for the week before D-Day, while the 3rd and 5th Marine Divisions watched from their crowded transports, the Fleet pounded the island point-blank with its heaviest weapons. However, as history has painfully recorded, what was hoped to be a walk in the park was anything but.

No one expected the Jap garrison, to which both retreat and reinforcement had become impossible, meekly to surrender, but it was hoped that the incessant bombing and shelling had wreaked so much havoc as to preclude any organized defense. What we had not counted on was the Jap's inordinate capacity to dig in, and what we found later on was an amazing underground encampment dug into and under the ridge, a labyrinth of vaulted chambers, ammunition dumps, hospital and command posts, messing facilities, all connected by an elaborate system of tunnels that together provided a perfect bomb shelter. So complete was their subterranean fortress that an examination of their medical records indicated that our massive pre-invasion assault had resulted in inflicting only 11 fatalities. So it was that when our Marines hit the beach, the Jap infantry popped up like prairie dogs out of their holes with their small arms, mortars and machine guns and within minutes turned that beach into a carnage. Up and down, back and forth our carrier planes ranged in close support with napalm and anti-personnel incendiaries, but nothing could dislodge them but flame-throwers and cold steel. Their defense was stubborn, inspired, heroic, and in the end, futile; but if Iwo Jima stands as a monumental testament to the valor of our Marines, as it well and truly does, in equal measure it speaks to the magnificent courage of the defenders and their willingness to pay the ultimate price.

Not for three weeks was the island declared secure, so laborious was the process of digging out the remaining defenders, for not one of those 25,000 willingly surrendered. But when finally our Seabees pronounced the air strips usable and the caves apparently flushed out, the great aerial hegira from the Marianas got under way. Initially Muldrow decided to send up only three planes as guinea pigs to test out the landing strip and other facilities; ours was the air strip running along the crest of the ridge, and we negotiated it without any difficulty, although it was evident the clay would be mighty slick when wet. As we crawled out of our planes to look around, we beheld a bewildering sight of frenetic activity.

Me (Jack) in front of *Prometheus Unbound* in Iwo Jima, 1945

The island was literally ringed with support transports, barging in petrol, ammunition, spare parts, water, food, and that panoply of necessities requisite to starting up an air base from scratch. From our vantage point on the ridge, we could see in every direction tent cities being erected with their outdoor kitchens. The Seabees in their bulldozers were concentrating on lengthening the two sea level strips for the Army P-51 Mustangs that were beginning to pour in, one of the primary reasons for taking Iwo in the first place. The whole island was alive with organized confusion, and for the first time I got some idea of the complexity of the logistical planning for an operation such as this. Who, for example, had loaded those transports, and where and with what and got them to the shores of Iwo Jima at precisely this moment. We aviators were the ultimate beneficiaries of this tremendous effort, and for the first time I began to appreciate what it took to keep us in the air.

While our plane crews set off to find our billets, Muldrow, Buzz and I flagged down a jeep and were driven to the invasion beach. The savagery of the fighting was everywhere in evidence, empty ammunition canisters, shell cases, bits and pieces of bloodied garments, gun emplacements blown to bits, everywhere the mute litter of battle. Among that litter were hundreds of tins of C-rations which the Marines, out of desperation or disgust, had hurled at their tormentors, and a sick joke had it that the Japs were much too smart to open them and partake. We looked gratefully at our flag flying on Mount Suribachi, but it was on this beach that the nut-cutting had taken place. The smell of the place said everything—the stench of sulphuric ash mixed with blood. The only thing redeeming about this dreadful scene was the knowledge that Tokyo was now only 750 miles away.

The dominant physical characteristic of Iwo was the sulphuric ash that covered every square inch of its surface, and every movement, be it vehicular or human, sent swirls of it into the air. Its fumes permeated everything, clothes, food, bedding, and if cleanliness is next to Godliness, we were headed straight to Hell. The tenting areas were assigned by squadron, and about 300 yards separated the Navy bivouac from that of the Army Air Force, a wide gulf because the service rivalry was intense and neither group was given to fraternization. Our clothes and mess gear were all G.I. issue; we pumped our water from barrels, and for ablutions we used our tin helmets for basins. Our bedding consisted of sleeping bags and blankets. In sum, it was the Sahara without an oasis, but we would have welcomed the desert sands instead of our volcanic gook.

Iwo had been declared secure, hence our presence, but it was not quite, and we were warned that there well might be nests of Japanese survivors still at large in the hills and caves that bordered our encampment and that we were not to move about without our side arms. Indeed, we slept that first night with them in easy reach, but there was no incident. The second night, however, was sheer, unadulterated bedlam. Sometime after midnight, a Jap platoon, armed with swords and hand grenades, slipped out of its cover and made a desperate banzai charge into the Air Force compound, slitting open the tents and lobbing in their grenades. The cacophony was awful as the whole place seemed to explode, and in the confusion the retaliatory small arms fire came from every direction. We literally groveled on our stomachs in the darkness of our tents, not daring to raise our heads as the bullets whistled by and wondered if our encampment would be next. It was the Jap at his best and worst, saving the last grenade for himself to gratify his death wish; and when dawn finally came, the grisly toll was 50 Air Force pilots blown to bits without ever knowing what hit them. It might just as easily have been us, and it brought on such an attack of jitters that there was a tragic sequel. Despite a doubling of the Marine guard on our perimeter, the next night we just lay on our bedrolls, '45s in hand, staring into the darkness and listening for any untoward sound. At some point one of our petty officers felt compelled to relieve himself, and when he stepped out of his tent he stumbled over a tent rope, and in trying to right himself he made quite a noise; in an instant he was dead, the shots coming from several directions.

The next morning provided another shock for the system. Muldrow, Buzz and I, along with our co-pilots and radiomen, went to the make-shift communications center to check on available facilities and frequencies. While there, one of the corpsmen asked if we would like to listen to their chief form of entertainment—Tokyo Rose, who broadcast every hour on the hour. To our utter amazement, her opening gambit of that day's recording went this way: "Two days ago, Commander Muldrow and the first elements of his patrol squadron landed on Iwo Jima. I would like to welcome him to our island, and to assure him that not one of his blue devils will ever leave there alive."

The corpsman just laughed at our astonishment and asked, "Have you ever heard a prettier voice?"

We only looked at each other, wondering just how secure was secure? But we left there with one bit of good news; the most powerful ultra-high frequency transmitter in the whole Pacific was being assembled to serve as our radio directional beacon.

"Your bird dog will be able to pick us up loud and clear right in the big middle of Tokyo Bay," chortled our happy corpsman.

And he was right. Indeed, as a navigational aid for the B-29s and for our purposes, Iwo could not have been more perfectly situated. Running due north right into the mouth of Tokyo Bay was a string of volcanic islands called the Bonins, which included Chichi-jima, Hachijo-jima, Miyake-jima, Kozu-shima, and Izu-Oshima, each of which provided an ideal radar fix. The B-29s, taking off from Guam, Tinian and Saipan, could form up over Iwo and then had the whole Japanese industrial heartland as their target area, due north to Yokohama and Tokyo proper, northwest to Nagoya, Kyoto, Kobe and Osaka, and farther west, the Inland Sea and the island of Kyushu. And Iwo, besides providing the bases for their fighter cover, was also a Godsend as an emergency landing field for the cripples returning from the mainland. Had it not been there, we should have had to invent it, and that is why the Japanese so hotly defended it.

The final string in our bow was the line of our submarines—our Dumbos, as we affectionately dubbed them, stationed at 100 mile intervals between Iwo and the mainland, with two of them always sitting on the bottom of Tokyo Bay. Their primary mission was air-sea rescue, and they would swing the line to the right or left so as to be directly beneath the line of flight to the target area, and they were also primed for offensive action should any targets of opportunity present themselves. They were privy to all our radio traffic and it was comforting to check in with them going up and back. It was monotonous duty for them, sitting motionless and silently just beneath the surface most of the time, but many an Army and Navy pilot owes his survival to their presence.

Gradually, a semblance of order began to emerge from the chaos of invasion, and as support facilities expanded, more units made their appearance until our normal strength stood at three squadrons of 4Y-2s and two squadrons of PV-2s for the shorter missions. For us, Muldrow's modus operandi was simple but efficient: since Iwo was now the forward area, Tinian became a backwater for R&R purposes, and so we would keep ten planes on Iwo and five in reserve on Tinian, rotating five crews a week, so each crew would spend two weeks up and one week back. On Iwo we flew a patrol every third day, with the following day off-duty, and the next day on stand-by, with each mission being preceded by a weather and then a tactical briefing. Since our patrols now penetrated the coastal areas of the Japanese home islands, our sectors were plotted out on a grid resembling a fully-opened fan in V-shaped units, but to keep the Japs off balance, not every sector was flown every day. The average patrol ran ten to twelve hours, and they were flown around the clock, the rule of thumb being never to show up at the same place at the same time, but to let the Jap know that his coastline was under constant observation.

For his part, the Jap had few tactical resources with which to oppose us. In the first place, Iwo was free from any threat from the air; his carriers had ceased to exist as a strike force, we were beyond the operational range of his land-based fighters, which in any event were being husbanded for defense against the B-29s, and he possessed no long-range bombing capability. True enough, the string of islands helpful to us as navigations aids were useful observation points for him, each one having radar facilities which we delighted in knocking out as quickly as he could repair them. His main reliance for information was his screen of picket boats, hundreds of small, speedy wooden craft, armed and each with a radio transmitter, operating from the outlying islands and spread in a huge fan-shaped arc south of the mainland. From an altitude they looked like water bugs dancing on the ocean's surface, but they were testy little creatures. We were at liberty to go after them as we chose, being forewarned that a direct hit from a low-level strafing run might well cause them to explode right in our faces. A far more effective tactic was to catch them moored in their home harbors, but they were far too numerous for eradication, and their offensive threat was nil.

 The great beauty of our initial operations out of Iwo was the absence of any Navy "gold braid." Admiral Hoover, the nominal area commander, and his staff were far to the south on Guam, and thus we were spared the purblind injunctions that inevitably emanate from poorly informed desk officers. Here, there was a perfectly relaxed chain of command, headed by whichever squadron commander happened to be the SOP. The daily patrol sectors were carefully coordinated and meted out from a master plot, and the only awkwardness was the occasional "jumping" of your sector by an over-zealous colleague thus alerting the enemy of your likely presence before you reached your apogee. This is not to suggest that this was all a piece of cake; the weather was our persistent foe, as was the attrition to our engines and instruments from the constant demands on them. Not infrequently our planes would return on three engines, or sometimes on two, or be porous from bullet holes with casualties among the crew; for some unknown reason co-pilots were the most frequent victims. But by and large we were accomplishing our mission of denying the Japanese fleet the opportunity for any surprise concentration by keeping it scattered and penned up in its myriad hiding places; and we were racking up a pretty good score in merchant shipping, picket boats and radar installations. And I was happy to have Charno's companionship once again, although in his determined fashion on his first patrol he had taken on a picket boat, the debris from which had knocked out his nose turret and killed his gunner. I was on the flight line to meet his battered aircraft, but despite getting it back in one piece, he was nearly inconsolable at the loss of his crewman.

It was on our first penetration of the Tokyo Bay area that Rivers displayed his irrepressible pride in his stewardship of *Prometheus*. He had somehow scrounged a hot plate to complete his galley, and the crew was forever on the lookout for provisions to stack our larder. We approached the mainland in pretty good cloud cover, but as I descended beneath it to get some visual familiarity with the area, I became increasingly on edge and instructed the crew to stay off the intercom unless sighting a bogey. As we sailed up the Boso-Hanto peninsula between Chiba and Choshi Point, the nesting ground of the Japs' crack night fighter squadrons, I heard the microphone button click and I nearly jumped out of my skin; it was Rivers with a question, "Boss, how do you want your eggs, fried or scrambled?" Such was our introduction to the lair of the dragon, but the tension was broken, although we postponed the sampling of our first hot meal until we were well back out to sea.

April 12, 1945 was not, however, such a red letter day. Returning from a sortie over the Inland Sea, I landed about mid-afternoon, and after taxiing to the flight line and cutting the engines, I cracked open my hatch and looked out to see tears streaming down the linesman's face.

I shouted down to him, "What in the world is going on?"

He looked up at me and said simply, "Roosevelt is dead."

I just sat there with my head in my hands, numb with disbelief, finally relaying the message to the crew. I thought of the three times I had met him in the company of Commissioner Splawn, that jaunty cigarette holder and infectious smile, and that sonorous voice that had lifted a whole nation out of its despondency and which had given my generation a cause. Now he had left us with the job not nearly finished. And who was this man Truman, a petty politician? What could he know about the prosecution of a war and the resurrection of Western civilization? Suddenly Iwo Jima seemed bleak and purposeless, and we had been cast adrift. But there was one man who might know something, and in my agony I went off to find him. George Charno was from Kansas City, and I remembered that his father held Senator Truman in high regard.

"Don't you worry, Hub," counseled George. "We could certainly be in worse hands. He is smart, and principled, and a fighter. He served with distinction as a cavalry officer in the First World War and his men worshipped him, so he knows what this is all about. He obviously lacks the polish and charm and charisma of FDR, but you listen to me—he is straight as a string, and it won't take long for the nation and the world to find out that he is one tough little cocker!"

So that night on this God-forsaken spot, two guys went to sleep, one hoping and the other knowing that our world had not come to an end after all.

After a two-week stretch on this stinking island, Tinian was our new version of Paradise. I would let Hale and Moskowitz, with much advice from Rivers, fly *Prometheus* down, while I became the navigator, which is to say that I made sure our radio direction finder was set on the right frequency, nor would I let them use the auto pilot unless we were in really heavy weather because they needed the flying time. Once there, good things were possible: we could luxuriate in a hot shower for as long as we pleased and get rid of that odoriferous sulphur, sleep on an honest-to-God mattress, get our laundry done, wolf down relatively edible chow, and have a proper drink with, believe it or not, ice or a cold beer. Our fifty cases of I. W. Harper were being dented, but the end was not yet in sight. One could even get a haircut, and here again my Goddess of Coincidence was still at work; the chief barber of the island was a tech sergeant named Alabama, who had been cutting my hair in Denton, Texas, since I was a kid. True to his trade, 'Bama was observant and garrulous, and he was like an English village postmistress as a fountain of information, for he soaked up the conversations of high and low, mostly high, as they frequented his chair. He told me where General Ramey, whose younger brother was my good friend in Denton, and his B-29 group were quartered, and I would jeep over there for old home week and chat with his colleagues like Rosie O'Connell, and once I was introduced to the great man himself, General LeMay. Parenthetically, I was and remain convinced that the Navy could fly rings around the Army Air Corps, but there was one critical area in which they were vastly our superior, the ability of their Generals to perform in the aircraft under their command. These guys could fly, and more often than not they led their missions, including the C-in-C himself. By contrast, many of our Admirals, especially those ensconced on air staffs, had got their wings late in their careers, attaining the designation as aviators by flying training like PBYs around Pensacola, and amassing just enough air time each month to qualify for their flight pay. Most of those who were land-based in the forward areas had never heard a shot fired in anger and hadn't a clue as to the performance and the limitations of our current operational aircraft. In terms of morale, imagine the difference in being led on a strike by the men who had designed it, or ordered out by men safely removed from the combat area who wouldn't know how to retract a landing gear.

'Bama was also a wizard at matching resources available for barter. If you had whiskey, he knew who had the good steaks, and for a modest fee in kind he would arrange the connection. Our I. W. Harper was a premium bargaining chip, especially with mess sergeants attending the brass. We reveled in building a fire in a shallow trench over which we laid an iron sheet and barbecued thick filets, accompanied by freshly baked loaves of bread with real butter and a wash tub brimming with bottles of cold beer. And of course I saw to it that our agent never lacked an invitation, and so for all parties concerned it was a marvelously useful relationship.

But as the repository of all the current scuttlebutt, 'Bama could also bear sad tidings. It was from him sometime later that I got my first intimation of a drastic revision of our modus operandi on Iwo. According to his sources, the mounting successes of our free-wheeling methods were so well known as to become a bone of contention among the Navy brass on Guam who, because of their removal from and indifference to the scene of action, were getting no credit for our daring-do. This was intolerable, a sloppy way to run a war, and a decision had been made (according to 'Bama) to establish a command staff on Tinian to bring the whole of our activities under its direct purview. Allegedly the commandant of this new outfit had already been named, some Rear Admiral by the name of Greer, whose record thus far was apparently so undistinguished that not even 'Bama's informants could get a line on him, beyond the fact that he was an Academy graduate and sported a pair of wings, two very ominous signs. In the event, this is exactly what happened, and thus I learned one of life's invaluable lessons: always trust your barber.

In due course, and with appropriate pomp and ceremony, Admiral Greer and his low left shouldered (so named because the Academy ring was allegedly so heavy as to cause the left shoulder to sag) desk jockeys arrived and installed themselves as a permanent feature of the Tinian landscape. ('Bama's sage comment was that their mess should yield some pretty fancy groceries.) Muldrow and the other irate squadron COs were summoned to receive instructions as to the new dispensation, and a deputy chief-of-staff and three flunkies were ensconced on Iwo to purvey orders. Now for one not familiar with the relationship, one should know that the animosity between staff and line officers had been endemic since the inception of organized warfare, and in the modern era the gulf was unbridgeable between those who drew up on paper the neat set-piece battles and those who had to implement such designs. Animosity reached the apogee of detestation in the First World War when Sir Douglas Haig and his staff, from their comfortable chateaux forty miles behind the front lines, designed and directed the massacres of his Majesty's forces on the Somme and at Passchendaele, thus signing the death warrant of the British Empire. A civilian counterpart would be the Board of Directors of the British East India Company, sitting in London and without ever having set foot in the place, issuing instructions to their agents on the Sub-continent half the world distant. Though not completely ordained, the result is often grim tragedy. In our tiny microcosm of the war, so it was with us.

Admiral Greer, unprepossessing in appearance, was in his early fifties, short, rotund, with a balding pate and a florid complexion which did not belie his fondness for strong drink; in happier times and with a beard and a bell, he might have made a passable street corner Santa Claus. One seldom caught a glimpse of him in the daylight, and I first laid eyes on him one evening at our al fresco theatre when, propped up by an aide at each elbow, he staggered into the VIP seats and promptly snored throughout the movie. At the outset, we hoped that he and his staff would be content to ride a good horse, but no, they were bent on doing something spectacular, apparently driven by the notion that with the B-29s in capital letters—and us in smaller print—grabbing all the headlines, they had to justify their existence. What they came up with was an absolute beauty.

Meanwhile, the war continued. On the night of one of General LeMay's spectaculars, we on Iwo would be lying on our backs watching Humphrey Bogart whistle at Lauren Bacall. We could hear the steady drone of aircraft engines coming up from the south and see the lights of the B-29s forming up, and at the same time we could hear the P-51s revving up their engines and see the flames spitting from their superchargers as they took off in support of their big brothers.

That was the signal for those of us who had air-sea rescue duty to gather up our crews and head for the briefing shack. There would be seven of us, each assigned to a Dumbo submarine, and after our navigators double-checked our rendezvous coordinates, we headed north below the parade streaming above us. At fixed times the Dumbos would surface, allowing us to home in on them with our radar, after which we would fly a 25 mile square box around them at 500 feet and await the B-29s to complete their mission and turn for home. With the initial contact we would exchange pleasantries, but from then on we maintained strict silence while we listened for any anguished cries of "May Day!" It was a lonely vigil but with enormous rewards for the air-sea teams when downed flyers were plucked from the sea. The plain fact was that the B-29s with their fire-bombing were wreaking massive destruction on Japan's major industrial centers, and the Jap was unable to mount any effective deterrent because of the limited range of his land-based fighters, that is, until our brilliant new staff on Tinian came up with a possible solution for him.

Poring over their maps and claiming fresh intelligence from sources that have forever remained undisclosed, our desk boys got it into their heads that the Jap was about to launch a daring counter-offensive against his tormentors. Equipping his fighters with wing tanks to increase their range, he was going to covertly transfer some five hundred of them from the mainland through an air corridor east of the Marianas to one of his last remaining island bastions at Truk, using Marcus Island as an intermediary staging base. From Truk, 750 miles southeast of Guam in the Carolines, he could commit his entire strike force to a surprise attack on the B-29s sitting defenseless on the ground at Guam, Tinian and Saipan, destroying so many of them as to render LeMay's Bomber Command impotent for the foreseeable future. To clinch matters, our staff knew the precise hour and day this Jap aerial armada would deploy from the mainland. So the obvious way to thwart this grand design was to interdict the Jap fighters at Marcus by launching our own surprise attack and catching them helpless on the ground in the process of refueling. For this job VPB-108 drew the assignment, but for obvious security reasons, the plan was not revealed to Muldrow until the morning the launch was scheduled.

Marcus Island (Minami-Tori-Shima) lay 800 miles due east of Iwo; it had the reputation of being a tough nut to crack because of its excellent anti-aircraft defenses, but it had been by-passed by us after an abortive air strike by the *Enterprise* early in 1942 in an effort to demonstrate that we still had carriers operating in the Pacific despite Pearl Harbor. Since then it had just sat there half-way between Wake and the mainland as a lonely sentinel with ennui its garrison's only enemy. The game plan called for Muldrow to lead two 3-plane sections, loaded with 100 pound fragmentation bombs, timed to reach Marcus just at daybreak, with the first section to sweep the island at 100 feet, dropping its bombs in salvo on the runways massed with Jap fighters, with the second section which I was leading to follow at a two minute interval to allow the debris to clear. We flew the last 100 miles at an altitude of fifty feet, hoping to escape radar detection, and as the island loomed ahead of us in the first light of dawn, we went up to 300 feet to get a running start to our bombing altitude. Then, with turret guns cleared, bomb doors open, and bombs armed, the first section began its run into the grey dawn. It was God-awful. The Japs had had us on their radar all the time and were just lying in wait; they opened up with everything they had and then pointed their weapons straight up to force our planes to fly through a steel curtain of flak; Muldrow's plane just disintegrated, Ebright on his right did a cartwheel into the sea, and Wallace on the left, with two engines out on one side, somehow managed to get out to sea and ditch. Now any way you reckon it, three minutes is not a great deal of time, but it was that interval that saved the second section; with better visibility than John had had, I looked at the island and saw its runways absolutely barren, empty, void of any sign of Jap aircraft, and I screamed to my wingmen to pull up and scatter an instant before we were to begin our run. I stood *Prometheus* on her tail and then fell off in some kind of wing-over and then climbed upstairs out of range of the Jap AA, where our section formed up again. We then circled Marcus as close as we dared to photograph its emptiness, all the while keeping Wallace and his life rafts in view so the Japs couldn't get to them. Before long one of our Dumbos surfaced, having been dispatched to the area the day before in the only sensible move in this whole charade, and picked up Wallace and what was left of his crew. So that is how the Marcus garrison, finally awakened from its three year torpor, justified its existence: three of our best aircraft, two and a half of our finest 12-man crews, one CO to whom we were all devoted, in an attack on a barren hunk of lava in the middle of nowhere. Not an enduring monument to staff planning; just plain murder. Not a word was spoken on the long flight back to Iwo.

For the next several days our grief was exceeded only by our anger; the staff officers on Iwo were hastily called back to Tinian, probably out of concern for their personal safety. In their stead came Captain Chink Lee, a grizzled combat veteran, the only active flyer on Admiral Greer's staff, and a man held in high regard throughout the Pacific Fleet, for reasons that soon became apparent. With hat in hand he went from crew to crew, freely admitting a grotesque staff blunder to which he had been privy, but counseling that the game was still on and that we simply couldn't holler "Foul" and walk off the playing field. In the privacy of Buzz's tent, he produced some steaks and a couple of bottles of Scotch, which we hadn't seen for ages, and let his hair down. Yes, it was a bad call which he regretted as much as anyone. Johnny Muldrow had been his friend, too, and that was all he was going to say on that score. No, a petition to Admiral Hoover for Greer's recall would not be appropriate because we didn't run this Navy by petition; to be sure there would be a shakeup in the staff, but Greer had friends in high places and I don't want you guys to get the tag of "cry babies." No, he wouldn't be able to wash Marcus from his record. This was not our first mistake or our last, and the best thing you guys can do is rally around Buzz and get on with your knitting.

No, the Marcus affair was not cut out of whole cloth; the reports we got made it plausible enough not to be ignored, and from where he was now sitting, he would have to conclude that the Japs had simply put out some bait to test our reaction, and we had swallowed it hook, line and sinker. So just remember that the Jap was a tough, wily son of a bitch who wasn't about to throw in the towel. Yes, he'd have another touch of Scotch. This, then, was no petty apologia, and we were assuaged by his candor and concern for our discomfiture, and we stayed with him until the Scotch was gone.

There could not have been a better replacement for John than Buzz, and we got back to business. Replacements for our planes and crews were in the pipeline, and we declined Captain Lee's offer to pull us all back to Tinian for an extra week's R&R. Weather was becoming an even more oppressive factor since we were in the typhoon season, and having ridden one out at Tinian that had blown two of our Quonsets away, we knew what to expect. I was scheduled for a dawn patrol one morning, and when I entered the weather guesser's tent for my briefing, I was surprised to see Buzz there. He told me that during the night one of our Dumbos had reported that in my sector for the day a crippled Jap cruiser was under tow along the coast below Nagoya which they were apparently trying to slip into the Inland Sea.

"It would be a fat target," he said, "and if the cloud cover's right, you might get a good crack at it, but apparently there's some weather out there."

"Just how bad is it?" he asked the aerologist.

"Sir, it's bad. I'd have to say its a typhoon, and I'd put it right now about two-thirds of the way between here and Osaka, moving east. And I can promise you plenty of cover over the coast, which will probably be socked in tighter than a drum."

Buzz persisted, and it was clear he wanted that cruiser, "Have you any records of a plane penetrating a typhoon?"

The reply was not encouraging, "Oh, yes Sir, we have records of planes going in but no record of one coming out."

That should have done it, but Buzz turned to me with the worst remark he could have made, "It sure as hell doesn't look good, Tex, so I'll have to leave it up to you."

"I'll have a go at it" was all I could say.

The result was the worst experience of my life. I briefed the crew on what to expect and told them to buckle up as tightly as they could, and we were not a happy bunch when I lifted *Prometheus* off the deck. I went up to 5000 feet and leveled off; it was grey ahead but the first hour was none too bad. Then it began to get darker and darker, and soon we were in it, bouncing all over the sky as Hale and I held onto the yoke for dear life. The rain was in sheets and the turbulence beyond my experience, and I really didn't know how much more beating the plane could take. After two hours of it I was ready to call it quits, when suddenly we burst out into the sunlight and smooth air with a calm sea below.

"Nice going, Boss," said Rivers, and I was about to jump with joy when reality struck; we weren't through the typhoon at all but smack in the eye of the son of a bitch.

But when that finally sank in, I knew that I had gone as far north as I was going to go, for even if we managed to get through it, we would have it all to do over again to get back home. So staying within the eye, I circled down to 500 feet hoping to find a little cushion and headed south, plunging back into the storm. There were two more hours of sheer hell, but finally things began to lighten up, and before too long we were well and truly out of it. Neither Moscow nor I had a clue as to our position because the needle on our RDF had been bouncing all over creation, but we surmised that we had been blown far to the east of our original course, and sure enough our bird dog settled down and pointed us in the right direction to the southwest. For once in its existence Mount Suribachi was a beautiful sight, and it was a weary but thankful crew that taxied up to the flight line. We had been at it for seven hours and we hadn't got close to that cruiser, but we had tried.

Buzz and Charno were on the line to greet us, but first I wanted to check my crew which had so dreadfully been beaten up; there were some angry-looking welts and Wingfield had a pretty deep cut in his arm, but mainly they were just thankful it was over. Then Buzz drove George and me in his jeep to his tent and poured me a stiff drink and just let me sit there. Gradually I began to unbend and tried to describe the ordeal. But when all was said and done, the heroine of the place was *Prometheus* which had somehow stayed intact. She had no way of knowing it, but her performance in that storm resulted in the formation of a new kind of squadron, the Hurricane Hunters, which to this day renders such a valuable service in the tracking of tropical disturbances. And our aerologist now had something to add to his records.

Because of the pounding by the B-29s, the Japs began beefing up their aerial defenses around their major coastal cities, and to counter this we began assigning two planes instead of the usual one to these "hot" sectors, and in these instances I usually worked with Buzz, and it was on one of these patrols that we had our greatest disappointment, but in the end one of our most productive days. We were making our way north towards the Tokyo area, and as was our usual wont, we were checking out the harbors of the island chain en route, which thus far had yielded nothing but a few fishing craft. As we neared Hachijo we went down to 50 feet, and when we swung up and over a ridge that encircled the harbor, there below us was a Jap destroyer we could have spit on. We passed over it in a flash, but he must have been less startled than we because he got his forward batteries into action as the black puffs of flak bursting around us gave evidence. I veered sharply to the right and Buzz swung up and to the left without sustaining any damage, but when we joined up again, we were two angry PPCs. Had we been prescient enough to have anticipated that critter, we would have had our bombs armed and ready to drop and put that destroyer out of its misery then and there. But we had missed a golden chance, and all we could do was report the DD's location, which brought one of our Dumbos into play that promptly sank him when he ventured out of the harbor. But all we got on that scorecard was an assist.

Farther north business picked up, and we had our second surprise of the day. The harbor at Miyako almost in the mouth of Tokyo Bay was packed and jammed with picket boats which had sought shelter from a violent storm front which had just passed through, and there was a new radar installation that had not been there before. We were carrying 100 pound fragmentation bombs, and this time we were ready. I went for the radar station while Buzz began his run on the harbor; and in the end we each made four passes at the picket boats with all our turrets blazing and with Buzz getting to use his 20 mm cannon. We exhausted our bomb loads, and with those wooden craft exploding in all directions, the harbor was covered with debris; later our photos confirmed that we had got at least fifty of them. But on the last pass Buzz took two hits, one knocking out his outboard starboard engine and the other exploding in his radio compartment, knocking out his command set, seriously wounding his radioman, and tearing a gaping hole in the fuselage. Thankfully, however, his plane was still airworthy, and we began the long, slow pull back to Iwo, checking in with each Dumbo as we passed over. Our only communication with each other was now by hand signals, but as long as Buzz kept flashing thumbs up, I knew he was making do. At Iwo he made a long, straight-in approach and a good landing, with the ambulances and fire equipment waiting for him. Our scorecard now looked a lot better with a lot of putouts recorded.

The Philippines were back in our possession despite a seven hour delay with the cameras grinding out God knows how many retakes before Dugout Doug was finally satisfied that his few steps through the surf and grand announcement to suffering mankind had been properly recorded for posterity. With Formosa by-passed, the next campaign was the seizure of Okinawa in the Ryukyus, 400 miles southwest of Japan's southwestern most home island of Kyushu.

Accordingly our patrols were concentrated to the west and northwest of Iwo, while a mighty invasion fleet moved up to encircle the island. After the by now accustomed aerial assaults and bombardment by the surface units, the landings began on 1 April 1945, simultaneously Easter Sunday and April Fool's day, but this time the Jap had radically altered his strategy and tactics.

In the first place, the landings on the relatively flat northern tip of the island were unopposed at the beachheads, with the Jap instead electing to defend from well-concealed positions in the rugged terrain farther south towards Naha, the capital. So within the first hours the only serviceable air strip in the north, Yontan, came under our control. In the second place, this invasion site was within easy range of the Jap's air force based on his home islands, and it resorted to the frightening new tactic of kamikaze with a vengeance, and for our Fleet it became a nightmare.

Thus the subjugation of Okinawa became a bloody tough proposition, and Yontan became an unbelievably congested airstrip, handling every kind of plane in our arsenal, from hospital evacuation transports to night fighters, around the clock. It was a bedlam of activity with incessant radio traffic from frustrated pilots begging for instruction from the tower; and to add to its woes, the Fleet put up smoke every night to defend against the kamikazes, and with a wind shift from the wrong direction, Yontan would be absolutely blacked out, and one could hear the coughing and sputtering of aircraft engines above as the night fighters exhausted their fuel and were forced to take to their parachutes.

It was in late May, with the issue still in doubt but with the ground combat having moved inch by bloody inch half-way down the island, that Admiral Greer wheedled an invitation from his old Annapolis classmate, Admiral John Mason Brown who was commanding a carrier task force, to visit his flagship at Okinawa, ostensibly to discuss matters of strategy but covertly to enable Greer to claim a battle star for having been present in a combat zone. The honor of transporting the old bastard fell to none other than Buzz Lefever, who, to the disgust of Tony Jackson, asked me to go along as his co-pilot. We took off from Tinian on a wonderfully warm sunny day, and a couple of hours out Buzz, making sure the auto pilot was firmly engaged, invited the Admiral into the co-pilot's seat and asked him if he'd like to take the controls. He accepted with alacrity, and not realizing the auto pilot was doing the work, he was proudly maintaining course and altitude; but the sun streaming in from the overhead on his bald head got the better of him, and pretty soon he was snoring away. After a little while Buzz turned off the autopilot, put the plane into a shallow dive and kicked the rudder smartly, with the resulting jolt awakening the Admiral with a start, who, seeing the altimeter winding down screamed to Buzz, "You take it, you take it." When Buzz obliged, the Admiral, now sweating profusely, excused himself and went back to his easy chair which we had provided in the radio compartment, and that was the last we saw of him up front.

When we reached Yontan and finally raised the tower, we asked for landing instructions and reported we had "scrambled eggs" aboard, to which the tower operator asked us to say again, which we did, and his reply was "Wait." It was strictly forbidden to mention anyone's name and rank on the air, so we were unable to identify our passenger to the tower, hence the reference to scrambled eggs, but in Navy parlance that reference has two meanings: either a high ranking officer with gold braid on his cap, or bombs loose in the bomb bay. Admiral Greer was listening to all this on his headset, and when the tower said "Wait," I saw him shake his head with a little smile on his face thinking that the tower was making sure the red carpet was rolled out and the reception party in place. But that was the last thing Yontan, overwhelmed with the exigencies of war, was thinking about, and we circled for ten minutes before the tower raised us again.

"Do your bomb bay doors work?" was the query. That surprised us, but Buzz checked to be sure before answering in the affirmative.

Then came the denouement, "Roger your affirmative. Fly a vector of 060 for twelve minutes and jettison your scrambled eggs."

The Admiral went crimson, and I thought he would perish from apoplexy; but in time we got everything straightened out and were permitted to land, and Admiral Brown did have an aide there to meet his thoroughly deflated guest. For VPB-108, it had been lovely to behold.

After getting rid of our guest, it was no easy matter to find a spot to park our 4Y-2; both sides of the runway and into the outfield were cluttered with planes of every description awaiting their various missions, and we had to taxi a considerable distance from Base Operations to find a clear spot which, as it turned out, proved to be a Godsend. A personnel carrier came out to pick us up, Buzz was duly shown to his quarters, and the rest of us were standing around waiting for some kind of assignment for the night. Happily we ran into some old buddies from a PV-2 squadron which had been redeployed here from Iwo, and they invited us to bed down in their tent area which was located about midway down the airstrip and off to the side of the parked planes. Four or five squadrons including Marine torpedo bombers and night fighters were bivouacked here in a line of tents along both sides of which a deep trench studded with machine gun emplacements, had been dug "just in case some of those buggers showed up without an invitation," a hangover from those ill-starred P-51 lads on Iwo. So the sights and sounds of war were everywhere: the artillery duels raging to the south, the airstrip alive with the noise of whining engines, the Fleet beginning to make smoke; but it was also a gorgeous night, with just a whisper of a breeze and a dazzling full moon in a cloudless sky.

"Bombers moon," somebody observed.

For the "benefit" of Admiral Greer, we had brought along several jars of whiskey, and thanks to Alabama, we had also picked up in Tinian a goodly supply of ground beef and buns, and combined with our PV-2 friends' provisions, including plenty of beer, we had the makings for a grand cook-out with the trench proving a splendid spot for our fire. It was one of those occasions when, gorged with good food and drink, everyone tried to exorcize whatever devils were plaguing him; someone produced a guitar and the ribald songs began. It was around 2100 hours when without warning every anti-aircraft battery ringing Yontan opened up seemingly, from the trajectory of their tracers, aiming at the moon. We looked up, and for an instant at about 5,000 feet a formation of five Japanese Sallys, twin-engine medium bombers, were clearly etched against the moon. The air raid sirens were now sounding all over the place, and we all jumped or fell into the trench, expecting the bomb detonations at any instant. But no bombs fell, and soon the tracer trajectory began to lower slowly in a sweeping circle as though tracking planes in a landing pattern. Suddenly there was a flash as one of the Sallys disintegrated in mid-air, and then there was another but still the circle of fire kept getting lower and lower.

"What in the hell are those monkeys trying to do?" asked someone huddled close to me, and suddenly the three remaining planes swept the length of the runway at about 500 feet, and as they veered off to the left, another one went ass over tea kettle but the other two looked like they were heading out to sea. The anti-aircraft fire which was damn near parallel to the ground had to break off for fear of hitting each other, and for a moment there was an eerie silence. But then we could pick up the drone of engines as they circled back right on top of us.

"Jesus Christ," someone shouted, "They're trying to land!"

They were indeed, and in the bright moonlight we could pick up the last two in their final approach. One undershot and ploughed into a line of our planes parked to the right side of the airstrip, but the other one touched down wheels up on the runway and screeched to a halt, and out poured a platoon of Jap soldiers each wearing a sword and with a huge pouch stuffed with grenades strapped to his belly. Sirens wailed, whippet tanks and assorted other vehicles got under way, and it is impossible to describe the chaos and confusion that followed, punctuated with indiscriminate small arms fire into which none of us dared to venture. The Japs had scattered among our jumble of parked aircraft, and in a moment we could see and hear the explosions as they lobbed their grenades into them. Geysers of fire erupted into the air as flames found petrol tanks, and the din was unbelievable. We just stood there in our trench with pistols and carbines at the ready, dumbfounded at the carnage. How long it lasted I was never quite sure, but I do remember pleading to high heaven for our plane to be spared. Adding to our apprehension was not knowing whether this was an isolated sortie or but the prelude to a determined effort to put Yontan out of business, and although things began to calm down, there was no sleep to be had. Many people have nights to remember, some filled with joy; this was mine, and the nightmare persists.

Dawn gave us our first chance to assess the situation; Marine jeeps were careening up and down with their bull horns blaring, "This field is not secure," but men of all ranks, pilots and crews checking on their planes, and just the plain curious were streaming on to the airstrip and its environs. I made a beeline for our plane with Buzz happily to find that it had been beyond the reach of the commandos, but our crewman who had been on watch was suffering from a bad case of nerves. Our losses amounted to 33 aircraft totally destroyed and as many others damaged from flying debris; we found the mutilated bodies of 10 Jap soldiers who had apparently saved their last grenade for themselves. Their uniforms were brand new from kepi to boots, with newly-minted yen and packs of cigarettes in their pockets, and their swords were burnished. We were standing in a group staring down at one body when a Marine sergeant suddenly threw his arms in the air and began shouting, "Booby trap, booby trap!" We all scattered like a flushed covey of quail, whereupon the sergeant stepped forward and relieved the corpse of its sword and uniform buttons and calmly walked away with his souvenirs.

Wild as it was, the incident at Yontan was a walk in the park compared to the slugging match to the south which was to continue for six more weeks before the last Jap defender gave up the ghost. But it was a frightening example of the Jap's fanaticism and addiction to the drug of kamikaze in defense of his possessions, and its implications for the future were ominous.

It had also got Admiral Greer much closer to actual combat than he ever intended, although he had probably passed out before the curtain went up. The next day we deposited him at Tinian and proceeded on to Iwo and its relative calm.

Editor's Addition

Despite the feelings Jack expressed in these memoirs for Admiral Greer, the Admiral thought enough of Jack's skills and accomplishments to award him a second Air Medal for the raid (herein described) on Miyako Harbor near the mouth of Tokyo Bay. Admiral Greer's citation, which details the basis for the award follows:

> In the name of the President of the United States, the Commander Fleet Air Wing Eighteen takes pleasure in

presenting the Gold Star in lieu of a second Air Medal to Lieutenant John Randolph Hubbard United States Naval Reserve for services as set forth in the following Citation:

For meritorious acts while participating in aerial flight in Japanese Empire Waters on June 12, 1945. As Patrol Plane Commander of one plane of a flight of two United States Navy Patrol Bombers he attacked enemy installations and shipping in the face of extremely hazardous topography and weather conditions, destroying a warehouse, dock installations, two cargo vessels and numerous fishing craft. His courage and skill were at all times inspiring and in keeping with the highest traditions of the United States Naval Service.

M. R. Greer,
Rear Admiral, U. S. Navy

CHAPTER 12
—
The Bombs and VJ-Day

By the end of June 1945, the prospects for a complete Allied victory over the Anti-Comintern Pact had never seemed brighter. In Europe, Hitler and Mussolini were no more, and the Continent had been freed of its Fascist enslavement. In the Far East, Japan's Southeast Asia Co-Prosperity Sphere lay in shambles: she had been driven out of Burma, Indonesia, and the Dutch East Indies, out of Hong Kong, Malaysia, and Singapore; and in Manchuria, the last of her occupation on the Asian continent, she was facing not only the Americans, British, and Chinese, but also the prospect of a Soviet invasion as well. In the maritime South and Central Pacific, the Jap had been dislodged from Tarawa, Eniwetok, Kwajalein, Guadalcanal, and New Guinea, from Palau, Yap and Ulithi, from the Marianas and Iwo Jima, and from the Philippines and Okinawa. And in the whole of the Pacific Basin, the Japanese fleet that had smashed Pearl Harbor had been reduced to a potpourri of surface and undersea craft which collectively possessed only a miniscule nuisance value. Now, with the surrender of Germany and Italy, the Allies' combined industrial, military and naval might could be concentrated against the last remaining obstacle, the Japanese mainland itself. This would be a patent mismatch, albeit a terrifyingly bloody and destructive ordeal to which no rational government would subject its citizenry.

But the long march up the Pacific had been agonizingly difficult, wearisome, and brutal in its attrition of men and material. Without exception, our pre-invasion estimates of time requirement and casualties had been woefully short of the mark. Time after time with their backs to the wall and no hope of survival, the Jap had never considered surrender but had fought until the last defender had perished, turning every island and atoll into a dark and bloody ground. As one example, our two-week forecast for subduing Peleliu actually became three frightful months with casualties exceeding projections by a factor of ten. And following the Okinawa example, it seemed clear that we were now facing not just a military cadre but an entire nation committed to kamikaze. The judgment was uncontestable and therefore inescapable: the invasion of Japan would be the bloodiest military operation in the history of mankind, reducing Verdun and Stalingrad to mere skirmishes. There were endless estimates of the casualties to be expected, the least sanguinary being at least two million for the Allies and for Japan, fifteen to twenty million. Since recent precedent had it that the Jap would never surrender his emperor and his homeland, we on the scene could operate only on the assumption that invasion was inescapable against a fanatical foe who preferred death to dishonor. Try that in the pit of your stomach.

Everywhere the physical preparations were underway, and in the Philippines, the Marianas, Okinawa, and Iwo, the islands seemed on the verge of sinking under the weight of the massive buildup. Sleep was constantly interrupted by the incessant clamor of hammer against nail as the evacuation hospitals began to take shape, accompanied by one glorious sight—the first contingents of the nursing corps arriving on this benighted forward area. Supply, ordnance, and fuel dumps took the shape first of foothills and then mountains. On Iwo, Quonset huts replaced our tents, roads were macadamized, and liberal applications of tar reduced the sulphuric dust. And as welcome as a nurse's face was, one of the Seabees' loveliest creations were twin, hard surfaced 10,000 foot landing strips; and just in time, for new planes and squadrons were pouring in. The Army's P-51s, for example, being augmented by Republic P-47s, and we in the Navy were up to five squadrons of PB4Y-2s and eight of PV-2s, with more en route. In short, we were getting ready for the final act, no matter how long it might take.

The immediate objective of our pre-invasion strategy was to keep the southern coastline of the five major Japanese islands—from Shikoku to the northeast to Kyushu to the southwest—under round-the-clock surveillance. The first element in the achievement of this objective was the assembling of the mightiest naval armada the world had ever seen. All the principal units of our Pacific Fleet—battlewagons, carriers, cruisers, destroyers, submarines, and the whole panoply of support craft, augmented by all the British Fleet units in the Pacific, were brought together to form the 5th Fleet under Admiral Spruance's flag, or alternatively the 3rd Fleet under Admiral Halsey's flag, whose radio call name was "El Toro." Flying over the middle of that vast assemblage of naval might presented the most awesome spectacle of my career: at 1,000 feet, it was impossible to see its head or tail, and the flight time across it at 150 knots was exactly nine minutes. It was there, of course, for all the Japanese to see as it plied its way up and down the coastline, with the BBs firing their 16 inchers at selected shore targets, and no sensible Jap could fail to grasp the hopelessness of his situation. The other element of surveillance was provided by the patrol bombing squadrons based on Okinawa and Iwo. For our part on Iwo, our sectors extended from Tokyo Bay to the tip of Shikoku, the flight time consuming a wearisome 17 hours, and by the end of July our squadron strength on Iwo permitted a patrol plane to takeoff every three minutes around the clock, with our crew's down time reduced from what had been a normal 48 hours to 24. Under such flight pressure, half of each squadron was rotated every seven days back to Tinian for a week's R&R. These flights to and from the Marianas were always instructive as we noted the steady stream of convoys headed north, although the sight of the hospital ships added a grim note to the proceedings.

On Tinian we shared the airstrips with the Army's B-29s, and so we were privy to the last, and what we hoped would be the decisive element on our pre-invasion strategy: the stepping up of General LeMay's aerial offensive against Japan's major cities. Here again was an awesome sight, whether on Tinian watching those huge, sleek birds stream down the runways, or on Iwo, lying on our backs and watching what seemed to be an endless procession of their running lights heading north before we manned our own planes to rendezvous with our Dumbo subs on our air-sea rescue operations.

So there was the nub of it. The most massive armada ever assembled, cruising up and down the Japanese coast virtually unopposed, its huge guns belching out the harbinger of things to come. The 24-hour aerial surveillance of that coastline, virtually unopposed. The increasing frequency of the fire-bombing of metropolitan Japan, virtually unopposed. The convoys disgorging men and material by the day. In sum, the combined resources of the United States, Great Britain, China, and the Soviet Union inexorably closing the vice on the beleaguered Japanese homeland. Please, God, answer the prayer on the lips of every man in the area: no invasion!

But despite what to us seemed overwhelming physical evidence, we could not dismiss the presumption that General Tojo and his militarists held Emperor Hirohito in thrall as they marched to a different drummer. Trying to get inside their heads, and with the nature of the war thus far, our most persistent scenario was that they would court invasion with no hope of victory, but that they had the means and the will to make that invasion so costly that the Allies would settle for terms far less than unconditional surrender, thus at least assuaging their warrior's code of honor. As for their will, the military faction held the Japanese rank and file so firmly in its grip that they could demand the ultimate sacrifice from every man, woman, and child; in other words, they could commit the nation to kamikaze, with the near debacle at Okinawa still fresh in our minds. As for the means, our frogmen in their nightly reconnaissance of underwater costal defenses, were appalled by the diabolical nature and extent of what they found. Our air intelligence was pretty confident of its estimate that the Japs still had some 3,000 front line aircraft stashed away in caves and underground hangars, all committed to kamikaze tactics, and that they would be launched at 500 an hour against our invasion fleet, to be augmented by swarms of one-man kamikaze submarines packed with high explosives. But most worrisome of all were the constant revisions upward of Japanese strength on the southernmost island of Kyushu, our obvious initial invasion target since it lay closest to our land-based staging area of Okinawa, and making it clear that the Jap would begin the defense of his homeland at the water's edge, as at Iwo Jima, rather than inland as at Okinawa.

But for me it was not the carpentry of the Seabees that disturbed my sleep, but rather recurring nightmares centered on invasion beaches. Some nights it was Purple Beach at Peleliu, others, the sands of Iwo Jima, both of which I had trod soon after the guns had been silenced. For an aviator covering an invasion in close support, the action is too swift, too kaleidoscopic to establish any personal affinity for the human beings slogging it out below, the sanctity of airspace shielding one like a cocoon from any visceral involvement with the carnage being wrecked on the beaches. Thus there is no way for the flyer, even though he has joined in the action in his own fashion, to comprehend the grisly reality of the earthbound scene of combat; indeed, few military fliers have ever been privy to the actual results of their efforts except for the briefest of moments, later abetted by their gun cameras, or from a considerable distance. My mistake after landing on captured airstrips was then to walk through the killing ground itself.

The world holds no sorrier sight than a newly littered battlefield. The earth churned to pulp and tinctured with red— the stench of bodies blown asunder by shrapnel or crisped by liquid fire, disgorging entrails and brains. Arms and legs and bits of uniforms, rifles, small arms, ammunition belts, rations and spades and heavy equipment scattered as by a hurricane. Shibboleths to patriotism and terror—a dreary litany to insanity and final testament to man's inhumanity. The crosses in Flanders Field begetting crosses on Iwo Jima. Crosses for the victors, that is. For the defenders of Iwo, dead to the last man, a gaping ditch in the sulphuric sand gouged out by bulldozers into which bodies and pieces of bodies were scrapped by other bulldozers. For our Marines of the 3rd and 5th Divisions: a table was set up in the open air heaped high with all the dog tags that could be recovered, behind which sat an officer and a yeoman with a list of names. To the right of the table were stacked the bodies like cordwood, and to the left were the coffins in goodly supply which had been part of the invasion paraphernalia. The officer would pick up a dog tag at random, read out the name to the yeoman who would make a check on his list, after which corpsmen would pull a body from the stack and place it in a coffin, duly noting on the outside the name, rank, and serial number from the yeoman's list, which in turn was transcribed on the cross which accompanied the coffin to the burial ground. What mattered whose body actually lay under the cross; all had paid the ultimate price.

And sometimes in the aftermath, tombs of unknown soldiers, citations for bravery and censors for cowardice, equally futile, meaningless, arrogant, for who is to stand in judgment of an individual's response to madness. But in truth, Peleliu and Iwo, the Philippines and Okinawa were miniscule slaughterhouses to what must lie ahead. That was our collective nightmare.

So July settled down to a routine of watching and waiting, with our stepped-up patrols along the mainland and air-sea rescue stints when the B-29s were on the prowl, relieved by the respites on Tinian. And so with our divertissements: reading, letter writing, mail call, softball and volleyball, the nightly beer call and movie. For the gambler, there were the never-ending bridge and poker games at any stakes one cared for; as a general rule we avoided the Army fly boys like the plague since they gambled on the assumption that every deal might be their last one, and with some justification. They were so undisciplined about fuel conservation that even a routine foray to and from the mainland, though totally unopposed, was a perilous proposition. But not to hear them tell it: invariably they had shot up 25 Jap planes on the ground at Atsugi, or a couple of dozen at Choshi, or a whole raft at Osaka, and they had the film to prove it, when in reality they were only keeping the Jap camouflagers busy as they populated their air strips with dummies made mostly of straw and paper. To use the Army figures, our invasion would have been unopposed from the air. And in passing, I might relate the most useless single tragedy that I witnessed during the war. Shortly after our beautiful hard-surfaced twin 10,000 foot airstrips had become operational, the first Army P-47 squadron arrived, having somehow found its way up from Tinian. Once over the field, they went through their insane fighter break-up pre-landing drill, and in a few minutes we could spot the squadron leader on his long straight in approach to nearly two miles of landing strip ahead of him. Believe it or not, he undershot, smashing headlong into the cliff at the front end of the runway. I can only suppose that he was awarded posthumously the Distinguished Flying Cross.

Tinian was always a welcome respite because it meant, among other things, hot showers, clean beds, laundry facilities, semi-decent chow, and an Officers' Club with plenty, plenty booze. And one also rediscovered the art of conversing with the opposite sex in the nurses' compound. As for exercise, my crew preferred softball, and with Hale on third base, Moscow on the mound, and me in left field, we had a standing challenge to any air crew in the Fleet. At night, Moscow and I literally cleaned up at the bridge table, and we easily withstood the challenge from the champs of Gen. "Rosie" O'Donnell's B-29 outfit. But for us the biggest asset of Tinian was the fact that our CASHU units (Navy jargon for aircraft maintenance) were located there, the importance of which was accented by the fact that within a six-month period, *Prometheus* required three new sets of engines, which accounts for the fact that in all our operational flying, I only lost one engine in mid-air.

But regardless of the divertissements, the specter of invasion never left our deeper consciousness. And its imminence began to take a measurable form when Buzz Lefever, our squadron skipper since Johnny Muldrow's ghastly demise at the Marcus Island fiasco, was summoned along with other squadron commanders to our Air Staff headquarters on Tinian presided over by the alcoholic Admiral Greer, whose cohorts had dreamed up the Marcus mess. Happily on this occasion this group of incompetents was not formulating policy but was merely passing along the word from higher echelons as to our unit's tactical role in the scheme of invasion. Our assignment was tersely worded: We were to fly a kamikaze barrier between the Japanese mainland and the invasion fleet, with tactical specifics to be issued just prior to D-Day. The objective was clear enough, if not the division of labor: all the Allied air power in the forward area—Navy, Marine and Army—were to stop the kamikazes short of the fleet. In the meantime, our aerial reconnaissance was given free rein to fly inland and go after any Jap airstrip we could find. For the PB4Y-2s with our radar, we figured the best times for this would be dawn and dusk. So now we had at least some concept of what we were in for.

Then at the end of July the rumor surfaced and began to spread. We on Iwo first heard it from our units returning from Tinian, and in its vaguest form it involved the presence of some "secret weapon." The genesis seemed to have been the observance of unusual security being clamped on a small area where certain B-29s were at roost, but after that it was pure scuttlebutt and its copious misinformation. A secret weapon indeed, the only purpose of which was to hasten the Japanese surrender. What could it be? A super bomb? Why would we need a super bomb given the firebombing proclivities of the B-29s? Maybe a new kind of chemical warfare? Could we, perish the thought, be about to usher in germ warfare? Speculation was as fruitless as it was endless, but there was one undeniable result: the rising hope that the invasion might be circumvented.

As a matter of fact, something was indeed up, and all the scuttlebutt was given a singular validity on 1 August on Iwo. At about 1600 hours a small detachment of Seabees, equipped with a bulldozer and an earthmover, assembled at one of the hardpan taxiways just off the northeast end of our runway and within spitting distance of our Quonset enclave; whereupon they proceeded to excavate a hole about 10 x 10 x 10 feet, then shore up the sides of which with steel plating. This accomplished, they then rigged a block and tackle apparatus designed to lower something into the hole which was then covered with more steel plating. With the excavation completed, a platoon of Marines armed to the teeth took up sentry duty around it. Yes, something was up, and those of us who had witnessed this activity from a discrete distance could only conclude that an ultra-top-secret something was going to be stashed away in that pit. Then at 2300 hours that night an Army transport plane accompanied by a fighter escort landed and taxied up to the excavation, and when its engines were cut it was immediately surrounded by another contingent of Marines. The Jeep shuttles picking up our flight crews returning from patrol were shunted well clear of the excavation area, but some of our chaps using their night binoculars were able to make out a large white object shaped like a hugely inflated football being gingerly removed from the hold of the transport and then lowered into the pit. Although there was some disagreement as to size and shape, the consensus was that it was some kind of bomb unlike anything we had ever seen but that it was much too small to pack much of a lethal punch. Yet the hyper security told us it was something special. As Buzz laconically remarked, "I don't care if it's filled with piss so long as it gets the job done." In the event, it was not long until we got the word.

It was on the evening of 5 August during the movie, which happened to be Bogart and Bacall in "The Big Sleep," that over the PA system came the order for the PPC's (Patrol Plane Commanders) of ZEBRA Squadron to report to the Briefing Shack on the double. Buzz and the other eight of us who were on Iwo at the time piled into Jeeps and were soon in our seats in front of the Briefing podium. The Briefing Officer was terse and cryptic: ours was an Air-Sea rescue mission along a heading of 310 degrees outbound from Iwo, take-off at 0500 hours.

Beginning of the mushroom cloud after the atomic bombing of Hiroshima, Japan, August 6, 1945

"Seven Dumbo subs will be positioned along that heading at 100 mile intervals from the mainland southeast; one plane homing on the first five Dumbos and flying the normal limited search pattern at 500 feet, with two planes each for the northern most Dumbos flying one pattern at 500 feet and the other at 2,000 feet. Weather should be CAVU with calm seas. UHF Mayday frequency, so and so, Dumbo frequency so and so. You will be on the lookout for three B-29s flying up your heading at 17,500 feet, returning altitude undetermined. You will maintain radio silence throughout, to be broken only by the Dumbos, who will also dismiss you. Hope you're not needed, but in any event, good luck. Dismissed."

So we got back for the tail end of the movie, after which we alerted our crews and reported to our bunks for a few hours sleep and wondering what this was all about.

Buzz had decided that he and I would take the Dumbo just off the mainland, so at 0500 hours on 6 August 1945 we led off on a crystal clear morning, climbed to 8,000, set our automatic pilots and settled into the four hour run to our rendezvous, which in the bright sunshine came up to periscope depth for our contact, and then slid back under while we began our search pattern. Then the monotony set in, with not a sign of the B-29s nor a peep from the Dumbo as the hours dragged by. Then suddenly—at 1216 hours to be exact—the whole damn world shook, and within minutes a shock wave tossed us around like confetti. At that juncture I was flying at the higher altitude, and it was my gunner in the top forward turret who spotted it first—a huge mushroom cloud rising in the northeast and seemingly reaching up to Heaven. Buzz came up to join me and we just circled in complete ignorance and amazement. Half an hour later our Dumbo dismissed us with the message that our birds were safe and headed home to roost, and so we proceeded back to Iwo completely unaware of how much history we had vicariously just been a part of: Hiroshima.

It is impossible to describe adequately the wave of excitement that swept the forward area after the official pronouncement that the Japanese city of Hiroshima had been obliterated by the detonation of an atomic device which had been dropped by one of our aircraft which had returned safely to base. It was simply beyond our comprehension despite the efforts of the embryo physicists and chemists scattered among our ranks to explain the mysteries of atomic fission to anyone who would listen. At least we now knew what that bedfellow was, lying in that pit which had appeared so harmless at first blush. My God, what if that thing went off prematurely!! But the conviction that now pervaded everyone's mind was that the Jap, faced with such an awful weapon, would surely surrender. Before the blast, the B-29s had showered the mainland with leaflets warning of terrible things to come, an admonition generally dismissed as propaganda by the Jap military faction. But now surely there could be no dismissal of the new leaflets calling for immediate surrender. It was all over, brother, all over. But the only signal emanating from Tokyo was silenced, and nothing changed in our routine of around-the-clock patrols.

At 2200 hours on the night of 8 August, the Marine sentries around the pit were heavily augmented, and a short while later three B-29s landed on our strip and taxied up to the area now illuminated by portable floodlights. Our cantonment was cordoned off, keeping us at bay from the scene of activity, but we knew the contents of that pit were being transferred to the bomb bay of one of those Super Forts. This time it was FOX squadron that drew the air-sea rescue assignment, and at 0200 hours on 9 August, our colleagues took off on a vector considerably to the west of Hiroshima, there to be joined along the Kyushu coast by elements coming up from Okinawa. In the event, this was the turn of the major port city of Nagasaki, with the same devastating result. Our group was now celebrating on two counts—first, that this bomb had been removed from our environs, and now the absolute certainty that the Jap dementia must now succumb to the hopelessness of the situation.

What we denizens of the forward area and the Jap did not know was that we had only two atomic bombs in our arsenal, and that we had no foreknowledge that either would detonate on schedule. As matters now stood, we could only hope that for decision-making purposes in the Emperor's palace, two were enough. That was apparently the case, for after evening chow on 10 August, the word swept across Iwo like wildfire that the Japanese had surrendered. There was bedlam from one end of the island to the other: shouts of hosanna filled the air, carefully cached booze was broken out, the small arms fire sounded like a massive fireworks display on the 4th of July, punctuated by flares of every description. In such a frenzy, the only really safe place to be was under one's bunk, and at dawn some twenty-odd fatalities could be counted among the enlisted personnel. So much harsher, then, the reality that this was all a false alarm!!

In ZEBRA Squadron, the PPCs had gathered in Buzz's Quonset, and noting that no official word had yet come from on high, we sent our co-pilots to alert our air crews that the flight schedule was holding. For the four of us who had just returned from patrol and had the next day off, Buzz broke out a bottle of Scotch, saying that just in case the rumor was true, we were entitled to strike a few blows for liberty.

11 and 12 August came and went with nothing but silence from the Jap, although we were told that their diplomatic representatives were making overtures in foreign capitals regarding the terms of surrender. As it turned out, my last combat patrol was on 13 August when I led a two-plane section on a sweep of Tokyo Bay to show the flag and report on any unusual activity. Heading due north at 8,000 feet, I vividly recall checking in with each of the six Dumbos along my route with the question, "Is this trip necessary?" Each reply was a variation of "Nothing new to report, so keep your dukes up." By this time the Bay area was old hat and the apprehension considerably less than on my first foray some five months ago, but today there was no telling what to expect. Would the Jap fighters be up in force for one last agonizing show of defiance, or were they still being reserved for the B-29s? Did they even know they were on the brink of surrender? I doubted it, and I signaled Morgan to close up, and with all our turrets manned, we began a slow descent into what appeared to be pretty good cloud cover at 4,000 feet above the Bay's entrance. Indeed, the cloud cover permitted us to go down to 3,000 feet, and as we swept the Bay's periphery, our radar detected no unusual surface activity. As we were coming abeam of Tokyo itself, we suddenly burst out of the clouds into the clear sunlight. As if on signal, a shore battery opened up on us, and with the angry puffs of flak bursting around us, we pulled every inch of power we had and scrambled up into the welcome clouds, leveled off at 8,000, set our "bird dogs" on the Iwo radio beacon, and got back without further incident. The Dumbos along the way still had nothing for us.

The ZEBRA section trailing us by an hour was not so fortunate, and what happened to one of its crews is instructive about the Japanese psyche. Rogers and Wallace were jumped by ten Zeros out of Choshi Point, and although they knocked down two of them, Wallace lost his port engines and was forced to ditch in the Bay close to Yokohama. As he later related the story, he and his crew were uninjured and picked up almost immediately by picket boats which took them ashore and turned them over to a squad of Jap Marines. Given the imminence of peace, they did not know what treatment to expect, but they soon found out: they were put in chains and steel bits were inserted in their mouths and tightened until their jaws broke; then they were turned over to the tender mercies of a crowd of civilians which had gathered to watch the sorry spectacle, and these kindly souls laid on them with clubs and bamboo poles, beating them to the ground almost senseless and then, men and women alike, took turns urinating on their prostrate bodies, and tormented them all through the night. But the next morning, with the announcement of their surrender, these same worthies in turn prostrated themselves before our battered crew, removing their chains, bandaging their hurts, all the while jabbering about the glories of Japanese-American friendship. What kind of people are these?

Given all that had happened during the last seven days, the announcement of the cessation of hostilities on 14 August 1945, Japanese time, was almost an anti-climax, but the collective sigh of relief from all the potential participants in the now-scrubbed invasion could be heard around the world. Never in the whole history of organized warfare had two bombs saved the lives of so many. Our most immediate activity was the writing of letters home assuring whomever that we were still among the living; and to that end Buzz mustered the squadron, congratulating everyone on his performance to date but warning against the relaxation of flight discipline and silly screw ups since we still had a lot of flying to do before we saw the home fires burning.

Privately, I could only reflect on the sorry prospects of my generation on that graduation day from The University of Texas of June 5, 1938 as we ruminated about the kind of world we would be stepping into—the prospects of which seemed dreary at best—and take enormous pride in the fact that we had rid the world of three of those then extant dictators—Hitler, Mussolini, and Tojo—with now only one to go. Little did I know how difficult that was going to be.

Editor's Addition

For his experiences and deeds in combat, in both the Atlantic and Pacific theaters of the war, Jack was awarded the Distinguished Flying Cross and four Air Medals. In addition he received other medals recognizing his participation in various theaters of the war. A letter from the Department of the Navy delineates his awards.

> Mr. John Hubbard was entitled to the following awards: Distinguished Flying Cross, Air Medal (w/3 gold stars), World War II Victory Medal, American Defense Service Medal, American Campaign Medal (w/1 bronze star), Asiatic Pacific Campaign Medal (w/3 bronze stars), Naval Reserve Medal, Discharge Button, and the Honorable Service Lapel Pin (Ruptured Duck).
>
> Mr. John Hubbard was also entitled to the Philippine Liberation Medal, which is a foreign award.

Adventures with a Historian 253

Medals awarded to John R. "Jack" Hubbard

The following are verbatim copies of the citations that go with the Distinguished Flying Cross and four Air Medals (one medal and three Gold Stars in lieu of the other three). (Thanks is here given to U S. Congressman Michael Burgess and his office for their assistance in obtaining these citations from the U.S. Naval Archives in St. Louis.)

- -

The President of the United States takes pleasure in presenting the DISTINGUISHED FLYING CROSS to LIEUTENANT JOHN RANDOLPH HUBBARD UNITED STATES NAVAL RESERVE for service as set forth in the following CITATION: "For heroism and extraordinary achievement in aerial flight as Pilot of a Patrol Bomber in Patrol Bombing Squadron ONE HUNDRED EIGHT in action against enemy Japanese forces in the Iwo Jima and Japanese Empire Areas from March 25 to August 7, 1945. Participating in twenty search missions during this period, Lieutenant Hubbard contributed materially to the success of his squadron, and to the infliction of damage on hostile installations. His courage and devotion to duty in the face of antiaircraft fire were in keeping with the highest traditions of the United States Naval Service."

For the President,
/s/ James Forrestal
Secretary of the Navy

Copy to:
Pers 101-101h
Public Relatinsm (sic), Navy Dept.
Ref: ComAirWing 18 Ser 0195 dtd 22 Sept 1945

The President of the United States takes pleasure in presenting the AIR MEDAL to LIEUTENANT JOHN RANDOLPH HUBBARD UNITED STATES NAVAL RESERVE for service as set forth in the following CITATION: "For meritorious achievement in aerial flight as Patrol Plane Commander of a Patrol Bomber in Patrol Bombing Squadron ONE HUNDRED EIGHT in action against enemy forces in the vicinity of the Japanese Homeland on June 12, 1945. Participating in a mission over enemy-controlled territory, Lieutenant Hubbard attacked hostile harbor installations and shipping despite extremely hazardous topographical and weather conditions and in the face of hostile antiaircraft fire to destroy a warehouse, dock installations, two large vessels and to damage other cargo ships and numerous fishing craft. His skill and courage were in keeping with the highest traditions of the United States Naval Service."

          For the President,
          /s/ James Forrestal
          Secretary of the Navy

Pers 101-101h
Public Relations Navy Dept.
Ref: Misc 51-J ComFltAirWing 18 dtd July 21, 1945

The President of the United States takes pleasure in presenting the GOLD STAR in lieu of the Second Air Medal to LIEUTENANT JOHN RANDOLPH HUBBARD UNITED STATES NAVAL RESERVE for service as set forth in the following CITATION: "For meritorious achievement in aerial flight as Pilot of a Patrol Bomber in Patrol Bombing Squadron ONE HUNDRED EIGHT in action against enemy Japanese forces in the Iwo Jima and Japanese Empire Areas from March 25 to April 22, 1945. Participating in five search missions during this period, Lieutenant Hubbard contributed materially to the success of his squadron, and to the infliction of damage on hostile installations. His courage and devotion to duty in the face of antiaircraft fire were in keeping with the highest traditions of the United States Naval Service."

          For the President,
          /s/ James Forrestal
         Secretary of the Navy

Pers 101-101u
Public Relations Navy Dept.
Ref: ComFltAirWing 18 Ser 0195 dtd 22 Sept 1945

The President of the United States takes pleasure in presenting the GOLD STAR in lieu of the Third Air Medal to LIEUTENANT JOHN RANDOLPH HUBBARD UNITED STATES NAVAL RESERVE for service as set forth in the following CITATION: "For meritorious achievement in aerial flight as Pilot of a Patrol Bomber in Patrol Bombing Squadron ONE HUNDRED EIGHT in action against enemy Japanese forces in the Iwo Jima and Japanese Empire Areas from March 25 to June 7, 1945. Participating in ten search missions during this period, Lieutenant Hubbard contributed materially to the success of his squadron, and to the infliction of damage on hostile installations. His courage and devotion to duty in the face of anti-Aircraft fire were in keeping with the highest traditions of the United States Naval Service."

For the President,
/s/ James Forrestal
Secretary of the Navy

Pers 101-101h
Public Relations, Navy Dept.
Ref: ComAirWing18 Ser 0195 dtd 22 Sept 1945

- -

The President of the United States takes pleasure in presenting the GOLD STAR in lieu of the Fourth Air Medal to LIEUTENANT JOHN RANDOLPH HUBBARD UNITED STATES NAVAL RESERVE for service as set forth in the following CITATION: "For meritorious achievement in aerial flight as Pilot of a Patrol Bomber in Patrol Bombing Squadron ONE HUNDRED EIGHT in action against enemy Japanese forces in the Iwo Jima and Japanese Empire Areas from March 25 to July 9, 1945. Participating in fifteen search missions during this period, Lieutenant Hubbard contributed materially to the success of his squadron, and to the infliction of damage on hostile installations. His courage and devotion to duty in the face of antiaircraft fire were in keeping with the highest traditions of the United States Naval Service."

For the President,
/s/ James Forrestal
Secretary of the Navy

Copy to:
Pers 101
Pers 101-H
Public Relations, Navy Dept.
Ref: COMAIRFLTWING 18 Ser 0195 dtd 9/22/45

- -

During his naval aviation career, Jack wrote many poignant and descriptive letters home to his parents and family. It seems fitting that a few excerpts be included at this point as he concludes the narratives of his experiences during the war, for they provide tender descriptions of the depth of his emotions and outlook for the future.

Jack wrote frequently to his parents during the war. The following is an excerpt from a letter written immediately after the cessation of hostilities in which he describes the mood of the combatants now that they can relax.

> I don't have to tell you how we here feel. There has been no marked celebration; rather it is like heaving a great sigh of relief, and the smiles are everywhere. No handshaking, no backslapping, no shouting, no party. But there is no mistaking the universal joy.
>
> I made my last raid Monday, revisiting some of my old haunts over the Tokyo area, and very luckily came through without a scratch. The skipper got a few holes in his plane. But one of the most satisfying hops I've ever flown (and my last operational hop of this war) was yesterday when I was covering the B-29 strike, and I located a P-51 pilot who had been shot down and brought one of our destroyers to his rescue. I say that's the way to end a war! I would rather have saved that boy than to have sunk a carrier.

On July 23, 1945, Jack's sister, Louise Hubbard Paine, gave birth to the first of three sons. The parents named the child John Randolph Paine in honor of Jack and also in honor of a brother of the child's father, both uncles bearing the given names of John Randolph. The following, written sometime in August 1945, is taken from Jack's response to Louise after being notified of the blessed event.

> Whenever the tide runs out, leaving the damp sand of my soul, whenever the night is fitful with the horrible anguish of yesterday, when today has no meaning with tomorrow remote, I read your letter and find peace. For me no more precious document ever existed. I'm grateful, not simply because I am alive, but because I can now see you and your Randy. It took courage equal to any I've seen in battle to bring forth a son into this world of ours, and the contribution you and Roz have made makes mine seem even more meager. I have thanked God many times for the way he treated you.
>
> It is when I consider the future of your boy that I am nigh overcome by the enormity of the task that lies ahead. The firing has ceased, for a time, at least, but the destruction, the human flotsam, the misery and pestilence, the atom still abide. I know I speak in generalities, but it is up to us to leave something better for those we leave behind. Yet this time there will be no separation, for ours is now the same kind of battle. Surely the stakes are high enough, for it is Randy who stands to win or lose.
>
> Kiss Randy goodnight for me.

On the occasion of his mother's birthday, October 12, 1945, the war is over, and Jack is waiting for the opportunity of returning home. His letter to his mother on that day speaks of his optimism and also of the strength he received from her during the dark days of the war.

> Today is your birthday, and it must be the happiest you have known in years. How long it has been since you could look this day upon a world at peace! How long it has been since you could think of me without a fearful mother's anguish.
>
> I wish I could say that all this is my doing, that the peace is my present to you. That is the only fitting gift I know. Instead I can tender only my meager contribution to the winning effort, and tell you that only because I am your son did I stand my ground. When every inner resource of strength had been drained, and it seemed that I must break and run, it was the thought of you that kept me going, that kept *Prometheus* in the air and brought her back again. So it is that the medals I bring home are yours more than mine, and I shall pin them on you.

Part III

—

Academic, Athletic, and Politically Eclectic Adventures

Jack (center) with former USC baseball players,
Brent Strom (#40) and Tom Seavers (#41)

CHAPTER 13

The Road Not Taken

U.S. Navy planes form up for their pass over of the Japanese surrender ceremonies in Tokyo Bay, 2 September, 1945

VJ Day ending World War II found me on Iwo Jima, a Lieutenant Commander in the U.S. Naval Air Corps, USNR, a Patrol Plane Commander of a four-engine, land based heavy bomber attached to Squadron VP-108. For the last six months we were herding Japanese fleet units north of the Marianas towards the Japanese mainland. In February we had covered the invasion of Iwo, and in April, Okinawa. Now we were back on Iwo, from which our daily patrols kept the Jap coastline under 24 hour surveillance. At night we would fly underneath the massive B-29 strikes against the major cities, establishing contact with our network of submarines in air-sea rescue operations. In July and early August we were flying a kamikaze barrier between our 3rd and 5th Fleets and the mainland, preparing for the invasion, but after Hiroshima and Nagasaki, it was over.

My squadron was not relieved until mid-October, which gave us the opportunity to assist in air cover for the formal surrender in Tokyo Bay on the USS *Missouri*. I then flew the old bucket of bolts to Hawaii, turned her in, disbanded the crew, and lay on the beaches for a week. I then hitched a ride on one of our aircraft carriers, the *Wasp*, disembarking at the Naval Air Station in Alameda, California, located on the east side of the San Francisco Bay. I reached home in Denton, Texas, on Thanksgiving Day. When I walked into my family home on the campus of TSCW, my father greeted me with, "You're late. Where have you been? Dinner was two hours ago!"

I was now facing the classic dilemma: a choice of careers. Before the war, the decision had been made. My father was a professor of English literature and a college administrator, so campus life with all its attendant intellectual accoutrements had been my pleasant lot. A well-stocked gene bank had apparently provided me with the requisite wits; I was our high school valedictorian, and I had been elected to Phi Beta Kappa after my junior year in college, which I had entered at age 15. So nature and environment, had conjoined to indicate clearly a life in academe, and all that was left was the selection of an area of concentration, which for me became modern British history and then to complete my dissertation. But that was before the war.

The problem on this Thanksgiving Day of 1945 was myself, and the Navy—and flying. My four and a half years in this war had been arduous, demanding, replete with challenge, not the least of which in my case was learning to live with fear. I had heard my share of shots fired in anger and had acquitted myself reasonably well, now wearing with considerable pride on my tunic under the wings of gold the Distinguished Flying Cross, four Air Medals, and a host of campaign ribbons. I had found the Navy an absolutely first class organization, and I enjoyed wearing the uniforms, the discipline, the camaraderie and membership in its elite branch. And now as inducement to stay in as a regular, I was promised an immediate spot promotion to the rank of Commander. But for me an even more compelling argument was the flying. Although I had never before been off the ground, I took to naval aviation as to the manor born, effortlessly, joyfully, and nothing I had ever experienced gave me more pure pleasure.

One has only to read young John Gillespie Magee's glorious sonnet, *High Flight* to know the enchantment of the skies.

> *Oh! I have slipped the surly bonds of earth*
> *And danced the skies on laughter-silvered wings;*
> *Sunward I've climbed, and joined the tumbling mirth*
> *Of sun-split clouds - and done a hundred things*
> *You have not dreamed of - wheeled and soared and swung*
> *High in the sunlit silence. Hov'ring there*
> *I've chased the shouting wind along, and flung*
> *My eager craft through footless halls of air . . .*
>
> *Up, up the long delirious, burning blue,*
> *I've topped the windswept heights with easy grace*
> *Where never lark, or even eagle flew –*
> *And, while with silent lifting mind I've trod*
> *The high untresspassed sanctity of space,*
> *Put out my hand and touched the face of God.*

Nor had I ever before engaged in any activity wherein I felt I could perform as well as any man alive. So here I was at age 26, single, in buoyant health, full of piss and high purpose and a beckoning honorable career in which I had already proved I belonged and which had lived up to its promise that "the pay is good and the life is glamorous." How could I desert that which I most enjoyed?

In the end, and after long discussions with my father, the obvious compelling argument emerged that it would be senseless, almost criminal to squander my already considerable academic investment. Finish the dissertation, get the Ph.D. and then decide. The Navy would wait. And in the year or so it would take, I could maintain my flying proficiency as a "week-end warrior" in a Ready Reserve squadron being established at Naval Air Stations all over the country, one of which was at Grand Prairie, Texas, a stone's throw from Dallas. So I was discharged from active duty in February 1946 and drove straight away to Austin and The University of Texas, arriving on the opening day of the Spring semester after an absence of nearly six years. The History Department was still housed in old Garrison Hall, and inquiries revealed to my relief that my old mentors were still on the faculty, with Professor Gutsch now serving as chairman.

I found him in his office where I had gone to pay my respects, still in uniform as per my reserve status. He gave me a most cordial welcome, not only remembering me but even my M.A.

thesis on the *Anschluss*, the German invasion of Austria in 1938 which I had written under his direction. After a brief résumé of my activities *ad interim*, I asked him if I might write my doctoral dissertation with him.

"I'll be delighted to have you," he said, reaching for a book on his desk and handing it to me, "but in the meantime you have two sections of the Freshman survey of Modern Europe and your first class meets in one hour. That is your text book." To my stunned protestations he replied, "Look, this campus is literally swarming with returning services people, financed by the G.I. Bill of Rights, determined to get their degrees, and we simply don't have enough faculty to cover the classes. You've got an M.A., a good one since you did it with me, plus two advanced years beyond that. So you're elected." His eyes twinkled. "It's really quite simple, Jack. "All you have to do is stay one chapter ahead of the students, and by the looks of the ribbons you're wearing, you should be brave enough to face a classroom."

So that's how it happened that in less than an hour of my having stepped on the UT campus that January of 1946 I found myself not only reinstated as a Ph.D. candidate but also a Teaching Fellow at the handsome stipend of $110 per month. The real reward, however, was the teaching experience itself, and I became so enamored of it that my career dilemma resolved itself.

My dissertation topic was the Spanish Civil War, 1936-1939, as a prelude to the greater conflict, but since Francisco Franco and his regime—who had come to power with the bloody aid of the Nazi Luftwaffe and the Condor Legion and had remained in dictatorial control of Spain until his death in 1975—would not permit research on that subject within Spain, I had to shift my emphasis to the British reaction to that crisis, which necessitated a research trip to the U.K.

In February 1948, Walter Richardson, Professor of British History at the Louisiana State University (LSU) in Baton Rouge, took a sabbatical leave to London, and I was invited to come over from The University of Texas to cover his classes for the Spring semester and the Summer Session to follow. I was then a Teaching Fellow at UT in the middle of my Ph.D. dissertation on British Public Opinion and the Spanish Civil War. It was a fortuitous arrangement for all concerned, for Lucy, my lovely wife of a year and a half, and I occupied Walter's apartment which was very close to the LSU campus; and upon his return in September, we then went to London and occupied his digs there while I finished my research at the Public Record Office, the British Museum, and its newspaper and periodical repository at

Colindale. It was also useful in other ways in that it broadened considerably my range of teaching, and it provided the opportunity to become well acquainted with the History Department at Tulane University, just 75 miles down the road in New Orleans, and where I was subsequently appointed to my first regular professional position.

In September we sailed from New York on the *Nieu Amsterdam*, the ship on which I had taken her maiden voyage in June 1938 for my first European venture following my graduation from The University of Texas. But this was ten years and one world war later, so I was eagerly anticipating this return to the continent and anxiously wondering what if anything remained of those places I so happily remembered from that golden summer a decade ago.

In London, the scars left by the blitz were a shock to the system, but among the people of that great metropolis was a buoyancy, an *esprit*, a confidence that was nowhere in evidence in 1938. Then there was a sense of dread as each evening at dusk the householders came out into the streets and faced the east, listening intently for the drone of German warplanes. Now there was a sense of quiet confidence, camaraderie, and pride born of having suffered together, surviving and winning the victory. And all this despite the utter drabness of austerity which had descended upon the land with its endless queues mandated by shortages of food and drink and consumer goods and all the niceties of life so well deserved by a courageous people after their long ordeal.

Our living quarters consisted of a modestly sized bedroom and bath in a flat in Bedford Court Mansions just off Tottenham Court Road north of Oxford Street and very close to the British Museum. Our hostess/landlady was a bouncy, cheerful Swiss matron, Mrs. Bucher, who, with her unwed daughter, Betty, owned and operated a beauty salon in the Strand. We took breakfast and dinner with them, and their principal hairdresser, Pop Palmer, was a frequent visitor for drinks after closing the shop. In brief, it was a very comfortable and compatible arrangement, and we were grateful to Walter Richardson for putting us on to it.

My first order of business was the British Museum, and armed with a letter of introduction from Professor Gutsch, I called on its Director, Mr. Francis, an exceedingly cordial man in his late 50s, with graying hair and twinkling eyes and a total lack of pomp. After explaining to him what I was up to and the materials I needed, he led me into the famed circular Reading

Room, where scholars from around the world had labored for so many years and where, incidentally, Karl Marx had written his famous treatise. The encircling wall was lined with card catalogues, which in their archaic format were Greek to me until Mr. Francis explained the system, showing me how to fill out a call slip and taking me to the desk in the center of the room where one turned in the slip and awaited the book. "For Americans," he observed, "this requires some patience, for we are not automated and it takes time, but we will find what you ask for." With that he invited me to his room for tea, and he told me an amusing story.

At the beginning of the war, he had gathered together all the cherished documents at the Museum and the Public Record Office such as the Magna Carta and had taken them to Washington and our Library of Congress for safekeeping. When the war was over, our Librarian of Congress, Mr. Luther Evans accompanied them back to London where a small ceremony was held at the entrance of the Museum marking their return. This was the first visit of Mr. Evans to the Museum, and after the formalities, he asked to see the procedure for securing a book from the Reading Room. After selecting a title from the catalogue and being instructed how to fill out the slip, he took it to the call desk, and Mr. Francis told him the item would appear in about twenty minutes. "Twenty minutes," Mr. Evans exclaimed, "My God, what a system!" To which Mr. Francis replied, "My dear sir, the Library of Congress may have the system, but we have the books."

Before I left, he penned a note to his opposite number at the Colindale depository for newspapers and periodicals and instructed me on how to get there: take the Northern Line of the Underground at Tottenham Court station and get off at Colindale, where you have a three minute walk from the station. Nothing could have been simpler, and I discovered that Colindale was only one stop from Hendon, which had been London's principal aerodrome before Heathrow and was now an RAF station. Lucy was going to help me with my note-taking, and our routine was now established: 10 to 4 at either the Museum or Colindale, with a break for a pint and a pub lunch.

London at the time was the headquarters for the U.S. Navy's Eastern Atlantic and Mediterranean Command under Admiral Richard L. Conolly, and since I was still actively flying in the Ready Reserve, I had brought some uniforms and my flying gear with me in the hope that I could pick up some flying time with some of our units scattered about. So I checked in with Admiral

Conolly's staff which was housed next to our Embassy in Grosvenor Square, and I was delighted to find that we had aircraft based at Hendon which were used for supply and personnel runs to the Continent and to transport the Admiral to our key bases in the Mediterranean such as Port Lyautey in North Africa, and yes I would be welcome as a co-pilot on some of these missions. As for my two-weeks active duty which I had failed to do thus far in 1948, perhaps that could be arranged, and in the meantime, I was welcome to join the Officers Mess and Commissary. Eureka—the answer to my austerity!

So there began another routine, since on Saturdays I was on call as co-pilot on the run from Hendon to Orly Field in Paris in one of our Beechcrafts or Douglas R4Ds (DC-3). It was about a two hour flight each way, and we would generally have a long lunch at a restaurant which fronted as an active black market just outside of Orly, where we could exchange dairy products and cigarettes for steaks and oranges, among other things, much to the delight of Lucy and the Buchers. As for the two weeks active duty, it came in dramatic fashion in the form of the Berlin Air Lift of June 1948 to May 1949.

When the Russians denied land access to Berlin, our reply was to establish air corridors to supply the city, and business really picked up for the British and American Air Forces, with the British corridor from Hendon to Hamburg to Tempelhof, and the American from Hendon to Rhein-Main to Tempelhof. And in order to say that it participated, the Navy dispatched two transport squadrons of four-engine Douglas R5Ds from Guam to Rhein-Main. I was again welcomed as an extra hand who gave regular pilots the day off, and so back and forth I went with mundane cargos of potatoes and coal but in a game that was eminently worth the candle.

In the meantime useful contacts were being made in London to help me with my research project. Because of the shortages in Britain, some friends in New York had given us a packet for an English friend of theirs whom they had met during the war. It contained paints and pigment, and fine brushes and was meant for one Angus Irwin, proprietor of the *London Illustrated News*, who had been an aviator in the Fleet Air Arm during the war and had been for a short while stationed in Washington. I contacted him shortly after reaching London and we arranged to meet for lunch at the Roya1 Aero Club at 119 Piccadilly, not far from Hyde Park Corner. He was a tall, handsome chap some ten years my senior, and aided by the similarity of our flying backgrounds, we hit it off well together. He maintained a flat in London, but he lived with his wife, Inez, in a solid country home at Preston, near Hitching, north of London, where he spent most of his time pursuing his hobby of painting. We saw each other with some frequency, and Lucy and I spent several splendid weekends with them. When he learned that we would be in London for about six months, he insisted that he sponsor me as an overseas member of the Club, which was speedily arranged. And so it was that subsequently for many years, the Royal Aero Club became my London home away from home.

The Club Secretary was an amusing Irishman who had been an RAF fighter pilot, and his administrative assistant was a well-formed but slightly over-ripe young woman in her mid-30s, Heather Pilkington, who had a croaking voice like a frog made even huskier when she laughed, as she frequently did. The three of us would sometimes have a pint in the office or at a nearby pub in Shepherd Market, and in due course I learned that Heather was the mistress of John Lloyd, head of the London bureau of the Associated Press. When I told her about my research interest in the late Spanish Civil War, she said that I ought to know John, who had many contacts in Parliament, the Foreign Office and elsewhere, and he might put me in touch with someone who was an expert on Spain and the British relationship and who might have even been there during the war period. So saying, shortly thereafter she arranged for us to have drinks with Lloyd at the AP offices in Fleet Street. He was a tall saturnine sallow man, who looked like he had a perpetual hangover, but he was cordial enough, and he offered to provide introductions for me to several people, one of whom in the Foreign Office later was extremely helpful. Heather left us to attend to some personal matters, and towards 6 p.m. Lloyd said, "I'm going across the way to the Press Club to have a drink with the best newspaper man in Fleet Street. Would you like to come along?" I did.

That newspaper man was Robert Lindsay, a ruddy faced, slightly built Scot with a receding hairline, a booming voice, a wealth of good humor, and, as I was soon to learn, a hollow leg. He worked for Reuters, and he enjoyed a wide reputation as a shrewd observer of things national and international, and who has earned the confidence of highly placed persons in both areas because of his good judgment and discretion. (Lindsay later became the chief press officer of General Gerald Templar when he commanded the British forces that stamped out the insurgency in Malaysia.) Lloyd explained to Lindsay my reasons for being in London, and since I would rely heavily on newspapers and periodicals, would he be good enough to instruct me in the mysteries of the British press and their controllers.

Over the course of the next week, Lindsay did just that, conducting a seminar for me that was the most instructive I have ever attended and which convened daily at 6 p.m. at the Press Club bar with his fixture of whisky and splash. The first sessions dealt with press bias. Unlike the United States where every newspaper claimed political objectivity where there was none, in Britain the political position of every leading daily was clearly delineated and well known to the reading public. For example, just to the right and to the left of center were the two most serious journals, the *Times* and the *Manchester Guardian*. As one went further to the right, he encountered the *Daily Telegraph* and the *Daily Express*, thoroughly Tory in their leanings, and on to the *Daily Mail* which was outrageously reactionary. Moving to the left after the *Guardian* was the liberal *News Chronicle* and then the unabashedly Labourite *Daily Herald*, both of which were owned by the Cadbury brothers, which earned them the sobriquet, of the Chocolate Press. At the extreme left was, of course, the *Daily Worker*. So if one wanted a fix on the whole spectrum of public opinion on any given day, he would have to read the editorial pages of nearly a dozen newspapers.

"Take, for example, your particular interest, the Spanish Civil War. If you read our press, you will find that the Franco forces were either bloody Fascists or the restorers of order, and that the Republican forces were either bloody Communists or the defenders of democracy. Now, it is up to the poor historian to sort out this mess, but don't blame it on us ink-stained wretches. I think that if you dig deep enough, you will find some legitimate basis for all these allegations."

My next lessons involved the proposition that for most of the owners and editors of the morning and evening London dailies, their primary mission was to entertain rather than instruct, and especially was this true in these ragged days of austerity, so there were no apologies for a tabloid mentality. As an example of this, Bob showed me the comic strip "Jane" in the *Daily Herald*. Jane was a lusciously formed blond who was daily depicted in some form of dishabille getting into or out of bed or shower. And on one day of the week, and very occasionally on two, she was shown in the buff, but no one except the editor knew which day this might be, so one bought the *Herald* every day so as not to miss this revelation of nature in all its glory. Then Bob told the story of Sir Stafford Cripps and the Austerity Budget of 1948.

Jack and bride, Lucy, in front of the Little-Chapel-in-the-Woods, 1947

Cripps was Attlee's Chancellor of the Exchequer, and the day before he announced his Budget that demanded even more belt-tightening by an already strapped British populace, he called in the editor of the *Daily Herald* and demanded that he publish the Budget *verbatim* since it would impinge on the lives of every person in the land. The editor reluctantly consented, and the next day Sir Stafford left to attend a week-long economic conference in Paris. On his return he rang up the *Herald* editor to ask how the budget measure had been received.

"Sir Stafford," the editor replied, "I did as you requested and printed every word of that budget, in five daily installments on the front page. I am sorry to report, Sir, that our circulation has fallen so drastically that I shall have to undress Jane every day for a week to get it back up."

In sum, our relationship with Bob and his wife, Trudy, became firm and fast. When Lucy and I returned to Texas, little did we know we would be seeing them again so soon.

Editor's Addition

During the timeframe Jack covered in this chapter and the next, (1945—1950), three very personal and emotional events occurred in Jack's life.

The first event was Jack's marriage to Lucille (Lucy) Luckett of San Angelo, Texas in January 29, 1947. He had met Lucy upon his return to The University of Texas where she was also a student, and they were married in the Little-Chapel-in-the-Woods on the campus of TSCW. Under the inspiration and direction of Jack's father, the Little-Chapel-in-the-Woods was built as a sanctuary for private meditation and prayer. TSCW students and faculty participated in the design and construction of the chapel. Dedicated in 1939 by First Lady Eleanor Roosevelt, the Little-Chapel-in-the-Woods has since been named one of Texas' outstanding architectural achievements.

Eleanor Roosevelt flanked by Jack's parents
at the dedication of the Little-Chapel-in-the-Woods, 1939

Upon his return to civilian life, Jack, like most of his brothers in arms, put the war behind him to focus on a future free from tyranny. For reasons unknown, Jack made little mention in his memoirs of the whereabouts and futures of the surviving members of his original Anacostia Volunteer Group (AVG).

When AVG member, George Charno, Jr. learned third hand of the death of Jack's mother, Alice Bertha Altizer Hubbard, (the second significantly personal event), he knew Jack would be grieving. When she died on August 14, 1947, following a long and painful bout with cancer, Charno sent the following letter to Jack. Of the many expressions of sympathy tendered the family, the editors feel that Charno's poignant eloquence embodies the depth of Jack's love for his mother and should be included with his memoirs.

August 19, 1947

Dear Hub,

> Dad received a letter today from Dean Nowatny with the very sad news that your mother had passed away.
> From the many long discussions together these past few years about practically everything in the world, I know how close you were to her and how deeply you loved her. Knowledge of this, and of you and your capacity for sensitive, human feeling, makes poignant your deep grief. I know you are now reflecting all the cherished moments of her living days, moments of happiness and laughter, tragedy and sacrifice, all intermixed and confused, but combined in a portrait of her and of the qualities you adored in her as a person, as well as a mother.
> When I think now of you, and of the things you have told me of your family, and the face, the enthusiasm and courage and high purposes, with which the Hubbards face the world, I have, too, a mental picture of your present reflections. Your friendship, and my vicarious acquaintance with all of you, is expressive of the life she led.
> Surely the sole function of any human life lies in the creation and preservation of values—that activity alone can give it significance. And so when I mark your approach to the matter of living and your record of activity, and recall the great deal you have told me of your father's devotion and service to his high profession, I necessarily realize how

deeply your mother's life affected those she touched and how she imparted to them and imbued them with a knowledge and appreciation of the profound values we treasure. Truly, then, her life was full and creative and genuinely significant.

Unfortunately each of us must continue after they who have created and enriched us have ceased. The burden is not lessened by an awareness that they have given us all we need to continue their heritage. If, in the name of a sincere friendship, I could now absorb some of the weight of your grief I would do so. You, and your family, have my heartfelt sympathy at your great loss, and your grief is mine.

Sincerely,

/s/ George Charno, Jr.

The third event occurred in early February 1950 when Jack's father announced his retirement as president of TSCW. This announcement coupled with his father's birthday caused Jack to pen the following letter in which he revealed a career aspiration that would eventually materialize but in different places.

Dear Dad,

Here I am late again with best wishes on your birthday, but since you are a veteran of my manifold lapses, I'm sure my delinquency occasioned no surprise. Nevertheless, Lucy and I tender our sincere hope it was a pleasant day for you.

The announcement of your retirement evokes a mixture of emotions. I can't say "Regrets", for there can be none in face of the stature of your accomplishments. Nostalgia, perhaps, and a wish to turn back the clock to the day you and I turned the corner in that Model T onto Oakland by old Capps Hall and I got my first glimpse of my future home. Remorse, too, when I consider how far removed I am from that cherished if secret ambition of being able to succeed you and somehow repay the many blessings that your abilities provided. A sadness that the end of every pleasant era must impose, yet a sadness so rich in memories that the retrospect which departure entails makes taking departure an almost welcome event. And therein lies the real measure of your contribution, for thousands of persons who read of your announcement looked back to the days of their association with you and your school and took pride in the keen sense of loss which they felt. And I am one of the proudest of them all.

These have been days of hectic activity for me. I go to press with the dissertation tomorrow, and of course I shall not rest easy until it is in the hands of my Committee. I was in Austin between semesters working with Riker and in the library. He was most complementary, but I feel sure that he remembers only a fraction of what he has read. I had a pleasant visit with George and got to meet his newest love, who seemed quite nice. Incidentally, both your sons will be up for degrees at the same time, D.V. I tried to call you, but the ice storm prevented my getting through.

When you get time, let me hear your future plans. Austin would be my first choice, but there is a great deal to be said about New Orleans.

Devotedly,

/s/ Jack

CHAPTER 14

Hi'yuh Tex: Scandinavian Research Adventures

With my Ph.D. finally in hand and after teaching stints at Texas and Louisiana State, I found myself ensconced as a boot Assistant Professor at Tulane University in New Orleans, Louisiana. It is, of course, an accepted axiom in the academic lexicon that if one would successfully negotiate the slippery pole of promotion, he must publish as well as teach. There are to be sure stars on each side of that equation, but the surest path to success is a happy equilibrium. Teaching for me had become almost second nature, but I had only the relatively modest research efforts required for my advanced degrees to indicate that I had any promise in that direction. Selecting the diplomatic background of the Second World War seemed foreordained by my recent experience, for I wanted to know with far greater definition why and how such an event took place which had consumed my generation. And in this endeavor I was shortly to encounter a surprising opportunity from a totally unexpected source.

As an undergraduate at The University of Texas, one of my roommates had been a young man of modest means from Sherman, Texas, George Franklin Smith, Jr., a brilliant student, an accomplished jazz musician (trumpet) and an ardent bibliophile whose destination was Law School. He was two years ahead of me, and we had met when I pledged his fraternity, Delta Kappa Epsilon. The year I got my M.A., he finished Law School with highest honors and passed the bar exam with flying colors. But the Depression was still with us, and George could not find an opening in any of the better law firms. Finally he was taken in by a small but decent establishment in Dallas as a kind of glorified clerk. When I got to Washington that summer I importuned Commissioner Splawn to see if he could find a slot for George, which he managed to do in the Bureau of Internal

Revenue. So George came up and joined the Revenue Service, and we became roommates again. When war came, he too enlisted in the Navy and spent the duration in the Judge Advocate's Office, specializing in tax matters, performing brilliantly, and gaining a wide acquaintanceship in the Washington legal fraternity. When the war ended, he accepted a partnership in one of D. C.'s best legal tax establishments.

Axel Wenner-Gren

One day George called me (in New Orleans) from Washington saying that he, accompanied by an associate counsel, was coming to New Orleans to consult with local lawyers concerning a tax matter centered in Louisiana, and could we have dinner together two nights hence. I managed to reserve the 1840 Room in Antoine's revered establishment for the gathering; there were eight of us, and I sat next to George's associate, Harold Weill, of the firm Leon, Weill and Mahoney of New York City. During a traditional feast of Creole specialties—Oysters Ellis, Crayfish Bisque, Pompano en Papillote, and Cherries Jubilee—we chatted about my relationship with George and our now divergent careers, about the quality of life in New Orleans, and about things in general. He then asked me about the courses I was teaching at Tulane and if I had any particular research interests. When I explained that I was much concerned with the diplomatic background of the late war, he put down his fork, looked at me with some astonishment and exclaimed, "What a remarkable coincidence! I have something I think would be of enormous interest to you. Do you know anything about Axel Wenner-Gren, the Swedish financier and industrialist?" When I replied that the name meant nothing to me, Harold began to brief me.

It seems that Axel Wenner-Gren—variously known as the Swedish Viking for his erect bearing and imperious mien, or the Swedish Croesus—as one of Europe's wealthiest men, began his empire with the acquisition of Kelvinator, maker of the Electrolux refrigerator and other appliances, and parlayed this into steel manufacturing, automobile production, and Bofors munitions, among other things. We all remember that Sweden, although technically neutral in both World Wars, was a strong supporter of Germany and a steady supplier of the necessities of war such as steel, ball bearings, and munitions of various kinds to help offset the Allied blockade. The market place had it that Wenner-Gren maintained a close relationship with Krupp and amassed still another fortune in helping to rearm the Wehrmacht after Hitler's rise to power. What we know for a certainty is that Wenner-Gren and a Swedish colleague, Birger Dahlerus, were frequent visitors to Germany after 1936 and were accepted into the highest circles of the hierarchy being, for example, favored house guests of Hermann Göring at his fabled shooting parties. Wenner-Gren met his wife-to-be, Margaret, a disappointed opera singer from Kansas City, on one of his Atlantic crossings aboard that wonderful old Cunard liner, the *Mauritania*, and after their marriage they began to establish self-contained residences with all the necessities for gracious living, including complete wardrobes—to obviate the need for tons of luggage on their travels—in such places as Rome, Paris, New York, Cuernavaca, Mexico—where he had installed the national telephone system—and the entirety of Bear Island in the Bahamas. Their principle abode, however, was a stunning townhouse in Stockholm, and they also had acquired from the bankrupt estate of the "match king," Otto Kruger, the lovely Häringe, formerly the summer palace of the Swedish royal family, some sixty miles southeast of Stockholm in a stately forest fronting the Baltic.

Mention of Bear Island in the Bahamas caused my mind to reflect back to America's early participation in World War II and to my experiences in anti-submarine warfare along our Atlantic coast. When the United States entered the war against Japan and Germany our first battle zones—after Pearl Harbor—were our Atlantic and Gulf coasts. From Portland, Maine, south around Florida and then north up the Gulf to the Mississippi River delta, German submarines ravaged our costal shipping. I was stationed at the time at our Jacksonville Naval Air Station in Jacksonville, Florida, and my first taste of combat was in flying anti-submarine patrols from dusk to dawn in our old PPY's, for the Germans never surfaced in the daytime. A blackout was ordered for the entire Atlantic coastline, but our national indiscipline at that stage of the game was so great that few people paid any heed to the lighting restrictions, with the result that the U-boats would surface close to shore and wait for our lumbering merchantmen to glide by silhouetted against the shore lights, and sink them with their surface guns, thereby preserving their precious torpedoes. I remember our perfect fury as we flew up and down the coast at the number of communities with their lights ablaze. It was like shooting fish in a barrel, and in short order there was not a stretch of beach from Maine to Florida that was not covered with oil slicks and debris from our sinking tankers. An example of German arrogance and efficiency were the remains of three tankers who were shelled and sunk with their sterns stuck out above the shallow waters of Jacksonville beach, in shooting distance from our Air Station. We later used them for bombing targets on our practice missions.

What I did not know at the time, as Mr. Weill continued his narrative, was that Bear Island was allegedly being used as a refueling and replenishment depot for the German submarines. When our Naval intelligence belatedly cottoned onto this proposition, Wenner-Gren was declared *persona non grata*, his considerable assets in this country were frozen, and his name was added to our blacklist of aliens sympathetic to the enemy. His protests were furious: if Bear Island was being badly used, it was without his knowledge; in all of Europe no greater champion of peace could be found, nor anyone who had tried harder to avert the tragedy, and he could prove it. He would sue the United States for the restoration of his good name. Although he was told by his advisors that the United States Government could not be sued without its consent, he was determined to pursue his appeal as far as the law would permit, and to that end, through his principal merchant banker in London, Boy Hart, and the head of his legal section, John Max-Muller, Wenner-Gren engaged Leon, Weill and Mahoney to prepare his defense.

"We filed suit," said Harold, "but of course it was never acknowledged and the whole thing became moot with the end of the war. Our point man in all of this was Eddie Leon. The crux of his argument was the undisputed fact that in 1938 and 1939 Wenner-Gren and his colleague, Birger Dahlerus, were engaged in some kind of shuttle diplomacy between Berlin and Downing Street carrying confidential, hand written memos between Hitler and Göring and Neville Chamberlain, trying to find some rapprochement that would avert Armageddon. In Leon's elaborate brief, two of those memos are replicated—one from Göring to Chamberlain, and Chamberlain's reply—and there is reason to believe that there are several more which Wenner-Gren photocopied and still keeps in his possession. An interesting part of all this is that the negotiations were apparently conducted without the knowledge of either Foreign Office, so no record will be found in either's official files. Needless to say, Wenner-Gren is still mightily galled by the whole affair and he recently produced an apologia titled *In Search of Peace* in which he manages to convince himself of his shameful treatment. So the next time you're in New York why don't you look in on us, talk to Eddie, and examine what we've got. If it piques your interest and you want to pursue it further, then we'll talk about the parameters of discretion."

For me, this conversation was worthy of the meal, or vice versa. I was excited. Not that I thought I had stumbled upon some vast treasure trove of revelation that would forever alter the judgment of history on these men and events. Rather, a snippet, a vignette, a fresh and different insight on the way the principal actors handled affairs of state at that critical time—surely worth an article in the *Journal of Modern History*, one of our professional Bibles. So at the Thanksgiving break I went to New York.

Harold was as good as his word introducing me to Eddie Leon and the three of us talked for a while, they giving me more details of the Wenner-Gren persona and bringing me up to date on his current activities. After getting my agreement to the ground rules they ushered me into the library and handed me the Leon brief. Yes, I could make notes for my own use, but there was to be no replication of the text and no attribution of the source. In sum, the central thrust of the brief was to portray Wenner-Gren as a man dedicated to peace—not as a Nazi sympathizer. True, he had easy access to the likes of Göring, and Goebbels and Hess, and even at times to the Fuhrer himself, but he only wanted to use these relationships to try to convince Chamberlain that these were reasonable men worth dealing with. The French would then follow suit. Surely the villainous, traitorous Poles were not worth a *cause celebre* when the real threat to the security of western Europe lay farther east in the guise of the well-armed Soviet hordes. England, France, Italy, and Germany must form a solid phalanx that Stalin would not dare attack. As an earnest promise of German sincerity, Hitler was prepared to offer Britain a 25-year non-aggression pact which would bind the two nations in mutual cooperation instead of deadly enmity.

It was all very plausible and well-argued, but there was nothing new in it. What interested me most were the replications of the two handwritten notes. The first was from Göring to Chamberlain, introducing Wenner-Gren and Dahlerus as trusted couriers who enjoyed the confidence of the Fuhrer; and the other was Chamberlain's reply welcoming this new and desirable means of direct communication. So there had indeed been a contact established between heads of state through the agency of the two Swedes. But how extensive it became, what views were exchanged, whether, for example, the subject of the Russo-German pact was ever raised, and what evidence still existed to support any of this were queries only Wenner-Gren could answer. The question for me was, "Would he?"

These were things that Harold and I discussed at lunch. I was in his debt for having whetted my appetite, but the brief itself was not much use to me except for its indication that interesting things may have occurred. Did he think that Wenner-Gren would be willing to receive me, knowing in advance the topic of discussion? I would meet him anywhere at his convenience, although I imagined that Stockholm would be best, since any extant documentation would most likely be kept there.

Harold replied that he hadn't a clue, but he said, "I'll be happy to make enquires through our London associates who know him far better personally and see him with much greater frequency than we do."

A slim chance at best, but it had already been an interesting experience.

It was about a month later that Harold called. There was a slight prospect that a meeting with Wenner-Gren might be arranged, but the operative word was "slight." The proposition was that if I should find myself in London in the reasonably near future I was to contact Boy Hart and John Max-Muller. If they agreed with Harold's assessment of me, they might be able to take the process a step further.

"In other words," said Harold, "my English colleagues are under orders to examine you thoroughly and report their findings to Stockholm. I hope you don't mind."

On the contrary, it seemed quite reasonable to me. If I were one of the world's richest men and a total stranger came knocking on my door, I would want to know everything there was to know about him before I offered my hospitality.

"It matches," I said to Lucy. "When the semester is over, why don't we just happen to find ourselves in London in early June."

That notion suited her right to the ground, for she was an inveterate traveler. On our research trip the previous academic year of 1948-49, we had fallen in love with London. If the Swedish venture came to naught, there was still the British Museum, Collingdale, the Public Record Office, and a host of friends and acquaintances. I so informed Harold, and we made plans to return to London.

On the first of June 1950, with my papers all marked and the grades turned in, we locked our apartment and headed for the airport. We had dinner in New York with Harold and his wife, and embarked the next day on what we thought was the most gracious old liner ever to ply the oceans, the *Ile de France*.

In London we took up lodgings with our landlady of the previous year, a Swiss matron who had a comfortable flat off Tottenham Court Road. The next morning with some temerity I made the telephone call to one John Max-Muller, Esq. Again Harold had paved the way. Max-Muller's tone was cordial and we made an appointment for lunch next day at one of his clubs, the Oxford and Cambridge. There we had a pre-prandial pint and a passable lunch which enabled me to lay down the party line. I was not a freak, nor a journalist, nor a sensationalist of any kind. There was not the slightest opportunity for any pecuniary advantage to me in all of this. I was not a spy, government or industrial. I was simply a professor of European history, much concerned with pre-war diplomacy, and after my fortuitous meeting with Harold Weill, now keenly interested in the role Mr.

Wenner-Gren may have played. If he was content to live with the stigma placed on him by my government and had decided to turn his back on the whole affair, so be it. If instead he still sought vindication, no amount of protest fulmination, or apologia on his part would do the trick. If he had profited from Hitler's rearmament, he could stand on his belief that the only use for those arms would be against the Soviet Union. If after the war began, he was sympathetic to the German cause, he was merely reflecting Sweden's historic position. The only issue I was concerned with was the scope and sincerity—and the evidence thereof—of his efforts to preserve peace.

That night Lucy and I had dinner with Max-Muller and his gorgeous wife at the Jockey Club, and we were invited for Sunday lunch at Boy Hart's country place. So apparently we had successfully cleared the London hurdle.

The following Wednesday I got the word. Would we be willing to travel on to Stockholm, but without any firm agreement on a meeting. I must remember that because of Wenner-Gren's far-flung business interests, he traveled a great deal and often at very short notice. He would, however, try to fit me into his schedule. So off we went, believing that we were at least one step nearer the end of the rainbow. At our hotel, I received a message from Wenner-Gren's private secretary informing me that Ambassador Procopé and his wife would pick us up for dinner at 8 p.m. Procopé, Hjalmar Procopé—that was a name I was vaguely familiar with if, indeed, he was the same person. As Finland's ambassador to the United States in the Thirties, he had cut quite a social swath in Washington and gained considerable notoriety when he presented a check to Secretary Hull repaying in full Finland's World War I debt—the only nation so to do. Of his present role I had no idea.

At the appointed time we met them in the lobby. There was no doubt about his identity. He was tall, handsome, suave, soft-spoken, a touch of grey in his hair—every inch the diplomat. And she, Brita, a Swedish beauty, much younger than he, also tall, willowy, perfectly proportioned with ash blonde hair, dancing brown eyes, and an infectious smile. They were obviously hurdle number three, and quite the most dazzling couple Lucy and I had ever met. They took us to Stockholm's Old Town to a subterranean grotto once used by pirates but which now housed the celebrated restaurant Den Gyldene Freden, where we managed the schnapps, beer, wine lobster, and goose with appropriate social grace.

Hjalmar on retiring from the Finnish Foreign Office had been retained by Wenner-Gren as his advisor on international relations. Brita was his second wife whom he had married right after the war. They divided their time between Stockholm and Helsinki.

As expected of me, I explained my presence and interest—no pecuniary interest, no axe to grind, no notoriety, simply a historian's concern with the record. It would be an impartial analysis that might or might not redound to his benefit, but I believed I represented his one best chance at vindication.

For his part Procopé told me more about the vast and complex Wenner-Gren ventures, his charitable gifts, his overseas capital ventures, such as in Mexico. He related the courtship of Margarita, the marriage, his utter devotion to her and reliance on her judgment—especially about people—despite her problem, which would become obvious to us should we ever meet her.

"He is not an easy man to deal with," concluded Hjalmar. "If he agrees to see you, he will act the bully, and if he succeeds in cowing you, you are through."

Brita offered to take us on a sight-seeing junket the next day, and on that pleasant note, we ended a really agreeable evening. Certainly we had not lost any ground.

Brita took us on a shore cruise down the Baltic to Saltzjöbaden, a lovely area where the Stockholm affluent maintained summer cottages on the meandering waterways. One must have endured the unrelieved gloom of a seemingly endless Scandinavian winter to appreciate the Nordic ecstasy when the sun reappeared, warm and lasting and glorious. All along the estuary we could see the bare bodies lounging on the cottage verandas, or diving and splashing in the water as though not to waste a single ray of light. It was a pleasant excursion, and I confess wondering at the sight of Brita in such circumstances. When we returned to our hotel late in the day, the note was awaiting us—lunch with the Wenner-Grens the following day. We had passed the fourth test.

The Procopés drove us to the town house, massive as a fortress, where we were met by a manservant in frockcoat who ushered us into a sunny atrium just off the main receiving area, dominated by an elegant, curving marble staircase leading to the upper floors. We stood sipping aperitifs as Brita described the carpeting, the period furniture, the tapestries, the art work, and the beautiful flower arrangements seemingly everywhere. Lucy claimed she was as nervous as I, but I doubt it. After a little while, we heard noises at the top of the stairs, and they, the

Wenner-Grens, began their descent, Margarita in the lead. It was slow business, for she clung tightly to the balustrade while measuring every downward step, and two footmen stood nervously at the bottom rung—just in case. But she made it.

Steadying herself, and with her husband by her side, she walked as straight as she could directly towards me, held out her hand and said, "HiYuh, Tex, welcome to our house," and turning to Lucy she said, "I understand you're also from Texas. Good girl. I've always liked Texans because they're full of piss and vinegar. They brag a lot, but that's part of their charm. Meet my husband."

Axel Wenner-Gren was as imposing as advertised: tall, erect, a wonderful shock of snow white hair, and the most piercing blue eyes I have ever gazed into. Nor did his appearance belie his studied formality and aloofness, with my thanks for our presence evoking no response whatsoever.

At lunch I learned something about Swedish dining protocol—but not enough. Ambassador Procopé was seated on Margarita's right and I on her left, with our wives in the same order beside our host, who uttered exceedingly brief words of welcome. It was then that the guests raised their glasses in a toast to the hostess and then to the host, "Tak, gemucht, tak, tak," and then during the course of the meal, each person toasted the others individually, our glasses kept replenished by the butler and his alert staff. Margarita mercifully bore the brunt of the conversation, regaling us—to the acute discomfort of her husband—with the story of their courtship aboard the *Mauritania*, saying that when she first laid eyes on the Viking, she knew he was for her and that he had very little to say about it. She also very quietly spoke a few words of encouragement to me, saying not to let him bully me, and I felt that somehow I had a friend at court. The luncheon ended with our host saying, "Professor Hubbard, if you will be in my office at four o'clock this afternoon, I shall speak to you."

Paying heed to alleged Swedish precision, I was in his office at the appointed time, where I was ushered into a small reception area in which his book, *In Search of Peace*, was on display, along with a current issue of *Life* magazine. The wine at lunch had worn off and I was just plain nervous. I waited and waited, and if his strategy of delay was designed to increase my unease, it certainly worked. It was nearly five o'clock before he fairly burst into the room, fixing me with those eyes as he paced up and down, red in the cheeks, and almost shouting, "Why do people keep pestering me? The newspapers are after me, the magazines, your Voice of America, and now you! Why, not two months ago *Life* offered me a million dollars for my story, and I laughed at them. I have said everything I want to say in my book, and that is enough. So why should 1 say anything to you, Professor?"

It was a heavy salvo but not as bad as I had feared, for he had ended his tirade with a question and so had given me at least, an opening. I blessed my rehearsals in New York, London and here with the Procopés, so my rejoinder was almost by rote. My only interest as a professional historian was a dispassionate examination of the diplomacy preceding the war. I had no pecuniary ambitions whatsoever, for my findings would be published only in historical journals. It was my understanding that he had worked diligently to preserve the peace by acting as a go-between between German and British principals in a last ditch effort to avert war, that he had in his possession certain documents now invaluable because they would never be found in any official archive since the negotiations he was privy to had been conducted outside the purview of either foreign office.

"Despite your efforts, sir," I continued, "the war did occur, but the war itself is not my concern. What I need to see is every shred of evidence in your possession of the Hitler, Göring and Chamberlain exchanges and your role therein. And there is the possibility—although obviously I can guarantee nothing—there is the possibility that my investigation may turn up facts that might help dispel the allegations about your true sympathies during the course of that war."

"Those allegations," he roared, "are a pack of lies fomented by your damn government! Let me tell you, young man, that I don't give a damn what your country thinks of me. I have operations all over the world, and no man is held in higher regard by the international business community. So I couldn't care less about opinion in the United States and especially those liars in your State Department!"

"Sir," I replied, "I understand your position perfectly well, and a man of your stature can easily brush aside those innuendos and accusations. But I would be terribly mistaken if they did not bring pain to Margarita, who so obviously adores you, and for her sake I hope I might turn up something useful as a credible third party. Your associates have attended to my legitimacy else I would not be in this room with you today. You know that I have no axe to grind and that I threaten no one. So in the last analysis, what have you got to lose by allowing me access to a small part or your life?"

He was about to make a rejoinder but apparently thought better of it. All he said was, "I'll think about it," and he walked out.

Lucy and I had dinner with the Procopés that evening, and I related my ordeal, confessing to my dissimulation in suggesting that I might come up with something that would allay the suspicions of his Nazi sympathies. The Ambassador would not even hazard a guess at Wenner-Gren's decision, merely reiterating the obvious: he was a man of strong convictions and could be stubborn as a mule. The answer, however, was not long in coming. The next morning Lucy and I received a handwritten note from Margarita inviting us to be house guests for a week's stay at Häringe.

We were collected by Margarita in her chauffeured Rolls, where she sat surrounded by flouncy pillows and with two of her adored poodles at her feet. As we drove through those glorious Swedish fields and forests bathed in sunlight, she explained the occasion for this sojourn in the country. Häringe, we were reminded had been the summer palace of the Swedish royal family. After it had reverted to private ownership, Axel had acquired it from the bankrupt Kruger estate and presented it to his wife as her twenty-fifth wedding anniversary present. This week it was to be the site of the annual meeting of the various national directors of Electrolux. They and their wives would be housed in the main castle, but we would be most comfortable in the newly constructed guest apartments in the rear of the castle proper. While the high-powered discussions by the business types were going on, our companions would be the First Secretary of the American division of the Swedish Foreign Office, the young Carl Henrik Pedersen and his *tres jolie* wife, Ingeborg, and her sister, Brigette, who was visiting them. The Procopés would join us on the week-end.

"And tomorrow," she continued, "will be a special day for Sweden."

Tomorrow, we learned, would usher in the kräftor season, when that unbelievably sweet and succulent Baltic crustacean ended its spawning season and became available in the marketplace, with flags raised all over the land depicting the red shell fish on a white background.

After some two hours we turned onto a wide, tree-lined avenue at the end of which appeared the long, white facade of the palace, set amid formal gardens ablaze with geraniums set against the green background of a thick forest—a picture post card come alive. We were met in the courtyard by the chief of the household staff who helped Margarita gingerly from the car and into the palace entrance. Our luggage was whisked away and Lucy and I were led by an attractive matron through a ground floor corridor to a rear entrance which opened onto a latticed passageway dripping in gladiolas to the new apartments two on each side and all detached. We were ushered into the first one on the right and found ourselves amid sheer unadulterated luxury— a sitting room in dark paneling with a huge fireplace, two spacious bedrooms with enormous baths, a small dining area off a complete kitchen, a bar stocked with every imaginable brand, and a mammoth Electrolux refrigerator where the schnapps and beer lay chilled, along with fruit juices, milk, mixers and the inevitable Coke. Our hostess on parting hoped we would be comfortable, and I am afraid my reply was that we would do our best. A maid appeared to unpack our luggage, and everything that was remotely soiled or wrinkled disappeared. Just beyond the apartment were two swimming pools, one with heated fresh water and the other fed by the frigid Baltic, and adjacent to them was the log cabin containing the saunas.

When we were alone, I said to Lucy in utter disbelief of our surroundings, "Honey, I don't know how this will all turn out. I've said everything I can say, and at least we've gotten this far. So from here on in, let's pretend that we deserve all this, and enjoy." With that, we opened a bottle of champagne.

Shortly thereafter, the Pedersens, with Bridgette, arrived. Never have I met three more handsome and vibrant people, and the rapport was instantaneous. We were all about the same age and endowed with equally high spirits. It all added up to a simply unforgettable week what with swimming, hiking, exploring, drinking, good conversation, tennis, and saunas with that mandatory ghastly dip into the Baltic. I realized that Carl Henrik was not there just to amuse us; he was to keep his eyes and ears open to detect any sign that I might not be what I seemed, in particular to discern any role that I might have in the government that was anathema to my host. Fair enough, and since there was nothing to hide I could, for better or worse, be my natural self. Indeed, in our long conversations together, it was I who was the learner.

Dinner that evening was an unpretentious affair: just the five of us in the informality of the Pederson suite, soup, cold cuts, potato salad and fresh fruit served by a butler and two maids to the accompaniment of a splendid white wine and champagne. Breakfast the next morning was prepared to order in our individual kitchens and served to us in bed. What luxury, but I was baffled: I had never seen or heard any of the staff come and go; they simply appeared and disappeared as if by magic. It was later that Carl Henrik, who had been a guest before explained that there was an under-ground passage connecting the apartments with the main establishment, and the entrance was through what I had taken to be a closet door in the kitchen. With this little matter cleared up, Lucy and I began to anticipate the event of the day—the inauguration of the kräftor season.

At noon a butler collected the five of us and led us into the lower reaches of the palace to a subterranean oval dining room in rustic decor with rough-hewn tables and well-padded chairs arranged in two tiers around an open hearth fire place in the center. The effect was that of a country tavern with a seating arrangement that enabled everyone to see everyone. On the tables were crystal decanters of chilled schnapps in buckets of ice, and the whole room was festooned with kräftor flags. In a few moments Margarita entered—slowly and unsteadily—in the company of the directors' wives, the men still being in session upstairs.

After the introductions, Margarita with some assistance was seated with Carl Henrik on her right and me on her left. After drinking the toast he proposed to our hostess, she declared the season open. We each then donned the huge bib which had been placed on our plate, and the feast began. First came a most divinely seasoned creamy kräftor bisque, followed by great silver platters of cold baby lobster in the shell. Washed down by ice cold beer, nothing ever tasted more heavenly, and one welcomed the interruption of a skoal to gather strength for another assault on those sublime crustaceans. After an hour of this I had reached my limit, so I was stunned when Margarita announced that it was time to proceed upstairs to the dining room for lunch.

The dining room maintained that standard of elegance that one had learned to expect in these surroundings. It was a long, tapestried room illuminated by chandeliers whose central feature was a magnificent oaken table down the middle of the room which could be lengthened or shortened according to the number of persons to be accommodated. This luncheon was the first time that all the guests at Häringe had gathered together, and the table was thus set for 30 people, 15 to a side. The same seating arrangement pertained, with Carl Henrik on Margarita's right and me on her left, with our wives seated by our host. But what astonished me was a sight I had never seen before and shall probably never see again: behind each chair stood a serving man or woman whose sole function was to see that his diner lacked for nothing. Really, now, who is going to believe this?

After the opening toasts, Margarita confided in me that I was to expect only light fare after our bout with the kräftors. It was light, all right, opening with chilled gazpacho, followed by mounds of diced filet migon moistened with a delicate version of béarnaise, white asparagus with hollandaise, and a green salad followed by a sorbet. After the dishes had been cleared for dessert, Mr. Wenner-Gren made a speech of welcome, saying how pleased he and Margarita were to have us all together and hoped we would enjoy our visit and each other, etc. etc. etc. All the while I was wondering how Carl Henrik would reply, since he was seated as the guest of honor, but when our host finished, there was silence. Wenner-Gren sat staring at me, and I looked quickly at Carl Henrik, who gave me a little flick of the head. My God, it suddenly dawned on me—I was the respondent. In my fluster I began to mumble something about the graciousness of our hosts, and what an unexpected pleasure is was for Lucy and me to have been included in such distinguished company, and how we would always cherish this experience, and thank you very much. I must have looked as foolish as I sounded, and the applause was just barely polite. Thankfully dessert was served immediately, during which Margarita turned on me with what I can only describe as a low hiss.

"Damn you, Tex, you're not very smart. And to think of all those good things I said about Texans. Obviously nobody told you, but I thought you would have figured it out by now. In Sweden, the guest of honor sits to the left of the hostess because there he is closest to her heart. At dinner tonight I'll give you another chance, and don't you dare make an ass of yourself—and me!"

The afternoon was given over to a long nap and then rehearsal. Carl Henrik apologized for not having explained the protocol and assured me that redemption could be gained. Gained it was, because that night I was ready. When my turn came, I talked about the community of nations and the interdependence of mankind as represented by the various nationalities at this table; about healing the wounds of the last war through such agencies as the Marshall Plan; about the grave menace to western Europe of the Soviets under Stalin, and how our policy of containment and the Cold War must be won; and how one man in this room had stood tall in his early recognition and denunciation of that menace; and finally I think I invoked divine providence to bless Sweden, the Wenner-Grens and

Electrolux, and please join me in that toast! It was a triumphant *tour de force*, but there was a sad note: by this time Margarita was out of it and beyond hearing anything I said, and amidst the applause for me, her husband and a butler helped her from the room. The best thing for me was that I did not have to occupy the seat of honor again.

In our daily contacts, Carl Henrik and I became comfortable with each other, and without badly stating it, the feeling grew that we could share and respect our confidences. On Wednesday afternoon after another light lunch, we took a long walk into the forest behind Häringe, found a quiet glade and sat amidst the green ferns to smoke a cigarette. I recited the scenario of my presence here and my objective, and I asked him to tell me just what kind of man I was dealing with. "Smart," "able," "driven by ambition," "opinionated," "stubborn," "ruthless," "controversial" were some of the words he used. There was no doubt that he had greatly admired Hitler and the Nazi movement. There was no doubt that he enjoyed a personal relationship with the Nazi brass, particularly with Göring and Hess, and that he was a fixture at Göring's shooting parties. Given his stature in international finance, his selection as a go-between to London came as no surprise. How many trips he made and with what messages are not certain, but there is no question of his reception by Chamberlain.

Now, being a messenger is one thing, but being an honest broker for peace is quite another. Did he, for example, ever argue with Göring and even Hitler that if the Red menace was to be stopped, then rapprochement with Britain was vital, even to the point of easing pressure against Poland? And in London, did he plead with Mr. Chamberlain that the great danger to Western Europe was Stalin, and to stop him a rapprochement with Germany and Italy was essential, even to the point of minimizing the guarantee to Poland? What was his opinion of the Molotov-Ribbentrop agreement: was it a shrewd bit of *real politik* to give Stalin a false sense of security, or was it evidence of Hitler's decision to crush Poland? In other words, did he actively try to influence decisions and events? Or did he merely carry back and forth scraps of paper? In the opinion of the Swedish Foreign Office, he merely did the latter; but even if he had done the former, what difference would it have made? So the official view had it that the only thing instructive about the whole exercise was that Chamberlain resorted to such a bizarre means of communication. The fact remained, however, that no one had yet been privy to Wenner-Gren's record of the affair, so there might indeed be something that I would find useful—if I ever got to see it.

As for his activities during the war, there was no doubt about where his sympathies lay or that he made immense profits from his traffic to Germany of finished steel, ball bearings, automotive vehicles, and sundry munitions from Bofors. Bofors, to be sure, was not Krupp, but at the time it did produce the finest anti-aircraft weaponry extant. Still, these activities did not brand Wenner-Gren as a criminal, for he was acting solely within the context of Sweden's official position of neutrality. A neutral can trade—or not trade—with whomever it chooses.

It should be remembered that Sweden's stance was consistent with her policy during the First World War, when all Scandinavia remained neutral. True, Sweden's sedulous cultivation of the new German Reich after 1871 had made her one of Germany's principal trading partners, and it was natural that she should have profited to a far greater extent than her neighbors during the 1914-1918 conflict. The British naval blockade may have sealed off the Baltic from the North Sea, but it was never able seriously to impinge on cross-Baltic traffic.

The Second World War, however, imposed a wholly different set of circumstances on Scandinavia. To begin with, when Russia invaded Finland during the Winter War of 1938, Sweden again declared her neutrality, and a British proposal to send a relief expedition overland through Norway and Sweden to aid the beleaguered Finns was abandoned because of Sweden's refusal to grant transit to the BEF. So on the one side, Finland lay beaten and battered. On the other side, both Denmark and Norway were subsequently invaded and occupied by the Nazis. So Sweden now stood alone, neutral and untouched, and prospering from her trade with Germany. In the end, after the war, all this earned for the Swedes the bitter hatred and unmitigated scorn of her neighbors, all of whom had been ravaged by the war while Sweden stood there fat and happy. (I well remember, for example, when Lucy and I were refused a table in a little bistro in the Tivoli Gardens in Copenhagen until someone pointed out to the proprietor that we were not Swedes.)

"So in that sense," continued Carl Henrik, "Axel Wenner-Gren is simply a victim of the opprobrium heaped upon his nation as a whole. Believe me, it is not pleasant to be hated, to be branded as a pariah by your neighbors, but in terms of national self-interest, which is every country's primary concern, after two World Wars, you will not find a single war grave on our soil. What you will find today is the most complete and humane system of social services ever devised by any nation. As the saying goes, 'You pay your money and you take your choice.'"

For the rest of the week it was fun and games for the five of us. Each meal was a culinary treasure, and the sauna blessedly relieved our systems of the abundance of champagne. One aspect of the hospitality we enjoyed never ceased to amaze me: each evening when our beds were turned down, if the seal had been broken on any bottle at the bar, it was replaced by a fresh one. Since my speech-making was over, I was always seated at meal time opposite Ingeborg, several places removed from the center of attention, while Lucy sat opposite Carl Henrik in the other direction. And another thing I learned is that skoaling an individual in Sweden is serious business. If I raised my glass to Ingeborg, then throughout the toast, I was expected to gaze as deeply into her eyes as humanly possible. And God, what eyes; I could feel them throughout my system. Nor was she loathe to reciprocate, and it was a wonder we ever managed a bite of food. But when I noticed that Lucy and Carl Henrik were not doing badly, my conscience, such as it was, subsided.

The climax came on Saturday night with a black-tie dinner in honor of the directors and their wives. The Procopés had driven up and we were delighted to see them, although he did not, look particularly fit. During the course of the festive meal I tried desperately to convey to both Ingeborg and Margarita how much I would miss them, but "Tak, gemucht, tak, tak" is hardly the language of love. Although it was a long affair, Margarita managed to sit it out, and with some grace, and we were all relieved when she took her leave. Indeed, after the coffee and brandy, everyone dispersed rather quickly, and it was then that Wenner-Gren asked me to join him in his office upstairs.

He offered me a chair and went to his side of the desk on which reposed an oblong carton made of thick cardboard. He opened the lid and pushed it over to me.

"Professor," he said, "I am taking you at your word. I asked my secretary to put together all the material in my possession which might be even remotely useful to you. As you can see, he has arranged the file in chronological order, and behind each date you will find everything pertinent to that time frame. I checked through it all this afternoon before dinner and I found it complete except, unhappily, for two of the most important transmissions from Berlin to London. Now don't be alarmed for I know exactly where they are—in my strongbox in Cuernavaca. Now it so happens that within a fortnight, Margarita and I will be opening our residence there for a lengthy stay; she finds her life much easier to manage there than in Sweden. So if you will give me back the file, I shall take it with me so I can include the missing documents."

I was at once elated and apprehensive. "Sir," I said, "I am so excited and grateful, but wouldn't it be just as simple for me to take the file now so I can begin to digest it, and when you get to Cuernavaca I could come down and collect the missing parts?"

"No," he replied, "What we have here is an incomplete file, and if anything should happen to me on the journey to Mexico, it would be useless to you. I am an orderly man, and I insist on handing to you the complete *dossier*. I will call you from Cuernavaca and you can come down and even stay with us for awhile, which I much prefer, but if that is inconvenient, I could send the file to you by special messenger."

Upon my assurance that I would appear in person on receipt of his telephone call, he closed the file, extended his hand, and wished me well in my endeavors. I, in turn, thanked him again for his gracious hospitality and for his willingness to cooperate, expressing my hope that I would turn up something useful for us both. I bid him good night and left his office empty handed.

In retrospect, I still wonder if I should have sensed that this would be the last time I would ever see or speak to the Steel Blue Viking.

Our adventures in Scandinavia, however, were not yet over. For background, we need to go back in time to our brief sojourn in London while on our way to Sweden. When Lucy and I stopped in London on our way to Sweden, we had a happy reunion with Bob and Trudy Lindsay, and in the course of it, Bob told us he has just returned from the first of a series of assignments to Finland to report on the progress of their preparations for holding the 1952 Olympic Games.

The award of the games to Finland had come as a great surprise, and serious doubts had been voiced in many quarters about that tiny nation's ability to host successfully such a complex extravaganza. And apart from the games, the venue posed other disturbing questions. Because of the lingering bitterness of the Winter War, and the Berlin Airlift, and now the Cold War; and because the Soviets had not participated in the 1948 Games in London, this would be the first direct confrontation between the Soviet Union and the West since World War II. Could the Iron Curtain be breached with impunity? Could little Finland, living cheek by jowl with the surly Bear be a truly neutral host, or would she be forced to turn the

Games into a Russian circus? Then there was the more mundane question of whether Finland would have in place in time all the necessary physical installations, and how she would find accommodations for the flood of visitors. These were the kinds of things Reuters was interested in, and Bob was to make periodic progress reports.

In his recital, I had never seen him so enthusiastic about any topic; he had been enchanted by Finland and its people, and his first impression was that they would be ready. And he told us of meeting a remarkable woman, Anne-Marie Snellman, widow of a Colonel of the Finnish army killed in the Winter War, who was now Chief of the small Associated Press Bureau in Helsinki.

"Her husband was apparently an authentic hero," continued Bob, "and she knows everyone worth knowing. She's not beautiful, but she's a real smasher!" And then he planted the seed. "Helsinki is an interesting city, and it's only an hour by air from Stockholm. Since you are going to Sweden anyway, why don't you pop over and take a look?" Good question.

This was, of course, before we had met the Procopés, but, later during one of our conversations with them in Stockholm, I broached the topic, saying that since we had come so far and were now so close, we thought it would be a shame to return home without having visited his native land. He, of course, agreed, saying that he would book our hotel and see to it that we received VIP treatment. When I asked him if he knew Mme. Snellman, he said he had only a casual, social relationship with her since he had not spent much time in Helsinki for the last several years.

"Everyone knows of her," he added, "but I doubt if many people really know her. Gossip has it that she is probably the most influential and powerful woman in Finland," he added enthusiastically. It was a sobriquet she well and truly merited as the long-time mistress of Urho Kekkosen, the storied Prime Minister who so ably steered his country between the twin shoals of dependence and defiance in his relationships with Stalin.

So that is why, after the Saturday night debacle at Häringe, Lucy and I found ourselves the next day on a FINAIR plane bound for Helsinki.

The airport abutted a beehive of activity, for adjacent to it a new airfield was being constructed, with bulldozers and hundreds of workers laying out longer and stronger runways to accommodate the heavies expected in 1952, and a commodious new passenger terminal was taking shape. Our hotel, which had once set the standard for elegance, was wonderfully comfortable.

It was Sunday, and we spent the rest of the afternoon, strolling around the city, which at this time of the year had almost perpetual twilight.

On Monday morning I telephoned Mrs. Snellman; I had letters of introduction from Lindsay and Lloyd and a note from Procopé, and Bob had already alerted her to our arrival. She invited us to lunch, and we taxied to her commodious flat, decorated with soft shades of brown, with a mélange of memorabilia dominated by a large picture of her late husband in uniform, a striking figure. She was of medium size and height in her mid-50's, with brown hair whisked with gray, lively brown eyes, rosy cheeks, and a firm set to her jaw. She exuded energy and her carriage and demeanor indicated a self-confidence that was at the same time attractive and formidable. She had converted part of her apartment into a fairly sizable office, where we were invited to sit and join her in a pre-lunch schnapps.

She was a graduate of Helsinki University, and her affluent parents had provided her with the means to travel extensively, so she knew the major world capitols and had visited much of the United States. She had begun a career as a free-lance journalist before meeting her husband, and after losing him had joined the Office of Information in the Foreign Ministry, where she remained throughout World War II. Afterwards she had struck out on her own, and on a London visit, she had met John Lloyd, who persuaded her to join the Associated Press. So here she was, trying to get organized for the demands of the Olympic Games.

When I told her briefly about my aborted research in Sweden, she remarked, "I don't wonder. All Swedes are swine, and Axel Wenner-Gren is simply the largest hog in the sty."

With that we sat down to a delicious lunch of kidneys with a good wine, and then she called in a young assistant fluent in English who was to be our escort. In the course of the next few days she arranged a meeting for me with the Rector of the University and with the American Ambassador, who invited us to an embassy soiree. She took us to her sauna which turned out to be coeducational to the embarrassment of Lucy, although I had no problem after my massive reclining in *chaise* by the indoor swimming pool sipping from a stein of ice cold lager and pretending to read my *London Times*. She also took us to her favorite restaurant, the Fiskatropen, on the outskirts of the city where the kräftor were still in season. We told her of our plans to leave on Friday, and she suggested that would not be a good idea. She had, she said, a cottage hidden in a stand of aspen on a secluded island about an hour's drive away, and she cherished the time she spent there because of the complete privacy.

Anne-Marie Snellman and Urho Kekkosen

"I want to take you there this weekend because I am having a guest you will find interesting."

On Saturday after lunch she picked us up at the hotel and drove out to the countryside through thick forests of pine and aspen and along meandering waterways until she turned off on a narrow side road which shortly ended at the water's edge. There were two rowboats pulled up on the bank.

"Look across," she said, "and you see my island."

We unloaded the provisions into one of the boats, got in, and I rowed the short distance across the inlet from which a path led through the trees to a log cabin. It was indeed a hideaway, and it would be impossible to imagine a more peaceful spot. While I toted the things in, she lighted a fire in the roughly hewn stone fireplace, and we were soon relaxing in deep wooden armchairs covered in fur and with all shapes and sizes of down-filled pillows. We all had taken a brief nap and were having tea around 5 o'clock when there was a soft rap on the door. Anne Marie rose to open it and stood aside for a tall, wiry man with a woolen stocking cap perched on his head, and dressed in a faded tweed jacket over an open shirt and trousers stuffed in a pair of walking boots.

It was Urho Kekkosen, Prime Minister of Finland, who had just returned from a historic meeting at the Kremlin. He embraced Anne-Marie briefly, giving her a small peck on the forehead, and then briskly shook our hands. Now I understood the suppositions of her influence. She had been his mistress for years, but they had been so discreet and so perfectly mannered in public that only a few intimates could have guessed anything but a casual acquaintanceship, and those who knew admired their probity.

During the dinner of cold ham and beef and sausages, and cold potatoes in dill and tomatoes, and then assorted cheeses, accompanied by schnapps and beer, the Prime Minister talked about his negotiations in Moscow. It was clear that if the Finns hated the Swedes, they loathed the Russians and to try to negotiate with them meant walking a thin line between compliance and defiance.

"The one thing I tried to establish, and the only thing that Stalin seemed to appreciate, was that we are not afraid of them, and if he wouldn't take my word for it, he had the Winter War to think about." He explained that the purpose of his visit was to get assurance of the continued normalization of relations and to express his concern for the Russian posture during the Olympics, when the eyes of the world would be on both of us. Stalin had assured him, he said, on the propriety of Russian behavior, unless provoked, that he looked forward to this new kind of relationship with the West, and that he was sure that Finland would acquit itself creditably as host to the world. Russian garrisons on the Finnish frontier would be reduced. Finland should know, however, that Russian athletes and officials would not join other participants in the Olympic Village. Russia would build her own, with her own workforce, and with an eye to her own security requirements.

"I suppose," said Anne Marie bitterly, "that they intend to rape our women in privacy!" And with that she proceeded to tell Lucy about the unbelievable horrors endured by women in territory occupied by the Russian army during the war. "We can never be sure" she continued, "when they will come again, so every woman I know wears one of these."

With that she held up a finger with a ring adorned by a single stone, which, when touched in the right place, springs open, revealing a capsule of cyanide.

The first item on the Prime Minister's agenda the next morning was a sauna, saying that he wanted to cleanse himself of the last vestiges of his Russian visit. As we sat there in the cubicle together with the sweat pouring out of us, he told me about his son, aged 20, who had graduated from Helsinki University with a singularly undistinguished record, and what to do now? I told him I would be glad to talk to the young man—which I did the next day—but from what he had told me, it might not be a bad idea to send him to London where Lindsay could help him gain admission to some good polytechnic where he could learn a skill, and that I would be happy to do the same should he come to the United States, for which he seemed grateful. When we had had all the heat we could stand, we left the sauna, and we saw the ladies with their backs to us sitting on a grassy slope leading down to a tiny beach. Kekkosen broke into a run, and with me in pursuit, we leaped over them on our way to splash in the sea. I later suggested to Lucy that I was sure that was the first time she had ever seen a Prime Minister's private parts come sailing over her head.

During lunch I asked the question that had been bothering me. I explained that while walking around Helsinki, I kept hearing thuds, like muffled explosions, and they seemed to go on day and night. Were these part of a building program designed for the Olympics? No, they were not. The Prime Minister explained to me that as part of the peace settlement with Russia at the end of World War II, Finland had been forced to cede a strip of territory 30 miles long and 15 miles in width, along the waterfront in the environs of Helsinki. The area was known as Porkkala, and after the defeat of Germany, the Russian navy had decided to convert that parcel of land into deep submarine pens which would give her much better access to the Baltic in support of her fleet units there. What I had been hearing were the dynamite blasts being used in the excavations, the intensity and continuation of which would seem to indicate deep pens, indeed, with plenty of protection on top.

"My God," I exclaimed, "it sounds like a miniature Alsace-Lorraine."

"There is the similarity of non-negotiability and seizure by force," conceded Mr. Kekkosen, "but Alsace-Lorraine was not on the outskirts of Paris."

With that, Lucy and I returned to New Orleans and Tulane to await the promised phone call from Wenner-Gren.

After waiting vainly for a month for that telephone call from Cuernavaca, I called Harold to ask his advice as to any further steps I could or should take. John Max Muller happened to be in his office at the time, and the two of them agreed that the affair was at an absolute dead end, convinced as they were that Wenner-Gren in reality had nothing of substance to offer me. Remembering Carl Henrik's candid observations, I had to agree. So although the hegira from the 1840 Room at Antoine's to the banquet hall at Häringe had been exciting, there was nothing at the end of the rainbow. To write the affair off as an exercise in futility, however, would be grossly misleading. For me, the ripple effects were astonishing.

To begin with, the story of the "Quest," as it came to be known, was spread fairly widely through meetings of various historical societies, and I acquired a kind of minor notoriety for diligence and resourcefulness in pursuit of a research objective. This led indirectly to an invitation to join the history faculty at Yale as a visiting Assistant Professor. The *doyen* of the modern European history group there was Hajo Holborn, a leading authority on the Reformation, but who had more recently published a slim volume called *The Disintegration of Europe*, a scathing denunciation of appeasement as a harbinger of the late war. It seems that my *curriculum vitae* reached his desk, and he noted my research interests and a brief account of my foray into Sweden, and being of Scandinavian origin himself, he approved my appointment. September 1952 found me in New Haven, and there began a wonderful apprenticeship to Professor Holborn.

We had breakfast together nearly every week-day morning at Bob & Eddie's, and he invited me to sit in on his seminars and to take an active role in the oral exams of his Ph.D. candidates. At the time, his ebullient daughter, Hannah, was about 12, and she was frequently to be seen skipping across the quadrangle outside Harkness Hall with her pigtails flying. In time she became an historian in her own right, then as Hannah Gray she was named provost of Yale, and she is just now concluding a distinguished tenure as President of the University of Chicago. It was while at Yale that I, too, fell from grace and began an academic administrative career that culminated in my selection as President of the University of Southern California in August 1970. A few years later when Hannah Gray went to Chicago, I invited her to give the commencement address at USC, and I awarded her an honorary degree which for me, at least, was a vicarious repayment to her father for his many kindnesses to me.

My relationship with the Max-Muellers and Boy Hart continued, and they were especially hospitable to us during my sabbatical year at Cambridge in 1962.

Carl Henrik Pedersen and Ingeborg came to San Francisco where he was posted as Swedish Consul General, but their stay was brief and ended tragically when she was almost destroyed in an automobile accident. They returned home and we have lost contact.

My closest friendship, however, developed with Harold Weill and his wife, Libby, and he subsequently played a crucial role in the career of my eldest daughter, Lisa. She had been with us for four years in India during my first posting there, 1965-1969. She then attended Scripps College in the Claremont group for two years, returned to India with the University of Wisconsin's Junior Year Abroad program at Delhi University, graduated from Berkeley with a major in modern European history, returned to India for a month on her own, and on her way home stopped in London and enrolled in USC's program there in International Affairs. After receiving the M.A. degree, she was ready to tackle the world, all options open but no target in sight except her desire to try her hand in the Big Apple. Given her background I thought the UN was probably her best bet, but I called Harold to tell him of her impending visit and to ask him to keep an eye on her. On her first day in New York, she called on him. He liked what he saw and introduced her to an old friend, John Marion, head of Southeby Park-Bernet, who hired her forthwith as a cut-and-paste girl in his catalog department. From there she worked her way up to become a licensed auctioneer and a Vice President of the Gem division, responsible for the United States west of the Mississippi, Latin America, and the Far East from Tokyo through Hong Kong to Singapore.

Hjalmar Procopé died of cancer in that summer of 1954 and Brita divided her time rather aimlessly between Stockholm, Helsinki and New York. But for a few glorious weeks, she was central to the high adventure of my Finnish Interlude II in 1952. So in the end, Axel Wenner-Gren gave me far more than either of us had bargained for.

CHAPTER 15

Finland and the 1952 Olympiad

The naming of Helsinki as the venue for the 1952 Olympiad required a liberal admixture of imagination and daring on the part of the International Olympic Committee (IOC). The awarding of the 1948 Games to London had been largely a matter of respect for Britain's enduring wartime performance and Churchill's leadership of the victorious coalition rather than a reflection of Britain's capacity to be an engaging host to the world. In 1948 it was simply too soon for the assuaging of the grievous wounds and colossal physical wreckage of the Second World War. That year found Britain, more than most, strapped with a regime of austerity designed to distribute even the few creature comforts at her disposal. It was far too soon for the revitalization of national athletic programs that had largely lain dormant since 1940. And in 1948, the Cold War was upon us, and the Soviet Union was in no mood to consort with former allies and enemies on the other side of the Iron Curtain in a Western European capitol. So the 1948 Olympic Games came and went practically unnoticed, significant only for reviving the Olympic cycle.

But Finland in 1952??? Without cluttering the issue with all sorts of geopolitical speculation, perhaps the compelling factor in the IOC's decision was simple geographic propinquity: the USSR had little to fear from participating in an Olympiad hosted by her tiny neighbor. As for the rest of the world, God knows Finland had earned everyone's admiration by her superhuman defense against the Russian hordes in the Winter War of November 1939 to March 1940, and then her subsequent defiance of a Nazi occupation at the outbreak of the larger hostilities. *Sisu* is the Finnish word for it; sheer, unadulterated guts is the crude English translation. And just for the record, Finland remained unique as the only country in the world which had paid in full her World War I debt to the United States. So to go to Helsinki for the Games would be simple but eloquent testimony to the respect in which the host country was held. But despite the plethora of physical and spiritual qualities, could the Finns with their tiny country and meager resources meet the excruciating physical, social, cultural and organizational demands of this most complex of international athletic *fora*? Wasn't this far more likely to be a Russian circus with the Soviet ringmaster dangling the strings of Finnish puppets? The world wondered but made ready to participate, no matter what the circumstances.

So did I as I remembered Anne-Marie's cordial reception and the unforgettable long weekend she arranged for us with Mr. Kekkosen at her country hideaway, which among other things resulted in my becoming an advisor for his son's quest for higher education. Thus it was that in an incredulous fashion, Lucy and I found us as welcome members of the Kekkosen-Snellman ménage.

So from my point of examination, my summer of 1950 had been joyous and fortuitous almost beyond description. A chance dinner encounter at Antoine's in New Orleans, Louisiana, had in the space of four months somehow led to the inner circle of governmental power in Helsinki. It was a hegira whose excitement was matched only by its improbability. But now what? I had no genuine intellectual interest in Scandinavia; neither by preparation nor predilection was this for me an area of concentrated research. But by the same token I did not want simply to turn my back on an interesting and important part of the contemporary scene, particularly with the 1952 Olympiad in prospect. And selfishly I did not want to just walk away from new friendships which had been so helpful. Upon my return to New Orleans and my teaching position in the History department at Tulane University, I tried to take stock. Certainly I had at my disposal some disparate ingredients. Could I concoct them into a potion which would assure my presence in some meaningful fashion at the Helsinki Olympics?

Just what were my assets? To begin with, there was motivation. The Olympic bug is virulent, indeed, and when one is bitten, as I was in 1932, the infection lasts for a lifetime. The 1936 Games in Berlin produced high drama, thanks to Jesse Owens, but the venue was off limits for most Americans. 1940 and 1944 were, of course, dark; and the renewal in London in 1948 was more an act of faith than a spirited athletic event. But Helsinki in 1952—my oh my!! The very name conjured up all sorts of possibilities for high drama, and on many levels of consciousness. With the possible exception of the Berlin air lift, here for the first time since the descent of the Iron Curtain were the principals of the Cold War to meet head to head in an athletic arena with national honor at a high premium. USA vs. USSR; the totalitarian East vs. the democratic West. A host country only recently beaten to its knees first by Bolsheviks and then by Nazis, yet emerging as a talisman to the whole world of the survival value of a glorious resistance against insurmountable odds. And there was a veritable thicket of unanswered questions. Could little Finland really pull it off in high style, or be forced to admit that she did the best she could with her meager resources? Could Helsinki and environs accommodate in fitting fashion the rich and famous and titled dignitaries and the simply curious who would flock in from every quarter of the globe? Would the multitude of athletic venues, all of which had to be built from scratch, be completed in time? Could all the shades of political opinion as represented by the various national athletic contingents blend happily together in the Olympic Village or would there be an undeclared war of "isms"? Would the Soviet Union really permit these bumptious people, symbols of resistance to totalitarian *diktat* to "do it their way" which, if successful, would make them impregnable to future coercion? In sum, there was clearly much more at stake in this event than demonstrations of athletic prowess. Clearly it was not beyond the realm of possibility that a significant chapter in the Cold War might be written in Helsinki in the summer of 1952: And if this be so, should not a trained, objective observer be on the scene? Besides, I had recently been there; I knew the territory; and I had reveled in the delights of Finnish hospitality.

So much for motivation. The question was, could I make the case? (It should be noted that throughout my life in situations such as this, I have never had any trouble with giving myself the benefit of the doubt.) What could I bring to the table? To begin with, I was a professor of modern European history, albeit hardly a name to be reckoned with. My research specialization up to now had been the diplomatic prelude to the Second World War. I had acquired some notoriety in the trade for brashness and persistence in my unsuccessful pursuit of the Wenner-Gren papers, and in the doing of it I had received a first-class introduction to Scandinavia. I had established some absolutely fortuitous personal contacts. On the newspaper side: John Lloyd, head of the Associated Press' London bureau; Robert Lindsay, Reuters ace correspondent now assigned to Finnish preparations for the Olympics; Anne-Marie Snellman, head of the Associated Press' Helsinki bureau. On the diplomatic side: Carl Henrik

Petersen, Deputy Chief of the American Desk in the Swedish Foreign Office. Hjalmar Procopé, *doyen* of the Finnish diplomatic corps, former Ambassador to the U.S., and presently Axel Wenner-Gren's personal advisor in international relations—and his elegant wife, Brita. On the political side: Urho Kekkosen, Prime Minister of Finland—and his son and his mistress, Frau Snellman. Singly and collectively, these were counselors who could, if they chose, keep me abreast of any significant geopolitical developments attendant to the East-West tug of war centered on the Olympic Games.

At any rate, these were some of the things on my mind when my classes resumed at Tulane in September 1950. I was, of course, eagerly awaiting the promised telephone call from Wenner-Gren in Cuernavaca, and its failure to materialize was a bitter disappointment. I was really not surprised at the decision of the Steel Blue Viking to dismiss the affair, but I had hoped that my operatic friend from Kansas City, Wenner-Gren's wife Margaret, who had been so very kind and gracious, would somehow carry the day. Still, it had been a fabulous summer with surprising ripple effects, one of which was planting the seed for my second Olympiad. My task, then, was to develop a cogent thesis of the upcoming Games as a historical phenomenon to be observed from a variety of perspectives. That it would be an athletic "happening" was seemingly assured by the ferocity and divergence of the personal philosophies involved: training regimens coaching techniques, mental discipline and so on. But that it might also be a political or geopolitical "happening" was also a possibility, and the *raison d'etre* for my presence.

It seemed crystal clear that I needed a good plan were I to get to Helsinki. What it might be I hadn't the foggiest, but the necessity for it never completely left my consciousness. I found myself going back and forth over the events of last summer, the people I had met and our conversations. I tried to visualize the milieu in which the Games would be held: confrontation; East vs. West; democracy vs. totalitarianism; religion vs. atheism; NATO vs. Warsaw Pact; the nervous hosts, fearing that their little country might be turned into an ideological battlefield, or that some act of commission or omission on their part might bring Soviet fury down on their heads. In spite of anything the IOC could say, there surely would be much more at stake than athletic prowess. Would a major political coup be possible? A major propaganda coup? If so, how and by whom? My imagination ran riot. But what had triggered these fantasies? Someone had said something to me. What was it? Who was it? And then I remembered.

Prime Minister Kekkosen and I were sitting in the sauna on Anne-Marie's hidden little island, and he was relating his recent talks with Stalin, and that the dictator had promised to cooperate in every possible way to ensure Finland's success as host to the world, but that the Russian teams and attending officials would not reside in the Olympic Village, but would rather construct their own quarters with their own technicians at a considerable distance from the other participants. Now it dawned on me. The Soviets were certain they could hold their own in the athletic competition. What brought them to the point of paranoia was the possibility of defection of their athletes to the West with the whole world looking on. Just one, especially a star, would be an acute embarrassment; more than one would be a calamity. It was possible, of course, for defection to be a two-way street; but the odds against anyone fleeing East were enormous, whereas westward look, the land was bright. Thus the Soviets' decision to eschew the Olympic Village and sequester their people against any possibility of fraternization.

Now in my mind's eye the Helsinki scene took on a startling new dimension: I could see more intelligence operatives scurrying around the place than athletes, with underground railroads being greased and on the ready, set against counter-defection surveillance, with the Finns caught in the middle. Imagine if you will the consternation if, say, the Soviet water polo team disappeared into the night and later surfaced somewhere west of the Iron Curtain. What then would Mr. Stalin say to Mr. Kekkosen? Unlikely, but perhaps in this kind of scenario I might be able to find a plan.

So it was that during the Christmas recess, I went to Washington. I had worked there between 1939 and 1941 as private secretary to the chairman of the Interstate Commerce Commission before beginning my active duty in the Naval Air Corps across the Potomac at Anacostia. I still had a lot of Texas friends in high places, so it was no trick at all to arrange an interview at the Central Intelligence Agency, which, as the relatively new successor to the wartime OSS, was scattered in temporary quarters all over the place. I was courteously received by a young officer who listened to the recital of my Scandinavian experience of the previous summer, and then I was passed along to an area specialist who made notes as I repeated my story. Then began a gentle probing as to why I had come to them, to which there was an obvious reply: only they could determine whether what I had done and the contacts I had made would be of use to them, and if they were, I was here to offer my services. At the end, I was asked to return the next day with a detailed written description of my activities in and around Stockholm and in Helsinki, with particular attention to the individuals—nationality, age, gender, position—who I had met and with whom I could easily reestablish a relationship. This I did in what was essentially a replication of my Carnegie application, and I was told that I would be contacted shortly. I was staying at the Virginia home of my old college roommate who was now a tax lawyer in D. C., and there I awaited the telephone call. It came the following afternoon, with a meeting scheduled the following morning.

At this session there were several people who asked me specific questions about the people whose names I had listed, with particular interest in Hjalmar Procopé and Brita, and Anne-Marie Snellman. After this session when I was alone with my "mentor," he broke the news. Yes, there was a possibility that I might be useful if I were still of a mind to do so. But before proceeding any further with any particulars, there was the matter of a security clearance. Would I agree to an exhaustive check, and if so, would I give him a list of references exclusive of my naval file, which had been sent for. All of this would take time, and needless to say, say nothing, not even to your wife. In the meantime there were some books I might find helpful, including H. G. Mortimer's classic, *The Wartime Uses of Propaganda*. Nor would it hurt to stay in casual touch with my friends abroad.

The second part of my plan was an application to the Carnegie Foundation for a research grant which might result in a scholarly journal article. The Foundation found my proposal novel, though perhaps better suited for a political scientist or sociologist, yet the strongest thing in my favor was an unusually eclectic set of contacts not generally at the service of scholarship. I was told that I should write up the grant request for submission to Carnegie, being as specific as I could about objectives, and that if Dean Roger P. McCutcheon—Tulane University Graduate School—would endorse it, I might just have a chance, but not to count on it. So said, and then done.

So my plan had been formulated and submitted, and all I could now do was wait. And some nine months later, in what I still consider as the most fortuitous coincidence of my life, both plans materialized within a two week period of each other in September 1951.

First, I was notified by the Carnegie Foundation that pending the availability of funds, I had been awarded a $750.00 travel grant to enable me to observe the reactions of East and West at the Olympic Games in Helsinki, with findings hopefully worthy of publication in a scholarly journal. Then, I was summoned to Washington at my early convenience. There I was informed that my security clearance had been completed, and then I was briefed on the Agency's growing preoccupation with the Olympics *per se*, that a special cell in which I would be a member was being formed to assess opportunities for political advantage that might surface and action appropriate to the circumstance. I would be given a personal service contract which would provide for travel and per diem between Washington and New Orleans, and which on 1 June 1952 would be converted to a ninety day full employment status.

They were delighted with the Carnegie grant which should provide adequate cover. So now all seemed to be in order for the summer of 1952—I was going to be a scholar and a Cold Warrior at one and the same time. My trips to Washington were infrequent, and I was always treated on a "need to know" basis. In other words, I was never privy to the general "game plan" nor did I have a clue as to the manpower resources allotted to it. Defection—theirs, not ours—was certainly of concern to us, but it was stressed that ours was not to be an aggressive campaign but rather one of positive response should overtures be made. Above all, we must not do anything that would compromise our hosts and complicate their delicate relationship with the Soviets. Our control officer in the agency was a graduate of Princeton of my vintage who came from a prominent Rittenhouse Square family in Philadelphia. The leader of our six-man Helsinki cadre was Sandy Simpson, a well-decorated former Marine Corps fighter pilot who had become active in the U. S. Olympic Committee and was the designated team manager of our track and field group. Another was a salesman with a trading group active in Scandinavia whose personal specialty was Florida orange juice. Another was a former big league catcher noted for his superlative linguistic abilities. It was not that we ever met together as a unit, but bit by bit we became aware of each other's existence. Our point man in Helsinki would be revealed to us after our arrival there. I was also glad to learn that as part of my cover and as an adjunct to my Carnegie grant, I would be an accredited journalist on assignment with *Harper's Magazine*. (There might be difficulty in explaining the Carnegie bit to the layman.)

Throughout the year I was assiduous in maintaining contact with Lindsay in London, Carl Henrik Pederson and Brita Procopé in Stockholm, and Anne-Marie in Helsinki, and especially so after the Carnegie development assured my presence at the Olympics. Lindsay's accounts of Finland's herculean efforts to be ready indicated a true national commitment, with every citizen expected to contribute. News from Brita was not encouraging; Hjalmar was having health problems and was spending considerable time in and out of clinics. Anne-Marie generously agreed to find digs for me among her friends, since a protracted stay in a good hotel was beyond my means. The Games were scheduled to begin on 14 July 1952, and it had been determined that I should arrive in Helsinki on 15 June in order to become thoroughly familiar with the layout. En route I would be stopping over in Washington, London, and Stockholm, so I planned to leave New Orleans right after the end of the spring semester. Finally the day of departure arrived. I must say that Lucy was being a wonderful sport about all of this, for having been with me through all the preliminaries in 1950, she desperately wanted to make this junket, but she needed to stay behind with our 9 month old daughter, Lisa.

Two days were spent in Washington going over the final bits and pieces, and then I was instructed to proceed to Philadelphia by train, getting off at high noon at the 30th Street station and proceeding to the bar in that cavernous waiting room. In due course Clem, my Agency controller, introduced himself. We strolled out the west entrance and sat down on an empty bench, where another person joined us. He was Sandy Simpson, down from his office at U.S. Olympic headquarters in New York. We chatted for barely ten minutes, but the meeting had served the purpose of introducing three of the principals to each other. We went our separate ways and I boarded the next train to New York, and I arrived at JFK and took my seat on one of Pan American's Boeing Stratocruisers for an over-night flight to London's Heathrow.

At least it was scheduled as a non-stop flight. The Stratocruiser was the latest and last of the luxury passenger airliners before the jet age, powered as it was with four Pratt and Whitney radial engines, sleeping berths for ten passengers, and a snug little bar down a short flight of stairs beneath the main passenger deck. I was looking forward to a couple of drinks, dinner, and a good night's sleep en route, being also pleased to note a very attractive group of stewardesses—this being before seniority took all the pulchritude out of the game. We were a couple of hours or so north of Boston when the #2 engine started acting up, and despite the Flight Engineer's efforts to rectify the situation, the pilot announced that we were forced to land at Goose Bay, Labrador.

Goose Bay was a military air base set in the north Canadian wilderness and having a broad and lengthy concrete air strip; it was known to my generation of flyers as a vital ferry stop during the Second World War, and it was still maintained by us in conjunction with the Royal Canadian Air Force as a principal cog in our North American Air Defense Command. We landed about 10 p.m. and after deplaning were ushered into a fairly commodious but plainly furnished waiting room, being told by an over-optimistic steward that we should be on our way shortly.

There were a few civilian ground personnel about, one of whom opened the small bar. The grousing by the passengers had already begun and reached a high pitch with the announcement an hour later that the engine required spare parts which would have to be flown in, that we must perforce spend the night in Goose Bay, and that another plane would be dispatched as soon as possible to resume our flight. While the baggage was being off loaded, a slow process, indeed, we were assigned spartan but clean billets in the barracks adjoining; breakfast would be served at 8 a.m. in the officers' mess. When might we expect to depart? That would depend on the availability of a relief aircraft, and an announcement would be made at breakfast. So it was a pretty surly group, each of whom with an urgent reason for reaching London on schedule that trudged off into the night, despite every solicitous effort on the part of the Pan Am crew. As for me, who apparently was the only person without an earth-shattering appointment the next day, I had a night cap and commiserated with the stewardesses who had taken a lot of guff.

They took a lot more the next day when our estimated time of departure was set for 7 p.m. The crew worked manfully all morning with messages to hotels and the reworking of flight schedules and all the problems incident to a long flight delay; but the air of exasperation and even hostility was so great that I made a public plea at lunch to get off of Pan Am's back—certainly we were all importuned, but for Pan Am this was a positive embarrassment and they were doing all that was humanly possible to alleviate the situation. So the afternoon passed with considerably less tension, and two of the stewardesses thanked me for my intercession.

After landing in London and that tedious bus ride from Heathrow into the city—this being before the M 1—I checked into the Royal Aero Club on Piccadilly (my "home away from home"), looked in at the Secretary's office for a quick pint with Patrick. His assistant, Joan (John Lloyd's mistress), arranged for me to meet Bob Lindsay for a pub lunch at the Cheshire Cheese in Fleet Street, and then asked the Club valet to draw me a steaming bath in one of those lovely, commodious English tubs. I must have soaked for an hour.

At lunch I got the bad news: Lindsay, who had just returned from Helsinki, would not be attending the Games. He had been posted as Principal Press Officer to the staff of General (William) Templar, who was to command a multi-national force to quell the insurgency in Malaysia, departing within the week for Kuala Lumpur. We would, however, have time for a dinner at his place with Trudy and the young Kekkosen, who had come back with him from Helsinki to take a look at London schools of technology. He brought me up to date on Finland's preparations, and said that Anne-Marie had already secured lodgings for me with one of her friends.

I had a nostalgic dinner at L' Escargot at No. 12 Greek Street, a venerable old bistro which had tried mightily to save face during the days of austerity, relying mainly on snails, jugged hare, horse meat, and some fairly decent red wines. I remembered it mainly as the place where, in 1948, I had lunched with Ernest Bevin, then Prime Minister Clement Attlee's Foreign Secretary, who had astonished me with his observation that Franco would be good for Spain by providing the stability with his heavy-handed authoritarianism by which she might recover from her tragic civil war. At any rate, the snails on this night were perfect and the entrecôte and pomme frits were finely accompanied by a really excellent Chateauneuf du Pape. Despite the jet lag, I was beginning to mellow. Here I was in my favorite place in the world with, by sheer good luck sated by good food and drink, and with delicious commitments ahead.

Shortly afterwards, Stockholm replaced London. I stayed over a couple of days at the invitation of Carl Henrik and Ingeborg, and we relived that week at Häringe. Carl Henrik had me down for a morning at the Foreign Office, but all I gleaned was a general nervousness that there might be some kind of political contretemps between East and West at the Games. I also learned that the Procopés were in town, poor Hjalmar having undergone surgery for prostate cancer some ten days ago. I finally reached Brita and arranged to meet her for lunch at Den

Gyldene Friedan, that wonderful restaurant in Old Stockholm where they had first taken us to dinner in 1950.

Brita was lovely as ever but understandably harried, and none too optimistic about her husband's chances. At any rate, she was taking Hjalmar to a nursing home on the outskirts of Helsinki in a week's time at his insistence; he wanted to be on his native soil, and he knew she wanted to be there for the Olympic festivities. "Won't everyone we know be there?" he had said. She also added that regardless of what I thought about him, Axel Wenner-Gren was taking care of all expenses attendant to Hjalmar's problem and had so arranged their income that she had no financial worries no matter whatever might happen. To which I replied, "It was probably at Margaret's insistence." I told her I would arrive in Helsinki before she did and that I could always be reached through Anne-Marie.

This was actually the first time we had been alone together, and I had not realized what a strikingly beautiful person she was, tall, perfectly formed, and with eyes and a complexion born of Scandinavia. So I must say that it was with feelings of relief and considerable anticipation when she promised she would find me as soon as possible.

On 15 June I took Pan Am's hour-long flight to Helsinki, arriving at noon, and I was pleasantly surprised to be greeted by Pan Am's *charge des affaires* of all its activities in Finland. When I asked him about the VIP treatment, he replied that I was now a company favorite after my help at Goose Bay. When I looked out over the airport and the tarmac I was struck by the frenzy of activity—people and machines scurrying all over the place and he explained that the Finns were feverishly putting the finishing touches on the expanded runways and new terminal to accommodate the rush of traffic that was already beginning to descend on the capitol.

"Indeed," he said, "somewhere out there with a pick and shovel is the president of the Bank of Finland who last week, after a long lunch, was apprehended for walking unsteadily down the street and sentenced to a fortnight of hard labor."

So Mr. Kekkosen and Co. were leaving nothing to chance in their preparations. The station manager arranged transportation for me into the city, suggesting that we meet for a drink the next afternoon at the terrace bar of the new Palace Hotel.

My first stop, of course, was the apartment cum Associated Press office of Frau Snellman. Her greeting was cordial amidst a beehive of activity, saying it would be at least an hour before she could take me to my lodgings so why didn't I take a stroll around the city.

A feature of Helsinki was the long parkway dividing the main thoroughfare through the central business district, as though the area in New York City between Fifth and Sixth Avenues down to 42nd Street was an extension of Central Park. There were footpaths, benches, band stands, and myriad little open-air bistros for snacks and coffee or a beer, an ideal place during those three precious sun-drenched summer months simply to sit and take stock. It also seemed to me a good place for casual trysts.

My Helsinki address was #10 Unions-gatten, a relatively new middle-class apartment complex just a twenty minute walk from the town centre. I occupied the guest room and bath, small but nicely furnished, in an attractive flat owned by a lumber exporter and his trim brunette wife of about my age who had grown up with Anne-Marie's oldest daughter. The husband, a most pleasant chap, was away from home frequently on inspection trips of timber holdings, sawmills, and export facilities, and he welcomed having a man around the house who could be vouched for by a Frau Snellman. I was to take breakfast there and occasional other meals as I saw fit. There was a daily maid who would do my cleaning and laundry, so I did not add to the housekeeping burden. In a city that was to be bulging at the seams for the next two months, I was happily ensconced.

That night I took my new hostess and Anne-Marie to dinner at her favorite establishment, the Grill Room at the venerable old Hotel Westmark, still the posh address despite the spate of new hostelries built since my last visit. I was introduced by her to the *maitre'd* as Professor Hubbard, her usual sobriquet for me, and he duly noted in whose company I was which proved most useful in the days to come. During the Games this Grill Room was the mecca for the visiting royalty and notables who invariably made their first public appearances here after arrival.

During dinner I tried to explain as carefully as I could to my guests my reason for being here. The Games as a sports spectacle, despite my enormous personal interest in them, were incidental to the interests of my sponsors, the Carnegie Foundation and *Harper's Magazine*, neither of which was concerned with the reportage of athletic events. But the Games as a magnet bringing together for the first time the principal players in the Cold War and all the political and geopolitical rivalries coincident to the Iron Curtain was what I, as an historian, was here to observe. Should the jumble of personal interrelationships inevitable in the

Olympic process produce human interest stories worthy of reportage, I would attempt to do justice to them. The Finnish people themselves, for example, and their ability to orchestrate effectively and peacefully such a complex congeries of potentially conflicting interests were the concern of a global audience, and this in itself if accomplished might well be the most significant story of the Games. To reiterate, my role was simply that of an observer, and I was already indebted to them for giving my assignment such a pleasant beginning. Anne-Marie and I bemoaned the absence of Bob Lindsay, who we were both so fond of, and I told her that I had had dinner at Bob's place in London with young Kekkosen, who I presumed was back in Helsinki. After dinner we took Anne-Marie home and returned to #10 for my first night in my new digs.

The next day I spent with the map provided me by Anne-Marie of the Olympic layout—the venues of the various events such as swimming, basketball, boxing and wrestling, gymnastics, fencing and the like, as well as the centerpiece of it all, the new Olympic stadium and the sprawling Olympic Village in close proximity. I was concerned not only with the location of the sites themselves but also with public access, routes and means of public transportation, the timetables for each event, and the modes and timing for the transport of the athletes to their venues of performance and back to the Olympic Village.

I learned firsthand about the tight security at the Village, being denied admission politely but firmly for lack of credentials which I had yet to obtain. Finnish Olympic officials were easily identified by their neat brown blazers over beige slacks, and I was told that most of them had voluntarily been in daily rehearsal for some two years for the myriad functions they would have to perform. It was evident from the beginning that "courtesy" and "cheerfulness" were their watchwords. As far as I could gather from this first cursory inspection, all was in readiness for the opening ceremonies assuming the completion of the work at the airport. Within a week the national contingents would begin arriving; already the press was evident in abundant numbers.

Promptly at 5 p.m. I took a small table on the outside terrace of the new and sparkling Palace Hotel, and in a few moments I was joined by the Pan Am station chief. He was Paul Jennsen, a native of Helsinki but who had spent considerable years in the U. S., having graduated from Rutgers University and then joining Pan Am in a minor managerial position at its NYC headquarters. He had apparently moved up the managerial ladder in good fashion when in 1948 Helsinki was awarded the 1952 Olympiad.

In the Pan Am system, then, the New York-Helsinki route was to assume a spiraling importance, what with the "toing" and "froing" with the preparations for the event. So in 1950, Paul was posted back to his native heath as Pan Am's answer to the ever-increasing demand on that terminal. I observed that his life must now be reaching frantic proportions, what with increased flights, VIP's, athletic officials, the press to be funneled through his airport.

"Yes," he said, "and beginning yesterday every flight is going to have its share of CIA types."

When I replied that I certainly had no knowledge of that kind of activity, he smiled and asked, "How is Clem?"

So that was it, and I confess admiration for a system that could have someone so strategically well-placed. After our drink, he then took me to his apartment, spacious but not ostentatious, gave me a key and a private telephone number, and said, "This is known as a place where the young jazz devotees hang out. You will see how it works."

The following morning Anne-Marie called to say that Brita was in town and had asked for my address and telephone number, which she had supplied.

"But I want to tell you, Professor, that everything is not as it seems. Given the pressures of the next few weeks, you and I are not going to see much of each other, and you will only see him, (Prime Minister Kekkosen), at official functions. So this weekend will probably be our last opportunity to talk freely. Be at my place at noon on Saturday and we will go to the island."

In the interim, Brita called to tell me that she had put Hjalmar in a nursing home, that the prospects were not good, and could we have a drink at her place and then dinner at the Fiskatropen on Friday? I saw no reason why not; indeed I was happy at the prospect.

Driving to the island, I told Anne-Marie about my evening with Brita. "Professor," she said, "I want you to be very discreet in your dealings with her. Everyone knows that her marriage to Hjalmar has not been a happy one, probably because of the age difference. But Hjalmar is still a folk hero around here, and I don't want it said that you are taking advantage of his illness. And besides, he did you a great favor two years ago, and you should not be seen as presuming on his friendship." For which I thanked her.

Late in the afternoon the Prime Minister rowed over in the skiff, and we immediately repaired into the sauna. He seemed remarkably composed for a man whose country was about to become host to the world. Indeed, he was immensely pleased with the efforts of his countrymen, people of every walk of life who had pitched in to do the needful. When I asked him if he was worried that the Soviets might try for some political advantage, he said no, quite the contrary. His main worry was that one of Finland's Western friends might try to do so. When I responded that it seemed inconceivable to me that any nation would do anything that might compromise the sensitive position of a Finland which had won the free world's unqualified admiration for her resistance in the Winter War, his simple rejoinder was, "But, Professor, that was before the Cold War."

Speaking of which, I said that since my arrival I had not heard any sounds of heavy blasting coming from the direction of Porkkala, which had been so much in evidence two summers ago, and did that mean that the Soviets had completed their naval base? He said he thought not but that they were merely taking a recess for the duration of the Olympics so as not to attract undue attention to its existence.

"It is obviously a very difficult situation for us."

During dinner I spoke of my gratitude to Anne-Marie for my comfortable lodgings, and I reiterated my willingness to counsel his son and help with whatever arrangements I could. This was my last private conversation with this truly remarkable man.

The following week I simply tried to blend into the Helsinki scene. I obtained my Olympic identity card and press credentials, and I checked out the bus and trolley routes that I would be using. I checked into our embassy and met with our counselor for Political Affairs, who generously suggested that we should compare notes as the Games progressed and who said he would see to it that I was placed on the Ambassador's social invitation list. Paul introduced me to the sauna at the Palace Hotel, where I explained to him my relationship with the Procopés, Anne-Marie, and the Prime Minister and my weekend on the island. He agreed that I should be very careful with Brita and for God's sake not to do anything that would get me on the wrong side of the fence with Anne-Marie. Later, with my identification papers in hand, he and I drove out to the compound where the Russian contingent would be housed and where it was agreed that I innocently seek admission.

The Soviet complex had been constructed in a pleasant, lightly wooded area some twenty miles west of Helsinki, and could be reached only by one access road from the city proper, thus assuring easy surveillance and just far enough away to discourage visitation. The area was enclosed by a tall and sturdy wire fence, through which could be seen its own practice track and field, swimming pool, and gymnasia. The living quarters were three-story dormitories with a kind of motel look about them. There was certainly nothing ominous or forbidding about the place, but it was clear that there was going to be no fraternization and practically no chance that anyone could scale that fence in either direction. Paul stopped the car outside the main gate and I got out brandishing my badges; but the guard would not even deign to look at them, explaining through a Finnish interpreter that the team had not yet arrived and that he was under orders to admit no one. I thanked him and we departed, noting the driving time back of some thirty-five minutes.

That evening Paul was holding what he called an "open house" for Helsinki's younger set. There was a very good amateur jazz combo-piano, vibraphone, and drums, all of which reminded me of Nat "King" Cole's early aggregation. There were schnapps and beer, a cold buffet of meats and cheeses, sporadic dancing and a lot of coming and going and light banter by a remarkably attractive group that I judged to be mainly in their twenties. There was a really striking brunette, slightly tipsy, whose father had just been posted as Finland's ambassador to Sweden, who was bemoaning the fact of having to live in a country she despised—yet another example of the almost universal contempt in Scandinavia of the Swedes, who had profited so handsomely from their trade with the Nazis when the rest had suffered so much from them. In an aside, Paul said that in general this was a nice group of kids with a lot of contacts that might be useful to us, so he had been having this kind of soiree about once a month.

I had no sooner returned to #10 when Brita called. She had just gotten back from the nursing home where she spent most of her days and Hjalmar had insisted that she take a break for a couple of days at their cabin which the Procopés had built years ago on a secluded promontory overlooking the Gulf of Finland, that I would love it, and would I go with her over the weekend? I told her I would have to check in the morning to see if any press briefings were scheduled that I shouldn't miss, and I would let her know tomorrow night. When I checked with Anne-Marie in the morning, she had no objections since we weren't likely to be seen by anyone.

"I've never been there but I know roughly where it is, and I think you will find the countryside interesting." And Paul had no objections if Anne-Marie didn't.

So late on Friday afternoon Brita picked me up, the back of her car laden with provisions. "We will really be camping out, but I just love the place." We were driving west south west, gradually ascending the hills that would bring us a view of the Baltic, passing occasional small lakes, and then turning off the main road onto a lane that took us deep into a dark forest thick with birch. After some time we crossed a small stream and emerged into a clearing where stood the log cabin; it was as lonely and secluded a spot as I had ever seen, as if its builder had wanted simply to disappear from this world. There was a chill in the air as we unpacked the car, for although this was midsummer, not much sunlight could penetrate the birch and the fir and the hemlock. Inside the place was just as primitive; there was no electricity but a number of oil lamps, water was drawn from a hand pump, cooking was done on a wood-burning stove, there was a large four-poster bed on which eiderdown quilts were heaped, a cot equally heaped, and a back door opening onto a short path to the outhouse. But the dominant feature of the cabin was a huge stone fireplace, and while I brought in the provisions from the car, Brita got a wonderful fire going which transformed the whole atmosphere of the place to something cozy and attractive. We sat there listening to the birch logs hiss and crackle, and I do not remember schnapps and beer ever tasting so good.

Dinner was delicious. We started with kräftor in a pungent dill sauce, then scrambled eggs with slabs of ham and thick slices of crusty bread. There was a cellar that served as a natural refrigerator that was also well stocked with wine; and we had literally left the world behind. Brita's mood, however, was anything but festive. It seemed clear that Hjalmar was not going to make it, leaving only the prospect of a slow, painful ending. During the last two years his infirmity had robbed him of all the grace and élan that had made him so charming and his career so distinguished.

"But even before that," she began to ruminate, "our marriage could hardly have been called a success." The wedding had taken place in 1937 when she was 23 and he, 59. She had been the daughter of a minor Finnish diplomat, and both she and her family were bedazzled by the attentions of this handsome, polished, distinguished statesman, just back from his much-publicized ambassadorial success in Washington. Even beyond the discrepancy in age, they had lived through dreadful times; their honeymoon had been interrupted by the outbreak of the Winter War and all the dread and horrors of the Russian invasion, only to be followed by the Nazi occupation and war again against the Russians under a different guise in 1941. Hjalmar was helpless, as are all diplomats in time of war, and crushed by his uselessness, unlike Anne-Marie's husband who had died in action. As Brita continued, her emphasis shifted, and Hjalmar became lost in her threnody of loathing against the Russians. She became livid in her depiction of their atrocities, of the suffering of her friends and family, of their unspeakable treatment of their captives and the women they could get their hands on. And now we are utterly helpless as their tiny neighbor, dominated by the whims of the Kremlin and the greatest beast who ever walked this earth. And now we have to be the gracious host to them during these dreadful Games. And now this and now that—and the depth of her anguish was frightening. Finally she subsided. "Tomorrow," she said, "I'll show you why I brought you out here." I gave her a stiff brandy, and we went to our beds.

She was up early the next morning, rekindling the fire and mercifully brewing coffee. After some cheese and bread, she produced a heavy green shirt, an old pair of trousers and some boots for me, and attired in like fashion, she loaded her camera and handed me a pair of binoculars. She took the lead and we disappeared into the forest along a barely perceptible trail; after a half-hour of this, the trees began to thin and the sun started to make itself felt. Before us lay a broad, flat stretch of land, covered with waist high grass and occasional wild flowers that seemed to stretch forever under a perfectly blue sky. Actually we were on a high escarpment which overlooked an inlet of the Baltic, beyond which stretched a long peninsula running to the southwest. At the extreme right of our ledge where the forest debouched onto the grassland, if one faced northeast, and with the aid of binoculars, there was a startlingly clear view of Helsinki and her environs.

We sat quite still, exchanging the glasses and peering through the grass at the peninsula. Brita finally spoke, "Well, there it is."

"There what is?" I replied.

"Porkkala!" she hissed.

After the Nazi occupation of Finland in 1940, followed by Hitler's savage attack on Russia, a co-belligerency of Finland and Germany against the Soviet Union had existed from 1941 until the end of the war in 1945. As part of Stalin's seizure of control of Eastern Europe, and its punishment for her participation, albeit forced, against him, and despite the protests of Great Britain and the United States, Finland was forced to grant Russia a 50 year lease on 150 square miles of Finnish territory centered on the

Porkkala peninsula. Russia's rationale was that Porkkala would provide her with a much better strategic position for the defense of Leningrad, plus an obviously much better access to the Baltic for her fleet.

So the Porkkala enclave was sealed off by a mini-Iron Curtain on the outskirts of Helsinki, and construction on a huge new naval facility was begun in late 1949. It was the constant thud of high explosives used presumably for the excavation of deep submarine pens that I had asked Mr. Kekkosen about on Anne-Marie's island in the summer of 1950. And it was at that time, in explaining Finland's chronic, abysmal discomfiture, he had asked me how President Truman and I would feel if the section of Virginia and Maryland from Mount Vernon through the Chesapeake Bay had been sequestered by an alien power.

"Take a look at those Russian bastards," said Brita, handing me the binoculars through which I could see the dust trails thrown up by trucks and hundreds of Russian laborers scurrying about like ants. She was crying again and was trying to vent her frustration by taking pictures until her film was exhausted, knowing full well that at that distance with that puny camera she would record nothing useful. Indeed, she later showed me hundreds of snapshots she had hidden in the cabin. "I'd give them all up for just one set of working drawings of that horrid place. I'd give anything up to embarrass them!"

We went back to the city on Monday, and that evening I reported into Paul at our sauna, bringing with me a dozen of her older pictures of the place on the off chance that someone might be able to make something of them. He took them but expressed doubt of their usefulness. Paul was a most attractive bachelor much sought after in the increasing pace of the Olympic social scene, and I suggested to him that he ought to add Brita to his ménage, for I believed there was no limit to her determination to harass the Soviets and he might want to keep tab on her after the Games were over. We also made arrangements to go to the airport together to greet the American team which was arriving on a Pan Am charter.

As the plane taxied onto the ramp of the handsome new terminal, Paul left me to attend to his duties and a group of newsmen. There were dignitaries galore, of course—the head of the Finnish Organizing Committee, the personal representative of the Prime Minister, our Ambassador, the mayor of Helsinki, and the like, even the president of the Bank of Finland, now dressed for the part. As our entourage disembarked and filed into the terminal for the welcoming ceremonies, I caught sight of

Sandy, looking smart in his blue blazer and white trousers. We nodded, and I was glad to know that our other team was assembling. It was later that evening at a reception hosted by Pan Am for our team officials that Sandy and I renewed our acquaintance as old naval aviators who had once flown out of the same base at Peleliu. Small world and all of that. He also met Paul in the receiving line. Two days later by commercial flight an American orange juice salesman showed up.

But in terms of popular interest, the most exciting event of the week was the arrival of the Russian team. Since it was well known that they would not be staying at the Olympic Village but in their own secluded quarters, thousands of Finns jammed the airport in hopes of catching a glimpse of these formidable participants. I was the only one of our group with any reason to be there. The Soviet was by a good deal the largest of any national contingent, two plane loads, in fact, and it was accepted by the cognoscenti that there would be more "managers" than athletes. The prime news was that they had left behind their world record holder in the shot put because of a "training injury," although it had been rumored for some time that he would not appear because of "political instability." After the official greetings and amidst lots of applause from the crowd—the Finns had been well-tutored—the entire party was whisked off in a caravan of busses, never to be seen as a unit again. The Games were about to begin.

There was nothing furtive or complex about the *modus operandi* of our little unit. Very seldom were we all at the same place at the same time, and then only by accident. We met to compare notes mainly at social events or at the sauna, but mostly we went our separate ways, talking and listening and trying to expand our contacts. Both Sandy and Paul had demanding professional commitments, and our commercial traveler spent his time within the business sector. I was our "free safety" able to move about freely with whomever I chose.

I spent a lot of time wandering about the Olympic Village chatting with athletes, officials, sportswriters and hangers on. I concentrated on team physicians and trainers in hopes of getting a line on any participant on any team who was unduly nervous and distracted or who seemed to have something more than his own individual effort on his mind. Security at the Village was hardly flawless. This was, for example, the first time that many Scandinavian women had ever seen men of color at close range, and I was astonished at the number of these blond beauties who would lean ladders against the fence which they would climb and jump over into the housing areas allotted to the various African delegations. To this day it remains a mystery to me how any members of the Brazilian soccer team could enter their matches with any vitality left in them. All in all, life in the Village seemed relaxed and easy-going; certainly it was not seething with political unrest, nor could I find a trace of any national disaffection.

One day Anne-Marie invited me to her place for one of her famous kidney in burgundy lunches, and I asked if I could bring my old wartime friend, Sandy, along. They got along famously, I was pleased to note, as he regaled her with all the vicissitudes of trying to keep our athletes' minds on the Games rather than on the abundant hospitality of our hosts. I also took him to #10 so he could have that locale firmly fixed, after which we strolled through the parkway in the town center and had an alfresco beer. It was then that he briefed me on how and when I would be introduced to the "safe houses" available to us. I was also keeping in touch with Brita by telephone, who reported no improvement in Hjalmar's condition.

The Opening Ceremonies were as colorful as the crowd in attendance from all over the world and the elegant stadium bedecked with flags and bunting. The President of Finland in his words of welcome expressed his hope that these festivities might make a real contribution to the theme of these Games which was, not surprisingly, world peace. The parade of the nations was, as always, impressive, as was the precision with which the program was carried out. Indeed, precision became the hallmark of this Olympiad, a tribute to the thoroughness of Finland's preparations. The climax came with the release of thousands of doves to emphasize the hopes that this gallant little country held for the rest of us. Then for the next two weeks, there were, as always, some surprising as well as predictably excellent performances.

The greatest upset was by the unheralded American, Lindy Remigino, who captured the gold in the Men's 100 meter dash. Fanny Blankers-Koen, the Dutch housewife, lived up to her billing by sweeping the women's sprints. But if the Olympics of 1932 in Los Angeles belonged to the brash 18 year old tomboy, Mildred "Babe" Diedrickson, and those of 1936 in Berlin belonged to the flawless Jesse Owens, these in Helsinki belonged to a skinny, scraggly, styleless Czech army lieutenant, Emil Zátopek, whose every agonizing step seemed destined to be his last. His announcement that he was entering all three of the premier distance races—5,000 meters, 10,000 meters, and marathon—seemed as nothing but foolhardy bravado, an outrageous bid for attention. But when he won all three of them, two in world record time, he became the toast of world track. No one in attendance will ever forget that toward the end of each race when that scrawny little man went into his ungainly agonizing finishing kick, every person in the stands was on his feet screaming in one tumultuous voice , "ZÁTOPEK! ZÁTOPEK! ZÁTOPEK!" Never was there a performance like it. Never was there a crowd reaction like it—and the odds are that there will never be again.

Emil Zátopek leading the marathon in 1952

There was another performance, far less dramatic and witnessed by only a handful of spectators that provided for me the most poignant spectacle in the five Olympic Games I have witnessed. In the finals of the pole vault competition, the USA's Reverend Bob Richards had already eliminated the field when he asked that the bar be raised for his attempt at a new Olympic and world record. He missed badly on his first two attempts, and before his last try, he sat dejectedly on the bench by the landing pit, his head in his hands. After some time he got on his knees, elbows resting on the bench, head still in his hands, obviously deep in prayer. Seeing this, the wizened little Russian vaulter who had won the silver medal, dressed in his unkempt sweat suit and wearing a jaunty little beret, came up to Bob and without hesitation, knelt beside him and put his arm around his shoulders, praying to whatever God he knew for Bob's success. That Richards cleared the bar was for me anticlimactic. I had just witnessed a spontaneous demonstration of what the Olympic spirit was supposed to be. And to this day I wonder at the fate of one of my few ultimate heroes.

Three days before the closing ceremonies, I was attending a late afternoon musicale at Paul's apartment when the call came from Sandy. It was our prearranged signal that something was up, "Hell of a party last night and I badly need a sauna." Within an hour Paul and I met Sandy at our accustomed spot, and within that heated torture chamber he told us that a Romanian pistol shooter had informed one of his American counterparts that he wanted to defect. Sandy through his own devices had checked him out, and it was true. We agreed that I should fetch him at the Olympic Village at 5 p.m. the next afternoon and get him to a safe house, after which we would decide how to get him out of the country.

The next day I left my usual seat at the stadium and wandered over to the Village around 4 p.m., went inside and chatted with a few people and wandered back to the main gate area about 4:45 p.m., where the Romanian was also to be. I was to be identified to him by the pork-pie hat I habitually wore. Just before 5 p.m. Sandy happened to stroll by. He stopped for a moment, nodded in the direction of a nice looking, swarthy young chap who appeared to be in his late 20's, and said softly, ""That's our man. He'll follow you out the gate."

So that was pretty much it. He followed me out the gate to the principal bus stop for the city, entered the crowded vehicle, and disembarked three stops later where a taxi which wasn't a taxi, driven by one of Paul's men, was waiting for us on a side street. Within minutes we were home free. Not a word had been spoken, and inside the "safe house" I was delighted to find that his English was passable, which simplified matters considerably. As instructed he had brought nothing with him—clothes, money, passport or any means of identification except his Olympic credential, which had got him out of the Village and which I immediately took from him.

"Except this," he said, opening his jacket and pulling from his waistband a beautifully burnished and crafted target pistol, his "most favorite possession" as he explained.

"My God," I thought, "the one thing we don't need to be caught with!"

With much reluctance he handed it to me, and I promised him we would try to get it back to him somewhere down the line.

"You're in good hands now. Just stay put."

His absence from the Village was not discovered until bed check that night, and when he failed to reappear in the morning, there was a mild hue and cry. Finnish security officials conducted a meticulous search of the premises. What was unexplained was that all his possessions seemed to be intact, except his pistol. One of his teammates volunteered that he had been depressed over his poor showing in the competition; and lacking any other evidence, this led to the official conclusion that he had probably committed suicide, somewhere outside the village.

I volunteered to stay around until our friend was safely out of the country, but Paul vetoed that notion, suggesting that our little group should leave as soon as possible. Indeed, he found a seat for our salesman on a shuttle flight to Stockholm the next day, and he and Sandy had somehow got a spot for me on the U. S. team charter leaving the day after the Closing Ceremonies.

That night Anne-Marie had a farewell "do" for her departing AP types, to which she also invited Sandy. Before leaving for her party I phoned Brita for my usual enquiry and told her of my departure date.

"My God," she gasped, "that doesn't give me much time. You must save the last night for me—I might have something for you." To which I happily agreed.

Anne-Marie was a perfect hostess and it was a jolly affair, and we outlanders all agreed that as exciting as the Games had been, the real heroes of the occasion were the Finnish people themselves, who had hosted the world in such a gracious and seemingly effortless manner as to belie the near impossibility of the challenge. *Sisu*, a new word for most of us, but one that we would hang on to. And in all of this newspaper banter, the case of the missing Romanian did not surface.

The last day was not a happy one for me; I simply hated to leave a place and a people who had been so kind and generous. My final lunch with my host and hostess was almost tearful, so fond had we become of one another. And there was really nothing adequate I could say to Anne-Marie. Of course, we would keep in touch, of course we would meet again. I even called the daughter of the Finnish Ambassador who was so reluctantly going to Stockholm, telling her to look up Carl Henrik and Ingeborg, who were at least two Swedes she would enjoy. And then I packed my gear.

Brita picked me up and we drove out into the country to an old rustic inn far removed from the Olympic frenzy. She was nervous and tearful and drank a lot; she, too, did not want it to end, leaving her practically alone with a dying husband. But finally she began to eat and perk up—who wouldn't with such a jolly proprietor, fire blazing in an open hearth, a dappled lake in front and a crescent moon over the fir and birches.

"Boy," I said, "you certainly kept this place a secret from me!"

"Oh," she replied, "we were going to come here, but I wanted it to be a festive occasion, not a farewell dinner. You know what I mean, festive, like I was a free woman and you weren't married and we had just discovered a peaceful world together."

I just stared at her, ordered another bottle of wine, took her hand and mumbled something like she and I had no control over her first two conditions, but as for the third, some of us, in fact, a lot of us, were working at it. I had seldom seen her smile, but even in distress, she was something to see. We decided to have our coffee and brandy on the little veranda overlooking the lake. Our boniface seemed in no hurry, and I assumed that she, like I, had the whole night before us.

After the waiter left us alone, she lit a cigarette, took a hefty swig of her brandy, and smiled. She was clearly excited.

"Jack," she said, "I've got it."

"Got what?" I asked.

"I've got a map of Porkkala that supposedly shows all the major installations and the proposed dispositions of the Russia fleet. I've glanced at it briefly but I can't make heads nor tails of it because all the notations are in Russian."

"By the Lord Harry," I stammered, "Where did you get it?"

"From a Russian engineer who works at the base who I met at a reception at the Soviet Embassy in honor of their Olympic team. He never left my side, convinced as he was that he was God's answer for Finnish women.

"We must meet again," I said to him.

"How can I call you?" he asked.

"You can't," I had presence of mind to say, "but I can call you."

"This is my number," he said, writing on a card. "Top secret!"

It was after our long distance view of the place and my obvious interest, she continued, that she decided to try. She called, they met, where and when unimportant, told him what she wanted and what she was willing to pay.

"It cost me," she said with a wry smile, "a lot of vodka and me. It may be absolutely worthless, but you take it and do what you can with it. I am so naïve in these matters, but it does seem to me that if it is real, they should somehow know that we have it. If they know that we know, it might make a difference."

With all this in hand, I dared not go to her place or to mine, so I walked inside and asked our accommodating host if he might be able to put us up for the night. He could. He had two available rooms.

Back in the city, Brita dropped me off at a busy intersection. We had said all we could say, and I simply slipped out of the car and melted into the crowd of pedestrians with my neat little package. At #10 I gathered my luggage, kissed my friends goodbye, and hailed a taxi to the Village, and just barely made the team bus to the airport. After clearing customs, I spotted Paul on the tarmac supervising ground operations. I walked up to him packet in hand, which my friends at #10 had wrapped in bright ribbons.

"You've been great," I said, "and here is a little token of appreciation. It's supposed to be an engineering schematic telling a great deal about Porkkala. If it really is, remember you didn't get it from a Finn, and maybe our people can rub the Big Bear's nose in it for awhile." We shook hands and laughed when I told him Brita would be expecting a call, and I went up the stairs, pausing at the top to wave goodbye, and stepped into the airplane.

My seat was between one of our weightlifters and Clyde Lovelette, the giant center on our victorious basketball team. It had been left vacant on the trip over to allow the behemoths some breathing room, and it was that space that had enabled me to come aboard. Needless to say, when I scrunched in between them, my companions were less than enchanted. The first thing I did was to check the stewardesses, but, alas, mine were not among them. We stopped at Shannon, Ireland to refuel, and some seven hours later we touched down in New York. Sandy and I had barely spoken to each other during the flight, but after clearing customs and collecting our gear, we joined forces in a taxi to Penn Station—we were headed for Philadelphia to meet Clem and spend the night before going on to Washington for our debriefing.

Lucy flew up from New Orleans to meet me and took in the sights while I was at the Agency. The debriefing was really quite simple, for there had been no deviation from the script and we had apparently handled our one chance to everyone's satisfaction. My Porkkala story hardly lifted anyone from his chair; the consensus seemed to be that nothing was likely to come of it, but "no harm, no foul." After it was over and I had signed my contractual release, Lucy, Clem, Sandy, the orange juicer and I had a roaring good farewell dinner at the Old Ebbitt

Grill. It had been a good show, a mere cameo, to be sure, but a good one.

The next day Lucy and I flew to New Orleans to gather our belongings and collect our year old daughter, Lisa, for the long drive to New Haven, where I was to join the History department at Yale in September.

Life magazine ended its extensive coverage of the 1952 Olympiad with a sardonic footnote. Despite all the dire prospects of angry confrontations and "dirty tricks" as the major nations met face to face for the first time since the Iron Curtain had dropped, the score at Helsinki in the political arena read:

EAST: 1 - A Romanian pistol shooter, missing.
WEST: 0 - All hands present and accounted for.

Editor's Addition

There were two Romanians who competed in the Shooting competition at the 1952 Helsinki Olympics: Penait Calcai and Gheorghe Lichiardopol. Gheorghe Lichiardopol, age 38 when he competed in Helsinki, again represented Romania in the Shooting events in the 1956 Melbourne Olympics at the age of 43. Mr. Lichiardopol died in 1991 at the age of 98. Penait Calcai, who was 28 years old when he competed in Helsinki, was never heard from again—at least not by the Romanian name of Penait Calcai.

Despite the fact that Porkkala was officially "the Porkkala Leased Territory", many Finns felt as though the Moscow Armistice, into which they were forced, made Finland an occupied country. This view appears to have been shared by the United States. In January 1954, the CIA reported, "The Finnish armed forces have no capabilities for offensive warfare and could not successfully defend Finland's borders. Soviet possession of the Karelian Isthmus, and occupation of Porkkala, only 10 miles from Helsinki, renders any significant defense of the capital and key southern ports impossible." So why on September 19, 1955 did the USSR execute an "Agreement between the Union of Soviet Socialist Republics and the Republic of Finland concerning the renunciation by the Soviet Union of rights to the use of the territory of Porkkala-Udd as a naval base and the withdrawal of Soviet armed forces from the said territory" when in March 1955 the CIA reported that "recently . . . Soviet defense activities on all Finnish borders have been speeded up"? Could it be that the engineering schematic Brita Procopé gave Jack was proving to be a valuable asset in the Cold War?

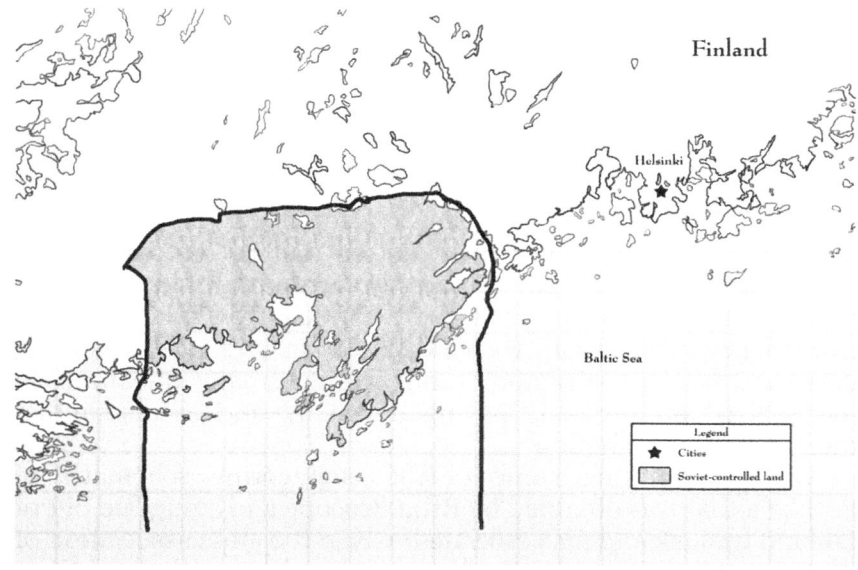

Map 6
Map of Porkkala (Inside black line is the area controlled by the USSR)

Documentation exists evidencing that Porkkala served not only as a Soviet naval base and watch tower, but as a gateway for Soviet deep cover operatives needing to traverse the Iron Curtain—at least one of which occurred in July 1952 right under the noses of the West simultaneously participating in the Olympics. The Soviets had lost the cover of Vienna when the Soviet forces withdrew from Austria in May, 1955. With the physical return of Porkkala to Finland in January 1956, only Berlin would be left as the point of least resistance for Soviet operatives. For Soviet deep cover operatives, it would be much more difficult to get to and from Moscow.

The official reason given by the Soviets for the return of Porkkala was that the installation was obsolete and too expensive to update. Some Finnish political scientists postulated that Porkkala's return was to show good faith so that the United States would remove some of its military installations that were near Soviet boarders, especially those in Turkey. Others referenced a British assessment that the return of Porkkala was one of the ways in which the Soviets hoped to discourage Sweden from joining NATO. That rationale seems somewhat illogical considering the general animosity that existed between the Swedes and Finns.

At the same time the Agreement (which was signed by N. Bulganin as Presidium of the Supreme Soviet of the USSR), to return Porkkala to Finland was being finalized, Khrushchev, and his followers (primarily Bulganin and Kaganovich), constantly emphasized Western aggressiveness in order to keep military expenditures high. They believed "that military strength as an adjunct to diplomacy should play a major role in foreign affairs, [and] argued for the need of increased military preparedness." Therefore, why would they voluntarily surrender Porkkala? In his memoirs referencing the return of Porkkala to Finland, Nikita Khrushchev wrote that "Helsinki could, in any case, easily be destroyed with missiles and bombs from a greater distance," so the Soviets left Porkkala having blown up and/or dismantled their military installation.

So did anything come of the engineering schematic of Porkkala that was obtained by Brita Procopé and smuggled out of Finland by Jack and his associates? Given the close association of the Procopé's with Urho Kekkosen (who along with Emil Skog signed the Agreement as President of the Republic of Finland), many would most likely say "Yes!"

1. Let us master the new equipments in an exemplary way. let us improve the level of military and political training, let us achieve new progress in tightening up military discipline and in the organization of service.

2. Artillerymen and mortar men of the Red Army! Using power and accurate fire let us smash the adversary's defences, destroy the enemy's manpower and fighting machinery.

3. Long live the first of May!

Building from Porkkala Russian Marine Base (1946—1956) and translation of graffiti painted on the wall

CHAPTER 16
—
Interlude at Yale

In the academic year 1952-1953, the Carnegie Foundation for the Advancement of Teaching was underwriting a series of collegiate undergraduate curricular revisions designed to vitiate what seemed to be a trend towards too much disciplinary specialization too early in the undergraduate experience. The program rubric was Directed Studies, a set series of courses for Freshmen and Sophomores designed to illustrate how the several customary academic disciplines, such as the Humanities, the Social Sciences, the Natural and Physical Sciences, Mathematics and the Arts depend upon and contribute to each other in forming knowledge into an integrated whole rather than as disparate branches of learning. The experiment was to be initiated at four universities—Yale, Harvard, Princeton, and Chicago—and it was billed as an honors program, which is to say that the students were hand-picked from an already select group consisting of 10% of two successive entering classes. A core faculty of 20 from its own ranks was designated by each participating university, to be augmented by five additional visiting professors at each university to be selected from a roster of former Carnegie Fellowship holders awarded for innovative teaching at other institutions. I was on that list, and my Dean at Tulane, Fred Cole, prevailed on his friend, the Dean of Yale College, William DeVanne, to select me for his Directed Studies faculty. So that is why Lucy and I, with our year-old daughter, found ourselves driving from New Orleans to New Haven in late August, 1952.

Thus began an intellectual and personal odyssey for me, the memories of which have never dimmed and which I still savor as one of the most rewarding experiences of my life. And whenever I think back on my career choice of the Naval Air Corps or academe, I count my blessings, for had I opted for the former, I never would have known Yale.

My first glimpse of its environs from our room on the top floor of the Taft Hotel made it abundantly clear that New Haven would never be confused with New Orleans for its innate charm. Apart from the village common with its stately elms and parish church, the signature of so many New England townships, there was nothing in view except a dingy, dirty factory city as bereft of aesthetic value as a frog is of hair. There is probably no less salubrious environment for an institute of learning anywhere in the world, and the sad history of town and gown relationships in New Haven is a dismal recital of continuing confrontations, some lethal, between an Italian-dominated blue collar labor force and the Eli preppies, between whom lies a gulf worthy of Ulster and Ireland. A legend has it that two Yale graduates, the Mellon brothers of Pittsburg, offered the Yale Corporation in 1932 a cash gift of $3,000,000 if it would desert New Haven and build a new campus out in the glorious Connecticut countryside, removed from all the hostilities of that terrible town. As the story goes, the Yale Overseers labored long and hard over the proposal, finally rejecting it on the grounds that the original university structure, Connecticut Hall, was so fragile in its dilapidation that it could not be moved, and hence Yale must perforce stay put. Whatever the reason, the decision meant that the agonies of the town and gown relationship would be perpetuated.

One of the salient (and surely the most expensive) characteristics of Directed Studies was the concept of team teaching. My assignment, for example, was to the two-semester survey course in Western civilization, in which the lectures would be shared by an American, a British, and a Modern European historian, together with a Political Scientist who would tie the loose ends together along the time line as they affected the emergence of contemporary systems of government. There were to be three lectures per week to the student group as a whole, which was also divided into four study sections over which one of us would preside twice a week for an *explication du texte* of original documents pertinent to the broad themes of the lectures, such as the Reformation, or the Enlightenment, or the American, English, French and Russian Revolutions. To assure continuity, each professor would sit in on all the lectures. Needless to say, for both students and professors the required reading was substantial. For the two years of the program, a student's schedule would look like this:

FIRST YEAR	
First Semester	**Second Semester**
Western Civ	Western Civ
Phys. Sci.	Nat. Sci.
Math	Music or Art Hist.

SECOND YEAR	
First Semester	**Second Semester**
Western Civ	Western Civ
Economics	Philosophy
Sociology	Research Project

The objective of all this was the presentation of the development of Western civilization as a continuum and an integrated whole.

Heading our Western Civilization team of three Yale regulars and me was Professor Thomas Mendenhall, a specialist in British naval history and also the Master of one of Yale's eight residential colleges, Berkeley. He was the first person I made contact with on arrival, and he invited me to his office the next day. As I made my way across the Commons to the Yale campus, crossing the grounds of Old College which now served as the residential quarters of the Freshman Class and onto the greensward of the modern configuration, my feeling was one of acute apprehension, the same one that had seized me that first day at Naval flight school: here I was at Yale, in the academic major leagues, and did I really belong?

My qualms were soon laid to rest by Professor Mendenhall. The History Department was housed in one of the Gothic piles called Harkness Hall, and when I entered his office, I stepped into an absolute masterpiece of disarray, with books, maps, charts, papers, periodicals covering the floor and scattered in every direction. He was attired in his sweat suit and rowing shoes: a skilled oarsman, he never missed a day, weather permitting, taking a run in his single scull to stay in shape even as some people jog. Nor did his appearance belie the gracious informality of his greeting: during the late war he had been in the "black shoe" Navy, doing sea duty in a battle cruiser but spending most of his time on assignment to the Office of Naval Intelligence, and although I was "brown shoe," a term denoting the Naval fly boys because of our penchant for wearing jodhpurs when flying, we both had been members of the Senior Service with a lot of sea stories to tell, so we should get along splendidly—which, indeed, was the case. He said that in a couple of days he would get our Western Civ team together for drinks at his Berkeley College digs so we could go over our syllabus and layout our lecture schedules. In the meantime, he suggested that I walk the campus to get my bearings, and that I call on Professor Ellsworth, the Chair of sociology and the chap who was administering the Directed Studies program for Carnegie, and that I look in at Yale's Housing Office which kept a listing of professors on leave who had their houses up for rent.

So I left Tom's office reassured, even jubilant, for if this was an example of the Ivy League's hospitality, I had nothing to fear about acceptance into the ranks. With Tom's help I had made appointments for that afternoon with the Housing Office and then with Professor Ellsworth, so I went back to the hotel to collect Lucy for a walking tour of the campus which we could manage with Lisa in a stroller. With map of the university in hand, we crossed the Commons and through the Old College and back to Harkness Hall, where my office was to be, and then made the circuit of the residential colleges such as Berkeley, where I told Lucy about my happy meeting with its Master, and then Timothy Dwight, Pierson, and the like, along with the various Schools, such as Law, Fine Arts, Forestry, and the Yale College administrative offices as well as that of the President, A. Whitney Griswold, who had been named to succeed Charles Seymour in 1950.

But the centerpiece of the campus outward from which all the life of Yale radiated was an imposing Gothic structure, replete with soaring vaults, frescoes and gargoyles, the Sterling Memorial Library, one of the most distinguished repositories of mankind's intellectual heritage in the world. It is told of the inauguration ceremony in the late 1930s held on a dais outside its finely chiseled entrance that the principal speaker became infatuated with his grandiose description of the architect's fidelity to the Gothic tradition, the striking facade, the huge weight of stone. Finally, the Librarian could stand it no longer, and wresting the microphone from the speaker, he pleaded, "But, sir, the Library is inside!" Needless to say, the Sterling became central to my academic activities as I immersed myself in the reading materials suggested by our Western Civ syllabus and painstakingly polished my lecture notes, as well as beginning work on a series of articles addressing the Spanish Civil War as a dress rehearsal for World War II.

The visit to the Housing Office paid immediate dividends, for we found the listing for four furnished homes of professors on leave for the academic year within a reasonable price range, as well as the addresses of the real estate agents involved. And our meeting with Professor John Ellsworth was equally rewarding. He was a dyed-in-the-blue Eli in his early fifties who, upon graduation from Yale, had joined his father's manufacturing business at its central office in Manhattan and had eventually taken over the enterprise. Yet it was Yale that remained his consuming passion, and he became one of the New Haven Railroad's steadiest commuters, returning to the campus at the slightest pretext and, of course, never missing a game at the Bowl. Out of his professional experience he had written a book entitled *Factory Folkways*, a first-rate sociological dissection of the mores within a for-profit industrial organization from the chief executive's chair down to janitor's closet, and it had been so acclaimed as a management bible that the Yale Department of Sociology had invited him to join its faculty. Thus was he enabled to return to the mother lode, although he was never able to rid himself of the reputation of an academic maverick because he had not earned a Ph.D. Thus when an odd program such as Directed Studies came along which would divert the energies of the pure scholar, John eagerly volunteered to become its director and take on its not inconsiderable administrative chores, fortunately for the Carnegie Foundation, me, and all the other participants. He welcomed my presence as an outlander, saying that fresh perspectives were needed to make this break from a traditional curriculum work, and his enthusiasm for the experiment was infectious.

Ellsworth also explained another facet of the residential college system which provided the lebensraum for Yale's undergraduates after their Freshman year, and which provided each Yale graduate with two precious lifetime loyalties, one to his residential college and one to his university. An adjunct to the system was the selection of all regular members of the Yale College faculty as Fellows in each of the residential colleges, making sure that all the academic disciplines were equally distributed. Custom decreed a monthly gathering of the Fellows at each college for cocktails and communion, after which they would join their undergraduate counterparts for dinner. It was a marvelous method for commingling intellectual interests at several levels. At the beginning of each academic year, the c.v.'s of new faculty appointees were distributed to the college Masters for their perusal and statements of preference, if any. Now according to Ellsworth, a Fellow of Pierson College, one of his colleagues who had read my c.v. was an Air Force Colonel, the commandant of Yale's NROTC units, and had noted that I was a Naval aviator in the Organized Reserve and who then insisted that I be selected by Pierson so that "between the two of us we can convince you chaps that the last war had been won in the air." From such specious reasoning do good things sometimes transpire; for although I could not have known it at the moment, my becoming a Pierson Fellow made all the difference in the world to what became a richly rewarding experience. At any rate, so ended a most productive first day at Yale.

The next day saw the solution to our housing problem. Following our leads from the Housing Office, we explored the environs of New Haven and got some notion of the lay of the land and the sea and the beauties of the Connecticut countryside. The first three addresses we looked at were beyond our resources or logistic limit, but in West Haven on a quiet street in a decent neighborhood we found what we needed: a modest bungalow owned by an Assistant Professor of Anthropology on research leave, and only a fifteen minute walk to a bus line that would deposit me half an hour later within a block of the Yale campus, which also meant that Lucy would not be stranded with Lisa without a car.

In retrospect, I am still mystified by my enormous good fortune. In the first place, just my being at Yale was the result of fortuitous circumstance, and then within two days after arrival, I found myself and my family comfortably ensconced in one of the world's great academic communities. Given my rearing and my father's experience, I had long been aware of the obvious fact that the key to any academic kingdom was the caliber of the faculty, the student body and the library, and the meaningful interaction of these three elements. All else was infrastructure: Trustees, Presidents, and other administrators, Staff, Alumni, physical plant, extracurricular activities, fund raising—useful only as they contributed to the central mission of the institution's teaching and research, the distribution and expansion of knowledge. And here I was a part, infinitesimal, to be sure, but still a part of a truly great congeries of intellectual talent and endeavor.

As to the Yale faculty, I shall confine mainly to that which I knew best, the Department of History, superb in its breadth and depth, but merely representative of the general strength of Yale College. Our Chairman at the time was Harry Rudin, whose field was Modern Germany, a compassionate man who presided over the most marvelous mélange of scholarly individualists that I have ever been associated with and of whom I was in constant awe. Typical of the man was that shortly after term began, he and his wife drove over to West Haven to make sure that I, the lowliest minion in his charge, and my family were comfortably situated, and then took us out for dinner, a kindness I have never forgotten. Then there were the giants, like Samuel Flagg Bemis, the master of historiography and the *doyen* of American Diplomatic historians; the quietly insightful practitioners of American and European Intellectual history, Ralph Gabriel and Franklin Baumer respectively; the triumvirate of Modern British historians, Thomas Mendenhall, Basil Henning and Archibald Ford, all disciples of the late great Wallace Notestein; the imperious George Pierson, the chronicler of Yale College; the gentlemanly David Potter, historian of the Old South and the American social scene; the formidable Hajo Holborn, undisputed authority on the Reformation, who left his field long enough to pen *The Disintegration of Europe*, a trenchant condemnation of the appeasement of Hitler which was destroying the Europe he loved, and who in his lighter moments liked nothing better than to preside over his accustomed table at Morey's. These chaps were good, as their international reputations attested, and they reveled in their stature, but unlike some other excellent academic departments I have known, they did not rest on their laurels but made sure that underneath there was a second echelon and a third echelon of promising teacher-scholars, such as the shy and introverted Robert Lopez, who as a relative youngster had few peers as a Medieval Economic historian, and Howard Lamar, the youthful and personable historian of the American West, whose popular courses the irreverent Eli undergraduates dubbed as "Cowboys and Indians." The "publish or perish" dictum and the three-year "up or out" rule assured that the struggle for tenure was furious, exacting and sometimes tragic, and that fresh talent was continuously being injected into the intellectual mix, and no one denied that perhaps the most exciting and intensive teaching came from this rung on the academic ladder. This was the stuff that had established the Ivy League's reputation and made it so attractive to the gifted products of our secondary schools. Certainly I had never been associated with more stimulating colleagues.

Every academic institution has its pantheon of faculty "characters," and at Yale one of the most colorful was Samuel Flagg Bemis. A burley man with a ruddy complexion and long hair askew, his appearance was distinguished by a tweed jacket with so many patches that its original shape and color were indeterminate, with trousers too short that plainly revealed his high-buttoned shoes. His physical movement was unmistakable, and I always stopped whatever I was doing when from my office window I spied him dancing across campus with his unvarying long strides in those shoes and hair flying as though he were perpetually late for a meeting. Another characteristic was his well-known conservative political preferences, which he never disguised in public but which never obtruded on his scholarship; indeed, had the John Birch Society been in operation then, he would have found its tenets far too liberal for his taste. In fact, the results of the Presidential election of 1928 was the last time he had known any political solace, but undaunted, from 1932 onwards he had unhesitatingly predicted a Republican landslide. The upset of 1948 had nearly crushed him, but here it was 1952, and there was hope again. This was also the year that the distinguished Ralph Gabriel, one of Sam's closest friends, was returning to Yale after a year's leave as Harmsworth professor at Oxford, and to honor this reunion at the beginning of the term, Sam had invited some members of the History faculty to his home for a welcoming dinner. My inclusion in that august company remains a mystery, but there I was in the Bemis living room sitting silently ill at ease among the Paladins. Over drinks Sam asked Gabriel to recount his experiences at Oxford and his opinion of the British approach to higher education. Gabriel happily complied, and at the end of his pleasant discourse, he asked a question.

"Sam. How did our department fare this past year?"

Sam reacted as though he had been stabbed through the heart, and he sat there glowering and speechless. Finally he was moved to reply.

"Ralph," he said, "Why did you have to ask me that question? But since you have, I must tell you honestly, however much it pains me, that our Department is a shambles. Three of our younger members have disgraced us, have made a mockery of our creed of dispassionate objectivity, have made a laughing stock of us in the Yale faculty, let alone what our colleagues in other universities must think, and who even as I speak continue to heap opprobrium on us! Never in my life have I witnessed more disgraceful professional behavior!"

"But, Sam," interrupted a stunned Mr. Gabriel, "whatever have these chaps done?"

"Well, Ralph, you know that we have a Presidential election in November, and these three young whippersnappers have actively entered the hustings and are working night and day in support of Adlai Stevenson. And not only that, they are recruiting among their faculty colleagues for workers in their campaign. Clearly they have forfeited the right to call themselves historians!"

If I judged correctly the reaction of the others in that hushed room, it was one of a kind of whimsical friendly sympathy for our bemused host. Be that as it may, we all sat as graven images and were much relieved when he ended his diatribe.

"But enough of this, Ralph. I don't want to spoil your return for we are all so happy to have you back. Let's repair to the dining room and enjoy dinner. I think you'll enjoy the wines I've selected."

So we all trooped into the dining area where a handsome buffet was laid out on the sideboards. But what absolutely dominated the room was the centerpiece on the dining table which consisted of a huge pyramid of "I Like Ike" buttons. Thus did I see the great Bemis at his eccentric best. And I must add that during the course of that year, I sat in as often as possible on his historiography seminar, and his mastery of the source material and literature of American diplomacy was breathtaking.

There was Rollin Osterweis, the wealthy scion of a long line of cigar makers, which was one of New Haven's cottage industries, an Associate Professor who had a treatise on nationalism and romantics in the Old South, but had turned to urban history, producing a creditable study, *Three Centuries of New Haven, 1638-1938*. Rollie was also director of Yale's outstanding forensic activities such as debate and declamation, an activity that his departmental colleagues looked down upon as an excuse for inattention to real scholarship, which bore heavily against him at promotion time. From the outset he was the soul of hospitality to Lucy and me, and we were frequent guests in his home, perhaps because I was a good listener to his furious denunciations of intellectual dilettanti. God knows what his colleagues must have thought when he later produced a volume commemorating the centennial of the First National Bank of New Haven.

Then there was Hajo Holborn, the tall, saturnine Swede who had authored the prodigious multi-volume *History of Germany* the first volume of which on the Reformation was seminal. There were later studies on the constitutional basis of the Weimar Republic, and his before-mentioned denunciation of the appeasement of the Fascist dictators. I had met him briefly during my initial introductions to the Department members, but a much closer relationship developed after a chance meeting at breakfast. Between my bus stop and the Yale campus was a popular eatery called Harold and Bell's, and when I first stopped in for coffee, he was there and asked me to join him, and thus began our four-day-a-week breakfast ritual; in effect he took me under his wing. I regaled him with my experiences in Germany in the summer of 1938 when I attended a Nazi Party rally in Nuremberg and was assaulted by the Condor Legion at Bacharach, and, of course, my war stories, and he in turn took a real interest in my research program, and invited me to attend and participate in the oral examinations of his doctoral students. He also paid me the supreme compliment of introducing me to the hallowed tables at Morey's and inviting me to join him there from time to time. (Hajo's daughter, Hannah, would later become a historian in her own right, and as Hannah Gray would serve with distinction as Provost of Yale, and then as President of the University of Chicago. So it was with profound pride and pleasure as President of the University of Southern California to invite her in 1975 to give our commencement address and to bestow on her an honorary degree. Thus I could finally express to someone who knew, cared and mattered my gratitude for her father's friendship at an important juncture in my life.)

As for that second vital element in the corpus of a university, the caliber of the students, the least thing that Yale or any institution of such distinction had to worry about was the number of applicants of high academic promise. Rather the Admissions Office had other problems as it sought social, cultural, ethnic, economic and geographic diversity, while paying assiduous attention, as any university with wits must, to its alumni legacies. Granted that the union of Ivy League-Seven Sisters gene banks was not likely to produce a high incidence of dullards but rather a plethora of precocity, too much inbreeding weakens any living organism. So the goal of the Admissions wallahs was to be true to Yale's traditional excellence while broadening its base. Surely I have had students just as good or even better than those I encountered at Yale in every university with which I have been associated; the difference, and it is significant, was that never before nor since have I met such a high average of intellectual promise. Frankly, I was just plain scared of facing such a critical audience, and never have I read more voraciously or prepared lectures more precisely, for this was, indeed, the complete antithesis of "just staying one chapter ahead of the class." But my fears were soon allayed, for they were remarkably generous in their reception of this outlander. The morning lectures were formal affairs, but in the afternoon discussion sessions there was much good-humored give and take, and as a relief from Hobbes or Locke or Malthus or Adam Smith, I was not loathe to interject sea stories from the late war, or describe aspects of the just-concluded Olympic Games, or how the North had to cheat to win the Civil War. All in all, they were an engaging, irreverent, provocative lot, and I cannot recall a moment spent with them that I did not savor.

It was Yale's head football coach who best described for me the essence of the contemporary Ivy League milieu. As both player and coach, Jordan Oliver was a veteran of the rough and tumble Big Ten and the National Football League, and there were many who thought that Athletic Director Ducky Pond's selection from such a background was bizarre at best. It was not that Yale lacked a football tradition, for hers had been considerable in the glory days of Albie Booth, Larry Kelly and Clint Frank, among others; but since the Ivy League's eminently sensible decision to abandon the subsidy of athletes in quasi-professional intercollegiate sports, gone forever were the chances of a Lou Little taking a Columbia football team with the likes of Cliff Montgomery and Al Barabas to the Rose Bowl for that classic upset of Stanford. So it was when I met him at a reception in President Griswold's home, I asked Coach Oliver how he had adjusted to this strange environment populated with simon- pure athletes.

He greeted that query with a hearty laugh and replied, "When I first arrived I called the squad together to explain my offensive and defensive philosophies, and I was busy with the x's and o's on the blackboard detailing how we would run our off-tackle sweeps. A hand went up from our All-Ivy League guard, who asked, 'Coach, are you suggesting that the blocking assignments for OT-Right are the antithesis of those for OT-Left?' So I have never again given a chalk talk without a thesaurus handy! In truth, I have never in my life so enjoyed the coaching profession, or competed on such a level playing field."

Given the fact that all my students had been hand-picked to participate in the Directed Studies curricular experiment, there was little to choose among them in terms of native wit, so it was the differences of demeanor that manifested themselves particularly in our discussion sessions that account for my selective memory of them as individuals. A few examples must suffice, although as a group we bonded together in remarkable fashion.

There was one student, David McCullough, whose command of the language stood out even among this gifted bunch, and whose felicity of phrase set him apart as a prose stylist even at his tender age. So David surprised no one who knew him then when he later captured literate America's attention with his fascinating chronicle of the building of the Panama Canal, which was to be followed by his candid portrait of Truman, which leaves most political biographies struggling in its wake.

Then there was Karl Taeuber, slight of stature, shy, soft-spoken, who devoured his reading assignments yet was hesitant to answer questions lest he show up his peers. There was never a doubt as to his aptitude for scholarship, yet he resisted my blandishments about the pursuit of history as a profession, saying that he was already determined to follow as best he might in the tradition of his parents, who had established themselves as truly distinguished demographers.

Jan Deutsch would have been voted by his peers "most likely to succeed" whatever his career choice. His parents were both classical scholars and teachers who had managed to escape from Hitler's Germany when he was just a tot, making their abode with distant relatives in an Atlantic City suburb, and ekeing out a living as tutors in Latin and Greek for affluent youngsters hoping to qualify for the better prep schools, a goal far beyond Jan's means. Rather he was a product of Atlantic City's public schools, and it was said he practically took up residence in the public libraries in the area when he was not earning his spending money pushing well-heeled tourists in their strollers up and down the Board Walk. A university scholarship had brought him to Yale. He was even-tempered, energetic, articulate, assertive, possessed of a superbly molded and eclectic intellect without the slightest trace of boorishness or false modesty. He liked and was liked by all of his associates, and he remains vivid in my memory for possessing the most exquisite set of personal tools in my experience. After our brief acquaintance, I lost intimate touch with his progress, but I was certainly not surprised some years later that at the same Commencement at Yale, he was awarded the Ph.D. in German History under the tutelage of Hajo Holborn, as well as his J.D. from the Law School. He subsequently joined the faculty of the Law School, but a ghastly automobile accident a few years later robbed him of most of his faculties.

Unwittingly, Deutsch was central to a strange and wonderful coincidence which befell me. From February to August, 1962, I took a sabbatical leave from Tulane University and my post as Dean of its woman's coordinate division, Newcomb College. By then my research interests had centered around the First World War, and I was chalking out a study of the British home front during that ordeal. So off to England with my family where I knew that the Cambridge University Library had arranged all of its massive holdings on that period in a separate wing, complete with its own card catalogue, making access a blessedly simple affair. The Library abuts on the rear of the "new" Clare College complex, and in the course of events I was invited for sherry with some of the Clare dons in their venerable refectory on the opposite side of the Cam; and on that occasion I was introduced to a University Professor, the world renowned Tudor scholar, Geoffrey Elton, many of whose works I had admired since my undergraduate days. And in the same spirit of scholarly comradery that I had so enjoyed at Yale, Elton, when he discovered that we had taken up lodgings only three blocks from his own home, invited Lucy and me over for after-dinner strawberries and clotted cream and a touch of Port. In our conversation on that occasion, the topic of Yale came up, where he had lectured on two occasions, and I then described my glorious year there, ending with the observation that there I had met the most remarkable student in my experience, one Jan Deutsch. Without another word, Elton put down his glass, rose from his chair and disappeared upstairs, soon to reappear with a letter which he handed me to read. It bore a New Haven postmark and was dated only a fortnight previously, and it closed with felicitations and the signature of Jan Deutsch. It seems that after receiving his B.A, Jan had spent the next academic year at Cambridge as a Clare Fellow, during which time he sat in on several of Elton's lectures and tutorials, and a relationship developed which spawned a fairly regular correspondence between them ever since. It was shortly after this surprising discovery in Cambridge of a shared admiration of one of Yale's best and brightest that Deutsch's near-fatal accident occurred.

But my most poignant memory of my students in Directed Studies involved young William Gillespie, scion of a Boston Brahmin family. Little had he done to attract my attention during the Fall semester, but in the Spring after the icy fangs and churlish chidings of that dreadful New Haven winter began to ebb and a glorious Spring with its warmth and greenery burst upon us, Gillespie's absences from our discussion sessions became noticeable for their frequency. One afternoon in class I expressed my concern that something dire must have befallen him only to be greeted by smiles from his colleagues, who informed me that he was a passionate and very talented striker of the golf ball and that one of Yale's blandishments, its own challenging 18 hole golf links, was more than Gillespie could resist. So I finally called him into my office and read him the riot act, explaining that I, too, was an addict who had never seen an ugly golf course, but that one of the marks of adulthood was establishing sensible priorities, and here he was, one of a select few, given this singular opportunity to discover the mystery and beauty of knowledge as an integrated whole, squandering it all by not doing his reading and joining in the lively discussions it inspired. I even said I'd be happy to play golf with him for modest stakes—but only on the weekends, and only if he'd give me two strokes a side. After that we saw more of him, and the denouement came in late May just before the end of term. I was about to enter the classroom for our final discussion session when he waylaid me in the hallway. He was obviously in a state of great excitement, and tears of joy were coursing down his cheeks: "Professor," he blurted out, "about three o'clock this morning I sat bolt upright in my bed, and it all came flooding in. My God, Professor, I'm integrated!!" He eventually was chosen as captain of the Yale golf team and, more importantly, graduated with honors; in later years he could be found in the Boston directory under the rubric, William Gillespie, M.D., FACS, as he enjoyed a distinguished career as a cranial neuro-surgeon.

It was in fact the residential college system which provided that vital nexus to a pleasant, satisfying, challenging, rewarding personal existence for the Yale undergraduate. There were 10 of them with an average population of 350, and they guaranteed each individual an equal start in the student hierarchy. The College was where he hung his hat, ate and slept, large enough to assure a meaningful variety of individual traits and experience, yet small enough to foster a clannish loyalty. Here is where the lifelong friendships were formed and nurtured, and the sweet memories rooted in the halcyon days of adolescence in full flower. Here was the security of belonging to a tangible and vibrant entity, a font for all the hi-jinks that lively imaginations could conjure up, a sense of pride and elitism which inevitably spawned friendly rivalry with other such groups and fueled the confrontations on the playing fields. Indeed, no Etonian ever played with greater spirit than these.

The College system provided the perfect format for an intramural athletic program designed under the maxim of a sport for every student and every student in a sport. In truth, the rivalry engendered between, say, Pierson and Berkeley or Saybrook and Timothy Dwight was a true microcosm of the traditional confrontations between Harvard and Yale. This was serious stuff. Intramural football, for example, was not of the flag variety, for these kids donned helmets and pads and cleats and really got after each other, and game officials were invariably hard pressed to limit the bodily mayhem. After the season, to be selected to the All-College team was not, to be sure, the equivalent of winning a coveted Varsity Blue but it was no pale reflection either.

The coaches for these teams came from the College's faculty Fellows, and it was not an assignment to be taken lightly, and some of them after years of service had become minor legends in their own time. My College, Pierson, had been blessed with one of these worthies in baseball, but his time for retirement had arrived, and our Master, with nowhere else to turn, gratefully accepted my offer to take over. What he failed to tell me was that fifteen of last year's twenty man squad had graduated. So it was that after our first practice, it was clear that I had far more bodies than talent at my disposal, but they were an enthusiastic bunch and it was not easy to reduce the forty-odd aspirants to the allowable twenty-man roster. So we opened the season as a pretty rag tag team, and selecting a starter from our pitching staff was the equivalent of playing Russian roulette; but we did have two gifted athletes, Stolzenberg in center field who was fast as a deer and could catch, throw and hit with power, and Meyers, a burly catcher who understood the game, was steady as a rock, and could also hit. We were divided into two five-team leagues, and by a major miracle we stumbled through our division undefeated; it was not that we made fewer errors but fewer that killed us, and not that we issued fewer walks but fewer at critical times. So we arrived at the championship game unexpectedly, the toast of our surprised Pierson colleagues, ready to face the winner of the other league, detested Berkeley, whose redoubtable Master, Tom Mendenhall, was my academic boss who threatened to disbar me from the profession if we defeated the reigning titleholders.

Not surprisingly, my starting pitcher started out as wild as a March hare, walking the bases loaded and uncorking a wild pitch, and somehow getting out of the inning only four runs behind when our opponents ran into a double play. The next inning began the same way and the score was 6-0, bases loaded, and only one out. I could see Mendenhall sitting on their sideline grinning from ear to ear, and poor Meyers was looking at me in desperation; but what to do, since my best pitcher was already out there and getting killed? But as all great managers, I was wont to make a move, and so I sauntered calmly up to the umpire and asked for time, and in a fit of inspiration, I waived in Stolzenberger from center field. "Young man," I said, "these cunny-thumbs can't hit a lick. Just make them swing the bat." He did just that, and with a vengeance, striking out all seventeen batters he faced! In the meantime, we scratched and clawed but managed only five runs, and so lost the championship. But Stolzenberg and I were instantly installed in Pierson's Gallery of Heroes, he for the greatest relief pitching in the history of organized baseball, and I for the shrewdest single managerial move in the annals of the game. Seriously, his performance was a topic of conversation for a long time to come. I later lost track of Stolzenberg, but Meyers went on to earn his Ph.D. in Sociology and some years later I had the pleasure of offering him a faculty position at Tulane, which he finally eschewed for one at Duke. But we had a fine evening together in New Orleans at Antoine's reliving THE GAME.

So my life at Yale continued to be a kaleidoscope of memorable experiences, but none did I enjoy more than the monthly gathering of the Fellows in the Pierson Library, presided over by our Master, Gordon Haight, who opened the proceedings with the usual words of welcome and a brief updating of the state of the College, and then, since this was the first meeting of the academic year, asked for the introduction of new members. The Air Force Colonel did the honors for me, and, since my academic credentials were so relatively spare, dwelt mainly on my war record, warning the group that Naval aviators were notoriously lacking in veracity when describing their deeds of derring-do, but that my saving grace was my shared conviction with him that General "Dugout Doug" MacArthur was beyond peradventure the vainest man ever to wear the uniform of his country, a remark which, as intended, evoked good-natured cries of "Shame" "Shame" from earthlings around the room. Obviously this was a light-hearted group that did not take itself too seriously. But with the end of the introductions, the serious business of the evening began with the mixing of the martinis.

This was more than serious business; it was a sacred ritual. The two senior Fellows who bore the coveted title of Grand Sommelier took their places at the sideboard where all the necessities were neatly laid out: the smoothest and driest ingredients in their crystalline carafes, the long tapered spoons standing in the tall silver mixing pitchers, the rows of stemmed goblets filled with ice, the anchovied olives, pearl onions and twists of lemon to accommodate any palate. We all then crowded around to watch the magical creation of that rarest of all libations, the perfect martini—dry! Each Sommelier took up his pitcher, removed the spoon, and poured in the essential liquids, measuring from memory, then added ice, and stirred ever so gently so as not to bruise. Then each of us emptied a now-icy goblet to receive the nectar. It was always for the Master to take the first sip, and upon his announcement of perfection achieved, the Fellowship was well and truly in session. The key, of course, was in the measurements, and our Sommeliers were long in memory and practice.

 An obvious pleasure for me in these gatherings was the meeting of a goodly cross-section of the Yale faculty under pleasantly informal circumstances. At the outset I had a useful conversation piece in describing the just completed Helsinki Olympics and Zátopek's heroics, a change of pace from the usual shop talk, so I was accepted as someone "interesting." Thus I got to meet, for example, Fleming James of the Law School, whose treatise on Torts had become a legal Bible, and whose brother, Francis, was a colleague of mine in British History at Tulane. The afore-mentioned John Ellsworth of Sociology was a Pierson man, as was Frank Baumer, in European intellectual history. Nor can I think of any other way that I would have come to know on such friendly terms William DeVane, the Dean of Yale College, one of the most prestigious positions in all of academe. I was immediately taken with him, nay, awed by him, his simple, forthright demeanor, his friendly approach, his exquisite choice of words softly spoken, the sense that he was nothing more nor less than the first among friendly equals engaged in the serious pursuit of the life of the mind. To me he was the quintessential academic statesman, with the same dedication but gentler in manner than my father. I still cherish the warmth of his initial reception and the easy rapport we subsequently established, abetted I am sure by that fact that since I was merely a visitor, he would not be making any of the critical professional judgments as to my academic future. Or so we thought at the moment. From time to time he would invite me to his office where, over coffee, we chatted about higher education in general, and in particular about our joint concern for how and when the institutions in the Deep South were going to face up to the inevitable task of integration. So I became envied by my younger associates for being able to consort so amiably with the College's Father Figure while they lived in holy dread of a summons to the Dean's office.

 The Pierson Fellowship was also the genesis of what became a minor baseball legend. After my libidinous introduction to that august body, the pre-prandial ritual had assured an expansive mood as the Fellows trooped down the stairs to join the undergraduates at dinner. Quite by chance I joined John

Ellsworth and Frank Baumer at a table with six students, to whom I was introduced as a visiting professor and, incidentally, as Pierson's new baseball coach for the coming Spring season. This set the tone of our dinner conversation, in the course of which we went around the table naming our favorite team. Ellsworth was a Brooklyn Dodger nut, but for Baumer and me it was the St. Louis Cardinals. Dinner ended, the undergraduates excused themselves while the three of us lingered over coffee, and I broached an idea. New York was but an hour and a half away on the New Haven Railway, so the next Saturday afternoon that the Cardinals came to Ebbets Field, why not go to the game and afterwards dine at a fine restaurant, all of which would put us back home by ten thirty at the latest unless we encountered other inescapable diversions. With that possibility in mind, we decided that this outing should be a stag affair, so that all we needed was the consent of our halves.

That was why some two weeks later at noon on a sunny Saturday we found ourselves on the subway leaving Grand Central for Prospect Park in Brooklyn on the banks of the Gowanus Canal. Lovely, rickety Ebbets Field; our seats were on the first base line, and the Cardinals prevailed in a thriller, much to Ellsworth's disgust. Afterwards, a cab driver dropped us off at his favorite watering hole noted for its generous drinks, where we enjoyed Happy Hour as we discussed our dining venue. We decided on Gage & Tollner, that venerable chop house on Fulton Street which had become a gustatory shrine for affluent Brooklyn burghers since its founding in the mid-nineteenth century. Inside, the dark mahogany paneling and the overhead gas light fixtures and whirring ceiling fans added to the ambiance of the black waiters in their black suits and crisp white shirts and aprons wearing proudly their gold length of service stripes on their coat sleeves. Ours was a patriarch who had been there for thirty-five years since leaving his native New Orleans, and his first words were a command that we must start with his famous version of a Cajun dry martini—as though we needed any bidding. There followed freshly shucked Chincoteagues on the half shell, she-crab soup and belly-broiled clams washed down with chilled Chablis, and finally an outrageous apple pan dowdy slathered with clotted cream, coffee and a goodly snifter of brandy. We just sat there in utter contentment, savoring the moment and saying little, but agreed that this was a bit of a do worthy of repetition. Happily for mankind, our loving families and future students, our return logistics were very simple: a few, carefully measured steps to Borough Hall, then the rattler to

Grand Central, and then on to New Haven, where our prescient wives had insisted on meeting us in the family vehicles at the station.

Thus began an unbroken succession of thirty-six annual baseball rendezvouses, with all but one in NYC. Mine was the logistic problem for in all that time I was resident either in New Orleans or New Delhi, India or Los Angeles none of which were exactly next door. But since we decided that any Saturday day game at any stadium would serve our purpose, the planning became relatively simple; at the beginning of each baseball season, we would consult the National and American schedules, marking the possibilities, and later I would let John and Frank know when circumstances would permit my presence in New York. As Dean of Newcomb College of Tulane University, I came to New York with some frequency for conferences or to shake the can at the myriad educational foundations headquartered there; in New Delhi my duties at our Embassy necessitated my coming in to Washington two or three times a year for consultations, one of which was bound to coincide with one of our possible dates; and in Los Angeles as President of USC, I was back on the foundation circuit with a vengeance. Once our date was fixed, our routine became inviolate. The University Club was my home away from home, and they put up at the Yale Club, since their sapient wives insisted that they return to New Haven on Sunday refreshed rather than worry about late Saturday night train schedules. So on the Saturday morning, I would leave the Club promptly at ten thirty, walk over to Park Avenue and down to the Pan Am building, and descend on the escalator into Grand Central at eleven sharp, where they would be waiting under the clock. We then repaired to a German *bierstube* on Third Avenue which had been recommended to us and which became our absolute favorite, where the draught Dortmunder Union in liter tankards and excellent sauerbraten provided a solid foundation for the rigors of the day, but only after we followed Frank's dictum that festivities must begin with a martini. Thus fortified, it was back to Grand Central and the subway to either Ebbets Field, the Polo Grounds or Yankee Stadium, then back to our respective digs for a shower and change of attire, and then reconvening at the bar of the Yale Club before dinner, the site of which each was responsible for in successive years.

Time, of course, wrought inevitable changes, few of which were for the better. There was, for example, the ruination of Third Avenue in the name of progress; first, the El was abandoned and torn down, and then on a black Saturday to our horror we found only a huge crater where our *bierstube* once stood as a prelude to some horrid high rise. Were that not desecration enough, there was the unthinkable and detestable defection of the Dodgers and the Giants to the West Coast, engineered by those monumentally greedy savages of tradition, Walter O'Malley and Horace Stoneham, leaving in their wake only the drab sterility and soon to be filthy Shea Stadium, with no history and only a rabble of baseball poseurs called the Mets, saved from self-immolation by the genius of Casey Stengel, whose bandy legs, baggy pants and wizened countenance were much in evidence on his frequent visits to the pitcher's mound with his hook. On the other side of the coin, as our annual visitations began to mount, we became known to the team owners, their general managers and administrative assistants, and our status was elevated to that of honored guests; we had but to inform the front offices of the date of our arrival, and our box seats and reserved table in the Stadium Club would await us, plus attractive young staffers to attend to our gustatory wishes throughout the game. The media even took notice, and we were interviewed several times on the radio and TV pre-game shows. Just why three Yale academics who could talk the baseball talk were such a curiosity we never really understood, but by the same token we never dared raise the question.

But of all the sights and sounds and kindnesses which our annual do had engendered, it was our 25th anniversary in August 1977 that was the most memorable. I had come to Los Angeles from my tour of diplomatic duty in India at the end of August 1969 to assume my new position of Academic Vice President and Provost of the University of Southern California, and through improbable circumstance before the year was out I found myself sitting in the Presidential chair. Early on I was enabled to indulge my new passion for gold by being inducted into an inner circle of the Los Angeles Country Club known as G(olf)-P(oker), a group of 50 members who gathered religiously every other Tuesday for lunch, a round of golf, then a happy hour of drinks and cards, followed by dinner which each member hosted in turn. Numbered among this august group was the afore-mentioned Walter O'Malley, owner of the now Los Angeles Dodgers, whose locker just happened to be next to mine. Never have I met a man whom I liked and admired more—a lawyer by training who was smart, shrewd, tough-minded, but withal congenial and a veritable font of Irish blarney, wit and charm. Once he became aware of my love of baseball, I found myself a frequent guest in his spacious box in Dodger Stadium on the loge level behind home plate, where drinks and an elegant repast were served during every home game. And it was there that I first became acquainted with his son, Peter, and daughter, Kate, the sole joint heirs of the Dodger empire after his death in 1976.

So it was Peter O'Malley who insisted that he host our 25th if I could persuade John and Frank to come west, and we settled on a date in August when there was a night game with, appropriately enough, the St. Louis Cardinals. Enhanced by its setting in the most beautiful and perfectly proportioned athletic venue in America, and enlivened by the presence of our wives and cronies of mine from G-P and the university, including USC's legendary Rod Dedeaux, the most successful collegiate baseball coach in the land, it was a wonderfully pukka affair. During the traditional seventh inning stretch, the stadium lights were dimmed and the Public Address announcer intoned the following words which were flashed on the huge message board in center field:

IN 1952 THREE YALE PROFESSORS WENT TO A BASEBALL GAME AT EBBETS FIELD, AND SINCE THAT TIME IN UNBROKEN SUCCESSION THEY HAVE ATTENDED A GAME EACH YEAR. TONIGHT MARKS THEIR 25TH ANNIVERSARY, AND YOUR LOS ANGELES DODGERS ARE HONORED TO PAY TRIBUTE TO THEIR DEVOTION TO OUR NATIONAL PASTTIME AND TO HOST

>PROFESSOR JOHN ELLSWORTH
>PROFESSOR FRANKLIN BAUMER

AND THE THIRD MEMBER WHO YOU KNOW AS

>DR. JACK HUBBARD, PRESIDENT OF USC.

PLEASE BID THEM WELCOME.

We rose to acknowledge the generous applause.

We ran the skein to 36, when John became too infirm to leave his home, after which Frank and I carried on until his death in 1993. 43 years of a fraternity spawned in Pierson College. Today (1996) when I am in New York I still go through the motions just to honor their memory, but it is a lonely exercise.

As is ever the case when one's daily routine is an unmitigated pleasure, the passage of time is much too swift, and I suddenly realized that the end of term was approaching pell-mell. For me this was a sad prospect, indeed, for I had never been so happy in an academic milieu which combined beautifully with my other love when on alternate Saturdays I could "wheel and soar and swing high in the sunlit silence" as a "weekend warrior" in the Naval Air Corps Ready Reserve. But Lucy's experience had been just the opposite—in a word, dismal; in West Haven she had mainly known snow-filled and icy streets, a recalcitrant furnace, an unreliable supply of fuel oil, and confinement with a just turned two year old daughter. So I dared not tell her that, like Creon's son, I was "hearing whispers in the street at night" that the History Department was on the verge of offering me a regular tenure-track position, or that the Pierson undergraduates had penned a missive to the Master that I ought to be considered as his successor. Nor to this day do I know what my response would have been had these eventualities come to pass, but I know for a certainty that a family crisis was averted by a telephone call.

The caller was Rufus Carrolton Harris, President of Tulane University, where I had served for the previous three years as an Assistant Professor of History. His question was brief and totally unexpected: would I accept an appointment to the deanship of H. Sophie Newcomb College, the woman's undergraduate liberal arts coordinate division of Tulane? This decision on his part had been made "on the basis of many considerations," his favorite phrase, and would I please talk to Lucy and give him a reply as soon as possible. (For those unfamiliar with the coordinate college configuration, this call would be the equivalent of one from the President of Harvard asking me to become the administrative head of Radcliffe College.) Besides Lucy, who was transported with joy at the thought of returning to her beloved New Orleans, I consulted two other people whose judgment I trusted implicitly! The first was my father, just completing his 25th year as President of the Texas State College for Women, who had made a career out of converting a curriculum based on home economics and the industrial arts which he had inherited into a demanding intellectual exercise in the liberal arts, thus plumbing the wealth of creativity latent in academic administration. He and Mr. Harris had long been close associates in the inner councils of the Southern educational establishment, and his advice to me was that I ought not forego this opportunity for tutelage under "one of the best men in the business."

My other consultant was, naturally, Dean DeVane, who invited me to his office to talk it over. There, I sought his opinion of whether, at this stage of my academic career, I could successfully combine meaningful scholarly endeavor that I so admired in my faculty colleagues and which I genuinely wanted to emulate with the demands of effective administration. He must have anticipated my question, for his ready reply was perhaps the most insightful piece of advice ever directed my way.

"Yes," he said, "the two can be combined," and he handed me a volume which had just come off the press, the 2nd edition of his seminal work on Browning, "for I made the extensive revisions of my first effort sitting at this desk. But you must remember that I was already a publishing scholar with tenure before I first sat in this Dean's chair. On that score you are still a neophyte, although Holborn tells me your research designs are well-conceived and that in time he is convinced you will be most productive. But there is another side to the academic coin that you may not have considered: in this business there are all too few administrators who really understand the essence of scholarship, and that he is just as committed to the search for truth whose work only closes up blind alleys of the past as the man who achieves some brilliant breakthrough. In other words, it takes the same kind of dedicated effort to tear down the wrong signposts for the future as it does to erect the right ones, and no administrator can effectively abet the pursuit of knowledge who does not grasp this singular fact. So, even though you have not yet donned the mantel yourself, you can be a boon to our profession if as an administrator you become the willing servant of scholarship and establish as your first priority the provision of the tools and the aura in which your faculty charges can thrive. We have enjoyed your presence at Yale and will certainly miss you, for it is not often that we see one of your age so abundantly full of piss and high purpose, but I say seize this chance and run with it."

So ended my interlude at Yale, the memories of which to this day remain fresh as the morning dew and one of the greenest of my pastures. And though I could not know it at the time, Mr. Harris' telephone call was the first of four from out of the blue that profoundly affected my career.

CHAPTER 17
—
The Newcomb Years

On 16 December 1870, Harriett Sophie, aged 15, died in the arms of her mother, Josephine Louise Newcomb, in New York City. Mrs. Newcomb (nee Le Monnier) had previously lost an infant son and then her husband, Warren, who had been a successful wholesale grocer operating out of Louisville, (Kentucky), New Orleans, (Louisiana), and New York City. An orphan herself, the widow spent the next thirteen years of life driven by the twin passions of enhancing the value of her late husband's estate of some $850,000 which had been bequeathed to her, and finding a suitable remembrance for her beloved daughter. By 1883 she had succeeded on both counts.

In the previous year, another benefactor of higher education in the South, Paul Tulane of Princeton, New Jersey, an eminently successful financial entrepreneur with various attachments to New Orleans, made a sizeable bequest which resulted in the creation of the Board of Administrators of the Tulane Educational Fund in New Orleans. Within two years by an Act of the State Legislature, this Board had subsumed the title and property of the University of Louisiana, a public institution, to create the Tulane University of Louisiana for Men, a private institution under the presidency of William Preston Johnson. Now it so happened that Johnson was a valued acquaintance of Mrs. Newcomb, and she decided to make an initial bequest to the Tulane Board of Administrators to establish under its prevue the H. Sophie Newcomb Memorial College, a degree-granting institution for women. Thus was born a novel arrangement in American higher education known as the coordinate college system, from which subsequently among others, stemmed the Radcliffe-Harvard, Barnard-Columbia, and Pembroke-Brown, relationships. Here for the first time in American academic history was a quasi-independent, separately endowed collegiate division for women with its own campus, its own faculty and administration, in control of its own admissions, curricula, and degree requirements, and yet financially and legally responsible to the same Board of Trustees and thus an integral part of a major university. Indeed, Newcomb's first administrative head had the title of President to indicate its unique nature, although subsequent heads had the title of Dean, a more realistic representation of its legal relationship with Tulane.

During its formative years, Newcomb was physically quite removed from Tulane, developing its own campus in midtown New Orleans, and its own curricula deemed useful and proper for the intelligent young white women of Louisiana but especially New Orleans: art, music, dance, drama and the other liberal arts such as literature, history and foreign languages. The Newcomb Chapel with its superb stained-glass windows was a small architectural gem. A highly responsible student government, an effective honor system, and a commencement exercise featuring a daisy chain became cherished Newcomb traditions. This sense of independence and superiority was obviously bolstered by the fact of its own endowment.

In the late 1920s handsome uptown properties were acquired cheek by jowl next to Tulane's main campus, and Newcomb College was moved bag and baggage, but propinquity did not mean union. The new campus lay out in the form of a horseshoe amidst a stand of stately live oak trees. At the top of the arc was the principal classroom and administration building, Newcomb Hall, resplendent in red brick and cream-colored cornices. Next to it in the same motif was an equally impressive building, our principal dormitory called Josephine Louise House. Next around the bend came the Gymnasium with its indoor swimming pool. And then anchoring that end of the Horseshoe was the School of Fine Arts, already known internationally for its pottery and glazes, portraiture and sculpture. Then directly across the greensward to the other end of the horseshoe was Dixon Hall, named after Newcomb's first and only President, which was the home of our music, dance and drama departments. The open space between Dixon Hall and Newcomb Hall lay in waiting for the Newcomb Chapel when funds permitted, whose stained glass windows were safely stored in the meantime in the Newcomb Hall attic.

All of this property in what was one of New Orleans' poshest residential areas had been acquired through eminent domain, and the principal artery which ran through it was Audubon Place, which was now attenuated to handle only campus traffic. One regal residence, however, #43, had been saved to become the home of the Newcomb Dean, and through the years it, too, became a symbol of Newcomb's independence and elegance, since Tulane's President was housed at a far less distinguished address some distance from the campus in the Garden District.

So now, with the exception of the Medical School, which remained downtown next to the gigantic public hospital built by Huey Long, all the major components of Tulane University were united on a single uptown campus which extended east to west from Audubon Park on St. Charles Avenue to Poydras Avenue. The Campus was divided almost in half by a public thoroughfare named Freret Street which ran north and south and had in many people's minds become the definitive line of demarcation with Newcomb on the east and Tulane on the west. Gibson Hall, which housed the President of Tulane, the Dean of the men's undergraduate College of Arts and Sciences, and the Dean of the Graduate School, was on St. Charles Avenue, as far west of Freret as it was possible to be, while Newcomb Hall was a considerable distance east of Freret. There were, however, along the Newcomb side of Freret, a number of buildings that served as points of union for the university community: the Library, the Student Union, and McAlister Auditorium; and later, as Tulane became more and more residential, men's dormitories and, ultimately, co-ed dormitories. But when I arrived in September, 1953, as Dean of Newcomb, the distance physically, intellectually, philosophically and culturally between Newcomb Hall and Gibson Hall was long, indeed, and my frequent toing's and froing's between the two were always the subject of much speculation on both sides of Freret.

The Newcomb College over which I first presided had 800 students and a faculty of 163, a very good ratio of one to the other. Newcomb controlled its own admissions through a Dean of Admissions and a Faculty Executive Committee which set the standards, among which were the relatively new College Entrance Board (SAT) examinations. Newcomb enjoyed an excellent reputation in the Gulf South as the best liberal arts college for women south of Sweet Briar in Virginia, and possessing several unique advantages. One was the city of New Orleans' colorful, historic, magnolia scented, culturally diverse, "the city which care forgot," a liberal education in itself. Another was Newcomb's coordinate position vis a vie a major university. A Newcomb student had her own campus, her own dorms, her own norms, her own student government, her own honor code, and she was seldom in direct intellectual competition with the opposite sex. Yet she was in no sense physically or socially isolated; she was an integral part of university extra-curricular life, she had a major library at her disposal, the visiting scholars and attractions of a major university, university-wide interest groups, and intercollegiate athletics. In brief, the best of both academic worlds and it is no wonder that the coordinate college system was so widely emulated in the East. All of this is to suggest the Newcomb application pool for admission made possible selectivity not common in the South and certainly not possible across Freret Street.

But from where I sat, Newcomb's greatest asset was its tradition for superb teaching. To be sure, three-fourths of the faculty had earned doctorates and were not unmindful of the importance of research and publication, but what they did better as a group than any other congeries of academics I have ever been associated with was teach the school. George Meyer and Mildred Christian in English Lit, Jerry Capers and Francis James in History, Cy Lee in Philosophy, Warren Roberts in Political Science, William Woods, Francis Livingston, Giovanni Cecchetti, the Le Breton sisters in Romance Languages, Margaret Groben in German, Dorothy Daspit in Physics, Peter Volpe and Milton Fingerman in the Biological Sciences, Peter Hansen in Musicology, Louise Snyder and Egydio Castro y Silva in Piano, Alfred Moyer and Pam Meyers in Art History, Pat Trivigno in Painting, Jules Struppeck in Sculpture, James Steg in Printmaking, and Mary Margaret Smith in Physical Education were all paragons of the pedagogical arts as well as splendid collegial companions. And the first among equals of this talented and dedicated group was the saintly and graceful Anna Many, Dean of Women, beloved by every student who set foot in Newcomb Hall, who by appearance, demeanor, and intellectual curiosity was the epitome of the gracious, mannered, liberated Southern aristocrat, a presence if ever there was one.

Now most of these things I had become aware of, at least vicariously, during my four years tenure as an assistant professor of History at Tulane, but not until after my sojourn at Yale when I came back to cross Freret Street and take up residence at 43 Audubon Place did I begin to know the sheer quality of the place. My inauguration festivities included a two-day Chautauqua on the Liberal Arts as the Key to Career Choices for Women (or something to that effect) the principal speaker at which was the attractive and vivacious Nancy Lewis, Dean of Pembroke, the coordinate college of Brown and one of the reigning icons of the so called Seven Sisters of the Ivy League. The proceedings ended with a gala dinner at Antoine's which featured the gathering together of all the heads of Newcomb College except the first,

Brandt Dixon, deceased. There was his successor, the venerable Pierce Butler, whose long tenure had set the tone for academic rigor. He was succeeded by William Hard, who seven years later left to become the President of Scripps College of the Claremont group in Southern California. He in turn was followed by the tall and elegant Logan Wilson, who after four years left to become Academic Vice-President of the University of North Carolina at Chapel Hill, and soon thereafter to become President of The University of Texas, my alma mater. In the two-year hiatus while searching for Wilson's successor, Anna Many had served as Acting Dean. One of my favorite photographs and certainly a landmark in Newcomb's history was the formal portrait of the four of us standing behind a beaming Miss Many. Thus began on a happy note the tenure of Newcomb's youngest and least experienced Dean.

But behind these pleasant civilities were serious doubts on the Newcomb side about the probity of its new Dean. Conventional wisdom had it that a relative unknown had been deliberately chosen by the Tulane administration and Board to emasculate Newcomb's collegiate personality and to bring it into line as simply another division under the Tulane masthead. And there were several disparate facts and situations which taken together made this supposition at least seem plausible. There was, for example, the historic separation of the two entities at the beginning and the concomitant development of distinctive institutional characteristics. There was the acceptance as common knowledge of Tulane's jealousy of Newcomb's far better reputation for a meaningful undergraduate experience than its male counterpart enjoyed. There was the unvarnished fact of Newcomb's far more demanding admissions policy. There was the powerful Newcomb Alumnae Association whose members were fiercely loyal to their college and many of whom were the social arbiters of Louisiana and New Orleans society. Then there were the periodic rumors that the Tulane Board was systematically dipping into Mrs. Newcomb's benefaction to finance other University programs, despite the fact that just before his departure, Dean Logan Wilson made a definitive disclosure of Newcomb's financial position which showed beyond peradventure that Mrs. Newcomb's largesse now provided only three-fourths of the funds requisite for operation and that Newcomb now relied on Tulane's other endowment resources to balance her budget.

There was also my personal history to be considered. It was common knowledge that my father had long been President of the Texas State College for Women, and that in the conclaves of Southern educators, he and President Harris and Roger McCutcheon, Dean of Tulane's Graduate School had become good friends, the inference being that they would mislead my father about Newcomb's true position in the educational firmament. There was the known fact that Fred Cole, Dean of Tulane's undergraduate college for men had personally recruited me for his Department of History and that he and I played handball together each day at noon. He was the most jealous of all because Newcomb's reputation and pride of place among New Orleans' cognceti so greatly overshadowed his own academic operation. Ergo, it must have been Cole who planted the seed with Harris, McCutcheon and the Tulane Board to send their man across Freret Street who would be a mere handmaiden to Gibson Hall. At any rate, it was no secret that neither the Newcomb faculty nor the Alumnae Association felt that it had any meaningful input in the selection process.

In any event, I was far removed from all of this and palpably ignorant of it. I was at Yale at the time, and the first inkling I had of my name being associated with Newcomb was a telephone call from President Harris asking me if I would consider the deanship. The only conversation with my father about the matter was his statement that he considered Mr. Harris the ablest university president of his acquaintance. But when I got back to New Orleans, it was Fred Cole who alerted me to the possible quicksand, as a good friend should.

So it was that once in office, I sedulously respected all the Newcomb mores as I understood them, and I had a magnificent administrative assistant in Mildred Mouch, a former Marine Captain who understood the meaning of loyalty and who was breaking in her third Newcomb Dean. There was, for example, a Chapel service at 8 a.m. each Friday morning over which I presided clad in my academic gown as were the Seniors present, and we sang the hymns and read the Scriptures selected by the student Chapel committee. Then, once a month the faculty gathered in its lounge to partake in the ritual of Cafe Brulot, presided over by the aristocratic Le Breton sisters, mainstays of our Romance Language and keepers of the sacred Creole recipe which demanded that if there be any variation in the ingredients, the brandy should not be shorted. And my first pronouncement from the chair was that the graduation ceremonies known as Little Commencement would remain unchanged wherein the Newcomb graduates would be preceded by the Junior class daisy chain and would then be individually announced and given their diplomas for the benefit of their parents and well-wishers, all this the day before the all-university commencement exercises. This was all very well and duty noted, but I needed something more, something distinctly for Newcomb, that would enhance her reputation as a leader in higher education for women and at the same time allay any suspicion about my loyalty to her cause. My first major interview with the *New Orleans Time Picayune* provided the occasion.

This very pleasant reporter, a former Newcombite herself, dutifully went through the litany of my educational background and soon came to the inevitable query of how I saw Newcomb's present place in the academic firmament and what changes had I in mind for its future. The interview resulted in an unusual headline the next day: "New Newcomb Dean Looks Forward to an Empty Campus."

What I had done was to outline my hopes for the establishment of what is known in the trade as a junior year abroad program, wherein selected juniors spent their junior academic year enrolled in a foreign university or institute of higher learning pursuing a carefully selected curriculum and system of evaluation that permitted the full transfer of academic credits back to the home institution. In this regard, Sweet Briar College for Women in Virginia had been a highly successful pioneer in Paris. But my motivation stemmed from personal conviction.

To this day I remember the astonishing change in my perspective and grasp of the world scene resulting from my first trip to Europe following my graduation from The University of Texas in June, 1938. As a major in modern British and European history, I had read voraciously as an undergraduate, but nothing could have prepared me for what I saw and experienced that summer. The fear in the British and French householders' eyes as they cocked their ears at dusk listening for the drone of an approaching Luftwaffe. The sense of foreboding at a Nazi Party meeting at Nuremberg while seeing and listening to the ravings of Hitler and Goebbels and Goering and Himmler. The sight and bombast of the pompous Mussolini prancing on the balcony of the Palazzo Venezia. The sight of Panzer divisions rumbling toward Czechoslovakia. These to be sure were melodramatic events in a dramatic era, but to have been able to experience them first hand was surely a defining moment in my life. At the very least I was convinced of the wisdom of Professor A. Li Burt's dictum that one can never know another country unless he gets inside it, and one can never know his own country unless he gets outside it. So at that age what more rewarding intellectual experience could there be than to reside and study abroad for a whole year. At least that was—and still is—my conviction.

What I did not say for publication was a concomitant conviction that although a Newcomb student was considerably above average in terms of intellectual gifts, she was by and large pretty provincial. At this time our student body was drawn almost entirely from Texas and the Deep South, where a certain gentility of manners often masked an almost complete ignorance of the world beyond. For many of our girls, taking up residence in New Orleans was a monumental adventure for one who had never before left home for any length of time or crossed a state boundary. Their magnolia-scented cocoons seldom produced much curiosity about a larger universe.

But my junior year abroad program was not to be for dilettantes. It was to be an honors program, an honest-to-God serious intellectual endeavor, qualifying for which was a major accomplishment. For the first two years at Newcomb a 3.5 grade point average on a 4.0 scale, and a 4.0 or a professor's certification in the major subject area. For a country other than the United Kingdom, a demonstrated language proficiency. There were to be a battery of psychological tests to measure stability under stress. There was to be an ongoing extracurricular seminar in United States history and civics and current events, because for the first time in her life the Junior Year Abroader would have to explain to an often critical audience just why and how we did things as we did, things which heretofore she had always taken for granted, and seldom if ever questioned. No two students were to be roommates abroad. In other words, baptism into the JYA experience would be not by sprinkling but by complete immersion. Preparation for it would begin the first day of the Freshman year. Finally, France and the Sorbonne had for several years been the loci for American JYA programs; we hoped to include Great Britain, Spain, Italy and Germany as well. Anticipating that our British contingent would always be the largest, I planned to base one professor-in-charge in London, and another in Paris for the Continent.

Having rashly gone public with my dream, I now had to convince the Newcomb faculty, and then the President of the University, and then the Board of Administrators of the efficacy of my proposal. This was accomplished despite much skepticism expressed in Gibson Hall. We then had to create the infrastructure to support the program, and so it was that in time JYA became the most prominent acronym on the campus. We had to set up a JYA Office, appoint a JYA Director, name a JYA Steering Committee, devise JYA admission forms and selection procedures, JYA family permission forms, and the like. So it was JYA this and JYA that which in fact served as a sort of smokescreen to cover my numerous deadly sins of commission and omission that first year. There were, however two positive developments.

The first was that we had on our faculty the first semester a visiting professor of British history from the University of Birmingham, D. C. Clarke, eccentric but witty and urbane, who became a magnet for our better students. In the course of the semester I talked to him at length about my JYA proposal. To my delight, he not only grasped its possibilities but also offered his own institution as a trial site, with himself a paterfamilias for our students, contingent upon the agreement of his own university authorities. Since to our knowledge no such arrangement had ever been worked out between an American and a British university, we agreed on a very modest start of sending only two students.

The second positive note was the fact that the French Line maintained a major regional office in New Orleans, whose longtime head, Captain Estache, was noted for his wit and hospitality and had become a fixture in New Orleans society. After a series of meetings with the Captain, we worked out an arrangement whereby Newcomb College would use the French Line exclusively for the transport of its students abroad, and that for every twenty-five roundtrip passages, one would be provided free, which to my mind would take care of our professors-in-charge. And as with most transactions in New Orleans, there was lagniappe, that little extra. Estache hinted that whenever the Newcomb Dean and his wife had to go abroad to oversee the operation, first class accommodations might be available at a very reasonable fee.

In sum, the parts were gradually assembled and put in place, and the JYA became operational for the academic year 1954-55 when we sent our first two students to the University of Birmingham. The results were mixed: one came back at the end of term ecstatic about her experience; the other succumbed to the blandishments of a young English swain, married him, and we never saw her again. One can imagine the shaking of heads and clucking of tongues, particularly among the older alumnae, about this mad Texas dean sending abroad our innocents to be ravished by the lascivious foreigner, and to think what was going to happen when we send our first group to France!

Indeed, much of that year had been spent in readying our first batch of students for France and in developing the French connections for their accommodation. We were going to divide the French experience between a six-week stint in a provincial city, Dijon, with nothing but language study and practice while residing with French families, before going to Paris for the regular academic term at the Sorbonne and its affiliates. As our Agent we engaged Madame Marie Alverhne, who had worked with Sweet Briar and Reid Hall, and it was she who handled our logistic problems, which were legion.

As for Britain, we were greatly encouraged by our one success, and now our task was to expand the number of institutions willing to host our students. While my wife, Lucy, and the head of our Department of Romance Languages, Professor William Woods, worked France with Madame Alverhne, I made the English circuit much aided by Professor Clarke who provided me with invaluable introductions. In the end, our UK lineup included Birmingham, Manchester, Leeds, Sheffield, Reading, Exeter, the University of London and its affiliate colleges, Glasgow, Edinbourough, St. Andrews, Cardiff and Aberwistrith, which enabled us generally to adhere to our policy of no more than two of our students at each institution. Later we added the University of Madrid, and especially its institute of Fine Arts, the University of Florence, and finally the University of Tubigen in West Germany. And not only was our geographic institutional spread impressive, but also the holiday periods provided an enormous opportunity for trans-national and cross-cultural travel. All student financial assistance applicable at Newcomb was applicable to the JYA, and the year abroad was almost always a fiscal wash with a year at the home campus.

Not all of our JYAers, to be sure, were paragons of social decorum, nor was our selection process flawless; there were a few rude recalls for academic or behavioral reasons, and there was one instance of a deep depression that led to suicide. But the overwhelming effect of the JYA program was the dramatic uplifting of the intellectual climate of the college. The returning JYAers were the object of everyone's attention, and they wore the badge proudly. They were generous in sharing their experiences, and they were invaluable in the selection, placement and indoctrination of the next batch. As seniors they generally selected honors courses, and their presence was distinctive in the student body as a whole. There were two groups, however, who found it difficult to adjust to this new sophistication range of interests and global perspective so alien to the Deep South—their parents and their boyfriends. Conversational gambits could be a trial.

Painting of Dean J.R. Hubbard by Pat Trevigno

And at the other end of the academic spectrum, the freshmen and sophomores exhibited an enhanced work ethic in keeping with a reward system so palpably attractive. Our language laboratories, for example, were seldom vacant. Another pleasant result of the program, and one not foreseen at the time, was that a handsome JYA brochure replete with photographs from abroad and fulsome quotes from participants became a standard part of our promotional admissions package with dramatic results: our admissions pool increased dramatically, allowing a much higher degree of selectivity, but even more importantly, the ratio of acceptances of our admissions invitation increased by a third. Until there was a marked expansion of our physical facilities, we were forced to set a cap of 1000 students from an ever-increasing admissions application pool. Finally, there was evidence from another quarter that we had done something special. The demand from the male undergraduates on the other side of Freret Street for admission to the program became so intense that shortly after I departed the scene, the JYA became an all-university phenomenon.

One of the legends springing from this whole endeavor is still fondly recalled by JYAers at Newcomb homecomings. It is known as the Madame Woods story. It was in the winter of 1956 that my wife, Lucy, accompanied by Professor Bill Woods chairman of our Department of Romance Languages, and I were going to Paris to see if we could improve the living arrangements of our French contingent and open up more opportunities for our Fine Arts majors. True to his word, Captain Estache had provided us with handsome quarters on the magnificent new France. It was frigid in New York at the time of embarkation, and I had contracted a terrible cold, and as soon as we went aboard I immediately repaired to my bed of pain. Fortunately for Lucy, Bill, a confirmed bachelor, was a great pal of ours and a gay blade, and he wined and dined and danced with her and accompanied her to the ship's galas, while I never left our stateroom and subsisted on soup and cheese. It was the third morning out about 8 a.m. and Lucy and I were still in bed when the knock came on our cabin door. "Entre," I said in my best French, and in stepped the Chief Purser. Looking at us as we lay side by side with the sheet drawn up, he said, "Dean Hubbard, the Captain requests that you and Madame Woods here join him for dinner tonight." Drawing Lucy closer to me, I replied, "Please tell the Captain that we would be delighted. But tell me one thing. Is Professor Woods included?" Without blinking an eye, he replied, "Certenment!" and took his departure. That, I would suggest, was savoir faire in spades. It was a delightful evening and even the Captain was amused when we got it all sorted out. Lucy still has her place card for "Madame Woods."

The antics of the new Dean of Newcomb College were, however, a mere sideshow to President Harris' much more serious agenda for Tulane University, the ultimate goal of which was an invitation for Tulane to join the Association of American Universities (AAU). The AAU was the institutional Phi Beta Kappa of higher education in North America. The organization began in the early 20th Century with the voluntary union of the principal members of the Ivy League. The presidents of these institutions would meet together once a year to discuss common problems and future prospects. After about ten years of this, the group deemed itself too provincial, and determined on a slow and careful expansion and geographic spread. The AAU was from the outset self-selecting, and the principal criterion for membership was the research potential of the institution, which spoke to the caliber of the faculty and its publications, the scope of its library holdings, the quality of its laboratories, the amount of sponsored research it attracted, the membership of its faculty in learned societies, and the like, all quantifiable measures of distinguished post-baccalaureate performance. Obvious clusters of excellence such as McGill and Toronto in Canada, Chicago, Northwestern, Berkeley, Stanford, Cal Tech, Duke, and North Carolina at Chapel Hill, gave the AAU a truly national representation, and it became the dream of every university president to bring his institution into that scholastic Valhalla. Now it seems that in the 1940's, the AAU wanted better representation among the private universities in the deep South, and there were two which seemed ripe for membership—Vanderbilt, in Nashville, Tennessee, and Tulane, in New Orleans. In practically every measurable aspect, they seemed evenly matched. Both, for example, had distinguished medical schools, both had increasing financial support from foundations and alumni, both had undertaken substantial physical renovation, and so on. There was really no way to choose, and since to elect both would have upset the AAU's carefully achieved regional balance, this erudite leadership determined on a Solomonic solution—flip a coin. Vanderbilt won, and when the decision was announced, its Chancellor, Harvie Branscomb—who I can attest was a consummate horse's ass—chortled to his friends that since he had now achieved one of his most cherished goals, his next for the rest of his life would be to keep Tulane out of the AAU.

In New Orleans, Rufus Carrolton Harris was on the very brink of apoplexy, and he vowed then and there to build a case for Tulane's membership that all the Branscomb's in hell could not countervail. His strategic plan was quite simple: recruit young, personable, aggressive deans to head the major academic divisions of the university, who with the few already in place would in turn concentrate their faculty recruitment with one objective—Tulane would henceforth be known for the quality of its graduate and professional programs. For his part, President Harris promised an intensive fund-raising campaign. Among his administrative holdovers was Fred Carrington Cole, a 41 year old Texan and historian, and Dean of the College of Arts and Sciences; Elizabeth Wisner, revered Dean of Social Work; and Max Lapham, known nationally as an able Dean of the Medical School and the doyen of campus administrators. Brought in fresh was the 40 year old handsome and scholarly Ray Forrester as Dean of the Law School; the 40 year old hard driving Lee Johnson as Dean of Engineering; the 38 year old visionary John Lawrence as Dean of Architecture; the 39 year old brilliant anthropologist Robert Wauchope to revitalize our Institute of Latin American Studies; and when the venerable Roger McCutcheon retired, the 38 year old Robert Lumiansky, one of the country's leading Chaucer scholars who as a tank commander had been assigned to General Le Clerc's Free French Armored Division which had liberated Paris in World War II, as Dean of the Graduate School. At age 35 I was the baby of the group. In effect, what Mr. Harris had done was to assemble an array of decanal young Turks and say to them, "Gentlemen, take us into the AAU." This prioritizing of graduate and professional work was a mission change of high order destined to alter significantly the whole personality of the institution, and it mitigated against the historic relationship of Newcomb College to Tulane University. My task therefore was to preserve the best that was Newcomb while fitting her comfortably into the new dispensation.

The burden of working out the new relationships fell upon Cole, Lumiansky and myself, the Deans who presided over faculty groups central to the new mission, and it was indeed fortunate that we were the closest of friends both professionally and socially, for there was a substantial amount of give and take involved. First we had to develop a new faculty profile; we could no longer afford the skilled pedagogue with no interest in research and publication, or the rocket scientist who couldn't be bothered with undergraduate teaching. Nor could the Arts & Sciences faculties at Tulane and Newcomb be mutually exclusive, for what sense did it make to offer a course for, say eight girls when the same subject matter was being offered by another professor for ten boys. The key was to reorganize all the academic disciplines on a university wide basis under a university chairman, and from these the graduate faculty would be selected. The individual faculty member might sit on either side of Freret

Street, with his courses cross-listed in both undergraduate and graduate bulletins and the students attending wherever the course was taught. As a professor of History, I sat in graduate faculty meetings presided over by Lumiansky, but in departmental meetings where the gut issues such as faculty recruitment, course offerings, promotion and tenure were at stake, the presiding officer was the university departmental chairman. Another point of union was the University Senate, made up of nominees from each collegiate division and which developed university policy positions for discussion with the administration and Board. All in all it was a system which required considerable acculturation and adjustments as experience dictated, but with liberal doses of good will it worked, and in 1960 we marched proudly into the hallowed halls of the AAU. I was informed later that the fact that Newcomb's admissions application pool was beginning to rival that of the Seven Sisters in the East in terms of quality and number did nothing to hurt our chances.

These were also the days when a far more poignant drama was being played out in the South—the integration of our school systems. As a London Times editorial pointed out, the violence emanating from Little Rock, distressing as it was, was still the harbinger of change. In the 1950's the battle was well and truly joined, and the dreadful ordeal and bloodshed of Edgar Medford at the University of Mississippi and the calling out of the State Guard to block Arturine Lucy from entering the University of Alabama (referred to as Bama) were manifestations of a struggle of increasing fury.

Among our most effective agents for change were our professional organizations such as the Mississippi Valley Historical Association and the Southern Historical Association. Every academic discipline had similar organizations on a national and regional level which without exception were fully integrated, and we boasted of it in every public pronouncement, as well as exhorting our home institutions to follow suit.

Progress was slow, but at least we had an accurate if peculiar way of measuring it—the hotel ground rules where we convened for our annual meetings. In the beginning, no black member would be permitted to set foot inside the hotel premises. Then we found an occasional one who would permit them to attend our discussions, but no food, drink or slumber. Each year a hotel blacklist was compiled and circulated among every professional organization, and the economic impact gradually began to take its toll, for a gathering of five to six hundred delegates for a week was a bonanza not to be ignored. Take the Bayshore Inn at Gulfport, Mississippi, a pleasant hostelry overlooking the Gulf with meager patronage during the off season. To attract two or three of our organizations during the slack periods was a fiscal infusion not to be ignored. So the local arrangements committee would canvass likely venues, and each year the restrictions became less rigid. The Bayshore Inn, for example went from a complete prohibition of blacks in the premises to permission to register as guests and attend the sessions, but no mixed dining and drinking in public.

Since Tulane was to be the titular host to the Southern Historical Association that year, our local arrangements committee, which included two professors from our local black universities drove over to Gulfport to test the water. No problems with registration or the selection of meeting rooms, and we were informed that our dinner would be served in a private dining room. We were six people, and after a couple of drinks in my room, we went down to dine and were ushered into Room A. There we found a table set for four, with two other chairs against the wall. Upon enquiry about this arrangement, we were informed that according to state law it was permitted for our black companions to be in the same room with us but they could not be served food in our company. With that we went back to our rooms in high dudgeon, ordered dinner from room service, and spent a passable evening. Fortunately we were able to find more suitable arrangements elsewhere.

But next year, 1959, the breakthrough was complete. Memphis State University was the host institution, and the stateliest of all the hotels in the Deep South, the Peabody, welcomed our association's annual meeting. At the formal banquet we had invited every black dignitary and his wife in the city, and the mixed seating was something to behold. It was nothing less than the irreversible beginning of the end of segregation in the South. We were warmly greeted by the mayor of Memphis, and the program was a discussion of just where we were in this matter of integration by a panel consisting of the president of the Memphis Bar association, the president of Fisk University, one of our finest black institutions, and the president elect of the SHA, Jim Silver, professor of History at the University of Mississippi and one of the most courageous and articulate opponents of segregation who had befriended Edgar Meador and hidden him under his bed during the time of troubles at Ole Miss. The final member of the panel was William Faulkner himself who's moving denunciation spoken almost in a whisper of man's pettiness and prejudice was the fitting climax to a memorable event in Southern history. At the SHA's meeting the next year in Ashville, North Carolina, Jim Silver's presidential address was a masterful dissection of the anatomy of segregation as practiced in Mississippi by state officials and the administrators of Ole Miss that resulted in many new faces and a far more humane approach to the problem. The *London Times* reported Silver's speech almost verbatim from a text supplied, I am proud to say, by me.

But what of my own institution? Here the process of integration was inexorable, and as a private institution its freedom of action was almost complete, but shielded as it was from the madding crowd by its private nature, its methodology was carefully muted. The opening gambit was a resolution passed unanimously by the newly-established University Senate delivered without publicity to the President and Board of Administrators of the Tulane Educational Fund that race and color should be forthwith eliminated as elements in the admissions criteria for Tulane and Newcomb College. In reply, the administration thanked the Senate for its thoughtfulness, assured it of its careful consideration, and that as a first step the resolution was being forwarded to University counsel.

Now it was a matter of record and therefore common knowledge that both Paul Tulane and Josephine Louise Newcomb had specified in their deeds of gift that their funds were to be used for the education of the white youths of Louisiana. And when the winds of desegregation in the South began to approach gale force, the Tulane and Newcomb heirs separately informed the Tulane Board that if the terms of the original deeds of gift were in any way violated, it would be sued not only for the principal but also for the accrued interest since the gifts were accepted. For the few members of the Board who were constitutionally opposed to the notion of integration, it was hoped that this prospect would put an end to the matter. But the substantial majority, many of who were lawyers, and all of our Jewish members, were undeterred. In New Orleans was based the 5th Circuit of the U.S. Court of Appeals, and it was decided to seek a declaratory judgment from that body. There was no indication of when the court would rule, but in the meantime, with as little publicity as possible, there was a lot of groundwork that needed to be done if the decision was favorable. In other words, if we got the opinion we needed, we wanted to be able to act quickly and decisively before any groundswell of opinion pro or con could develop. The first question was which division of the university was most likely to provide the warmest milieu for what would be undoubtedly a bewildering experience. I immediately volunteered Newcomb, for thanks to the JYA, we had undoubtedly the most cosmopolitan group of students on the campus. That settled, it was then incumbent on me to find the person who was not only willing but able to blaze the trail.

Always on a "what if" basis, I talked to a lot of people—JYAers coming back and going, our councilor to women, our key department heads, our psychologists, leading alumnae in the city, student class presidents, Mortar Board, Phi Beta Kappa, you name it, and slowly a profile began to develop. She should be a local girl and so not enter Newcomb as a stranger in a bewildering city. She should be a transfer student into the Sophomore class, since the direct progression from high school to college is traumatic enough under the best of circumstances. She should be a residential rather than a day student to be completely immersed in collegiate life, and she should have a roommate. She should be a science major rather than art or literature so that her academic progress can be more accurately measured than by subjective judgment. So any brilliant, personable, articulate, sophisticated, financially secure, color blind product of the middle class, not to mention courageous, would do nicely, thank you. My job was to find her.

There were two black universities in New Orleans, Dillard and Southern, one public and one private, the heads of each I knew very well. I invited them to lunch in the President's small dining room in the Student Center, and behind closed doors I took them into my confidence about Tulane's plans for integrating its student body, described the kind of person we thought we needed to begin the process, and asked for their help in identifying her. For these gentlemen, the future prospect of Tulane and Newcomb attracting the cream of the products of the black secondary schools in the area was not the most exciting scenario I could have painted for them, but they understood the larger issues as well or better than I, and they pledged their support.

About two weeks later President Jones of Dillard called to tell me he thought he might have the ideal candidate for me and would I please come to meet her in his office. She was indeed something special: 18 years old, in the second semester of her Freshman year, planning to major in bio-chemistry with a career goal to be a practicing physician, attractively well-groomed, articulate, and extremely nervous about our proposal. Her father, a graduate of Mehary Medical College in Nashville, was one of

New Orleans' ablest black physicians, and her mother was a graduate of Fisk University with an unlikely major in French literature, a not unhappy asset in New Orleans. She had an older brother who was a junior at Dillard majoring in History, and a younger sister who was a senior in high school, and we rather nervously speculated how unusual it would be if all three were involved in breaking the academic color barrier. At any rate , there began a series of meetings with daughter and parents quietly after hours on our campus, where we showed them our living and dining facilities, the Library and Student Union, the class rooms and laboratories. We talked about the importance as we saw it, of a roommate, which would deny her the luxury of feeling sorry for herself all alone in the wee hours. We told her there would be awkward, unpleasant happenings, because we had our share of "red necks" on our campus. We told her that she would undoubtedly receive favors because of the color of her skin, because so many of us so badly wanted her to succeed. But our constant litany was that we would ignore as much as humanly possible the fact of a "stranger" in our midst and assure the normalcy of her rite of passage. God and the 5th Circuit willing, she would enter Newcomb the following September at the beginning of the 1961-1962 academic session.

And that is what happened. Judge Skelley Wright wrote a masterful opinion for the Court of Appeals to the effect that mort main could not obtain in 1961 after the legacies of Mr. Tulane and Mrs. Newcomb had been used for years and years for the education of youth from outside the state of Louisiana and for students of color from outside the confines of the United States in our graduate and professional schools without the slightest demurrer from the heirs. Thus the crust of custom must govern the present situation and that today our admissions policies could not embrace the bias of geography and color as enunciated in the original deeds of gift. We at Newcomb who had private knowledge of the verdict were ready.

On 3 September 1961 the Wright opinion was released to the media. This also happened to be the first day of Newcomb's orientation of new students, an event which had attracted no media attention in the past, nor was this day an exception, since the media was blissfully unaware of what we had done in anticipation of a favorable verdict. Thus there was no media in sight except our own when at 8:30 a.m. as scheduled, Dr. and Mrs. James Patrick drove up to the main entrance to Newcomb College on Broadway Boulevard. Their daughter alighted from the car, and as they drove away, she walked through the gates to be greeted by a returning band of JYAers who, with guitar in hand, swept her into the faculty lounge for cakes and ale and a round of songs. So it was that New Orleans woke up that morning totally unaware of a little drama without fuss or feathers that would forever change the mission and personalities of her leading institutions of higher learning. It was only in mid-afternoon that the press and TV got some inkling of what was going on at Newcomb, only to be told that no media would be permitted on campus. To the furious responses from newsrooms and TV stations, our public relations people could plead they were acting under severe instructions, but the media never forgave me. What matter. Jack Stibbs, Tulane's Dean of Students, and our wives had a marvelous dinner at Manale's, plump oysters on the half shell, shrimp remoulade, crab meat Verdi, cerise Jubilee. No Oxford, Mississippi. No Tuscaloosa, Alabama. Mission accomplished.

The relative ease with which Tulane's desegregation was consummated without public furor I was willing to attribute to the cosmopolitan nature of the Crescent City laced with its Spanish, French, Creole, and Cajun strains at variance fundamentally with most of the traditions of the deep South. So to this day I am not sure why the segregation issue at a different level was so bitterly joined ostensibly by men of good will.

New Orleans was the home of the Isadore Newman School, one of the college preparatory experiences available in the country. Heavily endowed by one of New Orleans' Jewish merchant dynasties, it had grown into an ecumenical melting pot where wits took precedence over religious orientation, and where graduation in the top 10% of the class was a passport to any university in the country. With a spacious campus located uptown, it also had an athletic tradition that spoke to its concern for the whole person. There was traditionally a goodly representation of Tulane and Newcomb faculty kids that flourished there in a beautifully integrated intellectual and social experience. My three daughters, for example, felt more at home at Temple than they did with the Episcopalian heritage of their parents. Isadore Newman's scion, Dede, was a pillar in the community, and as owner of our finest department store, Maison Blanche, he saw to it that Isadore's creation remained in funds. He kept his personal distance from the school, however, preferring his seat on the Tulane Board as a broader base for community involvement.

But for the Jewish community, New Orleans was often an unthinking and cruel anomaly. The city's whole social season was centered in, on and around Mardi Gras, the Carnival of Bachannalia which preceded the abstinence of Lent and the climax of Easter. But Easter, Lent, Carnival, and Mardi Gras were all Christian observances, of which the Boston Club, as social arbiter and, indeed, dictator of the Carnival Crewes and parades and balls, sedulously prohibited a Jew from entering its premises. So for the Jewish community, the Easter season became a propitious time for a hegira to Europe, the Caribbean, New York, or wherever. I believe this is why the Jewish community cherished the Newman School, the finest exemplar of its kind for miles around, as a particular Jewish creation. Certainly the Jewish members of the Newman Board were proud of its existence, a feeling perfectly well understood by its two Gentile members, of which I was one.

The other was George Meyer, Chairman of Newcomb's Department of English, a long time and respected member whose two children were graduates of Newman. It was George who was one of the authors of the Tulane University Senate resolution on desegregation. And it was before our next Newman Board meeting had been called to order that George and I were asked about the feeling on the campus and what we thought the fate of the resolution might be. The conversation then turned to the general dilemma facing Southern education and the disgraceful events at Ole Miss and Alabama, when George quite casually wondered out loud whether it might be an appropriate time for the Newman board to take a similar action. The chairman of the Newman board was Louis Laemmle, the distinguished head of one of our best law firms, and a tireless worker for any proposal deemed to be in the best interests of our community, a man of unquestioned probity and compassion. So I was not prepared for his extreme discomfort with Meyer's proposal that seemed to him to be almost flippant, whereas this was a subject of complex ramifications that required the most careful study and which conceivably might compromise Newman's hard won reputation for excellence.

Thus was sparked a debate that was long and often raucous and bitter, and which spilled over at times in public gatherings causing acute embarrassment. For my part, I could not see how any man with Mr. Laemmele's intellectual gifts and good judgment could be so pig-headedly wrong, or how the Jewish community, given the long history of its persecution, could support bigotry in any form or fashion, and I was convinced that Mr. Laemmele did not speak for that community. What I do know is that though Meyer and I never let a meeting pass without raising the issue, we could never get a majority vote for changing the admissions policy because of the members' respect and friendship for the chairman. Shortly after I left these premises for India, he resigned, and my first message at our Embassy in New Delhi was from the new chairman, Moise Dennery, "You've won. Resolution follows." The first person to enroll under the new dispensation was black as the ace of spades, bright as a penny, and one of Newman's better quarterbacks.

So with a color blind admissions policy and membership in AAU, Tulane's progress under President Harris had been notable indeed, but in the doing of it, some egos had been bruised, some sacred cows dehorned, and some shibboleths trampled in the dust. Newcomb, for example, was no longer an undemanding haven for next year's crop of debutantes, and God knows who might wind up as your magnolia blossom's roommate. But a much broader and more vocal segment of the local populace had become enraged by what it deemed to have been the deliberate sabotaging of Tulane's ability to be at least competitive in intercollegiate athletics. What was more, that was exactly the case!

Tulane had for many years been a member of the Southeastern Athletic Conference, which boasted such powerful programs as those at Alabama, Tennessee, Auburn, Ole Miss and LSU, Tulane's arch rival from Baton Rouge some 70 miles up the pike. For years Tulane fielded reasonable football teams; in 1932 her team that included such names as "Iron Legs" Scafide, "Wop" Glover and Jerry Dalrymple had been invited to the Rose Bowl, only to be demoralized by the passing of Howell to Hutson of the Bama Crimson Tide. The annual donnybrook between the Tulane Green Wave and the LSU Tigers had generated such interest that both schools found themselves with 70,000 seat arenas. But in these intercollegiate groupings dominated as they were by the tax-supported state institutions, the private universities with their much more selective student bodies found it impossible to compete. Thus the Rice Institute in the Southwest Conference, Northwestern in the Big Ten, and Tulane in the Southeast became the whipping boys of their respective groups. What mitigated the fiscal situation for Tulane a little bit was that its stadium became the annual venue for the Sugar Bowl and once for the Super Bowl. One solution for the privates was simply to withdraw from the fray, as did the University of Chicago who in 1938 produced the first Heisman Trophy winner in Jay Berwanger, but whose storied President, Robert Hutchins, claimed that whenever he was inclined toward physical exertion, he lay down until the mood passed. Northwestern, Rice and Tulane, however, for their own reasons, eschewed this solution. Northwestern, backed by its alumni, refused to lower its admissions standards and decided just to ride it out. Rice, on the other hand, as the lone purveyor of such divertissement in the metropolitan Houston area and not wishing to decamp to its arch-rival in Austin, installed a Division of Physical Education, engaged a highly visible coach in Jess Neely and in effect hired a football team which at its peak won the conference championship and went to the Cotton Bowl where it defeated the University of Colorado Buffaloes with its legendary "Whizzer" White. In so doing, Rice, which boasted a superb science and engineering faculty rated by many as on a par with Cal Tech and MIT, deliberately negated its chances for election to the AAU.

Tulane attempted the Rice solution as demanded by a powerful member of the Board, Lester Lautenschlager, a former football great, whose lovely manse at the corner of Audubon Place and St. Charles Avenue, a stone's throw from Gibson Hall, was not only one of the poshest addresses in the city but also the watering hole for the sporting set. Les was solidly backed by his old Deke fraternity brother, Joseph Jones, the flamboyant chairman of the Board and the head of New Orleans' most powerful law firm. Thus were the courses in Physical Education greatly expanded with Richard Baumback—who quarterbacked Tulane's 1929 southern championship football team—engaged as Athletic Director, and one of our ablest, best known and beloved of our athletic alumni, Andy Pilney, resurrected as football coach. The net result was a few closer encounters with LSU and one genuinely exciting performer, Eddie Price, who enjoyed a notable career as a New York Giant running back. But that was about it, and that was the situation when the Young Turks began their quest for the AAU.

It was abundantly clear to us that the academically indefensible physical education program, even had it yielded any tangible results, would have to go lest we become a hydra-headed academic entity such as Rice. Knowing full well the risk he was taking, Mr. Harris bit the bullet and took to the Board a proposal severely limiting the scope of the physical education offerings and with Jones and Lautenschlager kicking and screaming every step of the way and finally carried the day when every dean on the campus appeared in support of the proposal. Clearly now the relationship between the President of the University and the Chairman of the Board of Administrators and his principal henchman was at best dangerously adversarial. Whereas Mr.

Harris had placed every last one of his chips into the AAU pot, Mr. Jones neither understood what membership would mean to Tulane's national and international reputation, nor did he care. So when the great gamble paid off, we had the supreme irony that Mr. Harris was a prophet without honor to his own Board. He remained just long enough to attend the next meeting of the AAU as its youngest member and thumb his nose at Mr. Branscomb, before resigning and returning to his roots in Macon, Georgia, as President of Mercer University, the institution that had started him on his administrative way as dean of its Law School. His last great victory was the quiet integration of that venerable institution.

Enter Joe Jones again who announced a great nation-wide search for a new leader worthy of Tulane's now exalted place in the academic firmament. We insiders had a candidate at the ready, John Weaver, Dean of the graduate school at the University of Iowa, a distinguished geographer who had visited us several times as Dean Lumiansky's guest. Our most logical candidate, Lumiansky himself, could not of course be considered because he was not permitted to enter the sacred confines of the Boston Club. For his part, Weaver was not deemed even worthy of another trip to the campus, which didn't bother him a great deal since he was slated to be the next President of the University of Wisconsin. Who Jones did turn up was about as nondescript a person that one could have found in higher education, a mediocrity named Herbert Longenecker, who at some time had been some kind of an official in the Ford Foundation and, ergo, in a position to channel unlimited amounts of Ford funds to Tulane. The road back to bare respectability was crystal clear and especially bitter to those of us who had worked so hard to rise above it. Our institutional espirit had been crushed. Even so, Joe Jones deserved a better denouement than shortly thereafter being burned to death with his wife in an early morning fire at his Metarie estate.

We were not rats but we certainly recognized that our ship was aflame. The first to leave was Ray Forrester, to become Dean of Boalt Hall, the law school of the University of California at Berkeley. Then Fred Cole, to become President of Washington and Lee, and then the first Director of the Ford Foundation's Council on Library Resources. Then Bob Lumiansky, lured first to Duke and then to Penn as chairman of the English Department, and then to the presidency of the American Council of Learned Societies, and with Barnaby Keeney, sometime president of Brown University, were the prime movers in the creation of the National Endowment of the Arts and its companion National Endowment for the Humanities. There was no doubt that Mr. Harris had a very keen eye for talent.

My position was egregiously bad. My contempt for the new President and his obese, insensitive wife was thinly disguised. My loyalty to Mr. Harris as against the Board was common knowledge. My position as Dean was considered impregnable because no one dared take on the powerful Newcomb constituency. But I had lost my leader and my closest professional and social companions and the excitement of our mission. It was clearly time to move on, but my problem was that the only place I really wanted to go was my alma mater, The University of Texas, and UT was not in the market.

I, my wife, and my three daughters (Lisa, Missy, and Kristi), loved Newcomb, and Newcomb had reciprocated. The occasion of my sabbatical leave of absence in the Spring semester of 1961 illustrated the symbiosis that had developed between us. Although most of my professional time was devoted to academic administration, I still fancied that my true profession was that of a teacher-scholar. The teacher in me worked wonderfully well, and I had never deserted the classroom, giving at least one graduate or undergraduate class each semester. But it was the scholarship that had perforce been neglected, even though there were still areas of research interest that clamored for my attention. One of them was—and still is—the First World War, and I was convinced that there was a useful book in my system dealing with the British home front and the almost criminal unreality of its comprehension of the actual frightfulness of the battlefield. And I knew that the most comprehensive gathering of material dealing with the British experience in that war had been collated under one catalog and housed together in its own wing in the magnificent library of England's Cambridge University. That was my leave destination.

Thanks again to Captain Estacy, we traveled en famille on the Liberte, and although it was a stormy January crossing, I managed not to miss a meal. I remember the dancing was mostly groping and hanging close, which was not all bad. We stopped for a couple of days in London to begin the kids' orientation to left-handed England and to visit our friends, Dr. Dennis Melrose, he of the first surgical team to use successfully the "blue baby" technique, and his gorgeous wife, Ann, a former model who, when the slightest bit tipsy, liked to ascend the stairs, turn holding out her glass, and proclaim, "Deeelicious" which she used to do for Pepsi ads. Then up to Cambridge with our sea freight in the middle of a winter that even the natives admitted was severe. We were at the mercy of a housing agent who had available a vacant half-bungalow at one extremity of Queen's Road exactly a mile from the Cambridge library. We snapped it up to get out of the cold, though it had no central heating. There was a small parlor, dining room and kitchen below, and upstairs, two bedrooms and, happily, two bathrooms. It was a pretty grim prospect for the next seven months, but thanks to Ann, who showed up with her station wagon crammed with blankets, portable stoves, sleeping bags, and one of the most welcome bottles of whisky in my experience, we began to make do. And so began one of the great family adventures of our experience.

To begin with, I took delivery of a Volkswagen Camper, which permitted us to explore the Fens on the weekends and to meander on the Continent during school holidays. So we were mobile. We then were introduced by neighbors to a sturdy, jovial, middle-aged widow who turned out to be maid, laundress, and baby-sitter extraordinary, which freed Lucy and me for overnights in London or whatever. We then found within walking distance for the kids the Milton Road School, considered to be an above-average educational establishment. Lisa, aged 9 and Missy aged 7 were enrolled in the Upper School presided over by the prim and proper Mr. Varley, while Kristy aged 5 entered the Lower School under the pious Miss Southerland. So in short order they were confronted with, among other things, a mysterious "times" table reckoned in pence, shillings and pounds. I remember one night at dinner asking about the day's experience at school. Lisa and Missy replied, "We played all day," but Kristie, looking up with tears in her eyes, said, "We prayed all day."

To try to stay in some kind of physical shape I elected to walk the two miles to the Library and back, and what a glorious walk it was, following the bank of the Cam through a lovely green park and then along the Backs and the gorgeous gardens of the Colleges. It was at Clare where I turned through the new quarter into the entrance of the imposing structure that was the Library with its immense tower dominating the landscape. There I was warmly greeted as was every lover of learning and directed to what I came to consider as "my" wing, crammed as it was with just about everything that had been written about the Great War. It was, in a word, overwhelming.

And as if this were not enough, I discovered that exactly half way between the Library and our modest digs there stood the Merton Arms, Arthur and Dorothy Houghton, Props., cheek by jowl to an imposing townhouse occupied by a younger Rothschild. Its location was ideal when I was in the mood for a pub lunch, and it was the perfect place for me after leaving the Library bleary-eyed each evening for the pint or two before my trudge up the hill toward home. It was here that in good time I was included in the goodly company of the pub regulars, one of the great privileges of my life.

But the greatest surprise and most rewarding experience of all was the warmth of my welcome into the community of scholars at Cambridge. As an example, I had been using in my course in 19th Century Britain a new and definitive survey by David Thompson, Master of Sydney Sussex, one of the residential colleges that made up the Cambridge complex. When I paid a courtesy call to tell him how useful I was finding his text, I found this jovial tall, amiable, out-going chap not much older than I fussing around his cluttered desk with some page proof, who brushed aside my praise and asked me if I would do him the great favor of critiquing some of the chapters in his new work on 20th Century Britain. Soon thereafter he and his charming wife had Lucy and me to tea, and later he asked me to dinner at High Table where we sampled some of Sydney's best claret. What an absolute tragedy was his shocking loss to cancer before term was out.

Then there was the flamboyant, red-headed Labour M. E., Dame Margaret Perry, ardent defender of women's rights and Mistress of Newnham, one of Cambridge's two residential colleges for women, whom I called on simply to compare notes about the administration of somewhat similar institutions. After convincing her that I was as ardent a champion as she of the fairer sex, she became my social arbiter in Cambridge. At one of her soirees, she seated me next to Sir Charles Darwin, Jr., son of the celebrated anthropological theorist, who regaled me with tales of his experience in the Great War which he managed miraculously to survive as an infantry officer. Dame Perry climaxed our relationship by agreeing to accept one of our JYA students although she could see no advantage in reciprocation.

Then there was the pleasant discovery that a near neighbor of ours was Geoffry Elton, the world-renowned Tudor scholar and fellow of Clare, who began a long association on both sides of the pond with an invitation to strawberries and clotted cream. His pride and joy, however, was a cellar which featured Jack Daniels Black Label Tennessee Sour Mash Bourbon Whiskey! His wife, also a historian, was working on a life of Lloyd George, and we frequently had lunch together in the Library canteen. Elton was a frequent lecturer in America, and they were our house guests on several occasions.

Altogether those seven sabbatical months flew by in an adventure experienced by the whole family. Over the years I have been able to lecture there, to attend seminars, to simply visit, and it became in every sense my spiritual home. And there is a codicil in my will directing that part of my ashes be taken to Clare Bridge and dropped into the Cam.

But I started out this description of my sabbatical leave as an incidence of my love affair with Newcomb. As earlier described, it was a long way between Gibson Hall and Newcomb Hall, and the most efficacious way for me to make the frequent journeys demanded of me was by bicycle, which I kept parked on a ramp by the steps leading to my office. Somehow it became an accepted custom that if any student wanted to get a message to me without the formality of making an appointment, she could leave it attached to my bicycle. Now when the timing of my leave became known, it was apparent that I would miss Little Commencement for the first time since my arrival, and I went to a Senior class meeting to apologize for not being able to wish them a personal farewell. Imagine my surprise then, a week before our departure in January for England, when I find attached to my bicycle seat a model of a Pan American airplane with an envelope containing an open round trip ticket London-New Orleans-London, and a note from Ann MacDonald and the Senior Class which said, "Valid only during the week of Little Commencement. Ta Ta." To this day I am still touched by the memory of that gesture.

There remained, however, a demonstration of Newcomb at her finest, although the denouement was an unmitigated tragedy. It was common knowledge that Professor William Woods, he of the "Madame Woods" story, University Chairman of our Department of Romance Languages, was a homosexual, a fact that produced hardly a raised eyebrow in New Orleans. He was the ideal academic citizen: a nationally respected scholar, a leading figure in the Modern Language Association, equally conversant in French and Spanish and had published in both. He would have won hands down any student poll for most popular professor, and hundreds of his former students were on record as to the effectiveness of his teaching. I could never have developed a JYA program of the quality and dimension of ours without him. He was by nature a gentleman, amiable, thoughtful, humorous, a wonderful traveling companion. He was a genuine bon vivant and racenteur, a good cook and respecter of food and wine, and his hospitality was always generous. He was Bill Woods, and everybody loved him.

Thus I was totally unprepared for the scenario that began to unfold on a Saturday morning when President Longenecker's secretary tracked me down in the grill room of the New Orleans Country Club and, with a touch of hysteria in her voice, informed me that the President wanted me in his office as soon as possible. When I arrived, there sat the President, grim faced, and Ashton Phelps, chairman of our Board's legal committee, grim faced, and a lieutenant of the New Orleans Police Department. It seemed that the previous night in a French Quarter bar Professor Woods had been inveigled by an undercover officer into making a lewd proposition, had then run amok while resisting arrest, and was now being held in jail without bail. The whole sordid affair had been tape recorded, a copy of which lay on the President's desk, having been brought to us by Lieutenant Jones, who also bore a message from the Chief of Police.

My first reaction, of course, was one of complete disbelief. This was too bizarre. This could not have been our Bill Woods. There must be a hideous mistake. But a playing and replaying of the tape left no doubt about the victim's identity. When after his incarceration it had been determined that the culprit was a Tulane and Newcomb professor, the upper echelons of the Police Department were notified, and in an attempt to save the institution acute embarrassment, the Chief had suggested a solution which had been relayed by Lieutenant Jefferson. Professor Woods must be relieved of his position, never again to set foot on the Tulane campus. He would be placed on permanent personal probation. And if he agreed to leave the community, the police would drop all charges against him. "An eminently fair and generous solution," opined Mr. Phelps, with Mr. Longenecker nodding in relieved and complete agreement.

They seemed astonished that I should voice an objection. Yes, the tape seemed to provide a positive identification. Yes, I understood that his academic tenure was no protection against proven immorality and malfeasance. But before we rush to judgment shouldn't we in all conscience first get him released from a cell full of drunks, pimps and junkies, give him a chance to clean up and regain his composure, and then hear his side of the story? Couldn't he be released to my cognizance? After all, we were not talking about a common criminal; we were talking about one of our own! He must be given a chance to defend himself. After all, our university's reputation for probity was on trial, too. My argument somehow carried the moment, and after a conversation between Phelps and the Police Chief and an expression of our gratitude for his concern for our institutional position, Mr. Woods was released on his promise to me to remain absolutely incommunicado. The session ended with Mr. Longenecker agreeing to call a special meeting of the Board on Monday, while I would convene an emergency meeting of the Newcomb Executive Committee on Sunday. Later that afternoon I spoke to Woods briefly, saying that I wanted none of his contrition but to keep his chin up and know that I would do my best.

The Sunday meeting of the Executive Committee opened, naturally, with universal expressions of shocked disbelief. But the tale of the tape, which I played for them, convinced us all that we had no rebuttal for the facts of the matter. Our friend had been caught red-handed, and the fact that he had been entrapped was no defense for the act, per se. I then carefully enumerated Gibson Hall's proposed solution to the matter, which at least had the merit of relieving Bill of a criminal record. Cy Lee was there, George Meyer was there, Dorothy Seago was there, and the more we thought about it, the angrier we became. There were not just our personal feelings of friendship and the deepest kind of sympathy for his chagrin. There was his impeccable scholarship, the marvelous effectiveness of his teaching, his dedication to the life of the mind that had propelled a long and distinguished academic career, his humane concern for his students and his faculty colleagues ... all this to be snatched from him for one compulsive act. No! No! No! We were not going to stand mutely by and see him forced to resign in disgrace and be forever exiled from the profession and the institution he loved. There was fire in Dorothy Seago's eyes, there were tremors in Cy Lee's voice, and there was a snarl of defiance from George Meyer. To hell with Gibson Hall's tidy solution! We were going to place Newcomb College and all she stood for in defense of our colleague, and let the chips fall where they may. And we were confident that if there had to be a showdown with Gibson Hall and the Board, our students and our alumnae would vociferously rally to our support. We spent the rest of the morning drafting our position in succinct terms, and I was instructed to produce President Longenecker in Newcomb Hall on Monday morning to instruct him about where matters stood so he could report to his Board that afternoon. Finally I drove to Bill's house since he was not answering his phone and told him to engage a lawyer as quietly and discreetly as he could, assuring him that he was not in this mess alone.

So it was that the Tulane President paid his first and only visit to my office in Newcomb Hall on Monday morning to meet with our Executive Committee. As the senior faculty member present, Dorothy Seago claimed the right to be our spokesman, and she minced no words. Making no excuses for or denial of Professor Woods' aberrant behavior, she simply demanded that his long and distinguished service to Newcomb and Tulane must now be taken into account. In the present circumstances, he merited no less than the following consideration: that he be given a medical leave of absence for one year; that he absent himself completely from the campus during that year; that he place himself in the hands of any or all members of the Tulane Medical School faculty competent to advise and counsel him, and that he faithfully follow any regimen which they might prescribe; and that at the end of the year he be thoroughly examined by whatever panel deemed competent for his physical and psychological aptitude to resume his career; and that given a favorable verdict, he be forthwith restored to his-academic rank and duties. He must understand that she was speaking not only for our faculty but for our students and alumnae as well, and she warned that he would be doing a serious disservice if he by so much as an iota minimized the intensity of our feelings and the unanimity of our position to his Board. Visibly shaken and white as a ghost, he thanked us for our candor and took his leave. That afternoon the Board, more to avoid a donnybrook than out of conviction, accepted our proposal, and a year later Professor Woods was restored to good standing. How distressing it was then, that several years later in a totally unrelated incident in front of his house when returning from the grocery store he was set upon by a street gang and beaten so severely that he never recovered.

Clearly my days and my usefulness were numbered. But it was not that I hadn't been sought after elsewhere. In fact, I had been engaged in a couple of extra-collegiate activities that had greatly increased my visibility as an academic administrator. One was as chairman of a regional selection committee of the Woodrow Wilson Fellowship Foundation, headquartered in Princeton, New Jersey, a national program for the award of handsome stipends for a first year of graduate study. My region consisted of the states of Louisiana and Texas, from which any graduate from a four-year accredited college could apply. My colleagues were the President of Southwestern Louisiana University, the Provost of Rice University, and the chairman of the English Department of The University of Texas. Every year we would hole up for a week reading applications to determine whom we would interview in New Orleans, Houston and Austin. One of our problems was to assure that a disproportionate of awards did not go to the graduates of Tulane, Rice, and UT, and we were reasonably satisfied with our even-handedness, receiving several kudos from Princeton in that regard.

A similar activity was my serving on the final selection committee of the National Merit Scholarship program, headquartered in Evanston, Illinois, where once a year a nationally representative group of academics, such as the Dean of Admissions at Radcliffe and the Dean of the Graduate School at Stanford, met to select a thousand scholars from the top 2% of the graduates of all the nation's secondary schools for tuition grants to the colleges of their choice. To assure a national spread of recipients, a quota was set for each state based on the number of secondary school graduates. It was exciting to dwell with these young minds, and another dividend was the broadening acquaintanceship among the committee members. I shall always remember the day when I was working on the State of New York applicants and I encountered the first perfect College Board scores—800, 800—I had ever seen. They were attained by a young man from Buffalo. I turned to his written statement, which began, "I want to be a physicist. In fact, I already am a physicist—please see Appendix A." Which I duly did and found three patents in the young man's name. Turning back to his statement, I read, "I want to attend MIT for my graduate work, but before I begin that I want to take the strongest liberal arts program that Harvard has to offer, because I do not want to grow up to be an ignorant genius." For some reason I felt that he merited an award.

At any rate and for whatever reasons, other institutions began to express interest in my services. My father had long since laid down the dictum that if anyone thought enough of me to invite me to come take a look at this situation, I at least owed him the courtesy of a visit. Ironically, my first such invitation was the most difficult for me to decline although I knew at the outset the situation was hopeless. The call came in September 1954, barely one year after my arrival at Newcomb, and it was from Logan Wilson, my predecessor and now the new President of The University of Texas. It seems that the College of the Desert in El Paso was going to be absorbed into The University of Texas System. It badly needed new management and a beefing up of its faculty and curricula. Would I please go take a look? "But Logan," I said, "I haven't even got the seat warm here. I can't do this to

Mr. Harris." "I understand how you feel," he replied, "but please go take a look." Which I did. An added inducement was the fact that Lucy's brother, now an orthopedic surgeon, had recently moved to El Paso, and he and his gorgeous wife were delighted with the community and were sure it would support a vigorous new administration at the college. I, too, was sure I could do the job and gain a passport to Austin that Logan promised me in two or three years. But I just couldn't do it. Mr. Harris had taken a mighty gamble with me, and he deserved better than this. In fact, Logan left Austin after five years to become President of the American Association of Universities and Colleges in Washington, D.C., and his successor at UT, Harry Ransom of Yale, and I became very good friends, but I had lost my one best chance.

Next came Wofford College in Spartanburg, South Carolina, a very decent liberal arts operation in a pleasant community, but not a place with any attraction for Lucy and my growing family.

Sweetbriar, that notable institution in Virginia and undoubtedly the best known college for women in the South, with a beautiful campus of sculptured boxwood and stately elms was the next institution that expressed interest in me. It had long been presided over in grand fashion by Meta Glass, from one of Virginia's most famous families and whose brother, Carter, had long been a fixture in Washington as Virginia's senior Senator. President Glass had long been a tower of strength and decorum in women's education, and to be even considered as her successor was high praise, indeed, especially in Virginia, The fact that my mother was an Altizer who had been reared in nearby Salem did not hurt my chances. But what I liked best was the ebullience of the young chairman of the Sweetbriar Board, the vigorous CEO of the Norfolk and Western railroad who represented a new breed of Southern entrepreneur. It would have been great fun to work with him, and he certainly made a most generous offer. But I did not like the school's relative academic isolation; there was no major institution nearby, and Sweetbriar was, after all, only a kissing cousin of the University of Virginia at Charlottesville. So I declined, gracefully, I hope, because it was a fine school and I was flattered to have been asked.

Next came an unexpected conversation with Bill Friday, the former President of the University of North Carolina at Chapel Hill and now the Chancellor of the North Carolina system. Friday was without question one of the most gifted and soundest academic statesmen ever produced by American higher education. With a fund of good humor and without any supercilious intellectual pretensions, he relied on a heaping portion of good common sense to deal with the manifold problems of academe. He was a master of human relationships, and at the AAU meetings, he made the Puseys of Harvard and the Brewsters seem like simpering choir boys. At any rate, I was in his office discussing some issue under consideration by the Southern Association when he abruptly changed the topic. "The Woman's College of North Carolina at Greensboro needs a new President, and you're my man. Interested?" Flattered, yes, for the opportunity presented to work with a man I so much admired. Interested, no, because if it had to be a woman's college, I held the best position in the country. I did, however, have a name for him: Otis Singletary, who was a bright young historian and now an assistant dean with Logan Wilson at Texas, and a comer without question. (Otis did accept Friday's offer; he later became Director of Lyndon Johnson's Job Corps, and then the long-time President of the University of Kentucky and the national president of Phi Beta Kappa.)

My last offer of a university presidency was a tale so bizarre that it would have been impossible to imagine and a denouement so prophetic that it would have been impossible to predict. It deals with the integration of the University of Alabama (Bama) and the recruitment of its legendary football coach, Paul "Bear" Bryant. Certainly one of the most disgraceful and repulsive incidents in the sordid story of the integration of Southern universities occurred in Tuscaloosa when Arturine Luck attempted to enroll at Bama. We all remember the hate-filled face of the embattled Governor personally blocking the entrance to the administration building and his calling out of the State Troopers to place the university and the town under a virtual state of siege. The president of the school had long since decamped and here lay the institution in tatters, its reputation as a civilized seat of learning shattered, and its mission of teaching and research disintegrating in the dust kicked up by the troopers' boots. It was a sorry spectacle, and it was there for the whole world to see.

In time the emotions began to subside, and to the rescue of this pathetic, beleaguered academic entity came one of Alabama's and the South's most beloved and effective academic statesmen. He was Oliver Carmichael, long-time President of the University of Alabama, and then for fifteen years President of the Carnegie Endowment for Learning in New York, and for the last five years, retired. In the university's darkest hour, he stepped forth as Acting President until a leader could be identified with the ability and stomach for the daunting task of rehabilitation. Now in an earlier, happier time, Mr. Carmichael had been President of the Alabama State College for Women at Montevallo, and we used to visit him there when my father left his complementary position at the Texas State College for Women on one of his summer treks. They became and remained good friends for many years, and I am reasonably sure that it was Mr. Carmichael who put my name in the Alabama pot at this critical juncture.

The search committee was dominated by the Governor's appointees to the State Board of Education, a hard-faced bunch if ever I saw one, and, of course, members of the University's Board of Regents, which included a bright young lawyer and Bama alumnus from Birmingham, who was to become my mentor and advocate. As one can imagine, the list of available applicants was not too lengthy. There was one Clanton Williams, a very mediocre president of a very mediocre University of Houston, but an alumnus of Bama who might be prevailed upon to serve. But he withdrew when he became convinced that everybody's favorite, General Mark Clark the controversial commander of Texas' 53rd Division in its march up the boot of Italy, and now the President of the Citadel Military Academy, was a shoo-in who would know how to restore discipline and hold the soft-headed liberal element in the state at bay. And there was I, who in my own mind was there only out of my father's and my respect for Mr. Carmichael, but who for some reason the search committee kept in the hunt.

I remember very well my last meeting before that august group. General Clark had spent most of the afternoon with them, and I had been walking around the campus awaiting what I had presumed to be a cursory handshake and dismissal. I stood for a time outside the President's house, a truly beautiful and faithfully restored pre-Civil War mansion, with its white pillars and broad balconies, a fitting centerpiece for this charming campus. This, I mused, was as close as I would ever come to being in residence. I had already been quite clear about the need for the unequivocal demise of Jim Crow, for diversity in student body and faculty alike, for the absolute requirement that the Statehouse keep its distance, and how we must all accept the inevitability of change, but that the tempo must be one of moderation and accommodation. No, I was not a crusader nor was I in a hurry, but there could be no equivocation about the goal of opening up this university to every student with the wits to benefit from the experience. At least I had been honest. So when I was finally ushered in for my final appearance, I was quite unprepared for the preamble from the chairman of the Board of Education that the selection committee, fully cognizant of the enormity of the task ahead, for the necessity to heal deep wounds, and recognizing the dangers of political interference in the inevitable task of reforming admissions standards in higher education in the state of Alabama, and being impressed with my deliberation and moderation, was pleased to offer me the leadership of this university by unanimous vote. When I recovered my composure enough to speak, I of course thanked them for this expression of confidence but that frankly it was so unexpected that I needed some time to digest it. The spokesman laughed and said he could readily understand my surprise. "I am sure you thought," he continued, "that we were so red necked that we couldn't abide anyone who could speak good English. Take all the time you need. But you should know that there is another problem that we deem important."

The problem: "The football fortunes of the Crimson Tide have fallen so low as to be an embarrassment to the university and the state. Why, I doubt if today we could give even the Tulane Green Wave a good game. (Chuckle) We intend to do something about it. Now, one of our own boys, Bear Bryant, began his coaching career here. He went on to do the impossible, make a winner out of the University of Kentucky, and now he is doing the same thing for Texas A & M. We want him back. So the first thing we want you to do as President is to go to Houston. We'll engage you a suite at the Shamrock Hotel, fill it with food and drink, and give you an ample expense account. Take all the time you need. Do what you have to do. But don't come back here without him. What we figure is that you and the Bear together can put this university back on the road to respectability."

My banker friend from Birmingham drove me to the airport, and he was as stunned as I. The Bear and me! Respectability! There was no secret about the brutality of Bryant's training camps or his willingness personally to physically chastise a lagging performer. Eligibility rules were made to be broken, and he would do whatever was necessary to win!

Editor's Addition

Jack was presented with the Star of Solidarity of the Republic of Italy by the Consul General of Italy in New Orleans on January 24, 1962, for his efforts in establishing Newcomb's Junior Year Abroad which fostered better understanding of Italy and Italians among Newcomb students and their families.

CLASS OF '66 GIVES PORTRAIT

A portrait of Dr. John R. Hubbard, former dean of Newcomb College, was presented to the college in special ceremonies at the Newcomb administration building.

Presentation was made by FLORENCE DE FROSCIA '66, former president of the Newcomb student body and a member of the 1966 Newcomb graduating class which arranged for the portrait.

Dr. Charles D. Hounshell, Newcomb Dean, accepted the portrait for the college.

Dr. Hubbard, who is currently in India on an assignment for the Agency for International Development of the U. S. Department of State, served as dean of Newcomb from 1953 until 1966.

The portrait was executed by Pat Trevigno, professor of art at Newcomb. It will hang in the faculty lounge of the Newcomb administration building.

TAKING PART IN CEREMONIES WERE PAT TRIVIGNO, THE ARTIST, DEAN HOUNSHELL AND FLORENCE DEFROSCIA.

Jack resigned from Tulane and Newcomb in 1966 when he accepted an extended position with AID in India. The Newcomb class of 1966 honored his years at Tulane with a portrait which continues to hang in the administration building.

An indication of the esteem with which Jack was held by the students and alumnae at Newcomb can be gleaned from the following letter, penned by Ethelyn Verlander, President of the Newcomb Alumnae Association, that appeared in the Newcomb Alumnae Newsletter dated Summer 1966. Written on the occasion of Jack's resignation as Dean of Sophie Newcomb College, Verlander asserts that the letter is a "consensus of opinion of the entire Executive Committee of the Newcomb Alumnae Association."

The Ideal Dean

What kind of person would the Alumnae like to see become the Dean of Newcomb?

1. The Dean should be a man because a man can be more forceful and is less likely to be swayed by emotion or sentiment. And matters that specifically require the attention of a woman can be capably handled by our Counselor to Women. Newcomb is a college for girls, and girls respond more readily to the guidance and direction of the opposite sex.

2. The principle quality of this man's personality should surely be administrative ability, which necessarily encompasses, in this particular position, a remarkable ability to get along with people—students, parents, faculty, staff, fellow administrators, alumnae, and emphatically, foundation representatives.

3. He should be a man with a keen understanding and appreciation of the youth of the day; one who could mingle with the students at their own level and still maintain his authority and their respect.

4. The dean should be of strong moral fiber and have an unimpeachable reputation for morality and integrity. After all, he is constantly before the eye of the students, an example for them to follow, whether consciously or subconsciously.

5. Our new dean should be a man of recognized academic prominence.

6. Since Newcomb's dean is required (?) to teach at least one class, then he should be able to teach his subject, not just have a thorough knowledge of it. A student can respect a teacher's knowledge of his field, but he cannot learn unless the teacher has the all-important ability to impart his knowledge.

7. Our dean should have some religious faith, preferably being a member of a recognized congregation. This, for two reasons: a) In such a position, the poor man may probably often need the solace of prayer and a firm belief in some better life; b) Newcomb's image might well be damaged if her dean were known to be an atheist or agnostic, in this community which so greatly respects religious belief.

8. Our new dean should be a man brought in from the outside, but preferable from a school of conservative reputation, not one involved in extremist student movements. It would be an advantage, we think, if our new dean could be a native Southerner or one who has taught for some time at a Southern University.

9. If possible, the dean's wife should be a person of grace and charm who could, by her presence, enhance the dean's social image.

Adding together all of these ideals, perhaps you have noticed that they give a fairly adequate description of Dean and Mrs. Hubbard. In lieu of them, may we hope that you can find their doubles?

Good luck!!

Sincerely,

Ethelyn E. Verlander,
President, Newcomb Alumnae Ass'n

CHAPTER 18

A Cajun Compliment

When in September 1948 I went to New Orleans as an Assistant Professor of Modern British History at Tulane University, one of the first persons to bid me welcome was Jack Stibbs, Associate Professor of English Literature and newly appointed Dean of Students. As an undergraduate at Michigan he had been a member of DKE—as was I from The University of Texas—and he had received his Ph.D. there, with a dissertation dealing with Sir Walter Raleigh as a man of letters. He had also been in the wartime Navy. Given our fraternal and service affiliations and academic interests centered in things British, we became close companions in short order. But the tie that really bound was our love for hunting the duck.

During my years in Washington at the ICC, one of my best friends had been Hallan Huffman, a transportation economist and, incidentally, a DKE from Minnesota, who was a great outdoors man. During the two hunting seasons we were together, we had spent every available weekend shooting ducks and geese at the wild fowl refuge at Matamuskeet off Cape Hatteras in North Carolina; but, given the war, I had not fired a sporting shot since early 1941.

So I was overjoyed to find myself in Louisiana at the lower end of the Mississippi flyway where, within an hour's drive from New Orleans, there began endless stretches of bayous, marsh, swamp, and rice plantations intercised by canals. This was Cajun country, a whole new world for me, inhabited by a hardy, colorful breed of fishermen, trappers, shrimpers and oystermen, bounty hunters living in huts and clapboard shanties usually perched on wood pilings, moving over and through the trackless marshes like water bugs in their hollowed-out wooden canoes called pirogues like poor men's gondoliers, and sharing this watery vastness with alligators, water moccasins, nutria rats, pelicans, ibis, herons, egrets—all denizens of the swamp. And each October this was the destination of millions of water fowl boring south along the Mississippi waterway to escape the freezing blasts of a Canadian winter: teal, redheads, canvassbacks, sprig, and, above all, the prized mallard piling down into the estuaries and rice fields of this primitive Eden. On a clear day one could hear the whirring of their beating wings and their honks and cackles that sent tingles up one's spine. Opening day would soon be here.

But to operate effectively, indeed, even to survive in this milieu required equipment and a set of skills wholly foreign to me and at which Stibbs was still a novice. But we had at hand an unlikely mentor with exceptional gifts. He was Jerry Capers, Professor of Southern History at Newcomb College, the women's coordinate division of Tulane, the progenitor of the Harvard-Radcliffe, Columbia-Barnard, Brown-Pembroke relationships. Jerry was a prolific scholar of Southern statesmanship in the era of the Civil War and Reconstruction, and students were attracted in droves to his stimulating, if unorthodox pedagogy, Monday through Thursday. But on Friday he disappeared into the marsh regardless of the season, for he was as much at peace in pursuit of the wily bass or crappie as he was in scouting out the feeding grounds of the greenheads. He was the most inelegant looking human being I have ever laid eyes on: short and wiry, seemingly nothing but skin and bones, his hands a mass of calluses from hours of propelling a pirogue through straggly reeds, his face toughened by the relentless rays of the summer sun or the chilled salt sprays in a winter wind under an unruly shock of salt and pepper hair, his teeth stained by the perpetual presence of an ancient briar pipe. It was difficult to imagine him holding a group of scholars at a Southern Historical Society meeting enthralled by a seemingly outlandish new interpretation of Henry Clay or Jefferson Davis. Because on Fridays, arrayed in muddy hip boots, patched dungarees held up by frayed suspenders over a tattered shirt, and a hunting cap torn by endless encounters with the sharp needles of scrub oaks, he was the swamp rat incarnate, the stealthy trapper of nutria, the renegade creeper of decoys. And because he had mastered the Cajun patois, he had never met a stranger in the swamp.

So to find two colleagues in what he deemed a stifling academic environment not only willing but eager to learn the folkways and the arts of survival in his mysterious wonderland was almost more than he could bear, and he adopted us like brothers. First he checked our clothing and especially our foul-weather gear, for it could be miserably cold and wet when the blue northers and rain squalls swept over the fens. Then our boating equipment, such as stout paddles for the pirogues and an outboard motor and extra petrol can for the rental skiff by which we would traverse the bayous, canals, and patches of open water. Then our hunting gear, such as decoys and plastic cases to keep our shotguns and shells bone dry. Then other odds and ends, such as an ice chest for beer and booze, waterproof plastic containers for matches and food stuffs, a compass and maps of the area,

"Life in the marsh is not simple," he admonished, "and there's no point in being any more miserable than you have to be."

So our hunting kits had taken on considerable substance. Fortunately I had on hand a Volkswagen Camper that I had acquired in Britain while on a research junket the previous semester, and it served perfectly as a storage place and transporter of our equipment. It had taken several days to assemble all this stuff, but when Capers was finally satisfied, he suggested we take a trial run the following weekend, although the opening of the season was still two weeks hence. Since Jack (Stibbs) and I couldn't leave until Saturday, Jerry, not being willing to waste his Friday, gave us directions to the boat landing where we would begin our expedition and said he would meet us there at high noon.

Saturday dawned cool and clear; we loaded the Camper, and after pleas from our anxious wives for sensible behavior, we were off. Our route out of the city took us through the old Chalmette battlefield where in 1812 Jean Lafitte and Andy Jackson had given the British what for, and on eastward for half an hour until we reached Bayou Lafourche and the boat landing where Jerry awaited us. He had already selected a sturdy flat-bottomed skiff for us and tied it alongside his on the rough-planked quay, to which we transferred our gear and hooked on the outboard motor. After parking and locking the Camper, and paying the rental for the boat, we started down the bayou with Jerry in the lead. Along the way we passed several cuts in the bayou that led to various fishing camps, and as we approached the sixth one, we slowed down and glided into the entrance which Jerry had marked for our benefit by tying a Tulane banner to a tall stand of reeds. We then threaded our way down a narrow passage through the toolies to an exit which Jerry had similarly marked, and ahead of us lay a stretch of open water across which lay the beginnings of the marsh proper. We headed due south, and after about half an hour Jerry pointed out the dim outline of what seemed to be a man-made structure rising out of the middle of nowhere.

"That's our landmark," Jerry shouted, and as we got nearer we could distinguish what seemed to be a large, ramshackle house perched atop a set of huge pilings driven down into the water. Attached to the pilings was a floating pier, above which in pyramidal fashion was board planking which formed a porch around the building. The whole thing was a mass of weather beaten gray, although above the entrance was an old sign on which one could barely make out the words, GREEN GABLES. Green Gables, indeed; the whole structure looked like it might collapse at any minute.

After tying up at the pier and stretching our legs, Jerry explained that depending on whether one was going into the marsh or coming out of it, Green Gables was the first or last outpost of civilization. From here on in one traveled by pirogue.

"The place looks like hell to you now, but I'll guarantee that when you're coming out of the swamp and have been paddling that pirogue for three or four hours, it looks like the Waldorf!" In fact, it was a trading post for the human denizens of the marsh, and a welcome stopover for hunters and fishermen bound for the interior. Inside was a bar, a short-order kitchen, and shelves stocked with basic canned goods and a few sundries. Here the trappers would bring their nutria pelts and deal with agents who appeared at given intervals. Here were jerry cans of petrol available, as well as crude wooden lockers for the storage of outboard motors, decoys and surplus gear. It was a welcome way station, and also a unique spot to observe the fascinating types of humanity—Cajuns, blacks, mixed breeds, renegade Anglos—who depended on these trackless waterways for their livelihood and refuge from civilization's norms.

Green Gables was presided over by a stout, fiercely imposing Cajun widow named Genevieve and her three daughters, the youngest and comeliest of which—faint praise—was named Marie. They tended bar, manned the kitchen, served the tables, and for anyone who felt the need and had the wherewithall, they provided other services in the bedrooms upstairs. The place was generally a bedlam of the coarsest language imaginable as they screamed at one another, bullied their customers and made snide remarks about their sexual preferences. They were, in sum, the foulest mouthed, toughest set of whores I have ever listened to or looked at. But meanness was not one of their sins; as one became accustomed to the din, if not the language, there was a note of essential good nature to most of it. And Jerry was their philosopher-king. He looked like a trapper and he could converse at their level in their patois, but he was different from their regular customers: he was citified, he was cleaner, he smelled better, and he had that mysterious aura of being associated with something called a university. So he was our talisman for acceptance.

It was here under Jerry's careful tutelage that we transshipped our gear from the skiffs to the pirogues. Now a pirogue is a sturdy little craft whose principle utility is its very shallow draft and a sharp keel that can slice through reeds, lily pods and mud flats with remarkable facility; but it is not very forgiving to shift in weight, so the trick is to carefully center the load, sit steady, and not attempt a snap shot or reach out suddenly for a dropped oar. For the neophyte, the going is tense and hard work; but for this outing and our benefit, Jerry chose a relatively easy route over mostly open water, and after an hour or so we paddled into a little estuary that led us to high ground dotted with scrub oak. And there in the middle of nowhere was a trapper's cabin perched up on stilts. The occupant was on his knees on a little landing pier repairing a trap, and he did not spot us immediately as we glided in; but when he did he reached for his shotgun and covered us until he recognized Jerry.

"Can't be too careful these days with these black scalawags jumping my traps."

Jerry had gotten to know the man, Baptiste by name, on his earlier forays down here, and he explained that we were looking for a place to blind up for Opening Day two weeks hence.

"Any birds here yet?"

"Some, a few more every day, mostly greenheads. One cold spell and de be here."

After settling down over a beer, Jerry and Baptiste discussed our strategy. It seems that the estuary cut this high ground into an island, and if we kept going up it for a couple of miles, it emptied into shallow open water.

"Good feeding ground, and plenty of toolies along the shore for your blind, and yore plumb outta sight from this place. But when you come back from the hunt, stop by on yore way in so I'll know I ain't got a pack o worthless scum on my land." With that agreed, off we went, and we found the spot as Baptiste described it.

Heading the pirogues into the mud bank and then pulling them into the reeds, we found enough dry ground with good cover to make our camp about thirty yards off shore. After unloading, Jerry took me out in a pirogue to show me how to set out our decoys, while Stibbs was hacking away at the toolies to give us more cover and a good line of sight. As sunset approached, the wind picked up coming from behind our backs right out over our decoys. We then covered our pirogues in the reeds, put out our sleeping bags and food and drink, and built a fire with kindling that Baptiste had given us.

It was my first sunset in the marsh, and God, it was beautiful with the crimsoned clouds and the wind kicking up little silver streaks in the water. Suddenly Jerry whispered, "Quiet!" A flight of ten mallards came whistling over us, turned into the wind and flopped down on our decoys. It was pure magic. The night sounds of the marsh were magic, too—the birds on the water cackling among our decoys; the shrill, plaintive cries of the nutria; the rustling of the wind through the toolies. For Stibbs and me it had been a long, tough day, and after a couple of drinks and the sandwiches we had brought with us, we moved our sleeping bags around the dying embers of our campfire, crawled in, and were lost to the world, leaving Jerry alone to contemplate the mysteries of life.

But he had us up an hour before daybreak. The marsh was awakening, too. Apparently more birds had come in during the night, for we could hear the cackles in increasing volume and the slap of stretching wings. We inched our way as close to the water's edge as our cover permitted and waited as the eastern sky began to brighten. And just as the sun peeked above the horizon—whoosh went the beating of the pinions. To the hunter of the duck, there is no sound or sight like the morning flight breaking water and beginning their climb into the skies. There is no thrill to match it.

"Well," observed Jerry, who had greeted the dawn a hundred times like this, "it looks like we've found our spot for Opening Day. Let's just hope someone doesn't beat us to it."

Then, reluctant to leave, we began yesterday's routine in reverse. I was sent out alone to retrieve the decoys, my acid test which I almost flunked I shipped so much water. Next, we cleaned up our little campsite, leaving it much as we had found it, loaded the pirogues and headed back up the estuary, stopping briefly at the trapper's shanty, leaving him a bottle of booze and imploring him to discourage any interlopers. Then back into the open water, setting a north-north-east course until the welcome sight of the Green Gables finally loomed dead ahead. There we parted company with Jerry, who wanted to do some fishing, but he helped us load up our skiff and pointed us due north to the big stand of toolies and the cut into Bayou Lofourche, up which we went to the boat landing and our camper. On the drive in, we stopped at a Cajun bar and grill right on the edge of the Chalmette Battlefield; never have a fresh, hot oyster loaf and a cold stein of Dixie beer tasted so good. Thus we got home dirty, tired—and exhilarated.

It was in this fashion that Stibbs and I opened the duck season for four straight years. Jerry was with us for the first two of them, but then his wife, a kind, gentle lady and a favorite in faculty circles, divorced him on the grounds that he cared more for the marsh than he did for her. After that he became more of a loner than ever, but by this time Stibbs and I had become seasoned veterans who could handle the waterways without him. Our string, however, was broken in 1952 when I left Tulane to join the history faculty at Yale.

At Yale I was in a young professor's heaven: wonderful students, wonderful faculty colleagues, wonderful library; but it was also at Yale during my very first year there that I "fell from grace" by accepting an offer to return to Tulane as Dean of H. Sophie Newcomb Memorial College and a promotion to Associate Professor. So in September 1953 I found myself back in the familiar surroundings of New Orleans, and with the opening of duck season only a month away. The first word of welcome came from Stibbs, who was still deaning the students, and the conversation was brief.

"Are you on for October 10?"

"Yes."

He then suggested dinner that evening for he had a wonderful story to relate. So he and Phyllis and Lucy and I went to Manale's for a kind of homecoming and my favorite menu, starting off with a couple of Brown's Martinis, followed by a dozen cold plump oysters, and then finishing up with Crabmeat Verdi and chilled with Chablis, all served by Katherine, the sweetest waitress in town.

His story went like this. Shortly after I had left for Yale, Tulane had appointed a new member to its Board of Trustees, John Doe, a prominent oil man from Lake Charles, whose wife was an active Newcomb alumna. At a Trustees' reception for its new member, Jack had been introduced to the Does by Bea Fields, our Director of Alumni Affairs, a classmate of Mrs. Doe at Newcomb and still good friends who had worked together on many university functions. During the course of the conversation, the subject of duck hunting came up, a topic that no one can speak with more enthusiasm than Dean Stibbs. To which Mr. Doe replied that they enjoyed pretty good shooting in the Lake Charles area and that the good Dean might like to sample it, a suggestion which elicited from Jack, "Sir, I am at your complete disposal." Now it so happened—and this later on from Bea—that Mr. Doe and his partner in the oil business also were rather large in rice and jointly owned a sizeable plantation southeast of Lake Charles in Plaquemines Parish near the little Cajun hamlet of Gueydan. And right in the middle of that plantation stood the Florence Club, the most storied duck hunting lodge in all of Louisiana, and to which Messrs. Doe and Smith invited twenty guests for each of the six weekends of the hunting season. These were friends, business associates, captains of industry and finance, ranking military officers and government officials—a select and distinguished group; and for those on the permanent short list, an annual affair not to be missed. Well, Mr. Doe had been as good as his word, and Jack was invited for the fifth weekend of the 1952 season. With his face wreathed in smiles and his voice filled with excitement, he described the experience as the most fabulous hunt of his life and one in which he did not disgrace himself at the bar, the dining table, or the duck blind.

So the questions before the house were clear: would Jack's invitation be repeated, and if so, would I be included? The key to that riddle was, of course, Bea Fields, and when we broached the topic to her the next day, she said that she would do her discrete best, adding that she knew that Doe had enjoyed Stibbs' company last year, and that my being the new Dean of Newcomb might intrigue his wife. But before any of this was resolved, I faced my first crisis with a member of my faculty.

The next afternoon Jerry Capers came into my office all smiles and full of kind words about my appointment, and then at some length he expressed his opinion about some of our colleagues and suggestions about how to deal with some of the potential trouble makers. He then came to the point.

"And I have some good news. I am going to be married."

"My friend, how wonderful," I replied with all sincerity, "and who is the lucky lady?" thinking perhaps it was one of his graduate students.

"It's Marie."

"Marie?" I said, trying to think of a Marie that we both knew. And then to my consternation it dawned on me.

"Jerry," I cried, "you surely can't mean Marie of the Green Gables!"

In a low voice he replied, "I do mean that Marie."

I was stunned. I stood up and started to pace the office, a thousand reasons racing through my mind about the absurdity of such a proposal. And then they started to spill out while he sat there without saying a word. It was not the good name of the college that worried me. It was not his reputation that worried me. It was not the scorn of his colleagues. It was not the opprobrium of insulted faculty wives. It was not the loss of confidence of his students. It was Marie. To bring her into the city was idiocy enough. But to force her into a university milieu was unadulterated lunacy. She wouldn't be able to handle it. She would be miserable, and so would the marriage. Worse than being senseless, it would be cruel. When I finally finished, I just stood there and glared at him, knowing that some of my arguments were answerable.

He just sat there and looked at me, and then with a little smile and a look almost of pity, he said, "Jack, I know that you said all these things as a friend, but I am bound to tell you that you cannot explain the caprice of the heart." With that he left, and we never mentioned the matter again.

The utter sadness and futility of that meeting was one of the most depressing experiences of my life, mitigated only by the novelty and demands of my new position, and by the fact that Jack and I had a fine Opening Day. By this time we had become quite familiar with the marsh and confident of our ability to traverse it, and each year we had gone deeper and deeper into its reaches to build our blinds; but going in and coming out, the Green Gables remained our oasis. I had fallen in love with Yale - but not with New Haven, and I was happy to be back in New Orleans with the divertisements its environs afforded. But Opening Day had merely whetted Stibbs' hopes for the season for he had drunk the milk of Paradise at the Florence Club, and would he ever know its enchantment again? There was thus far the doom of silence from Lake Charles, and he became grumpy and irritable, whereas in my ignorance I was far less concerned. With every mail delivery he would call—and curse, and he drove Bea up the wall with his interrogatories. Finally the tension was broken with the arrival of his invitation, along with mine, for the fifth weekend. Had Stibbs been a true believer, the Lord would have been duly praised.

Now in his element, Jack laid out our program. My camper would be ideal for the outing, for although we had not to worry about such items as shells and decoys, our guns, boots and duffle bags crammed with warm clothing would take up a lot of room. We would leave New Orleans on the Friday morning in time to reach Opelousas for an early lunch at Didi's and her Creole smothered chicken, a masterpiece of that cuisine. Then through Morgan City with its bayous filled with shrimpers and supply boats for the off-shore oil rigs, and on to Abbeville and Jean St. Pierre's for a mid-afternoon snack of crawfish and shrimp loaves, again washed down with that glorious draft Dixie, all of which should tide us over until dinner. Then by a back road due west through the beginning of the rice country until we reached Gueydan, where we would go due south on a narrow track to our destination, arriving there at about 5:00 p.m. Clearly Jack believed that getting there was half the fun, and that suited me right down to the ground.

So our count down began, and slow, how slowly our target date drew nigh; on the Wednesday night before our Friday departure, Jack insisted that we load the camper just to make sure that everything was in good order. It was the next morning, Thursday, that all hell broke loose. By special messenger there was delivered to me a memorandum from the President's Office addressed to all Deans and Directors announcing an emergency meeting to discuss issues so critical to the future of the University, that attendance would be mandatory. The place—the President's conference room; the time—Friday afternoon at 4:00 p.m., with the possibility of continuation on Saturday.

Within ten minutes an apoplectic Dean Stibbs burst into my office, his face livid and his hands shaking.

"What in the name of common humanity is going on?" he fairly screamed. "What is he doing to us? If we cancel the Florence Club at this late date, we'll never be invited back."

The "he" was Rufus Carrolton Harris, former dean of the law school and now in his tenth year as Tulane's president and one of the most respected academic administrators of his time. One of the reasons the spirit at Tulane was the envy of the land was his willingness and ability to spot promising but untested youngsters within the faculty and appoint them to key administrative posts, among whom were Jack and me. (I have always thought that one reason I had attracted his attention was our shared love for baseball. In those days the New Orleans Pelicans were a farm club of the Pittsburg Pirates, and as often as we could, Mr. Harris and I would take our seats behind third base and second guess managers like Danny Murtaugh.)

"But Jack," I said, "if whatever it is is as important as the President says, we don't have an option."

"The hell we don't," he blurted. With that he grabbed my phone and rang through to the President's administrative assistant, while I listened in on another line.

"Katherine, this is Dean Stibbs. It is imperative that Dean Hubbard and I see Mr. Harris as soon as possible!"

"Why Dean Stibbs, you sound upset," she purred, "I hope there's nothing wrong at home. Mr. Harris has someone with him right now, and then he has a luncheon meeting at the Boston Club, and this afternoon he is sitting with Mr. Jones and some other Trustees, and tonight he has to speak at an alumni dinner. So I don't see how I can fit you in today. And if this has anything to do with the meeting tomorrow, then I'm afraid nothing can be done about that."

I thought Jack would explode. "Katherine," he pleaded, "this is an emergency. You tell Mr. Harris that if he thinks the university is in trouble, I know that Hubbard and I are!"

"I'll do my best," she concluded, "but I wouldn't count on it." All of which left us twirling in the wind.

In any event, we got the call around 4:30 p.m.; the President had returned sooner than expected and he could give us ten minutes if we came right over. We raced and were ushered right in, to find him pacing the floor and rubbing his hands. Assuming his gravest look, he turned to face us.

"Gentlemen, on the basis of many considerations, this university faces the greatest crisis in my tenure here. What we decide tomorrow may well save us or sink us, and that is why I must have the advice and counsel of everyone on our senior staff. And I especially want the opinions of you two."

Our hearts plummeted, "But Mr. President . . ." Jack almost whispered, but that was as far as he could get, for apparently we were well and truly sunk. We must have looked it, too, for Mr. Harris could no longer contain himself; he opened his office door, which had been ajar, and in came Katherine and Bea, their sides splitting with laughter.

"Knowing how much those invitations meant to you," chuckled the good President, "this was a pretty mean trick, but your girl friends here talked me into it. Obviously you were the only two to receive that memo, which you could have discovered had you spoken to any of your colleagues, but you were so upset that you reacted like Ned in the first reader. Have a good hunt, bring Louise and me a couple of birds, and give my regards to John."

Leaving his office were two grown men who had never felt more sheepish—or elated.

The Florence Club was everything Jack had described. Driving south from Gueydan on the narrow track that was really the top of an enormously long dike, we passed through fields of rice standing two to twelve feet high, dotted by tall stands of toolies, and crossed and criss-crossed by irrigation canals—a vast green sea billowing in the gentle breeze. But the real spectacle was overhead with a sky filled with ducks and geese, diving, rising, circling to a symphony of mating calls. With each mile the cacophony grew until suddenly there it was, a sunny pleasure dome rising out of a primeval wilderness. The Club proper was a spacious, three storied plantation structure with stately columns supporting wide verandas which encircled the second and third floors. The ground floor contained the reception area, the game room with bar, two billiard and several card tables, and an elegant dining room with three long tables under spotless linen, each of which could accommodate ten people. On the top floors were the guest accommodations and the bath rooms. Behind the main building was a huge kitchen, a cleaning shed, storage facilities, and the living quarters of the household staff and the guides. The south side of the complex bordered on a major canal, and there was a long pier onto which the pirogues were pulled and to which were tied up a dozen swamp buggies, shallow drafted with powerful outboard motors, which could accommodate five people and their gear. But on the other three sides was the most amazing feature of all—a vast cleared marshy area that served as a feeding ground for thousands of duck and geese, a part of the officially designated bird sanctuary which extended for a five mile radius from the main house. To sit on one of the verandas and listen to and watch the comings and goings of these marvelous wild creatures was to gain at least some insight into the wonders of nature.

There was a standard routine at hunting clubs such as this. First came the Happy Hour during which introductions were made and acquaintanceships renewed. Then at 7:00 the black *maitre d'*, who along with the two cooks had been brought down from John's Lake Charles household, announced dinner. It was a sumptuous affair, beginning with Creole gumbo, then crawfish etouffee with red beans and rice, followed by thick filet mignon, jacket potatoes and avocado vinaigrette salad, and topped off by cherry jubilee. The wine flowed as did the conversation. Finally, over coffee and liquors, the great moment arrived: the drawing out of a hat for hunting companions and the assignment of blinds. With this ritual attended to, we repaired to the game room for Boo-Ray, Red Dog, billiards, or whatever. All I wanted was fresh air and to walk off that dinner, so Jack and I took a stroll along the dike. The birds were settling in for the night and their din had subsided, but you could feel their presence and still hear their subdued cackling and the preening of feathers. The wind had freshened and the stars were out in the clear night sky, which did not auger too well for the morning hunt, but it was an enchanting setting and I feared I might be too excited to sleep. On our return we had a nightcap and then, on Jack's advice, turned in, for the cowbells would start their clamor at 5:00 a.m.

It was a clear, brisk morning as we made our way to the dining room, some of us in better shape than others, for a breakfast of fluffy biscuits with eggs, bacon, duck sausage and grits and that bracing chicory coffee. Then onto the docks, where the boats were numbered according to the blinds, and we met our guide, who had already loaded our shell cases and thermos bottles and secured the trailing pirogue. My partner for the morning was John Mecom, a tall amiable Texan from Houston, large in oil and real estate, whose son had been a classmate of mine at The University of Texas. Once we settled in, the boat took off with a roar up the canal. That season they were using ten blinds, all of which had been artfully located years before, roomy, rock-solid affairs with telephone poles for piling, wonderfully camouflaged, and each facing a pool of open water where the decoys bobbed up and down. Inside there was dry flooring and a shooting bench wide enough for the two occupants to swing their guns freely, while behind was a platform on which the guide stood to work his magic with the duck call, with room underneath to stow the pirogue. Compared to those impromptu blinds we had scratched out of the marsh, this was the Royal Box; and to hunt with a guide was sheer luxury. These tough, weather-beaten, laconic Cajuns had been hand-picked by the game supervisor; they were long-time residents of the area and part of the regular work force for the ricing operation, but they lived for the hunting season when they could make those wild things in the air do their bidding. Crack shots, they only fired in support of a guest who was inept or having hard luck, or both; they hated to see cripples.

Mecom and I managed to knock down three out of the small morning flight in our area, but the rest of the morning was slow going, with a single here and there. The limit in those days was six per day and twelve in possession, and those thousands of birds in the sanctuary did not figure at all in this kind of hunting for they were too wise to leave, and we had to rely on newcomers into the rice paddies. But John and I didn't mind; the morning was gloriously fresh, our blind was in a wildly beautiful spot, and we had time for him to bring me up to date on many of my Houston friends, and I learned that his wife had gone to school at the Texas State College for Women when my father was president. But our guide, Etienne, minded; he would be disgraced if we came in with less than our limit, and he was working his duck call for all he was worth. Suddenly his call increased in frenzy as he touched my cap and pointed. There were two mallards barreling in from above our starboard quarter and seemed headed across our bow for a perfect passing shot. I got just the right lead and splashed them both into our decoys, and the pat on the shoulder from behind was all the approbation one could ask for. That filled me out and I put away my gun so my companion could have the blind to himself, and within the hour John got his limit too; so going back in were two pleased hunters and one very happy guide.

After lunch we all gathered in the game room for an off-the-record briefing on the situation in Korea by the Vice Chief of Staff of the Air Force and the Assistant Secretary of State for the Far East. Then most of us elected for a siesta in order to be ready for the grand dinner, which featured roast canard au orange among a host of other delights. In the lottery for the Sunday morning hunt, I drew the president of Louisiana State University, a pleasant and very able man whom I had known when I taught at LSU briefly before going to Tulane for the first time. I noticed that we all retired earlier than we had the night before.

Sunday brought us blue bird weather again and the shooting was slow, with three blinds failing to fill out, but no matter—just being out there was reward enough. When we got back in, everyone showered and changed clothes, and after coffee and Danish, we began our departures. Stibbs and I loaded the camper with our possessions, which now included two large waterproof cartons, each of which held 12 fat birds cleaned, gutted, and packed in ice. John came out to see us off and performed the kindest act of all when he said, "I'll see you guys here next year." We could have floated home but we stuck to terra firma, making just one stop at Morgan City for crawfish, oyster loaves, and a touch of Dixie.

Missing next year, of course, was the anxiety of waiting for the invitations, and in due course we were asked to appear at the Florence Club for the final hunt of the season on the sixth weekend. Seeing no reason to deviate from our flight plan of the previous year, we arrived late Friday afternoon well-fed and happy. One difference this time was the weather; a cold front was heading in our direction, the leading edge of which was already bringing increased winds and a dropping temperature, conditions which would discourage the birds from sitting idly in the rice paddies and preening themselves in the sun but force them into the air in search of more clement feeding grounds. In other words, duck hunting weather, following the maxim that the more uncomfortable the hunter, the better the hunt. So Saturday morning brought plenty of activity over the blinds with constant flights going this way and that, giving the guides plenty of opportunity to exhibit their skill with the duck call. Without exception the blinds got their limits, and the hunters returned cold and wet and sated.

There was another difference from last year's proceedings as far as Jack and I were concerned, one which for us was monumental. Just before the grand dinner, Doe took Jack and me aside.

"On the last hunt each year," he explained, "one guide is given his choice of blinds and hunters and is permitted 'to shoot for the camp,' which means that he can ignore the bag limits. We take those birds and distribute them among the guides and the help at the Club and to some of our neighbors and even to some of the game wardens, the idea being that when we shut the place down tomorrow, we won't leave any wasted birds around. Tomorrow it is Jules', the head guide's, turn, and he has asked that you two go with him, so you won't be in the lottery. But I don't want you to say anything about this beforehand. And you should know that since this is the last night, some of my friends are inclined to have a bit of a do, but you get your sleep because in the morning I want you bright eyed and bushy tailed."

What we didn't know, which John explained in town later, was that each guide kept a running tally on the guests: their deportment in the blinds, their concern with gun safety, their shooting skills, their general enthusiasm, and on the basis of that reckoning he selects his partners for this last shoot-out. So Jack and I retired shortly after dinner before the party really got going, which is not to say that we slept soundly, we were so excited.

When we got up at 5:00 a.m.—and there were very few of us stirring at that hour—it was as black as the inside of a goat and cold as a witch's tit. The main front had passed through during the night, but the trailing edge was still with us and there were rain squalls all over the place—duck hunter's weather with a vengeance. We really ploughed into that breakfast, and afterwards we donned every piece of foul weather gear we possessed getting down to the pier looking like Eskimos. There stood Jules clapping his gloves together, a big grin on his face, clearly relishing the prospect, and saying over and over, "Dem ducks de fly today!"

The blind he had chosen was the one farthest from the Club, and that run up the canal through a squall was not a memory I cherish. We tied up the boat and he poled up to the blind with amazing dexterity, and then his selection became clear: the wind was coming from directly behind us right into our decoys which were bobbing furiously in the roiling water. Fortunately there was enough space under our shooting bench to keep our shells dry, and we left our guns in their cases until just before daybreak. And this morning there was no fiery orb rising in the east, just gray, swirling clouds and patches of rain, although to the north a brightening sky marked the end of the front.

"Five minutes, genmen," said Jules.

Off came the gloves, out came guns, shells pumped into the chambers, and safeties on. And this time there were three guns at the ready. Whoosh came the morning flight right into us, three guns emptied, and as far as we could tell we had at least five in the water. Before we could reload, another flight came in and took our decoys, which moved Jules to say, "By damn, de lucky duck!" But no sooner said than here came another batch that weren't so lucky. And three more went down. And the same with the next flight. It had been so fast and furious that we had forgotten how miserably wet and cold we were until Jules called a halt. Back went on the gloves, and Jack and I stood up and began stomping our boots to try to get the circulation going. Jules mercifully passed around the thermos, and we discovered that some thoughtful soul had laced the coffee with, a goodly dollop of brandy which went right down to our toes. Given the action, we decided that we would take turns shooting with Jules first, Jack second, and me third. Jules let several flights go by and waited until two lost souls came into range to get his double. Jack, who was really on his stick, was not quite so selective, but he got his double out of a larger bunch. Neither said a word, but I just knew they had exchanged smiles. I wanted to reach for the thermos but decided to wait and was thankful I did, for the miracle might never have happened. In the distance I spotted a flight of six coming in our direction from 3 o'clock. They were at reachable height, and when they came in sight of our decoys I expected them to flair, but they kept boring in. So I jumped up and went BAM, BAM, BAM, and lo and behold, I had a triple, the third one falling in the reeds just behind our blind. Now, I have had a hole in one, in fact, two, but that is not a patch on the thrill of getting a triple with a pump gun and a three shell chamber.

"Jules," I said, with as much equanimity as I could muster, "pass me, the thermos."

And so it went. With each passing flight, the weather improved, and with the frontal system finally past, we found ourselves warming to the sun. Off came our heavy gear, and we took turns going out in the pirogue to pick up our birds, not an easy chore since we could only approximate where many of them had fallen. When we had forty odd in hand, Jules called a halt, saying the muskrats could have the rest. Now all that remained was to pick up the decoys which had served their purpose for this hunting season, the last act as it were, of this fabulous experience. But Jules was in no hurry, suggesting that we have a cigarette and finish the coffee. He stood on his little platform, his eyes scanning the heavens. Jack and I looked at each other quizzically; we had just finished the ultimate hunt of our lives, our guns were stowed, our birds were harvested--what was left? And then it dawned on us: we had had our hunt, but Jules had not had his; the action around our blind had been so furious that not once was there need for his magic flute.

"By damn," he said, pointing upward and reaching for his duck call. High overhead three birds were circling aimlessly, their wings flashing in the sun. Quack, quack, quack, quack, went Jules. Quack, quack, quack, quack, quack. We could see them break their rhythm slightly, meaning that they had heard. Jules stepped up his cadence, and they widened their circle, seeking the source of those calls of love. Jules was in his element as they began their descent; soon they were circling our blind within easy range as we tried to become invisible. Around they came again as Jules went into his trill. Again they came around, went down wind, turned, and glided with utter grace into our decoys. It was simply beautiful to watch, a symphony of one man in perfect tune with nature. Jules, head guide, before his hand-picked audience, at the very top of his game. Jack and I stood, and clapped in awe.

"Now we pick up decoys," he said.

Going back, down the canal, Jack and I could not resist taking a headcount of our birds: 47. After tying up at the pier, we staggered into the cleaning shed with our heavy burden, grinning from ear to ear. John was there to see how we had done, and he nodded in approval.

"Well, Jules," he asked, "should we invite these fellows back next year?"

"By damn, Mr. Doe," Jules exclaimed, "dem two Jacques shoot de gun!"

We had been anointed from on high, we had been knighted at the Round Table, we had been elected to the *Academie Francaise*, we were the chosen among the chosen. We had made the permanent short list of the Florence Club.

For the record, Jerry Capers did marry Marie. He brought her into the city, did his best to clean her up in mind and body, subjected her to the beauty parlor, outfitted her in smart attire. And to their everlasting credit, the faculty wives rallied around, doing their level best to put her at ease and feel welcome. But it was hopeless; she was a wild creature in unwonted captivity, and before six months were out she was back in Green Gables with the marriage annulled. Jerry's desperate bid to end his loneliness had failed, but he took it without apology. He became less ebullient, drank more than usual, and disappeared from time to time, but none of this seemed to affect his scholarly performance adversely. At the end of a year he remarried, and this time the shoe was on the other foot. She was the patrician cultured one, a distinguished art historian and chairman of our Department of Fine Arts and quite willing to share the blessings of civilization with him and provide the civilizing influence. I am told the marriage lasted five years before she called it a day.

CHAPTER 19

India (1965)
Huge Plans

Sitting at my desk in Newcomb Hall in early April, 1965 I received a telephone call from Clanton Williams, the aforementioned former president of the University of Houston and a casual acquaintance of mine in academic administrative circles. I, of course, knew of his brief candidacy at Alabama, but the last I had heard about him was his precipitous departure from Houston under circumstances which suggested an abrupt dismissal. Whatever the situation, he had since then hooked up with an old associate, Robert Dolly, who was now a Washington Bureaucrat sitting in the Agency for International Development overseeing international program initiatives in higher education. With Dolly's help, Williams had got himself named Chief Education Adviser to the AID mission in India. (In the U.S. Government scheme of things, it is the Department of State which develops the policies governing our foreign relations, and the Agency for International Development is State's operational branch responsible for the implementation of policy, particularly as it relates to the economic assistance to lesser developed nations. At this time, the two Agencies occupied the same premises, known as Foggy Bottom, in D.C., with State directed by Dean Rusk and AID by David Bell, a highly respected Harvard professor of international economics.)

Now thanks to some new agreements, our educational activities in India were to be greatly expanded, and Williams needed assistance, ergo he was in Washington to recruit a Deputy. Would I please come to Washington to discuss the situation.

I was very familiar with the background of the situation to be discussed. For the past fifteen years I had given a course on the British Empire, in which I had got the British in and out of India countless times. But my course syllabus ended in 1947 when the last British regiments marched through Victoria Gate on the Bombay (now known as Mumbai) bund (which is an embankment used especially in India to control the flow of water), furled their colors, boarded their transports, and sailed away after a 350 year love-hate relationship.

The old India was partitioned between the predominantly Muslim Pakistan and the predominantly Hindu India, as were the Indian armed forces, as Dominions within the British Commonwealth of Nations. In 1950, India completed a written constitution which embodied what she deemed best in the British and U.S. systems and as a Republic entered the international community as the world's largest democracy. From the U.S. they took an elected President and an elective bicameral legislature, the Rajya Sabha and the Lok Sabha. From the British the President, like the King, was a ceremonial figure, and the CEO was the Prime Minister who came from the political party commanding a majority in the lower house. The court and legal systems used the British precedent. Jawaharlal Nehru, the hi-caste Brahmin aristocratic product of Harrow and Cambridge, and who, with Gandhi, had led the All-India Congress in its opposition to the British Raj, became India's first Prime Minister, and the Congress Party the dominant force in Indian politics for the next forty years.

After Independence, Gandhi eschewed public office but remained India's spiritual leader with probably the most recognizable face in the whole world. He differed fundamentally with Nehru in the merits of Eastern vs. Western civilization. Nehru believed India must embrace and master the Industrial Revolution if she were to take a recognizable place in the society of nations, whereas Gandhi argued that Indian material wants were few and could be supplied by a cottage system and escape a competitive industrialist society which must inevitably result in self-destruction, to wit—the First World War.

In the event, it was Nehru who ushered in the London School of Economics' brand of state socialism as the cornerstone of India's economic system. If India was to compete in the contemporary economic environment, she found herself in need of a massive energy infrastructure which only huge public expenditures could provide. In the short term India's only salvation was a barter system with the Soviet Union in the exchange of agricultural products for industrial goods, plus Russian technical and financial assistance in the construction of massive dams and hydro-electric grids. In all this the United States took little notice.

But with the dropping of the Iron Curtain, the Berlin air lift, and the enunciation of the Truman Doctrine, the Cold War was joined in earnest, and India's growing geopolitical importance as the anchor of South Asia became manifest even to our Eurocentric policy makers. Here was India, a struggling democracy, on whose northern frontier stood a massive and truculent totalitarian congeries in the USSR, and on whose northeastern border, stood another, Red China, who by armed invasion in 1962 had seized a huge chunk of disputed frontier territory. To the east and southeast lived millions of politically uncommitted people who were watching these developments with one question in mind: which of these two systems, the democratic or the totalitarian, was more likely to put food on their tables and roofs over their heads? For our own strategic political and military health, then, it seemed incumbent upon us to try to shore up that massive but faltering experiment in democracy.

But India and the Indians were not easy to help. Given her propinquity to and dependence on the Soviets, India in her own inimitable rhetoric assumed a posture unsullied by the vulgarities of the Cold War by raising the shibboleth of non-alignment. A pox on the super-powers, but more pox on one than the other. After all, which one was it that loosed the bomb on Hiroshima? And as a result, after 1950 when Russia began to assemble its nuclear arsenal, that was regrettable but understandable in terms of national defense. It was one of her first Defense Ministers, the wildly articulate Krishna Menon, a continual apologist for the USSR, who loved to harangue the U.N. General Assembly about the venal capitalist West which in the name of international security refused to abandon its atomic weapons. Even in the mid-60s, when the U.S. Military Mission in India included Paul Tibbits, a Brigadier General in the Air Force and the pilot of the Enola Gay, the Hindu saddus and their whirling dervishes would gather each night outside his bungalow while burning him in effigy and shouting incessantly, "Murderer."

There was the further fact that many people in the West still shuddered in horror at the carnage and blood-letting between Hindu and Muslim at the time of Partition in 1947. Were these, then, to be the new apostles of peace? The net result of all this was that when in the 1960s it was realized that India might have a significant role to play in the Cold War, India in official Washington did not have a single champion—not in the White House, not on the Hill, not in the Pentagon, not in the State

Department. It took a natural calamity to force India into our national consciousness.

India's entire agricultural production, on which her increasing millions barely subsisted, depended upon the annual monsoon. For India the monsoon did not mean a sudden devastating storm but rather a steady and widespread rainfall over an extended period, particularly in the granaries of the central and north-western plains. It was therefore a tragedy of epidemic proportions when in two successive years, 1962 and 1963, the monsoons failed to materialize and left huge segments of the population facing starvation. And there was only one place in the entire world that had enough surplus grain to prevent it. Our response was unequivocal; in a remarkably short time a remarkable piece of legislation was passed by Congress and its implementation begun. The bill was known as Public Law 480, and its brief outline was this: the U.S. would ship and sell our surplus grain to India and the Government of India (GOI) would pay the U.S. Government for the grain in rupees, a non-redeemable currency of no value whatsoever outside of India. Congress would thereupon appropriate the requisite dollars to reimburse the American farmer. In such an arrangement the U.S, Government was obviously going to accumulate a huge rupee balance; the trick, then, was how to expend those funds in the best common interests of the two countries. The GOI understandably wanted a tight control over the areas and amounts, for by dumping we could simply inundate her planned economy. We, on the other hand, wanted to make sure our targeted areas were calculated to increase India's internal stability and her standard of living as examples of what could be done under a democratic regime. All very exciting, and all subject to intense negotiation, and the doing of it explains how India almost overnight became the greatest recipient of U.S. foreign assistance and a prized target in the Cold War.

Here, too, was the classic example of an effective symbiosis between State and AID in the crafting and implementation of foreign policy. But let it be understood at the outset that the official relationship between India and the U.S, was never an easy one; each side was prone to lecture the other, each side learned to despise the other's bureaucratic insanities; and the remarkable results achieved by the joint effort between 1964 and 1969 resulted not from a love affair but from an unsentimental perceived sense of necessity.

One batch of rupees which sparked little debate was the one set aside for what was known as "country uses," which is to say all the rupee expenditures incurred in maintaining the official U.S. presence in India: physical maintenance, salaries of Indian employees, housing, travel, both national and international, (since Pan Am as well as Air India would accept rupees for ticket payment), subsistence allowances, building construction, and the like. Then there was agreed upon three priority program areas—Agriculture, Family Planning, and Education—each of which qualified for project appropriation. The rationale was simple: if India could become self-sufficient in the production of cereal grains, and if the number of mouths to feed could be stabilized, then the standard of living was bound to increase. Education in many guises and on many levels was needed to supply the infrastructure in support of the first two objectives.

Thus was put in train a veritable beehive of activity under the rubric of assistance to India. AID/Washington was for South Asia, while AID/India came under the direction of the brilliant economist recruited from the President's Council of Economic Advisers, John Lewis, who worked with and under our Ambassador to India. As projects were negotiated with Indian officialdom, the personnel requirements would be forwarded to Washington, where Bill Macomber's (Deputy Director for South Asia), deputies would initiate the recruitment of the "experts" from both within the Government's bureaucracy and from outside on personal service contracts of varying lengths and conditions. In AID/India, Lewis presided over his own group of economists and financial experts, as well as the administrators of three project areas: the Chief Agricultural Adviser, the Chief Public Health Adviser, and the Chief Education Adviser, each of whom had his own staff of American and local assistants. This is the group to which I was being recruited, specifically as Deputy Chief Education Adviser to the AID Mission to India.

All of this personnel and planning was folded into the normal diplomatic mission, manned mainly by career foreign service officers and attaches from other federal departments such as Agriculture, Commerce, the Pentagon, the Library of Congress, the CIA, Labor, Culture and the U.S. Information Service, which included the Voice of America. All of this comprised the "Country Team" and was presided over by the Chief of the U.S. Diplomatic Mission to India, Ambassador Chester Bowles.

But except for the British experience in India, I knew little or nothing about all this when I had my first telephone conversation with Clanton Williams. That evening I absolutely confounded my family when out of the blue I suggested that we go live in India. The mere mention of India had conjured up visions of tigers and elephants and maharajahs and exotic dancing girls, and only after the squeals of disbelief subsided could I confide in them what little I knew. The girls were 9, 11, and 13 at the time, an adventuresome lot, as was their mother, and in the general excitement they urged me to go to Washington and find out what this was all about.

I was no stranger to Washington, having lived there for three years before enlisting in the Navy, and for a visitor, I had the best Washington address extant, the Cosmos Club, whose membership consisted of Nobel and Pulitzer Prize winners along with the intellectual leadership of the country. It is an address that has always stood me in good stead because the State Department takes note of things like that. Bob Dolly was not a complete stranger to me, since his brother had for many years been comptroller of The University of Texas and a good friend of my father. He and Williams explained that our education initiative in India was two-fold—institution building, and a massive overhaul of the curricula in engineering, mathematics and science at the collegiate level to introduce Indian higher education to the 20th century. As for institution building, there were nine agricultural universities, four teacher-training-colleges, and an institute of science and technology on the drawing boards. As for curricular revision, the plan was to introduce the new math, new physics, new biology and new chemistry into the Indian mix. All in all, huge plans and hugely exciting.

On the plus side we had practically an unlimited rupee budget to take care of the nuts and bolts. But would the Indian academic community permit such an intrusion into its accustomed teaching modes? Well, we could but try. My main problem with all of this was the scope of the enterprise, for these were plans that could easily constitute a man's career. I, on the other hand, was not at all prepared for any long haul. Could I, then, be of any real service to them for only one year, being reasonably sure that Tulane would grant me that leave. I received the answer from different quarters. First I sat with AID Director, David Bell, who spoke from his global perspective of the dangers of grand designs and unrealistic assessments of available resources. He then turned me over to Bill Macomber, Deputy Director for South Asia, to talk directly about India. He was an "old hand" known for his bluntness of address, later to become Ambassador to Turkey, and still later a long-time member of the Board of the Metropolitan Museum of Art. He had no use for Indian officialdom: "If you knew how those customs bastards held up our grain shipments at the docks waiting for bribes while their countrymen were starving, you'd be sick!"

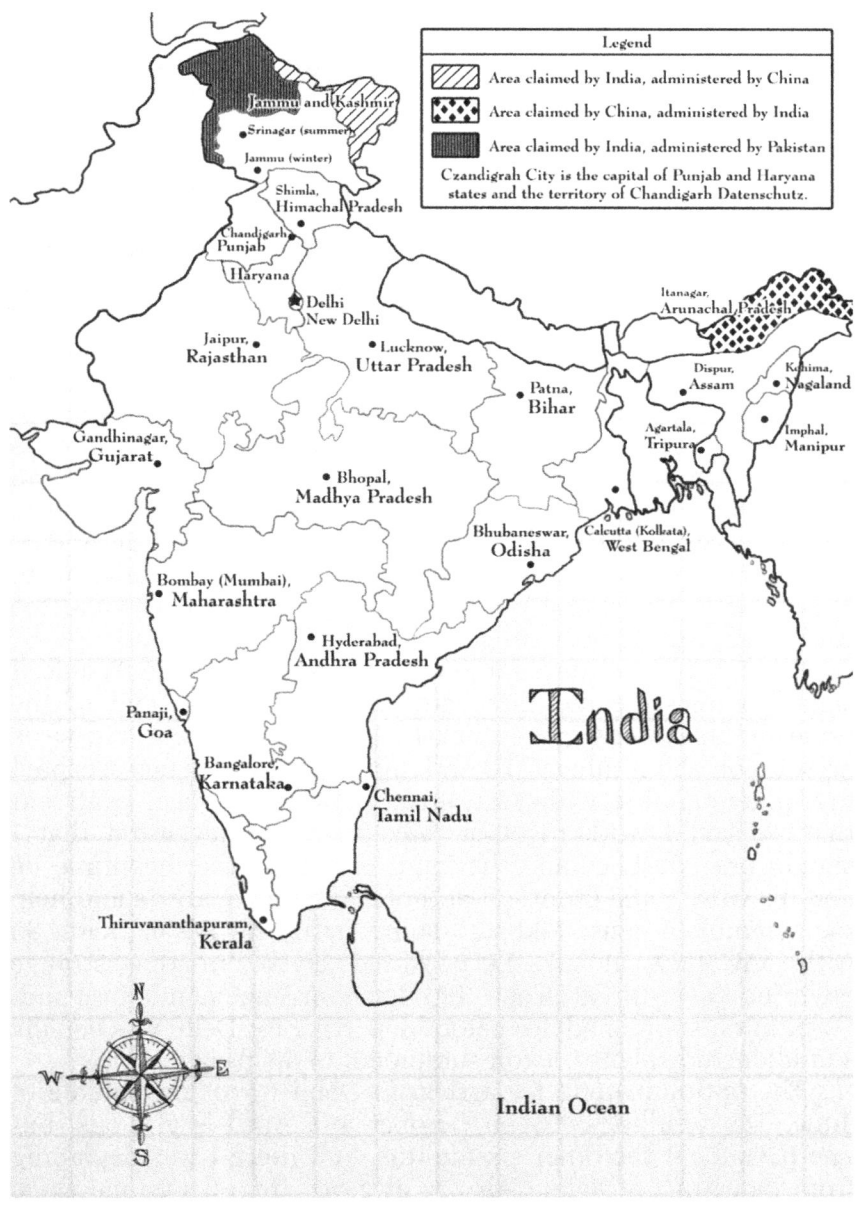

Map 7
1966 Administrative Map of India

On the topic of Dolly and Williams, he was equally candid. "I think they're both academic hacks who think they've found a gold mine and can't wait to cut their cronies in on the pie. So as to our academic initiatives, I am dubious on at least two counts. The first is India's receptivity. What do you think the reaction of our academic community would be if Red China suddenly appeared in our midst determined to overhaul our whole methodology? Secondly, assuming that we are welcome in India, can we get enough of the right personnel in place to effect any significant change? I personally would never have picked India for any such effort, but that is beside the point. We are there for humanitarian reasons. We have commanding resources at our disposal, and as professionals we must act reasonably to our own taxpayers and to the Indian community. I would rather burn all those rupees than fill a rat hole with them. We know we can change things for the better in agriculture. We have no experience, no benchmarks, and no illusions about family planning. We have serious doubts about education. So if you could give us a year of your time and take a really hard-nosed, on the scene look at our prospects in education, we in the Department would be most grateful. And so that there should be no doubt about your mandate, I shall inform Messrs. Bell, Dolly, and Williams here, and John Lewis and the Ambassador in Delhi of our conversation."

So after being granted a leave from Newcomb and Tulane, I signed a one-year contract with AID, and at the end of the semester in June, I came back to Washington for a two-week orientation about things AID and things India. Williams accepted my understanding with Macomber with good grace, confident that we could work together effectively. He suggested that I should precede Lucy and the family, while in the meantime he and his wife would scout out acceptable living quarters and help me assemble a household staff so necessary for life in Delhi. So with any luck at all, Lucy would arrive in this strange environment with at least the living arrangements in hand. Clanton's last bit of advice before departing for Delhi was equally sound: include plenty of golf equipment in my freight.

The optimum time for arrival in Delhi is not the middle of June. The weather between October and April is glorious, but one pays for it the other six months. Yet, there I was deplaning from Pan Am 1 at Palam Airport at 2:00 a.m. on 15 June 1965. Clanton and his wife were there to meet me, and thanks to our Embassy representative at the airport, it took only an hour to clear immigration and customs. I was then deposited at what was to be my home away from home for the next month, Claridge's Hotel.

The interjection of the AID programs and personnel into the normally calm routine of our diplomatic mission greatly altered the composition and pace of the American presence in India. In the first place, the local real estate wallahs were having a field day, for our requirements for housing and office space had trebled within the year. Already a new office building was under construction within the Embassy complex. And with our housing officers not too troubled about funds, our residential accommodations were generally quite satisfactory, located as they were in relatively new housing developments scattered around the diplomatic enclave. Our digs were typical, and had been reserved for us by the Williams as the most desirable available at the time.

Our address was 41 Golf Links (assi number), an upper middle class enclave in which two American Goodyear executives and the Afghan ambassador had taken up residence. The property fronted on a large maidan, or green park. The first floor of the residence was occupied by the owner, a well-to-do grain merchant (among other black market items) who had converted the second and third floors into a relatively spacious apartment consisting of a living room, dining room, kitchen, three bedrooms and two baths, while up a short flight of stairs was a bed-sitting room and bath which opened on a very attractive roof garden. So each of our girls had a room, and could double up if company came, while Lucy and I had a cozy little retreat all our own. Our dog could sleep on the roof garden. In the rear of the house were the servants' quarters; a bloc for the landlord's and a bloc for ours. The furnishings were all G.I. issue supplied by the Embassy and perfectly adequate, and of course the wives made all sorts of variations on the theme from the local markets.

As an aside, our arrival coincided with the outbreak of the second Indo-Pakistan war over the disputed boundary demarcations in Kashmir, and a blackout was imposed each night on Delhi lest the vaunted Pak Air Force make an unwelcome appearance. Furthermore, in the middle of our maidan, a series of zigzag trenches were dug to serve as air-raid shelters. And because of my distinguished record in World War II as a Naval Aviator, I was immediately appointed Air Raid Warden for Golf Links, issued a tin hat, flashlight and shrill whistle, and instructed to enforce the blackout. So each evening at dusk I would make my rounds, blowing on my whistle occasionally, and rapping on delinquent doors. Happily the Pak

Air Force never came anywhere near Delhi, but there were, nonetheless, nightly casualties—the sacred cows which wandered all over India undisturbed which had fallen into the maidan trenches. There was nothing in my contract about their survival.

Miraculously, as things sometimes seem to happen in India, the assemblage of a household staff took place with little input from me. The day after I had signed up for the Golf Links flat, there appeared in my office a nice looking young man in Western attire in his late twenties with huge black eyes, a moustache, and a dazzling smile.

"My name is 'Kushal'," he announced, "and I will be your bearer."

Now in the Indian household servant hierarchy, the "bearer" is the major domo, the factor factotum, the chief of staff, and if the household requires more than one, the senior wallah is designated as "head". He assembles the rest of the staff—the cook, laundry man, dressmaker, gardener, sweepers, whatever is required, and he is the principal go-between between them and the real head of household, the lady of the house, "memsahib." No household can function smoothly unless the head bearer and memsahib are on the same page. And if one is fortunate, the bearer can double as the driver, which makes it so much easier for sahib to get to and from his office, and for memsahib to get to the shops and markets, and for the children to get to and from school. It helped that Kushal could drive, and very well indeed in that indescribably hectic Delhi traffic. But how had he found me?

In embassy circles, with the constant change in diplomatic personnel, it was customary for staffs, in whole or in part, to be handed down to one's successor; and each embassy had its own roster of servants, some in the second or third generations, who were deemed loyal and efficient. This was particularly important in the case of head bearers and cooks, who had grown familiar with the ways and tastes, culinary and otherwise, of a particular national group. For example, Mr. Bowles' No.3 bearer was my head bearer 20 years later when I became Ambassador, and the two cooks were the same. But here in 1965 I was getting my first exposure to the Indian "grapevine" which I never fully understood but was often amazed by its speed and accuracy of information—shades of the Indian Mutiny. In this case, Kushal had been bearer for an IBM executive whose tour was up and was not being replaced. The laundress in Kushal's staff knew the dressmaker in Clanton Williams' household, who told her about the new American family coming in. Ergo, here was Kushal standing before me with his chits (letters of recommendation) in his hand. With the help and advice of others in India, I found myself with a posh address fully furnished and staffed while I had barely lifted a finger. Now all I had to do to be in business was to await the arrival of my family and my car, purchased in Washington, D.C. for delivery and resale abroad.

My first introductions were to Williams' office staff, two Americans and six Indians. We were housed in Pandara Flats, a relatively new middle class housing development where we had leased three units and converted them into office space, and which was only a stone's throw from Golf Links. The Americans were under direct-hire yearly contracts with AID, written by Dolly's office. One was Phil Haney, on leave from his professorship in the New Jersey Technical Institute in Trenton. He was Clanton's man for initiatives in technology. The other was Gordon Hiebert, who had earned his Ph.D. in Chemistry from Brown working under Professor Barton Springs, who was currently President Johnson's Science Adviser. Gordon was on leave from Brown, and was, of course, Williams' guru in the sciences. Williams as a political scientist and I as an historian did not figure in the "expertise" mix because the Government of India had made it clear that the humanities and the social sciences were beyond our purview, they being disciplines far more susceptible to "intellectual imperialism" than the hard sciences, engineering and technology.

Our Indian staff members were headed by V. R. Kheterapal, a Hindu with an M.A. in Management from Delhi University, and as well-organized a person as I have ever met; Gujral, an engaging Sikh; Hag, a shy and retiring Muslim; and three other Hindus. In these introductions I learned a great deal about India's attitude toward formal education. Gujral gave me his calling card which read D. S. Gujral, B.A., M.A. Honours (failed) which announced that he did hold a Bachelor's degree and that even though he failed it, he had been admitted to an M.A. Honours program which in itself put him a long leg up on most of his contemporaries. This, then, was the Education Division of AID/Delhi, and now it had a Deputy Chief.

John Pryor Lewis, aged 52, B.A. from Union College, Ph.D. in Economics from M.I.T., Harvard professor and member of the President's Council of Economic Advisers, had been recruited by his good friend and Harvard colleague, Dave Bell, to be the Director of AID/India. With surprising brilliance tempered by an uncommon admixture of hard common sense, articulate, friendly, witty, he possessed all the tools for an able administrator, a rare and classic case of the right man in the right place at the right time. And in a very real sense the future of our whole investment in India rested on whether John's economic pragmatism and belief in a market economy could sway that legion of Indian theorists who worshipped at the feet of Harold Laski and the London School of Economics. To have worked with Lewis in our Indian incarnation was one of the great experiences of my life.

It was he, then, who accompanied me to my first meeting with our Ambassador. Our Embassy in Delhi was Durell Stone's first architectural gem, establishing his reputation, and this graceful Doric structure of white marble and delicately filigreed transepts, fronting on a huge circular pond fed gushing fountains. My first walk up those marble steps through a stately entrance and under the shield of the United States of America was a thrilling experience. How many hundreds of times since then did I walk up those steps, often daydreaming that I was the Ambassador. Then to have it finally happen was one of the defining moments of my life—but that is for another chapter.

Chester Bowles was no stranger to India since he was just beginning his second tour as Ambassador. A graduate of Yale, Governor of Connecticut, member of Congress, director of Office of Price Administration (OPA) during the war years, he had first made a name for himself, and a fortune, as the co-founder of one of Madison Avenue's most successful advertising ventures, Benton & Bowles. Not so incidentally, in the Indian context, he had been captain of the Yale golf team and Connecticut's amateur champion, for it was he who taught me at the Delhi Golf Club how useful a diplomatic tool the game can be. He was a consummate public servant, and his wife, Steb (Dorothy "Steb" Stebbens Bowles), a consummate public servant's helpmeet; there was never a trace of condescension by either to anyone, from maharajah to the lowliest sweeper, and they were the shining exceptions to the contempt for India displayed by most of Washington's brass. No two people ever worked harder at their trade.

No man was ever blessed with more solid leadership than I enjoyed from Messrs. Bowles and Lewis. Thorough professionals, they were also eminently decent human beings. We had been thrown together quite by chance in this curious place to bring whatever talents and resources we could muster to bear on a critical problem facing one third of the earth's population: the enhancement of India's monumental experiment in democratic government. The fact that in all of this there were serious implications for the Cold War, now up in Vietnam, did not diminish the sincerity of our humanitarian objectives.

In our first meeting we discussed Macomber's injunction to me for a critical assessment of our initiatives thus far in education as to impact and feasibility. They did not know and did not dislike Williams, but given their Ivy League predilections, they seriously doubted whether the former president of the University of Houston, of all places, carried the academic credentials to command the attention of our major institutions of higher learning. And just incidentally, my storied year at Yale did nothing to diminish their expectations of me. So as far as the Ambassador and the Director of AID/India were concerned, my course of action was clear: find out what the GOI really wanted from us besides physical structures, if anything, and then determine if we could meet their expectations.

For me, a wonderful surprise was Gordon Hiebert. With his crew haircut and his bow tie, he looked much younger than he was, and his energy level was enormous. He had an equally lively wife in Dolores ("Dede"), and when life in Providence, Rhode Island, began to pale for them, he followed a friend's lead to AID and Dolly, and here they were in Delhi ensconced at Number 16B, Nizamuddin West, in the same enclave with the Williams. It was Gordon who gave me the lay of the education land.

Working with the Indian Ministry of Education, Williams had worked out agreements to supply American expertise in the fields of technology instruction and teacher training at the elementary and secondary school levels. To supply these "experts" AID/Washington had worked out contractual arrangements with individual American institutions which would cover all the rupee costs of transportation and maintenance plus the dollars for salary. As a carrot for the individual professor was a generous provision for home leave, and for the institution, generous travel grants which would permit institutional administrators to check on their minions' performance abroad. Thus far, the University of Houston's College of Technology under Dean Burke had signed on, as well as Ohio State's School of Education under Dean Severino. Negotiations were also being conducted with the University of Wisconsin's School of Engineering. The drill was for the dean involved to come out and sit with his Indian counterparts, decide on the subject matter areas to be addressed and the location, and then go back to recruit the necessary personnel. For example, India at the time had four regional colleges of education at Ajmer, Bhopal, Mysore and Kharagpur. The plan was to create in each one of them teaching laboratories (or what we sometimes call demonstration classes) wherein the Indian practice teacher under the supervision of the American master teacher would conduct actual classes for the youngsters in the community. Dean Severino had come out, made the circuit with Clanton and decided to begin with two Americans at each college; the program was now in its first year of operation. Similarly, Dean Burke had come out from Houston, traveled about with Phil Haney, and selected four technical institutes to begin the program with one American at each. So at this stage we had twelve Americans out in the field, not exactly what one would call a critical mass.

Gordon had helped brief these people on their arrival in Delhi about the mysteries of life in India, and in the doing of it he discovered that only two of the twelve were regular members of the departments which had recruited them. In other words, we were signing up academic mercenaries, non-tenured part-timers who were delighted with the emoluments which this program provided. It was not that Dean Severino, say, was deliberately providing shoddy merchandise, for what School of Education was so amply staffed that it could grant eight of its regular members a year's leave simultaneously? He was providing the best available bodies as per his contract. And when I asked Gordon about the sciences and mathematics, he just threw up his hands.

"Where," he asked, "Am I going to get enough chemists or biologists or physicists to make a difference? Where, indeed?"

But before I could try to digest that little conundrum, I had to find out how the Indians felt about our presence in the first place.

I had long felt that Washington, D.C. was the most capitol of all capitols, beginning with Capitol Hill itself and the long vista to the west down Constitution Avenue and its handsome Government Department buildings on each side of the Mall, the Washington Monument, the Reflecting Basin, the Lincoln Memorial, and the bridge across the Potomac to Arlington. My first view of the physical layout of the Government of India I found equally impressive. When the British decided to move their focus of power from Calcutta (now known as Kolkata), to the more centrally located Delhi, between 1920 and 1935 they literally built a new physical government complex that was stunning in concept, scope, and execution, in a vast open space just south of the teeming city that had been the capitol of the now-vanished Moghul Empire. Beginning on a plateau which provided an unobstructed view eastward to the Yamuna River, first came the sprawling Viceregal Palace (now known as Rashtrapati Bhavan, or Presidential Palace), which had housed the Viceroy and his host of satraps and which was now the official residence of the President of India, and where from its eastern pillared gates began the Rajpath, the path of power, a broad avenue, flanked by government office buildings in their piles of red sandstone, down the hill past the Houses of Parliament, and straight across the green valley through India Gate and on to the rotunda under which sat the bust of George V until Independence Day. This is the route of the Independence Day parade, the most colorful and complex spectacle of its kind in the world, in which dazzling vignettes of Indian communal life arrayed in riotous colors pass in review, interlaced with specimens of India's armed might and concluding with a fly-over by the Indian Air Force. All of this is preceded the evening before at dusk by the massed bands of the Army, Navy and Air Force performing that venerable British military rite, "Beating the Retreat," and ending with Gandhi's favorite hymn, "Abide With Me". The magnificent staging of all this leaves one limp with admiration and restores one's oft-sagging faith in India's future.

When one leaves the grounds of the Presidential Palace and heads east along the Rajpath, the first government building on the left houses the Ministry of Education, where took place my baptism into Indian bureaucracy. The Indian ministerial system is a carbon copy of the British: the Minister, who may or may not be of Cabinet rank, is nonetheless a political appointee of the Prime Minister and serves at his pleasure, coming and going as the political moods change. The Secretary of the Ministry, however, is a high ranking member of the Indian Civil Service, the equivalent of a British Permanent Undersecretary, and he is the chap who supervises the Ministry's bureaucracy and provides the continuity to the Ministry's affairs. He, in turn, is supported by all kinds of Additional Secretaries, Sub-Secretaries, and secretaries to Sub-Secretaries. To walk into a Ministry is to walk into seeming chaos. The corridors are dank and dirty, filled with a babel of voices from hundreds of peons rushing back and forth with stacks of files, restrooms stinking of urine, and offices crammed with petitioners.

The ritual is time honored: the visitor is ushered by a personal assistant into the inner sanctum of the official you came to see, if he remembered your appointment, and offered a choice of tepid tea or coffee and stale biscuits. As you ascend the bureaucratic hierarchy, however, the fare improves, and if the Secretary or the Minister, himself, be your host, the coffee will be warmer and you can expect cashews. On this morning I was to meet my first Indian Minister of any description, the Minister of

Education, and Clanton Williams was along to make the introduction. Educated at Eton and Christ, Oxford, V. K. R. V. Rao—known as "Alphabet" by his legion of critics—had the features of a hawk about to strike and spoke in a high-pitched staccato at the pace of a machine gun. I had, of course, carefully rehearsed my brief remarks about being new to India, to AID, to AID/India and so that I must seek his advice and know his priorities if India was to obtain the maximum benefits from the not inconsiderable amount of rupees at our disposal. He seemed to be studying me closely as he made a few tendentious remarks, and I got the distinct feeling that my Texas drawl was not going to be compatible with his clipped Oxbridge accent. He took up a pen, made a few scratches on a paper on his desk, looked out of a window, and began, to this effect.

"This is 1965, and in eleven more years your country will be 200 years old, quite a record for a country these days. I suppose your bicentennial will be marked by many celebrations with self-congratulations all around. India, on the other hand—her art, music, literature, painting, poetry, philosophy, mathematics, science, laws, customs, political institutions—stems from a civilization continuous and glorious for some five thousand years. Young man, what is there that you think you can teach us? However, I am sure that in time, you and the Secretary can find something useful to discuss. Good morning."

The Secretary and I found things to discuss quite easily. Prem Kirpal, with his patrician features and flowing white hair looked every inch the philosopher-king. In his early sixties, he was a product of Harrow and St. Johns, Cambridge, and then Elphinstone College, which had produced so many brilliant and able Indian Civil Servants. He had served widely and well in a variety of responsible posts, and by reason of his innate resources and political agility, he had risen almost unobtrusively to the highest bureaucratic echelons. Urbane, widely read, he had no problem with India's intellectual community; in fact, he was India's representative to UNESCO, and he spent as much time in Paris as he could possibly manage where he hoped to be deemed indispensable. All in all it was a most pleasant and constructive conversation in which he welcomed our presence and stressed that there was so much to do that we must waste neither time nor resources. At the end, he called in two of his Additional Secretaries, Chandiramani, whose portfolio included Engineering and Technical Education, and Chandrakant, who worked with elementary and secondary education. These, then, were the three men I would be working with most closely in the Ministry of

Education, and so in the space of an hour, I had gone from the depths of despondency to a feeling that I was going to be engaged in many useful discussions.

Another Indian agency, this one devoted entirely to higher education, was the University Grants Commission (UGC). The UGC, another British institutional transplant, was principal provider of funds for research and faculty enhancement at the university level; but rather than appropriate funds directly to the institutions which would foster all kinds of political bias, the GOI provided the funds to the UGC, whose Board, composed of academicians and distinguished laymen, allotted the grants on the basis of professional criteria which were under constant review. The chairman of the UGC, the most influential position in all of Indian higher education, was Dr. D. S. Khotari, admired as one of India's leading physicists, a distinguished former Vice-Chancellor of Delhi University, India's best, and an administrator as free from political bias as was possible to find in all of Indian officialdom.

As if to emphasize its independence, the UGC occupied its own building in a green park just off the busiest thoroughfare connecting New and Old Delhi, far from the Ministry of Education. Gordon Hiebert, who had already established a presence there, accompanied me for my introductions. First was the Secretary, B. R. Reddy, a veteran college administrator, whose brother was currently Vice-Chancellor of the University of Hyderabad, and who was known not only for his even-handedness but also for his sense of humor. Then there were his two Additional Secretaries, A. B. Chopra, curt, supercilious, unattractive, who handled the social sciences and was known to be in bed with the Russians, and Dr. R. D. Deshpande, a brilliant young biologist on leave from Delhi, whose concerns were mathematics and the sciences. I was then ushered into the Chairman's spacious offices. He arose and came out from behind his desk to greet me. Unimpressive in stature, almost shy in manner, dressed in his Nehru jacket, he bestowed upon me the warmest smile from the most pleasant countenance I had yet encountered in India. As I repeated my litany of ignorance about things Indian but with a desire backed by substantial resources to assist him in his priorities, he expressed his gratitude and delight with my circumspection. I forget just how he phrased it, but there was no doubt that I was in the company of a presence. The UGC, Khotari, Reddy, Deshpande—there was no doubt about it. Hiebert and I had found our spiritual home.

At about this time the new, ultra-modern, 5-star hotel The Oberoi, flagship of the Oberoi chain, opened its doors, its white marble facade towering over the Delhi Golf Club. Ground for its construction had been broken some four years ago, but at about the half-way point, construction and the supply of materials had been abruptly halted because the GOI decided that the first hotel of this modernity should be a product of the public, not the private sector. So for two years the Oberoi stood fallow, while across the city, overlooking the Diplomatic Enclave, there arose the massive and elaborate Ashoka Hotel, an example to the whole country of what state socialism could accomplish. That the elevators in the Ashoka worked only sometime was of no consequence: At any rate, one of the features of the Oberoi was a truly spectacular outdoor pool with a waterfall effect, and along one side of which was an al fresco coffee shop which served a very passable hamburger with chips which, accompanied by Indian beer, made a satisfactory lunch, accompanied by the splash of nubile bodies. It was there that Deshpande, Hiebert and I met at high noon twice a week to take stock of what we could most effectively do.

Here in August 1965 our educational activities in India looked like this:

1) *Agricultural Universities*

Already under construction or in the planning stage were nine institutions designed to work in direct support of our No. 1 objective in India: to help the country achieve self-sufficiency in its production of cereal grains. This was an immense, intensive effort on our part to increase the Indian farmer's productive capacity. It involved the introduction of new strains of hybrid wheat and rice and corn, the use of fertilizer, irrigation and water management, the sinking of tube wells, grain storage and pest control, transportation, agricultural economics and marketing technique, everything in the farmer's lexicon. We had agricultural technicians all over the place, at times two to three hundred strong, engaged in short courses and hands-on demonstrations. All of this short term activity was, of course, to be backed up over the long haul by the new agricultural universities. In effect, what we were trying to do was to transplant the American system of land grant universities, which collectively had made American agriculture the wonder of the world, to India; universities dedicated to the teaching of agricultural techniques, research in new methodologies and products, and the dissemination of these findings to the farmer in the field. These institutions were usually identifiable by the addition of the word "state" to their titles, such as Michigan State, Ohio State, Iowa State, Oklahoma State, and the like. To help plan the physical lay-outs, research facilities and curricula of these new Indian agricultural colleges, a consortium of three or four of our land grant schools were recruited, so that collectively they could supply for brief periods the expertise to train their Indian counterparts. All of these activities were organized and administered by inspired leadership from the American Association of Land Grant Colleges and Universities through AID/India's Agricultural Division, and were not the purview of the Education Division. The utilization of consortia of American institutions behind a single project was a device we used with remarkable success.

2)   *The Indian Institute of Technology, Kanpur*

During the formative years of her experiment with democracy, one of the major problems besetting India was the so-called "brain drain". Because of the dearth of any post-baccalaureate institutions of world class, India's brightest had to leave the country in droves to pursue graduate work, upon the completion of which they refused to come back in droves because the socio-economic complex of the time could not fully utilize their talents, and those that did come back were for the most part chronically under-employed.

It was the Soviet Union which first suggested a long-term solution. Since India did not have the expertise to build, equip and man a technical institution of world stature, she would build one for her, equip it, and staff it with Soviet academics until India could develop her own replacements. So in 1962 the Soviets completed the spic and span new Indian Institute of Technology, Bombay. Next, West Germany, recognizing India as one of the leaders of the developing world and seeking areas of useful collaboration, produced the Indian Institute of Technology, Madras. Then the U.K., embarrassed because the Colleges of Engineering which she had founded and nurtured were now deemed so inadequate, unveiled the Indian Institute of Technology, New Delhi. It was next UNESCO's turn, and here we can see the ambitious Prem Kirpal's handiwork, and that organization built and recruited an international faculty for the Indian Institute of Technology, Kanpur (IIT, Kanpur), just outside Calcutta (now known as Kolkata).

This curious competition was not one the U.S. could ignore if we were to have any voice in intellectual decision making, and when I arrived on the scene, the Indian Institute of Technology, Kanpur, was slowly rising out of a barren, dusty plain eight miles from what has to be the most desolate, unattractive industrial city in India. Why Kanpur, then? That is what happens when you are last in the queue and the most important personage in the region, Sir Rampant Singh, the wealthiest industrialist for miles around, pledges his undying support for the project.

The IIT, Kanpur project, no small undertaking, to be sure, was securely in the hands of a really distinguished consortium of our finest technical education practitioners—MIT, Cal Tech, Berkeley, University of Wisconsin, and Carnegie Tech. The technical details of the consortium were managed by Gil Oakley, a Boston-based educational consultant with lots of experience with institution building overseas, and he handled all the logistical matters with AID/Washington. The academic leadership for program and curricula developers was supplied by Professor William Estes of MIT. The purchasing agent at the site was the principal procurement officer at Cal Tech. And so it went. The American working group at Kanpur numbered on the average about twenty-five souls, including some seven or eight wives as what was to be faculty housing became habitable. Servants were assembled, and a weekly shuttle to the Embassy commissary was established. For reasons explained to me later, my first direct assignment by John Lewis was as the liaison officer between the Kanpur team, AID/Delhi, and Chandiramani at the Ministry of Education, whose office had overview of all the IITs.

Give the Soviets their due. By their initiative at Bombay, they had unwittingly sparked an international competition between aid donors that would result in not one but five splendidly equipped and manned institutions, each with a national sponsor that permitted India a quantum leap in scientific and technical education at practically no expense to herself. And our being last in line had, except for location, several distinct advantages. We could assess the strengths and weaknesses of our predecessors and profit thereby; we could offer distinctive academic programs, such as aeronautical engineering; our laboratories, computers and library would be state of the art. But what would make IIT, Kanpur stand out from the rest was a decision distilled from the collective wisdom of the consortium: there would be no American faculty members per se but rather a faculty recruited from among distinguished Indian practitioners of science, mathematics, engineering and technology who had gone abroad to meaningful assignments, especially in the U.K., the Commonwealth, and the U.S. who could be lured back by a) an appeal of sheer unadulterated nationalism, b) a relatively handsome compensation, and c) the prospect of having India's finest young minds as students, and a teaching and research and collegial environment the equal of anything they would be leaving behind. In effect, we would be engineering a brain drain in reverse. So from a variety of angles, AID and American prestige had a lot riding on the success of this project.

3) *The Regional Teacher Training College Program*

Conceptually there was certainly nothing wrong in trying to introduce teacher training into the syllabus of these four training colleges and their teaching laboratories presided over by "master" teachers who supervised trainees performing in actual classroom situations. The problem was one of sheer numbers. There were literally millions of Indian primary and secondary aged children with teachers without any kind of training available, and for the lucky ones more were taught under a banyan tree than ever saw the inside of a regular classroom. So even if Dean Severino and Ohio State could send us a steady supply of the greatest master teachers in existence, the ripple effect of their efforts in improving teaching at those levels would be invisible. We were not ignoring the problem, but its dimensions defied our solution.

4) *Technical Training and the University of Houston*

Phil Haney had done a pretty good job of getting around the country and identifying the practitioners of this sub-discipline of engineering in what we would term "Trade Schools" of which India had hundreds, some of which were quite good, others modest, and most of them hopeless. This was an area critical to the economy and the livelihood of millions, but from what we could see thus far, the caliber of "experts" the University of Houston was sending us was not the solution to anything. What to do?

5) *Literacy House, Lucknow, and Welthy Fisher*

Welthy Fisher was an American socialite from Philadelphia's Main Line, who had traveled extensively in India, was captivated by its charms and sympathetic with its short-comings. In Delhi, despite the new Oberoi and Ashoka, she would stay nowhere except her old hostelry, the Hotel Imperial, with its massive suites and aging but loyal staff who treated her almost with reverence. She became acquainted with Nehru and the Indian political mainstream, to which she announced her determination to tackle one of India's most intractable problems-- illiteracy. For some reason, she chose as her venue Lucknow, an active commercial city and learning center, whose British garrison became famous by withstanding a terrible siege during the India Mutiny in 1857. There the city fathers set aside the land on which she, with her own funds, erected Literacy House, which she staffed with help from Lucknow University. She dealt only with the lower classes, and the objective was to train illiterates who could then go out and teach others how to read and write. She raised funds for the project in the United States and where ever, and when she was in Delhi she never failed to let our Embassy know of her presence. Although absolutely hopeless—like our support of the Regional Colleges of Education—we could but applaud her vision and energy and dedication, and we supplied rupee support for a modest expansion of her facilities and their maintenance, made periodic inspections, and from time to time funded literacy "experts" from the U.S.

6) *The All-India Institute for American Studies, Hyderabad*

India's leading Shakespearian scholar was Sarup Singh, Professor of English Literature at Delhi University, formerly its Vice Chancellor, and probably the nation's best known academician in the liberal arts. His scholarly publications had been steady and significant over the years, especially in the U.K. where his non-traditional insights into the bard's works were most readily appreciated. Among Sarup's closest friends was Dr. D. S. Reddy, Vice-Chancellor of the University of Hyderabad, one of south India's most interesting cities long noted for its cultural ferment.

On my first tour to that part of India, I stopped in Hyderabad to pay a courtesy call on the Vice Chancellor, who resided in a spacious bungalow on campus. It was a hot afternoon, and I was ushered onto a long, shaded veranda where three terribly tired ceiling fans laboriously shifted the hot air. Moments later there bounced onto the veranda a spry little man, hair sprinkled with gray, brown eyes dancing behind thick glasses, and accompanied by his friend, Sarup Singh, whom I met for the first time. After the usual pleasantries, a bearer appeared with two pitchers of what appeared to be crushed watermelon and ice put through a blender. It was Sarup Singh who spoke, "Dr. Hubbard, what you see before you are two versions of Reddy's famous watermelon punch. But even though they look the same, I warn you, they are quite different. One is punch, but the other is PUNCH. If you wish to quench your thirst, partake freely of the first. But if you prefer something more Falstaffian, try the second which, I tell you, sir, is meant to be sipped slowly!" So after a very refreshing glass of the first, I sipped the other very slowly indeed. What I learned that afternoon was that with Reddy's encouragement, his university library had amassed the largest collection of Americana in Southeast Asia, and that students and scholars of things U.S. came from all over the region to use the Hyderabad resources. We went to the library where the whole first floor of one wing had been allotted to the American collection, which was impressive in scope. But from the sight of unpacked crates and boxes of books lying around, it was clear that the library, which had made many connections with suppliers including the Library of Congress in the United States, was out of space, and that cataloguing was now chaotic.

Suffice it to say, before that day was over the three of us had drafted the plan for the All-India Institute for American Studies, to be established on the Hyderabad campus, where Reddy said he had ample room, with its own library, research facilities, living accommodations for visiting students and scholars, as well as meeting rooms for seminars and symposia. Institutional memberships and fees could be worked out, as well as affiliations with various learned societies. And since two of the authors of the institute idea were among India's most respected academics, and since the principal beneficiaries of the institute would be Indian scholars and scholarship, we could not foresee serious objections by the Ministry of Education (MOE) or the University Grants Commission.

Now, just what did these educational activities amount to? At our final lunch in August 1965, we agreed on the following assessment.

1) *Agricultural Universities*

The whole agricultural effort was in concept, organization, and implementation brilliantly organized and on target. The present field work should result in dramatic increases in grain production, and when the universities grew up and were cranked into the equation, the long term benefits should be incalculable. The Education Division would respond happily to any requests made by the aggie wallahs, but mainly we would just stand on the sidelines and applaud.

2)   Indian Institute of Technology—Kanpur

Another spectacular concept, not ours, was one which became an issue of national prestige and one to which our very best institutions have responded in a consortium brim full of talent and ably managed. The only worry the MOE had was that we may try to upstage the efforts of the other nations who preceded us. At any rate, our IIT would be a gem, and the long term cumulative of the five of them could be crucial to India's survival.

3)   Regional Teacher Training Colleges

This is entirely the Education Division's baby, and a legitimate but meager effort to improve the quality of teacher training. It has no measurable immediate effect and no long term prospect of ameliorating India's chronic shortage of able elementary and secondary school teachers given the enormity of the problem. I would argue for the continuation of the program since it requires relatively so little of our time and resources, and it might just help as an example. But it is incumbent that we find the best possible practitioners to participate.

4)   Technical Training and the University of Houston

A complete washout from beginning to end. Abandon it as current contracts expire.

5)   Literacy House and Welthy Fisher

For cosmetic reasons, maintain the same level of support.

6)   All-India Institute for American Studies

The Soviets, the British and the West Germans all have variations on this theme in operation, but from the top to the bottom of Indian society there is nothing like the interest that American studies generates. It is a project that must be vetted in the MOE and UGC, but it could become a serious area of concentration in Indian higher education.

So, Items 1 and 2, with their enormous impact potential, are off and running. If Items 3, 4, and 5 disappeared tomorrow, few Indians would know or care. Item 6 is worthy of some thought. But where, gentlemen, is the plan to bring those thousands of teachers of engineering, mathematics, and the sciences with their antiquated syllabi kicking and screaming into the twentieth century? I understood in Washington that this was to be the major new thrust of the Education Division which justified adding a new staff position.

As a matter of fact, there had been discussion between the Education Division and the Indian side about the possibility of refresher courses for teachers in the scientific disciplines. The idea mooted was a variation of a long standing program in the U.S. by the National Science Foundation called the "Summer Science Institutes." These were six week affairs designed for teachers at the secondary school and undergraduate baccalaureate levels, using curricula developed by NSF in collaboration with the appropriate disciplinary learned societies, addressing what one ought to know at those levels and what one might be expected to work on at the graduate school level. Classes could be held at any high school or college with laboratory demonstration facilities. Faculty were generally selected from institutions in the region, many of whose younger professors had held NSF grants for the development of innovative new courses, and their salaries were met from tuition and fees from the participants. A successful passage was rewarded by an NSF certificate. Regional centers were established to receive applications from both attendees and lecturers so that the venues, subject matter and professorial staff could be announced a year in advance. Indeed, at present, with the appearance of the "new math," "new physics," and so on, these institutes for the last few years had been filled to overflowing.

Could such a program be tailored to fit India's needs? Would the Indian academic community welcome into its midst foreign practitioners whose avowed purpose was to minister to its shortcomings? Assuming everyone's endorsement, would such a program vast enough to make a difference on a national scale be logistically possible? The *sine qua non*, of course, was India's willingness to try, and despite Williams' assurances, I had to be convinced myself. So off I went to sit with Prem Kirpal at the MOE and Dr. Kothari at the UGC. Prefacing each discussion on the premise that American professors abreast of their disciplines would be available to preside over these short courses, would their Indian counterparts participate? Finally, for this program to have any long-term import, the Indian scientific community must be willing and able to sustain it themselves, so American participation would diminish as Indian capabilities increased.

A typical scenario might be this: for each 6 weeks institute designed for a batch of 50 Indian participants: 1st Year - 2 Americans to direct and lecture; 2nd Year - 1 American and 1

Indian to co-direct and lecture; 3rd Year - 2 Indians to direct and lecture, with 1 American observer. (As an aside, this was the kind of bell curve to which every American program planner of foreign aid was so addicted, which would enhance my chances of getting it approved.) If we look at, say, 25 Physics Institutes over a three-year span, we see 50 Americans the first year, 25 the second, and 25 the third, who will have been directly involved with 3,750 Indian participants, with each institute then standing on its own two feet. So given the number of academic disciplines involved, and given the Indian appetite, it was conceivable that we might have several hundred Americans in India each year for their six-week terms until Indian self-sufficiency had been achieved.

Prem Kirpal, seeing nothing in the program that would prevent him from making his appointed rounds in Paris, pledged the cooperation of the MOE. Dr. Khotari, mirroring some of Deshpandi's enthusiasm, was enchanted by the possibilities, insisting that success would depend upon a genuine joint effort by the GOI and AID which he would help to orchestrate. With these assurances, I was now ready to make my first report to John Lewis and the Ambassador. They both, along with John's program people, accepted the proposition that if we coupled a successful effort at modernizing India's scientific curricula with the benefits that were bound to accrue from the agriculture initiatives and the IIT development, we should have pulled off an exercise in foreign assistance comparable to the Marshal Plan. In the NSF science institute format, we had a viable means of reaching deep into the Indian intellectual consciousness with a methodology for change which she could then adapt and sustain for her own objectives. We now had the GOI's honest and enthusiastic endorsement of an effort in which they would join as a full partner. Now we had to close the loop by making a reality out of the assumption that the required number of American professors abreast of their disciplines could be identified and persuaded to come out to man those short courses. How could we do this? Contracts with individuals, as with individual institutions, were out of the question. The formation of new consortia to meet such a variety of needs would take forever to become productive. What was needed was an umbrella contractor, already in place, with a wide acquaintanceship with and influence within the American higher education community, and which could also grasp the importance of the task at hand. I could think of one agency that just might work—the American Council on Education, headquartered in Washington, D.C. and presided over by my old friend, predecessor as Dean of Newcomb

College, and one-time prospective employer, Logan Wilson, who had left his position of President of The University of Texas at the behest of many admirers to take the reins of this prestigious organization. A visit from me, according to Messrs. Bowles and Lewis, was very much in order.

Jack and Lucy Hubbard, US AID to Education, New Delhi, India 1966

In the meantime, my family had arrived—Lucy, a sprightly 42, three very active daughters, Lisa age 13, Missy age 11, and

Kristi age 9, and one hypersensitive female Hungarian sheep dog, a Puli named Bouksie, age undetermined. Lucy and Kushal circled each other like banty roosters for a week before deciding that they could co-exist, but we were onto our third cook in short order. But what in fact made it possible for us to be there was the presence of the American International School (AIS), which had just moved into an exciting new campus complex, designed by Delhi's leading architect, which abutted onto the western edge of the Embassy compound. AIS was not, strictly speaking, an official part of the U.S. Mission, but we watched over it like a hawk. It was divided into lower, middle, and upper divisions, classes ranging from K through 12; it was fully accredited in the U.S. and its graduates traditionally college bound. Its administrators were American, its faculty, half Indian and half American, recruited stateside with two year contracts. There were some 350 students, a polyglot group encompassing 22 nationalities, including a handful of Indians, for the school was open to all children in the diplomatic enclave who could handle the English language. There was also dormitory space for our consular families in Bombay, Calcutta and Madras, as well as for the missionaries scattered about. The school maintained an excellent library, nor were the arts and athletics neglected, with competition among the several very good Indian preparatory schools in the Delhi environs. Attendance at AIS was in and of itself a liberal education. Sometime later in payment, I suppose, for my transgressions in the American academic community, I was elected chairman of the AIS Board of Governors, which in the event was one of the most difficult postings of my career.

The route which I preferred between Delhi and Washington was via Air India through Moscow to London, and then via Pan Am from Heathrow to Dulles. I always looked forward to the brief stopover in Moscow mainly because the Air India station chief there was a really stunning brunette who, among other things, collected the passports of through passengers going into the terminal to buy mementos and/or vodka and then checked them back into the plane. I know she made particular note of those traveling on diplomatic credentials, and on this, my first trip, I managed to speak to her alone for a moment.

I whispered, "Ninotchka, if we ever can find the time, I'll tell what the CIA is up to in India."

She just smiled and said, "We must make the time, comrade."

Little did I realize what this would lead to in the future.

"No, Jack, the American Council of Education is not an operational body. Our primary concern is educational policy at the national level. Our business is to try to develop a consensus among our constituent members on the outstanding issues of the day as they pertain to higher education and so inform the Hill or the White House or wherever the arena of action is. We talk, we cajole, we lobby, we inform, but we do not act. We have no programmatic functions whatsoever." This was Logan Wilson in his spacious office in the headquarters of the American Council on Education on Massachusetts Avenue just below DuPont Circle. I had arrived in Washington the day before, checked in at the India Desk at AID and then repaired to the Cosmos Club to try to reset my biological clock. And now I was sitting with an old colleague, having my hopes dashed.

"Even if my Board so directed—which it assuredly would not—it would take me a year to build an organization within the council that could meet your needs. And if you go to any of the disciplinary organizations, like the National Academy of Science or the National Academy of Engineering, you will find the same operational incapacity. It is not that we find your project unimportant, because frankly I am fascinated by it; it is just that we exist for quite different purposes. But let me make a suggestion. As an historian, you probably have had no association with the National Science Foundation, but let me assure you that when it speaks every university in the country pricks up its ears because it funds so much of the basic research conducted in America, and every science department worthy of the name is beholden to it. Now you've been talking about NSF type institutes that you want to emulate in India. I'm not that familiar with NSF's organization either, but I do know that it has an Office of International Programs (OIP) though what it does I have no notion. So why don't you go to the source, as it were. They ought to be able to help, or at least advise you, if anyone can. It just so happens that NSF's Deputy Director, John Wilson, is one of my closest Washington friends; he's a psychologist by trade and he's on leave from the University of Chicago where he has long been President Thomson's right hand man. NSF has co-opted him to straighten out some administrative snarls, and he's really a great guy as well as smart. Let me give him a call. And how did you leave Newcomb?"

"Well, gentlemen, what do you think?" John Wilson had called into his office the Director and four of his colleagues who manned NSF's Office of International Programs to hear my exposition on India.

Wilson, himself, had stayed for the whole recital, and I could not have had a more attentive group. Never in my experience has there ever been a more fortuitous juxtaposition of interests which we discovered that day. It seems that NSF's contacts in Europe were fruitful, that she had established a working relationship with three Soviet Academies; that Red China's scientific community was making overtures of association, but that India remained a cipher, not from lack of interest but from lack of any real knowledge about the place. It was as though NSF and I had been groping blindly in search of each other.

John Wilson, who was every bit as congenial as the other Wilson had indicated, summed it up, "Upon receipt of an invitation from Ambassador Bowles, we will pay you a visit."

I suggested that Indian weather in November was reportedly very salubrious, thanked the gentlemen present, and fairly floated out of the premises. All of this was duly reported to the Desk, Dolly, and Macomber. I cabled the Mission in Delhi, *HAVE HOMERED WITH BASES LOADED. NSF HAS UMBRELLA UNDER WHICH WE CAN ALL FIT VERY NICELY.*

The stopover in Moscow was again very brief, but Ninotchka was still smiling.

The NSF team that arrived in mid-November consisted of Arthur Roberts, chemist and head of OIP, his principal program assistant, a nuts and bolts man without which a bureaucracy could not function, Paul Westfall, an eminent geologist who had just retired as Provost of the University of Illinois, Urbana, and a veteran organizer of international programs and who had signed on with NSF as a sort of ringmaster for this project, and a secretary quite familiar with governmental bureaucratic jargon.

The main objectives of the team were to gain an acquaintanceship with India, which none of them had ever visited, and within that context to produce a feasibility study of the possible areas and scope of NSF participation. The Ambassador in his eloquent fashion gave them an overview of American interests in India, and his estimate of where she was and what she might become in the community of nations. John Lewis briefed them on the tri-partite Agriculture-Family Planning-Education initiatives, and then had a reception for them to meet the principal players. They sat with Kirpal and his minions at the MOE, and they were enchanted by Dr. Khotari and his group and finding many similarities between the UGC and the NSF in their missions of supporting basic research in the colleges and universities of their respective countries. Hiebert and Deshpande were with them every step of the way, because in whatever guise NSF was going to appear, these two gentlemen would be key to their operation. My man Kheterapal sat in on all their meetings about Mission logistic support—travel, housing, commissary, medical—because he was going to be key to all such arrangements. We took them to the University of Delhi where they looked in on the science departments and especially the laboratories while heeding the admonition that Harvard was not typical of the American university scene.

For a break we took them to Agra where we caught the Taj under a full moon. It was a strenuous but most useful fortnight, with the team's enthusiasm visibly increasing as we went along; and by the time of their departure there was no doubt about their recommendation to their administration and board: NSF should become a principal partner in our Indian educational effort immediately.

It was an Indian educational effort of a different kind that led me to one of my most fortuitous associations. The Indian Constitution of 1950 specifically outlawed the caste system. Gandhi throughout his career had been the consistent defender of the "Untouchables" or their new designation under the Republic of the "Scheduled Classes." They were the harijans, the absolute dregs of society, the doers of all the menial and filthy tasks, hopelessly illiterate, often semi-savage tribals, existing at the very bottom of the societal heap. The GOI was going to considerable effort and expense to improve the lot of these unfortunates and turn at least some of them into productive citizens through the creation of special schools and social services. One such institution was called the Gujarat Vidyapith, located in Ahmedabad, a bustling cloth manufacturing city half way between Delhi and Bombay (Mumbai), and the capital of the State of Gujarat until the capital was moved to Gandhinagar, Gujarat's new capital city in 1970 some 32 kilometers north-east of Ahmedabad..

Founded in 1920 by Mahatma Gandhi, Gujarat Vidyapith was deemed a university in 1963 with funding from UGC. The principal objective of the Vidyapith is to prepare through education, workers with character, ability, culture, and conscientiousness necessary for the conduct of the movements connected with the regeneration of the country in accordance with the ideals given by Mahatma Gandhi which meant the dregs of society from the slums of slums were top priority. The teachers and trustees of the Vidyapith were required to regard Untouchables as a blot on Hinduism, and strive to the best of their ability for its removal, and not exclude a boy or a girl for reason of his or her untouchability nor tolerate any discriminatory treatment once admission had been accorded to him or her. Gandhi preached that the growth of the nation depended not on its cities but its villages, and therefore the bulk of the funds of the Vidyapith and large number of teachers were to be primarily employed in the propagation of national education in villages. In laying down the priorities of education, the needs of the village-dwellers were to be the principal consideration.

Shree Morarjibhai Desai, Chancellor of Gujarat Vidyapith

At the time of my introduction, Shree Morarjibhai Desai was chancellor of Gujarat Vidyapith. As we discussed the goals of AID/India and our proposed NSF science institute format, I watched him consume a breakfast consisting of nuts washed down with his own urine. Without rising, he shook my hand, nearly crushing my fingers, and said, "I recommend this diet. You'd never think I'm seventy years old and have never been sick a day in my life."

I would have agreed with anything that would have spared me another handshake. We chatted about the work being done here and how it might become a model for rehabilitation in other regions, and I suggested that he might want to visit Literacy House in Lucknow to see if their techniques might help, and that I would maintain an interest and be helpful to the enterprise in any way I could.

As I left he said, "Give my regards to your John Lewis. He is an earnest young man who thinks I learned my economics from Ricardo, and I have great respect for your Ambassador. I do not doubt your motives, but I think all of you are finding that India has a mind of her own."

Thus began a relationship that, in the event, saved the Indian Institute of Technology—Kanpur (IIT Kanpur) project in its darkest hour, and endured through his Prime Ministership from 1977—1979 and until his death at age 99, six years after I became Ambassador.

Embassy life suited the Hubbards right down to the ground. Being rank amateurs in this diplomatic setting, we found every day to be an adventure. And to experience it in a country as strange and wonderful as India had an appeal to each one of us, individually and collectively. We lived in a relatively small community of bright and interesting people, the core of which were the career diplomats, which most of us were not. For the men the work was important, challenging, and different, and for their families new sights, sounds, and companionships. All of us with various degrees of intent, tried to learn Hindi. The social scene revolved mainly about "at home" dining, with a new cook or recipe on display. The Embassy commissary stocked all the essentials at tax-free prices, including excellent selections of liquor, wine, beer, and tobacco. And everyone's larders were supplemented from India's bountiful stores: marvelous seafood from Bombay arriving in Delhi daily in refrigerated containers; goose, duck, partridge, pheasant, quail, venison acquired during hunting season and frozen fresh vegetables such as spinach of incredible taste and texture; pates and caviar from stopovers in Beirut and Tehran; the annual galas at the Embassy on the 4th of

July were notable for a grateful return to hamburgers and hot dogs.

The Embassy compound itself provided lots of opportunities for fun and games. There was a soft ball diamond kept busy every weekend by our own Little Leaguers and more senior teams from AIS, the Embassy and the community such as Goodyear, IBM, and Pan Am. Since baseball was the only sport I played with grace in college, I volunteered my services and immediately was named umpire in chief for league games. There was an Olympic-size outdoor swimming pool open from April through October where the boys and girls swimming teams from AIS trained early in the mornings and the whole Embassy could enjoy the rest of the day. There was an outdoor tennis court and an indoor bowling alley constantly in use. There was a movie theatre which three nights a week was the last repository for Hollywood's grade B offerings. There was a beauty shop for the ladies and a barber shop for the men, although I preferred my own barber who appeared on his bicycle at Assi(80) Number Golf Links promptly as 5:30 every other Thursday. (Incidentally, when I came back as Ambassador, it was his son who had become the chief barber at the Embassy shop.) There was a news kiosk which kept up fairly well with U.S. periodicals and the *International Herald Tribune* just three days late. There was AIS with its occasional recitals of music, dance and drama; here was also an opportunity of expanding one's relationships through meeting the non-American parents of your children's classmates. Finally there were the inevitable interest groups which sprang up, including bridge, modern dance, needlepoint, Indian cuisine, Indian fashion and the like.

An integral part of the Embassy, but occupying quarters in another part of Delhi was the United States Information Service, the overseas arm of the United States Information Agency, which harbored, among other things, the Voice of America, and whose mandate was to keep a healthy view of the American image before its international audience. USIS in Delhi, for example, published an absolutely first rate slick monthly magazine named *SPAN* depicting the many aspects of the Indo-U.S. relationship. USIS also sponsored global junkets of representatives of our creative arts, such as Isadora Duncan, Charlie "Bird" Parker, the Yale Whiffenpoofs, and the Merce Cunningham dance troupe. An unforgettable evening was the first return to India of a distinguished native son, the Bombay-born Parsee, Zubin Mehta, conducting the Los Angeles Philharmonic orchestra. The adulation heaped on the young maestro by American and Indian alike was a glorious moment of musical concert history.

Not very far from the diplomatic enclave and just off Lodi Road at the western entrance to beautiful Lodi Park was another cultural oasis known as the Indian International Center, which had been dedicated in 1962 by the President of India and the Vice Chancellor of the University of Delhi as a kind of glorified hostel and gathering place for the world's scholars concerned with things Indian. The location was so convenient and attractive that the Ford Foundation and UNICEF had established their Indian headquarters just next door. There was an administrative block cum library cum lecture halls cum small offices more like library carrels where visiting scholars could hang their hats. A few paces away was a motel-like structure built along the curving bank of a rivulet which watered Lodi gardens with some 100 single and double very comfortable sleeping chambers, each with private facilities, and two suites tacked on the western end. A few paces farther to the west were the social and dining facilities: on the ground floor a circular bar and service areas for tea, coffee and snacks consumed inside or outside on a beautiful day, and above all this, a spacious dining room that was undoubtedly the best food value in all of Delhi. Here indeed was a complex that well and truly ministered to a man's mind and body and soul. The place was usually administered by a retired senior civil servant/diplomat from the Ministry of External Affairs, and given acceptable intellectual credentials, sponsorship, and very reasonable annual dues, the entire establishment was made available to people of my ilk. So here was another venue for lectures and performances by a remarkable variety of talented people.

But to develop and enjoy these interests and activities—with much more to be related later—suggests plenty of leisure time and a long term assignment in India, and I had neither. After NSF came into the picture, I kind of tucked in the back of my mind a time table that suggested that if IIT Kanpur stayed on track and if we got the UGC/NSF/AID off and running, I should be able to get back to Tulane and Newcomb to open the 1966-67 academic year in September; but in the forefront of my mind was the certainty that for the massive assault on Indian higher education which we envisioned to be successful, a major international logistic miracle would be required. And, in the event, much, much more.

Cable traffic between Delhi and Washington increased exponentially. It was agreed in November that the launch date would be 15 April 1966, in New Delhi, with representatives of the two governments and the two academic scientific communities jointly announcing the most ambitious effort in bi-national intellectual acculturation ever attempted. The experiment would be unique in scale, scope and methodology, and we believed its announcement ought to be worthy of international attention. We did not want to stage a circus, but rather a spectacle in great good taste, and for the choreography to be eye-catching, we needed both governments' determination to put its best foot forward. And that meant joint planning with a vengeance.

In India, for the institutes in engineering, the site selection, subject content, and timing would be the responsibility of the Ministry of Education, and that meant Phil Haney and me working with Chandiramani and his designates. For the institutes in mathematics and the sciences, the responsibility lay with the UGC, and that meant Gordon Hiebert and me working with Dr. Khotari and Deshpande and the colleges and universities they designated. What we were doing was developing a roster of institute sites as to space availability, lecture and demonstration facilities, housing and dining facilities, ability to handle institute participants in batches of 50, and—of singular importance— living and hospitality arrangements for the American directors and, quite possibly, their wives. All of which for me resulted in the most interesting if exhausting aspect of the whole project— travel all over India, by every known means of transportation, from airplane to bullock cart, to remote areas that I normally would never have experienced, for we were working on the principle that it was far easier to take the institute and its American directors to a place in which it was relatively easy for the participants to congregate than to be moving batches of 50 participants all over the map.

Take Assam, for example. Tucked into India's northeastern extremity, squeezed between East Pakistan and the Burmese frontier, this remote, semi-tribal area was on no one's beaten path. Here was essentially a matriarchal society with a simple indicator of connubial bliss: if he returned to his abode to find his sandals placed outside the entrance, he could look for greener pastures. Its whole economy was based on its tea plantations, centered around Shillong. Its capital was Gauhati (now known as Guwahati), a motley collection of warehouses and government buildings, and its university whose scholarly pretensions, even by Indian standards, were practically non-existent, but which were the best the area afforded and was, as Dr. Khotari insisted, a deserving institute site.

The rub of it was that Deshpande, Hiebert and I rarely saw our families.

Then there was the Washington-Delhi traffic, by individuals and otherwise, like: Ambassador's Office—State Department—White House: No, President Johnson would not be present at the April ceremonies. The U.S. Delegation would be headed by his (President Johnson's) Science Advisor, Don Bunch, an eminent chemist, who would be bearing personal letters from the President to the President and Prime Minister of India. Ambassador Bowles, Prime Minister Gandhi, and The President of India would receive the U.S. Delegation and their ladies at the Rashtrapati Bhavan (Presidential Palace) following which Prime Minister Gandhi would receive the group for tea at her residence in Siliguri Gardens. Ambassador and Mrs. Bowles would receive the combined delegations and their ladies for cocktails and dinner at Roosevelt House. Amongst these cables was one from Arthur Roberts, OIP/USF addressed to me—John Hubbard, AID/India. "Will you join me on 18 January 1966 for briefing at its annual meeting of Board of Directors of NSF? Hope you could be here week in advance; so many details to discuss."

CHAPTER 20
—
India (1966-1969)
A Change of Plans

Mid-January is really not the time to fly to Washington from Delhi via Moscow. I can never remember a rougher transit, and how our Air India pilot found the Moscow runway in the middle of that blizzard is still beyond me. So Ninotchka gathered the passports from a thoroughly terrified and grateful list of passengers. The estimate on deplaning was that we would be grounded for at least three days.

I managed again to be the last to deplane, and as I handed her my passport, she smiled and said, "You see, comrade, I have found time for us. Wait at your hotel, I bring warmer clothes."

With that we were bussed into town to a very spartan tourist hotel used by Air India in such emergencies. Fortunately it had central heating. About two hours later, around seven, there came a little knock on the door, and in she came with a huge overcoat, a bearskin hat, and gloves.

Putting her finger to her lips, she wrote on a piece of paper, "First, I show you the bugs."

She pointed out three in the light fixtures and one very cleverly concealed in the headstand of the bed. She then produced from her satchel a transistor radio, found some music and went up to the headstand and turned the volume up to maximum. "That really drives them crazy!" she laughed, and we could now converse shielded by the volume of her radio. "Put these on," she said, motioning to the cold-weather gear she had brought. "Very, very cold outside, but we take a walk."

As we walked down one of the broad, practically deserted avenues, she explained that we were dining at the Hotel Majestic, a frantic place at the moment since it was housing most of the British delegation engaged in a summit meeting between Prime Minister Wilson and Khrushchev, but it had a decent dining room that should not be too crowded since the State Dinner was in progress at the Kremlin. We had what was known as a "leisurely" dinner with the unsurprising choice of borsht followed by beef stroganoff, both of which were surprisingly good, and a red wine that I was sure I would regret in the morning.

"Tell me," she said, "we know you're not one of the Embassy spooks, at least you're not on any list we have. And we know you're not a career diplomat. So what is an Education Adviser and who do you advise about what?"

So I went to some lengths to explain to her that given the increase of AID activity in India, of which I knew the Soviets kept close track of, mine was a new position in which my principal duty was to advise the MOE that its engineering curricula were out of date and that it was time to discard the old British syllabi. That's my cover, at any rate.

"And what about you?"

It seems she was half-Indian, a Russian father high up in the Party apparatus, and a husband a Colonel in the Soviet Air Force now observing our aerial activities in Southeast Asia and wondering like everyone else around the Kremlin how the U.S., in view of the French experience, could have got itself caught up in the same quicksand. And so much for my cover—couldn't I give her something more to report, since just keeping track of the official diplomatic travel through Moscow was not very exciting? Indeed I could: I was really advising the Ministry of Defense and the Indian Navy how to build a nuclear submarine! But that it would take time and patience for her to get at the details, beginning tonight.

After dinner we went down to the lobby, off of which behind closed doors was the transients bar, no Russians allowed. It was a large room with a long bar, a modest dance floor, a jazz trio belting out its version of Western standards, and tables occupied by a motley collection of ladies of the evening, who for a $50 bottle of cheap bubbly would give you a twirl on the dance floor and discuss any topic that came to mind. It was the B girls and Bourbon Street in Russian garb. Business at the bar, where we stood, was brisk, and I heard nothing but English spoken mainly, I assumed, from the British press covering the Summit, who ignored the girls in their attention to some good hard booze at fairly reasonable prices. Every drink at the bar or table was paid for in hard currency, the £ or the $, no exceptions. Ninotchka explained to me that establishments such as these were maintained in all the better hotels in Moscow and St. Petersburg, and although rarely was any information gleaned of operational benefit, they were good sources for foreign exchange, and they did keep some of the girls off the streets.

The good news on our way back to my hotel was that the snow had stopped; the bad news was that the London flight was scheduled to depart at high noon the next day.

The briefing of the NSF Board went very well indeed; it was clear that our project had captured their attention from the thoughtful questions they raised. The make-up of the NSF team to come out in April was discussed at length, John Wilson excusing himself for valid reasons but disappointing me no end. We agreed that the subject matter areas to be addressed by the institutes would be limited to engineering, mathematics pure, mathematics applied, physics, chemistry, and biology, and that these disciplines would be represented on the NSF team in April. As for the April agenda, there would be the two days of ceremonial functions in Delhi, followed by a week's retreat, including travel time, at a venue away from Delhi's distractions, wherein the Indian and the U.S. disciplinary experts would sit head to head to decide on subject matter areas to be included in the various institutes. By that time we should have a complete listing of possible institute sites and dates of availability, which would then leave us the arbitrary assignment of what, where, and when. With that in hand, the American side could begin its task of recruiting institute directors, while the Indian side began its recruitment of institute participants. With any luck at all we ought to be able to open with a flourish in April 1967. Finally, Roberts agreed to come back out with his two colleagues for ten days beginning the first of March to inspect potential institute sites so as to have some knowledge of the kinds of conditions our professors might confront to at least try to minimize the culture shock, extreme at times, that was inherent in the program. We also had to plan the post-Delhi retreat.

Just before departing Washington for Delhi, via New Orleans where I wanted to touch base for a few days and have at least one meal with Stibbs at Manale's, Macomber called me in. He said he had been discussing the matter with Lewis and the Ambassador, and would I consider extending my tenure in India. Bringing NSF aboard was a masterful stroke which portended a spectacular program development. The three of them would be far more comfortable if I would stay long enough at least to get the thing off the ground. NSF was prepared to insist on it if necessary. Williams had indicated to Dolly that he saw the handwriting on the wall and would be prepared to accept a proposal that he resign for reasons of his own choosing, so there would be no blood-letting. I replied that the last part of his statement was critical for me: Clanton had recruited me in good faith and he and his wife could not have been more helpful in our adjustment to India. He also claimed that holding NSF type institutes in India was his idea in the first place, and he might be right for all I know. At any rate, I would want him to be present in April for the inaugural and included in all the festivities and, I hope, thanked for a brilliant idea. I would, of course have to talk to the family, but so far as I could gather, they were all happy with their Indian experience. Personally, I most certainly wanted to see things under way.

New Orleans was a happy respite as I tried to share with old friends the excitement of the Hubbard family in their Indian venture. I had a useful session with Bill Hogan, University Chairman of History, and my best faculty friend since Lumiansky's departure, apprising him of the likelihood of my extending my tour in India and therefore resigning as Dean of Newcomb. In that event, he agreed to recommend the indefinite extension of my leave as professor of history, so that I would have a secure place to hang my academic hat. To all of this President Longenecker, delighted that he would be losing me as an administrative adversary, gave his blessing.

When the NSF group arrived on 1 March with its glorious weather, we first repaired to the UGC to look at the maps of India which had been prepared to indicate the principal academic centers and the density around each of the teachers of our selected disciplines. In India the major universities generally had several colleges in the area affiliated with them. What, for example, would be the approximate number of participating teachers of chemistry in the Madras area, physicists, biological scientists, mathematicians, engineers? Was space available for conducting simultaneous institutes? When during the academic year would the freeing up of batches of participants be less disruptive: Then there were the tougher logistical problems represented by the more remote, non-urban areas where over half the population of India resided in the villages. How many institutes and in what disciplines, for example, do you schedule for Vallabh Vidhyanagar, a kind of academic oasis in a remote part of Gujarat? Do we dare send American directors accompanied by their wives here or there? State by Indian state we worked, aided by consultants called in by the UGC, and finally on one large map with a lot of colored pins, we developed a master plan.

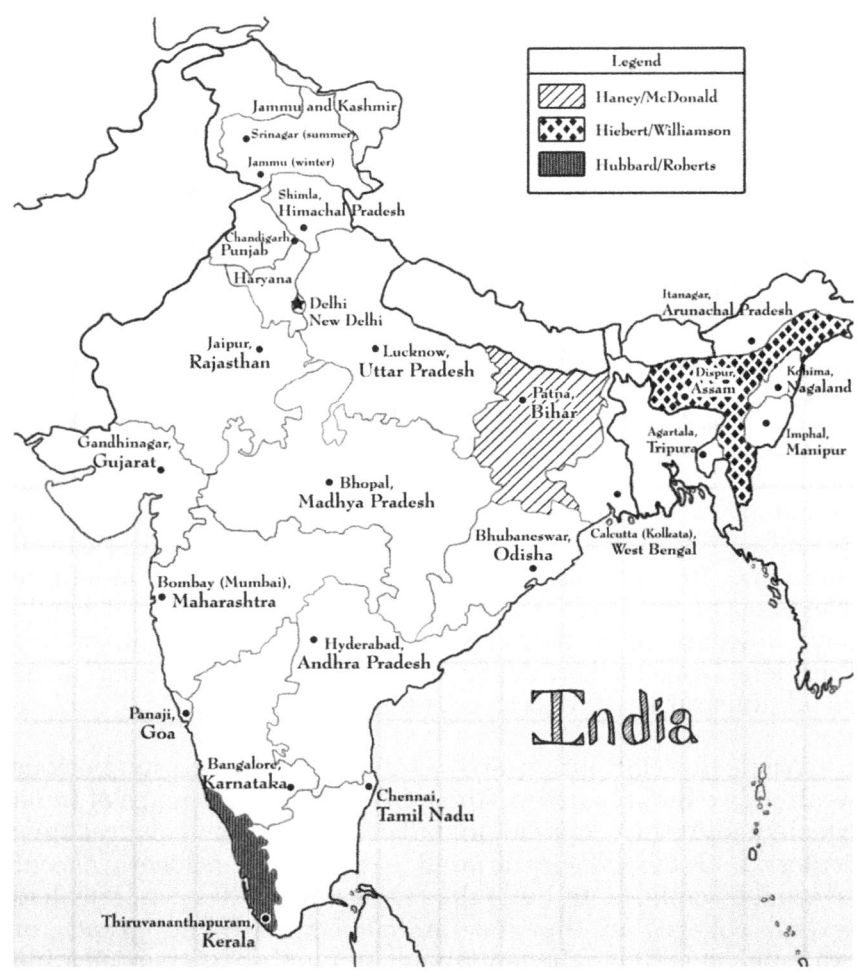

Map 8
Remote Destinations of AID Teams in 1966

Then we divided up the chores. Haney took McDonald, Hiebert took Williamson, and I took Roberts, our separate destinations being the remotest of our possible sites. Haney went to Bihar, probably the most backward state in India. Hiebert went to Assam. I took Roberts to inland Kerala, away from the Malabar Coast to regions only accessible by canals. We then reconvened in Delhi, agreeing on modest efforts in Assam and Bihar, but ruling out inland Kerala. We were sitting in the Chairman's office at the UGC, when the topic of our post-Delhi retreat in April was raised. Where was there a conveniently accessible, pleasant place with agreeable housing and dining arrangements for a variety of tastes and with at least five meeting rooms where some thirty odd Indian and American experts could confer face-to-face about the subject areas of the various disciplinary institutes? Deshpande, Hiebert and I had long since agreed that there was only one place in India at that time of year, perhaps only one place in all the world, that could meet our requirements—Kashmir, that storied summer playground of the British raj. But would our saintly guru, Dr. Khotari, whose idea of relaxation was a simple walk in Lodi Park, ever agree to such seeming ostentation?

From October through April, the Indo-Gangetic plain wherein Delhi sits has the most equable climate in the world. Through the winter months the temperature is steady at a daily high of 75 degrees to a low of 45. There is rarely a cloud in a perfectly clear blue sky. To tee off at high noon on any December day is to stroll in the sunshine and a gentle breeze, and the golf seems almost secondary to this gift of nature. But from May through September, one pays for the delights of winter. The Indo-Gangetic plain becomes a furnace, an unrelieved, sweltering oven, broken only by the monsoon in June, which brings the dripping humidity in its wake. Your insatiable golfer must alter his whole routine: he dare not tee off later than 6 a.m., play his first nine holes, then home to shower and breakfast and off to work, returning to the tee at 6 p.m. to complete his eighteen.

To my mind, one of the cleverest feats of Britain's 350 year ascendancy in India was finding ways to beat the heat. The answer lies in the utilization of "Hill Stations," which as the name implies, were elevated areas in the hills and mountains high above the fetid plains where the temperatures brought unfailing relief. Lying across northern India were the Himalayas, the world's most massive mountain chain, while down the eastern and western coasts almost to the tip of the peninsula ran the Eastern and Western Ghats. Now the Indian rank and file possessed neither the means nor the aptitude to relocate his livings twice a year. But for the ubiquitous British, the rotation between summer and winter climes was a rite as natural as tiffin. By the end of each April, for example, the whole vice-regal apparatus of government was physically moved first from Calcutta and then from Delhi to Simla [now known as Shimla], in the Himalayan foothills, and British hostesses vied with each other in the splendor of their parties announcing their arrival for the season. Among the Americans here in the 1960s, everyone seemed to have a favorite haven. In the south there was

Ootacamund and the Niligri Hills. The Bowles and their intimates preferred Dak bungalows in the Kulu Valley. There was Manali, there was Darjeeling. And there was Kashmir.

An hour and a half by air due north of Delhi lay the valley of Kashmir, and its capital Srinagar. Here in all its verdant glory were rice paddies, mustard fields, orchards, and groves of stately chinar trees that scented the pure air with a natural perfume. And just to the north of the town in the very center of the valley were two exquisite emerald lakes, Nagin and Dal, fed by crystalline mountain streams and emptying into a small waterway flowing through the city along whose banks lived seemingly half the population of Kashmir. Since ancient law and custom forbade the sale of any land to aliens, the British could not construct any holiday habitation; but determined to enjoy this earthly paradise, they resorted to a novel device, one destined to make the region even more famous—the Kashmir houseboat.

With an ample wood supply and skilled native artisans, the British designed flat bottomed, shallow draft boats that were virtually floating palaces. There could be one, two, three or more bedrooms each with WC (water closet aka bathroom), always a spacious dining area, parlor, and open-air veranda; and topside, a reinforced roof encircled with a railing and lined with potted plants and flowers that gave the whole affair the appearance of a floating garden. Attached to each houseboat by a mooring cable was another much plainer craft which housed the cook and his kitchen and the attendant staff, which would be pulled alongside during mealtimes. Also attached to each houseboat was its own shikara, your private water taxi with spring seats—another British innovation—and luxurious pillows on which you could stretch out full length while your own boatman paddled silently over to the Shalimar Gardens, or along the waterway to see the natives at work and play, or simply to the middle of the lake and let the oar drop while you napped or supped or decided to move again. Finally, there was a veritable flotilla of watercraft bearing the Kashmiri merchants and their wares; the jewelry wallahs, the paper mâché, the flower, needlework, the leather wallahs constantly gliding around so that memsahib, if she chose, need not leave the comfort of her veranda to have the glories of Kashmiri artisans spread out on the rug under her feet.

The British left a remarkable legacy when they departed, and tourists came from all over the world to fill the void. There were houseboats available for any purse, and since they were movable, a host could link together as many bedrooms as he required in any area of the lake he chose. Even at the peak of the season there was no sense of crowding or loss of privacy, but from May through September, those placid waters seemed alive with water beetles on the move, for the houseboat wallahs and the merchants had to realize enough income to take them through the year, because the winter closed the valley like a vise.

The Williams had introduced us to Kashmir in February, really too early in the year, for even though the sun is bright the air is chilled by the winds coming off the Himalayan snow packs, and the natives scurry around wearing their wool shawls under which they carried their little clay braziers of burning charcoal for warmth. The trip, however, was notable for our introduction to one of the most powerful families in the valley.

Mrs. Williams and Lucy were inveterate shoppers and they had heard through the grapevine—and the Indian grapevine is beyond peradventure an amazingly accurate source of information—about an establishment known as Butt Sons which reputedly produced among other things the best crewel work in the land. We found the shop on the main road north along the river front and were ushered upstairs to a small reception room. What were our interests—crewel, the finest Kashmir wool in its many guises, paper mâché, rugs, suits, please let our wishes be known, thank you—all this while being served Kashmir tea and cakes by our host who insisted that his father would be along any minute. And indeed, before long there was ushered in the patriarch of the family, Hadji Butt, a sprightly little man in his early seventies, flowing white beard and white hair under an Afghan hat, a snaggle-toothed smile that was really quite charming, and the most sparkling, mischievous blue eyes I have ever encountered.

"From the American Embassy right, oh my dears they have been my most faithful for years, and your great Ambassador Mr. Bowles, my dear, refuses to use any houseboat but mine, and oh yes we also have houseboats as part of our attempt to please distinguished like your good selves, and yes you must see a few of our wares here and let us know your wishes, and my dears, you will have lunch with me at Clermont where I modestly reside in my garden and where I moor my houseboats." And before we knew it the floor was covered with samples of the finest needlework we had ever seen. Butt Sons, were without parallel the most congenial thieves who ever existed, the only possible rival being Whispering Moses who had his ship at the other end of town.

Hadji Butt—Hadji, a title earned because he had made his pilgrimage to Mecca—would have been my candidate for the Readers Digest category of the most colorful character I have ever met. Sitting in the grass of his garden dominated by a giant chinar, he pointed out the many beauties it would hold in another month if the weather stayed fine. Gazing out over Lake Dal to the mountains and their ever-changing colors, he related some of the incidents of the Hadji. He introduced us to his four sons, all strikingly handsome, one who tended the houseboats moored in a line abutting the garden, two who minded the store in town, and one who commuted between Clermont and the diplomatic enclave in Delhi taking orders and delivering purchases. "Yes, there was passable telephone service to Delhi if one booked his call a day in advance." He brought out volumes of guest books with pictures and comments of the great and near-great who had visited Clermont and unfailingly promised to return. He introduced his two principal manservants, Biloo and Ardoo, who flitted about replenishing our plates and glasses. And why all this attention? Because we were the first visitors of the year, the harbingers of a new season, and our early appearance was an omen that Allah was going to bless his humble family and establishment in the days to come.

There was a final item that made this first junket to Kashmir so fortuitous. In driving in the Butt car, I noticed about 400 yards before reaching Clermont on the other side of the road a cluster of buildings that looked like a school, and at the entrance of which was a sign saying The Jammu And Kashmir Regional College Of Engineering.

I asked Hadji about it and he said, "Oh yes, my dear, it will open in mid-March and its principal is a very pleasant fellow and I would be pleased to introduce you." Then I asked if there were any other kind of tourist's accommodations beside houseboats. "Oh yes my dear, the houseboats are a Muslim monopoly, but most Indian tourists to the valley are Hindu and they feel much more comfortable at a very good and spacious hotel in Srinagar named Nedous." Everything seemed to have fallen into place for our post-Delhi April retreat. We had this glorious valley awake from its winter respite. We had a college campus as a venue for our discussions. We had a comfortable hotel for the Indian side, and we had houseboats to titillate the Americans. Maybe Allah also had a blessing for the NSF/AID India/UGC joint venture.

To our positive joy, Dr. Khotari thought Kashmir would be a splendid place for our gathering, and not only that, he would be there to open the sessions. With that knowledge in hand, the last phase of our preparations was to introduce our NSF friends to Kashmir and, with their approbation, to reserve all the spaces required for our April hegira. Young Bashir Butt called me on the way north, and I told him to have two cars meet the morning flight day after tomorrow and that we would be lunching that day with his father at Clermont. And that is how the six of us—Deshpande, Hiebert, Roberts, Williamson, Westfall, and myself—found ourselves sitting al fresco under that magnificent chinar enjoying a luncheon of freshly grilled brown trout and corn fritters with Hadji Butt. Mid-March is still just a tad early in Kashmir, but there were signs everywhere—in the leaves of the apple trees and the wisps of yellow beginning to show in the mustard fields and the buds opening in the Clermont gardens of the glories that would await us in April. The freshly scented air was already intoxicating, and Roberts et al were enchanted.

After lunch, Hadji took the group on a tour of his houseboats. There were six of them in a line, the largest, a three bedroom affair, at the southern end, followed by another three bedrooms, then three two bedrooms, and then at the northern end and farthest removed from the group, a cozy one bedroom boat, known as the honeymoon cottage. Hadji's pride and joy was the first one, ornately decorated inside as a Maharajah's hunting lodge, with two tiger skins on the parlor floor and dozens of lithographs of hunting expeditions and sporting events. It was aptly called the Ambassador's Lodge, and it was widely known for its opulence and heavily booked. But these six craft differed from the houseboat norm in that they were not mobile, all being securely moored to the bank of the lake. From these boats the view to the east was over the lake to the mountains, while to the west one looked onto the Clermont gardens. What was lost by this arrangement was any sensation of floating on the waves, a small price to pay in the eyes of most for sampling the famed Butt hospitality.

Then I outlined for Mr. Butt our plans for the gathering in April that we would house the Indians at Nedous, utilize the Regional College of Engineering for our meetings, and house the Americans on Lake Nagin. There followed the only real argument in our twenty odd years of association.

"But my dear Jack, did I hear you say Lake Nagin? My dear boy, Clermont is on Lake Dal!"

"I know that, sir, but for this affair I prefer Lake Nagin; its water is smoother, it is less crowded than Dal, and the views are just as spectacular. And there the houseboats are movable and we can make any configuration we want."

"Are you telling me, my dear young man, that my houseboats are not suitable? Not suitable? They are suitable for your ambassadors. They are suitable for the president of General Motors. They are suitable for British peers. They are suitable for Saudi sheiks. But they are not suitable for you and your celestial guests?"

"Please, my dear Hadji, let me try to explain."

SOME PROMINENT GUESTS WHO HAVE STAYED AT BUTT'S CLERMONT HOUSEBOATS

H.E. & Mrs. Nelson A. Rockfeller	Ex-Vice President of USA
H.E. Adelai Stevenson	Governor of Chicago- USA
H.E. & Mrs. Elsworth Bunker	U.S. Ambassador to India
H.E. & Mrs. Keneth Galbriath	U.S. Ambassador to India
H.E. Sir Paul Gore Booth	U.K. High Comissioner to India
H.E. & Mrs. Ronald Mitchner	Former Governer General of Canada
H.E. & Mrs. Chester Bowles	U.S. Ambassador to India
H.E. Kenneth B. Keating	U.S. Ambassador to India
H.E. & Mrs. Sir Morris James	U.K High Comissioner to India
H.E. & Mrs. John R. Hubbard	U.S. Ambassador to India
H.E. & Mrs. Bill Hayden	Former Governer General of Australia
H.E. & Mrs. Harry Burnes	U.S. Ambassador to India
H.E. & Mrs. John Guntler Dean	U.S. Ambassador to India
H.E. & Mrs. B. Olhart	U.S. Ambassador to India
Mr. George Harrison	Famous Sitar Player of Beatles Group
Mr. Pandit Ravi Shankar	Famous Musician of India
H.E. & Mrs. Jean Claude Winkler	French Ambassador to India

Partial Listing of Prominent Guests at Butt's Clermont Houseboats as Listed on www.buttsclermonthouseboat.com

I then said that we were talking about ten or twelve people, Americans on their first and perhaps only visit of their lives to India, and that I wanted them to have a *genuine* houseboat experience, and that meant not stepping from dry land onto the boat but stepping from dry land into a shikara and being rowed to the boat and helped aboard where they could hear the lapping of the waves and feel the movement of the wind. These people are absolutely key to the success of the program we have described for you which, if successful will mean that for the next several years we will have hundreds of American professors in India for at least six weeks, every one of whom will be encouraged to come to Kashmir and sit with the Butts before going home. So please my dear sir, what I want from you right now is to be my agent and bring the best houseboat wallah you know on Nagin here to talk to us. He was mollified, and about an hour later there drove up a well-accoutered Kashmiri gentleman who, after the shaloms were exchanged, said that he could provide a boat in time for tea at 5 o'clock, and we agreed on dinner after cocktails at 8, that we would be staying aboard the whole of tomorrow, leaving after breakfast the next day; furthermore, if we were pleased, and if his great friend and spiritual mentor, Hadji Butt agreed that the price was reasonable, he was prepared to provide six such boats or as many as needed beginning on 17 April for as long as needed. That accomplished, Hadji's staff called in their oarsmen and he invited us to board his shikaras and tour the lake while he went off to pray.

One of Butt's Clermont Houseboats

At 5 o'clock we were at the appointed landing on Lake Nagin. Desh had decided to go into town and check the facilities at Nedous Hotel and then rejoin us tomorrow. So the five of us boarded the two shikaras awaiting us; our destination, standing offshore about a quarter of a mile was a brand spanking new three bedroom houseboat named the Flower Garden. Maybe it was the angle of the sun, maybe it was how the flowers and the ferns were intermingled around the top deck; she just looked elegant. Our host greeted us, all smiles, and his footmen stowed our luggage; Gordon and I were sharing a room, as were Paul and Jim, while we left the master bedroom to our revered chief, an almost speechless Arthur Rowe. Yes, we would have tea on the top deck where the luxuriant floral display did nothing to belie the name of our floating odyssey. Ours was the only boat in the immediate area, and before us stretched the whole valley with both its lakes seemingly undisturbed, hemmed in on two sides by the magnificent mountains and their ever-changing hues, and there we were perched atop our own pleasure dome, and we just sat there and looked at each other and grinned.

Our host informed us that the Flower Garden had just been completed the week before, and that her "sister ship" would be in service in another fortnight. He felt sure he could sublet four more nicely outfitted three bedroomers for our use in April. We liked the relative seclusion of our present location, and decided that our little fleet should be anchored in a semi-circle, not too close together, but with each boat having its own shikara to allow visiting or to go ashore, or simply to drift. Indeed, since we had brought a few potables with us from Delhi and had secured some ice at Clermont, we decided to take our two shikaras out into the lake and lash them together for a small pre-dinner cocktail party. It was a glorious evening, calm and free, with a sunset that defied description as we lay back on our cushions and counted our blessings.

Dinner was more than passable with lamb kebabs, chicken tandoori and Kashmiri naan, and by the time we went topside again for our brandy and coffee, the moon had risen and all the stars of the eastern hemisphere had crowded down on top of us. The wind had picked up just a little, gently rocking the boats as the waves lapped the side. It was perfection, and we sat there too absorbed in our own thoughts to break the silence. Here were five of us, two of whom ten months ago had been total strangers and all of whom had never given India a second thought, now gathered together through intellectual curiosity to conceive and conduct a massive pedagogical experiment that might well determine the scientific future of this Asian sub-continent. Five individuals sitting on the roof of the Flower Garden on Lake Nagin in Kashmir, not one of whom was in this thing for any personal gain in a project that surely could qualify under Churchill's sobriquets of the Marshal Plan as "one of the least sordid acts of history."

I don't know how long we sat there; I only remember feeling compelled to rise and address my companions:

> *How now my co-mates and brothers in exile,*
> *Hath not old custom made this life more sweet*
> *Than that of painted pomp? Are not these woods*
> *More free of peril than the envious court?*
> *Here feel we but the penalty of Adam,*
> *The seasons' difference as the icy fang*
> *And churlish chidings of the winter's wind,*
> *Which, when it bites and blows upon my body,*
> *Even til I shrink from cold I smile and say,*
> *'This is no flattery: These are counselors*

That feelingly persuade me what I am!'
Sweet are the uses of adversity,
Which like the toad, ugly and venomous,
Wears yet a special jewel in his head;
And this our life, exempt from public haunt,
Finds tongues in trees, books in the running brooks,
Sermons in stones And good in everything.
As You Like It, Act 2, Scene 1
(Shakespeare)

Paul jumped to his feet and ended it when he intoned, "*I would not change it.*"

This burst the dam. Paul followed with a Hamlet soliloquy. Gordon surprised us with a Wordsworth sonnet and then Rowe with a touch of Robert Browning's *My Last Duchess*. It was formless, it was spontaneous, it was exuberant. We considered ourselves the luckiest five people in the world to be together, where we were, doing what we were doing. We even adopted a motto, to which we lifted our nightcap, "Never tire of doing good!" In retrospect, I think that was only half in jest.

The next day the NSFers stayed aboard and were treated to an endless procession of shikaras as the Kashmiri merchants displayed their wares, while Gordon and I, with Hadji's help, met with the Principal of the Engineering College who said he would be honored to have us meet on his campus in April. Deshpande rejoined us in the afternoon after having given his blessing to Nedous, which would also supply a bus to shuttle the Indian side back and forth to the Engineering College. So we returned to Delhi confident that we could pull it off in reasonably good style.

April 15th did arrive on schedule, and the festivities began. The American team numbered 13, headed by President Johnson's Sciences Advisor, and included one Nobel Laureate in Genetics, a distinguished biologist from Cornell who was also a member of the NSF Board, a mathematician whom I had known when he headed our department at Tulane before being co-opted by Duke, Taylor Ide, head of NSF's Engineering Division, whose brother was a high official in AID, and two equally distinguished professors of physics and chemistry, and three wives. All were housed either at Roosevelt House, the Ambassador's official residence, or at the Ashoka Hotel out of deference to our Indian hosts. And all were in their places at 10 a.m. in the Conference Room at the University Grants Commission when the session opened under the co-chairmanship of Ambassador Bowles and Dr. D. S. Khotari.

What all of us were skittish about was the predictable reaction of the left-wing Indian press egged on by the Soviets that all this was a classic example of intellectual imperialism on the part of the U.S. so Dr. Kothari's remarks bore heavily on the fact that it was India which had called this meeting to discuss a program greatly desired by India and how grateful he and his colleagues were at the unstinting response of the American academic community. He was followed by the Minister of Education, Triguna Sen, who was Alphabet Rau's successor, who spoke in the same vein. Ambassador Bowles responded with his usual generosity of sentiment. Don Biggs read President Johnson's personal message to the gathering, hoping that this joint project was the herald of a new era of good feeling between the world's two greatest democracies. John Lewis spoke for AID and this exciting new initiative in international development and in the end thanked Clanton Williams for his role in initiating the project. Then the Indian side and the American side introduced their academicians who would be working head to head on the course content of the institutes. Deshpande, Hiebert and I were sitting at the far end of our respective sides, quiet as mice and looking very unconcerned about it all. There followed a stand up buffet luncheon, Indian style, which permitted both sides freely to mingle, with the academicians holding center stage.

That evening there was the Ambassador's formal dinner at Roosevelt House, graced for a few moments by Prime Minister Gandhi herself in an unusually friendly gesture, which included a liberal sprinkling of vice chancellors and government officials. The next morning saw us at the Presidential Palace to be received by the President of India for coffee and a personally guided tour of the incomparable Mughal Gardens. Teatime found us at Mrs. Gandhi's residence/cum office where she, Mr. Bowles and the President's Science advisor led an informal discussion about India's educational system, which she concluded with an impassioned plea that the intellectual muscle of both countries could be brought to bear on one of India's most intractable problems—illiteracy. And then bright and early the next morning, off for Srinagar.

Four days before we had dispatched a driver and a truck full of sundries and goodies from the Commissary, and yesterday Gordon had flown up with Kheterapal and our office staff who were going to act as recorders at the various sessions. Dede Hiebert was coming along to help the three wives with their introduction to India. So when our main party arrived at the landing on Lake Nagin, there were tables set out under the trees laden with sandwiches and chips and tea and coffee and soda waters and cold beer and something stronger if needed; and there in the distance were our houseboats anchored in a half moon with the shikaras waiting patiently for their passengers. It was really quite a sight and much appreciated by a very happy group of pilgrims. Our office staff fitted quite nicely into one boat. We assigned the three couples to the newest boat.

I am convinced that all Kashmiris are born trout fishermen, but none more ardent than Hadji Butt, nor did I encounter two more skillful gillies than Biloo and Ardoo. When the British in 1906 began to stock these magnificent mountain streams with rainbow, cut throat and brown trout, only the brown took kindly to the environment, and the Kashmiris proved to be quite adept at fish culture, maintaining fish farms up and down the mountain chain and restocking the streams annually.

"You see," I told Hadji, "if you had all those science wallahs staying in your houseboats you'd be worrying about what to feed them tonight. Now all you have to worry about is how many trout we are going to eat for lunch?"

With that, he sent me off with his driver into town to procure the necessary licenses, while his sons rummaged around for warm clothes with which to outfit me.

That evening I turned in early on the Flower Garden, tremendously relieved that the meetings had been joined. Dr. Khotari had inspired them all with a sense of mission, and if he had not known the first thing about physics, our chaps would still have recognized a dedicated academic statesman. I was up at the crack of dawn and walked over to Clermont. (I will mention it now and many times again. My favorite time of the Indian day is sunrise when I can watch the mighty sub-continent open its eyes, stretch its limbs, and greet the dawn.) Dressed in warm Kashmiri garb and fortified by strong coffee and Biloo's doughnut balls, I was ready to go by sunrise when the four of us crowded into Hadji's car. Even his driver was happy, for he too had a fishing rod stashed in the boot. Hadji, of course, knew dozens of fishing beats but his favorite was the Kokernag, 8000 feet above the valley floor, and that was where we were headed for my introduction to Himalayan trout fishing.

For three hours we climbed steadily through the foothills up ever steeper grades, and I was amazed at the number of tiny villages clustered along the streams, wondering if their inhabitants ever encountered as much of the world even as

Srinagar. After three hours of this we pulled off onto a relatively level siding and there, clearly expecting us, was the forest ranger whose beat was the Kokernag, who greeted Hadji as a brother.

How he knew we were coming and where is beyond me, but he conscientiously checked our fishing credentials, and after gossiping with Hadji for a few minutes, pointed out where the last fishermen on this beat had had the best luck. But this was home to Biloo and Ardoo who could barely wait to get started.

The stream was a beautiful thing as it followed its rocky course downward. The currents were swift from the snows beginning to melt above, so rather than wade the angler worked his way slowly from rock to rock along the bank, pausing at pools that might be inviting to the big browns. Ardoo took Hadji while Biloo took me in tow, with the driver off on his own. Biloo was as agile on the rocks as I was clumsy, so the going was slow at first. He put away his rod so he could instruct me, standing behind me and holding my hand as I cast until I could pick up the rhythm. We came to a beautiful little pool that just had to have a fish lurking about. He took my rod and deftly put the fly right in the center and hastily gave me back the rod. Wham, the fly disappeared and I had on the end of my line a two-pound brown. Coaching me every step of the way, Biloo helped me work the fish in reach of his net, and I was no longer a virgin. Claiming that I needed some rest, I urged him to go off on his own, and it was pure pleasure to watch him glide along those rocks and work that beat with the deftness of a surgeon. And oh, how he enjoyed it, for that lovely toothless smile never left his face.

A little before noon our group reassembled, Biloo attending to the fire and Ardoo filleting a trout for each of us. Now every angler knows that there is no sweeter taste than to plop a catch fresh into the skillet with a little butter and lemon juice, like a sautéed walleye on a little island in the Lake of the Woods with a Mountie as a luncheon guest. And the setting: midway up the mountainside with the peaks soaring above us in the crisp sunlight that heightened their purple majesty, while below the valley was spread out before us, the trout streams now rivulets coursing gently through the rice paddies and mustard fields. The only sounds were the rustle of the foliage in the whispering breeze and the tinkling of the bell on some wandering goat. I sat with my back against the trunk of a stately cedar, my plate of perfect trout on my lap and a cold beer by my side which Hadji had thoughtfully provided. Could I but repeat one luncheon in my life, this would be it.

As soon as they had cleared away the remains of lunch, the gillies and the driver were back on the beat, while Hadji and I just stretched out and were blissfully asleep in a trice. We descended the mountain roads before dark and were back at Clermont for tiffin. Then laden with a dozen or so filleted trout, I walked back to Nagin and distributed my treasure, most of which I claimed to have netted.

The next day I set off to see more of the valley. To the east after a gentle rise of some 2000 feet was Pahalgam, a favorite area for hikers and campers with a modestly productive stream running through it. To the west was Gulmarg, the last part of the ascent to which was so precipitous that it could only be negotiated safely on mountain donkeys, and which in the winter was a ski resort and in the summer, the world's highest golf course. Then there was Ladakh and Tiber to the northeast. But I had never heard anyone speak of the area to the north and northwest of Srinagar, and that is what I decided to explore.

So with Hadji's car and driver and Biloo and a picnic hamper and a map, we drove north for about an hour on a metaled road out of Srinagar until we came to a rare intersection and headed due west. We were on a fairly smooth road gradually ascending through the foothills of the northwestern spur of the mountains, passing orchards and paddies and mustard fields, and little villages that dotted the route where our driver stopped frequently to chat with groups of attractive young maidens tending flocks of sheep and goats. We came rather suddenly to the crest of a steep, curling descent into a small, narrow valley with a lake at its center. I asked the driver to stop so I could stretch and relieve myself, and I found myself facing a fence which blocked a path onto the road. Wondering where the path led, I crawled through the fence with Biloo behind me, and we found ourselves on a shepherd's trail that skirted the top of a mesa that fell off sharply down to the lake and valley below. To the east another long valley led through the foothills towards the mountains in the distance. What we had stumbled upon was India's largest fresh water lake, Wular Lake, which varies in size from season to season, and was the source of more than half the total catch of fish in all of Kashmir. Biloo, of course, knew all of this, but allowed me to bask in the beauty of this unexpected surprise while we picnicked before heading back to Lake Nagin for our last night before returning to New Delhi and the full implementation to the plans that had been agreed to by UGC/NSF/AID.

I replaced Clanton Williams as Chief Education Advisor to the U.S.A.I.D. Mission in India in 1967, a year after the decision had been made that Williams would resign in a way of his own choosing. By 1968, the Summer Science Institutes were in full swing training Indian teachers in physics, mathematics, chemistry, biology, engineering, and polytechnics. A total of 370 institutes had already trained approximately 21,000 teachers.

To further the mission of training India's teachers, I encouraged the indigenous production of "academic hardware"—text books, visual aids, laboratory equipment, film strips, etc.—for use in schools and colleges throughout India. These tools were required if education was to become more than "rote learning". I envisioned the manufacturing and supply of "academic hardware" becoming a major domestic industry within India as it had in the United States. Hygrade Films of Bombay was the first manufacturer to undertake production in 1966. In 1967 Dynam Engineering Corporation of Bangalore, South India, began manufacturing.

The Indian Institute of Technology at Kanpur (ITT-Kanpur) and the four Regional Colleges of Education at Ajmer, Bhopal, Mysore, and Bhubaneshwar were my other major projects. Despite some rocky times, ITT-Kanpur has become an internationally recognized university and the birthplace of many high-tech companies—the most notable being Infosys which became the face of global data sourcing.

During my trips to the Regional College of Education in Bhubaneshwar, I would take a side trip to Calcutta (Kolkata) to play a round or two of golf at the Royal Calcutta Golf Club, the oldest golf club outside the British Isles, and where excellent courses with their attendant club houses were laid out. Polo was an Indian game, hunting and fishing were universal past times, but golf was peculiarly and passionately British. As time passed, however, more and more Indians began to cotton to the game, and after the Great War there were a great many titled and bemedaled members of the Indian armed forces who had earned their admission to the golf sanctuaries.

So when in the 1920s the British decided to move their capital from Calcutta to Delhi, one of the first orders of business was the laying out of the Delhi Golf Club, which the Hindus carved out of a vast Muslim cemetery with many of the tees, as they are to this day, sited on desecrated Muslim tombs. Many wells in the area provided an adequate water supply, and probably no golf courses in the world are so labor intensive, with hundreds and hundreds of peons, both men and women, available to tend meticulously to the fairways and greens. The cemetery was situated in the middle of a jungle, so that the rough through which the fairways wind is a place of utter despair, with thorny bushes and an impenetrable undergrowth from which one expects Rickey-Tickey-Tarvi to emerge any minute with a cobra locked in his jaws. And wildlife is a colorful if often aggravating part of the scene, what with peacocks crying out to each other as they preen their gorgeous plumage, monkeys quarreling in the trees waiting for the errant ball to come to a halt so they can pounce, and the ubiquitous Indian crow regularly dive-bombing the monkeys to make off with the ball themselves.

So it is that an essential part of the golfer's entourage is the aggi-wallah, or fore caddy, who stations himself far ahead of the striker of the ball to chase the plagued thing into the rough or to guard it from the predators. These aggi-wallahs are for the most part bare-footed, with skin as tough as a boot, and they learn early on how to nudge a ball in the rough or lift it between their toes so that when the golfer arrives, if there is any area where the ball can be struck, that is where it will be. In crucial matches or high-stakes games, the prudent golfer will engage aggi-wallahs to watch aggi-wallahs and discourage any such shenanigans. That is how I met Tej Pal.

If ever there was a ragamuffin it was Tej Pal. I had gone with Williams and Phil Haney for my introduction to golf in India, and when I first set foot on the sacred soil of the Delhi Golf Club I thought I was in bedlam. As one entered the gate, the club house was to the left and the car park to the right, where milling around were dozens of Indians in non-descript clothes and of varying ages waiting for their sahibs or for a new face which they would surround while seeking his favor. Clanton and Phil already had regular caddies and aggi-wallahs, and they had selected one for me, Karan Singh—not to be confused with the Maharajah of Kashmir—a fairly well dressed slender young man in his mid-twenties who allegedly could hit the ball pretty well himself. We shook hands and he took my clubs and was looking around for our aggi-wallah when we heard this commotion at the other end of the car park around which a crowd was gathering. A skinny bare-footed little kid about 12 years old who looked like he had never faced a square meal was just getting the tar beaten out of him by someone twice his size, although he was giving almost as much as he was getting. Karan Singh stepped in between them and dragged the youngster away still screaming imprecations.

Karan Singh shook him and told him to shut up and marched him up to me.

"Sahib, this is Tej Pal, our aggi-wallah if you want him. He's the meanest little devil out here, but he will take good care of our golf balls."

Thus began a thirty year odyssey in which I played the Delhi Gold Club hundreds of times, but never without Tej Pal in attendance as aggie-wallah, caddy, partner, or coach. He was mean as a snake, fierce in defense of sahib's ball wherever it might be lying. Others gave him a wide berth, especially as he began to grow and gain strength. When I left India the first time, he was 16 and already graduated to the caddie ranks. He was a bright kid, literate in Hindi and his conversational English was not bad, and he developed a beautiful golf swing. He took my middle daughter in tow and had her moving the ball very well indeed. He became a clerk for the Army and worked at a base adjacent to their golf course, and in his off time he became a teaching pro there. I always left a set of clubs for him in my absence and plenty of balls and shoes which I could bring in the diplomatic pouch.

At the end of my first tour in 1969, the Delhi Golf Club did me the high honor of a life membership, so I have never paid a green fee from that day to this. In those interim periods when I was getting back one or two times a year, my first message was to Tej Pal, who would appear as if by magic and whose first words in variably were, "How is Missy?" I cannot keep up with golf's technology, but every five years I see that he has a new set of clubs. At one stage he tried to make a go of it as a full time pro, attempting the small Indian professional circuit, but his putter failed him and he picked only chicken feed, hardly enough to support his wife and two children. So back to his clerical post with the Army and the role of a part-time teaching pro.

When I returned as ambassador, he loved it when my security men walked the fairways with us with their sub-machine guns at the ready; he claimed it made him feel like he was somebody. A laboriously written note from him at Christmas suggested some medical problem, so I don't know what his present situation is. What I do know is that I will never have a more faithful companion.

There was another aspect about golf in India that was fun, useful and important to me. Never before or ever again has golf been such a bargain as it was in the late 1960s. We could buy all our gear wholesale from outfitters in Hong Kong and bring it in via the diplomatic pouch. The monthly dues at the club, the green and caddy fees were miniscule, and the venerable pro, Shadi Lal, gave his limp-wristed lessons for a song. There was never a better time to take up and/or improve your game, and we Embassy wallahs played every chance we could get, or invent. The military attaches were usually quite adept at the game, since they had very little else to occupy their times, and even some of the spooks when they chose to walk in the sunshine were quite good at it. But one of the most avid, and certainly the most accomplished golfer in the Embassy was the Ambassador, former captain of the Yale golf team and Connecticut amateur champion. He utilized the game in two ways: First, as a pleasant, sociable way to gather information on Saturday, and second, to relax on Sunday.

It was a beautiful Saturday morning when we stepped onto the first tee at 9 a.m. only to see three Japanese foursomes, each with two women, between us and the first green. The problems of playing behind the Japanese were many and taxing: added to the fact that 80% of them were just plain hackers, they all had watched golf on television and were thus familiar with rituals of lining up a putt which they had to emulate, plus the fact that they would not concede a putt even though the winner of the hole had already been determined. And anyway, I had lost no love for them since the war. So I was striding back and forth with great disdain, and what I really wanted to do was shout at the top of my voice, "Remember Pearl Harbor!" and I just might have until I heard this quiet voice behind me say softly, "Jack." Fortunately the Golf Club possessed one golf cart and the Club Captain happened to be sitting in it watching all of this. I asked him if he would drive down and ask the Japs if we could play through. He did, and they waved us through and my incipient career was saved.

These Saturday sessions were generally fruitful, with many topics being discussed with different interpretations from different perspectives, sometimes quite lively and for me, always interesting. But however things were going, before the round was over, Mr. Bowles would steer the conversation around to Viet Nam, our policies and performance. As Ambassador, he was the official spokesman in India for U.S. policy, and it was his bounden duty, regardless of his own opinions, to explain and defend it to anyone who would listen. Sometimes his Saturday homilies were politely received with a "Thank you sir, I hadn't thought of that," but more often with questions and answers, the net result being that both the other Ambassador and the Indian knew exactly what our position was, and he in turn learned that that position was seldom heartily embraced by others. It was a very shrewd use of a day on the links, and a lesson that was to stand me in good stead later on.

Sundays were pure joy, no shop talk allowed, and it was wonderful to see how much Bowles still enjoyed the execution of a decent shot. By the time I got back, a certain skill at golf was almost *de rigueur* for the ambassadorial posting, and the competition between us was really quite keen, with trophies and silver plate and the lot.

Another diversion in which our Indian milieu provided us with spectacular opportunities was hunting, with birds of infinite variety and many species of horned ruminant. And for the really adventurous, there was the fabled Bengal tiger. Here again our military wallahs were usually in the van, although my experience in the Louisiana marshes put me right up there with the leaders. We in the Diplomatic Corps had a tremendous advantage over our Indian hosts because, apart from the maharajah class, the average Indian had neither the weapons nor the ammunition to allow him to take advantage of the bounties which his native heaths provided, whereas we could bring in by pouch everything we needed in ample quantities. The Indian peasant therefore usually welcomed us as we flushed the pheasant in his fields or built our blinds in his nullahs for the ducks and geese or stalked the neoguile and sambas in his hills because we would always down more game than we could possibly use and so leave behind generous amounts for his own consumption. So we had freezers full of venison and ducks and geese and chukar and partridge and pheasant, and wild turkey. And occasionally, in great secrecy, a fat peacock hen, for we had been tipped off surreptitiously by the Indian cognoscenti that the most toothsome bird in the land was the peacock, although it was a protected species under every game law extant. So it was that in November, some of our nimrods feigned color blindness as they slipped home with the Thanksgiving "goose."

To be in India and not hunt the tiger seemed to be a crime against nature, and I along with three members of an Internal Revenue Service team here on special duty to teach their Indian counterparts how to improve their tax gathering techniques, took off on safari to tiger country to the northeast along the Bengal border. We had engaged a Dak bungalow deep in the forest and an ancient, toothless guide who the ranger swore knew his business. It was story book! First we found the tiger's spoor, a distinct imprint of his paw along a game trail. Next we tied down a young bullock on the spot. Next, we built our machan (shooting platform) in the trees above the bait. That night, manning the machan in pairs, one with the .375 rifle, the other with a powerful single beam spot light, we began our vigil.

The first night resulted in nothing but cramps from the close confinement. But the second night about midnight the jungle came alive; the barking of the chital joined the twitter of the night birds. The tiger was on the prowl, and one could trace his movements as the jungle chorus swung from left to right. He found the bait, slashed its throat, and disappeared, just as the guide had said. The next night he would return, and our opportunity would come as he devoured his prey.

I lost the lottery, and my luckless companion and I were high in the trees above another clearing close by, cursing our fate while our other two friends took up their positions in the machan at sunset. And again around midnight the jungle chorus began, and the arc of sound came closer and closer. Then we could hear the crunching of bones in the tiger's jaws. The spotlight froze the tiger as he looked up from his grisly repast, and the rifle roared at almost point blank range. We had missed, and the beautiful creature had disappeared. But we could tell our grandchildren in all truth that we had tracked the tiger down in his native haunts and had come that close! Besides, how would we have divided the trophy?

And it was my addiction to hunting that led me to my second maharajah. This was Rao Raja Colonel Bahadur Sing, the Maharajah of Bundi, who presided over the principality of Bundi, a once powerful native state and fertile region in the Rajasthan desert. In the hierarchy of native princes with the Nizam of Hyderabad being accorded 24, Bundi rated an 18 gun salute. Not nearly as affluent as some of his royal colleagues, he nonetheless lived comfortably on the privy purse, an annual payment for life which Nehru had promised those princes who brought their territorial holding peaceably into the nascent Indian state. Augmenting this was the rental from his landed peasantry and investments in cement plants and other attempts at industrial modernization. The huge ancestral palace dominating the hillside overlooking the town of Bundi itself was half in ruins and uninhabitable, and certainly beyond his resources to renovate, but he lived with considerable panache in a spacious hunting lodge built by his father, long deceased, in a luxuriant sylvan glade beside one of the few spring fed lakes in the region. It was a veritable oasis, surrounded by rich irrigated farm land interspersed with patches of light jungle which teemed with game birds.

Phool Sagar Palace in Bundi, India

Phool Sagar Palace was a long, rambling affair, two and sometimes three stories in height, built in an elongated U shape, with one side housing the public reception salons, the game and trophy rooms, with heads and stuffed animals of every description and a profusion of tiger skins, and the dining and kitchen facilities. Along the back side were the family apartments, occupied primarily by the maharani, Bundi's estranged wife and her entourage, rarely if ever seen since she lived in purdah, and rumored to have been beautiful once but now obese. There were two dissolute children, a boy and a girl in their twenties, who seldom frequented the premises, preferring the jet set which still doted on royalty, no matter how jaded. On the other side two stories of guest suites opened out on lengthy galleries overlooking the inner courtyard. Each suite was decorated with portraits of men in uniform and pictures of battle scenes, ancient and contemporary, and each suite bore the name of a British general. Along the verandas, glass display cases contained an amazing collection of silver mugs and goblets given to Bundi by comrades in arms of every rank.

Phool Sagar Palace in its contemporary habiliments was the embodiment of the two things that made Bundi one of the most distinctive Indians of his generation. In the first place, he was the most decorated soldier in the Indian army that served with and under the British in World War II. Operating in the Southeast Asian Theatre of Operations under the general command of Lord Louis Mountbatten, Bundi led a tank brigade that was instrumental in stopping the Japanese advance at the Indo-Burmese border and subsequently forcing the beginning of the long Japanese retreat from the territory they had overrun since their invasion of Manchuria in 1936. Among the honors bestowed on Bundi was a short stint as aide-de-camp to King George VI before insisting that he be restored to combat duty.

The second distinction was that Bundi was the most redoubtable hunter of the tiger in this history of that activity. He was fearless, persistent, and a legendary marksman. He held every record in terms of numbers and heft extant. He was the subject of many film documentaries on the sport in India, the most notable probably being a series done with Peter Gunn and hosted by Curt Gowdy. Tiring of the lack of challenge in the one-sided encounters, he hung up his rifle soon after the war, and on the infrequent occasions when he was inveigled to resume the hunt, he was armed only with a bow and arrow.

We met Bundi at an Embassy function accompanied by one of Delhi's most attractive courtesans. He was small in stature, lithe, wiry, reminding me of a coiled spring. He took one look at Lucy and liked what he saw, and sometime later when we invited him and his friend to dinner at our humble establishment, he accepted with alacrity. That night I learned something else about him—he loved Scotch whisky but couldn't hold it very well. The evening ended in a shambles, with Bundi, deep in his cups, trying to force a diamond-studded cigarette case down Lucy's bosom, and it took his friend's and my combined efforts to rescue my child bride. Sometime later after sober reflection, he ran up a white flag by inviting us to Phool Sagar for a hunting weekend. I was enchanted, Lucy, less so, and only because two other Embassy couples were going would she accept.

To get to Phool Sagar, one boarded the Madrasi Express at a suburban station in New Delhi and disembarked three hours later at the town of Kota, some twenty miles from the lodge. We rode in a quite comfortable and private first class compartment, hermetically sealed from the bedlam that makes up most of the train, inside and on top. We were met by an ancient but serviceable Rolls Royce and a driver clad in what looked like once decent livery. As we entered the inner courtyard at Phool Sagar, Bundi's private army, consisting of ten retired veterans in rag tag uniforms tried to present arms without much success, but Bundi was on the carriage path to greet us. Our suite was named after

General Birdwood of World War I fame, and from then on it was held in readiness for us.

Bundi's day began at 11 a.m. when a bearer would come down the veranda with a pitcher of cold beer and begin filling however many silver goblets were required. The British call this little ritual "elevenses" after their pubs opening hours, and Bundi fancied himself British to the core. After lunch the men went off to hunt, while for the ladies there were pleasant walks and shikaras for lazing about on the lake. Lucy liked to take her camera and go with Bundi's secretary and record the fading glories of the palace.

Bundi's hunting vehicle was another Rolls cut down to fit a jeep-type chassis with oversize tires that made going cross country fairly easy. We kept one rifle and one shot gun each within easy reach in a gun rack attached to the dash. Birds abounded, but Bundi seldom if ever touched his guns, leaving the shooting up to me and any other guests that might be along. But I shall never forget one feat. Just the two of us were out cruising slowly cross country and really on the lookout for rabbits which were numerous in the area and a blight on the crops of his tenants. I had dropped my cap in the back of the vehicle, and when I turned to retrieve it, I saw this pheasant about 50 yards in the air bearing down on us and about to pass right over our heads. I yelled to Bundi, "Bandit at high noon." He never turned his head but instead stopped the car, reached for his shotgun, threw the barrel straight up and snapped off one shot. The pheasant dropped about twenty yards ahead of us. It was the quickest move and best shot I have ever seen.

It was on these junkets around his property that I saw one aspect of Indian life that normally I should have missed. Whenever Bundi saw peasants in the field he would stop the jeep and they would come up, prostrate themselves before him and then rise and come up to touch one hem in the garment he was wearing. Bundi would in turn chat with them, tell jokes, apparently, from the laughter, inquire about their families, and give each of them a little pat as they bowed their heads on leaving his presence. India was a democratic republic and had a written constitution to proclaim it, but on this parcel of land Bundi was still their lord and master, their maharajah.

Invitations were fairly frequent since I was an unfailing source of ammunition for his shooting parties and Scotch whiskey, none of which pleased Lucy in the slightest. But all was forgiven when we received a cryptic invitation telling us to bring formal attire and come down on Thursday for a long weekend with someone who he is sure we'll enjoy. Our Army, Naval and Air Attaches were also invited. It was on a Friday morning and "elevenses" were just getting under way on the veranda when we saw a long open touring car approach, and we could make out a driver and a man and a woman occupying the rear seat. As they drew nearer, the guards really snapped to, and when the car came to a halt, here was Bundi, dressed to the nines in his bemedaled regimental uniform, to open the door. Out stepped Lord Mountbatten and his daughter Pamela.

It seems that Granada Studios was filming a documentary of Mountbatten's career, and they were at the point in World War II when he commanded the Southeast Asian theatre. They wanted to interview Bundi on Mountbatten's qualities as a leader, and they wanted to interview Mountbatten on Bundi's qualities as a soldier, plus the two of them reminiscing about turning the tide for the Japanese. All of this was to end by Saturday afternoon, and that night would be the grand fete in honor of this most distinguished visitor. I, of course, simply could not believe my good fortune, for I was going to be able to talk about the last days of the British raj with the man who was Britain's last Viceroy who turned the keys over to Messrs. Gandhi, Nehru and Co, and who watched the last British regiment strike the Union Jack as it marched through Victoria Gate in Bombay to the transports which would take them home.

The gala held *al fresco* was a huge success; every notable in the region was there, the women wearing every last bit of jewelry in their possession, and the men resplendent in their white dinner jackets with every medal they had been awarded. A regimental band in full dress had come from Kota to serenade the gathering, and all day long two wild boars were slowly turning on the spit. And what made the affair so memorable was the graciousness and affability of the noble Lord, who found something to say to every guest; he and Pamela perfectly complementing each other as an adoring father and daughter. One of my favorite photographs has me holding forth on some topic while he stands there looking as though he were genuinely interested.

During the course of the evening I questioned him as closely as I dared about his relationship with and opinion of Nehru in negotiating the final settlement when the burning question was whether India retained her boundaries as a secular state with religious freedom for all, the fervent desire of Gandhi and the All India Congress, or whether predominantly Muslim areas be granted their own nationhood, as demanded by Jinnah and the

Muslim League. We know that Jinnah at one stage was sorely tempted to relent and accept Gandhi and the Congress leadership's offer to let him and his colleagues form free India's first government, but in the end finally insisted on the emergence of Pakistan (Pure Land) as a separate and independent entity. One explanation for Jinnah's adamancy that is gaining currency today is that he knew, along with everyone in Delhi's power elite, that Nehru was sleeping with Lady Mountbatten, so if the relationship between Nehru's overwhelmingly Hindu Congress and the British was that intimate, then no agreement regarding Muslim freedoms in a unitary Indian state could be trusted. But not the slightest hint about any of this to me, his most critical remark about Nehru being that he was the most patrician professed democrat he had ever dealt with and that he would have been a perfect British viceroy. This is the same man who years later in his autobiography admitted the saddest truth I have ever read about a marriage, saying that he and his wife spent theirs mainly getting into and out of other people's beds.

Poor Bundi never really recovered when Mrs. Gandhi, without any warning, canceled the maharajahs' privy purse, saying that it made a mockery of democracy to pay, simply because of the accident of their birth, handsome sums to a handful of useless parasites when half the nation lived on the edge of starvation. In a paroxysm of protest, he is said to have burned all his Indian army uniforms, and sometime later, not to have survived a drinking binge in New York.

Another aspect of diplomatic life in India that made the service so pleasant was that it was our government's bounden duty to observe all religious holidays, Catholic, Protestant, Hebrew, Hindu, Muslim, Parsee, Jain, Buddhist, or what have you, as well as national days, and at times it seemed to mothers that the kids were more often under foot than at school and that father lived on the golf course. Then there was the government vacation system.

Because of the lack of certain amenities and its geographic isolation, New Delhi in the State Department's lexicon was listed as a "hardship post," which meant that within every 12-month cycle, the employee was entitled to 30 days of R and R (Rest and Recuperation), with travel at government expense. For Delhi, the geographic limits within which the government would pay were Beirut to the west and Hong Kong to the east, two country fair destinations.

As a result of the Sykes-Picot agreement in 1916, Lebanon had been awarded to France as a Mandate of the League of Nations, and Beirut became known as the "Paris of the East." It was a lovely spot, with the Arab-French mixture reminding one of the creole culture in New Orleans, the chic boutiques, the elegant restaurants, the ultra-modern Phoenician Hotel and the more dignified St. George's and its beach on the Mediterranean shore. Adding to the luster of the trip to the west was that going and coming the airplane made a regular stop in Teheran and its $5 a kilo of the world's finest caviar at the airport.

Or if one wanted to go east, all one would find at the end of the line was Hong Kong, which the British had wrested from the Chinese in its disgraceful Opium War of 1838, and you could include Penang and Singapore in your airfare at no extra cost. Our introduction to the Peninsula Hotel, then and still the world's most nearly perfect hostelry, our first dance in Gaddi's, our first ride on the Star Ferry, lobster thermidor in the Mandarin Grill were experiences I have repeated dozens of times and never quite matched. The one note of dissonance was the fact that that gorgeous harbor was alive with the U.S. Navy's slate gray "men-o-war" en route to or returning from Viet Nam.

And there was more. At the end of a three-year tour abroad, "home leave" was mandatory, in which the State Department brought you and your family back to the United States for a thirty-day period for the purpose of re-charging one's emotional batteries and, more importantly, for refurbishing one's American perspective on what a well-ordered world ought to look like. To be understanding of and even sympathetic with a foreigner's point of view was one thing, but to "go native" and even join in an anti-American chorus was quite another. After all, our singular mission was the conduct of American foreign policy abroad, and "home leave" was designed to strengthen that perception. Even so, egregious misconceptions of a diplomat's basic loyalties were possible. In the whole history of American diplomacy, the United States never had a more consistent, able, and effective exponent of our foreign policy abroad than Chester Bowles, but his critics at State and on the Hill took perverse delight in their mawkish observation that sometimes it was difficult to tell whether Chester was our Ambassador to India or India's Ambassador to the U.S.

Editor's Additions

If Jack's last sentence leaves you wanting to "know the rest of the story", several correspondences between Ambassador Bowles and Washington explain Jack's ending comment as well as setting the stage for events in the future. Just twenty-five days after Lyndon B. Johnson became the President of the United States following the assassination of President John F. Kennedy, Chester Bowles wrote the following "Secret: Personal: Eyes Only" letter to President Johnson.

New Delhi, December 27, 1963.

Dear Mr. President:

I have not written to you directly about the situation confronting us here in South Asia, because I am keenly aware of the extraordinary burden so suddenly placed on your shoulders on November 22nd, and also because I feel that the cables sent from New Delhi give you a clear view of the existing situation as I see it.

Having worked for two years on the Washington end, however, I am also aware of the wide variety of problems that reach your desk, and since I understand that a decision in regard to my proposals will be made soon, I did want to fill in some background that the cables do not carry.

When John Foster Dulles decided in late 1953 to arm Pakistan as the "strongest available anti-Communist power in South Asia and the Persian Gulf area" I and many others who know the area well vigorously dissented for a variety of reasons—all of which, I believe, have been vindicated by events:

1. From the outset Pakistan would view the arrangement not as an alliance against the Communists, but as a source of United States assistance against India;

2. As fears of U.S.-strengthened Pak forces develop in India, the political strength of the anti-American, pro-Soviet, Krishna Menon group would be sharply increased to our grave disadvantage;

3. The likelihood of settling the Kashmir dispute (which was very nearly accomplished in February 1952) would be diminished to the disappearing point;

4. The Soviets, looking for an ultimate balancing factor to China in Asia, would be given a wide open opportunity for a close political, economic, and military relationship with both

Afghanistan and India with unpredictable but clearly unfavorable results to our interests.

Between 1954, when this pact was finally signed, and the election of our Democratic Administration in 1960, I wrote extensively and spoke in 43 states with this particular example of mistaken judgment by the Eisenhower Administration as a major theme. May I add in all fairness that the bold move by Herter and Dillon in 1958 to bolster India's economy in spite of Krishna Menon was a major factor in undoing some of the damage done by the Pak "alliance."

In October of 1962 we were suddenly confronted with the opportunity that many of us had been hoping for—an overt Chinese Communist action which would bring home to the Indian Government and people some primary facts of life of Asian politics, i.e., the inevitable political-economic rivalry of China and India and the danger an expansionist China holds for India not only along the 2,200-mile Himalayan frontier but also in Southeast Asia which flanks India's eastern approaches.

The Indians, who had refused substantial Soviet military aid in May 1950 and again in February 1957, were wholly unprepared for the Chinese attack and were, as you know, humiliatingly defeated. This situation forced the resignation of Krishna Menon, threw the Communist Party into disarray, knocked the Soviets off balance and (following our prompt assistance) established the United States as India's most reliable friend with an outpouring of public good will for our country which must be seen and felt to be believed.

If the Pakistanis had seized on this opportunity to establish a better relationship with India by a strong statement of support against China, or at least a beneficent neutrality, a wholly new atmosphere would have been created between Karachi and New Delhi in which some settlement of the Kashmir quarrel might have been achieved. But Pakistan chose to endorse China's border claim, assert that India had attacked China, and have Mao Tse-tung as a friend. Five weeks from now Chou En-lai will be welcomed in Karachi as a state guest.

I have many warm associations in Pakistan and indeed I have known on a personal basis every Pakistani Prime Minister and President since Liaquat Ali Khan. Moreover, I am fully sympathetic to the emotional strain which the Pakistanis are undergoing in regard to India's relatively orderly political development, the growth of her industries and her steady progress towards the status of a major power which inevitably downgrades Pakistan somewhat.

This, plus the fact that in their hearts the Pakistanis in spite of all this talk are good friends of America and the China gesture is more a gimmick than a commitment, leads me to feel that our aid to Pakistan should continue, and that we should seek in every reasonable way to quiet their fears—provided they are prepared at least to adopt a policy of neutrality in regard to the China-India conflict, and to work with us in establishing a better atmosphere on the subcontinent in which we can all deal more effectively with the basic problems of defense and development.

I think it is fair to add that under present circumstances the military aid we have given to Pakistan is wide open for attack by a Wayne Morse or some other critic of our foreign policy. Although the Mutual Security Act emphasizes that our military assistance is to be given for the purpose of combatting the Communists, the Pakistanis have made it clear that China is not a threat to her interests, and that their defenses are keyed solely towards India. The very nature of the highly sophisticated and mobile equipment which we have given Pakistan, equipment which is much better adapted to fighting Indians on the north Indian plains than to fighting the Chinese and Russians in the Himalayas and Hindu Kush, could be said by an unfriendly critic to bear this out. Pakistan can correct this situation only by assuming a new posture in regard to South Asian defense against China, and in the types of weapons which they seek from us.

One thing is certain. Contrary to the Pakistan view we do not have the power to decide whether or not India will build up her defenses. The only influence we can exert is over the sources of military equipment and to some degree the amounts obtained.

The Indians are thoroughly aroused against China and are deeply committed to the creation of an adequate defense force. They can accomplish this in cooperation with us (with an understanding as to ceilings, use of their own foreign exchange, modest purchases from the Soviets, and a greater willingness to work with us on the political containment of China in Asia)—or they can go down a different road with much greater purchases in the USSR, a bigger defense industry of their own and diversion of more of their own foreign exchange for defense purposes.

In South Asia at long last we have the opportunity some of us have been hoping for over the years, and which was the primary reason I returned to India, i.e., the building of a new relationship with India that will bring her growing industrial and military potential into focus against the Chinese Communists.

If I am to have even a reasonable chance for negotiating the basis for the new relationship I need a five-year military assistance commitment (properly hedged in regard to Congress), an adequate amount of annual assistance (no less than $75-$80 million including the British—a sum which is half that we give to Turkey or South Korea), and maximum flexibility in regard to items and timing.

Given these tools I will do my level best. Without them all we can expect is a continuing impasse, the gradual strengthening of the pro-Soviet Menon forces in India, and the loss of a major opportunity to further United States interests in Asia.

Believe me, I would not have written to you on this "eyes only" and personal basis if I did not feel that the situation and my long personal relationship to it warranted this direct approach. I feel the need for some contact with you, with whom I have never had an opportunity to discuss this situation or my relationship to it in any depth.

With my warmest regards and good wishes in all that you are striving to do,

Sincerely,

Chet Bowles

On January 21, 1964, President Johnson responded to Bowles' letter telling him to do the best he can "in ways which will minimize the risks to our relationship with Pakistan" (Johnson 1964). The President explained that the military aid requested by Bowles would not happen and that Bowles would "simply have to stretch the resources of diplomacy to restrain Indian appetites, while still getting the forward movement [sought]" (Johnson 1964). As it was, India was already the largest recipient of US foreign aid.

The USAID initiative of agriculture, family planning, and education of which Jack was a part, was in large part, the US's response to "stretch the resources of diplomacy". Militarily, the US continued to provide more military support to Pakistan than to India. As a result, throughout the 60's, 70's, and 80's India increased her reliance on the Soviet Union for military aid. The decisions made in Washington to provide military aid to India's enemies during these decades contributed significantly to the events that led to Jack's nomination as US Ambassador to India in 1988.

The following is part of a note penned to the Newcomb Class of 1966 upon his resignation as Dean of Sophie Newcomb.

> The essential fact is that the times are out of joint. The world as viewed from Newcomb Hall is quite different from the one I see from my window in Delhi. Here is a struggling democracy, in business for itself only since 1947—hence younger than most of you—embracing in a land area less than one-third the size of the U.S., one-seventh of the world's population, or some 500 million people. It is racked daily by every calamity that has ever befallen the human race; and this last year, compounded as it was by drought, war, and the sudden loss of a respected leader, has been a nightmare. Were this not enough, there is more. Confronting this mass of people is an even greater mass, richer by far in *lebensraum* and natural resources, and governed by quite different precepts. This is Red China, India's sworn enemy. Both are classed as underdeveloped nations, in Western parlance, but their approaches to the problems of development are diametrically opposed, India emphasizing the democratic process and China, rigid authoritarianism. Which nation will be more successful in bringing a fuller life to its people; which, indeed, will survive? It is this contest which all the rest of Asia intently watches, ready to take their cue from the winner. Africa watches. In fact, the whole world watches, and I would suggest that the future of everyone in this audience will be affected by the outcome.
>
> For obvious reasons, the U.S. has taken an overt stand in this affair. Our most pressing immediate concerns are to prevent famine, stem the population explosion, and stave off military exploitation. No one, of course, believes these things in themselves sufficient for the long-term solution. Rather it is accepted that the fundamental process of modernization is essentially a process of education. To be brief and blunt, this

is where I come in, for I have been asked to assume the direction of the U.S. Government's efforts to bring India's system of secondary and higher education abreast of the challenges it faces in the contemporary world. To this end, the Agency for International Development has been generous in its disposal of funds, and I was recently fortunate enough to enlist the support of the National Science Foundation as a full partner of AID in this endeavor. Last week we concluded a policy conference between an NSF team headed by President Johnson's science advisor and an equally distinguished panel of Indian scientists and educators. The session was opened on this note:

"There is no group of men meeting anywhere in the world whose concern at this hour has deeper significance than yours. And there is no hour more crucial in the history of mankind than the one in which you meet . . .

"India is a great and beautiful land, rich in promise. We know the problems you face in pursuing that promise. We also know the wisdom and energy which your most able Prime Minister, Madame Gandhi, and other leaders of your country are bringing to your great task. From our hearts we offer you encouragement; with our hands we offer you all the assistance that is ours to give."

The message was signed: Lyndon B. Johnson. In all humility I share the President's view; hence I had very little choice as to my personal decision.

John R. Hubbard

New Delhi
16 May 1966

As happens so often in life when one is able to venture further than ever imagined possible, Jack's experiences in India altered his idea of what the pinnacle of his career would be as evidenced in this letter dated November 29, 1967 which Jack wrote to his father.

Dear Dad,

Imagine my surprise the other night when I received a telephone from Denton. Bert said he had talked to you about Mathews' retirement from North Texas, and he was enquiring about my possible interest in the position. My answer was "Yes", I would consider the proposition; and I have since written him to that effect, but I also pointed out the difficulties involved.

My sentimental nature is of course attracted by the prospect of returning to the town of my youth and presiding over an institution which I once attended and in many ways emulating your career. On the other hand, I have had a plethora of college administration; Denton is still Denton; and North Texas is hardly my idea of academic heaven. At any rate, I would give it an honest look if anything concrete should develop. What I am not sure of is Bert's role in all of this; whatever happens, I certainly don't want to embarrass him.

Next week we shall be deluged with visitors. The NSF Board group arrives as the finale of my appearance before them in September. They will be here two weeks touring the country, and we have arranged an itinerary designed to show them the horrible conditions under which the educational process attempts to function. At the same time, Senator Allen Elleder of Louisiana makes his appearance. Ellender, a ranking member of the Senate Appropriations Committee and Chairman of the Agriculture Committee, is the *bête noir* of the State Department and the unrelenting foe of foreign aid. Consequently, the Mission is beside itself with nerves at the prospect of his visit, and this state of mind is best exemplified by the Ambassador's request that he be assigned to me. So he is going to stay with us, and Lucy, and the kids, and the dogs are supposed to shower him with love and kindness and feed him shrimp gumbo and red beans and rice and other Louisiana fare and hopefully he will leave convinced that there ought to be an American (or at least Louisiana) presence in India after all. Indeed, this assignment has gained for me considerable notoriety, for whatever that is worth. And, in truth, this is the kind of activity which makes Denton seem a little tame.

Lisa is coming out for Christmas; I didn't have a chance with my suggestion that she might well wait for summer. She has had a difficult academic adjustment to make at Baldwin and has done reasonable well. It is happily a demanding school, and if she survives, she should be well set for the future in that she will already have experienced that trauma usually first encountered by college freshmen.

Well, those Horned Toads have done it again; imagine their winding us as perhaps the most solid club in the league. And I must be getting old for I am kind of glad that A&M is going to the Cotton Bowl. The New Year's action here is going to center around the ability of Mrs. Gandhi just to survive in a tough and bloody league. I would not predict the score.

As ever,

/s/Jack

In an interview, Jack summed up his educational philosophy by saying that in the fear of false knowledge lay the beginning of wisdom. "We can think there is such a thing as Truth without thinking that we have it or are very near to finding it. What the teacher must bring to his craft, then, are the tools of reason and the passion for the search. It is the search that is exciting, and for an educated man, it never ends" (Kapuria 1968). Later in the same interview, Jack was asked what he thought about student unrest that was going on internationally, particularly in the US. Jack's response surprised his interviewers when he said, "It is a healthy sign of students taking their education seriously when they see themselves involved in current events. However, I deplore, most strongly, the nihilism that characterizes so many of these cases. They consider only the major attack; they rebel against the status quo without having any constructive ideas for an alternative"(Kapuria 1968).

Little did Jack know that a little over a year later he would be staring student protestors in the face as a university provost in California.

CHAPTER 21

Expanding the Liberal Arts at the University of Southern California

In my office in the West Building at the U.S. Embassy in New Delhi, India, on an April morning in 1969, the mail wallah brought a letter from one Dr. Paul B. Hadley, Special Assistant to the President of the University of Southern California (USC), informing me that USC was in the midst of a search for a Provost and Vice President for Academic Affairs (the #2 administrative position in the university). He said that he understood that I came back to Washington several times a year for consultations, and he asked me if the next time I came if I could spend a few days at USC.

Now the fact of the matter was that we were going to close down our major AID programs in agriculture, family planning, and education in July, to coincide with the departure of our Ambassador, Chester Bowles, who had been a prime mover in all these activities, and who had been largely responsible for the Government of India's willingness to cooperate with us so fully. The academicians among us, such as John Lewis, the Director of the AID Mission, and I had been recruited specifically for this Indian venture and were on leave from our respective institutions. Lewis, for example, a brilliant economist who had been on JFK's Board of Economic Advisors and had left the chairmanship of his department at Indiana University, was now being wooed by other universities such as Berkeley and Princeton upon the completion of this assignment. I had resigned from the deanship of Sophie Newcomb College, the woman's coordinate division of Tulane University and had taken leave of its History Department. Neither of us had had the slightest association with USC.

Under the circumstances, and given the hot pursuit of Lewis, I replied to Dr. Hadley that I appreciated his invitation, but I felt he probably had John Lewis in mind rather than John Hubbard. He, in turn, kindly replied that he knew which "John," and we made arrangements to meet after my next Washington consultation in May, though I said that he ought to know that the entire Hubbard clan enjoyed living in New Orleans and that I was looking forward to leaving academic administration (I had been Dean of Newcomb for 12 years) and regaining some intellectual respectability.

The visit went very well, indeed. Here was an urban university which had long been the intellectual center of a vibrant urban community, an institution best known for its excellent graduate and professional schools which surrounded a modest liberal arts college. Since my whole academic experience had been grounded in the liberal arts, I was impressed by the fact that a most attractive young physicist, John Marburger, and the very distinguished Dean of the Engineering School, a brilliant product of Berkeley named Zhorab Kaprelian, emphatically stated that they expected the new provost to concentrate strengthening the undergraduate offerings of the College by a serious upgrading of the liberal arts faculty; then only could we claim distinction as a distinguished university. Right then and there it seemed to me that if one of the leading scientists and the leading engineer felt that strongly about the role of the liberal arts, we had a legitimate shot at achieving distinction. The details of the appointment were pending a future visit to meet members of the Board of Trustees and a broader segment of the faculty and administration. So I returned to India with completely new prospects for my academic future. My family greeted the news with mixed emotions which I shared. Tulane and New Orleans had been good to us, and we would leave a host of friends. But four year's absence had loosened those bonds somewhat; and I reminded everyone that we had come to India with great ignorance and fear and trepidation only to find one of the most exciting chapters of our lives, and so God willing, California and Los Angeles and USC would do the same. The die was firmly cast when we arrived in Los Angeles in November 1969.

USC was founded in 1880 under the auspices of the Methodist church in a mustard patch south of the bustling town of Los Angeles. It is said that 1000 Angelinos were present at the ground breaking, remarkable in that they represented one-tenth of the population of the town. But as Los Angeles expanded exponentially to become the leading metropolis of Southern California, so did USC, which as the only bona fide university in the region responded to the ever increasing demands for trained manpower. Thus there was the creation of a host of professional schools: Medicine, Pharmacy, Engineering, Law, Public Administration, Dentistry, Education, Business, while the College of Arts and Science felt no such urgent demand for its product. Thus it was that at the central core of supplying the demands of a burgeoning community for goods and services was a critical mass of USC graduates. And thus was born the legend of the Trojan Family, which was indeed a reality buttressed by the fact that 85% of USC graduates to this day live within a fifty mile radius of the USC campus.

When inevitably the growing city enveloped the original campus there was a feeling among some that USC should move to more pristine surroundings so that she could pursue her intellectual goals without being submerged in the din and bustle and troubles of a growing metropolis. But at a meeting of the Board of Trustees in 1925 to address such a proposition, President Bovard emphatically stated that USC had been born in an urban environment, and it was to that environment that she owed her allegiance and her dedication to the solving of the city's problems.

By the time of my arrival in 1969, USC was no longer almost the sole supplier of executive manpower for Southern California. Across town in the late 1930s, UCLA (the University of California at Los Angeles), which had long been a teachers college, began to emerge as a full-grown member of the University of California's system and one of Berkeley's fiercest competitors as an advanced degree-granting institution. Certainly the State of California as a whole benefitted from such a development, as it did with the spread of the Berkeley system to other parts of the state. But apart from those, the state now had a marvelous configuration in its higher education establishment. In northern California, San Francisco was bounded on the east by Berkeley, a public institution, and on the south by Stanford, a private institution, two of the finest universities in the world. In southern California, Los Angeles had within its city limits UCLA, a public institution, and USC, a private institution, two of the finest urban universities in the world. Los Angeles could also be blessed by the presence of the California Institute of Technology in Pasadena, one of the world's premier research institutions, and by the Claremont group of seven fine colleges thirty minutes to the east. And although many people feel that California's economic primacy is based on its salubrious climate, the truth is that it is soundly based on the superb quality of its higher education facilities.

The president of USC at this time was Norman Topping, M.D., a graduate of the University, a distinguished epidemiologist who had found the answer to Rocky Mountain fever, and the vice president for media affairs at the University of Pennsylvania before returning to his alma mater in 1958. He had come to revive an institution that had been dead in the water for the past ten years because of the absence of any executive leadership occasioned by the illnesses of its then president, Fred Fagg, and the ensuing clumsy management of the Trustee committee which had tried to right the boat. Dr. Topping had succeeded in spades, and USC had regained the affection of the community and its standing in academic circles. He had a dedicated group of academic administrators but none with the charisma or the vision and the drive to take the institution to the next level of excellence. Hence, the search which had brought me there.

USC President Topping, Jack, & Board of Trustees Chairman Dart; 1970

I knew, but Topping did not know that I knew, that I was not his first choice for the post. That gentleman was a Chaucer scholar and head of the English department at Penn by the name of Robert Lumiansky. Now it so happened that Bob had been Dean of Tulane's Graduate School while I was Dean of Newcomb, and that he was my best friend in academe. He went on to become chairman of the American Learned Society in New York and hence one of the country's most esteemed scholars and, parenthetically, the man who had put my name in the USC pot. Dr. Topping's disappointment at not landing Lumiansky was acute, but he acquiesced in my appointment simply because Bob's recommendation was so enthusiastic. The net result of all of this was that it did not take long for Topping and me to thoroughly dislike each other. (Years later after his retirement, Topping, in a diatribe in his unfortunate autobiography, admitted all of this unhappiness with me.)

Despite the potential for the dissonance of a clash of personalities, my enthusiasm for my new institution and my position in it was undiminished. In the first place the roles of the President of a private university and its principal academic officer, the Provost, are quite different. The President with his Board of Trustees is responsible for operational and financial policies of the institution; in this regard, the President's constant and abiding concern is with fund raising, and everything he does morning, noon and night has a fiscal connotation. On the other hand, the Provost's primary concern is the intellectual health of the institution—the caliber of its faculty, student body, course offerings, and the vital interrelationship between the faculty, the students, and the libraries and laboratories. Put otherwise, the President must deal with the institution's many publics; whereas, the Provost is the day-to-day manager of the intellectual agenda, which for my money was the most rewarding position for anyone concerned with university administration.

In one sense, I was very fortunate to find that the Provost's office was a bare-boned proposition consisting of a faculty liaison officer, a clerical assistant, and a secretary who had been generously provided as the junior member of the President's clerical staff. It was a clear challenge to make of the position what I would and could. Clearly my first duty was to get to know the place—its schools and their deans -- and an enormous break for me was the fact that the main librarian, who was from the old school that believed that the main function of a library was to preserve books rather than share them, was more than ready for retirement. Thus my first major appointment, to everyone's approbation, was his successor.

While at Tulane, one of my closest associates had been a brilliant young associate librarian, (and incidentally, my handball partner), who had left to become the principal librarian at Rutgers University. An additional bit of luck was that both he and his wife were native Californians. Thus Roy Kidman became the head of our Doheny Memorial Library, and my tenure as Provost could not have gotten off to a better start.

Another fortuitous event for me was the fact that the first faculty member to call on me in my office was Richard Dale, our distinguished professor of ancient history and the current Chair of the department, who welcomed me, with his colleagues' blessing, as a fully tenured member of the department to teach as much or as little as my other duties would permit. As the Dean of Newcomb College I was also a tenured professor in Tulane's history department and I had taught at least one class each semester as well as directing graduate students. So to have that same kind of departmental and professorial affiliation was not only a source of much comfort but also of much pleasure. Most importantly, there could never be in any disagreement the accusation of the Provost versus the Faculty; the only relationship I would acknowledge between the two was "we."

Another part of my institutional orientation was to become acquainted with our athletic director and the coaches of our perennially successful Pacific 8 Conference teams. I could appreciate USC's pride in her athletic history, and as often as I could I would visit the practices where another form of university teaching was being demonstrated.

Under Jesse Hill, our athletic director and a successful coach in his own right, a group of collegiate coaches had been assembled whose collective team performances are unequaled in collegiate athletics. There was John McKay in football, Rod Dedeaux in baseball, Vern Wolfe in track and field, Peter Daland in swimming, Stan Wood in golf, George Toley in tennis, and Bob Boyd in basketball. Not only did I enjoy the association with coaches and players (I had a locker in the football coaches' dressing room), but I was also aware that in the perception of the Trojan Family, it did not impair town and gown relations to let it be known that USC's new principal academic officer had a keen grasp of the importance of intercollegiate athletics.

Perhaps it had all been foreordained that my first glimpse of a USC student took place in 1932 when my father brought me to Los Angeles for the Olympics and in the exhibition football game between the Eastern and Western collegiate football stars, there was Gus Shaver. My second exposure had been in 1952 at the Olympic Games in Helsinki where one evening I happened to be in the same bistro where USC's athletic director, Bill Hunter, was holding court.

So all in all the first five months had gone reasonably well, though it was a steep learning curve for the university community and its new provost.

My next major assignment I did not look forward to. Now it was customary for the Board of Trustees to repair to a resort in the Palm Springs area at the academic Spring Break, at which the university administration would give an account of itself—a show and tell of where we had been, where we thought we were, and what we hoped to accomplish in the next academic year. This year quite understandably I was to be the star attraction—where I hoped to take our academic programs, my plans for sponsored research, admissions, and city, state, and federal relations. But just as importantly, it was an opportunity for the Board to get better acquainted with the Provost personally, for in the recruiting process, very few of the Board members had participated.

Now it is an accepted fact that the USC Board of Trustees was one of the most powerful, influential, dedicated, and able a group of men and women ever assembled to guide the destiny of an academic institution. In local, state and national affairs many were preeminent, and it was an easy board to recruit to because anyone of any substance wanted to be associated with such a distinguished assembly. In relation to the university's fiscal health, the Board had a simple approach—give, get, or get off. Its Chair at this time was Justin Dart, the crusty CEO of Dart Industries, and it included the likes of Leonard Firestone, Henry Salvatori, Willard Marshal, Robert Fluor, Herbert Hazletine, Anna Bing Arnold, Virginia Ramo, Blanch Seaver, Asa Call, Gordon Marshall, John McCain, Forest Shumway, Gordon Huff, Frank King, John Wilson, Kenneth Norris, Paul Trousdale, and other like-minded types who individually and collectively represented the economic and political power of Los Angeles and Southern California. There was not a board room in corporate American or a political office in Los Angeles, Sacramento and Washington D.C. that members of this Board did not have access to. Its persona was seen as assuring that USC would be a staid and steady institution not given to flights of intellectual whimsy or rabid liberal political postures. It was this posture that attracted USC's most generous financial supporter.

When in the early 1970s Walter Annenberg decided to liquidate his media empire in Pennsylvania and move his base of operations and principal residence to the West Coast, he looked around for some non-institution over which to raise the family escutcheon. He became convinced that the membership of the

USC Board pretty faithfully represented his own personal and societal values, and his financial largess over the years until his death in 2001 was over 150 million dollars.

Such was the Board before which I was to make my maiden policy address, and I was reasonably sure that few if any of its members were convinced or had ever thought about the proposition that a strong liberal arts undergraduate curriculum was the *sine qua non* of a distinguished academic institution. But in the event I had no option, so firm was my conviction; and so I belabored my audience with a paper entitled, "Why the Liberal Arts?"—and that it was my intention to strengthen the College of Letters, Arts and Sciences, and in the doing of it, I did not intend to neglect our graduate and professional schools. We simply must have a stronger fiscal base from which to operate. I was not lynched, and indeed there were some remarks about never having thought about it in quite this way. But my address was by no means the highlight of this Trustee Retreat.

> **Note to Reader:** This marks the end of Jack's memoirs. He died before completing them. Everything that follows is written by the editors based upon documented research, personal interviews with people who knew Jack, private notes and letters, and personal recollections of communications between Jack and his brother, George. We have attempted to maintain Jack's writing style and voice by providing background settings for the events and activities to be discussed.

Although Jack had advocated expanding the liberal arts at USC since his initial interviews with the university the year before, the Trustees held reservations about the concept. If the Trustees had any doubts about Jack's position on the importance of liberal arts in higher education prior to his appointment, they were reminded of it when Jack delivered his position paper to the USC faculty shortly after assuming his duties as vice president for academic affairs and provost of the University of Southern California. This speech set the tone for Jack's tenure at USC and became the source document for many of his media interviews, for he never waivered from his personal convictions espoused herein.

> Ladies and gentlemen and especially those of you new to the USC community:
> Logic would argue that I should be sitting with you facing this podium rather than addressing you from it, for I'm among

the newest of the new. And my problem of getting acquainted with USC--its traditions, purposes, practices, personnel--is compounded by the fact that I come here off of four years in India. So not only do I confront a new institution but also what is for me a new region, Southern California, and in a very real sense, a new country.

Most of you at first hand, and I only vicariously, have witnessed the profound alteration in the social, emotional, and political fabric of the United States wrought in these last four years, among which the processes of higher education have figured so prominently. Indeed, the cacophony on some campuses was so nerve-shattering that some of my colleagues in India wondered at my sanity in desiring to come back into the seeming maelstrom. The din was heard round the world, to be sure, and, in the end it affected everything I was trying to do as education adviser to the American mission and the government of India. There our priorities were agriculture, family planning, and education, and since I was in charge of the latter my principal concern was the life of the mind. Our disciplinary efforts were concentrated largely in science, engineering, and technology--also vital to economic development--but our basic thrust was simple and applicable across the academic grid: the inculcation of an approach to learning rooted in free inquiry. To be very brief, we found an educational system imposed by the British long ago--and long since abandoned by them--which featured a syllabus approved by authorities external to the teaching situation, and student performance measured by an external examination which placed the highest premium on memorization. The results of that exam marked the student for life and generally determined his future. I can best illustrate this by describing my astonishment at receiving a calling card which bore the inscription: D. S. Gujral: B. A. Honors (failed), which means that somewhere along the line he had at least been admitted to an honors course rather than an ordinary pass course, and even his advertised failure put him a leg up on most of his peers.

So our effort in education--and I relate it here since it reflects my own philosophy and approach to academic affairs--was to take dead aim on rote learning and the idea of the infinite rectitude of professional dicta and the printed word. Our arguments were plain: knowledge cannot come just in the amassing of facts by a retentive memory. In the contemporary world, the only thing that can help is an attitude of inquiry which is reluctant to accept any knowledge as final except tools of reason and the passion for the search. The task of the educator, then is to disclose the formal principles of theory and the interpretation of procedures. Put otherwise, we tried to substitute aids for obstacles, the questions for the answers, the methods of research for the absolute. In all of this we were accused of advocating skepticism, but such was not entirely the case. Skepticism is a stage in the process of unlearning hoary beliefs, not an end in the pursuit of knowledge. Unhappily, the process of education requires as much time for unlearning as it does to master objectivity. We argued that it was the certainty of beliefs which must be placed under attack, for the fear of false knowledge is the beginning of wisdom. We should not accept either rumor or dogma, but we cannot remain skeptics. For we can believe there is such a thing as Truth without thinking that we have it or even that we are very close to finding it. Finally, we pleaded strenuously for a substantial liberal arts component in every curriculum concerned with science, engineering and technology.

I shall not belabor you here with examples of how we tried to apply these principles. Suffice it to say that there were days when we seemed to be more believed than scorned, and a few institutions were beginning to overhaul their curricula based on these precepts. But then the time of troubles of academe got up a full head of steam. The most raucous voices came out of the West, and the things we were advocating were essentially Western. Berkeley was no longer thought of as just an aberration. The Sorbonne, Berlin, Rome, Madrid--somehow we had all been poisoned. The climax, of course, was the picture of the guns at Cornell. After that was splashed in the Indian press, I had plenty of time for golf. And even if my advice had continued to be sought, what was I to say? In my four years in India, the U.S. academic scene was in the throes of turmoil and transformation, and I have not participated one jot. To miss the action is anathema to any professional, and that is one reason I am back.

So I speak to you today from what I hope is at least the middle of my reentry period. Becoming acquainted with the generalities and particularities of this country, this region, and this institution will take time. I shall need all the tolerance you can spare me. You are, however, entitled to know some of the benchmarks from which I proceed in my quest for understanding of the contemporary scene.

One term that kept recurring in the disjointed reports we received in India about campus troubles was "the establishment," which seemed to mean university administrators and trustees. The narrowness of that definition troubled me. I was born and reared on a college campus, and, except for the war years, I had in one way or another been associated with higher education ever since. And the only establishment, if that is the term we must use, I ever recognized or understood was the student body, the library, and the faculty, and the only reason for being of any educational institution was the constructed interchange between those three elements. In my view all the rest of the institutional panoply is infrastructure, absolutely essential to the operation, to be sure, but basically supportive in its function. Now having said that--and meaning it--I should add that I cannot abide the kind of campus politics that breeds division and polarity, that categorizes people as "you" and "us." We all perform different functions, but everything we do individually and collectively bears the stamp "USC."

You may have already gathered that I am devoted to the liberal arts and the humanizing role they ought to play in the development of an individual's personal philosophy. A friend of mine at Harvard contends that in that bright student body at least half are only half civilized, and he propounds this law: in proportion as young people grow brighter and better educated they become less civilized; in proportion as they become more widely and deeply informed about current events they become ignorant in the humanities, and that ignorance barbarizes them. Be that as it may, I believe that the liberal arts as intellectual disciplines are as important to our survival as human beings as is quantum mechanics.

It naturally follows then that I believe we can never be a really distinguished university without a really distinguished LAS college and graduate school to go along with the fine professional schools with which we are blessed. And how does a college claim that mantle of greatness? Ned learned it in the first reader. Only with a distinguished faculty that teaches the school superlatively well, whose concern for students is manifestly genuine, and whose research and writing can pass muster with any authority anywhere. To assemble such a group is a painstaking process but the *sine quo non* is and always will be the maintenance of high standards of performance. We must recruit to those standards, promote to those standards, grant tenure to those standards, and reward to those standards. Lowering them to accommodate individuals means simply that we have lost the struggle for greatness right then and there. We can be above average, even good, but we shall never be great if we do it. At LAS we happily have a vigorous new dean in Bob Linnell, and his coming has freed Chuck Mayo for full attention to the graduate school. Milton Kloetzel and I have assured these worthies of every support we can muster in establishing those conditions wherein great teaching and research can flourish, and among those conditions is the weeding out of those among us, if they exist, who are more concerned with rewards than performance.

And speaking of Dr. Kloetzel, he and I have been discussing with the Council of Deans the division of our labors, and while we are all aware of the pitfalls inherent in this situation, he and I are going to attempt, at the outset at least, a horizontal division of his concentration on research and graduate affairs and my primary attention on undergraduate matters. You and your deans will, of course, constitute a continuing board of review as to how well this essentially pragmatic, evolutionary approach to the matter works out.

Another area of intense concern to me, as my recent experience would suggest, is international education and the role this university can play in developing a world perspective in our students. I agree with A. L. Burt's dictum that no man can understand the world until he goes out in it, nor his own country until he gets outside of it. I would hope that we can launch more programs at both the undergraduate and graduate levels that will give an ever increasing number of our students experience in depth in other climes and cultures.

Now I realize that practically everything I have said up to this point can be classified under the head of pious platitudes. That charge I can readily accept. But if you and I are to work together effectively, I can only ask you not to underestimate my conviction in them as first principles.

In closing let me make just a few comments on how I see this university in this place at this time. The progress made at USC during the last decade under President Topping's leadership is in many respects absolutely phenomenal, and it is one of the most helpful auguries in the confused American academic scene today. As you well know, anyone who is fairly literate and has managed to stay out of jail and is foolish enough to want to attempt university administration has a variety of job choices, but there is no institution in this country with which I am acquainted whose portents for the future are brighter. Your presence indicates that you share this view. We sit in the region of Southern California so incredibly rich in all those elements that nurture a university's roots: intellectual vitality, ferment, curiosity, human and natural resources, raw wealth. We have a student body with wits and which is concerned. We have a Board of Trustees whose commitment to its responsibility and efforts to provide us with the wherewithal are unsurpassed anywhere. We have alumni whose devotion to this school is a revelation to me. President Topping and his planning staff have done a remarkable job in interpreting USC's aims to this community and in establishing that rapport which has resulted in an unprecedented fund raising effort. The physical campus has been literally transformed in the last few years, and the pace continues. You have just heard Dr. Kloetzel's recital of impressive accomplishments on other fronts. In sum, if institutional distinction cannot be achieved in this milieu, we ought to turn in our suits.

But as exhilarating as these prospects are, a few words of caution may be in order. No university can ever have enough money, so we shall always have to live with limited resources. That means the setting of priorities and getting the most out of our educational dollar, which I don't believe we're doing now because of the bewildering variety of ad hoc arrangements and activities which are unevenly applied and haphazardly pursued and which bleed off precious resources from our central concerns, such as the library, for instance. And as I look at all the new structures around us, I am reminded of the story, apocryphal perhaps, of the dedication of the Sterling Library at Yale. The guest speaker was eloquent in praising the architectural ingenuity, the weight of stone, the gargoyles, and the impressive Gothic façade, and finally the librarian could stand it no longer. He stepped to the rostrum and exclaimed, "But, sir, the library is inside!"

And who is inside USC? We are, and we are inside at a time in American educational history resplendent with conflict, confusion, confrontation, compromise, soul-searching, action, reaction, and sometimes just plain abysmal retreat. My exhortation to you in the midst of all of this sound and fury is to stand steady, to merit from those who are watching us and testing us the accolade so often heaped on USC's athletic teams: poise and pride. If this institution as a whole or if any of essential elements within it start to run scared, we may never recover. If we try to reset our sails at the buffeting of every noisy gust that sweeps across this campus; if in response to challenges all we can muster is panicking rededication to what we should have been doing all along rather than leadership; if we dilute the academic bill of fare and our standards in a puny plea for peace, then we shall abundantly deserve our demise. A great university, which is perhaps the most delicate and complex mechanism ever devised by man, is not built by political combustion but by the love we have of learning. And that love has thus far been able to transcend all the vicissitudes that American educational establishments have been heir to. Just in my lifetime I can remember the depression, the savage disruptions of war, the putrid anti-intellectualism of the Joe McCarthy era, the post-Sputnik jitters. Yet here today stands USC in fresh array and at the dawn of what should be its greatest achievements. And after this present turbulence we shall, if we are professionals, still be doing business: still worrying about false knowledge; still consumed by the passion for the search; still fiercely upholding academic freedom; still reposing our ultimate hopes in the dignity of the individual.

If we do not defend USC as a citadel of these values, who will?

If not now, when?

In his presentation to the Trustees a few months later, Jack stayed true to his passion and personal philosophy as he argued for the expansion of Liberal Arts, reemphasizing that a good liberal arts education was the pre-requisite for a world class research institution. Jack's message had a persuasive effect on a largely conservative group that had generally considered that the liberal arts faculty and students were the source of most of the university's problems (Trombley 1970). Many of the Trustees admitted that they had never considered things in that light.

John R. "Jack" Hubbard,
8th president of the University of Southern California

Although Jack made an auspicious beginning at that meeting, his presentation was by no means the highlight of the Retreat. In a manner befitting very conservative trustees of a private university, it was determined that Topping would formally announce his resignation immediately following the retreat (on Monday, April 27th), citing reasons of his own choosing—though everyone agreed that "health reasons" would be accepted without question by students, faculty, and the media. It was *fait accompli* that Jack would replace Topping as president with the charge to strengthen the university's undergraduate offerings while moving USC toward becoming an internationally recognized research institution.

'The Car Goes With the Job!'

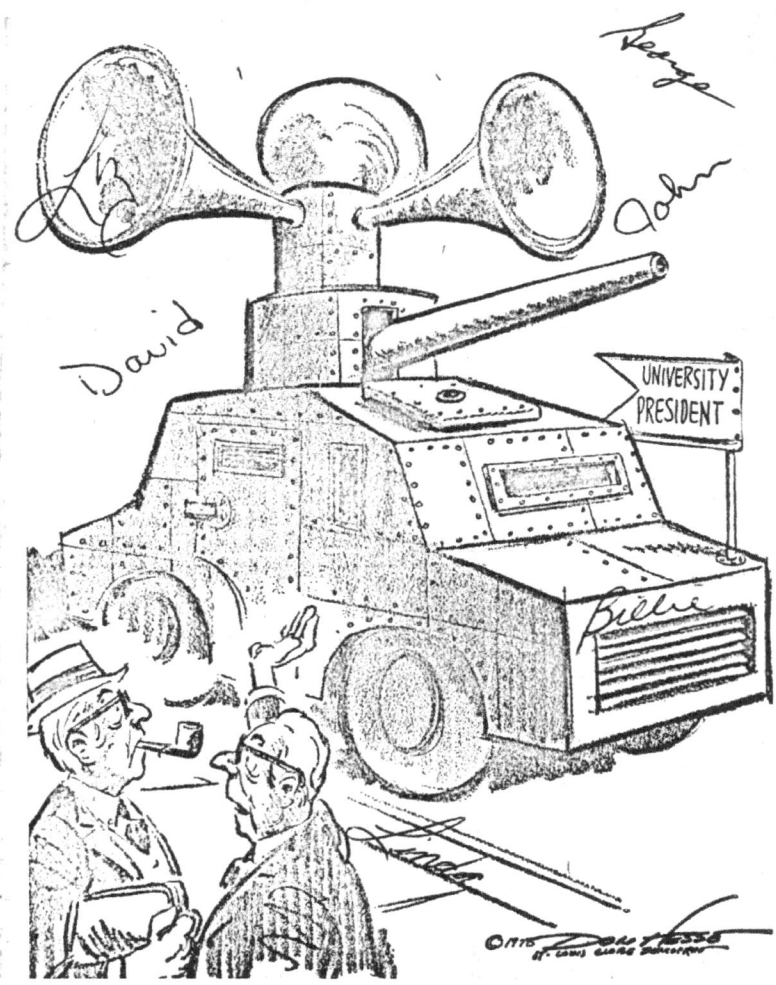

Congratulatory message sent to Jack from his brother's (George) family; 1970

In August 1970, following an "official search" by a committee comprised of students, faculty, deans, trustee, and alumni, Jack was unanimously recommended for the office of president. Jack was generally considered an academic progressive who encouraged innovation and was willing to consider—and make—

academic changes and who had a genuine feeling for the problems of youth. Jack told reporters that he was under no illusion that he was signing on for a prestigious joy ride. He said, "The nation's educators face a hard task in restoring the public's faith in the educational process, but it can be done. An instinctive love of learning will bring higher education through its current difficulties" (*Los Angeles Times* 1970).

Jack's advocacy of the liberal arts at USC stemmed from his deep seated conviction of the importance of the humanities in all phases of life. Throughout his life Jack not only preached the value of a liberal arts education, he embodied it beginning with his youthful exposure (recounted in an earlier chapter) to the great artists who performed in the auditorium of Texas State College for Women (now Texas Woman's University) where Jack grew up. When invited to be the main speaker at the convocation of a new president (Mary Evelyn Blagg-Huey) at Texas Woman's University in October 1978, Jack offered the following insights (*Pioneer* 1978):

> If the youth of today want to reinvent the wheel every day, then let them ignore the previous minutes of mankind. The humanities offer the opportunity to compress time, and—like it or not—we travel alone.
>
> It takes an incredible sensitivity found in the humanities to prepare students for the complexity and loneliness of today's world. If the youth of today can cope with the present and ponder the future, they will understand the past. We must have a well-defined sense of time and place. We must know our point of departure.
>
> It was in TWU's Main Auditorium that I gradually began to realize that the key to survival lies in an understanding of, and appreciation for, the arts and humanities.
>
> Fear of false knowledge is the beginning of wisdom. Substantial aids for obstacles and answers for questions are part of the professor's role, and unlearning is important as well as believing there is such a thing as truth without having it.
>
> If the technologists are to be simply obedient but devilishly clever devisors of whatever the state wants, it's pretty clear to me that the humanities and the social sciences are a waste of time. It is precisely in the acquaintance with, and understanding of, the intellectual heritage of the past as encompassed in the liberal arts that distinguishes between the free man with a free choice and the totalitarian automat.

The great human questions, all unresolved, are all matters of debate available in the record of mankind since the beginning of writing. To dwell with these minds ought to—and, I think, usually does—yield a more powerful personal philosophy than that found in the man who tries to run without them.

A harbinger of things to come was summed up in the congratulatory letter dated August 7, 1970, sent to Jack from Rufus C. Harris who had been President of Tulane University when Jack was Dean of Sophie Newcomb and as of the date of the letter was president of Mercer University in Macon, Georgia.

Dear Jack:

Henry Harold has kindly sent to me the article which appears in the Tuesday edition of the Los Angeles newspapers, announcing your appointment as President of the University of Southern California. Congratulations! And welcome to the fraternity! The photograph in the paper is excellent—I just hope you can manage to retain that happy countenance as you tread the battlefield which the college presidency has come to be! But it is a very satisfying existence, one which I would not exchange for any other.

I take great pride in your appointment, because as one who "knew you when," I am uniquely aware of the great capabilities of U.S.C.'s new President. The University is more than fortunate to have you at the helm, and I shall watch with much interest the progress which is sure to ensue during your administration. This latest phase in your distinguished career merely serves to confirm what I have known and said all along—you are one of the ablest college administrators in the country, and I am so pleased that this opportunity to utilize your abilities to the fullest has come your way.

With felicitations to you and Lucy, in which Louise joins warmly, I am

Yours very truly,

Rufus C. Harris

In the early 1970s, a "new depression" was identified in higher education induced by institutional excessive aspirations (St. John 1995). This was largely due to the rapid expansion of American higher education in the years following the Second

World War and the subsequent changing conditions of higher education (Gumport, et. Al. 1997). Jack, speaking about his tenure in a documentary film celebrating USC's century mark stated, "This [the 70's] was the decade, throughout this country, of retrenchment on the part of practically every university occasioned by the fact that we had won the race to the moon and the post Sputnik panic, and the boom in terms of resources to American higher education had ended. Well it seemed to me that this would be a good time strategically to become aggressive as a university."

Jack felt he could achieve the goals of USC's Board of Trustees as well as his own, but the first step was restructuring USC's administrative activities to fit his management style—the epicenter of which was broadening participation in the decision-making processes; to wit, he created various commissions comprised of administrators, faculty, and students. Three of these commissions were Academic Planning, Governance, and Student Life. The commission on governance would be instrumental in Jack's later problems.

In an interview published under the title "Keeping Pace with Excellence" in an undated issue of *USC Aspects*, Jack advanced the following thoughts about pursuing academic excellence:

> One of the great advantages of a private university is its freedom of choice in what it undertakes. Private universities must organize research activities based on cooperation with other institutions. They must redesign their organization structures to be more efficient. Private universities must learn to function as efficiently and as effectively as any well run corporation.
>
> In addition to limitation arising from finances, universities these days must struggle with a whole set of paradoxes before formulating plans for the future. They have been asked to perform new tasks while continuing traditional ones; to find a way of admitting all qualified individuals who seek higher education and at the same time maintain a close-knit academic community; to produce practical professionals as well as Renaissance men and women; to pursue knowledge for its own sake, to stand a critic's distance from society, and to leap into society's midst with solutions to moral and political questions.
>
> Obviously, no single institution can be all things to all men or ride off in all directions at once. Each institution must decide what it can and will do.

Regardless of specific purpose, all universities strive for an ideal called excellence. It seems to me that excellence should be defined by each institution in terms of the institution's real potential and that its appeal to faculty and students should be that it approaches excellence, not in all things, but in everything it undertakes to do.

USC may well become a model of how it is possible to translate enormously complicated problems into opportunities for new and innovative approaches to this business of higher education."

It has taken a considerable amount of time to develop this kind of approach to university management, but the most heartening aspect of the operation thus far has been the magnificent cooperation in terms of time and intellectual commitment of the faculty and student body.

But did Jack anticipate both the sheer number and the geopolitical magnitude of the obstacles he would have to surmount in order for his vision for USC to be successful? No. Of his first year as president, Jack said, "It was a year of trying to fill with at least a modicum of adequacy the commodious shoes which were my legacy; trying to weld an administrative team which could effectively and comfortably accommodate to my style of doing business; trying not to be overwhelmed by the vast panoply of demands I had never dreamt of. In short, trying to learn the business of being president of USC made it the kind of time I would not like often to repeat."

"The hardest sell," Jack told a reporter who noted that he was taking over USC in a period of real stress nationally, "is going to have to be with the general public which by and large seems to be losing its faith with the so-called educational establishment. The thing I'm counting on is an instinctive love of learning which we all share. That love so far has been able to survive all the vicissitudes involved in higher education—depression, war, post-Sputnik jitters, and now, campus unrest."

While Jack's arrival at USC in 1969 meant pursuing his vision of a stronger liberal arts core along with handling the normal issues of academia, it also meant dealing with the nationwide unrest and anti-war sentiment that pervaded almost every college campus throughout the nation. Within days of Jack's appointment as Provost in August 1969, half a million people invaded a farm outside of Woodstock, NY for a three day music festival intended to inspire peace, love, and harmony against the backdrop of the Viet Nam War. Anti-war demonstrations were proliferating on university campuses throughout the country, including neighboring UCLA, in competition with race riots on both college campuses and in city streets. By year's end, four major events occurred dramatically impacting academe: UCLA fired (Black) Assistant Professor Angela Davis for being a member of the Communist Party (September 23rd); The United States Supreme Court ordered the immediate desegregation of all schools (October 29th); President Richard M. Nixon signed into law the lottery for Selective Service Draftees (November 26th); and on December 1st the first draft lottery since 1942 was held determining the fate of thousands of young men. The early part of 1970 added two more dramatic events which roiled through quads, lecture halls, and student unions from sea to sea. On March 9th the Senate Subcommittee on Constitutional Amendments began hearing testimony on lowering the voting age from 21 to 18, and on April 29th the US invaded Cambodia. Further complicating matters, the Federal Government was shoring up its military and defense budgets with off-setting reductions in federal funding for higher education, and states were reducing funding to higher education because they were being required to shoulder a larger portion of federally mandated Medicaid.

On the USC campus, there were increasing numbers of student and faculty demonstrations and complaints, specifically from those within The College of Letters, Arts and Sciences who called the physical facilities inadequate and overcrowded, faculty salaries abysmal, the library collection spotty, and librarian services terrible. Mark Savit, the vice president of USC's Associated Students said, "We need money for the liberal arts and we need it soon or we'll be a group of professional and quasi-vocational graduate schools with a rotten core. We have a lot of encouragement for people in athletics, but we don't offer much of anything for academic achievement" (Trombley 1970).

When Heritage Hall, a new $2.3 million athletic department facility, was dedicated as part of the Homecoming festivities on October 25, 1969, within days of Jack's arrival in California from India, students picketed the ceremonies with signs which read, "Where does USC rank in academics?" and "$2.3 million for academics" (Trombley 1970). The demonstrators then carried their protest to Alumni Park where thousands of alumni were picnicking before the USC-Georgia Tech football game. Despite the fact that USC was a dry campus, several alumni who had enjoyed a bit too much liquid refreshment took umbrage with the protestor's disruption of the sacrosanct. Pushing and shoving turned into an all-out brawl. Although it didn't last very long, word raced across campus with the call for a mass rally and march into President Topping's office the following Monday morning. Protests, demonstrations, and meetings continued throughout the day, but President Topping refused to bow to student demands that the Dean of Students and chief of campus police be fired since blows had been struck by both students and alumni.

Suffice it to say that when Jack arrived on campus and officially assumed his new post as Provost a couple weeks later, the campus air was rife with tension. Jack had enough distain of admirals, presidents, and other positions of power and authority to know that he needed to reserve judgment until he had a better understanding of the lay of the land which required spending time with faculty and students as well as with his bosses—Topping and the Board of Trustees.

President Topping acknowledged that the humanities and social sciences had not fared as well as the hard sciences and engineering had, and in early April he let it be known that a formal announcement of changes to the College of Letters, Arts and Sciences would be made after the Board of Trustees retreat in Palm Springs scheduled for April 24–26, 1970. Topping also allowed the leak that Jack was expected to lead the revival of liberal arts at USC (Trombley 1970).

During the first several years of Jack's presidency, student protests and demonstrations against the Viet Nam War continued unabated across the nation. The USC students, however, though quite active and vocal, were not as radical as their counterparts at UCLA, Berkeley, or Stanford. Therefore, a Brother Lennie, an outside activist, decided the USC students needed proselytizing and conversion to the more extreme anti-war movements that were playing out on other campuses. For his USC rally, Brother Lennie chose to take his stand on a mound of dirt next to Tommy Trojan.

Tommy Trojan, the nickname for Trojan Shrine, is a life size bronze statue of an ancient Trojan warrior—the symbol of the fighting strength of USC's athletes—had been a favorite gathering spot since it was first unveiled in 1930 in honor of the university's 50th birthday. It is one of the most famous collegiate landmarks in the country, a source of school pride, and is often mistaken by outsiders as the school's mascot. (Traveler, a white stallion is the official mascot.) At the base of the front of the statue is inscribed the five attributes of an ideal Trojan: Faithful, Scholarly, Skillful, Courageous, and Ambitious. On the back side of the statue's base is inscribed a quote from Virgil, "Here are provided seats of meditatively joy, where shall rise again the destined reign of Troy." Brother Lennie could not have picked a more central and emotionally charged location from which to mount his soap box.

As the crowd of students increased, head football coach John McKay and his assistant coach, Marv Goux, looked down from the window of McKay's office at the gathering. Irate, Marv Goux rushed out of McKay's office, pushed his way through the throng, and confronted Brother Lennie demanding that he "get his ass off USC before he was physically thrown off." Goux was not only extremely patriotic and believed fully in the supremacy of the U.S. military, but he felt that any anti-war protest staged at Tommy Trojan was a personal affront to everyone associated with USC. While no one was physically injured, the verbal scuffle that ensued resulted in the call for Goux's dismissal—or at least some form of discipline from the university. The petition went all the way to the president's office, but Jack, true to form, determined to do what he thought was right regardless of public pressure. He took no action against Goux because he agreed with Goux's position and because no violence had ensued.

"Violence has absolutely no place on this or any other campus. It is inimical to the purpose of a university," Jack stated. "Universities are the life blood of this country and at the same time they are the most delicate, probably the most complex institutions ever created by man. Stress is no obstacle." Jack was fortunate in that he had not had to confront the violence playing out at other universities but he was not immune to the stress driven by the changing *mœurs*.

It is significant to note that while Jack was advocating the strengthening of USC's liberal arts offerings, the USC student activists were also advocating, from their own perspectives, additions to liberal arts at USC.

USC students were petitioning for changes to campus speaker policies and rules governing visiting hours in the women's dormitories. The Black Student Union demanded greater minority enrollment accusing the admissions office of violations of federal affirmative action rules, more financial assistance for Black students, and a greater selection of Black Studies courses (Trombley 1971). From another quarter, the Gay Liberation Forum (GLF) petitioned to become an officially recognized on-campus organization. After being turned down by USC's Board of Trustees, the GLF threatened Jack and the university with a civil rights law suit for "interfering with the rights of the individual" if

Jack did not give the University Senate's pro-GLF recommendation to the Board of Trustees at their next meeting and encourage them to approve recognition of the GLF (Kazanjian 2001). Feminists were accusing USC of sexual discrimination due to the low numbers of tenured female professors, disparity in pay between male and female staff, and the dearth of feminist studies (Murphy 1972). To make matters worse, these groups played off one another. If the Black students got the *Emancipation of the American Slave* class added to the curriculum, the feminists wanted a course in *Female Sexuality* added. If the GLF were successful in having *The Legal Rights of Gays, Lesbians, Bi-Sexuals, and Trans-genders* course added, the Blacks wanted *Judicial Oppression of the Black Male* added to the curriculum.

Needless to say, none of this sat well with the primarily conservative Board of Trustees and alumni. Many felt that academically unqualified minorities, supported by long-haired Anglos who advocated socialistic and communistic programs and armed with federal affirmative action regulations, were being admitted to USC and devaluing the value of a USC education. In the Fall of 1972, much of this came to a head via the School of Dentistry.

John Ingle, who had been dean of the School of Dentistry since the mid-60's, had been actively recruiting minority applicants and had increased the school's minority percentage in the freshman class that year to 10%. Critics from the dental school's fund-raising support group, the Century Club, the USC Dental Alumni Association, and individual dentists alleged that Ingle had transformed USC into a "second- or third-rate institution" because there had been "an alarming increase in the number of USC dental students who [had] failed the California board on their first attempt" and "the presence of minority students lower[ed] the academic standards expected of all students." Ingle was also accused with being pro-Jewish in his hiring of new faculty when there were already a predominate number of Jews on the faculty (Trombley 1972).

Although refusing to yield to these groups that pressured him to fire Dean Ingle, Jack later acknowledged that the "avalanche of mail critical of the dental school dean" made this one of the toughest decisions he had faced since becoming president. As an aid to properly understanding the situation, Jack organized a special advisory committee, composed of both supporters and critics of Ingle, to investigate many of the criticisms and accusations of discrimination in hiring.

According to Trombley, the investigation was leaked to the press, and the press wanted to know why Ingle was still dean when there were 70 allegations of wrong-doing and bad leadership against Ingle. "Not all the allegations have merit, have foundation in fact, or are being seriously considered," Jack told reporters. "At this point in time, the only other thing that I can add is that I will continue to maintain the complete academic integrity of the University of Southern California. USC will continue to make its own academic decisions and will not be coerced, dictated to or yield to any pressure groups" (Trombley 1972).

Ingle was "disheartened" by the allegations and ensuing disputes. He told reporters, "It has been pointed out to me, not only by the university people but by people outside the university, that my effectiveness has been pretty heavily damaged. When the report is released I will have to reach a decision about how effective I can be in the future even if I am vindicated. The school needs broad support and if I don't think I can harness that support I certainly won't stay on" (Trombley 1972). Ingle soon left USC, spending the next six years working for the Institute of Medicine at the National Academy of Sciences in Washington, D.C. In an apologetic scene that would be repeated by USC several years later after another ethnic related witch hunt, Ingle was awarded the highest honor USC's School of Dentistry bestows on an individual when he was inducted into the School of Dentistry's Hall of Fame in 2001.

It should be mentioned at this point that during Jack's tenure during the turbulent 70s, the historical record will show that the campus unrest at USC was much less than at most of the other major universities across the nation, and especially less than at UCLA, Stanford, and Berkeley. That didn't make the first few years any easier on Jack. "I remember one day when I was driving to work with a campus full of crises to confront. It seemed to me I might as well turn around and drive away. That's how much I dreaded walking into the office. But I glanced at a bumper sticker on the car ahead. It said to me: 'Do not repent. The end has been postponed.' That made my day."

Now anyone who knew Jack's heritage would know that Jack—and his brother and sister—were raised to treat all people with civility and respect regardless of race, creed, color, nationality, or native language. He would not cast dispersions on an individual or on a group as a whole unless he felt he had sufficient evidence to justify his actions. There was one area however which increasingly raised the hackles on the back of his neck—the demand for equal results regardless of effort. No student should expect to receive a degree from the university unless actually completing all of the requirements set forth for the desired degree. In Jack's opinion, all humans were born with the same potential. Where they ended up in life was entirely up to them—and the federal government definitely was not going to tell him that USC had to bestow degrees on the same percentage of minorities as were admitted. But for those who were trying, Jack would assist them to the best of his ability within the confines of presidential protocol.

"President Hubbard was an individual who inspired me and made me the individual I am because of his character," recalled Charles Young—one of the many great USC tailbacks and one who played thirteen seasons in the NFL after leaving USC. "He had time for a young black man navigating his way through USC. I was wholly unprepared for USC when I arrived, but President Hubbard allowed me to go into his office just to chat! How many other university presidents would do that? President Hubbard carried himself with distinction. He had panache. He was genuine. After a while, he would let his hair down during our office chats and let me see how genuine and great he really was and he was a large man—I mean his heart was large. He was everything I wanted to be."

"I remember how friendly President Hubbard was to everyone he would see as he walked across campus," recalls Sam Dickerson, wide receiver for USC who caught the game winning touchdown pass in the back corner of the end zone in the 1969 game against UCLA which led to the Trojan's record 4th consecutive appearance in the Rose Bowl. "He made you feel as though he had a personal interest in your success."

Yet, in some eyes, Jack and USC still were not doing enough. At the Baccalaureate Ceremony in June 1972 the address was given by the most distinguished Black Pastor in Los Angeles, the Reverend Dr. Thomas Kilgore of the 2nd Avenue Baptist Church. Dr. Kilgore blasted the university for its ineptness in dealing with the community. A few days after Dr. Kilgore's caustic remarks, Jack asked him to have lunch with him. "I was a bit upset with what you said the other night," Jack said to him. To which Dr. Kilgore replied, "Good. I was hoping I would upset somebody" (USC Media).

In response to Dr. Kilgore's comments, Jack met with Dr. Kilgore and asked him to help USC establish a community outreach program. As part of this new program, Jack set up a Chicano Task Force comprised of administrators, faculty, and students and instructed them to prepare a paper which would give his office direction regarding the needs of the Chicano students in the areas of financial aid, housing, and admissions. In recognition of the support Jack gave the USC Mexican American Alumni Association (MAAA) formed in 1973 under the leadership of Raul Vargas, the John R. Hubbard Award is awarded every year to a Latino student who deserves extra recognition for academic and community work. The John R. Hubbard Award was established in Jack's name because in 1974, he committed the university to a 2-1 matching program for undergraduate scholarships. For every dollar the MAAA raised, the university would provide two dollars for the fund. The scholarships have been awarded every year since 1974 to first generation, low-income Latino students who have achieved superior academic records and who provide volunteer service for the community.

John R. Hubbard establishing El Centro Chicano

If minorities constituted a growing part of the USC student body, the rich and famous were also significantly represented. USC was, and still is, often referred to as an "oasis in the ghetto." Derogatorily referred to as the University of Spoiled Children, a large number of USC students were children of the rich, famous, and influential. It was not unusual for a student from outside the Los Angeles area to be sitting next to the son or daughter of a movie producer, film star, politician, or captain of industry. Their lives were totally foreign to those who lived in the neighborhoods immediately adjacent to USC.

As the composition of the student body and curriculum changed with time, so did the physical campus and the USC Board of Trustees. Kenneth T. Norris replaced Justin W. Dart as Chairman in 1971. J. Robert (Bob) Flour became chairman of the Board of Trustees in 1972 and remained in that position throughout the remainder of Jack's presidency. Though still primarily conservative and republican, the board's membership was increasingly Jewish. The most prominent change was the addition of Walter Annenberg. According to Jack, when Walter Annenberg relocated his media dynasty from Pennsylvania to southern California in the mid 70's, he found that Californians were not as liberal and open-minded as they professed to be. He was denied membership at the golf club which he wanted to join because he was Jewish, but rather than sulk, he built his own golf club which was superior in every respect to the one to which he had been denied membership. Over the course of the next three decades, more than $150 million would be donated and endowed to USC by Walter Annenberg and the Annenberg Foundation.

In pursuing his vision of outstanding liberal arts programs, Jack proved eminently successful in attracting needed funding. "When I arrived on the scene at USC, I found a very distinguished music school, a good school of drama, and we certainly had the best school of cinema in the country. But all of these departments were miserably housed and I was just extremely fortunate in finding people who were interested in this kind of thing. They are sainted names around here: Anna Bing Arnold, Virginia Ramo, Eileen Norris, Walter Annenberg, and Blanche Seaver," Jack said when filming the USC documentary, *The Hubbard Years*.

During Jack's years as president, the Virginia Ramo Hall of Music was constructed. Across from it was built the Norris Cinema Theater. The Annenberg School of Communication and Journalism was flanked by the Bing Theater for Drama. Finally the Raubenheimer Music Faculty Building was built. Jack proudly proclaimed, "I don't know of any place in this country that has a performing arts complex quite like this and **every brick in all of these buildings is the result of private philanthropy**!"

In addition to his successes in attracting financial support, Jack championed a number of innovative areas designed to elevate USC's stature both domestically and internationally. When the Watergate scandal broke in Washington, it was soon learned that many of the key players were USC alumni—all fraternity men, all politically active during the 60's, and all of whom had been involved in student body election fraud (Stumbo 1973). Patricia Nixon, wife of President Richard Nixon, was also a USC alum. Several current and former members of the USC Board of Trustees were friends of the Nixons including Leonard Firestone whom President Nixon appointed as U.S. Ambassador to Belgium in 1974 and Walter Annenberg who President Nixon appointed as U.S. Ambassador to The Court of St. James (United Kingdom) which position he held from 1969 to 1974. While it is not clear who approached whom first, secret meetings commenced between Jack and the Nixons. A historian first and foremost, Jack immediately recognized the value of President Nixon's tape recordings and papers—both personal and official—for Jack knew that regardless of the outcome, history was once again in the making. If he could obtain exclusive rights to them on behalf of USC, the university would immediately garner new international attention as the key source of scholarly research into U.S. politics from the time Nixon first entered public office in 1947 until his resignation of the presidency on August 9, 1974.

In April 1975, following the approval of USC's Board of Trustees, the announcement of the USC-Nixon Papers agreement was made at the Rancho Mirage estate of trustee Walter Annenberg (Masley 1975). The crux of the agreement was that USC would raise funds to build a library on campus which would house President Nixon's tape recordings and personal papers, thus making them available for "historical research and public study." However, there was a caveat that would take several years to resolve. In December 1974, President Gerald R. Ford signed an act requiring that the Nixon papers be retained by the Government in Washington, but Nixon's lawyers had filed suit challenging the legislation. "If the statute requiring that Mr. Nixon's Presidential materials be retained in Washington is declared invalid, plans for construction of the library will begin immediately," Jack told reporters (NYT 1975). Unfortunately, suits were still pending when Jack announced his resignation in 1979.

Jack strengthened USC's international recognition especially in the Asian nations. By reaching out to the many contacts made in India during his earlier sojourn there as the State Department's chief education advisor, and by establishing new contacts in other Asian countries he encouraged the exchange of students and also of cultural programs. "Now I've always thought that our institutions of higher education in this country, if properly utilized, could be among our most effective diplomatic tools, and to bring foreign scholars and students into our educational mileu and to send them ours is damnably important." Trustee Virginia Ramo recalled how warm and friendly Jack was as they met with executives in China to encourage and facilitate such exchanges (USC Media).

From left, Gregor Piatigorsky, Jascha Heifetz, Virginia Ramo, and USC President John R. Hubbard at the dedication of the Virginia Ramo Hall of Music in 1974

Trustees and faculty alike were surprised by Jack's constant concern with things international and his encouragement of a remarkable series of alumni clubs around the world established to embody USC alumni. During one of his visits to Saudi Arabia Jack drove to the Red Sea beach cottage of a prosperous business friend where he was to be a guest at an informal dinner party his friend was giving for a group of USC alumni. The host was Ahmad Abdulla al-Sulaiman of Jiddah, one of the wealthiest men in Saudi Arabia and a close advisor of the king. His 25 guests were some of the more than 200 Saudi Arab businessmen, academics, and government officials for whom USC was alma mater. The purpose of the meeting was to set up a new chapter of the USC alumni association (Thomas 1979).

In addition to recruiting additional quality faculty, Jack recognized the wealth of talent that was potentially going to waste when members of the academic community retired. In 1977, Jack established a task force to prepare a recommendation for what is now known as the Emeriti Center. Formally established in 1978, Jeanette Brown, current executive director of the center called Jack a "true visionary for his foresight in the creation of the center. No other center in the country is as well established and as beneficial to its retirees and university as is the Emeriti Center at the University of Southern California." One of the things the Emeriti Center did was to provide a forum through which retired professors could continue to expand and mold the minds of USC's students. Jack was one of these professors. For thirty years after he retired as president, Jack continued teaching at least one class every semester. Course titles included, Undergraduate Studies in Modern European History—World War I; The Britain of the Victorians, 1815-1885; Undergraduate Studies in Modern European History—England in World War I; The British Empire & Commonwealth, British Empire to the Mid-Nineteenth Century; British Empire since the Mid-19th Century; and The Era of the First World War. There were times when he supported himself with his walker as his body become frail, but his mind stayed sharp allowing him to teach until he was 90 years old. As technology changed the manner in which young people communicated and "evaluated" their professors, several of Jack's students posted comments on "ratemyprofessors.com" such as, "If you want to have a true learning experience while at SC, take Hubbard's BE class. If you have a genuine interest in the subject matter, expect to sit spellbound as this master story-teller takes you back into history. I loved every moment with the admirable, accomplished and truly decent professor." Another student wrote, "This dude is awesome . . .he falls asleep during his videos and the only grade was a term paper at the end of the semester . . .loved this class." Yet another wrote, "Don't miss an opportunity to take a class from this knowledgeable, admirable, caring and genuine professor. With a remarkable set of life achievements and a story-telling style of teaching, you are sure to be delighted by this 'elder statesman'."

Despite all of his accomplishments while serving as USC's president—the growth in student enrollment, physical facilities, national recognition for research, and international recognition that took place during a very turbulent decade in our nation's history—it will be seen in subsequent chapters that he was involved with two controversies that would dog him through the remainder of his life. One dealt with athletics, the other with fund-raising.

CHAPTER 22
—
USC without Football?

In Memory Dr. John Randolph "Jack" Hubbard 1918—2011, 8th President of the University of Southern California

At USC's 2011 season opening game against Minnesota in the Los Angeles Coliseum, Jack was given a special posthumous honor in the form of a memorial signage overlooking the football field spanning the breadth of the end zone and standing approximately 10 feet high. Jack loved USC football. In fact he credits football with helping make USC the university that it is. While acknowledging USC's outstanding academic accomplishments, Jack also admitted, "Frankly, I have no idea of what SC would be without football" (Oates 1980).

When Jack arrived on campus in November of 1969, football coaching legend John McKay and USC's new Heisman Trophy winner, O.J. Simpson had advanced the reputation of USC football as one of the top programs in the nation. The USC Trojans were ranked #3 that year, one of the few years Jack's alma mater, The University of Texas Longhorns, was ranked #1. The Trojans had been victorious in their Homecoming Game against Georgia Tech, though the victory was slightly tarnished by a pre-game brawl in Alumni Park, and were well on their way to another undefeated season—marred only by a tie with archrival Notre Dame. It was a glorious time of year to arrive in southern California and what better way to segue back into American university culture than in the middle of football season with its accompanying pep rallies; marching bands; picnics; school pride flung in colors, stances, and atmosphere; and a winning football team that included four All-Americans: tailback Clarence Davis, defensive linemen Jimmy Gunn and Al Cowlings and offensive tackle Sid Smith (Moss 1987).

Yes, this was the perfect time in which to become reacclimated into American life after having spent four years in India.

Jack & Rod Dedeaux Greet the Japanese College All-Star Baseball Team

Jack had a deep and abiding love of athletics, not only as an end in itself, but also as an integral part of a complete education. In the spring after his arrival on campus, Jack made time in his schedule for visits to football spring practice and also to Rod

Dedeaux's championship baseball team. In fact, one of Jack's favorite diversions was sitting in the almost empty bleachers at Bovard Field, eating a box lunch, drinking a malted, and watching the varsity nine at practice. USC had launched dozens of major league baseball players since 1925 with pitcher Fay Thomas (New York Giants, Cleveland Indians, Brooklyn Dodgers, and St. Louis Browns) leading the way followed closely by right-fielder Red Badgro (St. Louis Browns before becoming a National Football League Hall of Famer), outfielder Jesse Hill (New York Yankees, Washington Senators, and Philadelphia Athletics), and shortstop Rod Dedeaux (Brooklyn Dodgers). Rod (actually Raoul Martial) Dedeaux had been the head baseball coach at USC since 1945, compiling one of the best winning records of any baseball coach in college baseball history. Jack loved watching Coach Dedeaux in action as he groomed his players for their next game.

Jack was frequently on the sidelines during both baseball and football practices, cheering and encouraging individual players and joking with the coaches. Jack became especially close to John McKay, John Robinson, and Rod Dedeaux.

This was the *fun* part of being Provost. As Jack said, he was responsible for the "intellectual health of the institution—the caliber of its faculty, student body, course offerings, and the vital interrelationship between the faculty, the students, and the libraries and laboratories." Coach John Robinson explained, "Jack considered each coach to be a teacher and as such was keenly interested in the caliber of their teaching and their facilities (or laboratories)." Jack knew that many college athletes would learn skills and life lessons in their athletic endeavors that would complement what they would learn in the classroom. "The teacher in him," according to Coach Robinson, "was always interested in the coaches as teachers and the lessons athletes were being taught."

A good example of Jack's interest in the holistic development of the athlete showed itself following a 1978 football game against Alabama. Although Alabama was ranked #1 in the nation, USC beat them 24-14. After the game approximately 50 kids surrounded Trojan tailback, Charles White, asking for autographs. When the ABC-TV escort tried to shoo the children away, White said, "I've got the time. I'm signing for every kid here" (Hall 1978). White talked to each child as he autographed his way to the end of the line. "I'm not sure Charles White would have been able to do that two years ago," Jack commented. "I don't think he would have known how to handle it then. That's what's so thrilling about all this—seeing a young man like Charles White mature into an outstanding, beautiful human being" (Hall 1978).

While the athletes were taught to practice intensely, to be well prepared, to work as a team, to learn from their mistakes, to always do their personal best, Jack would take special interest in the individual and personal development of the players—especially their ability to speak in public." As the Rev. Theodore Hesburgh, president of USC's rival University of Notre Dame, said, "A decade after graduation, almost everyone will have forgotten when and where and what they played. But every time they speak, everyone will know whether they are educated" (Green 1986). Jack wanted his players to be educated.

Pro Football Hall of Famer Anthony Muñoz, considered by many to have been the best offensive lineman ever to play for USC, recalls his speech class as being the hardest course of all during his college career.

"In 1979 I took a speech class in which I had to give a 45 minute speech then receive immediate feedback and evaluation from the other students and the professor. The idea of standing before a group of 15 or 20 fellow students and knowing they were going to critique everything I said was frightening." This from a person standing 6 feet 7 inches and weighing 280 pounds who could have made mincemeat of anyone in the classroom. Muñoz called it one of the most helpful aspects of his education at USC. He now is a much sought after public speaker addressing large audiences. "Even today as I reflect on my USC experiences, I'd much rather speak to a group of 1,500 than have to take that speech class again. That was the most difficult of all of my classes—but also one of the most beneficial."

Football is a long standing and deep seated tradition at USC. It is likely that no other school in the nation—with the exception of Notre Dame—is as rich in game day tradition as is USC. Fans, alumni, and students do not simply drive to the Coliseum, park their cars, imbibe in a tailgate picnic, then proceed to their seats. They arrive early in the day meandering through campus inhaling the excitement-filled fall air. They mill through the bookstore before heading to Heritage Hall where the Trojan band leads a pep rally that commences two hours prior to kick-off. From Heritage Hall, the gathering fans follow the band as it marches through the music school and over to the Alumni Rally in Founder's Park. From Founder's Park the band moves to the flagpoles in front of Bovard Auditorium and plays there, then it marches all the way to the Coliseum where it takes the field for the pregame show.

The band's pregame shows take place prior to all games, regardless of location. As part of the pregame show, drum major Tommy Trojan stabs the field with his sword claiming the field for his team, for Trojans and for Troy. The band really shines as it feeds off the frenzy of the crowd. By the time the team takes the field, their fans are ready for blood.

Jack and Coach John McKay
holding the Rose Bowl Commemorative Plaque

One of America's premier college football rivalries is the annual game between USC and Notre Dame. USC's rivalry with Notre Dame, which began in 1926, is viewed by many as the greatest intersectional football game in the nation, not only because both private schools are among the most elite football programs, but because the game is not required and there is mutual respect between the teams, coaches, and most of the fans. Many sports historians cite the 1931 contest at South Bend as the game that catapulted USC into the same elite circle with Notre Dame (N 2011). USC came from behind for "the biggest upset since Mrs. O'Leary's cow knocked over that lantern." After the game, USC coach Howard Jones took his team to the grave of Knute Rockne where they placed a wreath at the gravestone and observed a moment of silence. In Los Angeles, the game film played to packed houses for weeks in Loew's State Theatre (N 2011).

It was at the 1952 game in South Bend, played in sub-freezing temperatures, when the Notre Dame Alumni Club of Los Angeles introduced the Jeweled Shillelagh (pronounced "shuh-LAY-lee"), a trophy to be awarded to the winner of each annual bout. The Shillelagh is a Gaelic war club made of oak or blackthorn saplings from Ireland. It is said they are the only woods tougher than an Irish skull. Presented initially to victorious Notre Dame, the emerald shamrock and ruby-adorned Trojan head encrusted cudgel would forever "symbolize in part the high tradition, the keen rivalry and above all the sincere respect which these two great universities have for each other."

Both teams have spoiled the other's title hopes on multiple occasions, but they keep playing each other because both teams desire to take on the best of the best. The USC-Notre Dame rivalry has also been the source of many quotable quips, legends, and records. In 1966, for example, the Trojans suffered their worst defeat in history when the Fighting Irish ran over them with a 51–0 victory. In the locker room after the game, John McKay snarled at his team, "All those who need showers, take them" (Green 1986). The Los Angeles newspapers showed no mercy when they printed, "USC made lots of mistakes, not the least of which was showing up. To show you how bad things were, its mascot quit in the third quarter" (N 2011).

The rivalry has also produced its share of gaudiness. Red Smith, sports columnist for *The New York Times*, called the 1978 match-up the "gaudiest game in 50 years" concluding that if the two teams met on the field for another 50 years "they could not match the gaudy theatrics of Saturday's fourth quarter" (Smith 1978). The Shillelagh was presented to USC after a 37-yard game winning field goal with 2 seconds left in the game.

USC's 1974 game against Notre Dame is the one game most remembered. Known as "The Comeback Game" or simply as "*THE* Game," Notre Dame was leading 24-0 late in the first half and was thoroughly outplaying USC. Then the Trojans managed to score and ended the half trailing 24-6. "Years later, Nick Pappas, an aid to McKay, recalled McKay's halftime instructions to the team: He told them 'Here's what we're going to do. We get the second-half kickoff. Anthony Davis is going to catch it, you guys are going to block, and he's going to run it back for a touchdown, and that'll be the end of Notre Dame.' And it was" (Gustkey 2001). The second half opened with USC's Anthony Davis running the opening kickoff back for a touchdown, and the rout was on as USC demolished Norte Dame by scoring a total of 55 unanswered points in less than 17 minutes to win 55-24.

Pandemonium reigned in the USC locker room following the game with Jack there in the middle of the jubilant team. The scene has been described as chaos, and Jack was celebrating as much as anyone else.

"He didn't show the usual decorum of a president of a university," Pat Haden recalled. Another player, J. K. McKay, remembers noticing Jack with his hair going in the wrong direction.

After the game, the Rev. Theodore Martin Hesburgh, president of the University of Notre Dame said to Coach McKay, "That wasn't very nice," to which Irish-Catholic McKay replied, "That's what you get for hiring a Presbyterian! (referring to Notre Dame's coach Parseghian's faith)" (N 2011).

Anthony Muñoz remembers that game. "I was a sophomore in high school in 1974. I had listened to the first half of the game before I had to go to work. I remember thinking that it was just as well that I had to work since SC was playing so poorly. When my buddy picked me up after work, I couldn't believe it when he told me how SC had turned the game around. That was the day that I decided I was going to play for SC and no one else!"

The USC - Notre Dame rivalry has also spawned some of the social highlights of the season—second only to the pregame brunches prior to the Rose Bowl—which always made the society pages, such as the 1972 pregame party held for "more than 200 Trojan elite"—and a few visiting dignitaries from Notre Dame. "Dr. and Mrs. Hubbard served their guests cold salmon, ham, champagne, and lots of fresh fruits at the brunch. Speaking to his guests, Dr. Hubbard said, 'I wouldn't say that Notre Dame is worried about this game, but Father Hesburgh could not be with us because he had to be in Rome.' After the brunch, the Hubbards provided four busses to transport guests to the Coliseum" (Loper 1972). Private bets were made, egos were stroked, and liquor was liberally plied so that large checks would be written to the benefit of USC during the post-game celebrations of the victor.

Whether it was a brunch or a soirée, Jack and his wife, Lucy, with their refined southern upbringings and international entertaining experiences with dignitaries, were impeccably gracious host and hostess for these deep pocketed high society pep rallies. These functions—whose guest lists included the Robert Fluors, the Simon Ramos, the Bob Woods, the Charles Reeds, the Gavin Herberts, the Raymond Watts, the Fred Williams, the Dick Van Voorsts, the Roger Seavers, the Gywnn Wilsons, the Holmes Tuttles, the Albert Martins, the Edgar Bergens, and the Walter Annenbergs, to name just a few—would be held under large tents set up in the perfectly manicured back yard of the Hubbard's San Marino home, at USC's Town and Gown, or at the Beverly Wilshire. The more important the associated game, the more grandiose the function and the more spirited the libations to the Gods of Football.

USC has two other special rivalries, though neither is as gentlemanly as that with Notre Dame—cross-town rival UCLA and California's other private university of note, Stanford. The pre-game week shenanigans with UCLA frequently require 24-hour guards around the statue of Tommy Trojan protecting it from the marauding Bruins. Stanford is another story.

The Leland Stanford Junior University marching band is legendary among collegiate circles, but not for glistening uniforms or for marching and drill precision. It really never marches; the musicians just sort of scatter into its formations. And its scant uniforms usually consist of only a red vest or jacket even during formal events like the Rose Parade. Its musical salutes are oriented to left wing radical ideals and mockery of anything that has a shroud of decency or respect. Stanford has always been considered the Harvard of the West, but when its band was organized in the mid-sixties, Stanford was geographically part of the cultural revolution taking place in northern California with its Haight-Ashbury hippies and the extreme radical movements in Berkeley. Stanford's new band reflected its members' anti-authoritarian, acid rock, let's just have some fun, and make love not war mentality. It was a battle of the bands when the two schools played each other once a year. If the Stanford band didn't offend not only the Spirit of Troy (as the USC band was called) but USC players and fans also, its members felt as though they had failed in that week's mission.

During one particularly insulting half-time, the members of the Stanford band stood at attention while issuing the Nazi salute to USC as the Spirit of Troy marched onto the field. "They belong in a zoo," Jack commented to his brother who had earned one of his Master's degrees from Stanford. "They should be banned!" But since Jack couldn't ban the Stanford band, the USC marching band composed and choreographed a spoof—"Countermarch"—of the Stanford band in the late 70's. "Countermarch," which is performed only when USC is playing Stanford, contrasts the disciplined team precision of the Spirit of Troy with the Stanford band's free-wheeling individualism.

"The decade of the 70s can be considered glory years for USC athletics," said Tim Tessalone, USC's current Sports Information Director. Giving two reasons for his opinion, Tessalone referred to the many national championships won by USC during that decade and to the emergence of women's athletics stimulated in 1972 by Title IX. The list of national championships for that decade is summarized in the following table:

National Championships Won by USC Athletics in the 1970s	
Men's Athletics	
Sport	No. of Championships
Football	3
Baseball	6
Indoor Track & Field	1
Swimming Diving	4
Tennis	1
Track & Field	1
Volleyball	1
Women's Athletics	
Tennis	4
Volley ball	2

USC's athletic accomplishments in the 1970s become even more impressive when one considers additional criteria such as the large number of second place finishes in national competition, the number of All-Americans, and the number of Olympic performers. Especially impressive are the six national baseball championships in nine years won under Coach Rod Dedeaux. Five of those championships were won in consecutive years (1970-1974).

Intercollegiate athletics for women really got its start in the early 1970s as a result of Title IX. In 1972, John McKay, the athletic director as well as football coach, hired Barbara Hedges to supervise women's athletics, and the women have compiled an enviable record.

But football was still king.

Former USC baseball players, Ron Fairly and Tom Seaver; 1973

The 1970 football game that had a major impact on integration in the South was played in the first year of Hubbard's presidency at USC. Documented in detail by Steven R. Travers, that game made history and accelerated the desegregation of the University of Alabama and the Southeastern Conference (SEC).

USC coach John McKay, with the approval of Pres. Topping and Jack, had accepted an invitation from Alabama coach Bear Bryant to bring the USC team to Birmingham, Alabama, for what many have dubbed the Salt and Pepper game. Having already been integrated for several years, the USC team was composed of more black players than whites; whereas the Alabama team was all white except for one black player that Bryant had secretly recruited but was not yet on the team. One comment heard in the press box when USC took to the field was that it looked like the Grambling team (an all-black school in Louisiana) was playing.

USC's 42-21 victory became a telling demonstration of the general superiority of black players to whites. As the story goes, after the game Bear Bryant "borrowed" USC fullback Sam Cunningham, who had run for 135 yards and two touchdowns, and displayed him to the Alabama players as the epitome of a football player.

Wide receiver Sam Dickerson recalled that game. "I was raised in California, so I had never experienced the racial discrimination that existed in the South. When we learned we were going to play 'Bama, to us it was just another game. We noticed the extra security and all of the eyes staring at us, but we didn't realize we were making history at the time. We were there to play football and to bring home a win for SC. That was all. Looking back on it all these years later, I see that it was a really big deal."

The decade of the 70s was filled with great football players at USC. The debate still goes on as to which was USC's best football team of all time: McKay's 1972 team or Robinson's 1978 team. Some even suggest that Robinson's 1979 team was the best team. Regardless, 93 Trojans were drafted into the NFL between the 1971 and 1980 drafts, 14 of whom were first rounders: Marv Montgomery, Tody Smith, Charles Young, Sam Cunningham, Pete Adams, Lynn Swann, Steve Riley, Ricky Bell, Marvin Powell, Gary Jeter, Clay Matthews, Anthony Muñoz, Brad Budde, and Heisman Trophy winner, Charles White.

It would be inappropriate and misleading to ascribe credit to Jack for USC's outstanding showing during his tenure. But it would be equally inappropriate to ignore the support he gave to athletics during that time. Not only was he a friend, he was an active supporter. Jack would frequently ask the coaches, and sometimes the players, what they needed, and then he did his best to provide it. Sam Dickerson recalls, "President Hubbard would come up to us and ask us if there was anything we needed. We had the best of everything. When we traveled to away games we traveled first class, stayed in first class hotels, and ate first class food. He made sure we had the best."

Pat Haden, J. K. McKay, and Anthony Muñoz, football players in the 70s, remember seeing Jack frequently along the sidelines.

"I thought it was great," Pat Haden later recalled, "that you had the support of the president of the university." J. K. McKay also saw it as a good thing. "We knew he was there."

"He left us alone, but we and everyone else appreciated his visible support," voiced both Haden and McKay. Muñoz recalled the personal conversations on the sidelines that he had with Jack. "I spent a lot of time on the sidelines due to injuries, so I got to observe Dr. Hubbard more than some of the other players might have. The one thing I recall vividly was the love and passion Dr. Hubbard had for all parts of USC and that he really wanted to be part of the game."

O. J. Simpson, one of USC's Heisman Trophy winners, once told Jack, "It always made me feel good seeing you on the sidelines and enjoying what was going on and being a part of it. I think it was your enthusiasm and support that led to most of those successes." (USC Media).

At games as well as at practices, Jack was usually with the team. Unlike most university presidents who watched football games and entertained friends and visitors in their stadium boxes, Jack preferred to be on the sidelines, and he frequently had friends and guests with him. When alone, he would mingle with the team, and he would even sit on the bench with them.

Frequently it was Bob Fluor, chairman of USC's Board of Trustees who accompanied Jack. As soon as the game would start, Jack and Bob would entertain themselves by yelling and harassing the officials. According to Coach Robinson, "They really had fun."

"Sure I was yelling," Jack acknowledged when questioned by a reporter following one of USC's games. "I never believe in sitting on it, but I was just teasing. I know the coach knows best" (Hall 1978). Coach Robinson acknowledged that Jack "really gets into it."

Following his appointment as president of the university, Jack continued visiting the practice fields. On one occasion, Jack and Bob being unable to make it to practice by ordinary means, had a helicopter drop them onto the practice field.

> In his early years as president, Jack was very respectful of the head coaches and their assistants. Charlie Young described the situation, "They, the coaches and their assistants, had proven track records and Dr. Hubbard was the new boy on campus, still wet behind the ears, learning his way." While at first both the coaches and the players were somewhat uncomfortable with Jack's vocal and often lighthearted and jocular interaction with them—after all he was the president of the university—they quickly realized that not only was Jack genuinely interested in them as individuals, he truly loved the team sports in which they were participating. As a boy, he "found that team sports are more enjoyable than anything individual . . . [He had] felt since then that nothing humans do is more beautiful than some kind of disciplined activity in unison" (Oates 1980).

As the years went by, Jack would spend more time on the practice field and in the locker room. John Robinson, hired as John McKay's assistant coach in 1972, recalled the first time he met Jack which was at spring practice. "Dr. Hubbard would come out and watch practice as an escape from the office. He watched the drills and the coaches. He enjoyed kidding around with both the coaches and players. I immediately learned what his sense of humor was like."

Jack had his own locker in the coaches' locker room which made it convenient for him to work out and play racquetball with some of the assistant coaches. Even after retiring as President, Jack continued to frequent the locker room and practice fields. Despite all of the time Jack spent on the sidelines or in the locker room, he did not try to micro-manage any of the athletic programs at USC—nor did he neglect them.

A year after John McKay left USC to coach the NFL's new expansion franchise, the Tampa Bay Buccaneers, Jack told the *Los Angeles Times* Sports Editor, Steve Clow, "I considered John as one of the best personal friends I had here. Like everybody else I hated like sin to see him go, but you've got to remember, he was here 16 years. I didn't blame him for leaving. He had an offer that he himself admitted was far beyond what anybody could normally anticipate. He went with my blessings.

"Now the great problem was finding someone who was willing to step into McKay's shoes. And we were lucky because we had a variety of good choices—people on his own staff then, as well as Robinson, who had been here for three years before leaving for a year."

During that same conversation, Clow asked Jack whether or not he had consulted with John McKay before naming John Robinson as McKay's successor as there was speculation that McKay had named his own successor and Jack had ignored him. "I knew his [McKay's] opinion of every man who had ever coached with him. That would have been the height of madness. He had commented on the competencies of a variety of them . . . You've got to make a decision. I made it and thus far the record speaks for itself.

"One reason that universities have gotten into deep trouble with the NCAA and other constituencies has been the neglect of the president in terms of actually knowing what's going on—they delegated that. I take that charge very seriously. It's not that I have any particular expertise, but I am as concerned with the leadership in that area as I am with any academic wing of the university. It all goes back to my original proposition—if we're gonna participate, we ought to do it right."

And do it right they did as USC continued its gridiron dominance.

"John McKay had been the head coach for a long time. He had winning teams, and he was pretty much left alone and allowed to manage his teams as he saw fit," John Robinson remembered. For a while, Robinson was an assistant coach under McKay, and it was on Jack's visits to the practice field that he began to notice Robinson. Jack liked the way Robinson handled his responsibilities as a coach and as a teacher.

"When McKay left USC, I was then an assistant coach with the Oakland Raiders and very much a dark horse," Robinson recalled. "I received a phone call from Jack during a layover he had at Dulles Airport. He told me I was his guy and asked me if I'd be SC's new head coach. 'Hell yes!' I said. Jack said we'd work out the details later. He continued on his trip, and I made plans to return to college football."

Generally speaking, the alumni were incredulous about Robinson's selection as coach. "Who is he?" was the general reaction. The letters poured in criticizing Jack for hiring this unknown coach. "Then we played our season opener against Missouri," recalled Robinson.

"I thought I was a gonner after that first game," Robinson said. "We were expected to win without much resistance. We were favored by 7 and we were playing in the Coliseum."

Missouri led the Trojans 30-10 at the half and ended with a 46-25 victory over USC—the worst drubbing in USC's history for an opening game. It was also the most points scored against the Trojans in an opener (Schrader 1976).

"In my office after the game, Jack and Bob Fluor were white faced and in shock," Robinson said. "We all just sat there for a long time waiting for everyone to leave—until we thought it was safe to go outside. The only thing I could say was that this was my fault, and it would never happen again."

Angry letters now poured in. One particular letter summarized them all. It spoke of the idiot of a coach and of the even bigger idiot who had hired him. One sports writer wrote: "How could one man ruin a team so fast?"

Jack never wavered in his support of Robinson. At a meeting of the Monday Morning Quarterback Club a week later, Jack showed the irate letter and read it to those in attendance. Then as the weeks went by with USC being the winner each week, Jack continued reading the letter to the group, but now with a different expression on his face.

True to his word, Robinson didn't let the Missouri debacle happen again. USC won all the rest of its games that season. It went on to beat Michigan 14-6 in the 1977 Rose Bowl—the game in which Jack made a $10.00 bet with President Gerald R. Ford that USC would beat Michigan—and they finished the season ranked #2 in the nation. After the game, President Ford sent Jack an autographed $10.00 bill to satisfy their wager.

Jack with President Gerald R. Ford

The Spirit of Troy showed itself in grand fashion after Robinson's opening loss. On the day before the next game, the USC band showed up at the practice field playing "Fight On" and other stirring selections. "I didn't know what was going on," Robinson said in an interview. Soon a girl was out on the field dancing with one of the players. Then before Robinson could collect his wits, the band members and all the players were dancing. The team's practice ended at that point. The episode had its desired effect for the team was victorious the following day.

The band continued appearing on the practice field on the day before a game, and thus began a tradition which Coach Robinson said is still going on.

Along with being an ardent supporter of athletics, Jack also maintained his business acumen with regard to college football.

Although he naturally wanted USC to win all its games, he especially wanted them to beat Notre Dame.

"I always found it easier to ask for large donations after we had beaten Notre Dame," he often commented.

"In my ceaseless quest for funds I've found I get a far better reception after we've beaten Notre Dame or won a game that's put us in the Rose Bowl. People know what I'm after. And almost invariably their opening gambit is, 'Great game,' or, 'Gee.' After a defeat, those who represent a college feel like apologizing. Winning puts everyone in a better mood. People become proud of their institution. It makes for a more congenial atmosphere ... Invariably, the first question I get from an alumnus anywhere is: 'Are you going to the Rose Bowl this year?'" (Oats 1980).

"I don't think that has changed any," commented Pat Haden, USC's current athletic director.

In a 1980 interview reported in the Los Angeles Times, Jack said, "College football is more than a game—it's an event. It comes under the rubric of tradition: the pregame parties, the band marching over to the Coliseum, the song girls, the card stunts, the horse. On a Saturday morning at SC during the football season, as many as ten different support (fund-raising) groups will gather on campus for brunch. The fiscal well-being of the university is tied up with these people—and their appearance on campus is tied up with the spectacle that it is a Saturday afternoon football game. The catalyst is the game."

By 1976, Jack was seeking additional funds and cutting costs wherever possible to the point of threatening to break up the PAC-8. He was "fed up with the financial beating his Trojans were taking" in dealing with the Northwest schools, namely Washington State, Oregon, and Oregon State. The reason? Ticket receipts distribution. Under the rules at that time, each team received 50 percent of the net take for each game in which they played. Because of the huge disparity in game attendance, that meant that when USC played in Corvallis, home of Oregon State, for example, the Trojans would be lucky to pocket $40,000, but when Oregon State played at the Coliseum, they usually took home $80,000.

In addition, the relative weakness of the northern teams was such that the PAC-8 was not recognized as one of the nation's stronger conferences.

Objecting to these disparities, Jack saw only two solutions: leave the conference or strengthen the conference. He chose to pursue the latter.

Jack talked UCLA into joining USC in a push for the admission of Arizona and Arizona State into the PAC-8. Larger gate receipts would be forthcoming at those two nearby schools. Then USC and UCLA prevailed on Stanford and California to vote with them for the addition of the two Arizona schools, otherwise USC and UCLA would pull out of the PAC-8 (Hruby 1976).

Family Reunion: brother George and sister Louise with Jack before the January 1, 1979 Rose Bowl Game

Jack also wanted the rules changed so that the visiting team received a flat guaranteed amount. "There is no way three Northwest schools could make it. They would have to throw in the towel and search for a new conference (the WAC?). It's unfortunate the Pac-8 is falling upon hard times. But when one realizes Washington State hasn't been to the Rose Bowl for 45 years, it's obvious something is badly out of balance" (Hruby 1976).

The end result was that in 1978 Arizona and Arizona State were brought into the conference, and the PAC-8 became the PAC-10. In a later comment to his brother, George, Jack facetiously commented, "I saved the conference."

As mentioned earlier, Jack never bothered nor interfered with the team. Not, that is, until the 1978 game against the University of Hawaii.

In the 1978 season, USC's last regularly scheduled football game was to be played against the University of Hawaii. Ranked #3 nationally, USC had just beaten UCLA and Notre Dame, they had won their conference title, and they were headed to the Rose Bowl. To the USC community, the Hawaii game at the end of the regular season was little more than a meaningless practice game and one they would have preferred not to play. But they were committed to the established schedule.

Scheduled several years in advance, a promised sum of $35,000 seemed acceptable for bringing the USC team to Hawaii. But inflation had taken its toll, and in 1978, $35,000 would not pay transportation for the team. Calling the president of the University of Hawaii, Jack asked for more money.

"No," was the curt response. "A deal is a deal."

Then when Jack learned that Hawaii was raising the ticket prices for that game, he called again asking for more money, only to get the same refusal. By the time the team landed in Honolulu, Jack was already in a foul mood.

After having had such a successful season, the USC team experienced a mental let down in Hawaii. This was one game in which the entire team was traveling together. "Even the injured players like me got to go," recalls Anthony Muñoz. "It was time for us to spend a couple days relaxing on the beach for a well-earned break before the Rose Bowl. As such our heads were not in the game as much as they should have been."

Hawaii had a better team than expected and USC was playing poorly. USC's quarterback, Paul McDonald, was out with an injury. Anthony Muñoz was also out with an injury. To make matters worse, it appeared that the officiating was very biased in favor of Hawaii. When the first half ended, twelve penalties had been called against USC and only one against Hawaii. Throughout most of the second half the final outcome of the game was still in doubt.

Suddenly, this game, which had seemed so unimportant, was now of major importance, and Jack was in an even worse mood. A victory by Hawaii would send USC's national ranking plummeting. Aspirations for another national championship would be gone, and expected monetary donations would be significantly reduced. Jack was not only mad, he was fearful. Late in the game with USC leading by only 14-5, USC intercepted a Hawaii pass, but for reasons never fully understood, the referee gave the ball back to Hawaii. Jack blew up.

Storming out onto the field, Jack yelled, "You are a disgrace to your profession," along with a volley of other words that are unprintable.

"I can still see the referee's face," Coach Robinson chuckled some 33 years later.

The official immediately threw his flag and penalized USC 15 yards.

"I tried to hide myself behind the bench hoping that Coach Robinson wouldn't see me," Jack later recalled.

Rising to the occasion, the Trojans stopped Hawaii's drive, then scored again to finish the game with a 21-5 victory. They went on to beat Michigan in the Rose Bowl, and they won the national championship for that year.

Coach Robinson recalls the Hawaii game.

"Jack and Bob Fluor were on the sidelines and in the locker room at all of the games. They were great fans and the team members loved having them on the sidelines. They would yell at the officials and the officials that knew Jack would come over and kid with Jack. The UH game was different. At UH the officials were an anomaly in that they were all locals. Our quarterback was hurt. We weren't playing very well and UH had a good team. Jack was getting madder with each penalty we received. I said, 'I think the officiating defies comment,' which I should not have said, because the next thing I knew Jack was screaming at the official who was a Hawaiian native who in turn threw the penalty flag. We were penalized 15 yards for a personal foul—made by Jack, not one of the players. We finally pulled it out and won the game, but it was the last time the officials were all from Hawaii."

When asked about the incident a month later, Jack said, "Well I felt there was a prejudice on the part of the local officials and I expressed it to one of the officials. I suggested that I doubted whether he could operate successfully in a Pop Warner League" (Moran 1979). It was rumored for many years that Robinson assigned an assistant coach to "keep Jack under control" at all future games, but Robinson said, "That's not true. I'd just say, 'Now Jack, don't get any damn penalties for us'."

Another myth that has grown out of the incident should also be set right. No, Jack was not ejected from the game.

Even after retiring as university president, Jack continued his visits to the practice field where he remained on friendly terms with all the coaches, especially with R. C. Slocum whom Robinson hired as an assistant in 1981. Jack's background was the University of Texas (the Longhorns), and Slocum's background was Texas A&M University (the Aggies). The two schools were arch rivals in everything from State funding, to faculty and sports—especially football. Texas was where the "refined city folk" obtained their higher education in fields such as engineering, business, and the humanities such as history.

A&M was attended by "dumb farm boys" who studied such topics as bovine reproduction, the genetics of the fire ant, and water capture and irrigation. In Texas, one was either a Longhorn or an Aggie, and like Trojans, it was a lifelong designation and distinction.

Like all good Longhorns, Jack was an eager purveyor of Aggie jokes—especially jokes about Aggie football players. Jack loved telling Aggie jokes to anyone who would listen. When he served on the Board of Directors of El Paso Natural Gas he was asked to open the meetings with an Aggie joke, such as: "What do they call a half-witted Aggie? Gifted!" During the 1981 season when R.C. Slocum was the defensive coordinator and linebacker coach at USC, Jack would seek him out at every opportunity with a new Aggie joke. Jack would even pin Aggie jokes to Slocum's locker or send him messages with jokes.

The Aggies were in Waco playing Baylor Bears. The skies had been ominous all day and tornado warnings had been posted. Late in the 4th quarter, with the Bears up by 3, the tornado siren started blaring. The Bears immediately left the field to take safe shelter. Three plays later, the Aggies scored the winning touchdown.

The Aggies and the Longhorns were playing their traditional Thanksgiving Day rivalry. The game was at College Station's Kyle Field. The Aggies' star running back was failing his math class and had to pass his exam in order to play in the game. The professor, head coach, athletic director, and A&M's president got together and decided to ask him one question at the beginning of the game. If he answered the question correctly, he passed and could play. However, if he answered incorrectly he failed and would be academically ineligible. On game day everyone is anxious about the question.

After the coin toss, the player and his professor go to the center of the field and over the loudspeaker the professor asks the question "What is two plus two?" The Aggie thinks and thinks, finally he asks the professor if he can use a calculator. The professor says "No, your time is up". In desperation the Aggie shouts into the microphone "Four!"

With that Kyle Field erupts into the chant of "Give him another chance! Give him another chance!"

Slocum later went on to become a legendary football coach and a College Football Hall of Fame member with 14 seasons as head coach of the Aggies at Texas A&M.

John McKay also showed a keen sense of humor while serving as USC's Head Coach, and this may help account for the close friendship he and Jack had for each other. McKay was often criticized for letting running back O.J. Simpson carry the ball too much. In response to those criticisms, McKay said, "Why not? The ball isn't that heavy. And besides, he doesn't belong to any union" (Green 1986). McKay taught all of his running backs that "a runner must understand that there's one bad thing about carrying that football—it attracts a crowd" (Green 1986). Simpson was good at evading such crowds.

College football is a business as well as a sport. In 1979, football revenue contributed as much as $3.5 million to the USC athletic department's annual budget of $4.5 million (Moran 1979). When asked whether big-time football really belonged in an academic setting, Jack responded, ". . . My first USC budget was $70 million. The next one will be $300 million. For whatever reason, football is the activity that does the best job of attracting those who can help us. And the task of the administration is to channel their interest into other areas of the university," (Oates 1980).

Responding to critics who said USC was nothing but a football factory, Jack said:

> One reason they say that is that athletics receive an inordinate amount of publicity. You can't win the number of national titles we've won (60), you can't be on the tube as frequently as we've been on without somebody saying 'My God, they're just a professional farm club.'
>
> And that poses an image problem—just the one you've enumerated. You counter that as best you can by pointing out that the university's medical school has been designated as a comprehensive cancer center. You talk about your music school. What music school had both Heifetz and Piatigorsky as regular members of the faculty? And so on.
>
> The problem is that none of these things commands as much of the attention of the daily newspaper reader or the daily TV viewer as sports. But my ultimate answer to the critics is that USC is a member of the Association of American Universities—the Phi Beta Kappa of American universities—and you don't get there except through the high caliber of your academic performance.
>
> So I really don't worry, because I know that knowledgeable people know about our relative strengths as an academic institution (Clow 1977).

From the beginning Jack had an interest in grooming the football stars for public appearances, and he achieved varying degrees of success. For example, running back Charles White was initially very shy according to Coach Robinson, whereas running back Marcus Allen was very friendly and outgoing. Jack knew the political and financial value of having star athletes mingle with fans, especially potential donors. O.J. Simpson and other football stars were often invited to accompany Jack at fundraising functions and to participate in media events. "A good athletic program is indispensable as a kind of glue that holds the university and community together. It keeps the alumni and our other friends interested in the university—actively interested," Jack told reporters. "It opens many doors." (Oates 1980).

"Because the Los Angeles area has such a mobile population," Jack continued, "there are not too many persons who were born here, comparatively, and when they come to California from wherever, they're strangers to all our institutions, including our schools. The first thing that calls their attention to a university is its athletic program, by and large. As they learn about us, they become interested in other things about us."

Jack wanted USC's athletics programs to be both clean and vigorous. When hiring John Robinson in 1976, Jack stated that "we will win with integrity." There were, however, occasional violations of NCAA eligibility rules that occurred during Jack's tenure as President in the 1970s, but no link has been discovered connecting Jack to purposeful rule violations. Still, many people accused Jack of being complicit in the student athlete academic eligibility scandals that made national headlines in 1980.

In order to maintain eligibility, some athletes would enroll for summer classes at junior colleges then transfer the units to USC. The junior colleges, which had less stringent requirements, also had an "understanding" with some of the coaches regarding certain athletes. This was going along swimmingly until 1980 when the press learned that a track & field athlete had submitted forged transcripts to USC. This student's transcript showed "that he had taken both extension and regular summer school courses at the Thousand Oaks school in the summer of 1977" in addition to units from Compton College at the same time (Cohen 1980). "That was physically impossible," explained Steve Travers. "It is physically impossible to be in a class in Thousand Oaks and at the same time be in a different class in Compton which is almost 70 miles away. Someone just plain messed up."

The transcript scandal came right on the heels of the revelation that 34 students—most of whom were on the 1980 Rose Bowl championship squad—had not attended three fall (1979) speech classes for which they had received credit. "This was one area of concern for President Hubbard," said Coach Robinson. "President Hubbard was interested in each player's individual development, but he was especially interested and wanted to foster each player's ability to speak in public." When it was learned that his championship football players had not attended the speech classes, Jack ordered a "make up" course to be given. Unfortunately, 26 of those players turned in work for the "make up" course that was not their own resulting in the order of a "make-up" course for the "make-up" course (Reasons 1980). As this scandal came to a head, athletic department coordinator Jeff Birren and debate coach John DeBross became the fall guys and ultimately resigned (Reasons 1980).

Selling football tickets for profit was a violation of NCAA rules. In those years, a player was given four tickets for family or close friends, but the tickets were not to be sold for profit. At virtually all schools, however, players were guilty of violating this rule with the NCAA paying no attention. But when the NCAA decided to start enforcing the rule toward the end of the 70s, USC, along with many other schools, was found guilty of another rules violation.

The scandal that really riled the press as well as members of the U.S. Congress actually was not an NCAA infraction at all. It had to do with the revelation that in the 1970s over 330 athletes had been admitted to USC even though they did not meet USC's normal minimum enrollment requirements which were a high school grade-point average of 2.7 on a 4.0 maximum scale and combined Scholastic Aptitude Test scores of 800. The U.S. Senate's Foreign Relations Committee used the controversy in 1988 as one of two reasons for balking on Jack's confirmation as U.S. Ambassador to India, and it was mentioned in several obituaries published following Jack's death in 2011.

Defending himself, Jack said "such athletes had been required to meet the standards for eligibility that were set by the Pacific-10 Conference and the National Collegiate Athletic Association, rather than the usual U.S.C. requirements" (Moran 1980).

Both the Pac-10 and the NCAA had eligibility rules to which all student athletes had to abide. The Pac-10 required an athlete to pass 36 quarter hours of degree credit or 24 semester hours, depending on the institution's system, during the year preceding competition with the exception of freshmen (Cohen 1980). The NCAA's "normal progress" rule required that an athlete "maintain satisfactory progress toward a baccalaureate degree or the equivalent" (Cohen 1980). Non-athlete students were not required to meet either standard set by the Pac-10 or the NCAA. It was reported that some people, including UCLA chancellor Charles E. Young, considered these two sets of rules "completely ridiculous" (Cohen 1980). It was felt that it was the Pac-10 and NCAA rules requiring student-athletes to make greater progress towards a degree than the average student that led to the abuses of athletes trying to pick up credits off the parent campus during off seasons. Admitting student athletes to USC who did not meet USC's normal academic standards, but did meet the Pac-10's and NCAA's eligibility requirements was done, but this was not a violation of either the Pac-10's or NCAA rules. Having been admitted, however, they attended summer school classes and they took remedial courses as needed to meet USC's academic standards. It was a practice common to all schools in the conference except Stanford. According to Coach Robinson, "We recruited a lot of athletes who couldn't get into Stanford."

Jack took the viewpoint that this was a way of offering an education to many who otherwise would not have had the opportunity. The practice was not limited just to athletes. When the scandal regarding the academic eligibility of the athletes was receiving national attention, Jack defended his policies and practices which allowed the athletic department to choose its athletes without the threat of veto from the admissions office. Jack explained that the policy was part of the university's attempt to admit disadvantaged students who did not meet the usual minimum requirements for enrollment. "It wasn't a question of condoning anything," he told reporters. "I saw it in the context of freshman access. I am proud of the minority access program" (Moran 1980). He explained that the athletes had been required to meet all of the standards set by the Pac-10 and NCAA even if they did not meet those set by USC for non-athlete freshmen.

Coach John McKay responded to the charges that he had recruited academically ineligible players during his tenure at USC with, "If this story were true, I'd have had a lot better teams . . . I interpret this story by the people at Southern California as an attempt to clean their souls by blaming it on people who are no longer there, and I resent it" (Smith 1980).

In 1980, it was the media, not the players, that was so critical of the situation at USC. When asked for his understanding of the criticism, Anthony Muñoz opined, "When you're the best, you have a big target on your back."

An example of the media coverage is a *New York Times* article by sports writer Red Smith:

The situation at U.S.C. is an example, a glaring example, of a malaise that is depressingly common in college sports. As the committees investigating Southern Cal phrased it: "The major spectator sports have taken on an existence and momentum entirely of their own and drifted away from the procedures and academic philosophies of the institutions which spawned them."

In other words, teams and sports and players have an existence apart from the university they represent. Intercollegiate competition began as recreation for undergraduates. It has become an industry with its own budget and only a tangential relation to the college. In many cases the players are not equipped to handle college classwork, so they don't go to class or pretend to work toward a degree. They are semipro hires, at starvation wages, to represent the college on the field. As long as they show up for practice, they can get lost between games.

On this level, the only measure of success is the score. It becomes necessary to win, at whatever cost. If this means dragooning muscular illiterates, employing their muscles for three or four years and then discarding them that is unfortunate but that's the way it is. That's the way it will be as long as winning is paramount (Smith 1980).

Graduation was always a USC goal for all students including athletes. Sam Dickerson made it his goal: "When I left the pros, I went back to SC to finish my degree. I thought I only had 2 classes left before I could graduate, but they changed the catalogue and courses, so it took me a lot longer, but I finally made it and graduated."

A report, which was prepared at the request of James H. Zumberge who succeeded Jack as president of USC, stated that "although the retention and graduation rates of U.S.C. student athletes during the last decade has been approximately the same as for the undergraduate student body as a whole, only a small number of athletes admitted as exceptions have ever graduated from the University" (Moran 1980).

Jack responded, "Obviously, our ideal is that everybody who enrolls here gets a degree. Not just athletes, everybody. But that isn't the way it works. There isn't a university president in the nation that's been more active than I. While I won't publicly list names, I wonder if some players who are now professionals knew where the library was" (Moran 1980).

Every effort, however, is made to encourage graduation of athletes. According to former Coach Robinson, summer school attendance has become a staple for USC athletes, and it is anticipated that all seventeen seniors on USC's 2012 football team will graduate.

Jack also believed that some educational exposure was better than none, which was the alternative for many under-privileged kids recruited by schools across the country to play football. "It's only a game, of course. It's only a game that can open the door to only everything" (Hall 1978). In the 1978 game against Alabama, tight end James Hunter had played exceptionally well by blocking up a storm and catching a pass. In an interview after the game, Jack referred to Hunter as a prime example of an athlete who otherwise would not have made it to college.

Jack said, "Can you imagine how thrilled and proud his mother must have been watching on television? It hasn't been easy for them. She's a deaf mute, a wonder woman. But they've had it very rough. They lived in a shack, actually a shack. Isn't it exciting? Look at Hunter now. He's found his way. This is why we do it. James Hunter is what this is all about. It's what college football means" (Hall 1978).

One may wonder if Jack, with his passion for sports and especially for football, maintained a proper balance of priorities as leader of the university. When asked where he thought USC would be without football, Jack's response was, "Frankly, I have no idea of what SC would be without football.

"For all their success, USC athletic teams today, however, are no more than a 'handsome auxiliary' to one of the nation's fine academic institutions.

"The greatest thing we have going for us now is our increasing academic reputation. We have become in the last decade or so one of the major research institutions of the United States. And this progress has been accomplished by steadily increasing quality in the three ingredients that make a university: faculty, students, and library" (Oates 1980).

USC without football??? "UNTHINKABLE!!!" declared Jack Hubbard.

CHAPTER 23
—
USC - A Bastion of Independence

John Randolph "Jack" Hubbard,
8th President the University of Southern California

As president of a private university, one of Jack's unceasing concerns was the university's fiscal stability. "From my first day in office, new financial realities were being imposed on higher education throughout the nation." It was critical that USC remain independent—free from governmental oversight and controls that were hamstringing public universities. "It seems to me that USC was able to grow so strong and to achieve so much over the years for one reason more than any other. That reason is its freedom. Freedom to assess itself. Freedom to act. Freedom to create. Freedom to decide what needed to be done. These freedoms are characteristic of a truly superior independent institution.

"In higher education, freedom naturally requires the existence of a number of institutions which are not ruled by state or federal governments. Indeed, people who provide funds for private institutions do so in part because they cannot in good conscience allow the government to make all the decisions about education. In this pluralistic society of ours, there is no national make of car, no national brand of coffee, no national church, and there should be no single kind of higher education."

As it was, Jack resented the fact that 5% of USC's annual budget was being spent on paperwork required to prove compliance to bureaucratic rules and regulations such as Title IX. "Stated in simplest terms, inflation and government regulations have pushed costs up sharply, and private higher education cannot realistically raise its tuition nor increase the number of qualified students paying existing tuition rates to make up the difference."

Jack continually acknowledged alumni loyalty and financial support. "For example, membership in the various [alumni] support groups, whose members pay no less than $100 annually, is approaching 11,000 members. It's generally recognized among colleges and universities that USC has the foremost support group program of its kind in the nation.

"Look at the alumni. They won for their alma mater a national award carrying with it a prize of $4,000. This was the United States Steel Foundation award for sustained performance in alumni giving. That's the equivalent of an "Oscar" in alumni fund-raising."

Jack also reminded students, faculty, and the public alike that none of the new physical facilities built during the 1970s would have been possible without the University's strong Board of Trustees. "These men and women have contributed tens of millions of dollars to the University over the years. Furthermore, they have spent an amazing number of hours working in committees and in other ways in USC's behalf."

But more money was needed—$300,000,000.00 more.

On April 20, 1976, Jack kicked off a major funding drive, entitled Toward Century II, at a gala banquet in the Century Plaza Hotel. His prepared remarks, which eloquently equate educational excellence with financial resources, are presented here in full.

> The record of our first 96 years up to this point in time, 20 April, 1976, has been written: and the most eloquent testaments of the service rendered to date by USC are the careers of her graduates and their manifold contributions to the society in which they live and have lived.
>
> Of all of USC's fine institutional characteristics, perhaps most important is our fiscal stability. One of my predecessors as President - Dr. Joseph Widney - refused to accept a salary because of the University's financial problems, and I am enormously relieved to report that his sacrificial act in no wise established a precedent. But his act was symbolic, and the University in everything it does demands fiscal rectitude. USC, with an endowment by far the smallest in this country of any institution of our size and complexity, has nonetheless never operated at a deficit, and in that fact we stand alone. Simply put, we manage within our means. But we do not wish to be perpetually in the position of post-Civil War Charleston, S.C., which reportedly was too poor to paint and too proud to whitewash.
>
> So, if our fiscal record is one of our prides, the paucity of our endowment is our constant sorrow. I believe I can present our position in its starkest form by comparison. We have at USC 24,000 students and an endowment of $60 million, the income from which annually provides barely 3% of our operating budget, which for next year will be $175 million. Stanford, for an operation smaller than ours, has an endowment of $321 million; Yale, at half our size, $461 million; Harvard, $1.2 billion. Even Berkeley, which as you know relies on State appropriations for its major requirements, has an endowment, twice the size of ours, which is free and clear. Put another way, our endowment per student is $2,500; Princeton's endowment per student is $60,000. Yet we all sit together in the Association of American Universities, the elite of American higher education, because the quality of our academic performance is judged to be roughly equivalent by our peers. But by any measurement, our competitive position is precarious, indeed.

Through careful planning by all segments of the University, we know what our essential thrusts for the future must be to stay in that league: new concepts of quality liberal education in harmony with rigorous graduate and professional training; graduates able to play key leadership roles in an era characterized by rapid change; the continual replenishment of those rare and invaluable human resources, the master teachers; research geared to society's problems and the discovery of new truths; multidisciplinary centers of excellence, bringing a variety of expertise to bear on paramount issues.

There is, of course, much, much more to our academic master plan. Suffice it to say, the University of Southern California can stand poised to enter its second century as the very model of an urban private university, secure in its financial and intellectual integrity, if you will but help. The dollar target for Century II is $265 million, or something in excess of a quarter billion dollars, dollars designated for the most part for people and programs; in short, for endowment. A staggering sum? You might think so, until you consider the alternatives.

Looking at USC's past and present, the most significant point for me is the fact of our independence. Indeed, I believe it would be more accurate to say "our fierce independence." And what I am talking to you about is, purely and simply, the cost of preserving that independence, and why it is vital to everyone as individuals that we do so. One set of percentages will illustrate the problem, and our Bicentennial year provides an excellent base for comparisons.

In 1776, some 140 years after the founding of Harvard University, nearly 100% of our college students were enrolled in private institutions—there were virtually no other. But with the advent of the land grant college and university system and until 1945, enrollment in higher education was evenly divided between the public and private sectors. This arrangement provided this country with marvelous diversity and balance, and it gave the college-bound student freedom of choice. The setting of standards traditionally came from the private sector, and the public segment had to measure up to those benchmarks to lay claim to academic excellence before establishing new ones, a process which quite literally kept both sides intellectually honest.

In this kind of institutional interplay lay a magnificent example of the American competitive system. But after the Second World War, with the floodgates to higher education wedged open by the G.I Bill, the balance was rudely altered in favor of the public sector, and today the private segment claims only 23% of the college population.

Now ponder those figures for a moment.

What was once a stimulating and productive division of responsibility for nurturing the life of the mind in this country has now been reduced to the spectacle of massive regiments of government-supported institutions ranged against the little platoons of independence. Why is this so? Why are things so difficult? We know we are deserving and intrinsically valuable—our record is writ large. Why does not everyone share our enthusiasm—and support us as we make the enormous contributions to our nation and the world of which we are capable?

Well, one very good reason is that the trends I refer to are those that threaten the private segment of the American existence across a broad front. The verbal vanguards are "egalitarianism" and "resource allocation," concepts which when skewed and abused lead only to what De Tocqueville described as the tyranny of the majority. I refer to the tendency which has evolved that alters drastically the meaning of a legitimate quest for equality so that now the argument in some quarters is that equality of opportunity is not enough and equality of end result must be guaranteed. Thus, increasing numbers of Americans are dismissing the virtue of an equal start in life in favor of demanding an equal finish.

But there's the rub.

Show me any nation that has adopted a monolithic and collective system of higher education and I will show you a nation wherein individual initiative has lost pride of place as personal virtue. That this shall not happen to this country is what the little platoons are all about.

USC's very existence, as that of Brandeis and Notre Dame and Cal Tech and the Ivy League, is eloquent testimony to the fact that pluralism still exists in this country, that the state does not possess a monopoly over public services, that our youth still has a choice.

Do not tell me that there is some all-pervading omniscience in Washington or Sacramento that knows better than I how to run this University, that can perceive more clearly than I what its standards and contributions ought to be, or whose sense of the fitness of things is more enlightened and humane than mine. And in this sense I equate USC with modern America. If our little platoons do not stand steady, then we are simply asking to be destroyed by the zeal of our own rapacious breed of social engineers.

A pox on them.

Ladies and gentlemen, that is why the success of Century II is so damnably important. USC must flourish as a bastion of our independence.

As we succeed, I know that on its 100th birthday in 1980, the University will engage in celebration not only of the century ended, but of countless centuries beginning—and while a birthday is not of universal consequence, nothing is more important to the future of civilization than the future of education.

This was Jack's opening salvo for the formal inception of USC's program entitled **Toward Century II**, a campaign that at its conclusion had generated more than $306 million for university programs and endowment. It was one of the first three capital programs in academic history to exceed $300 million (Sage 1995). However, obtaining this remarkable amount during an economically challenging period in our nation's history proved to be far more personally taxing than Jack could ever have imagined. The political backlash would dog him for years.

But first some background.

"On October 6, 1973—Yom Kippur, the holiest day in the Jewish calendar—Egypt and Syria opened a coordinated surprise attack against Israel. The equivalent of the total forces of NATO in Europe were mobilized on Israel's borders. On the Golan Heights, approximately 180 Israeli tanks faced an onslaught of 1,400 Syrian tanks. Along the Suez Canal, 436 Israeli defenders were attacked by 80,000 Egyptians" (Bard 2000).

The United States, under President Nixon and Secretary of State Henry Kissinger, called for an immediate ceasefire which was rejected by the Arab states. Three days later, on October 9th, Kissinger responded to Prime Minister Golda Meir's plea for military aid saying, "The President has agreed—and let me repeat this formally—that all your aircraft and tank losses will be replaced." This decision not only allowed Israel to send hundreds of additional tanks and planes into battle, but set into motion a major shift in U.S.-Israeli relations (Dorf 1998).

In response to the United States' resolve to resupply military equipment and weapons to Israel, members of the Organization of Arab Petroleum Exporting Countries (OAPEC) declared an immediate oil embargo and price increase against the U.S. which lasted until the Spring of 1974. The raging Viet Nam War's top priority position for massive petroleum consumption left President Nixon little choice but to cut back the amount of gasoline each state was allowed to access. The most populous states, such as California, felt the brunt of the shortages.

During the 50's and 60's Americans developed a love affair with the automobile—and the bigger the better. Facilitated by President Eisenhower's interstate highway system, millions experienced a new sense of freedom as the Norman Rockwallesque road trip became the norm. The United States was the greatest country in the world for the American Dream had evolved to include not one, but two automobiles in every garage. The ever increasing volume of individual vehicles on the roads reduced the desire for mass transit—except in cities such as New York and Chicago where mass transit already existed. Gasoline was required to keep the country moving. Suddenly American motorists were reduced to rising at the crack of dawn in order to be first in line when the gas station opened on their allotted fueling days in order to fill their tanks before the station ran out of gas. Those who didn't rise early often had to wait in long lines for gasoline.

Key Economic Realities Impacting USC's Operating Budget and Funding Requirements During the 1970s				
	1970	**1974**	**1976**	**1979**
Average price of a gallon of regular gasoline	$0.36	$0.53	$0.59	$0.86
Annual rate of inflation	6.5%	13.9%	8.7%	13.3%

Even after the embargo officially ended, the price of petroleum products continued to escalate impacting virtually every industry and every consumer's pocketbook. Additionally, Washington mandated very unpopular changes, such as year round "daylight savings time", in an effort to reduce the amount of fuel American's consumed and to curb the double digit inflation the country was experiencing. Almost overnight the members of OAPEC became the richest countries in the world and Americans' "public enemy number 1."

With a natural empathy for the underdog Israelis coupled with the disturbing effects of inflation and Arab controlled petroleum production, the prevailing mood across America was pro-Israeli and anti-Arab. Jack, however, sought not to favor one ethnicity over the other. Through his efforts Walter Annenberg contributed huge sums of money to USC development. Jack looked to the Arabs as another source of significant funding.

During this period of national unrest, Jack was very quietly developing a symbiotic relationship with the Shah of Iran, His Imperial Majesty Mohammed Reza Pahlavi, Aryamehr (Light of the Aryans), Shahanshah (King of Kings). With excess oil income, Iran was actively investing and providing philanthropic aid internationally. Jack wanted some for USC. "In August the Shah endowed a million-dollar chair in petroleum engineering at the University of Southern California" (The Shah 1974). This was a personal gift from the Shah. The H.I.M. Shahanshah Aryamehr Pahlavi Chair of Petroleum Engineering, established at USC in September, was to "serve as the focal point of a program to train Iranian petroleum engineers and further the exchange of technology between Iran and the United States" (News 1976). By early 1979, the Iranian Government had given an additional $5 million in grants to USC (NYT 1979).

Iranians, like Indians, prized titles, especially academic ones. Jack understood that proclivity. It would not cost USC anything to bestow honorary degrees for the Shah's endowment. It was simply *quid pro quo* and if stroking the egos of the Shah and other wealthy Iranians could pave the way for future endowments which USC desperately needed, so be it. On April 26, 1975, Jack and USC professor George V. Chilingar, a personal friend of the Shah who would later that year be named as the first professor to fill the H.I.M. Shahanshah Aryamehr Pahlavi Chair of Petroleum Engineering, traveled to the Shah's palace in Tehran to present the Shah with an Honorary Doctorate of Laws degree (Smith 1979, Speich 1979).

Following the ceremony, Jack told his brother, George, the Shah held a celebratory banquet at his palace. After the banquet, the Shah announced that everyone would adjourn to the lower level for the evening's entertainment. Jack thoroughly expected to be swept away with rapturous dancing girls. Instead, they were ushered into a theater, where the lights were dimmed and the party watched *the* USC v. Notre Dame football game from beginning to end. This was the 1974 game—ranked the number 1 game in the Notre Dame vs. USC rivalry. "Defending national Champion Notre Dame rocketed out to a 24-0 lead with only a minute to go in the first half, apparently on the way to an easy win," wrote Bill N. correspondent for bleacherreort.com. With six seconds left in the first half, USC scored its first touchdown. They would return the opening kick-off of the second half for another touchdown establishing the momentum that took the Trojans to a 55-24 victory.

Jack presents an Honorary Doctorate of Laws degree to the Shah of Iran, 1975

A month later, (May 20th), in a private ceremony in Jack's office, Jack awarded a similar degree to the chairman of the National Iranian Oil Company, Manoutchehr Eghbal. Jack's trip to Tehran was not kept secret, but there was little fanfare on either side of the Atlantic in order to keep it under the radar of the press. The degree awarded to Eghbal was done so in the privacy of Jack's office rather than awarded at commencement as was the usual USC tradition (Smith 1979, Speich 1979). All of this was quiet history until the witch hunt began in the Fall of '78.

"Now I had traveled extensively throughout the Middle East—quite frankly I was hoping to find some funding," said

Jack, "and every day there were headlines about the Middle East largely triggered by emotion and bias—nobody had any real notion of the history of the region." During his tenure as president of USC, Jack made several trips to Saudi Arabia. "I met what seemed to me an astounding number of Trojans. It was then and there that I determined in my own mind (that) we ought to beef up our expertise in the Middle East . . ." (Speich 1978).

When Jack announced the Toward Century II capital campaign, he was adamant that all funds raised be private funds so that USC could remain a private university. It was only natural that he would look towards the Middle East for additional endowments. Increasing numbers of students from OPEC nations were attending American colleges and universities—their tuition, fees, and other bills paid in full by government scholarships. "We as a university have had at least a 25-year relationship with Iran. We helped their university start its school of business administration . . . We have the largest segment of Iranian students of any university in the United States," Jack told reporters when questioned about the large amount of money USC was receiving from the Iranian government. "USC's ties with Iran are a perfectly normal, natural inter-university, intercultural relationship" (Speich, Townsend 1979).

In addition to the Iranian students, who comprised almost half of the foreign students enrolled at USC, a number of the sons of Saudi royalty had been educated at USC. Upon graduation, in many cases, they had returned home to assume top positions in the Saudi government (Speich 1978). University deans and presidents from across the country—Princeton, Chicago, Harvard, Utah, Texas, Pennsylvania, UCLA, Georgetown, Columbia, and MIT to name a few -- traveled to the Middle East to meet with the Arabs and Iranians (Smith 1979). They were the money men.

American multi-national companies, such as Fleur Corporation and Arabian American Oil Company (now Saudi Aramco) founded by Standard Oil of California (Chevron), recognized the growing urgency of improving cultural understandings of the Middle East. If multi-national companies were to flourish in the changing global economy, they needed to be able to hire employees who not only had the technical skills required, but also had the language, historical, and cultural knowledge required to build and maintain relationships with their Mid-eastern counterparts. Much of this was being accomplished through a new phenomenon on American campuses—the Arab or Middle East Study Center (Smith 1979). The first such center had been established in 1947 at Princeton, followed by Harvard in 1955 and UCLA in 1956 (Gottesman 2004). Even Jack's alma mater, The University of Texas, had established a center in 1960. After all, Texas had plenty of experienced oilmen and if the crude oil wasn't going to come from Texas, Texans were going to go where the crude was being pumped. They knew the demand was not going to dissipate, despite Washington's inane legislations, regulations, and PR attempts.

Jack shakes hands with Prince Fahd as King Khalid looks on

About this same time, the Saudi Arabian minister of Industry and Electricity, Ghazi Abdal Rahman al-Gosaibi, a USC alum, approached J. Robert "Bob" Fluor, president of Fluor Corporation, with hopes that Bob would be able to help improve Saudi Arabia's poor image in the United States. Bob had been chairman of the Board of Trustees at the University of Southern California since 1972 and was a good friend of Jack's.

In May 1978 the Saudis financed a secret meeting in Santa Barbara which was attended by executives from 40 major US companies then doing business with Saudi Arabia. Bob Fleur was responsible for bringing the executives to the table. At this meeting, the concept of the Middle East Study Center at USC was unveiled. With the help of committed funds from Saudi Arabia,

Fluor asked the executives of 40 major US companies that dealt with the Saudis to fund a $22 million Middle East Studies Center at USC. This amount would go a long way towards the university's Century II capital campaign goal of $265 million—especially those portions of the funds which would be endowments. This would be one of those rare win/win/win situations. USC and its students would win with a new fully funded Middle East Studies Center that would rival those at Texas, Princeton, Chicago, Harvard, Utah, Georgetown, Pennsylvania, Michigan, and New York University—and more importantly done without the assistance of federal funds and interference from Washington. Saudi Arabia would win through positive public relations regarding their educational philanthropy timed to coincide with political overtures to newly elected President Jimmy Carter. The U.S. corporations would win by donating funds to a new foundation established specifically for raising funds for USC's Middle East Studies Center which the corporations controlled—instead of the USC trustees controlling the funds, plus having the center at USC run by William Beling, a former official of the Arabian American Oil Company who had been instrumental in getting the Saudis to make a $1 million endowment in 1976 for the King Faisal chair of Islamic and Arab Studies (Smith 1979).

Beling was part of the rare breed of professorial talent Jack was trying to recruit to USC. He had both scholarly and academic credentials fortified with real world experience. William Beling earned a Ph.D. in oriental languages from Princeton in 1947 then did postdoctoral work in the Middle East and at the University of Basel (Switzerland). He spent ten years as an executive with the Arabian American Oil Company before joining the faculty at Harvard prior to moving to USC (Princeton 2010). Beling knew all of the key players. He understood the strategic intricacies of Fluor's vision. Fluor, representing the USC trustees would bring in the corporate commitments while Beling organized the academic side. Jack, with his penchant for thinking outside the proverbial box, allowed the plans to proceed. It was an innovative solution to one of USC's growing problems; inflationary costs exceeding stagnant revenue with financial oversight by an extremely conservative board.

A significant portion of the funds that were being raised through the Towards Century II campaign were earmarked by the respective donors for specific uses. The largest gift, from trustee Ambassador Walter Annenberg, was to fund the Annenberg School of Communications. Other funds were earmarked for the library, for the Widney Alumni House, for cinematic production, for a computer sciences center, for specific scholarships, etc. (Progress 1981). It was not unusual for each major donation to a university to have its own written agreement in which the institution accepted the donor's terms and conditions. The arrangements Fluor and Beling were making, though a bit unorthodox, were not much different than those made by Washington when federal funds were obtained by a university. For Jack, dealing with an outside (of USC) foundation was far more palatable than dealing with Washington. The foundation proposed by Fluor was far less threatening to USC's independence than was Washington.

"Well I had spent considerable amounts of time in the Middle East—quite frankly I was hoping to find some sources of income—and every day there were headlines having to do with the Middle East and they were triggered largely by emotion, by bias, and nobody had any real notion of the history of the region and that was largely the genesis for my idea of trying to establish a center for Middle Eastern studies at this university" (USC Media).

When the Center was announced via a USC press release, its stated purpose was "to provide research and related services concerning the area (Middle East) to the nonacademic community, and to prepare students for academic, business, and governmental careers relating to the Middle East." There was immediate criticism and backlash against the planned center especially from Neil C. Sanberg, then president of the American Jewish Committee who claimed the center would "eventually be influenced and directed by the Arabs and their American business allies". The American Jewish Committee further charged that grants and contracts from the Arabs "may be used to skew university curricula, underwrite biased anti-Israeli programs, and support on-campus propaganda" (Smith 1979). An editorial in the October 27, 1978, issue of *The Heritage*, a Jewish newspaper called for Jack's resignation stating that in finalizing the agreement for the proposed Center "he has compromised himself."

"And the press began to have a field day with us," intoned Jack. "Bob Fluor, the chairman of the board was known for his interest in that region where they were doing massive construction work, and the press put two and two together and got five suggesting that Mr. Fluor and Hubbard were somehow in the employ of the Shah or King Faisal, and that we were leading the University of Southern California down the sinister path and becoming a front for Arab penetration into the United States, and as always happens, the more we denied it, the worse it got" (USC Media). Jack told both the American Jewish Committee and the media, which were running this story coast to coast, that he hoped to establish a King Solomon chair at the Middle East Center and to have strong ties between the center and Hebrew Union College in Los Angeles (Speich 1978). Neither group was appeased.

An editorial in the *Los Angeles Times* on November 6, 1978, summarized the major issues that had unfolded during the prior weeks:

> Those who are most closely involved in plans for a new Middle East Center at the University of Southern California have stressed that it will be dedicated to objective scholarly research and teaching, and subject to customary academic controls over curriculum and faculty appointments. This may indeed be the intent. But the manner in which the proposed $22 million project has been handled so far has given rise to contrary suspicions, not least on the USC campus itself.
>
> The Middle East Center is to be financed by contributions from a number of American corporations that do business in Saudi Arabia. The Saudi government, while it has given public support to the appeal for corporate support of the center, is reportedly not itself directly involved in the financing. The Saudis two years ago did endow the King Faisal Chair in Arab and Islamic studies at use in the International Relations department. The occupant of that chair, Willard A. Beling, is the designated director of the Middle East Center.
>
> Formerly an official of the Arabian American Oil Co. in Saudi Arabia, Beling also heads the Middle East Center Foundation, which is raising the money for the new project. His appointment to the King Faisal Chair was made in consultation with the Saudis. "I got the chair from the Saudis," Beling said in an interview last month, although USC President John R. Hubbard says that Beling was his choice for the position. A confluence of views between Hubbard and Saudi officials on the appointment was not, of course, impossible. But if the Saudi voice in his selection was as determinant as Beling suggests, then a major question of proper procedure and academic integrity is inevitably raised.
>
> Major universities are traditionally inhospitable to efforts by donors to have a voice in naming the occupant of an

endowed chair. The reasons are straightforward and sensible. University research is supposed to be committed to the search for truth, wherever the quest leads. An endowment made conditional on the selection of a certain person could tend to raise doubts about the integrity of the scholarly research to be conducted. This in turn reflects on the intellectual seriousness of the university. Strings-attached donations are unusual at best, compromising at worst.

The background of Beling's selection to the chair has added fuel to the controversy over the Middle East Center. But that controversy would exist in any case, given the close connections between the financing corporations and Saudi Arabia, and given the contract governing the establishment of the center that was drawn up between the USC board of trustees and the Middle East Center Foundation.

The contract is curiously ambiguous on the all-important issue of how the center will be controlled. Read one way, the contract gives USC traditional control over how the curriculum and the faculty for the center will be chosen. Read another way, it gives the five-member governing board of the center a decisive voice over subject matter and personnel. Again, the issue of academic integrity is raised.

The executive committee of USC's faculty senate has passed a resolution deploring and rejecting the procedures by which the center was established. President Hubbard's own Advisory Council —composed of faculty members, students, staff members and deans—has similarly condemned the methods by which the center project evolved. Hubbard himself has called the contract governing the establishment and management of the center "convoluted" and has endorsed a subsequent "memorandum of understanding" that seeks to give USC customary controls over the center.

Last week the executive committee of the Board of Trustees, among whose members are a number of corporate officials who took the lead in proposing and financing the Middle East Center, gave its approval to the memorandum of understanding. But a memorandum is not the same thing as a contract. Given the questions about the contract's susceptibility to different interpretations, the question naturally occurs of why Hubbard and the trustees simply did not move to have the contract rewritten, to make it unmistakably clear that customary academic standards would prevail.

The importance of the Middle East in world affairs and in U.S. foreign relations, its rich historical past and present political significance, are reasons enough for efforts aimed at expanding American knowledge and understanding of the region. But studies of the Middle East or anything else at a university must, if that university is meeting its responsibilities, be governed by basic academic imperatives. Intellectual independence in scholarly pursuits must be assured. There must be complete freedom from the influence of financial supporters. There must be no departure from the high and necessary standards that are meant to insure free inquiry and unbiased development of knowledge.

It may indeed be the case, as we said at the outset, that the proposed Middle East Center at USC is intended to and would satisfy these requirements. But the circumstances surrounding this project have given some cause to think otherwise. The bases for those suspicions have yet to be adequately dealt with by USC.

Dr. Robert Biller, Dean of Public Administration at USC during the turmoil of the late 70's noted, "Events really overwhelmed Jack and the university around this incredible dilemma that was experienced around the Middle East Center" (USC Media).

One of Jack's nephews, John K. Hubbard, was a graduate student in physical therapy at USC when the media frenzy and public outcries erupted. John recalls, "I'd get telephone calls in the middle of the night from people telling me what a traitor I was for selling out my country and SC to the Arabs. I'd tell them they didn't know who they were talking to and they would say, 'Oh yes I do. You're the #!@#!!@ president of SC!' I'd then tell them that they were idiots because if I was the president of SC, I wouldn't be living in the ghetto like the poor student I was and I wouldn't have a listed phone number. Then I'd hang up on them and wait for the next call to interrupt either my sleep or my studies."

The media and general public weren't the only groups crying foul. USC's President's Advisory Council comprised of representatives from the student body, staff, and deans, passed a resolution condemning the procedures Jack followed in the establishment of the Middle East Center (Speich 1978). John LeBlanc, a management professor and dean of the faculty senate, said, "Administrators and trustees do not establish academic units unilaterally . . . in back rooms."

"A university is not a corporation. The heart and soul of the university is its faculty. You take the faculty out of a university and you will still have a corporation but you don't have a university," said Kenneth Owler Smith, associate director of the School of Journalism (Long 1979). In response, the trustees approved a memorandum of understanding assuring that the center would be completely controlled by the university, which the faculty said was not enough. "The credibility of USC as an academic institution is now in jeopardy before the world," read a faculty senate resolution. "To restore our academic integrity, we believe that measures far more sweeping . . . are now imperative" (Smith 1979).

"There were many of the academic community that were deeply worried that in the center as originally framed that the Saudi government might have found itself in the position able to impact academic choices at the University of Southern California." Biller continued, "[They] didn't understand what the guarantees against that were in the way that center was planned, and in the face of that they felt it was necessary to prevent its formation.

That was a hard time for Jack. It was a hard time for the institution and I think it represented the trough of his presidency. It was a great dilemma. In retrospect, that negative point will, I think, clearly continue to pale by comparison to his positive accomplishments of the quality that was being nurtured during that period that will be with us for a long time" (USC Media).

"My first semester at USC was the fall of 1978. Many of my professors were openly antagonistic towards me simply because I was Jack's nephew," recalls John K. Hubbard. "They implied that I was somehow going to try to circumvent the system. I never asked for nor expected any special favors when I enrolled at SC; however, I did not expect to have to work twice as hard as all of the other students just because my name was Hubbard. I just wanted to complete my master's degree, get a job, and get on with life. I didn't like being singled out, but at least I wasn't being vilified. The verbal and media beatings Jack was receiving were pretty brutal. Early on I wondered if he would still be president when I graduated in 1981—and he wasn't."

"None of us disagreed about having a [Middle East] center. It was the way the center was going to be established." Board member Virginia Ramo summarized the Board's position: "We did have a difficult time when we were discussing the Middle East situation at the university. There were so many people on the Board who were unhappy with the way the Board—or some members of the Board wanted to establish that particular center. Jack presented his viewpoint to us, the Board chairman at the time who was Mr. Bob Fluor presented his point of view, and we all agreed—I don't think anyone disagreed—that we shouldn't at least study the Middle East situation because after all some of our students would eventually be working for corporations who would be doing business with the Middle East and so we ought to understand the people who lived in that region—their business habits, their customs, so none of us disagreed about having the center established" (USC Media).

Lost in all of the brouhaha was the fact that the proposed Middle East Center would put the university $22 million closer to its Century II goal of $265 million—which to date was far short of its goal. Too much credence was being given to Palestinian activist Edward Said's book, *Orientalism*, in which he argued that it "was incumbent to fight against the hegemony of America and its client Israel, and that just as the peoples of the region would no longer submit to a world order designed solely to serve American interests, so too in the academic world, it was incumbent on scholars to actively promote the new native forces and support their aims on the campuses" (Gottesman 2004). In the end the board voted against the establishment of the Middle East Center.

As if the controversy over the proposed Middle East Center wasn't enough, there were allegations that SC's Iranian students were involved in some of the protests and violence taking place in Beverly Hills and there were conflicts at the university's School of International Relations. Fund raisers resented what they regarded as an attempt by Jack to take over their efforts—and take credit for them. Other trustees criticized Jack's general business management of university affairs, leaving too much to Vice President Zohrab Kaprielian. Still other members of the board, faculty, student body, and media were not placated regarding the Middle East and USC's academic integrity until Jack announced his "retirement."

The *Daily Trojan*, USC's student newspaper since 1912, severely criticized Jack in January of 1979 because "he has declined to state whether or not he plans to stay on at the university ... Throughout the Middle East Center controversy, he remained all but silent ... [He] had little to say during the heated conflicts that shook the university's School of International Relations ... He has issued no statement on his position concerning the university's alleged Iranian student unrest ... And now, recent reports reveal that Hubbard is one of several candidates being considered for the post of chairman of the 1984 Olympics organizing committee ... His silence is deafening in a time when the university so needs strong leadership ... [H]e should take a decisive step to see that his name is struck from consideration for the Olympic post ... It is unfair for Hubbard to use the university as a pawn in his own personal search for a new job ... It is this ignoring-the-problem-long-enough-then-maybe-it-will-go-away philosophy that is going to spell a slow death for this university ... A change in leadership is needed for the university to get back on the track ... It is not only that you cannot run a university like a corporation, but also you can not run it like an arrogant Captain Bligh either ... Some faculty members feel it is necessary to offer a 'sacrificial lamb' to show the outside world we are 'paying for our sins' ... Either he should step forward and take the reins, steering the university to a renewed sense of credibility and commitment or he should quickly step down."

On February 7, 1979, Jack formally submitted his resignation as President of the University of Southern California effective August 1980. In accepting Jack's resignation, Bob Fleur made the following statement. "I know that I speak on behalf of the entire University community—alumni, faculty, staff, students, and members of the board—in expressing our recognition and appreciation of the many important gains made by USC, in both its intellectual life and community service during President Hubbard's tenure." The Council of Deans adopted a resolution stating that when Jack announced his impending resignation, "publicity irrelevant to the significance of this announcement muted entirely what should have been the public response."

Even after Jack was no longer president, rumors, allegations, and accusations plagued him for years. One of the more ludicrous rumors which surfaced in February 1980 was that in 1975 Jack and then Los Angeles Mayor Tom Bradley secretly helped free some undercover agents of the Shah of Iran who had been arrested after breaking the neck of an anti-shah demonstrator (Secter 1980). A letter supposedly written by Iranian Ambassador to the U.S. Ardeshir Zahedi on Iranian Embassy letterhead to Amir Asadollah Alam, the minister of the Imperial Court in Tehran asked Alam to "please show him (Hubbard) a very particular friendship [when he visits the Shah next week] because of the help that the professor has furnished us" (Secter 1980). Jack, Mayor Bradley, and Ambassador Zahedi each stated this rumor was false. Anyone who knew Jack knew that he abhorred violence and its perpetrators.

As Jack handed over the mantle of leadership to USC's 9th president, Jim Zumberge, he looked forward to focusing on his first love—teaching British history. He was deeply moved when many of his nemeses in the Middle East Center debacle rallied behind the endowment of the John R. Hubbard Chair in British History established in his honor and his installation as the first holder of the chair on December 18, 1980. In response to this honor, Jack made the following remarks:

> My response to this happy affair could take a variety of forms. This occasion is, for example, in its simplest and purest guise a manifestation of friendship unsullied—and unparalleled in my experience. It is something that exists, yet defies adequate description; and I can only plead to Messrs. Skirball, Pardee, Horton, Sink, and all the goodly company of men and women who made this chair possible, that they understand the depth of my feeling and forgive the paucity of my lexicon of gratitude.
>
> This is also an example of one of the marvelous qualities of our American way of life, one that stamps us as unique in the world and makes possible so many of the freedoms, albeit diminishing, that we continue to enjoy. I am talking about private philanthropy, and how it deepens and enriches the texture of our daily affairs, and which is at the very core of institutions such as USC. Thus this chair, and all others like it, stand as a visible symbol of our citizenry's commitment to the life of the mind, their dedication to the idea of a university, and their confidence in USC's capacity to fulfill its imperative mission. By this gift, everyone in this room takes fresh heart in our educational endeavor.
>
> Since my retirement from the Office of the President and from some thirty years of academic administration, the usual question put to me is what am I going to do with myself. And my standard reply has been that I shall try as best I may to

regain some measure of intellectual grace. Such a reply, certainly, is not intended to demean administration and those who perform that essential function. Jim Zumberge and Tom Bradley and I know that there is such a thing as creative administration; but we also know that all too often we are at the mercy of events rather than in control of them, and that the one thing persistently denied us is time for quiet reflection. The presidency of a major university is one of the most demanding roles I know anything about; and I have long held that the academic community is best served by that president who is a willing servant of scholarship.

Jack at the dedication of John R. Hubbard Hall, Student Administrative Services, September 2003

For scholarship is what this place is all about. And as I contemplate my return after all these years to its pursuit, my feelings are a curious admixture of hesitancy and high anticipation. Perhaps I can best illustrate this sensation by going back to Geoffrey of Monmouth and the Arthurian legend, a not inappropriate analogy, I suppose, for a chair in British history. The story has it that Merlin, sage, conjurer, maker of kings, is fleeing before the enemies of his infant protégé, and he has arrived in Britanny where the ancient stones lie in serried ranks across a vast area of rough country, bringing the baby Arthur for hiding and shelter. And while he is waiting to be called to the king, he finds the ancient harp on which he had learned to play as a youth. In the evening as he sat in his rude hovel before the fire, he took up the harp and tentatively touched the strings. It was like remembering love after a long sleep; or returning again to poetry after years in the market place, or to youth after resignation to drowsy and stiffening age, recalling what you once thought life could hold, after telling over with muddied and calculating fingers what it had indeed offered. This was music made after long silence. His soul flexed its wings, and, clumsy as any fledgling, tried the air again. He felt his way, groping through chords, for the passion that slept there in the harp, exploring, testing, as a man tests the dark ground which once he knew in daylight. Whispers, small jags of sound, bunches of notes dragged sharply. The strings thrilled, catching the firelight, and the long, running chords lapsed into the song.

Whether my harp of scholarship produces any refrain worth hearing is still in the lap of the gods. And even if it should, what matter? The satisfaction of one individual's intellectual curiosity? A book or two more upon already crowded shelves? No, certainly not these things in themselves. What does matter is the effort, the calling to add vitality to the humanistic tradition, the ennobling of which is one of the sacred trusts of any university, The cultivation of the liberal arts, the arts becoming free men. When was our civilization more in need of these?

As I have mused in another context, despite the marvels of space exploration, the dynamism of Cybernetics, the communications revolution, ours is not yet an age of science. Men are still driven by greed and confused by guile, rather than moved by the wisdom inherent in our expanding knowledge. Whether reason, honesty, justice, compassion can contrive survival values equal if not superior to the blind forces of nature which have shaped man's past is also in the lap of the gods. Still, we cannot deny the possibility. And we can nourish the hope that primitive man, who somehow learned to stand erect, grew a brain worth having, formed speech and song out of a hiss and a roar, and stepped out of his cave to explore and master his universe may someday develop a less myopic view towards his kin.

It is in nurturing the speech and song of free men with a free choice in an open society that this chair and this university are dedicated. To the donors, let me say simply for my colleagues, you have strengthened our resolve, you have added another string to our harp; and for this golden opportunity to lapse into song, we are profoundly grateful.

Twenty-three years later, another honor would be bestowed upon Jack by USC when the Student Union was renamed John R. Hubbard Hall—Student Administrative Services. With the exception of the year he spent back in India as U.S. Ambassador, Jack was part of the USC tapestry from 1969 to 2010 spending a total of 40 years transforming the mush within students' skulls into cognitive matter and always proclaiming, "Fight on!"

John R. Hubbard Hall, Student Administrative Services

CHAPTER 24
India (1988—1989)
A Dream Come True

Jack (right) with First Lady Pat Nixon and actor John Wayne

As President of the University of Southern California, Jack hosted dignitaries, prominent business leaders, and celebrities covering the continuum of political ideologies that existed during the 70's—Ray Bradbury, Hubert Humphrey, Japanese Prime Minister Takeo Miki, Alan Cranston, George Romney, Byron (Whizzer) White, Benjamin Spock, Cesar Chavez, Nelson Rockerfeller, Casey Stengel, Gloria Steinem, Edmund Muskee, Art Buckwald, David Brinkley, Richard and Pat Nixon, John Kennedy, Jr., Neil Armstrong, Art Linkletter, Gerald R. Ford, Groucho Marx, Fred Astaire, John Wayne, Kirk Douglas, Nelson

Eddy, the King of Sweden, Henry Kissenger, Ronald Reagan—to name but a few. In his official capacity as USC's president, Jack served on numerous commissions and boards including the Commission on Federal Relations of the American Council on Education, Council on Federal Relations of the Association of American Universities, and Trustee of the Association of Independent California Colleges and Universities. As a historian, Jack held memberships in the Conference on British Studies, American Historical Association Organization of American Historians, Southern Historical Association, and Anglo-American Historical Society, and always he was a DKE—Delta Kappa Epsilon, along with Omicron Delta Kappa, and Phi Delta Kappa. The majority of these connections were made after his arrival at USC—and were added to the plethora of national and international dignitaries and notables with whom he had hobnobbed most of his life. Therefore Jack was not a neophyte to politics and political connections and their roles in both personal and professional arenas. So it is not surprising that Jack's old colleague, Morarji Desai, as the new Prime Minister of India, asked Jack to make a private trip to India to brief him before his meeting with President Jimmy Carter in January 1978.

Now it just so happened that USC had drawn a bye for the PAC-10 berth at the January 1, 1978 Rose Bowl—having lost to Alabama, Notre Dame, California, and lastly to the Washington Huskies—and was relegated to the lowly Bluebonnet Bowl on December 31, 1977 against Texas A&M. It was a good time to fly to India—a country he had grown to love—instead of commiserating with Trojan alums and board over their disappointing season.

Morarji Desai, whom Jack had met when Desai was chancellor of Gujarat Vidyapith, was one of India's original freedom fighters when India was seeking its independence from Great Britain. A strict follower of Mahatma Gandhi and a moralist, Desai used his prime ministership to help the people of India become fearless to the extent that even if the highest most powerful in the land commit a wrong, the humblest in the land should be able to point it out to him, and to understand that no one, not even the prime minister is above the law of the land. Desai also used his position to call upon the United States to "establish a new economic relationship . . . with their technology and affluence" to help India's villages become economically resilient (GOI FAR 1978).

President Carter, on behalf of the United States, responded to this request with the announcement of joint research and development projects, one of which was "developing renewable energy resources, especially solar energy" (GOI FAR 1978). "There is no shortage of sunlight in India," President Carter stated in his address to the Indian Parliamentary Group on January 2, 1978, in the Central Hall of Parliament, New Delhi. ". . . but the lack of a massive existing infrastructure tied to fossil fuel use will make the application of solar and solar-related energy vastly easier here than it will be in my country. Moreover, the inherently decentralized nature of solar energy makes it ideal as a complement to your government's stress on developing self-reliant villages and communities" (GOI FAR 1978).

Dr. Ramakrishna explains a solar cell operated sprayer design to Jack, 1988

When Jack returned a decade later as ambassador, he was given a demonstration of one of the ingenious designs to which President Carter's commitment gave birth—a solar powered sprayer for use in agriculture. The aggi-wallah would strap on an aluminum frame atop of which was a solar panel. The energy collected via the solar panel then fueled the sprayer through which fertilizer and/or pesticides were applied to orchards and fields.

When Jack announced his retirement from the office of president of the University of Southern California, he told reporters that he would "return to grace." "I fell from grace in 1953," he said, "when I entered the ranks of educational administration. I happen to be a professor of history and I have never ceased teaching. I would also love to read and write some books" (Speich 1979). He had the titles President Emeritus and Professor of History (with tenure) which meant that professionally he was set for life. However, he was emotionally beat up, he was drinking too much, his marriage was on the rocks, and he needed a break. There really wasn't a better location in his mind than India—even if only for a brief period—so when the opportunity presented itself to be a Fulbright Professor in India for a year, he jumped on it.

The Fulbright Program was established by an Act of Congress in 1946 under legislation introduced by then Senator J. William Fulbright of Arkansas. The Fulbright Program is an international educational exchange program administered by the U.S. Department of State's Bureau of Educational and Cultural Affairs. On February 2, 1950, in New Delhi, Prime Minister Jawaharlal Nehru and U.S. Ambassador Loy Henderson signed the agreement which established a bilateral Fulbright commission in India, one of the first in the world. Known as the United States Educational Foundation in India (USEFI), the commission has played a pivotal role in promoting educational exchange between the two countries. In 1963 Foreign Secretary M. J. Desai and U.S. Ambassador John Kenneth Galbraith signed a revised agreement which provided a broader and more flexible scope for educational exchange. Eventually, the Fulbright Program would augment, then supplant the USAID educational program in India which Jack had been instrumental in establishing.

Following the end of the Fall 1980 semester, Jack took leave from USC and returned to India as a Fulbright Professor until the Fall 1981 semester when he returned to teach British and Modern European History at USC.

Jack also became a member of the Indo-U.S. Joint Sub-commission on Education and Culture in 1980. This sub-commission was part of the State Department's Bureau of Educational and Cultural Affairs which focused specifically on India. He was appointed U.S. Chairman of the Indo-U.S. Sub-commission on Education and Culture in 1982 by President Ronald Reagan which position he held until his appointment as U.S. Ambassador to India in 1988. This assignment allowed him to travel to India twice a year.

"The Subcommission engages in a myriad of intellectual and cultural exchanges, and it successfully pursues these endeavors regardless of the political climate between our two countries,"

Jack wrote in his 1988 summary of his Indian experience. "Its most notable recent activity was to provide the infrastructure of staging the brilliant Festival of India in this country which resulted from the State visit of Mrs. Gandhi to Washington in 1982. It was I who persuaded the Prime Minister to include the West Coast on her itinerary, and I was her host in Los Angeles. That was also the occasion when I first met Mrs. Gandhi's son, Rajiv Gandhi; we had a long discussion stemming from the fact that we were both aviators at one point in our careers. I have met him with some frequency since then in Washington and Delhi."

Throughout the Cold War India received a majority of its military support and infrastructure support from the Soviet Union. While the United States continued to view India as a strategic point in the Cold War, in events in Southeast Asia during the 1970s, and in events in South Asia during the 1980s, the only relationship that consistently worked between the United States and India were the educational programs originated by U.S.AID in the sixties and cultural exchange. As Jack wrote in his memoirs of his time in India from 1965—1969 (Chapter 19), it was in the interest of the U.S.'s strategic political and military health that we try to shore up India's "massive but faltering experiment in democracy." As he continued, "India and the independent minded Indians were not easy to help."

India had its own view of its democracy and recent independence. As Prime Minister Shri Rajiv Gandhi, (Mrs. Gandhi's son who became prime minister in 1984 after his mother's assassination), explained in his Jodidi lecture at Harvard University on October 18, 1987, "Independence was no gift of the British: it was won by the biggest mass movement in history. It was a battle which sought to spill no blood. Yet, was as tenaciously fought as any other. . . . The movement culminated in Mahatma Gandhi's non-violent, peaceful, mass satyagraha which overthrew the colonial order. For the men and women who fought for our freedom, there was never any doubt that Independent India could only be democratic" (GOI FAR 1987).

One of the ways in which India exercised her independence was by refusing to kowtow to the desires of Washington. India viewed herself as a sovereign nation with the right to establish social, military, political, educational, and cultural relations with whomever she pleased as viewed in the best interest of the country's development. India proudly claimed itself non-aligned.

At the International Seminar on Non-alignment and World Peace held in New Delhi on August 7, 1987, Prime Minister Shri

Rajiv Gandhi said, "... our freedom movement developed strength against British rule, not against the English man. Our creed was non-violence, our bedrock was secularism. From that has developed our philosophy of Nonalignment. Nonalignment is our framework of interaction with the contemporary world keeping in harmony with our ancient ideals.

"While those who believe in Cold War or in the balance of power live in paroxysm of hate, they paint others in devilish colours and themselves as paragons of virtue. We, on the other hand, urge reason and understanding, tolerance and compassion, cooperation and not rivalry, coexistence and not confrontation.

"After the searing experience of two centuries of colonialism, we could not hitch ourselves to the bandwagon of others. We could not circumscribe our own opinions and our options to those chosen by others. To be free, we had to be free to speak our minds. We had to be free to control our destinies, we had to be free to determine our friends, we had to be free to choose our direction, and we had to be free to influence the direction that the world was taking" (GOI FAR 1987).

Thus, in both public and private, India had been and was continuing to exercise these freedoms much to the chagrin of the United States, the pleasure of the Soviet Union, the delight of Palestine, the consternation of Afghanistan, the concern of Israel, and the apprehension of Pakistan.

As India increased the quantity and quality of its educated scientists and engineers during the 1970s, there was an increasing interest from India in the exchange of high technology knowledge, tools, and products with the United States. Washington tried to manage this through the Indo–US Joint Commission on Economic, Commercial, Scientific, Technological, Educational, and Cultural Cooperation which was funded by the Department of State.

This commission had several sub-commissions. There was the Sub-Commission on Science and Technology, the Sub-Commission on Agriculture, the Economic and Commercial Sub-Commission, and the Sub-Commission on Education and Culture. Each sub-commission was co-chaired by a representative from India and a representative from the United States. The individual chairing each sub-commission was selected by their respective government. In the U.S., the selection was made by the Department of State. Jack was U.S. co-chair of the Sub—Commission on Education and Culture from 1980 to 1988 which necessitated his travel to India at least twice a year. The co-chair from India from 1985–1989 was the internationally renowned astrophysicist, Jayant V. Narlikar, whose first work provided the first reliable theory describing the continuous creation of matter within the framework of Einstein's "General Relativity Theory" and later developed the "white hole concept" as exploding sources of energy to explain some of the violent phenomena in the universe.

In June 1983, the Indo-U.S. commission set a goal of making 1984 and 1985 years of special emphasis on Indo-U.S. collaboration. The goal was to strengthen relations between the U.S. and India with special attention given to joint commission activities by President Reagan, Prime Minister Rajiv Gandhi, and the late Prime Minister Indira Gandhi. Despite the highest level of support for the Sub-Commission on Education and Culture's activities, there was an undercurrent of "lack of confidence" running between the members from the two countries which made it difficult to accomplish anything of significance. Commission members from the U.S. were never confident that Washington would actually fund any of the activities and collaborations being planned. Members from India questioned the ulterior motive of the U.S. Was the U.S. really going to increase educational and economic opportunities for Indians or were they really only interested in cultural exchanges not dissimilar to the Bolshoi Ballet's periodic performances in New York City, Washington D.C., and Los Angeles. The co-chairs, Hubbard and Narlikar, did their best to increase the degree of confidence among their respective members while making the offered assurances credible on both sides. In the end, the sum of the Sub-Commission on Education and Culture's activities was the "Festival of India" in the United States, the "Festival of the United States" in India, and "plans to expand exchanges and to establish collaborative programs and seminars in science, education, the arts, and sports" (Minutes 1986).

During the Indo-U.S. Joint Commission meeting held in Washington on February 6, 1986, during which the activities of the sub-commissions since the June 1983 meeting were reviewed, George P. Shultz, U.S. Secretary of State and India's Minister of External Affairs, Bali Ram Bhagat, recognizing that "strong ties between Indian and American scholars of the social sciences have been a continuing positive element in Indo-U.S. relations", encouraged Hubbard and Narlikar to have their members recommend means of facilitating the proposed programs and seminars (Minutes 1986). In typical Washington fashion, this "encouragement" did not mean funds would be available with which to implement the proposed programs and seminars. On the U.S. side, each year's programs were contingent upon congressional earmarks. In 1996, the proposed earmarks failed and the Joint Commission ceased to exist as a function with the Department of State.

The one area of the Indo-US Joint Commission that served India especially well was science and technology. In his memoirs, John Gunther Dean, US Ambassador to India 1985–1988 noted that "among the many ways our Commercial Section directly assisted Indians and American businessmen, was that the Embassy issued a booklet listing some 300 projects of U.S.-Indian cooperation actually in progress. Once it became known how many U.S.-Indian joint ventures were in progress, especially in Science and Technology, companies from other countries as well as new American companies became interested in following the American pioneers" (Dean 2010). In October 1988, India took receipt of its first Cray XMP-14 Super Computer for installation at the National Center for Medium Range Weather Forecasting (NCMRWF) on the premises of the Indian Meteorological Department in New Delhi (GOI AR 1988). India hoped to obtain a Cray YMP-132 for the Indian Institute of Science, Bangalore (GOI AR 1988). Dean went on to write, "The Reagan Administration also gave U.S.-Indian cooperation in high Technology a big boost when the White House approved the sale of a CRAY super-computer to the Indian Meteorological Service. Robert Dean, a namesake but no relative, who worked on the White House staff at the time on high technology issues, was most helpful in obtaining top level clearance for the sale of such high technology to India. The sale of this item was an exception, at the time, of U.S. willingness to export its top technology. In the meantime, U.S. authorities have learned that if the United States will not permit the export of American high technology items, foreign countries will fill the gap from non-American sources" (Dean 2010).

During the mid-eighties in the years leading up to Jack's appointment as U.S. ambassador to India, political rhetoric coming out of New Delhi increasingly rubbed Washington the wrong way on multiple occasions because of India's pro-Palestinian and anti-Israeli stance. Washington was also becoming increasingly concerned with India's advancements with nuclear technology and their increasingly friendly relationship with the Soviet Union and build-up of military weapons.

After the end of World War II Great Britain began to divest itself of its colonial holdings granting independence to several nations. The Republic of India was established in August 1947 and the State of Israel in May 1948. While India recognized the "State of Israel," full diplomatic relations were not established until 1992. During most of the forty-three years between 1948 and 1992, "strained" would be the best adjective to describe Indo-Israeli relations. Both Mahatma Gandhi and Jawaharlal Nehru had fervently opposed the partition of Palestine and the creation of a Jewish state in that territory. They also had anti-Western and anti-imperialist world views which played a key role in the country's stance toward Israel during the entire period of the Cold War (Kandel 2010). Additionally, the Indian government was concerned about maintaining unity between its Hindus and Muslims (Falk 2009).

India did purchase a few weapons from Israel during the Sino-Indian war in 1962 and the Indo-Pakistan wars in 1965 and 1971 and cooperation between India's Intelligence Agency, the Research and Analysis Wing (RAW), and its Israeli counterpart, the Agency for Intelligence and Special Operations (the Mossad), was long-standing since the mid 1960's (Gerberg 2010). However, India was reticent to acknowledge any communiques with Israel. For example, on February 24, 1987, the official spokesman of India's Ministry of External Affairs made the following official statement: "Responding to queries about a London report in the *Telegraph* newspaper of February 24, the Spokesman said that the insinuation in the report that India had contacts with Israel on the question of Pakistan's nuclear facilities was totally false and baseless" (GOI FAR 1987).

All other relations between the two countries mirrored the Cold War. At the banquet held August 3, 1987, in honor of Chairman of the Palestine Liberation Organization, Yasser Arafat, India's Prime Minister Shri Rajiv Gandhi said, "Israel must pay heed to international opinion. It must halt its aggressive and expansionist policies. It must concede the national rights of the Palestinian people. Israel must withdraw totally and unconditionally from all occupied Arab territories" (GOI FAR 1987). India continued this rhetoric in February 1988 after the PLO Ambassador, Mr. Khalid El Sheikh, apprised Prime Minister Gandhi of the "heroic resistance of unarmed Palestinians in occupied territory in the face of brutal acts of repression being perpetrated by the Israeli authorities." Gandhi condemned Israel for the "atrocities and reiterated the unequivocal support of the Government and the people of India for the just Palestinian cause" (GOI FAR 1988).

On August 20, 1988, India's Minister of State for External Affairs, Shri K.K. Tewari, spoke in New Delhi on Jerusalem Day in commemoration of "the sacrilegious attempt nineteen years ago to burn down the holy Mosque of Al-Aqsa." After reminding all who listened to his speech that Jerusalem has special significance for the "three great monotheistic religions which originated in West Asia—Islam, Judaism and Christianity" and The League of Nations mandate for Palestine granted to Great Britain in 1922, Mr. Tewari concluded his speech with India's party line.

> On this important occasion I would like to reiterate India's deep sympathy for the plight of the Palestinian people and its firm commitment to the restoration of the just and inalienable national rights of the Palestinian people including the right to self-determination and an independent state in their homeland.
>
> India in this context renews its call for Israeli withdrawal from all occupied Arab territories including Jerusalem and for restoration of the Holy City and the glory of its religious places so that people of all religions can practice their faith freely. Peace can be founded only on justice and tolerance, not on illegal occupation and violence" (GOI FAR 1988).

At the same time that India was calling for Israel to withdraw and return all occupied Arab territories, India was also learning all it could about fighting terrorism from the Mossad (Dean 2010, Gerberg 2010). India had Muslim minorities, which they feared could be radicalized. India had to deal with the violence in Kashmir, and was fully aware that the Hindu-Muslim rift could encourage radical Islamic fundamentalism in India. The country was concerned about radical Islamic fundamentalism at home, which could encourage domestic terror, extreme secessionist Muslim movements in Kashmir (in 1990 the uprising in Kashmir was at its peak), and possible terror by proxy initiated by Pakistan. India also had to consider the possible takeover of its neighbor Pakistan by radical Islam, and potential implications of this for India's national security (Gerberg 2010).

Ever since the creation of Pakistan as the primarily Muslim portion of the former India by Great Britain, as part of their divestitures of colonial holdings, India has felt a constant threat from Pakistan. When the U.S. chose (in 1987) to supply Pakistan with "Copperhead Short-range 155 mm laser-guided anti-armour projectiles" which India felt could be used against her, certain sections of the Indian bureaucracy outside of the Prime Minister's office sent an *Aide-Memorie* to the U.S. Embassy in New Delhi expressing their concern and asking Washington to reconsider their decision. The rationale for the request was that New Delhi said that those particular weapons were not suitable for deployment on the Pakistan/Afghan border, but would be more suitable for deployment on the plains of Pakistan which could only mean that India was the real target (Dean 2010).

Meanwhile, in Washington no one was pleased with the events or the people in New Delhi, India. India's acquisition of a Soviet nuclear submarine seemed to be the last straw in Washington's concurrence both at the White House and on Capitol Hill that changes needed to be made at the U.S. embassy, specifically the removal of the U.S. Ambassador to India. The current ambassador, John Gunther Dean, was not managing affairs in India the way Washington wanted them handled. The primary duty of a U.S. ambassador is to represent the United States' foreign policy in the country to which they were assigned which implies getting the government of their host country to follow that policy. In this area, Dean was relatively ineffective because, by his own admission, he often disagreed with Washington (Dean 2010). New Delhi definitely disagreed with Washington and wasn't afraid to say so.

On October 19, 1987, Prime Minister Shri Rajiv Gandhi speaking at a lunch hosted by the Foreign Policy Association, Asia Society, and the India Chamber of Commerce in New York said, "... We came to independence in a world frozen into the power blocs of the Cold War. To have become an appendage of either bloc would have been to trade in our newly won independence ... we wished also to be free to adopt internal and external policies of our choice ... we sought no allies, only the dissolution of all alliances." In speaking specifically about both the United States and the Soviet Union, Gandhi continued, "It is true that our [India and the U.S.] shared perceptions of democratic values have not always translated into shared perceptions on international issues. ... In education, science and culture our cooperation has been fruitful and significant. The Soviet Union remains a tried and tested friend. They have always been with us in moments of crisis. Their cooperation has been generous in building key sectors of the economy. Their cooperation has also been significant in building our defense capabilities, yet has not stood in the way of our diversifying our sources of defense procurement. They have consistently respected our views. Our relations are a model of peaceful coexistence" (GOI FAR 1987).

India's blatant defiance of Washington's desire for them to reduce their reliance on and relationship with the Soviet Union should have been quelled by Ambassador Dean. This was the Cold War and the Soviet Union was the enemy. Dean had failed to dissuade India from building nuclear power plants (with the assistance of the Soviet Union) and most recently from "leasing" a nuclear submarine from the Soviet Union, (which wasn't delivered until February 3, 1988), therefore Washington would have to take matters into its own hands and condemn India's nuclear proliferation.

On December 7, 1987, Shri K. Natwar Singh, Minister of State for External Affairs made the following statement in Parliament:

> Last week the U.S. Congress has considered some actions on South Asia which, if enacted, would have adverse implications for our bilateral relations with the United States. . . . the circumstances of congressional action have made it imperative to emphasize the improvement in Indo-U.S. relations requires a better appreciation of India's point of view. Financial flows or technology transfer are not the totality of the relationship nor can they be used as levers to force policy changes upon us. A healthy relationship between two sovereign democracies has to be built on mutual interest, trust and confidence. Devoid of these elements our relationship with the U.S. cannot retain its present level much less prosper.
>
> It is regrettable that the Senate Committee has thought fit to equate India's peaceful nuclear programme with Pakistan's relentless pursuit of a weapons-oriented programme. We cannot, and will not, accept this distorted view of the reality in our part of the world (GOI FAR 1987).

Washington also blamed Dean for the failure of the 1988 covert operation by the U.S. to obtain sensitive information about a Soviet nuclear submarine leased to India the prior year for the purpose of training the Indian Navy in the use of technically advanced naval vessels. In Dean's oral history, he explains the situation.

> . . . Naturally, our navy wanted to know more about the submarine leased from the Soviet Union to India, and this led

to a covert operation to obtain detailed plans and drawings of this vessel.

The incident occurred when an Indian Navy Captain was arrested at Bombay International Airport before boarding a flight for the United States in possession of detailed technical data on the Soviet nuclear submarine. Apparently, Indian Intelligence had tracked the Indian naval officer—or was he a double agent—and, in any case, I was asked to meet with the Prime Minister who confronted me with the facts. I did my best to smooth ruffled feathers, and fortunately Mr. Gandhi was sufficiently experienced in international relations to know that information on the Soviet vessel was a legitimate target for our Intelligence agencies. I urged that the apprehension of the Indian officer before leaving India with the drawings should not adversely impact our over-all U.S.-Indian relations. At the same time, I protected vis-a-vis Washington the American official who had been in charge of this case at the Embassy. He left the post quite rapidly, but has enjoyed an interesting career after his service in India (Dean 2010).

While Washington was blaming Dean, Dean blamed Washington for India's understandable action. "The failure of the United States to provide weapons and parts to India when requested or needed meant that India turned to those countries which provided and sold arms "without political strings attached to it" (Dean 2010).

It wasn't just the Soviets. New Delhi was also hob-nobbing with the PLO, the arch enemy of Israel whom the U.S. had sworn to protect and defend. "We welcome you to your 'second home', as you yourself have described India", was the way Prime Minister Gandhi began his speech on August 3, 1987, at the banquet in honor of Chairman Yasser Arafat. "You are to us much more than an honoured guest; you are a brother and a friend. . . . This visit further cements the special relationship and understanding which exists between the people of Palestine and the people of India. . . . Our great leaders who fought for the freedom of our country regarded the struggle for our freedom as integral to the larger worldwide struggle for the restoration to all subjugated peoples of their right to self-determination and of their right to an independent homeland.

"Palestine belongs to the Arabs . . . we reaffirm that the Palestine Liberation Organization is the true representative of the Palestinian people." Gandhi continued his speech by describing the injustices done to the Palestinian people and acknowledging the noble efforts they had made towards a peaceful solution which continued to elude them. The reason for their lack of success "is primarily due to the obduracy of Israel. And, in turn, Israel's intransigence has been encouraged by the external support it receives. Israel must pay heed to international opinion. It must halt its aggressive and expansionist policies. ... Israel must withdraw totally and unconditionally from all occupied Arab territories." After describing all of the support India would give the Palestinian people in international forums, Gandhi concluded his speech by inviting all in attendance to raise a toast "to the health and wellbeing of our distinguished guest and brother, His Excellency Yasser Arafat, Chairman of the Palestine Liberation Organization; to growing friendship and cooperation between the Palestinian and Indian peoples; and to the early success of the Palestinian revolution" (GOI FAR 1987).

Skirmishes between the Israelis and the PLO continued unabated. On February 6, 1988, the PLO Ambassador, Mr. Khalid El Sheikh, called upon Prime Minister Gandhi to "apprise him of the heroic resistance of the unarmed Palestinians in occupied territory in the face of brutal acts of repression being perpetrated by the Israeli authorities." Gandhi "strongly condemned the Israeli atrocities and reiterated the unequivocal support of the Government and the people of India for the just Palestinian cause" adding that world public opinion was "incensed at the senseless violence against Palestinians in Israeli bondage" (GOI FAR 1988). When the Palestinian leader Abu Jihad was assassinated in April 1988, the Government of India condemned the murder and again reaffirmed "its solidarity with and support for the brave struggle of the Palestinian people under the leadership of the PLO for justice, freedom and human dignity including their inalienable right to an independent state in their homeland" (GOI FAR 1988).

Jerusalem Day, in commemoration of the attempt to burn down the holy Mosque of Al-Aqsa in 1967, was observed on August 20, 1988, with a speech by Shri K.K. Tewari, Minister of State for External Affairs. During his speech in which he reviewed the historical, religious and cultural role of one of the oldest cities in the world he said, "the Israeli occupation of the Holy City of Jerusalem and efforts to Judaize it have resulted in many acts of violence and desecration against this revered shrine and against other places of worship.

"On this important occasion I would like to reiterate India's deep sympathy for the plight of the Palestinian people and its firm commitment to the restoration of the just and inalienable national rights of the Palestinian people including the right to self-determination and an independent state in their homeland.

"India in this context renews its call for Israeli withdrawal from all occupied Arab territories including Jerusalem and for restoration of the Holy City and the glory of its religious places so that people of all religions can practice their faith freely. Peace can be founded only on justice and tolerance not on illegal occupation and violence" (GOI FAR 1988).

By late 1987 Washington was beginning its search for Dean's replacement. Secretary of State George P. Shultz had tentatively decided that the State Department intelligence chief, Morton I. Abramowitz would become the next ambassador in India (Barr 1987, Goshko 1988). The White House was not convinced that Abramowitz was the best candidate for this sensitive posting and congressional conservatives such as Sen. Jesse Helms questioned whether Abramowitz showed sufficient anticommunist zeal to work at the top levels of diplomacy (Goshko 1988). No one in Washington, however, disputed the fact that a change had to be made in India. Israel was too important to too many people in the U.S. to allow the insolence being espoused by India to continue unchecked.

Now the duties of a U.S. ambassador are 1) to be the eyes and ears of the government he serves in any particular country; 2) to maintain the most amicable relations with the sovereign to whom he is accredited and with its ministers; and 3) to protect and defend, if necessary, persons and interests of his fellow countryman abroad. A U.S. ambassador must be thoroughly acquainted with the foreign policy of Washington and the White House regarding international matters in general, and specific policies regarding the sovereign in which the ambassador is posted. The ambassador is to keep officials in Washington informed of all important developments in the country in which they are representing the United States.

In the case of India, Washington's foreign policy which the ambassador was to foster was not restricted to India. Because Washington viewed India as the focal point of the stability of South Asia in the late 1980s, its foreign policy for India included considerations regarding Pakistan, Afghanistan, and the Soviet Union, with Israel woven throughout. Unfortunately, Washington's policies regarding each of these countries often contradicted themselves.

Afghanistan was fighting the Soviets and had been for almost a decade. Afghanistan's freedom fighters—Islamic fundamentalists under the leadership of Gulbuddin Hekmatyar—

received the majority of their weapons and funding from the CIA (Prados 2001). The war had extracted a heavy toll from the Soviet Union not only in hard costs and human lives, but in overall confidence in Moscow. As it became clearer that the Soviets would soon begin to withdraw their troops, the differences between Pakistan and India over the kind of Afghanistan that should emerge after the war became marked. In Ambassador Dean's opinion, "the United States had more sympathy for the Pakistani vision than [for] the Indian viewpoint" (Dean 2010).

Ambassador Dean recorded that throughout 1987 and 1988 "[t]he American Embassy in New Delhi exchanged significant messages with its counterpart in Islamabad. Both embassies analyzed the problem the same way. Both American embassies saw the orientation of the future Kabul Government of importance to both Pakistan and India, but also to the U.S. and the Soviet Union" (Dean 2010).

As mentioned earlier, India considered Pakistan to be its greatest threat even though the British had tried to alleviate the potential problems by partitioning off the primarily Muslim portions of India into Pakistan on the West and Bangladesh on the East. Unfortunately, the state of Jammu was part of Pakistan, but India claimed it should be part of India. The state of Kashmir was part of India as India felt it correctly belonged, but Pakistan disputed the status. Pakistani incursions into Kashmir to incite Muslims in India were escalating in the late 1980s. On February 18, 1988, the official spokesman of the Ministry of External Affairs in New Delhi responded to Pakistan's President Zia's latest statement on Kashmir and Muslims in India, saying, "President Zia has, once again, chosen to spit out venom and make totally unacceptable references to Kashmir and Muslims in our country. He claims to be on peace offensive with India, but rarely misses an opportunity to arouse passions on both sides. He says he wants normalization of relations with India, but does not shy away from using force in Siachen. . . . While he does so, we have no option but to remind him that Jammu and Kashmir are an integral part of India and that the only issue which remains to be resolved is that of vacation of Indian territory occupied illegally by Pakistan and that we should settle this issue like other issues in accordance with the Simla Agreement" (GOI FAR 1988).

Thus was the quagmire when the White House, and prominent members of the American-Jewish community, quietly asked Jack if he would consider accepting an appointment as the U.S. ambassador to India. Elated at the possibility of a dream coming true, Jack began the arduous process of vetting—preparing and submitting a summary of his Indian experience to the White House on January 28, 1988. Within two weeks the White House had prepared Jack's dossier. Additional documents were compiled and on March 22, 1988, a packet was submitted to the Committee on Foreign Relations, United States Senate for the evaluation of Jack's nomination as Ambassador to India. Of particular interest among all of the questions to which Jack responded in writing were:

> Q: Have you ever been publicly identified, in person, or by organizational membership, with a particularly controversial national or local issue? If so, please describe. (Reference to "particularly controversial" is intended to focus on issues that could be used, even unfairly, against you.)
>
> A: No
>
> Q: Have you ever submitted oral or written views to any government authority (executive or legislative) or the news media, on any particularly controversial issue other than in an official government capacity? If so, please describe. (Reference to "particularly controversial" is intended to focus on issues that could be used, even unfairly, against you.)
>
> A: No
>
> Q: Have you ever had any association with any person or group or business venture which could be used, even unfairly, to impugn or attack your character and qualification for this position?
>
> A: No

Jack, and the White House, would soon be faced with skeletons that Jack thought had long since been cremated.

1988 was also an election year with democrat Massachusetts governor Michael Dukakis running against republican Vice President George Bush. Some in Washington, on both sides of the aisle, felt as though Ambassador Dean should be left in place until after the election. Senior State Department officials claimed that Dean had been informed in early Spring of 1988 that he should prepare to leave India soon but Dean claims in his memoirs that he knew nothing of the impending change in his assignment until the Fall (Washington 1988, Dean 2010).

On April 27, 1988, two days after *The New York Times* reported that Jack was being considered as the next U.S.

Ambassador to India (Washington 1988), "Embassy New Delhi alerted the State Department to India's determination to begin reinserting its traditional role in Afghanistan. This meant that: "in the long run India will not permit exclusive Pakistani influence in Kabul." The Embassy reported that: "the Government of India was deeply concerned over the emergence of Islamic fundamentalism of the Gulbuddin variety and what impact this may have on India's Muslims, on the Pakistani regime and the rest of the region." Therefore, India seeks a more balanced government in Kabul. A similar assessment appeared in the respected *TIMES OF INDIA* in its April 26, 1988 issue signed by S. Nihal Singh: "India is doing its bit to ensure that the future government of Afghanistan is secular, rather than fundamentalist, in its orientation. Apparently, New Delhi believes that Washington, for its own reasons, is inclined to share Pakistan's desire to see a fundamentalist dispensation in Afghanistan" (Dean 2010).

Ronald Reagan was governor of the state of California when Jack became president of the University of Southern California. During this time they met and became friends. In 1980, when Reagan was running for the United States presidency, Jack was a prominent supporter. During the Reagan campaign Jack also met Robert H Tuttle, the Beverly Hills auto dealership magnate, who became President Reagan's Director of White House Personnel. Both Reagan and Tuttle knew Jack as a scholar of Indian and British history with extensive in-country experience and two decades of established relations with the Government of India, Indian culture, and the peoples of India which began in 1965 when Jack was in India with AID, further developed during the seventies when he was president of USC, and continued as he co-chaired the Indo-US Sub-commission on Education and Culture. Therefore as they were seeking a replacement for John Gunther Dean as U.S. Ambassador to India, it was not that much of a stretch to consider Jack for the position. Tuttle recommended that Reagan seriously consider Jack for the post. The *coup de grâce* however, was a very, very strong letter of recommendation to President Reagan from Walter Annenberg, former U.S. Ambassador to the Court of St. James (United Kingdom) and Chairman of USC's Board of Trustees—the long awaited fulfillment of the promise made to Jack when he resigned as president of USC. Jack also understood the importance of getting India to change its position on the PLO and establish full diplomatic relations with Israel. Perhaps if it had not been an election year, there might not have been the push-back from the Senate towards his nomination.

But I'm getting ahead of myself.

During the first half of 1988, U.S.-Pakistan relations and U.S.-India relations were becoming increasingly contradictory. Juxtaposed against India-Pakistan and India-Afghanistan relations during this same time period, turbulent rumblings were rippling throughout the region. The U.S. governmental officials and U.S. contractors were carefully eyeing the region for both strategic positioning and profits. Unfortunately, the desired results, including Pakistan's interest in purchasing an M-1 tank, were not actualized as illustrated by the following incident as recorded by Dean in his memoirs:

> When Ambassador Raphael reported on June 6, 1988, from Islamabad that President Zia had decided against the purchase of the M-1 tank, it came as quite a surprise to us in New Delhi. The news was not well received In Washington. It was at a small dinner for Congressman Wilson, on June 5, 1988, at Zia's residence, that the Pakistani President told the Congressman that he had decided that the price of the tank had moved beyond Pakistanis' means. So the Government of Pakistan would not purchase the M-1. The Government of Pakistan would focus its efforts on the decision to move ahead with the AWACs sale.
>
> But the advocates for the sale of the American M-1 tank to Pakistan had their supporters, both in Washington and in Islamabad. They organized a demonstration of the tank's capabilities in Pakistan in August 1988. It was attendance at that demonstration of the fire-power of the M-1 tank on August 17, 1988 that cost President Zia and most of his Senior Generals their lives.
>
> Zia had reluctantly agreed to fly to Bahawalpur that fateful morning of August 17 to see a lone tank fire off its cannon in the desert because Major General Mahmood Durrani, the Commander of the Pakistani Armored Corps, and his former Military Secretary, were extraordinarily insistent on his attendance. General Durrani argued that the entire army command would be there that day, and implied that if Zia were absent. It might be taken as a slight. As it turned out, the demonstration was a fiasco. The much vaunted M-I tank missed its target.

At 4:00 p.m. on August 17, 1988, I received the first of several phone calls from Prime Minister Gandhi's Personal Secretary, Ronen Sen, informing me that apparently the C-130 Hercules transport plane in which President Zia was travelling had crashed on take-off from the military air base, outside of Bahawalpur. Every 15-20 minutes I received update reports from Ronen Sen on the situation in Pakistan. When I alerted my C.I.A. staff and the Intelligence Agencies represented on my staff to the news received from the Indian Prime Minister's Office on events in Bahawalpur, they were completely uninformed. It was the first news of the tragedy for all of them. As for Ambassador Patricia Burns, she wondered who was the American General in Zia's plane who was killed, since on that day two American generals were in Pakistan. Was it the resident Head of the Military Assistance Section of the American Embassy in Islamabad, or the visiting General from Washington? After the second or third phone call from Ronen Sen, it was clear that American Ambassador Arnold L. Raphael and General Herbert M. Wassom, the Head of the U.S. military aid Mission to Pakistan also were on Zia's plane which had crashed. But why were they on Zia's plane? Both officials from the American Embassy had flown up to Bahawalpur on the embassy plane to witness the M-1 tank demonstration. Why had they not returned on their own aircraft to Islamabad? Didn't they travel with body guards? If so, what happened to them?

From 4:00 p.m. until about 10:00 p.m. that same evening of August 17, I received reports from Ronen Sen on what happened at Bahawalpur. After the completion of the demonstration of the American Abrams Tank, President Zia invited both Ambassador Raphael and General Wassom to fly back with him in his specially-equipped C-130 Hercules transport plane. Zia and his two top generals sat in the front, the V.I.P. section of an air-conditioned passenger "capsule" that had been rolled into the body of the C-130. The remaining two seats in the section were given to Zia's American guests: Ambassador Raphael and General Wassom. Behind the V.I.P.s, eight Pakistani generals packed the two benches in the rear section of the capsule. In the cockpit, which was separated from the capsule by a door and three steps, was the four-man flight crew.

After Zia's plane—Pak 1—was airborne, a controller in the tower of Bahawalpur asked the Commander of the plane—Mash'hood Hassan—his position. Mash'hood radioed back: "Pak One, stand by" but then, there was no further response. Those on the ground became alarmed, and efforts to contact Mash'hood quickly grew desperate. Pak One was missing only minutes after it had taken off. Meanwhile, at the river, about nine miles away from the airport, villagers looking up saw a plane lurching in the sky, as if it were on an invisible roller coaster. After its third loop, it plunged directly toward the desert, burying itself in the soil. It exploded and, as its fuel burned, became a ball of fire. All thirty-one people on board Pak One were dead. This version was also transmitted to me by phone by Ronen Sen. In the course of that evening of August 17, 1988, Ronen Sen also mentioned that one of the satellites in space had observed, and perhaps even filmed, the way Zia's plane took off, lurched like on a roller coaster, and then crashed as described above (Dean 2010).

As Dean received additional information over the next few weeks from the Indians, from the US Embassy in Kabul (Afghanistan), from his own staff and ambassadorial colleagues at other embassies in New Delhi, and from Washington regarding the plane crash and the death of President Zia, he felt as though he needed to take the unusual step of flying back to Washington to brief top U.S. authorities on his findings—the death of President Zia had been an assassination not an accident. On September 10, 1988, (three days after President Reagan announced his intention to nominate Jack to be the new ambassador to India), Dean cabled Washington asking authorization to return to Washington to consult with U.S. political leaders in the White House and in the State Department. Dean's intent was to apprise them of his evaluation of the status quo and let them know that in his opinion Washington's tilt toward Pakistan and its determination to court Afghan fundamentalist resistance movement was putting "our good relationship with India" at risk. Permission was granted and Dean went to Washington for what he thought would be a week but instead turned into six weeks (Dean 2010).

Dean left New Delhi accompanied by a CIA officer. His ticket was reserved by the CIA under the name of John Gunther and the CIA helped him clear police and customs formalities under that name both in New Delhi and in Washington. Dean took these precautions of hiding his identity because he had concluded that "Zia's assassination was a 'contract' led by one of the more important intelligence agencies of the world, and having been twice a target of assassination attempts in [his] professional career, [he] did not know who might not approve of the role [he] played in New Delhi" (Dean 2010).

> I had been alerted that the Reagan Administration was planning to appoint Mr. Hubbard from California as Ambassador to India, as my replacement. Apparently, the Reagan Administration could not wait and had suggested a recess appointment for Mr. Hubbard, thereby circumventing Senate approval just weeks before the November elections. In numerous messages from New Delhi I had clearly indicated that it would be preferable to await the election in November, so that the new American Ambassador would come to India with the endorsement of the U.S. Senate. Especially after the assassination of Zia, I thought nothing precipitous should be done which might appear as disapproval of our policy toward Pakistan or India. Certainly, I fully agreed in my messages that a new American Ambassador should be sent after the elections in order to deal with the changing situation in South Asia and in Afghanistan (Dean 2010).

Unbeknownst to Dean, Secretary of State George Shultz sent a memorandum to President Reagan dated August 19, 1988, which read:

> Attached for your approval is the nomination of John Randolph Hubbard, of California, to be Ambassador Extraordinary and Plenipotentiary of the United States of America to India. He would succeed John Gunther Dean who will be resigning.
> Agreement to Mr. Hubbard's appointment has been received from the Government of India.
> Mr. Hubbard has been accorded security clearance based upon a full field investigation by the Department's Bureau of Diplomatic Security. All questions relating to potential conflict of interest have been resolved.

When Dean arrived in Washington that fateful September, he quickly learned that the firm appointments he thought he had with Secretary Shultz and Vice President Bush were not going to happen. Instead he saw the head of the Intelligence and Research Division at State, Mort Abramowitz, whom Secretary of State George Shultz wanted as Dean's replacement, and the Director General of the Foreign Service, George Vest. Neither was very interested in his assessment of the evolving situation in South Asia. Instead he was asked to see the medical unit of the State Department for his sanity was being questioned. Dean had made the mistake of suggesting that pro-Israeli circles might have been in collusion with anti-Zia elements in Pakistan and with disgruntled Indian Agents in bringing about the August 17, 1988, crash of Zia's plane. He doubted that the CIA was directly involved but did believe the American establishment was involved in the cover-up of the crash. As Dean wrote, by questioning his sanity with reports from psychiatrists and different medical doctors, appointments with whom had been made by the State Department Medical unit, the Department of State was able to take away his medical clearance.

> I was sent to Switzerland, to our house in the mountains, for 'recuperation'. I received orders to stay there until I received word to return to New Delhi to pack up our personal belongings and leave post. In short, I was not allowed to return, from Washington, to my post because "my health" did not permit it!
> I flew from Washington to Switzerland, where I reported to the Swiss police. My wife and one of our sons joined me for the "forced rest period." This strange "confinement to quarters" lasted until the end of October, about 6 weeks. Then, I was authorized by telephone to return to New Delhi, pack our personal belongings, and take leave from the Indian authorities. During the 6 weeks in the Swiss mountains, I received periodic phone calls to ascertain that I was still there. An Assistant Secretary of State, with a highly placed State Department Administrative Assistant, even came from Washington to our resort to ascertain that I was really at the chalet and that the house belonged to us. That is a real demonstration of confidence in your ambassador (Dean 2010).

Back in Washington, the confirmation of Jack's nomination as ambassador was being held up by the Senate Foreign Relations Committee. The Democrats wanted to wait until after the election, because if Michael Dukakis won the election Reagan's nominees would probably never be heard from again. If

George Bush won the election he could resubmit the nominees. But the Democrats' objections to Jack went beyond the lateness of his nomination, and on September 20, 1988, they informed the President that there would be no hearings that year on John Hubbard's nomination as Ambassador to India.

Jack had been, and remains, USC's most colorful and controversial president. During his tenure as university president in the 1970s, Jack had obtained sizable donations for the university from the Shah of Iran and from Saudi Arabia. He was accused of sacrificing academic integrity for oil money. The fact that the USC trustees had resolved those issues back in the seventies, seemed irrelevant to Democrats on the Senate Foreign Relations committee. The Democrats also wanted to explore another scandal at USC during the 1970s in which more than 300 scholastically unqualified athletes had bypassed normal admission procedures with Jack's knowledge and approval (Goshko 1988). As football legend Charles Young said, "It doesn't surprise me that they [the Senators] chose to hold up President Hubbard's nomination due to USC athletics. When you're the best team in the nation and you have been the best team in the nation for decades, someone is always going to try to bring you down. Fight on!"

Jack being transported to present his ambassadorial credentials to the President of India

Congress adjourned at the end of October. Dean was released from house arrest at the end of October and was given permission to return to New Delhi to pack up his belongings. President George Bush was elected on November 8, 1988. John Randolph Hubbard was appointed Ambassador Extraordinary and Plenipotentiary (India) November 22, 1988 by President Reagan with President-elect Bush's knowledge. Waiting until after President Bush's inauguration when he had time to hand select an ambassador to India wasn't an option. Marlin Fitzwater, the White House spokesman, said that the appointment represented an urgency. India was the most obvious example where there was a change in government in neighboring Pakistan and Soviet troop withdrawal in Afghanistan currently in process (Berke 1988). Chairman of the presidium of the Supreme Soviet of the USSR & General Secretary of the C.P.S.U. Central Committee H.E. Mr. Mikhail S. Gorbachev had made a state visit to India on November 18, 1988 (GOI FAR 1988). New Delhi was awash with KGB and CIA, but no U.S. Ambassador.

Jack greeting India's military leaders
as part of the ceremony welcoming him as ambassador, 1988

Jack's appointment was a recess appointment by President Reagan on November 22, 1988, when the Senate Foreign Relations committee failed to confirm his nomination. "This appointment is a dream come true. It's just wonderful. It's like coming home. It's a distinctive honor to be the president's representative in this country. India is one of the most fascinating places in the world—so culturally, linguistically and geographically diverse that you never get tired or bored" (Eftychiou 1989). He understood that he might only be in India for a few months if newly elected President George Bush chose not to reappoint him. "Take the worst-case example," Jack speculated. "Say I have to resign—the new administration does not want me to continue. My successor has to go through an approval drill which could take months. I would stay in India certainly until he was named." Until otherwise notified by President-elect George Bush, Jack looked forward to being "the eyes and ears of the United States" in India. He especially was excited with the prospect of applying lessons learned from his former relationship with Ambassador Chester Bowles of cultivating "the most amicable relations with the sovereign and its ministers" on the golf course.

U.S. Ambassador John R. Hubbard
presenting his credentials to India's President R. Venkataraman

December 27, 1988 was a cold overcast day in New Dehli. But even though one's breath was visible, Jack dressed in his best grey suit without the benefit of an overcoat. This was his day—his dream had come true. The day's formalities included a military processional in advance of Jack's transportation to Rashtrapati Bhaban in an ornate horse-drawn open-air carriage with driver and footmen in full regalia, inspection of Indian troops, the US and Indian national anthems, concluding with palace trumpeters announcing the arrival of Ambassador Hubbard followed by

President R. Venkataraman. The actual presentation of credentials made to President R. Venkataraman was succinct. In accepting Jack's credentials, President Venkataraman reiterated India's call for nuclear disarmament.

With all of the rights and responsibilities of an ambassadorship, Jack had, among other obligations, the duty to represent to India's Prime Minister Rajiv Gandhi, the United States' foreign policy, especially its official position regarding Jews, Israel, Palestine, and the Palestinian Arabs—regardless of his personal opinion. He now had a greater appreciation of the predicament his old friend Chester Bowles had been in two decades earlier as he defended the U.S.'s position in Viet Nam to India's government. Jack had to remind Gandhi that his quest to quell the "Jewish evil" that was lurking in Sri Lanka probably was not in his—nor India's—best interest. Regardless of whom Mossad was training and to whom Israel was selling arms, the U.S. was Israel's ally and would defend her against any opponent.

Following protocol, Jack prepared and submitted his letter of resignation to newly inaugurated President George Bush on January 20, 1989. It read:

Dear Mr. President:

In keeping with established custom, I hereby tender my resignation as Ambassador to India to become effective at your pleasure.

Sincerely,

John R. Hubbard,
Ambassador

This resignation was kept by the White House in a sealed envelope until the end of September 1989.

President Bush had decided that he wanted the ambassadors in each country to follow a certain pattern. If the prior ambassador had been a political appointee, he would nominate a political "friend" to be ambassador in that country. If the prior ambassador has been a career foreign service officer, he would nominate a "career foreign service officer" to be ambassador. In the case of India, Jack had two strikes against him. Not only had he been a political appointee, he had been a recess appointment without senate approval. John Gunther Dean, on the other hand, had been a career foreign service officer. Therefore President Bush decided to nominate William Clark, Jr., a career diplomat, to replace Jack as ambassador to India.

Dated October 30, 1989, President Bush wrote:

Dear Ambassador Hubbard:

It is with deep regret that I accept your resignation as United States Ambassador to India.

Your achievements in this position reflect an outstanding commitment to public service. You have worked diligently and effectively to promote American foreign policy goals in South Asia. Your personal efforts in developing a close working relationship with senior Indian officials, including my friend Rajiv Gandhi, have immeasurably strengthened ties between the United States and India. I am deeply grateful for your outstanding contributions to both the Reagan and Bush Administrations, and I commend you for a job well done.

Barbara and I wish you every success as you return to private life and in whatever future endeavors you undertake.

With warm regards,

Sincerely,

George Bush

Jack's mission in India terminated on November 15, 1989.

Editor's Addendum

On May 21, 1991, Rajiv Gandhi was assassinated by a female suicide bomber reportedly in retaliation for shutting down Israeli arms trade in India and Sri Lanka causing the loss of significant income to the arms dealers.

In a surprise diplomatic move in January 1992, full-fledged diplomatic relations were established between the Republic of India and the State of Israel. Stephen P. Cohen (in his book *India—Emerging Power*) maintains that the main reason for the change in Indian policy on Israel was Israel's counter-terror experience: "The dangers from Islamic extremism were so great that it was worth risking domestic Muslim opposition". Ali Khan likewise stated succinctly: "Both countries shared a strategic perception of threat of fundamentalism" (Gerberg 2010).

Chapter 25

Sunset

Jack's daughter, Kristie, said, "Dad's professional and personal life is not easily summarized," as evidenced by the volume of this work. Were we to end this book with his return to the United States from his duties in India, we would be neglecting the last twenty years of Jack's life.

The University of Texas named President Hubbard its "Distinguished Alumnus" for 1978. Presenting the award is Texas President Lorene Rodgers (right), with Mrs. Lyndon Johnson, a Regent of the University, at left. Hubbard earned three degrees at Texas between 1936 and 1950, with time spent in between for military service and teaching positions.

Jack receives Distinguished Alumnus award
from The University of Texas, 1978

Jack loved teaching. He continued teaching at least one British History class a semester at USC until he was 90 years old. His students loved and admired him. Charles Young still warmly recalls how Jack not only arranged for him to get married at Town and Gown, but attended his wedding. "Dr. Hubbard will never know what a profound impact his presence at my wedding had on me. He had leveled the playing field."

Most of his colleagues respected him. He remained Trustee Emeritus on the USC Board of Trustees until his death. Jack loved sports. He continued attending USC football games and other sporting events up to the last year of his life, and he had become a Trojan first and a Longhorn second. In 1978, the University of Texas chose to honor Jack with their annual Distinguished Alumni Award. However, Jack had never paid his alumni dues and therefore was not a member of the Texas Exs. Since the award had already been announced and Jack had already agreed to accept it, someone else stepped in and paid Jack's dues in full.

The Hubbard Family, 1938;
Aunt Mercy, Dad, Mother, George, Louise, & Me (Jack)

Jack's Trojan conversion was even more pronounced as he and his brother, George—also a Texas alum, discussed the upcoming Rose Bowl in which USC would play the University of Texas on January 1, 2006. On the field at the same time would be the top three Heisman Trophy finalists—Reggie Bush and Matt

Leinart from USC and Vince Young from Texas. USC was favored and led Texas until the final minutes of the game when Vince Young made an unbelievable run into the end zone with 19 seconds to play. Texas beat USC 41 to 38. Jack did not speak of that game again to his brother. Jack did invite George to come out to California and attend other USC games with him.

In their earlier years Jack and George were not particularly close as brothers—due largely to their 10 year age difference and their different chosen professions. Jack was an educator and George had chosen a technical career with IBM. However, during the last 15 years of Jack's life, he and George developed a strong familial relationship. Impressed with some of the books George had written and published, it was during one of these later life visits that Jack handed George the manuscript of his memoirs and asked George to edit it and see to it that it was published.

In his final days, at Jack's request, George would sit at his side in the hospital and read to him scores and write-ups of the prior day's baseball games. On August 21 2011, surrounded by his three daughters and his brother, Jack passed on.

Elegy

Let them bury your big eyes
In the secret earth securely,
Your thin fingers, and your fair,
Soft, indefinite-colored hair,—
All of these in some way, surely,
From the secret earth shall rise;
Not for these I sit and stare,
Broken and bereft completely;
Your young flesh that sat so neatly
On your little bones will sweetly
Blossom in the air.

But your voice,—never the rushing
Of a river underground,
Not the rising of the wind
In the trees before the rain,
Not the woodcock's watery call,
Not the note the white-throat utters,
Not the feet of children pushing
Yellow leaves along the gutters
In the blue and bitter fall,
Shall content my musing mind
For the beauty of that sound

*That in no new way at all
Ever will be heard again.*

*Sweetly through the sappy stalk
Of the vigorous weed,
Holding all it held before,
Cherished by the faithful sun,
On and on eternally
Shall your altered fluid run,
Bud and bloom and go to seed;
But your singing days are done;
But the music of your talk
Never shall the chemistry
Of the secret earth restore.
All your lovely words are spoken.
Once the ivory box is broken,
Beats the golden bird no more.*

Edna St. Vincent Millay

Bibliography

Note: This bibliography applies only to those portions of the book written by the editors.

'Afghan refugee teaches Hindi to tots in India', *UNHCR*, The UN Refugee Agency, 20 February 2008, viewed 13 March 2012, <http://www.unhcr.org/news/NEWS/47bc36204.html>.

'Afghan refugees in India become Indian, at last', *UNHCR*, The UN Refugee Agency, 10 March 2006, viewed 16 December 2011, <http://www.unhcr.org/news/NEWS/441190254.html>.

Agreement between the Union of Soviet Socialist Republics and the Republic of Finland concerning the renunciation by the Soviet Union of rights to the use of the territory of Porkkala-Udd as a naval base and the withdrawal of Soviet armed forces from the said territory, 19 September 1955, viewed 24 November 2011, <http://heninen.net/sopimus/1955_e.htm>.

'Athletic Dept. Abused USC Admissions', *The Washington Post (1974–Current File)*; 14 October 1980, ProQuest Historical Newspapers The Washington Post (1877–1995) pg. D1.

'Article I—No Title', *Los Angeles Times (1923–Current File)*; 9 August 1970, ProQuest Historical Newspapers Los Angeles Times (1881–1988) pg. E5.

Antczak, J 1978, 'More than 35 Iranian students riot in downtown demonstration', *Daily Trojan,* 19 September, p.1.

Bard, M, 'The Yom Kippur War', Jewish Virtual Library, viewed 25 May 2012, <http://www.jewishvirtuallibrary.org/jsource/History/73_War.html>.

Barr, S 1987, 'State Dept. Preparing to Shuffle Diplomats', *The Washington Post*, 31 December 1987, p. A17

Beling, W 2010, February 3 Memorial, *Princeton Alumni Weekly*, viewed 18 March 2012, <http://paw.princeton.edu/issues/2010/02/03/sections/memorials/5492/index.xml>.

Benkin, R, *An India-Israel-United States Alliance: The Last Great Hope for Humanity*, Portal to the Hindu World, viewed 19 December 2011, <http://www.bangladeshihindu.com/an-india-israel-united-states-alliance-the-last-great-hope-for-humanity/>.

Berke, R 1988, 'Lame-Duck Appointments by President Touch Off Questions About Timing', *The New York Times*, Nov. 24, viewed 22 December 2011, <www.nytimes.com/1988/11/24/us/lame-duck-appointments-by-president-touch-off->.

Brabakk, J 1998, 'After the Cold War: Structural changes and Israeli-Palestinian rapproachement', The fourth Nordic conference on Middle Eastern Studies, The Middle East in globalizing world, Oslo, 13—16 August, viewed 17 December 2011, <http://www.smi.uib.no/pao/brobakk.html,>.

Clark, A 2003, 'The New Push for Middle East Studies' *Saudi Aramco World*, Vol. 54, No. 1, last viewed 28 May 2012, <http://www.saudiaramcoworld.com/issue/200301/the.new.push.for.middle.east.studies.htm>.

Clow, S 1977, 'Hubbard discusses the sporting life', *Daily Trojan*, April 15, 1977

Cohen, J, G. Reasons 1980, 'UCLA's Chancellor Fears for Intercollegiate Sports', *Los Angeles Times*, (1923—Current File); 27 July. ProQuest Historical Newspapers Los Angeles Times (1881—1988) pg. A3.

Del Nagro, M 1976, The Week; 20 September, *Sports Illustrated, SI Vault*, viewed 23 March 2012, <http://cnnsi.printthis.clickability.com/pt/cpt?expire=&title=The+Week+-+09.20.76+-+SI+>.

Dorf, M 1998, 'Yom Kippur War changed U.S.-Israel ties', 25 September, *Jewish News of Greater Phoenix*, viewed 25 May 2012, <www.jewishaz.com/jewishnews/980925/womkippr.shtml>.

Eftychiou, C 1989, 'Ex-USC President Chosen by Reagan to be Ambassador', *The Daily Trojan.*

'Escape from War', *The Times of India*, October 4, 2001, viewed 16 December 2011, <http://timesofindia.indiatimes.com/articleshow/487390023.cms>.

Falk, J 2009, 'India's Israel Policy: The Merits of a Pragmatic Approach', *Stanford Journal of International Relations*, Spring, viewed 19 December 2011, < sjir.stanford.edu/pdf/Israel.pdf>.

Fluor Corporation, viewed 28 May 2012, < http://www.fundinguniverse.com/company-histories/Fluor-Corporation-Company-History.html>.

Gerberg, I 2010, 'India-Israel Relations Strategic Interests, Politics and Diplomatic Pragmatism', Israel National Defense College, February, viewed 19 December 2011, <web.hevra.haifa.ac.il/~ch-strategy/images/…/**India-Israel** relations.pd…,> .

Goshko, J 1988, 'Political Realities Intrude on Shultz's 'Big Switch'; Plan to Tap Envoys for Top State Posts Shelved', *The Washington Post*, Sept. 1, p. A21, viewed 22 December 2011, <http://pqasb.pqarchiver.com/washingtonpost/access/73625909.html?FMT=FT&FMTS=A,>.

Goshko, J 1988, 'Too Late to Switch Envoys, Senate Democrats Contend', *The Washington Post*, Oct. 7, p. A21, viewed 22 December 2011, <http://pqasb.pqarchiver.com/washingtonpost/access/73635014.html?FMT=FT&FMTS=A,>.

Goshko, J 1988, 'Helms Blocks Diplomatic Promotions; Senator Apparently Hopes to Force Confirmation of Ambassadors', *The Washington Post*, Oct. 20, p. A21, viewed 22 December 2011, <http://pqasb.pqarchiver.com/washingtonpost/access/73637668.html?FMT=FT&FMTS=A, >.

Gottesman, L 2004, 'Middle East Studies in the U.S.: Combating Academic Anti-Semitism', *Campus Watch*, Fall, viewed 28 May 2012, <www.campus-watch.org/article/id/1360>.

Green, Lee, <u>Sportswit</u>, Ballantine Books, 1986.

Gumport, P J, Iannozzi,M, Shaman, S, & Zemsky, R, *The United States Country Report: Trends in Higher Education from Massification to Post-Massification*, viewed 4 April 2012, <www.citizing.org/.../Trends%20in%20HE%20from%20Mass%20to%.>.

Guskey, E, J Crowe 2001, 'Legendary Coach John McKay Dies', *Los Angeles Times*, 11 June, viewed 25 October 2012, < http://articles.latimes.com/print/2001/jun/11/news/mn-9034>.

Hall, J 1978, 'Only a Game', *Los Angeles Times,* 29 September. ProQuest Historical Newspapers Los Angeles Times (1881—1988) pg. E3.

Hastings, C 2008, 'Lord Halifax tried to negotiate peace with the Nazis', *The Telegraph*, 30 August, viewed 27 February 2012, <www.telegraph.co.uk/news/uknews/2650832/Lord-Halifax-tried-to-negotiate-peace-...>.

Hillinger, C 1978, 'With Nixon Papers Seized, Plans for Library Up in Air', *Los Angeles Times,* 5 November. ProQuest Historical Newspapers Los Angeles Times (1881—1988) pg. F1.

Hruby, D 1976, 'Is The Pac-8 Breaking Up?', *San Jose Mercury*, 2 November, pg. 53.

'Hubbard emphasizes humanities', *The Daily Lass-o*, 13 October, 1978 Vol. LXV, No. 23, p. 1.

'Hubbard Humanistic', *The Pioneer,* October 1978, Volume 1, Number 10, p. 4.

Jalonen, O 2001, 'What if?', viewed 24 November 2011, <www.finlit.fi/booksfromfinland/bff/401/jalonen1.htm>.

Kandel, A, Indo-Israeli relations in the post-cold war period, viewed 17 December 2011, <http://www.weeklyblitz.net/535/indo-israeli-relations-in-the-post-cold-war-period>.

Kapuria, VM 1968, 'Profile: Dr. John Randolph Hubbard', *Participant Journal Indian-American Technical Cooperation Programme*, June, p. 25.

Kazanjian, P 2001, 'In 1971, trustees denied gay group official status', *The Daily Trojan*, 11 April, Vol. 142, No. 56, p. 6, viewed 10 March 2012, < www.usc.edu/student-affairs/dt/V142/N56/10-in1971.56d.html>.

Kempster, M and R. Ostrow, 1978, 'Arab Gifts to U.S. Colleges Stir Suspicion and Unease', *Los Angeles Times*, 26 November. ProQuest Historical Newspapers Los Angeles Times (1881—1988) pg. A1.

Long, C 1978, 'Hubbard discusses tuition, crime and academics on KABC radio', *Daily Trojan,* 19 September, p.1.

Long, C 1978, 'Hubbard plans 1980 retirement, but . . .', *Daily Trojan,* 2 October, p.1.

Long, C 1979, 'Critics say change in leadership needed', *Daily Trojan,* p1.

Loper, M 1972, 'USC President Holds Pregame Party', *Los Angeles Times,* 4 December. ProQuest Historical Newspapers Los Angeles Times (1881—1988) pg. D8.

Loper, M 1975, 'USC Fans Celebrate at Dansant', *Los Angeles Times,* 1 January. ProQuest Historical Newspapers Los Angeles Times (1881—1988) pg. B7.

Masley, P 1975, 'Nixon Data Promised to Southern Cal', *The Washington Post (1974—Current File)*; 21 April. ProQuest Historical Newspapers The Washington Post (1877—1995) pg. A1.

Moran, M 1979, 'At U.S.C., the Rose Bowl Means Hollers, Dollars and Scholars', *The New York Times*, 31 December.

Moran, M 1980, 'Former U.S.C. President Defends Policies', *The New York Times*, 17 October, B5.

Moss, Al, Pac-10 Football, Bison Books Corp., 1987.

Murphy, J 1972, 'Feminists Put the Heat on USC, UCLA', *Los Angeles Times*, (1923—Current File); 2 November. ProQuest Historical Newspapers Los Angeles Times (1881—1988) pg. D1.

Nawroz, General (Ret) M Y & Grau, LW 1996, 'The Soviet War in Afghanistan: History and Harbinger of Future War?', June, viewed 16 December 2011, <http://www.ciaonet.org/cbr/cbr00/video/cbr_ctd/cbr_ctd_52.html>.

N, B 2011, 'Notre Dame vs. USC: The Best 25 Games in the Rivalry', 20 April. *Bleacher Report*, viewed 13 March 2012, < http://bleacherreport.com/articles/670257-notre-dame-vs-usc-the-best-25-games-in-the-rivalry>.

Nelson, V 1978, 'Viewing the gains, losses at breakfast', *Daily Trojan,* 2 October, p.1.

'News of Members', *AIPEA* Newsletter, No. 12, June 1976, p23, 26 viewed May 2012, <www.aipea.org/.../AIPEA%20Newsletter%20n.%2012%20Jun%2076... >.

'Nixon Library Plan Hailed at U.S.C.', *The New York Times,* 27 April 1975.

Oates, B 1980, 'USC Without Football? Hubbard Finds It Unthinkable', *Los Angeles Times*, (1923—Current File); 4 March. ProQuest Historical Newspapers Los Angeles Times (1881—1988) pg. OC_B1.

Prados, J 2001, 'U.S. Analysis of the Soviet War in Afghanistan: Declassified:, Volume II: Afghanistan: Lessons from the Last War', *The National Security Archive*, October 9, viewed 17 December 2011, <http://www.gwu.edu/~nsarchiv/NSAEBB/NSAEBB57/us2.html>.

Paterno, J 2011, 'Someone Exploits a Loophole, and the NCAA Adds New Rules', 19 May, viewed 22 March 2012, <http://www.statecollege.com/news/print.php?article=753284>.

Pathik, C 1968, 'Summer Science Institutes Help Develop New Technologies of Teaching Physics', *Participant Journal Indian-American Technical Cooperation Programme*, June, p. 20.

Penait Calcai, SR/Olympic Sports, viewed 25 November 2011, <www.sports-reference.com/olympics/athletes/ca/penait-calcai-1.html>.

Rand McNally Maps, *Atlas of the World*, 1987.

Reasons, J and Cohen, J 1980, 'USC Ousts Debate Coach in Case Involving Athletes', *Los Angeles Times*, (1923—Current File); 22 February. ProQuest Historical Newspapers Los Angeles Times (1881—1988) pg. B11.

Reasons, J and Cohen, J 1980, 'USC Athletes Must Retake Makeup Class', *Los Angeles Times*, (1923—Current File); 10 April. ProQuest Historical Newspapers Los Angeles Times (1881—1988) pg. B1.

Reasons, J and Cohen, J 1980, 'Transcript Scandal Hits USC', *Angeles Times*, (1923—Current File); 1 May. ProQuest Historical Newspapers Los Angeles Times (1881—1988) pg. B3.

'Return of Porkkala by Soviets 50 years ago had strings attached', *Helsingin Sanomat—International Edition*, 24 viewed November 2011, <www.hs.fi/english/print/1135218495524>.

Reuveny, R and Prakash, A 1999, 'The Afghanistan war and the breakdown of the Soviet Union', *Review of International Studies*, 25, 693-708, viewed 16 December 2011, <faculty.washington.edu/aseem/afghanwar.pdf>.

Robertson, L 1978, 'US 'suffocating' colleges, USC president says', *Fort Worth Star-Telegram*, 13 October, p. 1d.

'Rudolf Hess', *Spartacus Educational*, viewed 27 February 2012, <www.spartacus.schoolnet.co.uk/GERhess.htm>.

Sage, Wayne, 1995, 'USC Announces Billion-dollar Campaign; Funds Will Implement Strategic Plan for World-Class University', 15 September, *Business Wire*, viewed 17 March 2012, <www.thefreelibrary.com/_/print/PrintArticle.aspx?id=17441405>.

'Saudi Arabia 1976', viewed 28 May 2012, <http://astheysawit.info/12413-1976-saudi-arabia.html>.

'Saudi Arabia 1977', viewed 28 May 2012, <http://astheysawit.info/12730-1977-saudi-arabia.html>.

Schrader, L 1976, 'Mizzou Shows "Em Up, 46-25', *Long Beach Independent, Press-Telegram*, 12 September, viewed 13 March 2012, <www.mmbolding.com/Missou/Missouri1976.htm>.

Secter, B and Watanabe, T, 1980, 'Secret Iranian Aid by Bradley Alleged' *Los Angeles Times*, (1923—Current File); 28 February. ProQuest Historical Newspapers Los Angeles Times (1881—1988) pg. OC_A5.

Sherman, M, 'Indo-Israeli Strategic Cooperation as a US National Interest', Policy Paper No 89, Ariel Center for Policy Research, viewed 17 December 2011, <www.acpr.org.il/pp/pp-089-shermanE.pdf>.

'Sixty years ago: Parliament within range of Soviet guns', *Helsingin Sanomat—International Edition*, viewed 24 November 2011, <www.hs.fi/english/print/1076154119137>.

Smith, R J 1979, 'Middle East Investments in American Universities Spark Campus Confrontations', *Science*, 203 (4379), p. 421

Smith, R J 1979, 'USC President Resigns Amid Campus Quarrel', *Science*, 203 (4384), p. 990

Smith R 1978, 'Gaudiest Game in 50 Years' *The New York Times*, 27 November.

'Southern Cal President Quitting But Denies Any Link to Disputes', *The New York Times*, 11 February 1979.

Speich, D 1978, 'USC Establishing Mideast Center With Corporate Aid', *Los Angeles Times,* 22 October, ProQuest Historical Newspapers Los Angeles Times (1881—1988) pg A1.

Speich, D 1978, 'Middle East Center Prompts Bill Proposal', *Los Angeles Times,* 27 October. ProQuest Historical Newspapers Los Angeles Times (1881–1988) pg OC A7.

Speich, D 1978, 'Saudi Donation to USC Seems to Have Strings', *Los Angeles Times,* 29 October. ProQuest Historical Newspapers Los Angeles Times (1881–1988) pg A3.

Speich, D 1978, 'Panel Endorses Mideast Center Control Change', *Los Angeles Times,* 3 November. ProQuest Historical Newspapers Los Angeles Times (1881–1988) pg OC A2.

Speich, D 1978, 'USC Panel Oks Firmer Reins of Mideast Center', *Los Angeles Times,* 3 November. ProQuest Historical Newspapers Los Angeles Times (1881–1988) pg E8.

Speich, D 1978, 'USC Board Acts to Build Integrity of Mideast Center', *Los Angeles Times,* 9 November. ProQuest Historical Newspapers Los Angeles Times (1881–1988) pg E1.

Speich, D 1979, 'USC Quietly Honored Shah With Degree', *Los Angeles Times,* 7 February. ProQuest Historical Newspapers Los Angeles Times (1881–1988) pg OC A1.

Speich, D, & Townsend, D 1979, 'USC Chief to Quit; Defends Links to Iran', *Los Angeles Times,* 8 February. ProQuest Historical Newspapers Los Angeles Times (1881–1988) pg SD_ A1.

St. John, E P 1995, 'Hard Decisions: Retrenchment and The Faculty Role', *The NEA Higher Education Journal,* /prod/ta/S95Bdoc:S95 4/11/95 REPRO, viewed 4 April 2012, <www.nea.org/assets/img/PubThoughtAndAction/TAA_95Spr_01.pdf>.

Stumbo, B 1973, 'Every Year at USC Is a Watergate', *Los Angeles Times,* 17 May. ProQuest Historical Newspapers Los Angeles Times (1881–1988) pg I12.

'The Shah Is The Shadow Of God: Iran: Oil, Grandeur And A Challenge To The West', *Time,* 4 November 1974, viewed 26 May 2012,< http://www.ostomaan.org/articles/news-and-views/8276>.

Thomas, K 1979, 'America as Alma Mater', *Saudi Aramco World*, May/June, Volume 30, Number 3, p2, viewed 15 June 2012, <http://www.saudiaramcoworld.com/issue/197903/america.as.alma.mater.htm>.

Trombley, W 1970, 'USC Takes Giant Strides Under Topping', *Los Angeles Times,* 5 April. ProQuest Historical Newspapers Los Angeles Times (1881–1988) pg B1.

Trombley, W 1971, 'Campuses Optimistic That Calm Will Prevail', *Los Angeles Times,* 12 April. ProQuest Historical Newspapers Los Angeles Times (1881–1988) pg A1.

Trombley, W 1972, 'Dean of USC Dentistry School Under Fire', *Los Angeles Times,* 6 October. ProQuest Historical Newspapers Los Angeles Times (1881–1988) pg A3.

Trombley, W 1972, 'Won't Yield to Pressure Groups, USC Head Says', *Los Angeles Times,* 12 October. ProQuest Historical Newspapers Los Angeles Times (1881–1988) pg A3.

'U. of Southern California To Build a Nixon Library', *The New York Times,* 21 April 1975.

'University must be presidential priority', *Daily Trojan,* 10 January 1979.

'USC and the Middle East', *Los Angeles Times,* November 6, 1978, ProQuest Historical Newspapers Los Angeles Times (1881–1988) pg. C6.

'USC Gets Another Excellent Leader', *Los Angeles Times* (*1923–Current File*); 6 August 1970, ProQuest Historical Newspapers Los Angeles Times (1881–1988) pg. A6.

'USC Seeking Papers Gift From Nixon', *The Washington Post* (*1974–Current File*); 13 April 1975. ProQuest Historical Newspapers The Washington Post (1877–1995) pg. 3.

Verlander, E 1966, 'The Ideal Dean', *Newcomb Alumnae Newsletter,* Spring, Vol. 16, No. 2, p.7.

'Washington Talk: Briefing; One Last Ambassador?' *The New York Times*, April 25, 1988. *Infotrac Newsstand*, viewed 29 November 2011, <o-go.galegroup.com.library.cityofdenton.com/ps/i.do?id=GALE%7CA175845228&v=w.1&u=txshrpub100108&it=r&p=STND&sw=w>.

Weinskopf, H 1978, 'An Upsetting Time For The Top Ten', 23 October, *Sports Illustrated, SI Vault*, viewed 23 March 2012, <http://cnnsi.printthis.clickability.com/pt/cpt?expire=&title=Highly+ranked+USC%2C+Mic>.

West, R. 1980, 'Academic Aide at USC Quits in Sports Scandal', *Los Angeles Times*, 8 March. ProQuest Historical Newspapers Los Angeles Times (1881–1988) pg SD 16.

Government Records and Documents

Agreed Minutes, Feb. 6, 1986, 'Indo-U.S. Joint Commission Meets', *US Department of State Bulletin*, April 1986, viewed 10 December 2011, <http://findarticles.com/p/artickles/mi_m1079/is_v86/ai_488371/>.

Dean, J G, 'Oral History—India', Jimmy Carter Library & Museum, 2010, viewed 3 December 2011, <www.jimmycarterlibrary.gov/library/oralhistory/clohproject/dean.phtml>.

George Bush Presidential Library, WHORM Category Name: Diplomatic Affairs—Consular Relations, Document Number: 081904SS.

George Bush Presidential Library, WHORM Category Name: Diplomatic Affairs—Consular Relations, Document Number: 000094.

Government of India (GOI), *Annual Report, 1978*, Foreign Affairs Record, Ministry of External Affairs Library, viewed 11 December 2012, < http://mealib.nic.in/?2013>.

Government of India (GOI), *Annual Report, 1988–89*, Ministry of External Affairs Library, viewed 25 November 2011, <http://mealib.nic.in/?2024#The>.

Government of India (GOI), *Annual Report, 1989–90*, Ministry of External Affairs Library, viewed 25 November 2011, <http://mealib.nic.in/?2023>.

Government of India (GOI), *Foreign Affairs Records—1987 - 1989*, Ministry of External Affairs Library, viewed 15 December 2011, <http://mealib.nic.in/?2013>.

Letter from Ambassador Chester Bowles to President Lyndon B. Johnson, Foreign Relations of the United States: 1961–1963, Volume XIX, South Asia, Document 350, viewed 22 May 2012, <http://history.state.gov/historicaldocuments/frus1961-63v19/d350>.

Letter from President Johnson to the Ambassador to India (Bowles), Foreign Relations of the United States: 1964–1968, Volume XXV, South Asia, Document 7, viewed 23 December 2011, <http://history.state.gov/historicaldocuments/frus1964-68v25/d7>.

'Nomination of John Randolph Hubbard To Be United States Ambassador to India', September 7, 1988, viewed 8 December 2011, <www.reagan.utexas.edu/archives/speeches/1988/090788a.htm>.

'Nomination of William Clark, Jr., To Be United States Ambassador to India', *The American Presidency Project*, last viewed 3 December 2011, <www.presidency.ucsb.edu/ws/print.php?pid=17595>.

Telegram from the Ambassador to India (Bowles) to the President's Special Assistant and Chief of Staff (Moyers), Foreign Relations of the United States, 1964–1968, Volume XXV, South Asia, Document 360, viewed 23 December 2011, <history.state.gov/historicaldocuments/frus1964-68v25/d360>.

Telegram from the Ambassador to India (Bowles) to President Johnson, Foreign Relations of the United States, 1964–1968, Volume XXV, South Asia, Document 525, viewed 23 December 2011, <http://history.state.gov/historicaldocuments/frus1964-68v25/d525>.

U.S. Department of State, Office of the Historian, viewed 23 December 2011, <www.history.state.gov/departmenthistory/people>.

Additional documents obtained from the Central Intelligence Agency, Department of State, the office of Congressman Michael Burgess, and the Bureau of Naval Personnel Retired Records received under the Federal Freedom of Information Act.

University of Southern California Records

Videos

USC, "The Hubbard Years", History Media Institute,

In Memoriam: USC President Emeritus John Randolph "Jack" Hubbard, 92, <http://uscnews.usc.edu/obituaries>.

Progress Report, Toward Century II / 1880–1980–A $265,340,000 Fund, University of Southern California/Sept. 1981.

The History Department of the University of Southern California, Ceremony Marking the Establishment of the John R. Hubbard Chair in British History and the installation of John R. Hubbard as holder of the chair, December 18, 1980.

Personal notes left by John R. Hubbard among his USC papers.

CPSIA information can be obtained at www.ICGtesting.com
Printed in the USA
BVOW11s1035150714

359210BV00008B/64/P